Lecture Notes in Artificial Intelligence 2473

Subseries of Lecture Notes in Computer Science
Edited by J. G. Carbonell and J. Siekmann

Lecture Notes in Computer Science
Edited by G. Goos, J. Hartmanis, and J. van Leeuwen

Springer-Verlag Berlin Heidelberg GmbH

Asunción Gómez-Pérez
V. Richard Benjamins (Eds.)

Knowledge Engineering and Knowledge Management

Ontologies and the Semantic Web

13th International Conference, EKAW 2002
Sigüenza, Spain, October 1-4, 2002
Proceedings

 Springer

Series Editors

Jaime G. Carbonell, Carnegie Mellon University, Pittsburgh, PA, USA
Jörg Siekmann, University of Saarland, Saarbrücken, Germany

Authors

Asunción Gómez-Pérez
Universidad Politécnica de Madrid
Campus de Montegancedo, s/n, 28660 Boadilla del Monte, Madrid, Spain
E-mail: asun@fi.upm.es

V. Richard Benjamins
Intelligent Software Components, S.A. (iSOCO)
Francisca Delgado, 11 - 2°, 28108 Alcobendas, Madrid, Spain
E-mail: richard@isoco.com

Cataloging-in-Publication Data applied for

Die Deutsche Bibliothek - CIP-Einheitsaufnahme

Knowledge engineering and knowledge management : ontologies and the semantic
web ; 13th international conference ; proceedings / EKAW 2002, Sigüenza,
Spain, October 1 - 4, 2002. Asunción Gomez-Perez ; V. Richard Benjamins
(ed.).

(Lecture notes in computer science ; Vol. 2473 : Lecture notes in
artificial intelligence)
ISBN 978-3-540-44268-4

CR Subject Classification (1998): I.2, H.4, H.3, C.2, J.1

ISSN 0302-9743
ISBN 978-3-540-44268-4   ISBN 978-3-540-45810-4 (eBook)
DOI 10.1007/978-3-540-45810-4

http://www.springer.de

© Springer-Verlag Berlin Heidelberg 2002
 Originally published by Springer-Verlag Berlin Heidelberg New York in 2002
Typesetting: Camera-ready by author, data conversion by Boller Mediendesign
Printed on acid-free paper   SPIN: 10871348   06/3142   5 4 3 2 1 0

Preface

This volume contains the papers presented at the 13th International Conference on Knowledge Engineering and Knowledge Management (EKAW 2002) held in Sigüenza, Spain, October 1-4, 2002.

Papers were invited on topics related to Knowledge Acquisition, Knowledge Management, Ontologies, and the Semantic Web. A total of 110 papers were submitted. Each submission was evaluated by at least two reviewers. The selection process has resulted in the acceptance of 20 long and 14 short papers for publication and presentation at the conference; an acceptance rate of about 30%. In addition, one invited paper by a keynote speaker is included. This volume contains 8 papers on Knowledge Acquisition, 4 about Knowledge Management, 16 on Ontologies, and 6 papers about the Semantic Web.

This was the second time (EKAW 2000 being the first) that the event was organized as a conference rather than as the usual workshop (hence the acronym: European Knowledge Acquisition Workshop). The large number of submissions (110 versus the usual 40-60) is an indication that the scientific community values EKAW as an important event to share experiences in the Knowledge Technology area, worthy of being organized as a prestigious international conference. Knowledge is the fuel of the upcoming Knowledge Economy. Therefore, we believe that conferences such as EKAW, that focus on Knowledge Technologies, will continue to play a major role as a platform for sharing and exchanging experiences and knowledge between key players in the area.

Another point to highlight is the appearance of the Semantic Web as a topic at EKAW 2002. We received 24 submissions in this area of which we could accept 6. The Semantic Web envisions a web where software can automatically process content in order to achieve *task delegation* as opposed to the current *information retrieval* paradigm. Topics traditionally dealt with at EKAW are key ingredients for building Semantic Web technology, such as ontologies, knowledge modeling and representation, languages and tools, knowledge management, and knowledge acquisition. Therefore, the Semantic Web is an excellent opportunity for the community to capitalize on our expertise in Knowledge Technology, built up over the last 15 years.

We would like to thank the International Program Committee for their enormous effort in the review process (many reviewers had to evaluate up to 10 papers). In all, 46 additional reviewers were called upon to complete the review process in time. We are also grateful to EKAW's Steering Committee for their advice on strategic decisions.

Inexpressible are our thanks to Angel López who designed and implemented a web-based system to manage the whole review process, without which we never would have made the deadlines. We thank Mariano Fernández-López for organizing the tutorials and workshops; Oscar Corcho for organizing the demo sessions; and Jose Angel Ramos for his help with managing the registration process. Last but not least, we are very grateful to the local organizers.

July 2002

Asunción Gómez-Pérez
V. Richard Benjamins

Conference Organization

Conference Chair
Asunción Gómez-Pérez   Universidad Politécnica de Madrid (Spain)

Conference Co-chair
V. Richard Benjamins   iSOCO (Spain)

Steering Committee
Nathalie AUSSENAC-GILLES   IRIT- CNRS Toulouse (F)
V. Richard BENJAMINS   iSOCO (ES)
Joost BREUKER   University of Amsterdam (NL)
Rose DIENG   INRIA-Sophia-Antipolis, (F)
Dieter FENSEL   Free University of Amsterdam (NL)
Brian GAINES   University of Calgary (CA)
Riichiro MIZOGUCHI   Osaka University (JP)
Enrico MOTTA   Open University (UK)
Mark MUSEN   Stanford University (USA)
Nigel SHADBOLT   University of Southampton (UK)
Rudi STUDER   University of Karlsruhe (D)
Frank VAN HARMELEN   Free University Amsterdam (NL)

Program Committee
Stuart AITKEN   University of Edinburgh (UK)
Hans AKKERMANS   Free University Amsterdam (NL)
Nathalie AUSSENAC-GILLES   IRIT- CNRS Toulouse (F)
Brigitte BIEBOW   LIPN, Université Paris-Nord (F)
Joost BREUKER   University of Amsterdam (NL)
Olivier CORBY   INRIA-Sophia-Antipolis (F)
Paul COMPTON   University of New South Wales (AU)
Ying DING   Free University of Amsterdam (NL)
Rose DIENG   INRIA-Sophia-Antipolis (F)
John DOMINGUE   Open University (UK)
Jerôme EUZENAT   INRIA Rhône-Alpes, (F)
Dieter FENSEL   Free University of Amsterdam (NL)
Mariano FERNANDEZ-LOPEZ   Universidad Politécnica de Madrid (ES)
Yolanda GIL   ISI, University of Southern California (USA)
Nicola GUARINO   Consiglio Nazionale delle Ricerche (I)
Udo HAHN   Universitaet Freiburg (D)
Knut HINKELMANN   University of Applied Sciences Solothurn (CH)
Catholinj JONKER   Free University of Amsterdam (NL)
Rob KREMER   University of Calgary (CA)
Frank MAURER   University of Calgary (CA)
Robert MEERSMAN   Free University Brussels (BE)
Riichiro MIZOGUCHI   Osaka University (JP)
Martín MOLINA   Universidad Politécnica de Madrid (ES)
Hiroshi MOTODA   Osaka University, (JP)
Enrico MOTTA   Open University (UK)

Mark MUSEN	Stanford University (USA)
Daniel E. O'LEARY	University of Southern California (USA)
Enric PLAZA I CERVERA	Spanish Scientific Research Council, CSIC (ES)
Ulrich REIMER	Swiss Life (CH)
Chantal REYNAUD	University of Nanterre, Univ. of Paris-Sud (F)
Alfonso RODRIGUEZ	Universidad Politécnica de Madrid (ES)
François ROUSSELOT	LIIA-ENSAIS, University of Strasbourg (F)
Marie-Christine ROUSSET	University of Paris-Sud (F)
Guus SCHREIBER	University of Amsterdam (NL)
Nigel SHADBOLT	University of Southampton (UK)
Derek SLEEMAN	University of Aberdeen (UK)
Rudi STUDER	University of Karlsruhe (D)
Mike USCHOLD	Boeing (USA)
Frank VAN HARMELEN	Free University of Amsterdam (NL)
Gertjan VAN HEIJST	Oryon KMD BV (NL)
Mike WOOLDRIDGE	University of Liverpool (UK)

Tutorial and Workshop Chair
Mariano Fernández López   Universidad Politécnica de Madrid (Spain)

Demo Chair
Óscar Corcho   Universidad Politécnica de Madrid (Spain)

Local Organizers
Asunción Gómez-Pérez (UPM)
Mariano Fernández-López (UPM)
Óscar Corcho (UPM)
Ángel López Cima (UPM)
Socorro Bernardos Galindo (UPM)
José Ángel Ramos Gargantilla (UPM)

Additional Reviewers

Harith Alani	Koichi Hayashi	Heiner Stuckenschmidt
Trevor Bench Capon	Yannis Kalfoglou	Arthur Stutt
Mercedes Blázquez	Hideaki KANAI	Kaoru Sumi
Peter Brockhausen	Yoshinobu Kitamura	Valentina Tamma
Jeen Broekstra	Manuel Lama Penin	Rainer Telesko
Robert Colomb	Jerome Lang	Farouk Toumani
Ernesto Compatangelo	Peter Lucas	Raphaël Troncy
Jesús Contreras	Ralf Molitor	Maria Vargas-Vera
Oscar Corcho	Kieron O'Hara	Robert Woitsch
Antoine Cornuejols	Juan Pazos	Tetsuya Yoshida
Monica Crubezy	Stephen Potter	Daniela Zbinden
Martin Dzbor	Luc Schneider	Jijuan Zheng
Pete Edwards	Stefan Schulz	
Aldo Gangemi	Peter Spyns	
Nick Gibbins	Steffen Staab	
Siegfried Handschuh	Martin Staudt	
Steve Harris	Ljiljana Stojanovic	

EKAW 2002 Sponsors

Universidad Politécnica de Madrid (UPM) http://www.upm.es/	
Facultad de Informática, UPM http://www.fi.upm.es/	
iSOCO (Intelligent Software Components, S.A.) http://www.isoco.com/	
Ministerio de Ciencia y Tecnología http://www.mcyt.es/	
OntoWeb http://www.ontoweb.org/	
AAAI (American Association for Artificial Intelligence) http://www.aaai.org/	
IBROW http://www.swi.psy.uva.nl/projects/ibrow/home.html	

Table of Contents

Ontologies

Semantic Web

Invited Paper

Extending a Lexical Ontology by a Combination of Distributional Semantics Signatures*

Enrique Alfonseca[1] and Suresh Manandhar[2]

[1] Ingeniería Informática, Universidad Autónoma de Madrid, 28049 Madrid, Spain.
Enrique.Alfonseca@ii.uam.es
[2] Computer Science Department, University of York, YO10 5DD York, U.K.
suresh@cs.york.ac.uk

Abstract. Ontologies are a tool for Knowledge Representation that is now widely used, but the effort employed to build an ontology is high. We describe here a procedure to automatically extend an ontology such as WordNet with domain-specific knowledge. The main advantage of our approach is that it is completely unsupervised, so it can be applied to different languages and domains. Our experiments, in which several domain-specific concepts from a book have been introduced, with no human supervision, into WordNet, have been successful.

1 Introduction

Lexical semantic ontologies are now widely used for Natural Language Processing, and several of them are available for English and other languages, such as WordNet [Miller, 1995] and EuroWordNet [Vossen, 1998]. However, they are usually very general, and their enrichment with domain-specific information requires a high degree of supervision. This has motivated the appearance of knowledge acquisition methods for building domain-specific ontologies automatically.

Maedche and Staab [2001] define *Ontology Refinement* (OR) as the adaptation of an ontology to a specific domain or to some user's requirements, without altering its overall structure. An important problem inside OR is the placement of the domain-dependent concepts in the ontology. Applied to lexical ontologies, if we have an ontology $\mathcal{W}$ and a set of domain-specific documents $\mathcal{D}$ containing some unknown concepts and instances $\mathcal{U} = \{u_1, u_2, ..., u_n\}$, we have to find, for every unknown concept or instance u_i, its maximally specific hypernym s_i in the ontology.

This paper reports a system that extended WordNet with new synsets learnt both from Tolkien's *The Lord of the Rings* and Darwin's *The Voyages of the Beagle*. The unknown concepts that were learnt include locations, rivers, seas, animals, races and people. The classification of these concepts in the taxonomy is performed in a fully unsupervised way. The only input it requires is an initial ontology (we use WordNet) and a collection of documents. It will find unknown

---

* This work has been partially sponsored by CICYT, project number TIC2001-0685-C02-01.

A. Gómez-Pérez and V.R. Benjamins (Eds.): EKAW 2002, LNAI 2473, pp. 1–7, 2002.
© Springer-Verlag Berlin Heidelberg 2002

concepts in the documents and attach them to WordNet. We show that a Distributional Semantic (DS) model can be a good starting point for locating the right places in the ontology for placing the learnt synsets, and we present a way in which different DS metrics can be combined.

1.1 Related Work

We can group related systems in two groups. *Deterministic systems* are those that provide, for each unknown concept, one or several hypernyms all of which are supposedly correct. One of such systems, described by Hearst [1998], obtains regular expression patterns from free texts by looking at pairs of (hypernym, hyponym) that co-occur in the same sentence, and then uses them to learn new hypernymy relations. However, she notes that these extracted relations contain a high degree of noise. Kietz et al. [2000] quantified the error rate of hand-coded patterns as 32%, so he concludes that the concepts had to be ultimately revised and placed in the hierarchy by the user. A different approach is that described by Grefenstette and Hearst [1992].

Non-deterministic systems are those that provide a set of likely candidates, only some of which are correct. Hastings [1994] describes one such framework, Camille, that learns nouns and verbs. He has beforehand concept ontologies for nouns and verbs about the terrorist domain, and verbs are annotated with selectional preferences, e.g. the object of *arson* is known to be a *building*. If an unknown word was found being the direct object of *arson*, it can thus be classified as a building. Hahn and Schnattinger [1998] describes a similar approach. These systems do not return a single hypernym, but a set of plausible hypotheses.

2 Algorithm

Our aim is the enrichment of WordNet with new concepts learnt from general-purpose texts. Let us suppose that we have found a new term u that is not in WordNet. The aim is to find the place where it should be attached to the ontology. The algorithm we use performs a top-down search along the ontology, and stops at the synset that is most similar to u. The search starts at the most general synset s, and compares u with s and with all its immediate hyponyms. If s is more similar to u than any of s's children, then u is classified as a hyponym of s. Otherwise, we proceed one step downwards to the most similar hyponym. For a detailed description please refer to [Alfonseca and Manandhar, 2002b].

2.1 Similarity Metrics

The tools we used to compute the semantic distance between synsets are all based on the DS model, which assumes that there is a strong correlation between the semantics of a word and the set of contexts in which that word appears, and which has produced good results when applied to fields such as Information Retrieval and summarisation.

We have used the following tools:

- A *topic signature* of a concept c is the list of the words that simply co-occur with c in the same context (we have used the same sentence), and their frequencies.
- A *subject signature* of a nominal concept c is the list of verbs for which c appears as a subject.
- An *object signature* of a nominal concept c is the list of verbs and prepositions for which c appears as an argument.
- A *modifier signature* of a nominal concept c is the list of adjectives and determiners that modify c inside a Noun Phrase.

The intuition behind our procedures is that, if two words are semantically related, their signatures will also be similar. They can be automatically collected for every concept in an ontology, by collecting documents from Internet and collecting the frequencies as described by Agirre et al. [2000]; therefore, the classification procedure can be made fully unsupervised. As an example, Table 1 shows the highest frequency words in the signatures of the concept *<person>*.

In order to compare the topic signature of an unknown concept u and the signatures of a set of WordNet synsets $\{s_1, s_2, ..., s_n\}$, the raw frequencies of the synsets' signatures have be changed into weights, to decide which words do provide support that they are in the context of a synset, and which ones are equally frequent for all synsets [Alfonseca and Manandhar, 2002b]. In a few words, for each decision of the algorithm, the following steps are followed:

- Take the synsets that will be compared to u.
- For each synset, add up the frequencies of the context vectors of all its hyponyms in WordNet, and smooth the frequencies by adding 1 to every frequency value.
- For each one of them, use the rest as a contrast set to change its frequencies into weights. We have obtained the best results with Xi^2 (see [Agirre et al., 2000]).
- To calculate the similarity between u's list of words and frequencies, and a synset s_i's words and weights, perform the dot product of both vectors [Yarowsky, 1992].

2.2 Combining the Similarity Measures

Each signature (topic, subject, object and modifier) provides different similarity values that have to be combined. Let us suppose that we are classifying an unknown concept u, and that we have n choices to take: $\{s_1, ..., s_n\}$ and m signatures. Let us call $P_{sig_j}(s_i)$ the similarity value obtained from the signature sig_j, normalised so all the similarity values obtained from a given signature sum to 1: $\sum_{i=0}^{n} P_{sig_j}(s_i) = 1$. We combine the metrics with a weighted sum, by giving a weight to each of the kind of signatures: $P(s_i) = \sum_{j=0}^{m} weight_j \cdot P_{sig_j}(s_i)$

The baseline experiment was calculated by giving them the same weight $\frac{1}{m}$. In our experiments, we calculated the weights that produce a weight distribution P that is equidistant to the partial distributions P_{sig_j}. The distance metric

Topic signature			Subject signature			Object signature			Modifier signature		
Word	**Freq**	*weight*	**Word**	**Freq**	*weight*	**Word**	**Freq**	*weight*	**Word**	**Freq**	*weight*
Rights	314	23.16	be	23	0.71	of	77	0.38	innocent	16	8.28
Human	162	12.89	have	14	4.24	to	54	3.15	contact	10	9.51
that	161	0.00	use	10	15.09	for	45	3.31	live	8	3.34
Resources	136	19.19	write	6	20.51	in	29	1.11	own	6	5.62
Irights	109	19.94	live	5	4.59	be	23	0.32	indigenous	6	7.28
Department	102	21.77	make	5	6.37	with	15	0.82	other	5	0
Chromosome	96	24.82	kill	4	24.60	on	14	1.30	same	5	6.70
information	65	11.04	work	4	24.60	from	14	2.23	controlling	5	10.25
Center	63	16.04	hold	3	12.65	that	11	0.00	first	3	7.57
Health	63	15.86	produce	3	5.14	as	10	0.06	human	3	2.76
not	56	0.00	suffer	3	11.29	by	9	0.35	right	3	6.36
has	56	3.75	wish	3	16.56	say	6	12.45	whole	3	6.88
have	55	1.98	get	3	12.65	seek	6	13.41	particular	3	5.15

Table 1. Topic, subject, object and modifier signatures of the concept $<person>$. The words shown are the top frequency words and their weights.

chosen to compare distributions is **relative entropy**, also called **Kullback-Leibler distance**. Therefore, we calculated the weights $weight_j$ such that the final distribution P is equidistant (with the minimal distance) to each weight distributions P_{sig_j}, using $D(p||q)$ as the distance metric. These weights are calculated with a simulated annealing procedure. They are initialised as $\frac{1}{m}$, and then we proceeded changing them, slowing down, until the distances $D(P_{sig_j}||P)$ all converge to the same value (if possible). Finally, the synset chosen by the algorithm is $\text{argmax}_i P(s_i)$. Table 2 shows the similarity metrics produced in the first two decisions when classifying the concept $<orc>$, using the topic, subject and object signatures.

3   Experiments and Results

We have calculated the topic, subject, object and modifier signatures for the top 1,200 synsets of the WordNet taxonomy which is rooted by *entity*. This was done automatically by downloading the documents from Internet using the procedure detailed by Agirre et al. [2000].

For learning some new concepts, the domain-dependent texts were processed with our own *ad hoc* shallow parser, and the most frequent unknown words and sequences of words (collocations) were extracted: a total of 46 concepts that appeared 50 or more times in the texts, so we had enough contextual information to classify them. We also hypothesised that every appearance of an unknown common noun (e.g. hobbit, orc, etc.) refers to the same concept, i.e. that they are not polysemous. This did not always occurred (e.g. in Darwin's text *York Minster* was a person; and *St. Yago* was both a person and a place), so this is a shortcoming that should be addressed in the future.

We have used four different metrics. The first one, *accuracy*, is defined as the portion of correctly classified concepts. We have distinguished two measures of accuracy: *strict accuracy* is the percentage of times that the hypernym proposed by the program was the one we expected (as classified by a human), and *lenient*

synset	First decision: entity synset Id	P_{sig_1}	P_{sig_2}	P_{sig_3}	total	synset	Second decision: being synset Id	P_{sig_1}	P_{sig_2}	P_{sig_3}	total
being, organism	n00002908	0.40	0.23	0.29	0.3207	human	n00005145	0.64	0.80	0.40	0.6161
causal agency	n00004753	0.38	0.24	0.23	0.3121	animal	n00010787	0.24	0.18	0.41	0.2790
location	n00018241	0.11	0.17	0.17	0.1383	host	n01015823	0.00	0.01	0.05	0.0243
body of water	n07411542	0.09	0.12	0.20	0.1112	parasite	n01015154	0.01	0.00	0.04	0.0192
thing (anything)	n03781420	0.00	0.11	0.02	0.0457	flora	n00011740	0.00	0.00	0.04	0.0169
thing (object)	n00002254	0.00	0.11	0.02	0.0442	(34 more)	...	...	...	...	...
(16 more)	...	...	...	...	...						

Table 2. Similarity values for each of the decisions that have been taken when classifying the unknown concept $<orc>$. The similarities correspond to the topic, subject and object signatures (in that order), and the combination of the three of them. In the first place, when deciding between $<entity>$ and its children, the chosen one was $<being,\ life\ form>$. In the second decision, the winner was $<human>$ (both were correct)

Method	Accuracy strict	len.	L.A.	C.D.	C.P.
Uniform	13.04%	23.91%	0.34	71.09%	1.98
Entropy	13.04%	28.26%	0.38	73.44%	1.95

Table 3. Comparison of two methods to combine the results provided by the signatures.

accuracy is the percentage of times that the system proposed a hypernym that can be considered valid, although it is not the best one (e.g. if a *man* was classified as *grown man*).

Other metrics that we can measure on our top-down algorithm are **Correct decisions** (C.D.), the percentage of times that a correct decision was chosen at each iteration of the algorithm; and **Correct position** (C.P.), which measures, at each step in the search, when the different children synsets are ordered according to the signatures, the mean position of the correct one. Ideally, this metric has to be as low as possible. Finally, **Learning Accuracy** [Hahn and Schnattinger, 1998] takes in consideration the distance, in the ontology, between the proposed hypernym and the correct one. Please refer to [Alfonseca and Manandhar, 2002a] for a detailed description.

Keeping constant the number of signatures at three: topic, subject and object, we tried the two methods to combine them: the baseline, using a uniform weight, and the simulated annealing, using relative entropy. Results are displayed at Table 3. The procedure that uses relative entropy to find an *intermediate* distribution improved all the metrics when compared to the uniform weighting.

Next, we tested different combination of the signatures. Table 4(a) shows the results. The signature that produced the worst results was the modifier signature: the learning accuracy is the smallest, and the mean position of the correct concept at each decision is very high, nearly 1.5 over the next mark. Also, when used with the others, the modifier signature greatly degrades the results. A manual examination of the signatures seems to indicate that the modified

Method	Accuracy strict	len.	L.A. C.D.	M.P.
Topic	6.52%	17.39%	0.30 68.21%	2.30
Modifiers	16.28%	21.74%	0.29 62.96%	4.47
Subject	10.87%	23.91%	0.30 68.80%	3.06
Object	17.39%	28.26%	0.38 71.43%	2.63
T+S+O	13.04%	28.26%	0.38 73.44%	1.95
TSOM	10.87%	21.74%	0.35 70.31%	2.00

System	Accuracy strict	lenient	L.A.
T+S+O	28.26%	36.96%	0.44
	single	set	
[Hastings, 1994]	19%	41%	-
Hahn [1998]	21%	22%	0.67
Hahn [1998]-TH	26%	28%	0.73
Hahn [1998]-CB	31%	39%	0.76

Table 4. (a) Results using different signatures. (b) Comparison with related systems.

signature has a low quality, with a high degree of words which are not adjectives. The other three signatures produced acceptable results, and the best mark was attained by combining them all. Most of the errors were produced at the lowest levels of the ontology, when deciding between semantically similar synsets such as <man> and <woman>, for which the context is not much help.

Some characteristics of WordNet complicate the task, such as the fine-grained senses and the lack of multiple inheritance. For example, geographical locations (e.g. continents) are classified as *object*, while political locations (e.g. countries) are classified as *location*. However, the context of these two kinds of entities are very similar, and they are very different to the context of other *objects* such as *artifacts*. Our algorithm "incorrectly" classified concepts such as mountains or woodlands as *locations*.

Table 4(b) shows results obtained by our system, labelled T+S+O, compared to similar work. There are some important differences, and thence the results are not really comparable. First, the ontologies used in each approach are different, which can have dramatic consequences on the evaluation. Secondly, the other systems are not deterministic. In Table 4(b), the column labelled **single accuracy** shows the percentage of outcomes in which the systems returned a unique hypernym and that one was correct (like our own algorithm); and the **set accuracy** is the percentage of times that the system returned several outcomes among which was the correct one.

4 Conclusions

We have presented here a fully unsupervised method for extending lexical ontologies with unknown concepts taken from domain-specific documents. It can be applied to different domains as it is; and, if we have a shallow parser available, to different languages. It allows the attachment of new concepts to any intermediate level in an ontology, not only at the leaves; and it can tackle large ontologies, such as WordNet. It has been used for generating hypermedia courses using text summarisation as described by Alfonseca and Rodríguez [2002].

Compared to previous approaches (c.f. [Hahn and Schnattinger, 1998, Hastings, 1994]), it requires less resources, as all the signatures are collected automatically, and it does not need a previous encoding of selectional restrictions or article scripts.

The main drawback of our system, as it is now, is that the signatures need to have a certain size in order to provide reliable classifications. An unknown concept that only is cited once will provide a signature with at most a few entries, and the classification will probably be wrong, so an open line for future work is to improve it for low-frequency terms. It has also low precision when classifying concepts that are semantically very related, such as *man* and *woman*. Finally, it still cannot discover whether an unknown word is a synonym of a word already in the ontology.

References

E. Agirre, O. Ansa, E. Hovy, and D. Martinez. Enriching very large ontologies using the www. In *Ontology Learning Workshop, ECAI*, Berlin, Germany, 2000.

E. Alfonseca and S. Manandhar. Proposal for evaluating ontology refinement methods. In *Language Resources and Evaluation (LREC-2002)*, Las Palmas, 2002a.

E. Alfonseca and S. Manandhar. An unsupervised method for general named entity recognition and automated concept discovery. In *1st Conf. on Gen. WordNet*, 2002b.

E. Alfonseca and P. Rodríguez. Automatically generating hypermedia documents depending on the user goal. In *Workshop on Doc. Compression, AH-2002*, 2002.

G. Grefenstette and M.A. Hearst. Method for refining automatically-discovered lexical relations: Combining weak techniques for stronger results. In *Weir (ed.) Statistically based natural language programming techniques, Proc. AAAI Workshop*, 1992.

U. Hahn and K. Schnattinger. Towards text knowledge engineering. In *AAAI/IAAI*, pages 524–531, 1998.

P. M. Hastings. *Automatic acquisition of word meaning from context*. University of Michigan, Ph. D. Dissertation, 1994.

M. A. Hearst. *Automated Discovery of WordNet Relations. In Christiane Fellbaum (Ed.) WordNet: An Electronic Lexical Database*, pages 132–152. MIT Press, 1998.

J. Kietz, A. Maedche, and R. Volz. A method for semi-automatic ontology acquisition from a corporate intranet. In *Workshop "Ontologies and text", EKAW'2000*, 2000.

A. Maedche and S. Staab. Ontology learning for the semantic web. *IEEE Intelligent systems*, 16(2), 2001.

G. A. Miller. WordNet: A lexical database for English. *Communications of the ACM*, 38(11):39–41, 1995.

P. Vossen. *EuroWordNet - A Multilingual Database with Lexical Semantic Networks*. Kluwer Academic Publishers, 1998.

D. Yarowsky. Word-sense disambiguation using statistical models of roget's categories trained on large corpora. In *Proceedings of COLING-92*, pages 454–460, 1992.

Acquiring Knowledge and Numerical Data to Support CBR Retrieval

Stefania Bandini, Sara Manzoni, and Fabio Sartori

Department of Computer Science, Systems and Communication (DISCo)
University of Milan - Bicocca
via Bicocca degli Arcimboldi, 8
20126 - Milan (Italy)
tel +39 02 64487857 - fax +39 02 64487839
{bandini, manzoni, fabio.sartori}@disco.unimib.it

Abstract. This paper illustrates a Knowledge Acquisition and Representation tool (KARM) to support the design in a restricted and specific domain (i.e. the design of tyre treads for motor racing). The main goal of the KARM tool is to allow the acquisition and representation of track knowledge in terms of its morphology, and meteorological features. Two ways to analyze the geometric structure of tracks are combined into KARM; the first one is based on the acquisition and representation of qualitative knowledge (the *block view technique*), while the second one is based on the analysis of quantitative knowledge (*P–Race Telemetry*). Moreover, two fuzzy based modules that allow the representation of uncertain and imprecise knowledge about weather and asphalt conditions will be pointed out.

1 Introduction

The process of acquiring and modelling core knowledge concerning a specific domain is a very important research topic. Many Knowledge Based Systems (KBS) have been developed to deal with several knowledge fields [10], but the phase of knowledge acquisition and representation is still the main problem of this type of tools [7]. Knowledge engineering methodologies, such as CommonKADS [1] and MIKE [2], have been proposed as standard and generalized solutions to solve this problem.

Anyway, the knowledge acquisition and representation tasks can often be tackled more precisely with specific tools, due to the specific nature of involved knowledge, that can not always be captured exploiting methodologies designed for heterogeneous domains.

This paper presents the Knowledge Acquisition and Representation Module (KARM) of P–Race [3], a system based on CBR [11] technology that supports the experts (i.e. *race engineers* and *compound designers*) of an enteprise providing tyres to motor racing teams. *Race engineers* analyze the track where a race will take place and make assumptions about its geometric profile and conditions, in order to obtain a characterization of the circuit from the tyre wear point of view.

A. Gómez-Pérez and V.R. Benjamins (Eds.): EKAW 2002, LNAI 2473, pp. 8–13, 2002.

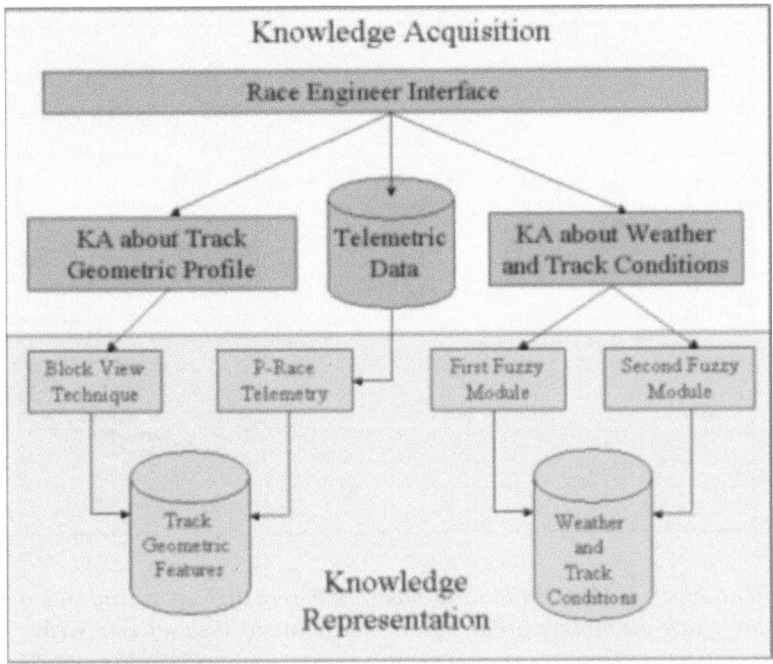

Fig. 1. *The general architecture of KARM*

Compound designers exploit race engineer considerations to design the rubber compounds to be adopted for a given race. Motor racing is a very dynamic field: track geometric features and conditions change frequently (e.g. due to the adoption of new safety rules), and so the knowledge on them. Thus, a KBS to support the activity of race engineers and compound designers must guarantee easy and continuous knowledge acquisition and representation.

The general architecture of KARM (see Figure 1) includes a graphical interface devoted to acquire knowledge of race engineers, and two modules for the representation of knowledge on track geometric features and track conditions. The description of track morphology is based on the *block description*: a block is an abstraction of a significant sector from the tyre wear point of view. This description can be made by the race engineer (*block view technique*) or through a numerical method based on car performance data (*P–Race Telemetry*).

In order to acquire and represent the qualitative and uncertain knowledge concerning track conditions, two fuzzy based modules are important components of KARM. The use of fuzzy techniques to acquire and represent knowledge in CBR systems has been widely adopted in many knowledge fields, as weather prediction [9], finance [6], traffic control [8] and so on. In the case of the motor racing domain, the integration of KARM into the P–Race system allows the use

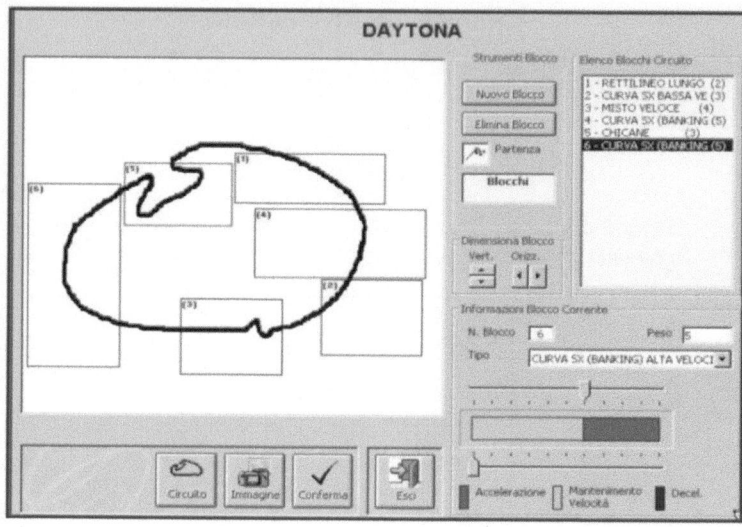

Fig. 2. *The block view technique: a block is a rectangle pointing out a relevant part of the track geometric profile, from the point of view of tyre wear.*

of race engineer knowledge in the computation of similarity among tracks, in order to retrieve solutions to old problems and to adapt them to new situations.

2   Acquisition and Representation of Knowledge about Geometric Features of Tracks

The definition of the geometric profile of a track is based on the so called *block description*: a track is an ordered set of blocks, each one representing a relevant part of it. The block decomposition of a track can be based on both qualitative (*block view technique*) and quantitative (*P–Race Telemetry*) approaches: in the first case the knowledge source is the race engineer, in the second one it is a set of numerical data acquired through a telemetering system.

A block is mainly characterized by two attributes: *type* and *weight*. *Type* reflects the morphologic nature of the block and can assume one of a given set of values (e.g. straight, left bend, right bend, chicane and so on). *Weight* is an integer value expressing an evaluation of the wear suffered by tyres on the block, on a range from 1 (very low influence) to 5 (very high influence). Block view technique and P–Race Telemetry value these parameters in a different way. In the first case, the expert exploits a graphical interface (Figure 2) to directly identify the most significant blocks of the track. According to its own experience, the race engineer estimates the attributes type and weight.

In the second case, P–Race Telemetry creates a block description of tracks based on the concept of *Curvature*. Curvature in a point of the track is the value

$\frac{a_y}{v^2}$, where a_y and v are respectively the tangential acceleration and the speed of a car in that point, and they are observed by a telemetering system. According to the value of curvature, P–Race Telemetry can value both the attribute type (the curvature of a straight is approximately null, the one of a bend has an absolute value greater than zero) and the attribute weight (the greater is the curvature of a block, the greater is its influence on tyre wear). P–Race Telemetry manages blocks as sequences of points with similar curvature values: a mathematical formula based on the mean deviation is used to determine if a point of the track belongs to a block, comparing its curvature with the curvature of the block.

The representation of knowledge aims to define the relation between track and tyre wear, exploiting the block description obtained during the knowledge acquisition phase. To this aim, KARM builds the track *block typologies*, classifying blocks according to their type. Then, KARM evaluates the influence of each block typology on tyre wear, as the mean value of the weight of all blocks belonging to it. The result of this representation is a qualitative characterization of track geometric structure from the tyre wear point of view.

3 Acquisition and Representation of Knowledge about Weather and Track Conditions

The simple morphologic description is not sufficient to completely characterize the main features of a track. Climatic and geographic characteristics of the track or the nature of its asphalt are important sources of information too. A fuzzy based system, shown in Figure 1, has been designed and implemented for acquiring and representing knowledge on these topics.

The acquisition of knowledge is focused on five parameters: *asphalt conditions, weather conditions, asphalt temperature, type of asphalt* and *weather conditions*.

KARM uses *linguistic variables* to represent each of them: a graphical interface allows the user to input the values. By using sliding cursors a race engineer can indicate a qualitative value for each input, within an integer range. A set of fuzzy rules implementing a *concept frame* transforms the final position of the cursor in a linguistic value. A *concept frame* for a linguistic variable *var* is the pair (U_{var}, C_{var}), where U_{var} is the range of possible values a race engineer can assign to it (i.e. the position of the sliding cursor) and C_{var} (conceptual domain) is the set of linguistic values the variable can assume. The binding between a value of U and a point of C is given by one or more *fuzzy sets* (i.e. *membership functions*). The conceptual domain is the union of all fuzzy sets defined for a specific variable.

The fuzzy system is composed of two modules: every module is a set of rules activated by a set of conditions. The first fuzzy module helps race engineers to choose the best type of tyres (slick, intermediate or rain) for a race. The choice is made on the basis of track and weather conditions. The second fuzzy module determines the level of wear (very low, low, medium, high, very high)

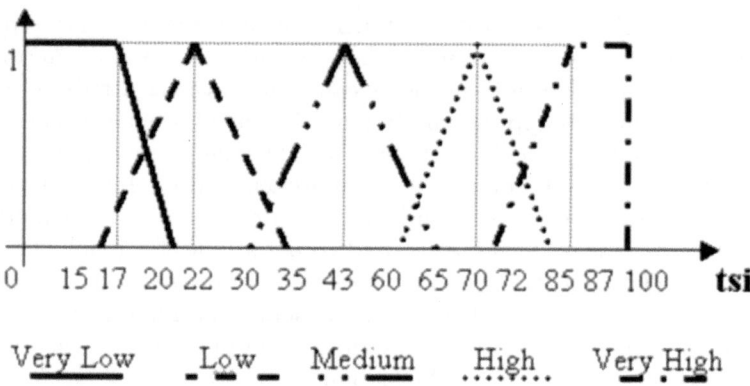

Fig. 3. *Concept frame of the linguistic variable representing thermal severity index*

suffered by tyres because of the track influence, according to asphalt type, asphalt temperature and weather conditions.

Two other linguistic variables allow KARM to represent the type of tyre and thermal severity index. Figure 3 shows an example of the concept frame related to the linguistic variables adopted by KARM.

4   Concluding Remarks

The P–Race system is the result of a project deriving from the co-operation between the *Department of Computer Science, Systems and Communication* of the *University of Milano - Bicocca* and the *Motorsports Department* of *Pirelli Tyres*. It is currently in use and supports the decision making process for the main championships in which Pirelli provides tyres to racing teams.

The modular architecture of the P–Race system is characterized by a set of components dedicated to specific tasks. The KARM module presented in this paper is an example of such modules. Another significant example is the *Adapter Module* [4], that supports compound designers in the chemical formulation.

The most significant benefit derived from the development of KARM is the possibility to provide a good characterization of tracks when either qualitative or quantitative information on them are available. In the former case, the block view technique provides a very detailed level of expressivity in the description of track profile features, modelling the core knowledge of a race engineer. In the latter case, P–Race Telemetry and the analysis of car performance data give a user independent geometric representation of tracks. Other important features of KARM can be summed up as follows:

– the combination of fuzzy techniques and CBR approach [5] allows the P–Race system to design a similarity relationship among tracks, helping the

user to choose the right rubber compounds for a race on the basis of solutions adopted in the most similar past events;
- the integration of KARM with the CBR core of the P–Race system allows the use of track knowledge representation (i.e. *block description, type of tyre* and *thermal severity index*) during the retrieval phase: different tracks from the geometric profile standpoint may be similar because of weather or asphalt conditions;
- the characterization of tracks is a subjective task: race engineers may have different opinions about it, so one or more meetings among race engineers are usually necessary to reach a common point of view. KARM is a useful tool to be used during these meetings that provides a standard representation of track knowledge;
- the KARM approach could be applied to the description of racing paths different from tracks, in order to support the design of rubber compounds for other types of competition (e.g. *rallies*).

References

1. Akkermans, H., de Hoog, R., Shreiber, A., van de Velde, W.,Wielinga, B., *CommonKADS: A Comprehensive Methodology for KBS Development*, IEEE Expert, pp 28-37, 1994.
2. Angele, J., Fensel, D., Studer, R., *Developing Knowledge-Based Systems with MIKE*, Journal of Automated Software Engineering, 1998.
3. Bandini, S., Manzoni, S., *A Knowledge-Based System for the Design of Rubber Compounds in Motor Racing*, Proceedings of 14th European Conference on Artificial Intelligence (ECAI) 2000, W. Horn (ed.), IOS Press, Amsterdam, 2000.
4. Bandini, S., Manzoni, S. *CBR Adaptation for Chemical Formulation*, in Aha, D.W., Watson, I. & Yang, Q. (Eds.), Proceedings of the 4th International Conference on Case Based Reasoning (ICCBR01), *Case–Based Reasoning Research and Development*, LNCS/LNAI 2080, Springer Verlag, 2001.
5. Bandini, S., Manzoni, S., *Application of Fuzzy Indexing and Retrieval in Case Based Reasoning for Design*, Proceedings of the 2001 ACM Symposium on Applied Computing (SAC), March 11-14, 2001, Las Vegas, NV, USA, ACM, 2001, pp 462-466.
6. Bonissone, P. P., Cheetham, W., *Financial Application of Fuzzy Case-Based Reasoning to Residential Property Valuation*, Proceedings of the 6th IEEE International Conference on Fuzzy Systems, Vol. 1, pp 37-44, 1997.
7. Cairò, O., *The KAMET Methodology: Contents, Usage and Knowledge Modeling*, in Gaines, B. and Mussen, M. (eds.), Proceedings of the 11th Banff Knowledge Acquisition for Knowledge-Based Systems Workshop (KAW'98), SRGD Publications, Department of Computer Science, University of Calgary, Proc-1, pp 1-20, 1998.
8. Gomide, F., Nakamiti, G., *Fuzzy Sets in Distributed Traffic Control*, 5th IEEE International Conference on Fuzzy Systems - FUZZ-IEEE 96, pp 1617-1623, New Orleans - LA - EUA, 1996
9. Hansen, B.K., Riordan, D., *Weather Prediction Using Case-Based Reasoning and Fuzzy Set Theory*,Workshop on Soft Computing in Case-Based Reasoning, 4th International Conference on Case-Based Reasoning (ICCBR01), Vancouver, 2001.
10. Hayes-Roth, F., Jacobstein, N., *The State of Knowledge Based Systems*, Communications of the ACM, 37(3) March 1994, pp 27-39.
11. Kolodner, J. *Case–Based Reasoning*, Morgan Kaufmann, San Mateo (CA), 1993.

An OO Model for Incremental Hierarchical KA

Ghassan Beydoun

Department of Mathematics and Computer Science
American University of Beirut
850 Third Ave., 18th Floor, New York N.Y. 10022-6297
U.S.A., fax: (219) 583 76 50
ghassan.beydoun@aub.edu.lb

Abstract Using a database management system (DBS) to build a knowledge base system (KBS) is sometimes desirable because DBS systems allow management of large sets of rules, control of concurrent access and managing multiple knowledge bases simultaneously. In this paper, we describe how to build a KBS using a database management system DBMS for its schema evolution ability. This allows the use of an Object Oriented DMBS (OODBMS) to manage the consistency of an incrementally built hierarchical knowledge base (KB). The underlying knowledge representation scheme, which we use, is our Nested Ripple Down Rules (NRDR).

An NRDR KB evolves into a hierarchy of concepts where each concept is defined as a collection of hierarchical rules with exceptions. To modify a concept definition, exception rules are added by a domain expert, they are never deleted or modified. This eases maintenance and development of a concept definition, but may cause inconsistencies to occur in the KB. We analyse the relation between cases and rules as the knowledge base evolves and as these inconsistencies occur. We explore what specific features an OO database model should accommodate to be used to implement an NRDR KB. The aim is that this in turn allows the use of the built-in mechanisms to manage the consistency of an evolving NRDR conceptual hierarchy. The significance of this paper is two folds: first, it describes an efficient mechanism maintaining consistency of an evolving classification hierarchy, using built-in schema evolution features of an OODBMS. Second, it proposes an intelligent interface for an OODBMS, to allow intelligent classification queries over stored objects.

1. Introduction

In [3], we introduced a substantial extension to the incremental knowledge acquisition (IKA) framework of RDR [8], Nested Ripple Down Rules (NRDR). NRDR eases the IKA process by allowing experts to introduce their own terms, and operationalise these terms while they are incomplete. The resultant NRDR KB is a conceptual hierarchy, where a concept (term) introduced by an expert is defined by a set of rules. NRDR addresses RDR's inability to uncover the underlying domain model used by the expert [9].

Interactions between NRDR concepts add extra effort in maintaining an NRDR knowledge base. In [4], we provided a probabilistic analysis to quantify this added effort. We showed that it quickly decreases as the accuracy of the knowledge base increases. In this paper, we describe how OO technology can be used to manage this

A. Gómez-Pérez and V.R. Benjamins (Eds.): EKAW 2002, LNAI 2473, pp. 14-20, 2002.

effort to deal with NRDR inconsistencies. We observe that NRDR concepts can be viewed as classes in an object-oriented database. In turn, instances of any NRDR concept are viewed as objects belonging to different classes simultaneously. These objects migrate between classes in (during the development of NRDR KB), and they potentially become inconsistent with respect to past classifications by the expert. Problematic objects can then be detected by an NRDR interface over an OO Database system with which can accommodate the dynamic relation between instances and their descriptions. Existing NRDR development policies [6] are enforced by the interface.

We illustrate our ideas in the domain of fitting Air Conditioning (AC) systems. This task normally requires the expertise of AC engineers who consider the specification of the AC system, the space features and the user requirements. They then decide whether or not the AC system can fulfil the user requirements in the given space.

2. Constructing Class Hierarchies with NRDR

Experts struggle to express themselves as they explain (justify) their expertise. To ease this difficulty experts use intermediate abstractions that they (re) use in further explanations. For example in chess, experts introduce notions like *"centre development"* to justify some of their opening moves. When asked to explain such intermediate concepts, experts often fail to provide a complete explanation that always covers their use, instead they provide an operational solution sufficient for the purpose of explaining the context on hand. Moreover, expert articulation of intermediate concepts may depend on his articulation of other concepts, which may not yet be made explicit or completely defined. NRDR adapts the incremental KA process to match the expert's natural tendencies, in introducing explanatory intermediate terms. This enables the expert more easily to express his/her knowledge and to build an operational KB more effectively.

To represent every concept in NRDR, an RDR tree is used, to allow experts to deal with exceptions and refine the definition of their concepts readily. The root node of the tree contains the default rule: "If *true* then *default conclusion*". Every case classification starts at this root node. Every other rule can have

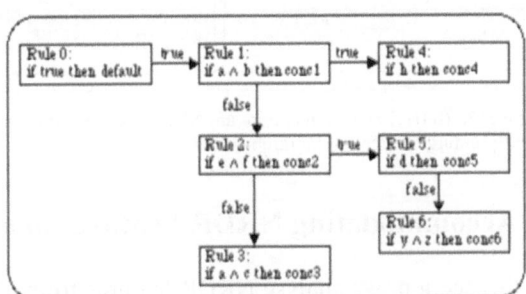

Figure 1. An RDR tree. Rules 1, 2, 3 are exceptions of rule 0.

two branches to other rules: a false-branch and a true-branch (figure1). The true branch of a rule is taken if its condition is satisfied, otherwise the false branch is taken. This is repeated until a terminal node *t* is reached. If the condition of *t* is satisfied then the conclusion of the rule in *t* is returned. If the condition of an exception rule (true-branch child rule) is satisfied it overrides the conclusion of its parent rule. If a false-branch leads to a terminal node *t,* and the condition of *t* is not fulfilled, then the conclusion of the last rule satisfied on the path to t is returned by the KB. When the expert disagrees with the returned conclusion, the KB is said to *fail* and requires modification. An RDR tree is incrementally constructed by adding new leaf nodes when the expert wants to correct a KB failure. Rules are never deleted or modified. Child nodes are treated as exceptions to the parent rule, each rule has only a local effect, which simplifies the KA process.

Conclusions of rules in an NRDR concept (RDR tree) have a boolean value indicating whether or not the concept is satisfied by a given case. Defined concepts can in turn be used as higher order attributes by the expert to define other concepts. No recursive or circular definition of concepts are allowed. The concept hierarchy of our NRDR example is also shown in figure 2 (right) where A is the highest level concept. An NRDR KB is said to fail and requires modification if the expert disagrees with the conclusion returned by any of its RDR trees. Two maintenance issues arise here: firstly, given a case that requires an NRDR KB to be modified, the modification can occur in a number of places. The choice of refinement depends on the expert's judgment. Secondly, localized updates in the hierarchical KB can cause the expert to inadvertently introduce inconsistency to the KB with respect to past seen cases. For example, if the expert modifies the RDR tree of a concept D which is used in the definition of a higher concept A, this may cause classification of past seen cases by A to change. Following every KB update, inconsistencies are checked and have to be fixed by the expert. In the next section, we discuss what features an OO model should have to allow implementing NRDR concepts.

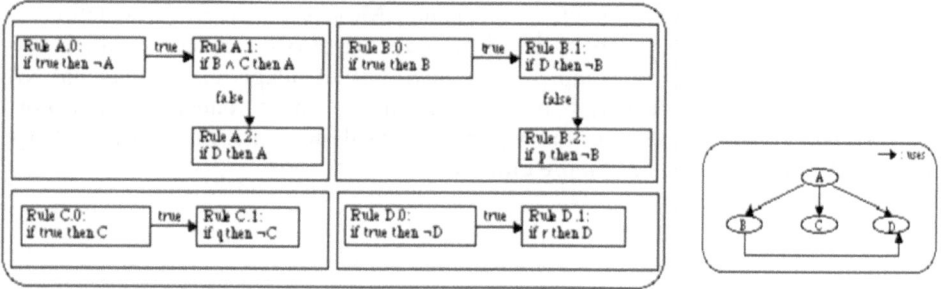

Figure 2. (left) Each concept in an NRDR KB is represented as a separate RDR tree. **(right)** The corresponding conceptual hierarchy.

3. Accommodating NRDR Features in an Object Orient Model

In this section, we analyse NRDR features from a semantic and structural point view. That is, we overview the entities which constitute an NRDR knowledge base, and we explore the relation between these entities as the knowledge base is developed. In particular, relations between cases and rules in an NRDR knowledge base are analysed and mapped to an OO framework.

Unlike RDR, in NRDR, the scope[1] of a rule is not stable [6]. Cases in the scope of the rule can travel as the condition of the rule changes due to an update elsewhere

---

[1] The scope of a rule is the set of cases for which the condition of the rule is satisfied during the usage of the KB. These cases are used to maintain the KB consistent.

in the KB. As a case is classified by an expert, the case can be given more than one description. That is, the same case can belong to scopes of different rules simultaneously, where these rules belong to different concepts (corresponding to the different descriptions given by the expert). Modeling NRDR concepts as classes in an OO system requires a similar dynamic relation between classes and objects. Indeed the view of an object as modeling a world entity and a class as a fixed set of these entities is to be revisited. In modeling our NRDR concepts, classes must describe facets or views of the world which are liable to change and are context dependent. For example, a staff member at a university may also be a student. The class hierarchy no longer should describe relations between the world entities. Instead the class hierarch is a reflection of the way we conceptualise the world, and this class hierarchy depends on the designer of the hierarchy in as much as it depends on the world. This is consistent with the situated view of knowledge as articulated in [7].

This view of classes is evident in modern object oriented database systems, which accommodate features to allow for changes in the class hierarchy during the lifetime of the database. Such systems also accommodate a dynamic relationship between objects and classes. These features are often bundled under the facility of *Schema Evolution* of a database management system. For example in the OO database management system, F2 [2], an object can belong to many classes simultaneously. Such objects are called *multi-objects*. Each object of a multi-object $M_o = \{o_{C1}, o_{C2}, ..., o_{Cn}\}$, M_o, denotes a facet of the entity and carries data specific to its corresponding class Ci. If an entity possesses an object in a class C, then it entity also possesses objects for all the ancestors (direct and indirect superclasses) of C. A case can be described by any concept in an NRDR KB, so a case is viewed as a multiobject.

The relation between objects and classes can further be conditioned by special symbolic rule of the form *"if condition then object belongs"* which are called *specialization constraints*. This feature is also in the schema evolution toolbox of F2. These features make F2 a suitable system which can be used to implement an NRDR KB as we illustrate in the next section.

3.1. NRDR Class Hierarchies in an OO System

In an OO database management system objects are considered at three levels: database objects, schema objects and meta-schema objects. To represent an NRDR class hierarchy, new meta-classes for NRDR concepts and rules are needed. Depending on the system, further meta-classes might be required. In F2, for example, all three meta-classes are required. Introduction of new meta-classes is a routine activity in database systems using a Data Definition Language [1].

An NRDR KA domain, K, becomes in an OO database system a root class D. A case K is an object in D. Each concept in K has a corresponding subclass C in D. Each such C has two boolean attributes: c_{value} and c_{expert}. For each object in D, c_{value} is the answer of the KB, c_{expert} is the answer of the expert. c_{value} values are automatically set by the database system. This behaviour can be implemented by triggers[2] of the classes. c_{expert} values are set by the domain expert. For an object not directly classified by the expert, c_{expert} has an undetermined value. A rule of an NRDR concept is

---

[2] A *trigger* is a procedure which gets executed automatically by a database management system when certain interactions between the user and the system take place.

represented in an OO database management system as a subclass R of C. Condition of this rule is represented by the set of specialization constraints defined on R. The scope of this rule in K is the set of objects that belong to R.

An NRDR concept $C1$ can have a concept $C2$ in the condition of one its rules r. $C1$ is evaluated using backward chaining (see section 2). Correspondingly in an OO database management system, attributes corresponding to the knowledge base classification (e.g c_{value} above) should be automatically maintained. This can be accommodated with existing triggers. A method *UpdateKBAnswer* (object in the meta-class *Method*) that updates the boolean value for the KB answer for a given case is also required.

4. NRDR in Domain of AC Installation

Our task here is to check whether an air conditioner (AC) system is suitable for a given setting. This setting depends on the dimensions and location of the room to be air-conditioned and the manufacturer specification of the available AC system. The KB is developed with the help of an AC installation engineer.

An AC system is suitable to a given room if it can cool the room adequately during the summer at its efficient running capacity. An AC which is too large can be a waste of a budget, and an AC which is too small will not provide adequate cooling. The adequacy of a system depends on inherent features of the system, e.g. its power (measured in B.T.U), it also depends on the room. A larger room or one with a sunny aspect requires an AC with more BTU. Further, some AC systems are designed for heavy duty - non-interrupted running, some are not. Whether heavy duty systems are required or not depends on the aspect and the volume of the space involved. The knowledge of matching an AC to the space requires training and study of the specifications of available AC systems in the market.

An NRDR concept maps to a class in an OO system such as F2, a rule of this concept is mapped to sub-class of is corresponding class. For example: the KB starts with the default rule *"if true then unsuitable"*. In an OO system such as F2, this corresponds to the following initialisation steps:

1. create a class *"unsuitable"* with all available objects added to it.
2. create a sub-class *unsuitable0* for the default rule of the concept *unsuitable*.
Since the default rule is always satisfied, no constraint is required.

Each added class (e.g. *unsuitable*) must have two attributes which correspond to the classification of the KBS and the expert advise. These get compared by a trigger which controls the interface to the database. Following the addition of any class a consistency check is carried out (see section 2).

To acquire the rest of the domain knowledge, we enlist the help of an AC engineer with five years experience who develops our knowledge base. Table 2 shows example training cases. Cases were automatically generated. A subset of these was manually classified by our expert. 40 training cases were randomly sampled for the expert to use to build a classification knowledge base. 100 randomly cases were used for testing. The performance of the system was then monitored by our expert. The expert extends the KB each time he disagrees with the trace (or part of it) returned by the KB.

Case no.	Brea.	Length	volume	Aspect	location	year	make	power
1	5	2	30	North	0	2000	Fugistu	3000
2	5	6	90	East	4	2001	Ge	3000
3	3	5	45	East	2	1999	Fugistu	6000
4	3	4	36	North	5	1999	Fugistu	6000
5	5	2	30	South	7	2002	Fugistu	12000
6	4	6	72	West	9	2002	Fugistu	9000

Table 1. Subset of AC cases. Each case is two parts, the first part contains the specification of the setting (location dimension, volume, aspect and height within the building. The second part contains features of the AC (its make, year and power).

It should be noted that the domain model here is simplified. For instance, attributes with respect to location have been simplified, they could potentially include architectural aspects of the building. The specification of the available AC's can also be extended and made to be interfaced to a database of commercial systems. Instead of a room denoting the space to be air-conditioned, a building with its specification can be used in the cases representation. These extensions would make the domain substantially more complex and commercially usable. However, our simplified view of the domain illustrates the useability of the NRDR approach by an expert without computing training. The expert was able to introduce intermediate concepts with ease, and the knowledge base matured to 52 rules and 11 concepts. The depth of the hierarchy was 4 at its deepest. The knowledge base results were 98% accurate on 200 randomly chosen cases. In the next section, we conclude this paper with a broad discussion of the work presented and a preview of future possibilities.

5. Discussion and Conclusion

In this paper, we described how to view an incremental knowledge acquisition scheme from a schema evolution perspective in an OO Database System. This scheme, NRDR, guides expert to produce a conceptual hierarchy which reflects their conceptualization of their domain of expertise. Implementing NRDR with an OODBMS results in a generic expert system shell which is completely domain independent. Using such an NRDR implementation for a new domain is a simple a matter of introducing the cases feature-vector representation to the DB system.

From an inheritance perspective, the resultant knowledge representation of NRDR supports multiple inheritance with exceptions (A concept X in an NRDR KB can be used to define a number of high level concepts). From an ontology perspective NRDR is an ontology with two relations between concepts: *Is-A* and order or dependence/priority between concepts which define the NRDR hierarchy. In this limited ontological framework, we contribute to ongoing research of ontologies and multiple inheritance [10]. More specifically, our approach circumvents some of technical challenges by using a mature object oriented technology of existing DBMSs.

From a purely DBMS perpsective, our work extends the services of an OODBMS to allow the capture and sharing of expertise. Building an NRDR KB using different experts is an important possibility which warrants future exploration.

Current extension of this work is extending the domain of air-conditioning system to cover more features concerning location, and building attributes. This will then be sufficiently complex to be of commercial interest and to be also used as a testbed for providing an empirical assessment of incremental KA monitoring technique which we presented in [5]. Further possibilities for future extensions include weighing potentials for our framework as a mediating step for informed labeling for training examples. This is in a wider knowledge refinement framework which can include machine learning as in [11].

Acknowledgment
Implementing the NRDR F2 interface was undertaken in collaboration with L. Al-Jadir and F. Moukadem. This research is supported by the AUB Research Board.

References

1. Al-Jadir, L. and G. Beydoun. *Using F2 OODBMS to Support Incremental Knowledge Acquisition* . in *International Database Engineering & Applications Symposium (IDEAS02)* . 2002. Canada.

2. Al-Jadir, L., *et al. Evolution Features of the F2 OODBMS* in *4th International Conference on Database Systems for Advanced Applications (DASFAA95)* . 1995. Singapore: World Scientific.

3. Beydoun, G. and A. Hoffmann. *Acquisition of Search Knowledge.* in *The 10th European Knowledge Acquisition Workshop (EKAW97)* . 1997. Spain: Springer.

4. Beydoun, G. and A. Hoffmann. *A Holistic Approach for Knowledge Acquisition* in *11th European Conference on Knowledge Acquisition and Management (EKAW99)* . 1999. Germany: Springer.

5. Beydoun, G. and A. Hoffmann. *Monitoring Knowledge Acquisition, Instead of Evaluating Knowledge Bases* . in *12th European Conference on Knowledge Acquisition and Knowledge Management (EKAW2000)* . 2000. France: Springer.

6. Beydoun, G. and A. Hoffmann, *Theoretical Basis of Hierarchical Incremental Acquisition.* International Journal of Human Computer Interactions, Academic Press, 2001. 54 (3): p. 407-452.

7. Clancey, W.J., *The Knowledge Level Reinterpreted: Modelling How Systems Interact.* Machine Learning, 1989. 4 : p. 285-291.

8. Compton, P. and R. Jansen. *Knowledge in Context: a strategy for expert system maintenance* . in *Second Australian Joint Artificial Intelligence Conference (AI88)* . 1988.

9. Richards, D. and P. Compton. *Knowledge Acquisition First, Modelling Later* . in *10th European Knowledge Acquisition Workshop (EKAW97)* . 1997. Spain: Springer.

10. Tamma, V.A.M. and T.J.M. Bench-Capon. *Supporting Inheritance Mechanisms in Ontology Representation.* in *12th International Conference on Knowledge Engineering and Knowledge Management (EKAW2000)* . 2000. France: Springer.

11. Wiratunga, N. and S. Craw. *Informed Selection of Training Examples for Knowledge Refinement.* in *12th International Conference on Knowledge Engineering and Knowledge Management* . 2000. France: Springer.

Experiences with Modelling Issues in Building Probabilistic Networks

Linda C. van der Gaag and Eveline M. Helsper

Institute of Information and Computing Sciences, Utrecht University,
P.O. Box 80.089, 3508 TB Utrecht, The Netherlands
{linda,eveline}@cs.uu.nl

Abstract. Building a probabilistic network for a real-life application is a difficult and time-consuming task. Methodologies for building such a network, however, are still lacking. Also, literature on network-specific modelling issues is quite scarce. As we have developed a large probabilistic network for a complex medical domain, we have encountered and resolved numerous non-trivial modelling issues. Since many of these issues pertain not only to our application but are likely to emerge for other applications as well, we feel that sharing them will contribute to engineering probabilistic networks in general.

1 Introduction

More and more knowledge-based systems are being developed that build upon the formalism of probabilistic networks for their knowledge representation. Halfway through the 1990s, we started with the construction of such a system in the field of oesophageal cancer. The system's probabilistic network was built and refined with the help of two experts in gastrointestinal oncology. It captures knowledge about the characteristics of an oesophageal tumour, about the pathophysiological processes underlying the tumour's growth, and about the possible effects of the various available therapies. When a patient's symptoms and test results are entered, the network assesses the stage of the patient's cancer and prognosticates the most likely outcomes for the different treatment alternatives.

Building a probabilistic network involves three basic tasks, for which usually domain knowledge is acquired from experts. As a probabilistic network in essence is a graphical model of a joint probability distribution over a set of statistical variables, the first task in its construction is to identify the important variables to be captured along with the values they may adopt. Once these variables have been decided upon, the relations between them have to be analysed and expressed in a graphical structure. The last task is to assess various numerical probabilities. As building a probabilistic network is a creative process, the three tasks are typically iterated in a cyclic fashion.

For building knowledge-based systems in general, sophisticated knowledge-engineering methodologies are available [1]. Such methodologies are still lacking, however, for building probabilistic networks. Also, literature on network-specific

A. Gómez-Pérez and V.R. Benjamins (Eds.): EKAW 2002, LNAI 2473, pp. 21–26, 2002.

modelling issues is quite scarce. The literature that is available, typically ac-
knowledges the assessment of the probabilities required for a network to be the
most daunting among the three engineering tasks [2]. Moreover, it is often stated
that the construction of the network's graphical part is rather straightforward.
In building the oesophagus network, however, we found that this task can also
be far from trivial. In fact, we had to address various intricate modelling issues.
Some of these were related to engineering knowledge-based systems in general,
but many of them pertained specifically to building probabilistic networks and
were for example related to eliciting and capturing the independences between
the statistical variables. We expect that the modelling issues that we encountered
in the construction of the graphical part of our network are likely to emerge in
other applications as well, and we feel that sharing them will contribute to the
advancement of methodologies for engineering probabilistic networks in general.

The paper is organised as follows. In Section 2, we briefly describe the field
of oesophageal cancer and introduce our probabilistic network. In Section 3, we
review the general set-up of the knowledge-acquisition sessions with our domain
experts. In Section 4, we address some of the modelling issues that we encountered in the construction of the graphical part of the oesophagus network. The
paper ends with our concluding observations in Section 5.

2   The Oesophagus Network

Due to various factors, for example related to drinking and eating habits, a tumour may develop in a patient's oesophagus. This primary tumour has various
characteristics, such as its length, its cell type, and its circumference. The tumour typically invades the oesophageal wall and upon further growth may invade
neighbouring organs. In time, it may give rise to secondary tumours, or metastases. The extent of these metastases and the depth of invasion, summarised
in the cancer's stage, largely influence a patient's life expectancy. These factors
are also important in deciding upon an appropriate therapy from among the
different treatment alternatives. The effects aimed at by these therapies include
improvement of the, often impaired, passage of food through the oesophagus.

The state-of-the-art knowledge about oesophageal cancer and its treatment
has been captured in a probabilistic network. Such a network is a graphical model
of a joint probability distribution over a set of statistical variables [3]. It includes
an acyclic directed graph that models the variables of the distribution by means
of nodes. The arcs in the graph with each other capture the probabilistic independences between the variables: two variables are independent if every chain
between the two variables contains either an observed variable with at least one
emanating arc, or a variable with two incoming arcs such that neither the variable
itself nor any of its descendants in the graph have been observed. With the variables are associated conditional probabilities that describe the strengths of the
influences between the variables. The oesophagus network currently comprises
over 70 statistical variables for which more than 4000 conditional probabilities
have been specified [4].

3   The Set-Up of Knowledge Acquisition

The oesophagus network was built with the help of two experts in gastrointestinal oncology from the Netherlands Cancer Institute, Antoni van Leeuwenhoekhuis. Over a period of more than five years, many knowledge-acquisition sessions were held by a single knowledge engineer, who is the first author of the present paper.

The acquisition was conducted in a cyclic fashion. After each session, the knowledge engineer carefully analysed the elicited knowledge and modelled it, as far as possible, into a segment of the probabilistic network in the making. Upon analysing the elicited knowledge, often various indistinctnesses and gaps were found. The results of the analysis were therefore used as input for the next session that thus started off with a structured interview. The second part of the session consisted of an unstructured interview addressing a new fragment of the experts' domain. This fragment was pre-selected by the knowledge engineer, based upon a tutorial overview given by the two experts in the first session.

During the structured interviews, detailed questions were asked of the domain experts. These questions were sometimes asked directly, such as the precise meaning of a term. More often, however, structured case descriptions were used; we elaborate on the use of such descriptions in Section 4. Also during the structured interviews, the knowledge captured thus far was carefully reviewed. In the early sessions, the graphical structure of the network was used directly as a means for communication between the knowledge engineer and the two domain experts. Unfortunately, however, the experts often appeared to misinterpret the structure. This observation contrasts the literature on probabilistic networks, in which it is commonly suggested that these networks are easy to understand because of their graphical structure [3]. In the later sessions, therefore, the structure of the network was discussed indirectly, once again using case descriptions.

4   Modelling Issues

As we have argued in our introduction, building a probabilistic network for a real-life application involves various engineering tasks. Among these is the task of constructing the network's graphical part, which in essence amounts to identifying the probabilistic independences between the represented variables and capturing them in an acyclic directed graph. In this section, we focus on this task of building the graphical structure and share some of our experiences.

4.1   Causality as a Guiding Principle

Since our domain experts did not have a background in probability theory, eliciting independences from them directly was deemed infeasible. We therefore decided to use a heuristic guiding principle for acquiring knowledge about the relationships between the variables. To this end, we exploited the notion of causality. Typical questions asked during the interviews were "What could cause this effect?" and "What manifestations could this cause have?". The thus elicited causal relations were expressed in graphical terms by taking the direction of causality for directing the arcs between the variables. The notion of causality appeared to match our experts' way of thinking about tumour growth and about the effects of the various treatment alternatives. Since it was used merely as a guiding principle during knowledge acquisition, the resulting graphical structure had to be validated and refined in terms of independence, however. A careful review of the structure proved the heuristic principle to be serviceable.

4.2   Correlations

Our domain of application involved not just causal relations between variables but also relations that could not be interpreted as causal. For example, the location of an oesophageal tumour and its cell type are strongly correlated, yet neither can be considered a cause of the other. Such non-causal relations required a more elaborate analysis before they could be expressed in graphical terms.

The correlation between a tumour's location and its cell type originates from various pathophysiological processes. A tumour in the upper part of the oesophagus, termed a proximal tumour, is generally the consequence of toxic damage of the oesophageal wall. The tumour then consists of the squamous cells that are typical of the oesophageal wall. A tumour in the lower part of the oesophagus, called a distal tumour, usually is the result of frequent reflux which causes gastric juices from the stomach to enter into the oesophagus. The squamous cells of the oesophageal wall are then gradually replaced by the cylindrical cells of which the wall of the stomach is composed. We thus have that proximal tumours generally have squamous cells for their type, and distal tumours have cylindrical cells. As the processes influencing location and cell type are not modelled explicitly in the network, the causalities involved are also not represented.

A correlation between two variables is represented in a network's graphical structure by an arc that in essence can be directed in either way. The two directions may give rise to different independences, however, that must be carefully examined before deciding upon the arc's final direction. In our network, the arc between location and cell type could be directed in either way. We decided to point it from location to type. The main consideration underlying our decision was the way the experts talked about their domain. They indicated for example that, for deciding upon a therapy for a patient, the tumour's location is of crucial importance; the cell type is merely a derivative concept.

4.3   Indirect Relations

By building upon the notion of causality, knowledge acquisition was focused on the direct relations between the variables. These relations were then combined into a graphical structure from which indirect relations were read. Figure 1 shows an example segment of the oesophagus network modelling such an indirect relation. It expresses that the length of an oesophageal tumour influences

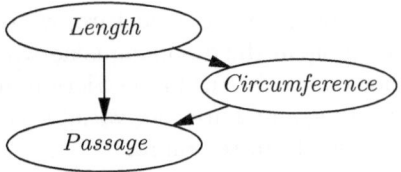

Fig. 1. The influences of the tumour's length on the patient's ability to swallow food

the patient's ability to swallow food, both directly and indirectly through its influence on the tumour's circumference. Such indirect relations had to be carefully reviewed in terms of independence.

The network segment from Figure 1 expresses that the three variables involved are mutually dependent and, moreover, that any two of them remain to be so given an observation for the third one. To validate these dependence statements with our domain experts, we used case descriptions to help them access the relevant knowledge [1,5]. The following case was posed, for example: "Suppose that you have a patient with a circular tumour and that you have made an assessment of this patient's ability to swallow food. Can knowledge of the tumour's length change your assessment?". If the experts would have answered this question in the negative, then the direct relation from the tumour's length to the patient's ability to swallow food would have been a re-statement of the indirect one, and could have been removed from the structure. The experts' responses to the various case descriptions revealed that many of the acquired direct relations were in fact superfluous. Our domain experts apparently had difficulties distinguishing between direct and indirect relations in their domain.

4.4 The Trade-Off between Richness and Efficiency

Building a probabilistic network for a real-life application often requires a careful trade-off between the desire for a large and rich model to obtain accurate results from reasoning on the one hand, and the costs of construction and maintenance as well as the complexity of reasoning on the other hand.

Various considerations may underlie a decision not to incorporate a specific variable or relation in a network under construction. One of these considerations pertains to the feasibility of obtaining all probabilities required. In the oesophagus network, for example, the process by which a tumour gives rise to metastases in a patient's lungs and liver, is not represented explicitly. Modelling this process would have required a new statistical variable that captures whether or not cancer cells are being transported through the blood vessels. However, as it is hardly feasible to establish whether or not cancer cells are present in the blood, the experts cannot have experiential knowledge that would allow for reasonably reliable assessment of the probabilities required. Also, obtaining probabilities for a single variable conditioned on numerous different contexts, in general is highly infeasible. As the number of probabilities for a variable is exponential in its number of predecessors in the graphical structure, we restricted the number of incoming arcs for each variable in the oesophagus network, in close consultation with our experts. Another reason for such a restriction in general is the observation that a large number of incoming arcs per variable contributes exponentially to the computational complexity of reasoning.

5 Conclusions

While for building knowledge-based systems in general sophisticated, detailed knowledge-engineering methodologies are available, no such methodologies exist as yet for addressing the intricate modelling issues to be resolved upon constructing a probabilistic network. As we developed a large probabilistic network for a complex medical domain, we built up some experience with addressing these issues. In this paper, we focused on the construction of the graphical part of our network. In contrast with the suggestion often found in the literature, we noticed that this engineering task can be far from trivial. We handled the various problems that we encountered in various different ways. To support the acquisition of knowledge about the independences between the statistical variables, we exploited the notion of causality. For resolving the detailed modelling issues, we used structured case descriptions. Since we noticed that our experts had difficulties interpreting the graphical structure of our network, we used case descriptions also for reviewing and validating the modelled knowledge. As we expect that many of the issues that we encountered are not restricted to our domain of application but are likely to emerge in other applications as well, we hope that sharing our experiences will contribute to engineering probabilistic networks in general.

Acknowledgements. We are grateful to Babs Taal and Berthe Aleman from the Netherlands Cancer Institute, Antoni van Leeuwenhoekhuis, who provided the domain knowledge for the construction of the oesophagus network.

References

1. G. Schreiber, H. Akkermans, A. Anjewierden, R. de Hoog, N. Shadbolt, W. Van de Velde, B. Wielinga, *Knowledge Engineering and Management: The CommonKADS Methodology*, MIT Press, Cambridge, Massachusetts, 2000.
2. M.J. Druzdzel, L.C. van der Gaag, 'Building Bayesian networks: "Where do the numbers come from?" Guest editors' introduction', *IEEE Transactions on Knowledge and Data Engineering*, **12**, 481 – 486, 2000.
3. F.V. Jensen, *Bayesian Networks and Decision Graphs*, Statistics for Engineering and Information Science, Springer-Verlag, New York, 2001.
4. L.C. van der Gaag, S. Renooij, C.L.M. Witteman, B.M.P. Aleman, B.G. Taal, 'Probabilities for a probabilistic network: a case study in oesophageal cancer', *Artificial Intelligence in Medicine*, **25**, 123 – 148, 2002.
5. A.C. Scott, J.E. Clayton, E.L. Gibson, *A Practical Guide to Knowledge Acquisition*, Addison-Wesley, Reading, Massachusetts, 1991.

IKRAFT: Interactive Knowledge Representation and Acquisition from Text

Yolanda Gil and Varun Ratnakar

USC Information Sciences Institute
4676 Admiralty Way
Marina del Rey, CA 90292
gil@isi.edu, varunr@isi.edu

Abstract. We propose a new approach to develop knowledge bases that captures at different levels of formality and specificity how each piece of knowledge in the system was derived from original sources, which are often Web sources. If a knowledge base contains a trace of information about how each piece of knowledge was defined, it will be easier to reuse, extend, and translate the contents of the knowledge base. We are investigating these issues with IKRAFT, an interactive tool to elicit from users the rationale for choices and decisions as they analyze information used in building a knowledge base. Starting from raw information sources, most of them originating on the Web, users are able to specify connections between selected portions of those sources. These connections are initially very high level and informal, and our ultimate goal is to develop a system that will help users to formalize them further.

1 Introduction

Large knowledge bases contain a wealth of information, and yet browsing through them often leaves an uneasy feeling that one has to take the developer's word for why certain things are represented in certain ways, why other things were not represented at all, and where might we find a piece of related information that we know is related under some context. Although the languages that we use are quite expressive (e.g., KIF, MELD), they still force knowledge into a straightjacket: whatever fits the language will be represented and anything else will be left out. Many other things are also left out, but for other reasons such as available time and resources or perhaps lack of detailed understanding of some aspects of the knowledge being specified. The challenges that arise in understanding, reusing, extending, translating, and merging knowledge bases [Burstein et al 00.; Chalupsky 00; McGuinness] may be due in no small part to the impoverished products that we create as knowledge base developers. When the knowledge base needs to be extended or updated, the rationale for their design is lost and needs to be at least partially reconstructed. The knowledge sources are no longer readily available and may need to be accessed. While it is the case that entire knowledge bases can be reused and incorporated into new systems, it is harder to extract only relevant portions of them that are appropriate in the new application. Parts of the knowledge base may be too inaccurate for the new task, or may need to be

A. Gómez-Pérez and V.R. Benjamins (Eds.): EKAW 2002, LNAI 2473, pp. 27-36, 2002.
© Springer-Verlag Berlin Heidelberg 2002

modeled in a different way to take into account relevant aspects of the new application.

We believe that knowledge bases should contain the fine-grained, detailed analysis, assumptions, and decisions that their developers made during their design. They should record in enough detail what were the original sources consulted, what pieces seemed contradictory or vague, which were then dismissed, what additional hypotheses were formulated in order to complement the original sources. Knowledge engineers have a sense for what topics or areas within the knowledge base they are more confident about, either because they spent more resources developing them, because they found better sources, or because as knowledge engineers had assessed the end result as more complete and consistent.

This information turns out to be also key to put the answers of a knowledge-based system in context. Consider, for example, our experiences with a system to estimate the duration of carrying out specific engineering tasks, such as repairing a damaged road or leveling uneven terrain. Users invariably wanted us to explain where the answers came from in terms of the sources we consulted and the sources that we chose to pursue when they suggested alternative models. They wanted to know whether common manuals and/or sources of expertise were consulted, which were given more weight, whether practical experience was considered to refine theoretical estimates, and what authoritative sources were consulted to design the content of the knowledge base. In other words, the analysis process that knowledge engineers perform during the implementation phase is part of the rationale of a knowledge base, and needs to be captured in order to justify answers to users.

Our goal is to capture the results of analyzing various information sources consulted by knowledge engineers as they design the detailed contents of a knowledge base. This paper presents our work to date on IKRAFT, a tool that enables knowledge base developers to keep track of the knowledge sources and intermediate knowledge fragments that result in a formalized piece of knowledge. The resulting knowledge base is enhanced with pointers that capture the rationale of its development. There are several other potential benefits to including this rationale within a knowledge base, such as supporting its maintenance, facilitating its integration with other knowledge bases, and transferring (and translating) knowledge among heterogeneous systems.

The paper begins motivating our work with a description of how knowledge bases are built. We then describe the approach we are taking in IKRAFT, and show with several examples how users can keep a trail of sources and intermediate knowledge fragments to support each item in the knowledge base. We finalize with a discussion of the implications of the approach and conclude with our plans for future work.

2 Creating a Knowledge Base

In order to illustrate why it is important to capture how each individual piece of knowledge in the knowledge base came about, we use a brief example taken from previous work on building a knowledge base from a chapter of a biology textbook. We describe the process of formalizing knowledge with three steps. These steps can be found in typical descriptions of knowledge engineering [Buchanan et al. 83; Stefik 95; Schreiber et al. 00]. Our description sets aside other steps concerning knowledge base development, such as feasibility studies, integration within the organization, refinement and maintenance. Our focus here is on the steps that involve a single developer set to the task of creating formal definitions given a set of sources that have been previously compiled (through interviews, literature research, or other consultations). We also assume the developer is not following any particular knowledge engineering methodology (such as CommonKADS).

STEP 1: Selecting relevant knowledge fragments

"…The first step a cell takes in reading out part of its genetic instructions is to *copy the required portion of the nucleotide sequence of DNA – the gene – into a nucleotide sequence of RNA. The process is called transcription* because the information, though copied into another chemical form, is still written in essentially the same language – the language of nucleotides. Like DNA, RNA is a linear polymer made of four different types of nucleotides subunits linked together by phosphodiester bonds. It differs from DNA chemically in two respects: (1) the *nucleotides in RNA are ribonucleotides* – that is, they contain the sugar ribose (hence the name ribonucleic acid) rather than deoxyribose; (2) although, like DNA, *RNA* contains the bases adenine (A), guanine (G), and cytosine (C), it *contains uracil (U) instead of the thymine (T)* in DNA. Since U, like T, can base-pair by hydrogen-bonding with A, the base-pairing properties described for DNA also apply to RNA…"

STEP 2: Composing stylized knowledge fragments

- ribose
    - it is a kind of sugar, like deoxyribose
    - it is contained in the nucleotides of RNA
- uracil
    - it is a kind of nucleotide, like adenine and guanine
    - it can base-pair with adenine
- RNA
    - it is a kind of nucleic acid, like DNA
    - it contains uracil instead of thymine
    - it is single-stranded
    - it folds in complex 3-D shapes
    - nucleotides are linked with phospohodiester bonds, like DNA
    - there are many types of RNA
    - RNA is the template for synthesizing protein
- gene : - subsequence of DNA that can be used as a template to create protein
- protein synthesis
    - non-destructive creation process: RNA and protein created from DNA
    - its speed is regulated by the cell
    - substeps: (ordered in sequence)
    1) RNA transcription
        - a DNA fragment (a gene) is copied, just like DNA is copied during DNA synthesis
        - the result is an RNA chain
    2) protein translation
        - RNA is used as a template

STEP 3: Creating knowledge base items

… (defconcept uracil :is-primitive nucleotide :constraints (:the base-pair adenine))
(defconcept RNA :is (:and nucleic-acid (:some contains uracil))) …

Fig. 1. Steps in Creating a Knowledge Base

The steps are illustrated with an example in Figure 1, Here the developer is trying to extract and represent a description of the protein synthesis process through its substeps and the entities that participate in that process.

In the first step, the developer selects original sources (in this case only one is shown, but typically there would be several) and selects from them relevant knowledge fragments. Source text will typically contain the relevant information embedded within details that may be irrelevant to the developer or commentary from the author. In the second step, the developer restates the knowledge fragments in terse English. Typically these new fragments are phrased as unambiguously and briefly as possible. They may be organized in a list of items and sub-items. The developer may combine two or more fragments into one sentence, or break a fragment into several sentences. This step is akin to making a summary when studying for an exam. The developer will often go back to step one to gather more documentation and knowledge fragments as he or she makes sense of the fragments listed. Step two can be done in several iterations, each iteration containing more stylized fragments.

Finally, the third step involves formalizing those fragments into the target language and syntax. Notice that some of the fragments extend existing definitions that are assumed to be already known, and as a result their formalization needs to take into account existing definitions.

Notice that the final formalization of the knowledge does not necessarily contain all the information in the original knowledge fragments selected or in the restated fragments. The developer may decide to formalize only those portions, or perhaps the formal language was not expressive enough to represent certain aspects of the knowledge.

Looking at the figure, it is easy to see where each assertion in the formal definition comes from, what portions of the stylized fragments are formalized, and where in the initial sources the information came from. Unfortunately, the knowledge fragments selected in step one and those composed in step two shown in the figure are never captured in the knowledge base, only the resulting formal definitions included are.

We believe that knowledge bases should include this information, i.e., that the final formalized knowledge items should point back to previous knowledge fragments considered by the developer, and ultimately to the source documents where the knowledge was drawn from. There are many benefits to this approach:

- **Knowledge can be extended more easily.** The formalized, final expressions may not necessarily contain every detail in every knowledge source, but if the need arises the developer is better positioned to track down additional knowledge missing. One could even consider natural language processing tools that would enable the system could use some automated tools to extract that knowledge itself, since it has access to the sources and to stylized fragments that are likely to contain information in the boundaries of the knowledge that was formalized the first time around. Today's knowledge bases are best (more efficiently) extended by their developers.

- **Knowledge can be reused at any level of formality**. Reusing and translating today's knowledge bases means reusing and translating expressions in different formal languages, which can be challenging [McDermott 01; Chalupsky 00]. Here, intermediate knowledge fragments can be reused and formalized in a new language without having to go through the original developer's language as an intermediate step. Moreover, during reuse of intermediate knowledge fragments can be further detailed and extended incorporating other sources to create different final formalized expressions.

- **Knowledge can be integrated and translated at any level to facilitate interoperability**. Translation is often used to enable integration and interoperation among intelligent tools. Today's translation tools have to deal with the different levels of expressivity and modeling styles of the source and target systems. One can envision developing translators that operate (or are supported by) the stylized knowledge fragments, either automatically or semi-automatically depending on the difficulty of the expressions used by the developer. Also, symbols would be annotated with their intended meaning, which is key when two systems may be using the same term differently. The rationale and meaning of different pieces of knowledge can be available to support translation and interoperation.

- **Intelligent systems will be able to provide better justifications**. We find that many users are reluctant to accept the solutions presented by the systems and ask for explanations not of how the system derived an answer automatically but instead ask for explanations of why the system starts out with a certain fact or belief. When users are shown the reasons for certain assumptions and the fact that certain sources were consulted to make that assumption they are reassured in the competence of the system to provide those answers. Capturing this trail within the knowledge base will enable the system to generate these kinds of justifications and explanations.

- **Content providers will not need to be knowledge engineers**. Although only those trained in the art of designing, modeling, and writing formal expressions can write the final formal knowledge items, anyone can contribute to the initial steps of the process. Many people in diverse disciplines acquire the analytical skills that suffice to organize and digest knowledge sources. The intermediate knowledge fragments shown in Figure 2 were not created by a knowledge engineer, one could argue that they may be more reusable than those shown in Figure 1 that were created by a knowledge engineer. In fact, if the knowledge base is in their area of expertise, they are likely do a much better job at re-expressing knowledge items than knowledge engineers. This would make knowledge base creation a true collaboration between domain experts and knowledge engineers where each is contributing at the stages of the process where they have relevant skills.

Protein : - unique amino acid sequence. - this sequence provides it a unique structure.
DNA :   - a sequence of 4 types of nucleotides, linked by phosphodiester bonds.
             - stores genetic information. - double stranded helix
RNA :   - sequence of 4 types of nucleotides linked by phosphodiester bonds,
             - like DNA. - short copies of nucleotide sequence of the DNA.
             - passes genetic information.
Transcription : - Part of DNA is copied to the 'RNA
Translation: - Nucleotide sequence of the RNA generates the protein

---

Fig. 2. Knowledge Fragments that were not created by a knowledge engineer.

3   Overview of IKRAFT

IKRAFT allows users to create new items in the knowledge base from multiple sources, while keeping track of the knowledge sources and intermediate knowledge fragments that were used in deriving the new item.

After collecting enough relevant sources, the user can now make statements to summarize salient parts of the sources with the Statement Editor. This is easily accomplished by highlighting parts of the source (or sources) and summarizing those parts in a statement. Later, when the statement is clicked, the parts in the sources where this information was gathered from are highlighted.

Each statement is parsed by an NLP tagger, which identifies nouns and verbs in the sentence. The nouns are referred as objects, and verbs as events. These objects and events are checked with those in the database. The user is then shown with a list of objects and events which do not occur in the database. They can be defined by the user with the Object Editor. The user is also shown the list of objects which do occur in the database. If the definitions in the database are not what the user wants, then another definition for the same object can be made by the user.

Also, when the user clicks on an object, the statement where the word came from is highlighted. This is useful in finding the context in which the word is used.

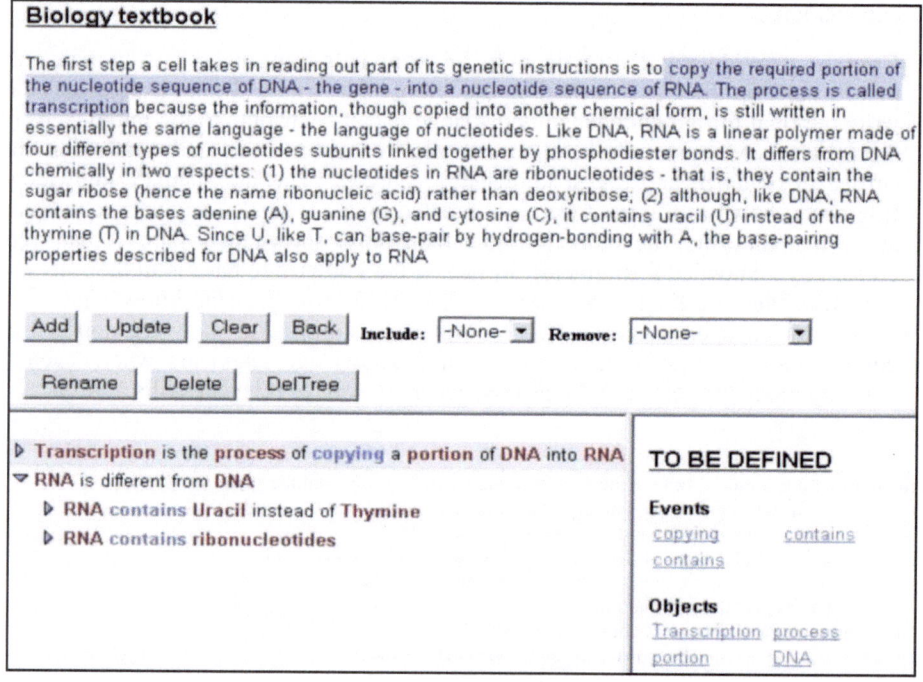

Fig. 3. IKRAFT allows a user to keep track of knowledge sources and intermediate knowledge fragments used in creating a new item in the knowledge base.

Figure 3 shows how the trail of knowledge sources and fragments are captured by IKRAFT as a user represented the scenario described in Figure 1. The knowledge fragments are represented as a collapsible tree structure of statements in the bottom left frame. The objects that have to be defined, and those that are already defined (not visible) are shown in the bottom right frame.

Our current prototype implementation addresses steps 1 and 2 in Fig 1. Supporting the formalization stage (step 3 in Fig 1) will be addressed by future work.

4   Using IKRAFT

In this section, we show an example created using IKRAFT. It is summarized in Figures 4 and 5.

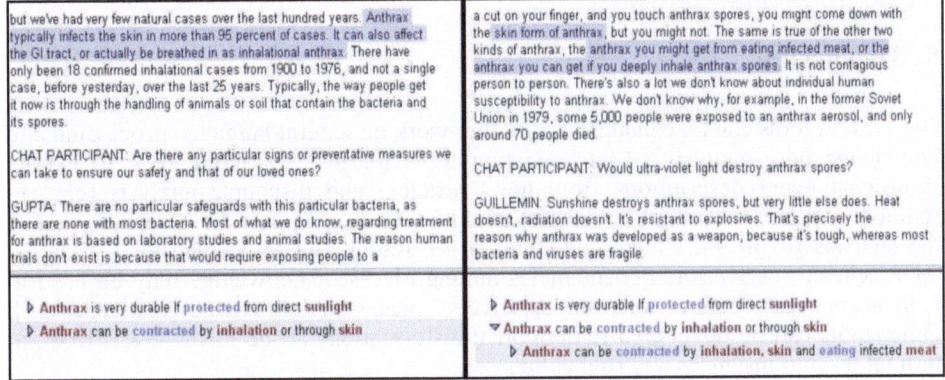

Fig. 4. Demonstrating supplementary information from different sources

This example displays a user trying to find out more about Anthrax. The user has three different sources of information. The first one is from a news article, and the other two are from interviews of experts in the area. In Figure 4, the user summarizes the information from one of the interviews to conclude that Anthrax can be contracted by inhalation and through skin contact. Later, he finds supplementary information to this in the other interview, and concludes that it can also be contracted through ingesting infected meat.

Figure 5 shows the user finding out about the durability of Anthrax spores. The newspaper article provides the information that Anthrax spores are extremely durable as long as there is no sunlight. However it is not clear if the spores are destroyed in sunlight or not. This is made clear by one of the other sources that they are indeed destroyed by sunlight.

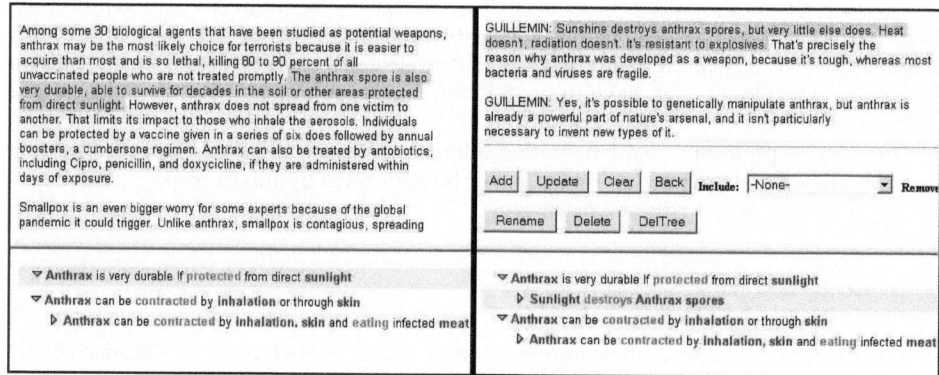

Fig. 5. Demonstrating clarification

5 Discussion

Our current tools can be enhanced with other work on natural language processing and knowledge base analysis. Many existing tools for text extraction (e.g, to extract significant event descriptions from news articles) and discourse analysis (e.g., to segment text into meaningful portions) could be used to support these earlier steps of the analysis [Croft 99; Cowie and Lehnert 96; Radey and McKeown 98]. Existing approaches to derive interdependencies among pieces of knowledge may be used to help users create connections among diverse pieces of knowledge [Kim and Gil]. Other tools can be developed to support transformations at the lower levels (e.g., to turn tables into instances and role values).

The approach presented here has many relations to software engineering methodologies to capture the rationale for knowledge-based development [Schreiber et al 00], and to higher-level languages and frameworks to develop knowledge-based systems [Fensel et al. 98]. However, these methodologies are often aimed at software and knowledge engineers and are not very accessible to other potential knowledge base developers, such as end users and/or domain experts.

The overhead that may be incurred in creating knowledge bases using this approach is, in our view, not as significant compared to the analysis efforts that developers already undergo. It may even save developers time if others can look up the rationale trail instead of asking them directly detailed questions about the portion of the knowledge base they are developing. As in any issue that creates overhead during development, it depends on the motivation and ultimately payoff to the developers in terms of facilitating maintenance and reuse by others.

The Semantic Web [Berners-Lee et al 01] will provide an ideal substrate to ground knowledge bases into their original knowledge sources, and to contain the progressively defined pieces of knowledge and the connections among them. More and more every day, knowledge originates and ends in the Web, and we find ourselves extracting knowledge from the Web, processing it inside of a knowledge base, then putting the results back on the Web. It only makes sense to integrate knowledge bases (their content and their reasoning) more closely with the Web. Currently, IKRAFT represents the links to the sources and knowledge fragments in its own language. In future work we plan to turn IKRAFT into a Web-based annotation tool, where these pointers would be converted into annotations in a suitable markup language. If the final knowledge base is published as a Web resource, it will be linked to other Web resources that represent the original documents, as well as intermediate knowledge fragments that can be turned into Web resources as well. Using IKRAFT may perhaps allow web users that are not AI experts to contribute to knowledge base development, at least in the initial stages as presented in steps 1 and 2 in Fig 1 in this paper. Others who are more savvy about knowledge representation techniques may take on the subsequent formalization stages (step 3 in Fig 1). Many knowledge bases will finally be open source, and one can only hope they will be adopted, extended, and used by much larger numbers of people than they are today.

6 Conclusions

Knowledge base developers may consult many sources presenting contradictory or complementary information, analyze the different implications of each alternative belief, and decide what and how to model the knowledge. In essence, developers often capture in the knowledge base only their final beliefs about some body of knowledge. The rationale for modeling the knowledge the way it appears in the knowledge base is not captured declaratively. Only consistent and complete information is captured. No indication of inconsistent but possible statements is added to the knowledge base.

In ongoing work, we are developing a knowledge base using IKRAFT to represent terms in the geosciences domain. We plan to measure whether the rationale capture by IKRAFT is useful by measuring how users access the rationale from the application as they try to find out how and why terms were defined as they appear in the final formal representation. We also plan to use IKRAFT to develop a knowledge base using two kinds of users: a user that is an experienced domain expert and that performs the first two steps outlined above, and a user that is a knowledge engineer and formalizes the statements input by the first user. An interesting possibility would be to explore how our framework would support collaborative knowledge base development by larger groups of users, both experts and knowledge engineers.

Intelligent systems should be able to access the roots and rationale of the knowledge they contain. This is the approach that we have taken in developing IKRAFT, a tool to allow users to link knowledge bases to their original sources and other knowledge fragments that result from the analysis of the knowledge base developer. This approach would create a new generation of knowledge bases that will be more amenable to updates, reuse, migration, and interoperation.

References

1. Berners-Lee, T.; Hendler, J.; and Lassila, O. 2001. The Semantic Web. Scientific American 78(3):20–88.
2. Burstein, M., McDermott, D., Smith, D. R., Westfold, S. 2000. "Derivation of Glue Code for Agent Interoperation". Proceedings of the International Conference on Autonomous Agents 2000. Barcelona, Spain.

3. Chalupsky, H. 2000. "OntoMorph: A Translation System for Symbolic Knowledge". Proceedings of the International Conference on Knowledge Representation and Reasoning, KR-2000, Breckenridge, CO.
4. Cooke, N. J. 1994. "Varieties of Knowledge Elicitation Techniques", International Journal of Human-Computer Studies, Vol. 41.
5. Cowie, J. and Lehnert, W. 1996. "Information Extraction". Communications of the ACM, 39(1):80--91, Jan 1996.
6. Croft, W.B. 1999. "Combining Approaches to Information Retrieval," in Advances in Information Retrieval: Recent Research from the CIIR, W. Bruce Croft, Ed. Kluwer.
7. Fensel, D., Angele, J., and Studer, R. 1998. "The Knowledge Acquisition and Representation Language KARL", Knowledge and Data Engineering, 10 (4).
8. Kim J., and Gil, Y. 2000. "Acquiring Problem-Solving Knowledge from End Users: Putting Interdependency Models to the Test." Proceedings of the Fifteenth National Conference on Artificial Intelligence (AAAI-2000), Austin, TX.
9. McGuinness, D. L., Fikes, R., Rice, J., and Wilder, S. 2000. "An Environment for Merging and Testing Large Ontologies". Proceedings of KR-2000, Breckenridge, CO.
10. Radev, D. and McKeown, K. 1998. "Generating natural language summaries from multiple online sources". Computational Linguistics, 1998.
11. Schreiber, G, Akkermans, H., Anjewierden, A., de Hoog, R., Shadbolt, N., Van de Velde, W., and Wielinga, B. 2000. "Knowledge Engineering and Management: The CommonKADS Methodology". MIT Press.
12. Shum, S.B. 1996. Design Argumentation as Design Rationale. Encyclop- edia of Computer Science and Technology (M.Dekker Inc: NY).
13. Stefik, M., 1995. "Introduction to Knowledge Systems". Morgan Kaufmann.
14. Swan, R. and Jensen, D. 2000. "TimeMines: Constructing Timelines with Statistical Models of World Usage", Proceedings of KDD-2000

TRELLIS: An Interactive Tool for Capturing Information Analysis and Decision Making

Yolanda Gil and Varun Ratnakar

USC Information Sciences Institute
4676 Admiralty Way
Marina del Rey, CA 90292
gil@isi.edu, varunr@isi.edu

Abstract. TRELLIS provides an interactive environment that allows users to add their observations, opinions, and conclusions as they analyze information by making semantic annotations about on-line documents. TRELLIS includes a vocabulary and markup language for semantic annotations of decisions and tradeoffs, and allows users to extend this vocabulary with domain specific terms or constructs that are useful to their particular task. To date, we have used TRELLIS with a variety of scenarios to annotate tradeoffs and decisions (e.g., military planning), organize materials (e.g., search results), analyze disagreements and controversies on a topic (e.g., intelligence analysis), and handle incomplete and conflicting information (e.g., genealogy research).

1 Introduction

In a world of overwhelming on-line information access and global communications, more and more people are asked to provide faster and more accurate answers based on up-to-date knowledge that is increasingly more disseminated in vast amounts of information sources. Research in text retrieval, extraction, and summarization, is aimed to sifting out relevant information to users [Croft 99, Cowie and Lehnert 96, Rader and McKeown 98]. Research in knowledge management and CSCW tools focuses on delivering information to interested parties in relevant formats [Smith and Farquhar 00, Ackerman & McDonald 96]. These tools can help users to manage all the information so they can make their decisions with reasonable accuracy and time bounds But users need support after they have made a decision, reached a conclusion, or made a recommendation. He or she will be often required to: 1) explain and justify their views to others, 2) update the decision in light of additional information or new data, 3) expose the intermediate products of the final recommendation to others that may be analyzing related information to make similar decisions. Our approach is to enable users to annotate the rationale for their decisions, hypotheses, and opinions as they analyze information from various sources. Once this rationale is recorded, it can be used to help users justify, update, and share the results of their analysis. This paper presents TRELLIS, an interactive tool that helps users create these annotations. TRELLIS includes a language for annotating information analysis, which can be extended by users to suit their needs. Additional information about how TRELLIS

A. Gómez-Pérez and V.R. Benjamins (Eds.): EKAW 2002, LNAI 2473, pp. 37–42, 2002.
© Springer-Verlag Berlin Heidelberg 2002

represents and reasons about information sources can be found in [Gil and Ratnakar 2002].

The paper starts by describing our markup language to annotate information analysis, followed by an overview of the TRELLIS architecture and its functionality. We then show a use case scenario for intelligence analysis for feasibility of a special operations plan. We finalize with a discussion of contributions and plans for future work.

2   A Vocabulary to Help Users Annotate Information Analysis

The language that we propose uses the following basic components to describe this information. A *statement* is a piece of information or data relevant to an analysis, such as "The average water temperature in March is 63 degrees". A statement may have been extracted or summarized from a *document*, which is often a Web resource (text, imagery, or any other format) indicated by a URI or could also be a user-provided document such as an email message or a note relating a conversation. A statement can also be created by the user to introduce a hypothesis, conclusion, or observation that will be used in the analysis.   Every document has a *source description*, describing its creator, publisher, date, format, etc. Each statement and its source can have a *source qualification* specified as a degree of *reliability* and *credibility*. Reliability is typically based on credentials and past performance. Credibility specifies the probable truth of a statement. Reliability and credibility are not the same, for example a completely reliable source may provide some information that may be judged to be not very credible given other known information.

A *compound statement or a unit* is composed of several statements related by a *construct*.   Constructs reflect how individual statements are related in the analysis. For example, a causal construct is used to form the compound statement: "The average water temperature in March is 63 degrees" results in "unlikely use of divers". A *likelihood qualification* is a subjective informal indication of the analyst's reaction to a statement (or compound statement). This can indicate surprise, dismissal, saliency, accuracy, etc. A *reason* can be used to justify a compound statement, a source qualification, and a likelihood qualification.

These basic components are used to create *units*, such as the one shown in Figure 1. The basic structure of a unit is:

> *statement* {and *statement*}* *construct* {and *statement*}*
>   is {not} *likelihood-qualifier* because
>   according to *source-description* which is
>   *reliability-qualifier* because *statement* and
>   *credibility-qualifier* because *statement*

The user may or may not provide all the components, only a statement is required to form a unit.

An analysis is composed of many such units. They can be *linked as subunits* of one another. Units or statements can be left with no links to the overall analysis, and in that case they can be specified as *attachments* to the analysis. This is useful to indicate that they have been considered by the user but do not appear in the derivation of the final analysis (for lack of time, or because the analyst found better options to justify their conclusions. An analysis can be done with an overarching *purpose*, which is often a question or request that the information analyst starts with.

---

water temperature unsustainable for SDV divers
  is elaborated in
    average March water temperature is 55-60 degrees
    and
    platoon requires minimum water temperature of 65 degrees
  according to source
    Cmdr Smith *which is*
      completely reliable (A)
        because Cmdr Smith has 15 years experience with JSOC
      and
      probably true
        because Cmdr Smith has been platoon cmdr for 3 years

Fig. 1. An Example of a Basic Unit that Captures a Portion of the Analysis Regarding Water Temperature

We provide a default set of constructs. This default set can be extended by the user to incorporate new constructs useful in the particular topic of the analysis. Our default set of constructs is drawn from argumentation and discourse relations [Mann and Thompson 85, Pollock 94], logic connectives (drawing mostly from natural deduction, sequent calculus and tautologies), action representations (including temporal and causal relations) [Myers and Wilkins 96, Allen 84], and object representations (parts and roles) [Gruber 91]. In developing the default set of constructs, our concern was not completeness (since the user can extend the default set), nor precise semantics (since users would not necessarily be able or willing to follow the pre-specified meanings), nor computability (since, at least initially, we were not intending to automate or verify of the derivation of the analysis). Instead, our aim was to select a set of constructs that were understandable to end users and had the potential of being useful in a variety of analysis and situations. For example, to specify disjunction we did not include "or" as a construct and give it semantics, as would be done with a logic system. Instead, we included two constructs that indicate whether the disjunction is intended to be an exclusive or. The default set of constructs, grouped into three practical categories, include:

- *Discourse relations*: provides background for, depends on, stands though contradicted by, conceding, can be interpreted through, evaluated by, restates, summarizes, in contrast with, is solved by, shows how to do, is elaborated in (set and members, abstract and instances, whole and parts, process and steps, object and attributes, generalization and specialization), is motivation for, depends on, otherwise, causes, causes choice of, resulted in, choosing S1 results in S2, happened and resulted in, is purpose of.
- *Logic connectives*: not S1, S1 and S2, S1 or S2 but not both, S1 or S2 or both, S1 therefore S2, if S1 therefore S2 then not S2 therefore not S1, if S1 therefore S2 then S2, if not S1 and S1 or S2 but not both then S2, if not S2 and S1 therefore S2 then not S1.
- *Temporal relations*: is before, is after, meets, is met by, overlaps with, is overlapped by, starts, is started by, is during, contains, ends, is ended by, equals.

Users can also indicate partial knowledge by choosing from a small set of general constructs that include: related to, temporally related to, unrelated to.

We followed a similar path to design our initial set of likelihood qualifiers, drawing from modal logic [Lemmon & Scott 77]. Our initial set includes definitely true/false, probably true/false, maybe true/false, likely, impossible, surprising, shocking, reassuring, believable, absurd, accurate, dismissable, and salient.

3 TRELLIS: Capturing Information Analysis and Decision Making

Figure 2 shows the components of TRELLIS.

A user typically starts searching the Web for a certain document using the Search Tool, or indicating a pointer to a specific Web resource that contains useful information.

The Statement Editor is used to add statements about these documents. A Statement is normally a short statement, backed up by a document or user text, and by information on its source. All metadata that is allowed for the source comes from the Source Description Schema. See [Gil and Ratnakar 2002] for details.

An issue with web resources is that they are not persistent. We have found it useful to have a Caching Module to cache any online resource that is added to the system.

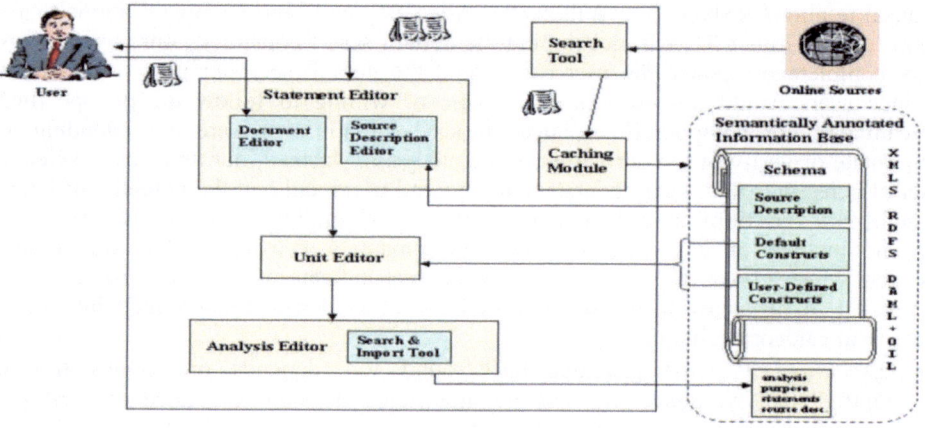

Fig. 2. The architecture of Trellis

The Unit Editor is used to add or edit units of knowledge in the system. It helps users compose statements and constructs into compound statements, and to add likelihood, reliability and credibility. These constructs are defined in the Schema. Users extend the schema when they define their own constructs specific to the domain being worked upon.

The Analysis Editor is used to organize the various units in a tree structure, which represents the reasoning pattern in reaching a conclusion for a given purpose. There is also a Search/Import utility for the Analysis Editor, which can be used to search analyses of other Trellis users for certain keywords either in the purpose or individual units. Any part of the other user's analysis can be imported into the current analysis.

TRELLIS is available on-line at trellis.semanticweb.org. In order to demonstrate the versatility and coverage of TRELLIS to annotate information analysis, we show here analyses created in a wide range of situations. Portions of the analyses discussed in this section are summarized in Figure 4. All these examples can be browsed on-line from the above Web site logging in as guest.

A genealogy example helps illustrate how TRELLIS helps annotate analysis of contradictory information. It shows how to capture an analysis of the date in which a user's family event occurred, in this case when an ancestor left Europe for the US. Another example concerns military planning and decision making. Here, a commander is trying to decide on the feasibility of using an SDV platform (Seal Delivery Vehicle) by analyzing weather conditions. Our last example captures the analysis of a user searching the Web in order to find a hotel for a trip to San Diego.

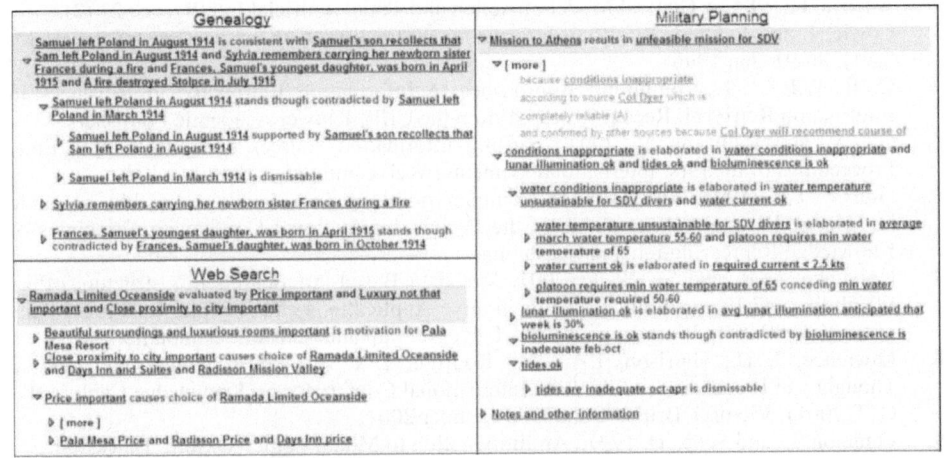

Fig. 3. Examples of Annotations in TRELLIS

4 Discussion

SEAS [Lawrence et al 01] shows an alternative approach to support intelligence analysis. Users define argument templates that contain questions to support the argument and an inference structure to derive the conclusion from the answers to the questions. The system contains a sizeable amount of patterns about early crisis warning for national security analysis. The approach emphasizes the use of shared patterns as well as support for automated inference on demand. TRELLIS has more generality but does not provide as much support for sharing and automation.

Collaboration is often supported through annotations. Web annotation and document annotation tools enable users to add commentary to documents [Koivunen & Swick 2001; Nagao et al 2001]. The emphasis of these approaches is more on collaboration, while our work has a more specific focus on information analysis for decision making. Other annotation tools provide a structured vocabulary such as the one used in TRELLIS to annotate debates and arguments [Lawrence et al 2001; Shum et al 2000]. These tools provide more ontologies and templates that the users must follow in order to enforce sharing and understanding by a specific user community.

TRELLIS provides an interactive environment that allows users to add their observations, opinions, and conclusions as they analyze information by making semantic annotations to documents and other on-line resources. This is in essence a knowledge acquisition problem, where the user is adding new knowledge to the system based on their expertise as they analyze information.

References

1. Ackerman, M.S. and McDonald, D.W. 1996. Answer Garden 2: Merging Organizational Memory with Collaborative Help. In Proceedings of CSCW'-96.
2. Allen, J. F. 1984. A General Model of Action and Time. Artificial Intelligence 23 (2).
3. Cowie, J. and Lehnert, W. 1996. Information Extraction. Communications of the ACM, 39(1): 80-91, Jan 1996.
4. Croft, W.B. 1999. Combining Approaches to Information Retrieval," in Advances in Information Retrieval: Recent Research from the CIIR, Kluwer Academic Publishers.
5. Gil, Y. and Ratnakar, V. 2002. Trusting information sources one citizen at a time, Proceedings of the First International Semantic Web Conference, Sardinia, Italy.
6. Gruber, T.R. 1991. The Role of Common ontology in achieving sharable, reusable knowledge bases. In Proceedings of the Second International Conference, Principles of Knowledge Representation and Reasoning.
7. Koivunen, M.R. and Swick, R. 2001. Metadata Based Annotation Infrastructure offers Flexibility and Extensibility for Collaborative Applications and Beyond. In: Proceedings of the K-CAP 2001 Workshop on Knowledge Markup and Semantic Annotation, BC.
8. Lawrence, J. D.; Harrison, I.W.; and Rodriguez, A. C. 2001. Capturing Analytic Thought. In Proceedings of the First International Conference on Knowledge Capture (K-CAP 2001). Victoria, British Columbia, October 2001.
9. Lemmon, E. and Scott, D. 1977. An Introduction to Modal Logic. Oxford: Blackwell.
10. Mann, W. C. and Thompson, S. A. 1988. Rethorical Structure Theory: Toward a Functional Theory of Text Organization. Text 8(3).
11. Nagao, K., Shirai, Y., Squire, K. 2001. Semantic Annotation and Transcoding: Making Web Content More Accessible. IEEE MultiMedia 8(2): 69-81.
12. Pollock, John L. 1994. Justification and Defeat, Artificial Intelligence, 67 p. 377 – 407.
13. Radev, D. and McKeown, K. 1998. Generating natural language summaries from multiple online sources. Computational Linguistics, 1998.
14. Shum, S.B., Motta, E., Domingue, J. 2000. ScholOnto: An Ontology-Based Digital Library Server for Research Documents and Discourse. Journal on Digital Libraries, 3 (3).
15. Shum, S.B. 1996. Design Argumentation as Design Rationale. Encyclop- edia of Computer Science and Technology (M.Dekker Inc: NY).
16. Smith, R. and Farquhar, A. 2000. AI Magazine, Fall 2000.
17. Wilkins, D.E., Myers, K.L. 1995. A Common Knowledge Representation for Plan Generation and Reactive Execution, Journal of Logic and Computation, 5 p. 731-761.

Web-Based Document Management for Specialised Domains: A Preliminary Evaluation

Mihye Kim and Paul Compton

School of Computer Science and Engineering,
University of New South Wales, Sydney NSW 2052 Australia.
{mihyek, compton}@cse.unsw.edu.au

Abstract. A Web document management system has been developed aimed at small communities in specialised domains and based on free annotation of documents by users. Knowledge acquisition support includes suggesting terms from external ontologies. Preliminary evaluation in a domain of research topics in Computer Science supports the utility of the approach, The most interesting result suggests that although an established external taxonomy can be useful in proposing annotation terms, users appear to be very selective in their use of terms proposed.

1 Introduction

There is a widespread belief, manifest through the Semantic Web initiative[1], that to make full use of the resources on the World Wide Web, documents will need to be marked up according to agreed ontological standards. Our aim has been to explore the possibility of document annotation systems that do not commit to *a priori* ontologies and expect that documents will be annotated according to pre-defined ontologies. Rather our aim is systems which support the user in freely annotating a document and the ontology evolves as a consequence. Rather than this being totally *ad hoc*, we would like the system to assist the user to make extensions to the developing ontology that are in some way improvements.

Our first attempts at incremental development of document management systems were based on selecting keywords that discriminate between documents [1] and was based on earlier knowledge acquisition techniques [2]. A limitation of this approach is that it does not directly organise the knowledge in a way that is suitable for browsing. The system outlined below uses the lattice-based browsing supported by Formal Concept Analysis.

The aim of this paper is to provide some preliminary information on how actual users interact with such a system. The application domain for this study is annotation of researchers' home pages according to their research interests, so that they can be more readily found by prospective research students, industrial partners and so on.

---

[1] http://www.semanticweb.org/

A. Gómez-Pérez and V.R. Benjamins (Eds.): EKAW 2002, LNAI 2473, pp. 43-48, 2002.
© Springer-Verlag Berlin Heidelberg 2002

2   Method

The core technology in our system is Formal Concept Analysis (FCA) [3,4]   In FCA a concept is specified by its extension as well as intention. This results in a lattice structure, where each node is specified by a set of objects and the attributes they share. The lattice can be quite sparse as a node is added only if the attributes at the node distinguish the objects from those at another node.

A number of researchers have advanced this lattice structure for document retrieval [5,6]. Several researchers have also studied graphically represented lattices for specific domains such as medicine, e-mail management, flight information and libraries [7-10].

The difference in our approach is mainly in the way the system is used rather than its underlying FCA basis. The system we have developed is aimed at multiple users being able to add and amend document annotations whenever they choose. The system is Web-based with documents represented by their URLs (see Fig. 1). We have previously described the main features of this system [11]. It can be explored at: http://pokey.cse.unsw.edu.au/servlets/RI. The following outlines some of the features relevant to the evaluation results.

2.1   Annotation Support

To assist in finding relevant keywords, a user can select from the keywords used by other researchers with whom they may share interests. After the user has selected some terms they are presented with a display of terms that co-occur with the selected terms somewhere in the lattice. As well, users are shown terms suggested from external taxonomies. In the present study the terms are from the ACM computing classification taxonomy[2] and ASIS&T thesaurus for information science[3]. If the user's terms occur in one of these hierarchies, the system shows all the parents of these terms up the hierarchy, but in a simple list without specifying the relations. The user is free to select none, some, or all of these parent terms to annotate their document. The result is a new taxonomy that is made up of parts of other taxonomies that users perceive as most useful along with other terms they add. We believe this may provide a very simple but powerful way of validating and improving on the ontological standards that are being established.

2.2   Browsing and Searching Support

Browsing is based on showing a web page with the hyperlinks and keywords for the immediate parent and child nodes of the current node as shown in Figure 1. As well as navigating the lattice, users can select terms from a list or enter terms into a text box. If the entered term is not a keyword a conventional text word search is carried

---

[2] ACM (Association for Computing Machinery); http://www.acm.org/class/1998/ccs98.html
[3] ASIS&T (American Society for Information Science and Technology);
http://www.asis.org/Publications/Thesaurus/isframe.htm

out. A sub-lattice containing only the documents that contain these text words is then displayed.

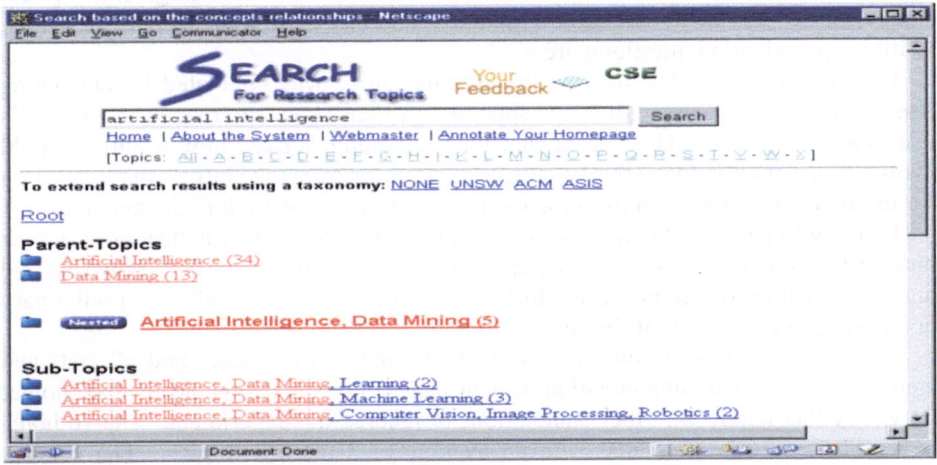

Figure 1. This shows the main features of the lattice-browsing interface in a domain of researcher home pages in a Computer Science school. The numbers in brackets indicate the number of researcher home pages at each node. The URLs for these researchers can be accessed via the folders on the left. The researchers for the current node are also listed at the bottom of the screen (not shown). The "nested" button gives a Conceptual Scale view as appropriate. The taxonomies available are towards the top of the main screen.

Figure 1 is an example of the advantage of lattice browsing. Users who search for Data Mining under Artificial Intelligence find that there are only 5 researchers in this area. However this node has 2 parents and so the lattice view makes it obvious that there in fact 13 researchers in the School who do research in Data Mining. Most of these researcher are under Data Bases rather than Artificial Intelligence.

A hierarchical display is also available. This is accessed via nested pop-up menus showing the subclasses below the current node. This display is generated using the Conceptual Scale extension to FCA [12,13]. A conceptual scale gives a view of a sub-lattice formed from objects that have specified attribute-value pairs.

The user can also view the lattice using one of the imported taxonomies available – in this case the ACM, ASIS&T and a local UNSW taxonomy. This recreates the lattice assuming that any document annotated with a term that occurs in the imported taxonomy also has all the parent terms for that term. One can browse this lattice or alternatively one can navigate the hierarchy at any stage as above.

3 Evaluation

The School of Computer Science and Engineering has used traditionally used simple research topic indices to help prospective research students and collaborators find

School researchers[4]. We chose this as an evaluation domain as it seemed likely that researchers would be motivated to add appropriate annotations to attract prospective students. Secondly there would be sufficient students browsing, looking for supervisors to provide a reasonable evaluation, and that these students may be willing to fill in an evaluation questionnaire.

To stimulate researcher interest the starting lattice was populated by annotating researchers' home pages with terms specified as their research areas in the School's research topic index. This meant that then we could not see how a lattice would evolve from scratch. Once the system was set up for research staff it was opened up for use by PhD students. In this case their home pages were not initially annotated.

To carry out the evaluation we logged all actions of users whether browsing or annotating home pages. We also set up some evaluation forms for both browsing and annotating which we invited users to fill in. The following results are preliminary and cover just one aspect of the study.

To date 76 annotated home pages are registered in the system and 52 staff and students have carried out annotation of their pages. Of course this means that another 24 were either happy with their annotations or ignored the experiment. The 76 home pages of have been annotated with an average of 8 research topics. The concept lattice contains 367 nodes with an average of 2 parents per node and path lengths ranging from 2 to 7 edges. The 52 researchers who actively annotated their home pages used 480 terms. 446 (93%) of these were terms that were already used to annotate other pages, while 34 (7%) of the terms were newly entered into the system. A total of 193 terms were suggested from the imported ontologies. Of these only 19 terms (4%) were used for annotation. The annotators were interviewed to investigate the reasons for the low uptake. The proposed topics were seen as applicable but too general in specifying a research area.

The relevance of terms suggested from ontologies can be seen in Table 1. The table shows the numbers of researcher home pages retrieved using the various terms in the left column with and without imported taxonomies. Recall that the lattice shows all the researchers who use a particular term, and that this number can be increased by importing taxonomies and considering that pages are implicitly annotated by any terms in the taxonomy that are parents of terms selected by the researcher. These would be the results if the researchers were obliged to conform to that ontology.

One can observe that ASIS&T and ACM taxonomies have different ideas of what constitutes Knowledge Engineering, but that UNSW researchers agree with the ACM. However they do not agree with the ACM about Learning or Operating Systems. However, there is a high degree of consistency with terms such as Knowledge Representation and Data Bases. These results suggest not just random variations, but specific and relatively consensual decisions about the value of the various terms available.

---

[4] (http://www.cse.unsw.edu.au/school/research/research2.html).

Table 1: retrieval of home pages without and without imported taxonomies

Terms	Number of researcher home pages retrieved		
	Lattice only	ACM taxonomy	ASIS&T taxonomy
Artificial Intelligence	37	46	43
Data Mining	16	16	-
Machine Learning	22	-	22
Knowledge Engineering	3	3	29
Knowledge Representation	17	17	19
Learning	4	18	-
Information Retrieval	8	8	9
Databases	10	10	11
Software Engineering	7	10	-
Operating Systems	2	7	-

4 Discussion

We do not have sufficient data to make strong claims about the value of a lattice-based approach to browsing. However, the case in Figure 1 provides an example of the power of lattice based browsing – a hierarchical pathway found only a small number of documents, but other related documents were readily found with lattice browsing.

The most interesting result from this study is in the use of the imported taxonomies. Standardised global ontologies are increasingly seen as the solution to many problems related to document and knowledge management. The results here suggest that within a small community, even a quite diverse community, selective use will be made of a more global ontology. The results suggest such ontologies are of value as a resource, but that in small communities and specialised domains people will prefer to pick and choose what is of value from an ontology. It should be noted that the researchers were not annotating documents for their own use but specifically to assist people outside the community who would be expected to have a more superficial knowledge of the terms used.

These accidental results confirm our original motivation for this project – that there is a clear need for tools which allow small communities to flexibly and freely develop their own document annotation and retrieval systems. However, as standards for representing ontologies take hold, these small community systems should be able to very flexibly import ontologies and make selective use of their resources. In turn the use these communities make of external ontologies and the extra terms they add will provide useful feedback on the external more standardised ontologies may be usefully evolved.

Acknowledgement: This research has been supported by an Australian Research Council (ARC) grant and is part of Mihye Kim's PhD project.

References

1.   Kang, B. H., Yoshida, K., Motoda, H. and Compton, P. Help Desk System with Intelligent Interface. Applied Artificial Intelligence, 11 (1997) 611-631.
2.   Compton, P. and Jansen, R. A Philosophical Basis for Knowledge Acquisition. Knowledge Acquisition 2 (1990) 241-257.
3.   Wille, R. Restructuring Lattice Theory: An Approach Based on Hierarchies Of Concepts, In: Ivan Rival (ed.): Ordered set. Reidel, Dordrecht, Boston, (1982) 445-470.
4.   Ganter, B. and Wille, R. Formal Concept Analysis: Mathematical Foundations. Springer, Heidelberg (1999).
5.   Godin, R., Missaoui, R. and April, A. Experimental Comparison on Navigation In a Galois Lattice with Conventional Information Retrieval Methods. International Journal of Man-Machine Studies. 38 (1993) 747-767.
6.   Carpineto, C. and Romano, G. Information Retrieval Through Hybrid Navigation of Lattice Representations. International Journal of Human-Computer Studies. 45 (1996) 553-578.
7.   Cole, R. and Eklund, P. Text Retrieval for Medical Discharge Summaries Using SNOMED and Formal Concept Analysis. In: Australian Document Computing Symposium. (1996) 50-58.
8.   Cole, R. and Stumme, G. CEM - A Conceptual Email Manager. In: Proceedings of the 8th International Conference on Conceptual Structure (ICCS 2000). Darmstadt. Springer-Verlag (2000) 438-452.
9.   Eklund, P., Groh, B., Stumme, G. and Wille, R. A Contextual-Logic Extension of TOSCANA. In: Proceedings of the 8th International Conference on Conceptual Structure (ICCS 2000). Darmstadt, Springer-Verlag (2000) 453-467.
10. Rock, T. and Wille, R. TOSCANA-System zur Literatursuche. In: G. Stumme and R. Wille (eds): Begriffliche Wissensverarbeitung: Methoden und Anwendungen. Springer, Berlin-Heidelberg (2000) 239-253.
11. Kim, M. and Compton, P. A Web-based Browsing Mechanism Based on the Conceptual Structures. In: Conceptual Structures: Extracting and Representing Semantics. Proceedings of the 9th International Conference on Conceptual Structures (ICCS 2001). Stanford University, California. USA (2001) 47-60.
12. Ganter, B. and Wille, R. Conceptual Scaling. In: F. Roberts (ed.): Application of Combinatorics and Graph Theory to the Biological and Social Sciences. Springer (1989) 139-167.
13. Stumme, G. Hierarchies of Conceptual Scales. In: B Gaines; R Kremer; M Musen (eds): 12th Banff Knowledge Acquisition. Modelling and Management. Banff Canada, 16-21 Oct., SRDG Publication, University of Calgary (1999).

From Informal Knowledge to Formal Logic: A Realistic Case Study in Medical Protocols

Mar Marcos[1]*, Michael Balser[2], Annette ten Teije[3], and Frank van Harmelen[1]

[1] Vrije Universiteit Amsterdam, Dept. of Artificial Intelligence
De Boelelaan 1081a, 1081HV Amsterdam, Netherlands
[2] Universität Augsburg, Lehrstuhl Softwaretechnik und Programmiersprachen
86135 Augsburg, Germany
[3] Universiteit Utrecht, Institute of Information and Computing Sciences
P.O. Box 80.089, 3508TB Utrecht, Netherlands

Abstract. We report our experience in a case study with constructing fully formalised knowledge models of realistic, specialised medical knowledge. We have taken a medical protocol in daily use by medical specialists, modelled this knowledge in a specific-purpose knowledge representation language, and finally formalised this knowledge representation in terms of temporal logic and parallel programs. The value of this formalisation process is that each successive formalisation step has contributed to improving the quality of the original medical protocol, and that the final formalisation allows us to provide machine-assisted proofs of properties that are satisfied by the original medical protocol (or, alternatively, precise arguments why the original protocol fails to satisfy certain desirable properties). We believe that this the first time that a significant body of medical knowledge (in our case: a protocol for the management of jaundice in newborns) has been formalised to the extent that it becomes amenable to automated theorem proving, and that this has actually lead to improvement of the original body of medical knowledge.

1 Introduction

During the last years a high number of medical practice guidelines or protocols[1] have been produced from systematic evidence-based reviews [1]. They are "systematically developed statements to assist practitioners and patient decisions about appropriate health care for specific circumstances" [2]. Medical protocols contain more or less precise recommendations about the diagnosis tests or the interventions to perform, or about other aspects of clinical practice. These recommendations are based on the best empirical evidence available at the moment. Among the potential benefits of protocols, we can highlight the improvement of healthcare outcomes [3]. More precisely, they can help to promote high quality practice, recommending interventions of proved benefit and discouraging those that are not supported by good evidence. They can also be used

---

* On research leave from the Dept. of Computer Engineering and Science, Universitat Jaume I, Castellón, Spain.
[1] In this paper we use the terms guideline and protocol indistinctively. However, the term protocol is in general used for more specific versions of a guideline.

A. Gómez-Pérez and V.R. Benjamins (Eds.): EKAW 2002, LNAI 2473, pp. 49–64, 2002.

to reduce variations in care. Finally, protocols can be useful to improve cost efficiency, thanks to the standardisation of healthcare. Indeed, it has been shown that adherence to protocols may reduce the costs of care upto 25% [4].

In order to enable their potential benefits, protocols must fulfill strong quality requirements. This is true not only for the final product, the protocol, but also for the development process. Medical bodies worldwide have made efforts in this direction, e.g. elaborating appraisal documents that take into account a variety of protocol aspects, of both protocols and their development process (see [5] for a comparison of appraisal instruments). However, these initiatives are not sufficient since they rely on informal methods and notations. We are concerned with a different approach, namely the quality improvement of medical protocols through formalisation. Currently, protocols are described using a combination of different formats, e.g. text, flow diagrams and tables. The underlying idea of our work is that making these descriptions more precise, with the help of a more formal language, will expose parts where the protocols are ambiguous, incomplete or even inconsistent. By pointing out these anomalous parts, and the reasons why they could be problematic, we expect to obtain useful indications for the improvement of the protocols. This idea is widely acknowledged in fields like software engineering, where formal methods are used as a tool for early detection of specification and design errors, but has been largely unexplored for medical protocols.

However, the formalisation of medical protocols can be tackled at different degrees of formality. In this paper we aim at a fully formal specification. The research question that we try to answer is: *can medical protocols be formalised in terms of logic? and can this formalisation contribute to the improvement of their quality?* In order to answer this question, we have carried out a case study on protocol formalisation. The main contribution of this paper is to show (1) that it is possible to formalise medical knowledge to a high degree of formality; (2) that this process must be divided into a number of steps, each increasing the degree of formality; and (3) that each step in this process uncovers problems in the protocol. An early report on similar problems in protocols can be found in [6]. It is important to notice that our work differs in significant aspects, namely that we aim at a much higher degree of formality, and that we focus on the verification and validation of the original protocol rather than the design of an enhanced version thereof.

For the purpose of our case study, a choice had to be made on the target formalism(s) as well as on the medical protocol to be used. Concerning the formalisms, we have first used a special purpose knowledge representation language suited for medical protocols–Asbru, and afterwards the logic of the KIV theorem prover. As for the medical protocol, we have selected one devoted to the the management of jaundice in newborn babies. Figure 1 illustrates the process of our case study, and also the structure of this paper. First the jaundice protocol is discussed in section 2. Then the Asbru language and the model of the jaundice protocol in this language are described in section 3. The next step in the formalisation process is to translate the Asbru protocol to the fully formal calculus of KIV. This step is described in section 4. In each of the previous two sections we also discuss the benefits of the corresponding formalisation step, as well as the difficulties we encountered. Finally, section 5 concludes the paper.

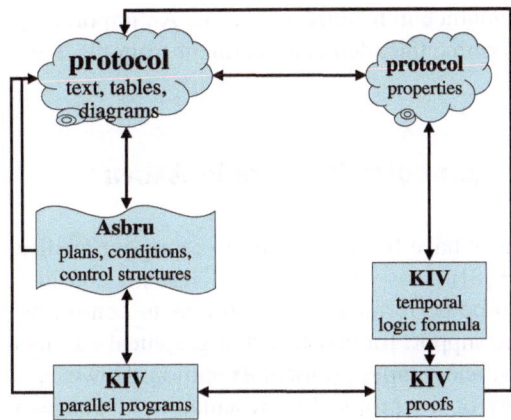

Fig. 1. The formalisation process of our case study.

2   The Jaundice Protocol

Jaundice (or hyperbilirubinemia) is a common disease in newborn babies. Under certain circumstances, elevated bilirubin levels may have detrimental neurological effects. In many cases jaundice disappears without treatment but sometimes phototherapy is needed to reduce the levels of total serum bilirubin (TSB), which indicates the presence and severity of jaundice. In a few cases, however, jaundice is a sign of a severe disease.

The jaundice protocol of the American Association of Pediatrics[2] (AAP) [7] is intended for the management of the disease in healthy term[3] newborn babies. The main reason for choosing this protocol was that it is considered a high-quality protocol: the jaundice protocol of the AAP is included in the repository of the National Guideline Clearinghouse[4].

The guideline is a 10 pages document which contains knowledge in various informal forms, namely:

- text (this is the main body of the protocol),
- a list of factors to be considered when assessing a jaundice infant (for instance, family history of significant hemolytic disease),
- two tables, one for the management of Hyperbilirubinemia in the healthy term newborn and another for the treatment options for jaundice breast-fed infants, and
- a flowchart-like notation representing the steps described in the guideline.

The protocol consists of an evaluation (or diagnosis) part and a treatment part, to be performed in sequence. During the application of the protocol, as soon as the possibility of a more serious disease is uncovered, the recommendation is to exit without any further action. The rationale behind this is that the protocol is exclusively intended for

[2] http://www.aap.org/policy/hyperb.htm
[3] Defined as 37 completed weeks of gestation.
[4] http://www.guideline.gov

the management of jaundice in healthy newborns. An important part of the protocol is the table used to determine the adequate treatment from the TSB value and the age of the infant.

3   Modelling the Jaundice Protocol in Asbru

A number of languages have been proposed to represent medical protocols and their specific features (see [8]). Most protocol-based systems consider protocols as a composition of actions to be performed and conditions to control these actions [9]. Most of them provide some support for text-based or graphical editing of protocols, text annotation of protocols, and simple protocol execution. However, although the trend is changing lately, many of the protocol representation languages in the literature (e.g. GLIF [10]) are not formal enough. For instance, they often incorporate many free-text elements which do not have clear enough semantics. Exceptions to this are PROforma [11] and Asbru [12]. In this work we have chosen Asbru, firstly because it is more precise in the description of various medical aspects, and secondly because Asbru protocols are more declarative, and thus they are more amenable to formal analysis.

3.1   Asbru: A Knowledge Representation Language for Protocols

The main aspects of Asbru are: (i) in Asbru a medical protocol is considered as a plan skeleton with sub-plans in the sense of the AI planning literature, (ii) the possibility to specify the intentions of a plan in addition to the actions of a plan, (iii) the possibility to specify a variety of control-structures within a plan, and (iv) a rich language to specify time annotations. Asbru allows us to represent medical protocols in a precise way. Below we will give a short description of the Asbru language (see [12] for a more detailed description).

Plan A medical protocol is considered as a hierarchical plan. The four main components of a hierarchical plan in Asbru are (1) intentions, (2) conditions, (3) effects and (4) plan-body. Furthermore a plan can have arguments, and has the possibility to return a value. Next we will briefly discuss each of these components.

Intentions Intentions are the high-level goals of a plan. Intentions can be given in terms of achieving, maintaining or avoiding a certain state or action. Such states or actions can be intermediate or final (overall). For example, the label "achieve intermediate-state" means that sometime during the execution of the plan, a certain state must be achieved. "Achieve overall-state" means that at the end of the plan execution, a certain state must be achieved (e.g. at the end of the plan execution, bilirubin levels must be normal). In the same way, "achieve intermediate-action" means that sometime during the plan execution, a certain action must have occurred (e.g. the bilirubin level must have been measured). Notice that in total there are twelve possible forms: [achieve/maintain/avoid] [intermediate/overall]-[state/action].

Conditions There are a variety of conditions that can be associated with an Asbru plan, each of which determines a different aspect of a medical protocol. Asbru has the following conditions:

- filter conditions: These must be true before the plan can be started. For instance, "the blood-type of the mother is not known".
- setup conditions: Like the filter conditions, these must also be true before the plan can be started, but in this case they can be achieved with additional actions, i.e. by executing other plans.
- suspend conditions: When these are true, the plan will be suspended.
- reactivate conditions: These conditions determine when a suspended plan has to be restarted.
- abort conditions: Such conditions determine when a started, suspended or restarted plan must be aborted.
- complete conditions: These conditions determine when a started or restarted plan can be considered successfully completed.
- activate conditions: These can have the values "manual" or "automatic". If the activate mode is manual, the user is asked for a confirmation before the plan can be started.

Effects Effects describe the expected effect of a plan on the values of observable medical parameters (e.g. administration of insulin decreases the blood glucose levels). Effects can have associated a likelihood to state how likely they are to occur.

Plan-body The plan-body contains the actions and/or sub-plans that will be executed as part of the plan. A plan-body can have one of the following forms:

- user-performed: an action to be performed by the user, which requires user interaction and thus is not further modelled.
- single step: an action which can be either an activation of a sub-plan, an assignment of a variable, a request for an input value or an if-then-else statement.
- subplans: a set of plan steps to be performed in a given manner. The possibilities are: in sequence (SEQUENTIALLY), in parallel (PARALLEL), in any possible sequential order (ANY-ORDER), and in any possible order, sequential or not (UN-ORDERED).
- cyclical plan: a repetition of actions over time periods.
- loop construct: a repetition of actions, either in the form of the for loop of conventional programming languages, or iterating on the elements of a list or set.

In the case of subplans, besides the specification of the ordering (SEQUENTIALLY and so forth), it is necessary to specify a waiting strategy. The main aspect here is the so called continuation specification, which describes the plans that must be completed so that the parent plan can be considered successfully completed. For instance, it is possible to define whether all the subplans should be executed (ALL) or not (e.g. ONE or NONE).

Time-annotations Many elements in an Asbru plan (intentions, conditions, effects and plan activations) can have a time annotation. A time annotation specifies (1) in which interval things must start, (2) in which interval they must end, (3) their minimal and maximal duration, and (4) a reference time-point. Any of these elements can be left undefined, allowing the specification of incomplete time annotations. The general scheme for a time annotation is:

([earliest-starting-time, latest-starting-time],
 [earliest-finishing-time, latest-finishing-time],
 [minimal-duration, maximal-duration],
 reference-point)

The use of a time annotation in the context of a plan activation determines the span of time and duration that the plan under execution should have. For example, the action follow a folic acid treatment for 3-4 months, starting in first month of pregnancy, could be expressed as:

Folic-acid-treatment ([week 0, week 4],   "start in the first month"
                        [week 12, week 20],   "end in 3rd, 4th or 5th month"
                        [12 weeks, 16 weeks], "do it for 3-4 months"
                        conception)   "counting from conception"

However, time annotations associated to conditions indicate the period of time during which the conditions are to be evaluated. Once this time has elapsed, there is no possibility for the condition to become true. In case it is necessary to monitor continuously a condition, a special time annotation can be used: NOW.

3.2 Asbru Model of Jaundice Protocol

Figure 2 shows the global structure of the jaundice protocol as a hierarchy of plans. The most important entry point of the protocol is the plan "Diagnostics-and-treatment-hyperbilirubinemia" (the three "Check-for-..." plans are Asbru artifacts to model checkups at temporally specified intervals). Figure 2 shows that "Diagnostics-and-treatment-hyperbilirubinemia" is divided into a diagnostics and a treatment subplan, to be executed sequentially.

The diagnostics stage is again subdivided into four sequential subplans. One of these plans is "Jaundice-determination", which has four optional subplans among which one of them is required. The protocol specifies that one of the corresponding methods has to be applied to determine if jaundice is clinically significant. This has been modelled as an any-order plan with a waiting strategy ONE, which enables the execution of any of the subplans and states that only one of them is needed. In addition, each subplan has a manual activate condition which requires a confirmation by the user and thus enforces a manual selection.

The treatment phase consists of two subplans (see label (-)): "Regular-treatments" and "Exchange-transfusion". One of them, the "Regular-treatments" plan, contains the main treatment procedure. However, it is possible that this procedure is aborted at some point (when its abort condition becomes true), at which point the "Exchange-transfusion" plan is triggered: it is the emergency action to be taken when the "Regular-treatments" plan aborts. In such an emergency case, the prescriptions of both intensive phototherapy and exchange transfusion must be done, in parallel. In parallel with the treatment plans in group (-), further cyclical actions specify that two important parameters must be measured every 12-24 hours.

The "Regular-treatments" plan has also a quite complicated control structure. This plan consists of two parallel parts: the study of feeding alternatives and the different

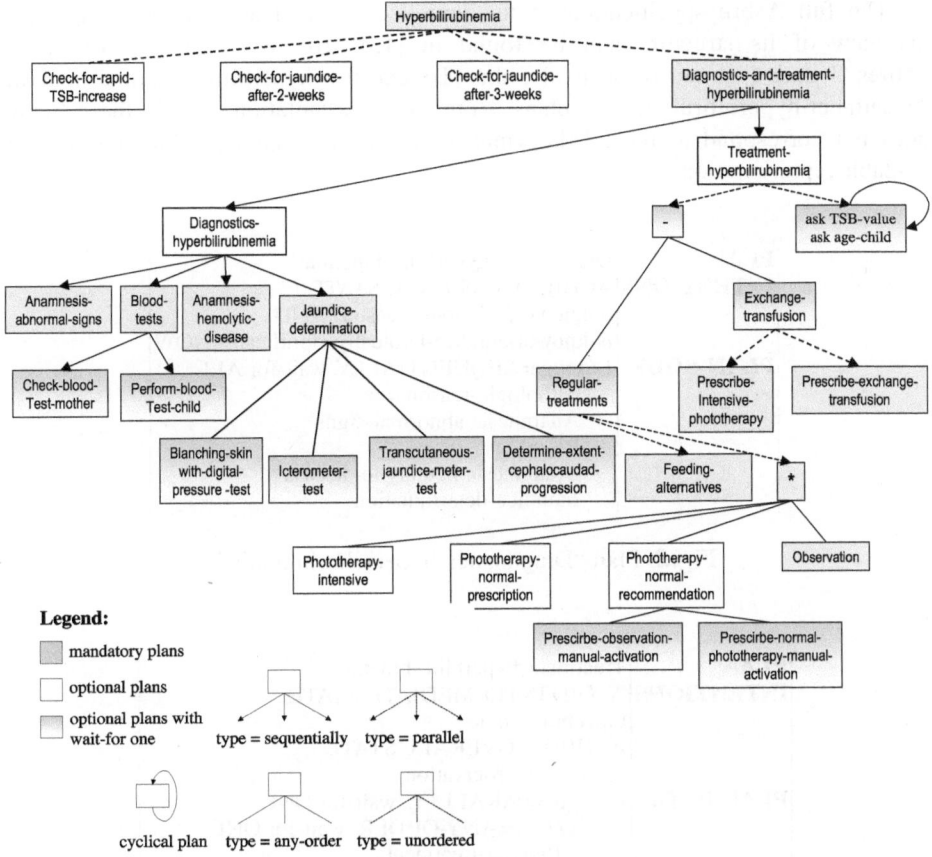

Fig. 2. Overview of the jaundice model in Asbru.

therapies (see label (*)). The plans in group (*) can be tried in any order, one at a time. The intentions of "Regular-treatments" plan are both avoiding toxic bilirubin levels and attaining normal (observation) ones at the end. The plan completes when the feeding alternatives and the therapies complete. The latter in turn depends on the completion of observation (compulsory). It aborts when either bilirubin raises to transfusion levels or intensive phototherapy fails to reduce them sufficiently, pointing to a pathologic reason.

The main surprise from this description is the richness and complexity of the control structures that are found in a medical protocol like the jaundice one: steps are executed in parallel or sequentially, in either a specific or an unspecified order; some steps are compulsory and other steps are optional; some plans are triggered when other plans abort; etc. The Asbru language contains a rich set of modelling primitives to represent these complicated control structures. Notice that these control structures (which apparently appear naturally in a realistic medical protocol) are much more complex than those found in typical programming languages or in planning languages.

The full Asbru specification of the jaundice protocol as well as a high-level overview of its structure can be found in [13]. To give a flavour of Asbru, figures 3 and 4 show, respectively, the "Diagnostics-hyperbilirubinemia" and the "Treatment-hyperbilirubinemia" plans. Notice that the notation used in these figures does not correspond to the XML syntax of the Asbru language, but it is a more readable representation[5].

PLAN	Diagnostics-hyperbilirubinemia
INTENTIONS	ACHIEVE OVERALL-STATE:
	is-known(pathologic-reason) AND
	is-known(jaundice-clinically-significant) NOW
PLAN-BODY	DO type=SEQUENTIALLY, wait-for ALL
	pathologic-reason = no
	Anamnesis-abnormal-signs
	Blood-tests
	Anamnesis-hemolytic-disease
	Jaundice-determination

Fig. 3. Plan "Diagnostics-hyperbilirubinemia".

PLAN	Treatment-hyperbilirubinemia
INTENTIONS	AVOID INTERMEDIATE-STATE:
	bilirubin = toxic
	ACHIEVE OVERALL STATE:
	bilirubin = observation
PLAN-BODY	DO type=PARALLEL, wait-for ONE
	DO type=ANY-ORDER, wait-for ONE
	Regular-treatments
	ON-ABORT Exchange-transfusion
	Exchange-transfusion
	CYCLICAL-PLAN
	DO type=SEQUENTIALLY, wait-for ALL
	ask TSB-value
	ask age-child
	retry-delay min = 12 h, max = 24 h

Fig. 4. Plan "Treatment-hyperbilirubinemia".

3.3 Benefits of Asbru Modelling: Detection of Protocol Anomalies

During the Asbru formalisation of this protocol, numerous anomalies became apparent. In a general sense, we have used the term anomaly to refer to any issue preventing a satisfactory interpretation of the original protocol. Below we give examples of the different types of anomalies we found. For presentation purposes we have grouped them into three general categories: ambiguity, incompleteness, inconsistency and redundancy.

---

[5] The full XML version of the protocol can be found in http://www.protocure.org/.

Examples of ambiguity: A problem we encountered during our modelling exercise in jaundice was determining whether the terms "jaundiced", "clinically jaundiced" and "clinically significant jaundice by medical judgement" have the same meaning or not. These are terms that are used in the flowchart form of the original protocol, but not defined elsewhere. In the Asbru protocol these different terms are translated into the single variable "jaundice-clinically-significant". See, for instance, the intentions of plan "Diagnostics-hyperbilirubinemia" in figure 3.

Examples of incompleteness: An example of incompleteness anomaly is the following: the original protocol contains a table with "factors to be considered when assessing a jaundiced infant". One of these factors is "Rapid increase in the TSB level after 24-48 h". However, what "rapid" exactly means is missing in the protocol. We have solved this problem by looking for the information in other protocols, and have given the rate value 0.5 mg/dl/h. This value is used e.g. in the filter condition of plan "Check-for-rapid-TSB-increase" (see figure 5).

PLAN	Check-for-rapid-TSB-increase
INTENTIONS	ACHIEVE OVERALL-STATE: is-known(possibility-of-G6PD) AND is-known(possibility-of-hemolytic-disease)
CONDITIONS	Filter: (TSB-decrease = no) NOW AND (TSB-change > 0.5) NOW
PLAN-BODY	DO type=SEQUENTIALLY, wait-for ALL possibility-of-hemolytic-disease = yes IF age = day2 THEN possibility-of-G6PD = yes Exit-possibility-of-G6PD ELSE possibility-of-G6PD = no Exit-possibility-of-hemolytic-disease

Fig. 5. Plan "Check-for-rapid-TSB-increase".

The rate of TSB increase is important for the treatment. The guideline says "Determination of the rate of rise of TSB and the infants age may help determine how often to monitor bilirubin levels and whether to begin phototherapy". To solve the imprecision of this sentence, we interviewed an expert, who provided us with the information that this monitoring should be done every 12-24 hours. This can be seen in the retry delay specification of the cyclical part within "Treatment-hyperbilirubinemia" plan (see figure 4).

Examples of inconsistency: We found an inconsistency concerning the applicability of the guideline. The guideline is meant for "healthy newborns" according to the title. The protocol specifies that "clinically jaundiced children of <= 24 hours old are not considered healthy". However, elsewhere in the protocol (in point 5 of the Evaluation part), an action is advised for exactly these children (i.e. the children to whom the protocol is not supposed to be applied): "A TSB level needs to be determined in infants noted to be jaundiced in the first 24 hours of life".

The previous inconsistency occurs only in the text version of the guideline and not in the flowchart form, where a simple exit condition is specified for these children. Our Asbru protocol models this version of the guideline.

Redundancy: Another type of anomaly is redundancy. We did not find any occurrence of this type of anomaly in the jaundice protocol. However, we did find redundancies during the Asbru modelling of a protocol for the management of diabetes mellitus type 2, developed by the Dutch Association of General Practitioners[6] [14].

To give a better idea of the extent of uncovered anomalies, some numbers follow (see [15] for more details and examples). In the case of jaundice protocol, we found 1 ambiguity, 10 incompleteness anomalies, 6 inconsistencies and no redundancy. Regarding the diabetes protocol, we identified 4 ambiguities, 38 incompletenesses and 2 redundancies, but no inconsistency.

3.4   Experiences and Difficulties

Next we summarise the lessons learned during the modelling of the informal guideline as an Asbru protocol. First of all, not all of Asbru's features described in section 3 were needed to model the protocol. This experience has been confirmed after the modelling other protocols. In particular, the following Asbru constructs were never used: setup, suspend and reactivate conditions, and effects. This has led us to the definition of Asbru-Light, a strict subset of Asbru containing only the features used in our case-studies until now.

Secondly, it was a significant surprise for us that even high quality protocols such as the jaundice protocol of the AAP contain significant numbers of anomalies, including serious problems such as inconsistencies. This already proves that the first step of our formalisation process is worth the significant effort it takes.

Although it is not described in this paper, we have used an interpreter of Asbru-Light to "debug" the jaundice protocol: by running the interpreter on case-data we could check if the protocol behaved as intended. It turns out that using the interpreter is necessary for improving the Asbru model. Of course, such a debug-run cycle is only possible after the protocol has been sufficiently formalised.

A final observation is the significant increase in size when going from the informal, original version of the protocol to the formal version thereof. The original 10 pages of the AAP protocol turned into 40 subplans, taking about 18 pages in the intermediate notation used in the figures above, and more than 2000 lines of XML in the machine readable version of Asbru. We have observed the same effect in our other case-studies.

4   Formalising the Jaundice Protocol in KIV

In the second stage of our formalisation case-study we have used the KIV verification tool [16]. KIV is an interactive theorem prover with strong proof support for higher order logic and elaborate heuristics for automation. Currently, special proof support for temporal logic and parallel programs is being added. In contrast to fully automatic

---

[6] http://nhg.artsennet.nl/standaarden/M01/start.htm

verification tools, the use of KIV interactive tool allows for the verification of large and complex systems, as it has been shown by its application to a number of real-world systems (distributed systems, control systems, etc.).

4.1   KIV

KIV supports the entire software development process, i.e. the specification, the implementation and the verification of software systems. Next we will briefly describe the relevant aspects of KIV for Asbru specification and verification needs.

For specification, three aspects are important: specifications can be structured, and both functional and operational system aspects can be described. A specification is broken down into smaller and more tractable components using structuring operations such as union and enrichment, that can be used to combine more simple specifications. For functional aspects, algebraic specifications are used to specify abstract data types.

Complex operational behaviour can be specified using parallel programs. Programs in KIV can contain assignments ($v := \tau$), conditionals (**if** φ_{pl} **then** ψ_1 **else** ψ_2), loops (**while** φ_{pl} **do** ψ), local variables (**var** $v = \tau$ **in** ψ), nondeterministic choices (**choose** φ **or** ψ), interleaving ($\varphi \parallel \psi$) and synchronisation points (**await** φ_{pl}).

For a better support of Asbru, additional basic constructs have been implemented: interrupts (**break** ψ **if** φ_{pl}), for modelling different plan conditions, and synchronous parallel execution ($\varphi \parallel_s \psi$), as well as any-order execution ($\varphi \parallel_a \psi$), for a more direct translation of plan bodies. With the help of these constructs, the main features of Asbru-Light can be translated one to one. Others still need to be encoded using additional program variables.

Concerning the verification, we use a variant of Interval Temporal Logic (ITL) [17] to formulate properties about Asbru plans. This logic is first order and allows finite and infinite intervals. In this paper we will restrict ourselves to the temporal operators always ($2\,\varphi$), eventually ($3\,\varphi$), next ($\circ\,\varphi$), and **last**–which is true only in the last step of an interval.

Single transitions are expressed as first order relations between unprimed and primed variables (v and v'). A primed variable represents the value of the variable in the next state. For example, the formula $v = 0 \wedge (2\,v' = v + 1) \rightarrow 3\,v = n$ states that, if variable v is initially 0, and the value v' in the next state is always incremented by one, then eventually the variable will be equal to an arbitrary natural number n.

In KIV, the proof technique for verifying parallel programs is symbolic execution with induction. Details can be found in [18]. Since programs are treated as formulas –for both, the semantics is a set of traces– they can be arbitrarily mixed. This gives rise to a modular proof technique, which is very important for the verification of Asbru plans as they tend to be large.

4.2   KIV Formalisation of Jaundice Protocol

In order to formally examine Asbru plans in a first attempt, we have translated them into parallel programs. The translation of the Asbru model into KIV has been done in a structure preserving way, by mapping each Asbru plan into a KIV specification. This has been possible thanks to the modularisation facilities that KIV provides. Thus, the structure of the jaundice protocol in KIV roughly mirrors the Asbru model shown in figure 2. This is one of the key ideas of our formalisation strategy, because it gives the possibility to obtain some feedback from the specification and verification phases in terms of the Asbru model, and to exploit this structure during proof attempts.

Following this idea, Asbru plans have to be translated into different types of KIV programs. For the moment this translation has been performed manually. Table 1 gives some of the translations of Asbru constructs into KIV programs that we have used in this process.

Table 1. Translation of some Asbru constructs into KIV.

Asbru	KIV
filter condition φ NOW body	**await** φ; body
filter condition φ body	**if** φ **then** body
complete condition φ body	**break** body **if** φ
abort condition φ body	**break** body **if** φ
<<name>> (*plan activation*)	<<name>>#(...) (*procedure call*)
do type=sequentially P1,... Pn	P1;... Pn
do type=any-order P1,... Pn	P1 $\|_a$ ... Pn
do type=unordered P1,... Pn	P1 $\|_s$ ... Pn
wait-for Pi body	**break** body **if** *some expression on* Pi-state

The example in figure 6, corresponding to the plan "Diagnostics-hyperbilirubinemia" of figure 3, serves to illustrate the kind of translations that have been obtained. In this example we can see that the KIV translation closely follows the structure of the original Asbru plan, except for an additional interrupt (break) construct. This construct has been introduced to model the waiting strategy of the plan, which is "wait-for ALL". This implies that all the subplans must complete successfully so that the parent plan can do so. Conversely, as soon as any of the subplans abort, the parent will abort too. The latter has been modelled with the help of specific plan state variables which are explicitly set within the subplans. Other translations, however, did not result in a version so close to the Asbru plan. This is due to the encodings necessary to represent the Asbru elements not directly supported by KIV.

Currently we are working on the verification of several protocol properties. Properties are expressed in the above described variant of ITL. For instance:

$$Diagnostics-hyperbilirubinemia\#(\ldots) \wedge (2\ time'' = time' + 1) \rightarrow 3\ \textbf{last}$$

is a property expressing the termination of the previous program/Asbru plan. It states that, if the program $Diagnostics-hyperbilirubinemia$ is executed, it will stop sometime in the future. The always formula in the antecedent is used to model the environment, in which time changes from one state to the next.

Termination of (sub)plans is a basic property necessary to prove the termination of the protocol. Although it might seem a not very interesting property in itself, our

```
Diagnostics-hyperbilirubinemia#(var patient-data, time,
     jaundice-clinically-significant, pathologic-reason)
begin
  var anamnesis-abnormal-signs-state = inactive,
       blood-tests-state = inactive,
       anamnesis-hemolytic-disease-state = inactive in begin
    break begin
       pathologic-reason := false;
       anamnesis-abnormal-signs#(; time, pathologic-reason,
           anamnesis-abnormal-signs-state);
       blood-tests#(; patient-data, time, pathologic-reason,
           blood-tests-state);
       anamnesis-hemolytic-disease#(; time, pathologic-reason,
           anamnesis-hemolytic-disease-state);
       jaundice-determination#(; time, jaundice-clinically-significant)
    end
    if   anamnesis-abnormal-signs-state = aborted
       ∨ blood-tests-state = aborted
       ∨ anamnesis-hemolytic-disease-state = aborted
  end
end
```

Fig. 6. KIV translation of "Diagnostics-hyperbilirubinemia" plan.

experiences until now show that it can serve to identify assumptions implicitly made in the protocol. These assumptions could be used e.g. to improve the description of the applicability conditions of the original protocol.

Another promising property is ensuring that the intentions of a plan follow from the intentions of its subplans. Although Asbru intentions are not included in the KIV formulation, they can be used to verify if the composition of subplans complies with what is intended in the plan.

As part of the IST Protocure[7] project, we are investigating other properties more significant from the medical point of view. Amongst them, we can cite the use of indicators issued by medical organisations, which define a variety of features that specific protocols should comply with.

4.3 Experiences and Difficulties

In the following paragraphs we briefly describe the experiences in the second stage of our formalisation case-study, and in our first verification attempts.

First, the KIV formalisation step has taken considerably less effort than the Asbru modelling one. This is mainly due to the structure preserving strategy we have followed. Thanks to it, the formalisation roughly consists in the translation of Asbru plans into KIV procedures.

Second, concerning this translation, a limitation of the current approach is that it is not automatic. Besides, in some cases it requires many creative tricks to adequately

[7] http://www.protocure.org/

encode the Asbru constructs not directly supported by KIV. As result, sometimes the KIV translation suffers from a weak resemblance to the initial Asbru protocol. These problems will be solved if verification turns out to be profitable, by means of a direct KIV support of Asbru syntax allowing for a direct translation of arbitrary Asbru models.

We cannot strictly say that the formalisation in KIV has contributed to the improvement of the original protocol, as in the case of its Asbru modelling. As for the verification, after the completion of the first proofs we can say that it is feasible and that it serves to detect implicit knowledge, such as underlying assumptions. We are confident that it is possible to use the jaundice formalisation and KIV for the verification of more significant properties like the ones mentioned before, which could actually be used to improve the original protocol.

5   Conclusions

It is of course well known that many forms of knowledge can be represented in languages that are formalised to a certain extent. Indeed this is the entire premise of fields such as knowledge engineering and knowledge representation. However, we would argue that it is a non-trivial result that is has turned out to be feasible to formalise a significant piece of realistic medical knowledge to such an amount of detail that it can be used as the basis for mechanised theorem proving (a much greater level of formality than is used even in common mathematical publications). This shows that the traditional gap between practical knowledge engineering and academic formal knowledge representation can indeed be bridged even for realistic applications.

Naturally, such an achievement comes at a price: a significant amount of effort is required for such a formalisation effort. Although we are not in a position to make strong quantitative statements, the case-study reported has taken close to a person-year to complete.

However, we would argue that this price is worth paying. A number of anomalies were uncovered in the original medical guideline, even though this guideline is representative of the best quality that the medical profession can offer. All of these anomalies were uncovered in the first stage of our formalisation (from original guideline to Asbru). The most important contribution of the second stage of our formalisation (from Asbru to KIV) until now has been to disambiguate any remaining unclarities in the Asbru model that resulted from the first stage: a number of semantic problems with Asbru were uncovered, and finally resolved by providing a fully formal semantics of Asbru in KIV. To date, we have only very limited experience in using the KIV formalisation in formal proofs of properties of the protocol. We expect that this usage of KIV will uncover further anomalies in the protocol.

A final observation is that of the two steps in our formalisation process (from original guideline to Asbru, and from Asbru to KIV), the first step was by far the most labour intensive. This step involved most of the conceptual analysis that was required for the formalisation. Consequently, we would argue that this stage of the formalisation process would benefit from being split up in a number of smaller steps, each yielding its own model, in ever increasing degrees of formality.

Acknowledgements

This work has been partially supported by the European Commission's IST program, under contract number IST-2001-33049–Protocure. We also want to thank Hugo Roomans and Geert Berger, for their contribution to the Asbru modelling of the jaundice protocol, Tibor Bosse, for his work on the interpreter of Asbru-Light and his efforts in debugging the protocol, and all other Protocure members: Silvia Miksch, Andreas Seyfang, Wolfgang Reif, Cristoph Duelli, Kitty Rosenbrand, Joyce van Croonenborg, and Peter Lucas.

References

[1] Weingarten, S.: Using Practice Guideline Compendiums To Provide Better Preventive Care. Annals of Internal Medicine **130** (1999) 454–458

[2] Field, M., Lohr, K., eds.: Clinical Practice Guidelines: Directions for a New Program. National Academy Press, Washington D.C., USA (1992)

[3] Woolf, S., Grol, R., Hutchinson, A., Eccles, M., Grimshaw, J.: Potential benefits, limitations, and harms of clinical guidelines. British Medical Journal **318** (1999) 527–530

[4] Clayton, P., Hripsak, G.: Decision support in healthcare. Int. J. of Biomedical Computing **39** (1995) 59–66

[5] Graham, I., Calder, L., Hébert, P., Carter, A., Tetroe, J.: A comparison of clinical practice guideline appraisal instruments. International Journal of Technology Assessment in Health Care **16** (2000) 1024–1038

[6] Musen, M., Rohn, J., Fagan, L., Shortliffe, E.: Knowledge engineering for a clinical trial advice system: Uncovering errors in protocol specification. Bulletin du Cancer **74** (1987) 291–296

[7] AAP: American Academy of Pediatrics, Provisional Committee for Quality Improvement and Subcommittee on Hyperbilirubinemia. Practice parameter: management of hyperbilirubinemia in the healthy term newborn. Pediatrics **94** (1994) 558–565

[8] Elkin, P., Peleg, M., Lacson, R., Bernstam, E., Tu, S., Boxwala, A., Greenes, R., Shortliffe, E.: Toward Standardization of Electronic Guidelines. MD Computing **17** (2000) 39–44

[9] Miksch, S.: Plan Management in the Medical Domain. AI Communications **12** (1999) 209–235

[10] Ohno-Machado, L., Gennari, J., Murphy, S., Jain, N., Tu, S., Oliver, D., Pattison-Gordon, E., Greenes, R., Shortliffe, E., Octo Barnett, G.: Guideline Interchange Format: a model for representing guidelines. J. of the American Medical Informatics Association **5** (1998) 357–372

[11] Fox, J., Johns, N., Lyons, C., Rahmanzadeh, A., Thomson, R., Wilson, P.: PROforma: a general technology for clinical decision support systems. Computer Methods and Programs in Biomedicine **54** (1997) 59–67

[12] Shahar, Y., Miksch, S., Johnson, P.: The Asgaard project: a task-specific framework for the application and critiquing of time-oriented clinical guidelines. Artificial Intelligence in Medicine **14** (1998) 29–51

[13] Roomans, H., Berger, G., Marcos, M., ten Teije, A., Seyfang, A., van Harmelen, F.: Asbru Protocol for the Management of Hyperbilirubinemia in the Healthy Term Newborn. Technical Report IR-495, Vrije Universiteit Amsterdam (2002) To be published.

[14] Rutten, G., Verhoeven, S., Heine, R., de Grauw, W., Cromme, P., Reenders, K., van Ballegooie, E., Wiersma, T.: NHG-Standaard Diabetes Mellitus Type 2 (eerste herziening). Huisarts en Wetenschap **42** (1999) 67–84 First revision.

[15] Marcos, M., Roomans, H., ten Teije, A., van Harmelen, F.: Improving medical protocols through formalisation: a case study. In: Session on Formal Methods in Healthcare, 6th International Conference on Integrated Design and Process Technology (IDPT-02). (2002)

[16] Balser, M., Reif, W., Schellhorn, G., Stenzel, K., Thums, A.: Formal system development with KIV. In Maibaum, T., ed.: Fundamental Approaches to Software Engineering. Number 1783 in LNCS, Springer (2000)

[17] Moszkowski, B.: A temporal logic for multilevel reasoning about hardware. IEEE Computer **18** (1985) 10–19

[18] Balser, M., Duelli, C., Reif, W., Schellhorn, G.: Verifying concurrent systems with symbolic execution. Journal of Logic and Computation (Special Issue) (2002)

KMsim: A Meta-modelling Approach and Environment for Creating Process-Oriented Knowledge Management Simulations

Anjo Anjewierden[1], Irina Shostak[2], and Robert de Hoog[1,2]

[1] Social Science Informatics, University of Amsterdam,
Roetersstraat 15, 1018 WB Amsterdam, The Netherlands,
anjo@swi.psy.uva.nl
[2] Faculty of Educational Science and Technology, University of Twente,
PO Box 217, 7500 AE Enschede, The Netherlands,
{shostak,hoog}@edte.utwente.nl

Abstract. This paper presents a new approach to modelling process-oriented knowledge management (KM) and describes a simulation environment (called KMSIM) that embodies the approach. Since the beginning of modelling researchers have been looking for better and novel ways to model systems and to use appropriate software to create simulations. The application of the approach and KM-SIM make it possible to create realistic business models (BMs) and simulate the consequences of KM interventions and events. The validity of the approach and tools is being evaluated in the game KM Quest.

1 Introduction

With the ever growing interest for knowledge management, it is unavoidable that the demand for a more formal approach increases in parallel. After the first flush of ideas, whose main function it was to create awareness, more precise and hands-on methods are called for (see for example [9]). This holds in particular for models that show how knowledge and knowledge processes can influence organisational effectiveness (see [5], [4] and [8]). This "show how" becomes even more valuable when these influences can be simulated in a business model (BM), as this is the only way one can capture and understand the dynamics of knowledge. The need for modelling and simulating knowledge management relevant business models raises the question whether additional tools are required beyond the standard simulation environments already available.

This paper describes KMSIM, a set of tools which have been specifically designed to support creating and simulating knowledge management relevant business models. It is argued that the need for these tools can be derived from the nature of knowledge management as a discipline, the peculiar properties of knowledge relevant business models and the intended users of the tools. The tools were developed in the context of the KITS project. The goal of this project is to develop a comprehensive game-based collaborative learning environment for knowledge management called KM Quest [1]. An essential part of this environment is a knowledge management relevant business model that simulates the behaviour of a (fictitious) company. This model has been developed and partly validated with the tools described in this paper.

A. Gómez-Pérez and V.R. Benjamins (Eds.): EKAW 2002, LNAI 2473, pp. 65–79, 2002.

The paper consists of four sections. In Sect. 2 the factors driving the need for a specific and new set of tools are discussed. Sect. 3 describes the architecture of the simulation environment based on the requirements. The last two sections describe the functionality provided by the tools from the point of view of creating business models (Sect. 4) and simulating and validating these models (Sect. 5).

Acknowledgements We would like to thank the three anonymous reviewers whose comments we have tried to take into account. Work partially supported by the European Community under the Information Society Technology (IST) RTD programme, contract IST-1999-13078 (KITS). The authors are solely responsible for the content of this article. It does not represent the opinion of the European Community, and the European Community is not responsible for any use that might be made of data appearing herein. Partners in the KITS project are University of Twente (NL), University of Amsterdam (NL), CIBIT (NL), ECLO (UK), Tecnopolis (I) and EADS (F).

2   Factors Driving the Design of the Tools

2.1   Knowledge Management Has an "Object"

Knowledge management, as a branch of general management disciplines, has an "object" that is different from the "objects" that are the focus of other sub-disciplines. There are many simulation environments that allow one to model various kinds of business processes, including manufacturing, public systems, and service systems simulations (for example Powersim®). Most environments, however, do not provide for treating knowledge as a *simulated entity*. Rather, in these environments the simulated entities are the *implicit result* of applying knowledge in a specific domain. Knowledge is not considered an object on which different actions can be applied, for example to model "stocks" and "flows" of knowledge.

To illustrate this idea, consider a manufacturing simulation which allows one to get answers to questions like "How can work-in-process inventory and cycle time be reduced while increasing throughput?" or "When should the next piece of equipment be purchased and how many people are needed to work with this equipment?" In this simulation knowledge about manufacturing processes is *applied* while simulating inventory, amount of labour, time are *not taken as a simulated entity* in contrast to knowledge management simulations. "Stocks" and "flows" of domain-specific knowledge compose the area of interest of KM simulations. For KM simulations it is important to quantify, measure and model "manufacturing knowledge" as a simulated entity, which can be done by introducing variables such as level of competence in manufacturing and speed of knowledge gain in manufacturing. As an example of one of the first knowledge management simulations we can mention *Tango!* [2]. Apparently the business model underlying this simulation does not handle knowledge as a separate entity, but operates directly through employees on key performance indicators of a company. So, the nature of the object of knowledge management in terms of stocks and flows requires a set of tools that allows the modeller of the knowledge management relevant business to map the "paper" representation of this model with a minimum of effort on a simulation engine.

2.2 Nature of the Knowledge Management Relevant Business Model

The model that is introduced in this paper was developed for KM training and is applied in the game KM Quest. To support this function the business model should satisfy the following basic principles:

- A business units' output depends on the *level of knowledge* and the *level of knowledge usage* (or utilisation). The output of work would be more valuable if people in the company possess better and use/apply (more recent, novel, advanced) knowledge. However this result could be counteracted by non-effective organisation of work processes, and vice versa. The ideal situation consists of effective organisation of work processes and highly skilled, highly knowledgeable employees.
- Certain changes outside or inside a company should influence its knowledge household – individual and organisational knowledge.
- An important assumption is that knowledge can be seen as a quantifiable object and can be measured in relative terms.
- There is a natural depreciation of knowledge due to volatility, instability, and ageing of knowledge. If in a company nobody takes care of renewal, gaining, and retention of knowledge, the company will in the long run not be able to compete with market conditions.

These considerations play a fundamental role in our modelling approach. Thus, in the model knowledge "stocks" are introduced as the level of competence(s) and knowledge "flows" are introduced as the efficiency of processes involving knowledge, such as knowledge gaining, development, utilisation, transfer, and retention.

Simply stated, any event that happens outside or inside the company and any interventions taken inside the company can have an influence on the knowledge processes – knowledge flows. These also influence the "state" of knowledge in the organisation – knowledge stocks, which influence business processes and determine their quality. Finally, the business processes contribute and generate the values of the key organisational effectiveness variables like profit and market share.

Based on what has been said above, our modelling approach resulted in a four-level model consisting of:

Organisational effectiveness variables These variables reflect the competitive characteristics of the company and are represented by variables like market share, profit, level of sales and so on.

Business processes related variables These reflect the quality of internal processes and "how well" work is done within the company. Examples are: average time of bringing a new product to the market and production level.

Knowledge related variables These variables reflect the relevant knowledge domains (e.g. marketing, research, production) and represent the level of competence in each domain.

Knowledge processes related variables Reflect the properties of processes involving knowledge in the organisation (e.g., speed of knowledge gaining, effectiveness of knowledge transfer).

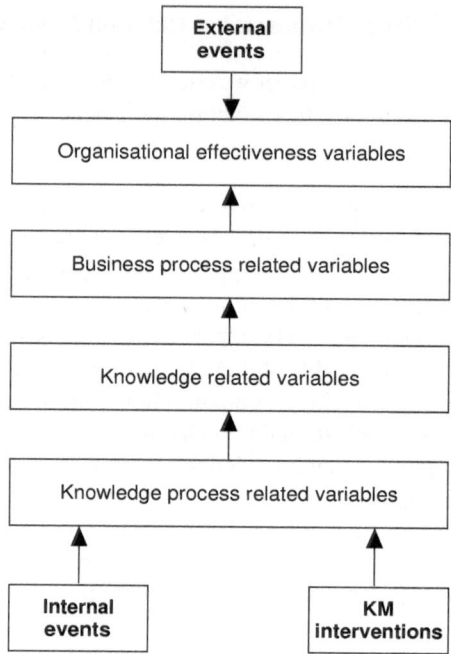

Fig. 1. Conceptual structure of the business model

The general structure of this knowledge management relevant business model is shown in Fig. 1.

Events and interventions are important components of the model. In our view, events are any changes outside or inside a company that happen independently from management of a company. Interventions are actions taken by management in order to prevent or to react to events and are aimed at improving the *knowledge household* of a company. These interventions become *knowledge management* interventions and differ from managerial interventions by its operational object(s).

However, knowledge is something that is difficult to measure in absolute terms. So, it is impossible to perform actions that (immediately) increase the "amount" of knowledge, i.e. quantitative characteristics of knowledge. On the other hand, it is relevant and possible to change the quantity of other objects such as raw materials, time, amount of labour, investments, which are the subjects of other managerial interventions. One can argue that managerial decisions concern not only these tangible, physical objects, but also include decisions about strategic development, market policy and strategies, partnership policy, and so on. Those decisions are qualitative and based on and impacting knowledge that is needed for a company to improve its value. Simpler examples include the decisions to conduct training programmes or ICT implementation. Those decisions lead to qualitative changes in the organisation and, in many cases, cannot be measured directly and more importantly they affect the *knowledge household*.

As a consequence we should treat interventions not as a quantitative, but as qualitative entities and which require a very specific implementation in the simulation.

Summarizing what was discussed above and referring to the classification of models [6], and the types of interactions that can occur between discretely changing and continuously changing state variables [7], both discrete and continuous components must be present in our simulation model, in particular the ones listed below:

- State variables change continuously with respect to time. Knowledge related variables exhibit decay behaviour and consequently influence the state of other types of variables;
- Discrete events (in our terminology - events and KM interventions) cause discrete changes in the value of continuous state variables;
- Continuous state variables achieving threshold values may cause a discrete event to occur. Threshold values of knowledge related variables could be conditioned to enable occurrence of several events. This feature of the model is relevant for the game and probably not applicable in reality, since events are unpredictable in many cases. Despite this fact, events still can be generated to consider several scenarios.

In addition we assume that the state of the business is never monitored on a permanent basis as is done both on aircraft and in many industrial processes. Usually some kind of reporting takes place at fixed points in time (monthly, quarterly, yearly). This should also be reflected in the model: it should be able to provide reports about relevant variables at pre-determined time intervals.

2.3   Practical Requirements for Tool Support

Apart from factors derived from the topic (knowledge management) and the business model, also factors reflecting the intended users of a tool are important. In general, the quality of a tool depends to a large extent on how the vocabulary of the user is made available in terms of tool functionality. The operationalisation of the functionality should be hidden from the user as much as possible.

In the KM Quest context the main concern is the need for modifying business models. As only rarely a single model can serve different purposes, one expects that people want to tailor a model to their own organisational context or even build an entirely new model. People having the knowledge to modify or build those models, usually don't have the skills needed to implement it in a simulation engine. Thus what is needed is a fairly simple and easy to learn way of creating running simulations. The technical skills we expect from users are more or less similar to the skills needed to use spreadsheets. Satisfying this requirement makes it possible that a business model can be created or modified, and simulated interactively without any technical training. Some further, more detailed, requirements are:

- Dedicated support for creating, modifying and maintaining BMs, interventions and events
- Vocabulary of the BM modeller and the tools is identical
- No limits in terms of complexity of the model and all common mathematical modelling constructs

- Automatic error detection where possible
- Extensive support for simulation, visualisation and validation

We are not aware of an existing simulation environment that is sufficiently close to what our model requires, in particular the notion of interventions and events acting on the BM variables. Using a general purpose simulation or programming environment is not an option, given the intended users.

From a historical point of view, we would like to note that in the KITS project initially extensive tool support was not deemed necessary. It soon became apparent that the nature of BMs in general and the additional complexities of connecting KM interventions to such BMs made dedicated tool support a necessity.

3   Architecture

In this section we provide an overview of the architecture of the tools. The main architectural decision is to maintain two representations of the BM. The first representation is a *specification* in terms of the meta-model. This specification can be edited and browsed by a set of model entry tools. The second representation is *operational*, and is a translation of the specification into storage, computational statements and control structures. The operational representation, called the BM engine, computes successive states of the BM and is used by the simulation and validation tools. Obviously, the translation from specification to engine is completely transparent to the user (Fig. 2).

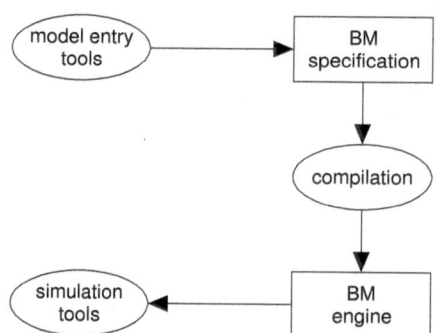

Fig. 2. Representations and tools involved in the architecture of KMSIM

The requirements are realised in detail through seven tools which are briefly described below. There is an additional tool to make the BM engine available as a server over the internet, following from a requirement of KM Quest. All tools are implemented in XPCE-Prolog [10].

Model entry (three tools) A BM can be created, modified and viewed using three model entry tools for the variables, interventions and events respectively (Sect. 4).

These tools allow the specification of the BM in terms the modeller will be familiar with: status of variables, ranges, constraints on variable values, notions of decay and depreciation, influence over time, delay and effects of interventions and events. In addition, some administrative aspects can be entered (domain within the company, precision for visualisation, description).

Charts design Charts are an important way to convey values of BM variables to the user. A high-level chart design tool supports the definition of visually attractive charts. The simulation tool automatically links values to the charts. The charts design tool is not further discussed in this paper.

Simulation Interaction between a user (model developer, validator, game player) and the BM is possible in a simulation tool (Sect. 5). The user can activate and de-activate interventions, issue events and view the effects on the BM variables as charts, numerically (HTML, XML) or as a comprehensive visualisation of all knowledge process related variables (called the *knowledge map*).

Validation and tuning support A very important aspect of a simulation environment is to provide assistance for tuning and validating the model. These tasks are supported by a tuning tool (which randomly generates events and interventions and checks whether user defined assertions are met) and a tool that traces the behaviour of the model graphically (Sect. 5.2).

Embedding A special version of the BM engine, called the BM server, can be run as a server on the internet in which it communicates using XML as input (specifying events and interventions) and outputs the BM state in XML and charts as bitmapped images. The BM server is used as part of KM Quest.

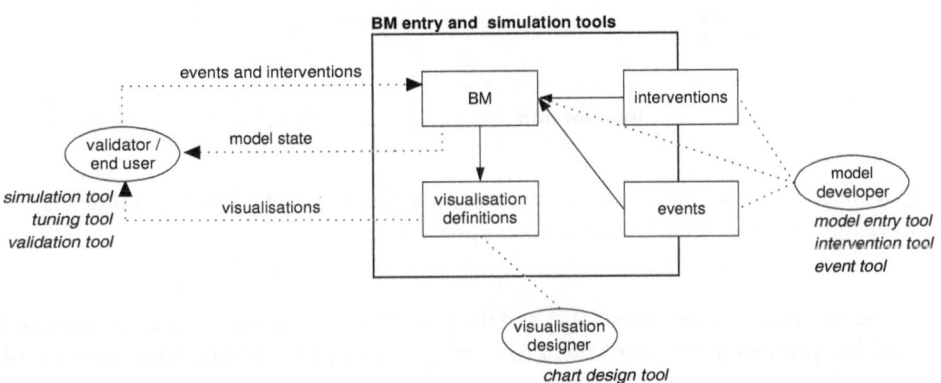

Fig. 3. Tools in KMSIM as seen from the roles of those interacting with them

Fig. 3 shows the roles of the various users involved with the tools. The *model developer* uses the model entry tools to create a BM and associate KM interventions and events with the BM. A *visualisation designer* defines how variables in the model are shown to the user. The *validator* uses the the simulation, tuning and validation tools to verify the correctness of the BM. Often the model developer and the validator will be the same person. And finally, the *end user* interacts with the BM engine embedded in the KM Quest game.

4 Model Entry Tools

The "core" BM represents a model of a company. The variables part of the BM are related to the business process (e.g. production level, number of employees), the knowledge process (e.g. competence in marketing), and the organisational effectiveness (profit, market share). The relations between these variables are such that the organisational effectiveness of the company deteriorates (*decay*) when no attempts are made to improve the knowledge process through interventions.

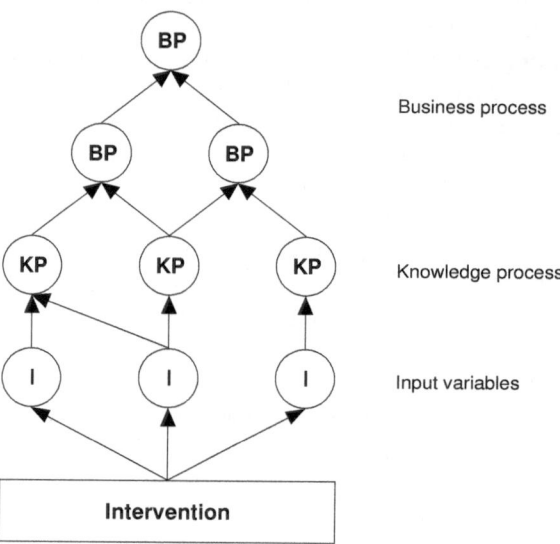

Fig. 4. Interventions (and events) influence input variables, which in turn influence the knowledge process variables and business process.

The link between the "core" BM and the knowledge management interventions and events is represented by a set of *input variables*. A "complete" BM therefore consists of the "core" BM and the input variables (see also Fig. 4). Because there are no randomised elements in the BM, it will always display the same behaviour when no interventions are implemented and no events occur.

Interventions and events are defined in terms of how they affect the input variables.[1] This makes it possible to define interventions and events independently of the BM. A BM that can be simulated therefore requires: (1) a BM consisting of variables representing the business and knowledge processes, input variables that distribute the effects

---

[1] External events can also affect the organisational effectiveness variables directly, for example when a competitor brings an innovative product to the market and thereby gains market share.

of interventions and events over knowledge process variables; (2) a set of interventions; and (3) a set of events. Different simulations can be created by replacing the interventions and/or events, without changing the BM.

4.1 Business Model Entry Tool

The BM entry tool supports the creation and modification of a business model. Each variable in the model has several attributes (see Fig. 5) defined in an ontology. Most of the concepts in this ontology are fixed, some, for example the domains in the company (marketing, research) can be changed by the user. One of the attributes is a *formula* which explicitly specifies how the value of the variable is computed and implicitly defines the influence relation between variables. An important aspect of the nature of the BM is the notion of time. This is modelled in discrete periods, which are called *cycles* in the tool.

The initial state of the model (cycle 0) is bootstrapped by computing constants. The constants represent a particular business case and can be used to "scale" the model for companies of various sizes or currencies.

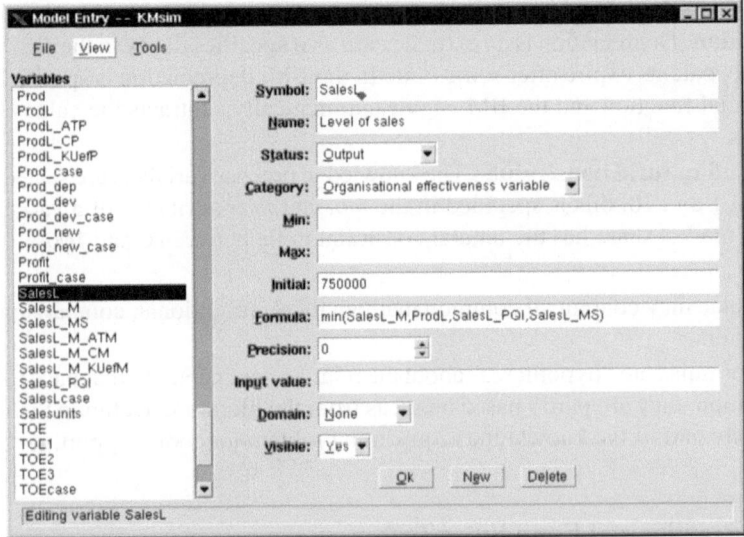

Fig. 5. Business model entry tool

A subsequent state of the model is computed by ordering the variables on their dependency on other variables. Once all dependent variables are computed, the formula associated with a variable is applied by the BM engine. Some examples of how BM notions are mapped onto formulae are given below:

Decay As explained in Sect. 2 the decay of knowledge process variables is fundamental to our meta-model. We can model the decay of knowledge utilisation with the

formula KU = KU * C1 (where C1 is a constant, e.g. C1 = 0.94). The BM
engine translates this formula to $KU_c = KU_{c-1} * C1$, where KU_c stands for the
value of KU in the current cycle and KU_{c-1} for the value in the previous cycle.
Because of the propagation of values from knowledge process (via knowledge and
business process variables) to organisational effectiveness, the overall performance
of the company will also exhibit decay.

Propagation of influence An example of influence between variables is the formula
for competence in marketing: CM = KG + KD + KR. The level of competence
depends on knowledge gain (KG), development (KD) and retention (KR). Here, all
variables are computed using the same cycle, which implies that KG, KD and KR
have to be computed first and that the computation is $CM_c = KG_c + KD_c + KR_c$.
A visualisation of influences and computation order can be seen in Fig. 8.

Relative change and delayed influence Relative change and delayed influence can be
computed by referring to a previous cycle using the notation V - V[-1] which
is the difference between the value during the current and the previous cycle (computationally $V_c - V_{c-1}$).

Constrained values Values can be constrained by other values. For example, the sales
level is constrained by the production level and sales level based on market share
(see example in Fig. 5).

Depreciation Depreciation is an extreme case as it specifies decay in the *future*. For example, patents expire after some time. In the BM, depreciation is specified through
a special function and the BM engine automatically subtracts the values for future
cycles.

Scaling and natural constraints The knowledge process variables are scaled to lie between 1 and 10, this is specified in the *min* and *max* attributes of a variable. Similarly, market share has the natural constraint to lie between 0 and 100%.

Formulae may contain all common mathematical, conditional, comparison and logical operators.

The formulae are "hypotheses" about the relative dependencies that have to be tested
by simulation, they are partly based on ideas from the literature. Defining the formulaes
is obviously part of the knowledge acquisition problem the tools support.

4.2 Intervention and Event Entry Tools

Interventions (Fig. 6) and events consist of a control and a computational part. The control part states whether the intervention or event is possible and the computational part
states which input variables (see Fig. 4) are affected. Events are slightly more complicated than interventions as they may depend on the current state of the model, whereas
interventions do not. For example, the event "intranet breaks down" requires that the
model is in a state in which the intranet is installed (through an intervention). Events
therefore may have enabling and disabling conditions. If these conditions are not specified, the event can always occur. Otherwise interventions and events are specified in
precisely the same manner and we will only consider interventions in this section.

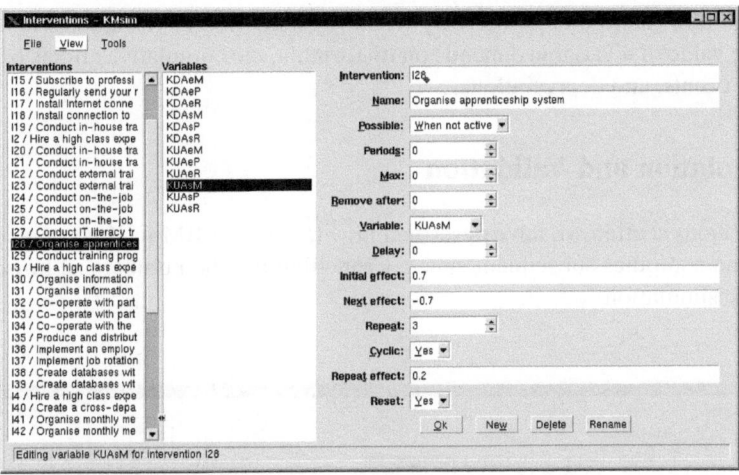

Fig. 6. Intervention entry tool

The control and computational aspects of interventions are:

Control aspects The control aspects deal with the possibility, frequency and duration
of an intervention. An intervention can be unavailable because it has already been
implemented (e.g. installing an intranet). An intervention can be implemented a
limited number of times (*Max*), there has to be some time between subsequent implementations (*Periods*) or the intervention is automatically removed after a certain
number of cycles (*Remove after*).

Computational aspects For each input variable (middle browser in Fig. 6) affected
by an intervention, the effect has to be specified. Unfortunately, a simple formula
does not suffice here, as the effect may be distributed over time in complicated
ways. For example, installing an intranet has immediate effect on expenses (i.e.
buying equipment), but there are additional expenses periodically (i.e. hiring staff
to maintain the intranet). The effect of interventions (and events) is specified using
the following vocabulary:

Delay Many of the KM interventions do not take immediate effect, there is a *delay*
of some cycles.

Initial effect The initial effect of an intervention is usually positive (e.g. knowledge development increases).

Next effect But, this effect disappears completely or partially.

Repeat and repeat effect Effects can repeat every so many cycles (e.g. paying for
subscriptions).

The BM engine treats the effects of interventions similarly to depreciation. When
an intervention is implemented the future changes to the input variables are computed
and these values are used when computing subsequent states of the model. These future
effects are not applied when an intervention is undone.

It may now also be apparent why existing simulation environments could not be used. The value of a variable depends on its formula, the cumulative effects of interventions and events, and depreciations.

5 Simulation and Validation

In the previous section we have described how to create a BM in KMSIM and how the BM engine computes subsequent states. Crunching out the numbers is, however, only part of the simulation.

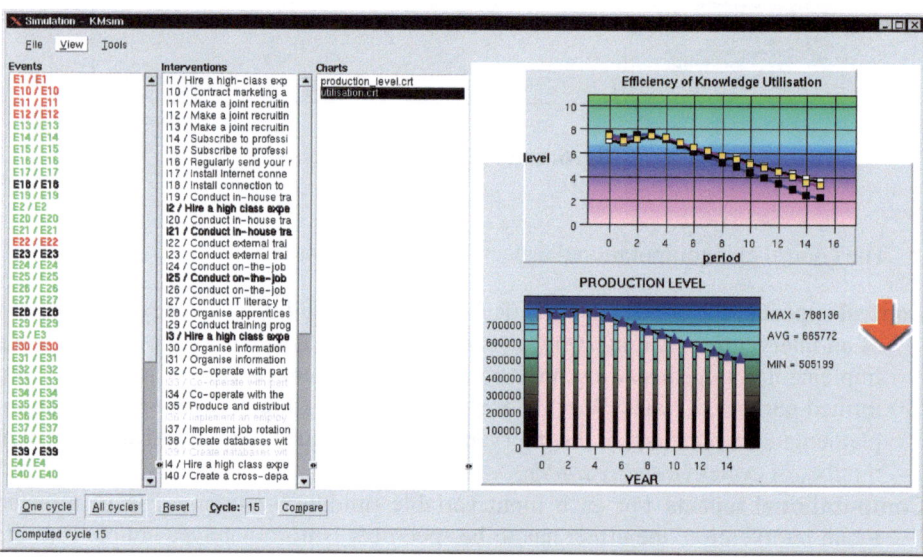

Fig. 7. Simulation tool. The two clickable browsers on the left display the events and interventions. Colour coding is used to indicate whether they are possible or active. The results are shown on the right. At the bottom are controls to run a simulation.

5.1 Simulation

There are often several reasons for simulating a BM. The BM modeller needs simulation to study the effects of interventions and events on the behaviour of the model. The main motivation for simulation for the BM modeller is to validate and tune the model.

In KM Quest the learner is only provided with a partial picture. The learner can ask for the past values of *output variables* (organisational effectiveness and business process) which are displayed using charts defined by the chart design tool. A complete simulation involves a little more. The state of the model at any point in time includes the values of the BM variables and the status of interventions and events.

Fig. 7 shows the interactive simulation tool. The status of interventions and events (active, possible) is displayed using a colour coding scheme. When validating the model developer uses the simulation tool to implement interventions and to issue events. The tool can visualise the BM variables in various ways: they can be shown in charts, as HTML tables (for later reference) or as a so called *knowledge map*.

5.2   Validation and Tuning

Visualising the BM itself is mainly useful for the model developer. The most obvious visualisation is a graph that displays the influence relations between variables (Fig. 8).

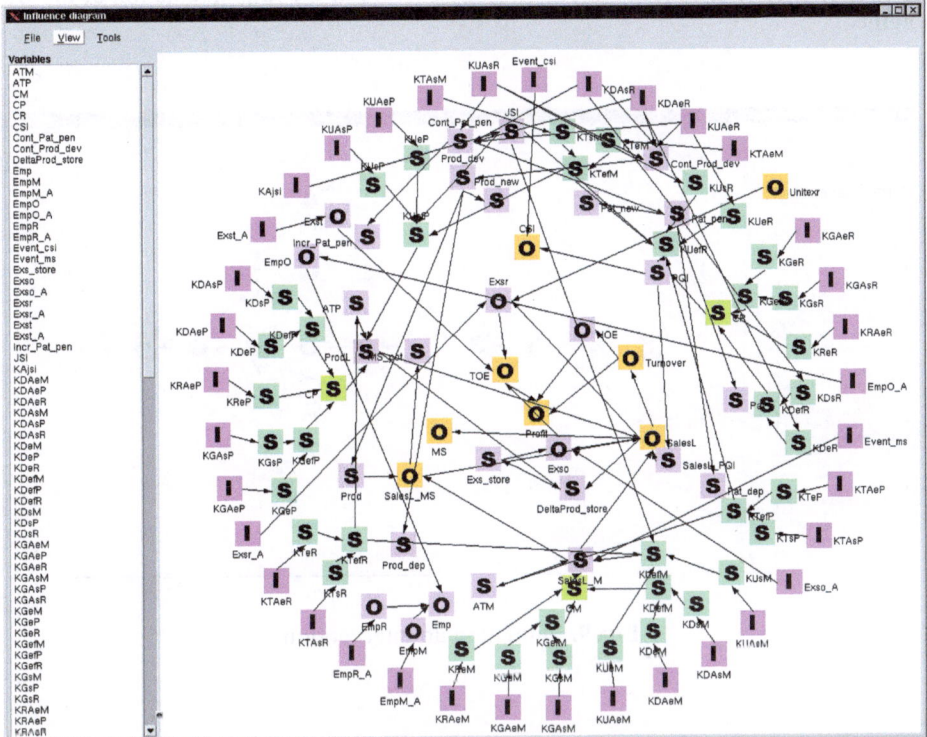

Fig. 8. Influence graph. Vertices represent variables (I=input, S=state, O=output) and edges represent influence. Colour is used to indicate whether the variable reflects organisational effectiveness, business process, knowledge process or knowledge.

For compactness, the graph is displayed as a sphere where influence extends inwards. Algorithms to draw such graphs dynamically can be found in [3]. The vertices in the graph are colour coded and indicate the status of the variable. The visualisation makes the organisation of the meta-model clear. The outer ring contains the input variables (which are influenced by interventions and events), the second ring mainly contains knowledge variables and the inner rings contain the business process and organisational effectiveness variables (for some reason *Profit* is in the centre). The graph has turned out to be a very powerful tool for finding "obvious" errors in the model.

Fig. 9 shows a simulation of an intervention; note the use of KMSIM's visualisation features. The vertices again represent variables in the BM. On the left are the input variables affected by the selected intervention and all vertices are decorated with a symbol indicating the value relative to *not* implementing the intervention. For example, *Profit* (on the very right) is lower (▼) as a result of the intervention, whereas most other variables are higher (▲) or the same (•).

Although the validation tools are aimed at validating and tuning the BM, they also turned out to be of practical value for finding errors in the implementation of the BM engine.

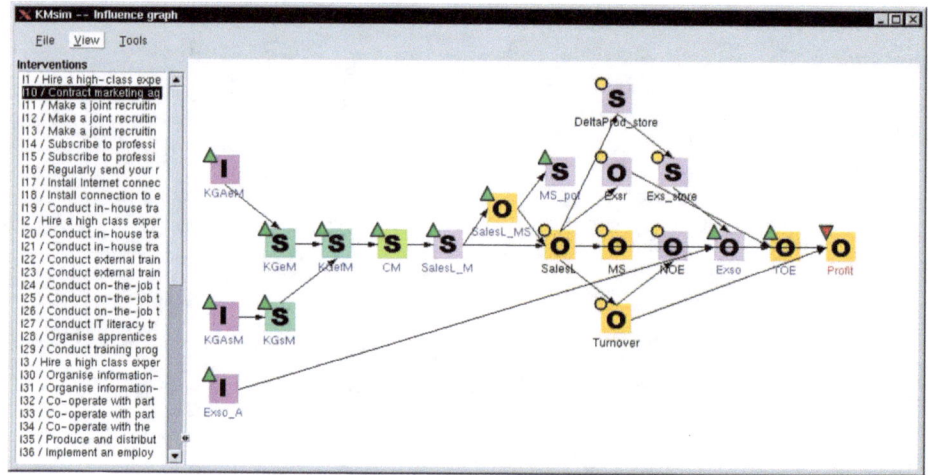

Fig. 9. Validating an intervention

6   Conclusions

The designer of tools is caught between the devil and the deep blue sea when faced with the choice between generality and specificity. Making a tool very general increases its applicability but decreases its support for the user because it will contain less "content" about the application domain. Making it very specific decreases its applicability because it can only be used in a well defined limited context but increases its support for the user because it will contain more "content" about the application domain.

The natural tendency is to go for generality: this will appeal to a larger market. As a consequence many simulation support tools are not too far removed from ordinary "visual" programming tools (e.g. Powersim®[2]), which makes them still difficult to use for domain experts without any programming experience. From a knowledge acquisition and knowledge creation perspective these domain experts are the people who really matter. In domains where acquiring and creating knowledge by means of systematic empirical investigations is either very time consuming, hard or dangerous, simulation is the preferred way to validate theoretical models on their plausibility. So, supporting domain experts in areas where these kind of limitations apply with easy-to-use tools for building, inspecting and running simulated versions of their models, can be seen as a key area for knowledge acquisition. By necessity tools that serve this purpose will be on the "specific" side of the continuum outlined above. In our domain this specificity is derived from the nature of the domain, the nature of the models that must be build and the intended users.

The domain described in this paper, knowledge management, and the tools developed are a clear demonstration of the power of this approach. Of course, more experience with the toolset is needed. For example, the range of users should be expanded, more research has to be done concerning actual ease of use, flexibility over a wide range of different business model types will be investigated. However, the application of the tool in the KITS project has significantly speeded up the creation and validation of a critical aspect of the learning environment: the business model represents in an active way the company the learning is dealing with. At the same time, the availability of the tools will make creating versions of the business model, fitting very specific requirements, much easier and this will contribute to the commercial value of the KM Quest environment.

References

[1] KMQuest simulation. See for more information www.kmquest.com.
[2] Tango! simulation. See for more information www.tangonow.net.
[3] G. Di Battista, P. Eades, R. Tamassia, and I. Tollis. *Graph drawing: Algorithms for the visualization of graphs*. Prentice-Hall, Upper Sadle River, 1999.
[4] T.J. Beckman. The current state of knowledge management. In J. Liebowitz, editor, *The knowledge management handbook*, pages 1.1–1.22. CRC Press, Boca Raton, 1999.
[5] T.H. Davenport. Knowledge management and the broader firm: strategy, advantage and performance. In J. Liebowitz, editor, *The knowledge management handbook*, pages 2.1–2.11. CRC Press, Boca Raton, 1999.
[6] A. Law and W. David Kelton. *Simulation modeling and analysis*. McGraw-Hill, Boston, 2000.
[7] A. Pritsker. *Introduction to Simulation and SLAM II*. John Wiley, New York, 1995.
[8] R. Reinhardt. Knowledge management: linking theory with practice. In D. Morey, M. Maybury, and B. Thuraisingham, editors, *Knowledge management: Classic and contemporary work*, pages 187–221. MIT Press, Cambridge, Mass, 2000.
[9] A. Tiwana. *The knowledge management toolkit: Practical techniques for building a knowledge management system*. Prentice-Hall, Upper Sadle River, 2000.
[10] J. Wielemaker and A. Anjewierden. Programming in XPCE-Prolog. Available from www.swi-prolog.org, 2002.

---

[2] It should be mentioned that this environment also has a kind of "meta-model": system dynamics.

Skills Management in Knowledge-Intensive Organizations

V. Richard Benjamins, José Manuel López Cobo, Jesús Contreras, Joaquín Casillas,
Juan Blasco, Blanca de Otto, Juli García, Mercedes Blázquez, Juan Manuel Dodero

Intelligent Software Components, S.A.
Spain
www.isoco.com
{richard, ozelin, jcontreras}@isoco.com

Abstract. In order for organizations to survive on increasingly competitive and global markets, adequate management of intellectual capital is essential. Although increasingly more information is found in electronic formats, turning this information into valuable knowledge is still the responsibility of people by applying it in professional situations to generate value. In this paper, we describe an approach and software tool to accompany organizations in the Knowledge Economy, where intellectual capital is the principal asset for organizations. In our approach we view people as sellers of knowledge, while departments, projects, profiles, and organizations are viewed as knowledge buyers. Together they constitute a knowledge market where the goods to be traded are competencies. The identification of knowledge gaps forms an important event to undertake action to compensate for the lack of competencies (training, new hiring, promoting, etc.).

1 Introduction

We are in the midst of the Knowledge Economy [10]. Although intellectual capital does not (yet) appear on companies' yearly balance sheets, and it is not subject to audits, many organizations recognize that intellectual capital is among their most strategic assets. Intellectual capital mostly resides in people in terms of their expertise, skills, and experience. This is one of the reasons for the high acquisition prices that are paid for companies whose main asset are very smart people.

The success of any company depends on the clever definition of its strategy (select market, define products and services, fix size and resources, select alliances, etc.) and the capacity to intelligently execute it (involving people, technology and processes, etc.). This paper contributes to improving the people and technology part. Management of skills [6], [1], [8] is an important tool to maintain the balance in real time between the needs of an organization and the capacities of its people (time-to-competency).

'If we only knew what we know', Jerry Junkins, CEO of Texas Instruments, said. An organization that is capable of knowing what skills it possesses, is able to better adapt to the ever-changing environment in which we operate today. 'Do we have the right

A. Gómez-Pérez and V.R. Benjamins (Eds.): EKAW 2002, LNAI 2473, pp. 80-95, 2002.
© Springer-Verlag Berlin Heidelberg 2002

skills to face the coming technological changes?' 'Do we need to acquire another company in light of the new UMTS technology?' 'Is our Paris office as prepared for B2B business as our London office?' Those types of questions are bothering top management on a frequent basis. However, not only at a strategic level such insights are important, also at a more tactical level we can identify many benefits. For example, improving the process to find the optimal (in terms of knowledge) person for a particular task or project, taking into account such constraints as availability, interests, experience, office base, etc. Or, to support the decision with real time information whether to hire a new employee or to promote and train an existing one could mean important savings. Also at the human resource level important wins can be made. For example, promoting the adequate person to a higher position would create a motivated person, whereas a new hire for that same position could cause frustration for the 'not promoted' employee. At an individual level, providing employees the possibility to manage and monitor their skill and interest level, to see the evolution in time, and to enable calculations of knowledge gaps between current and desired positions, will likely improve employee involvement and motivation.

In this paper we describe a web-based software product to manage skills in knowledge-intensive organizations. The product provides value for different types of people in an organization, including HR managers, top management, staffing, project managers and knowledge workers. In Section [2 The approach: a knowledge market], we describe the approach we have taken. Section [3 The software program] describes technical aspects of the product. Section [4 Practical experience] reports on some practical experiences with the tool, and finally, Section [5 Discussion and conclusions] discusses the results and concludes the paper.

2 The Approach: A Knowledge Market

We use the metaphor of a market with offer and demand, where people are sellers of knowledge, and organizations (departments, profiles, projects) are its buyers. Skills are the goods to be traded[1] with more or less value depending on the skill level (beginner, expert, etc.). Buyers and sellers are brought together through a mechanism that values the goods based on a weighted multi criteria approach.

2.1 Demand and Offer of Competencies

Important concepts in a market include: sellers, buyers, goods, and the value of the goods for which they are transferred. The last one is reflected in the compensation measures of organizations for their employees, and not considered in this paper

---

[1] Actually, skills are a peculiar kind of goods because it has many distinguishing characteristics from traditional assets such as increase while using (rather than decrease), no loss if transferred to another, etc.

The Goods – The Competencies

A skill reflects the knowledge and/or capacity a person has to perform a certain task. Skills can refer to job-specific knowledge, such as 'Java' in an IT company and 'financial products' in a bank. Often such skills are called hard skills. The more socially oriented skills, such as 'communication' and 'motivation' are usually referred to as soft skills. Skills can be organized in a skill hierarchy, where higher-level skills are more general than lower-level skills. Higher-level skills are used to categorize the lower-level skills. It is not the case that a parent skill is defined by its children skills; rather it is the other way around: the children are defined through their parent. Fig. 1 illustrates a skill hierarchy for a non-existing company.

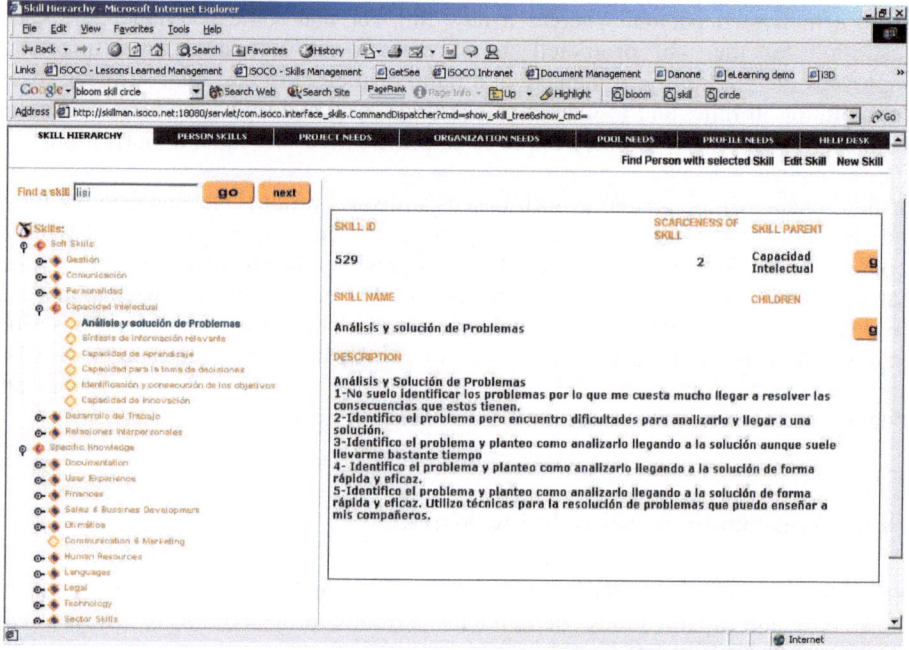

Fig. 1. Skill hierarchy with description of skill levels.

As can be seen in the left part of Fig. 1, there are soft skills and specific (hard) skills, each of which is sub-divided into more refined skills. The right part illustrates an explanation of what the different levels of a skill mean in terms of capacities. 'Scarceness of skill' reflects how difficult it is to find the skill on the labour market. Such skill hierarchies can be obtained from various locations, for free or paid, or developed in-house. Soft skills, in any case, are more or less standard for most organizations. Concerning hard skills, it is interesting to mention the possibility to have 'sector-specific' hard skills, such as for the IT sector, the financial sector, etc. that could be reused across organizations of the same sector.

The Sellers – The People

Skills are owned by people. In the knowledge economy, knowledge workers apply their skills to perform tasks that are part of projects of assignments. In this sense, people can be considered as knowledge sellers, whereas the projects are knowledge buyers. The values of the skills are expressed in levels, reflecting their rate of mastering. On a five-point scale, the levels could mean: 1:beginner, 2:can work with significant support, 3:can work independently, 4:advanced, 5:expert. Other scales are possible (e.g. 3-point, 7-point, 10-point) depending on the granularity needed. It is important that the persons who associate skill levels to people (the persons themselves, their peers, managers, HR) apply the same criteria, otherwise the results will reflect more personal opinions rather than intellectual capital. Apart from levels, people usually have a degree of interest in a skill expressing their attitude towards elaborating the skill. Fig. 2 illustrates the skills of a particular person acquired through self-evaluation.

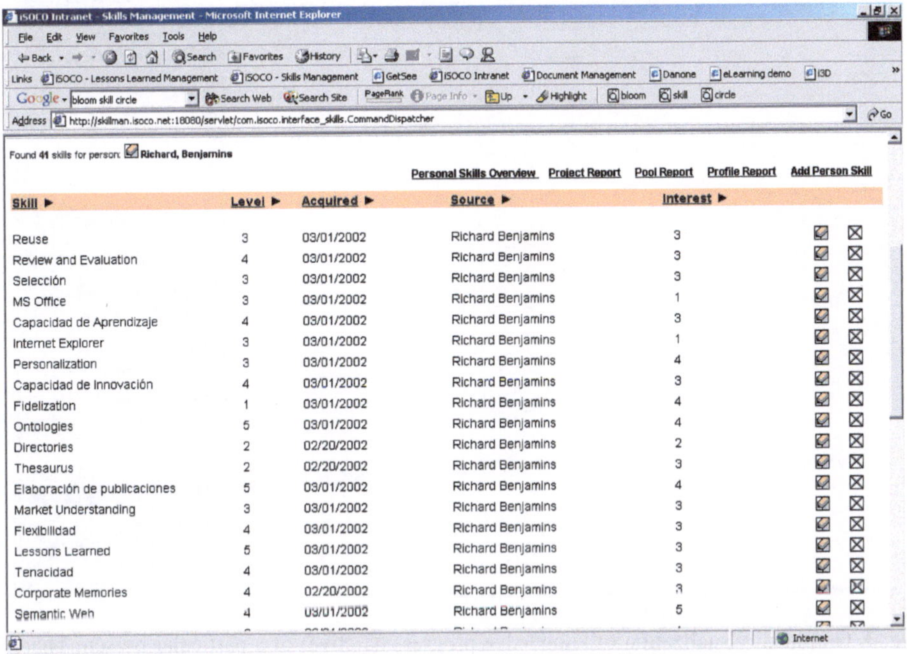

Fig. 2. Skills belonging to a person with their corresponding level, acquisition date, source and interest level.

As can be seen in Fig. 2, a skill and interest level are associated to a person, as well as the date and the agent (source) of the action. The date is especially important for viewing the evolution over time of a person's skills, which is a tool to support professional career management. Fig. 3 shows the progress of a particular person. The figure is a visual presentation of one level of the hierarchy (languages). The application allows one to navigate through the hierarchy, thereby showing at each level the corresponding progress.

The Buyers – Projects, Departments, Profiles

Continuing the metaphor of a knowledge market, buyers of skills are projects, departments, profiles, and the organization as a whole. Those entities need the skills of people in order to function well. Instead of specifying what skills are offered, in this case, one specifies what skills are required by the project, department, etc. The vocabulary used to express those requirements is defined through the skill hierarchy. Thus for example, a project could need a specific skill like 'databases: level 3' with importance: 5 (on a five-point scale). This would mean that for the particular project, intermediate knowledge of databases is required, and the importance that this skill be present in the project team is very high (i.e. its non-presence may lead to severe problems in project execution).

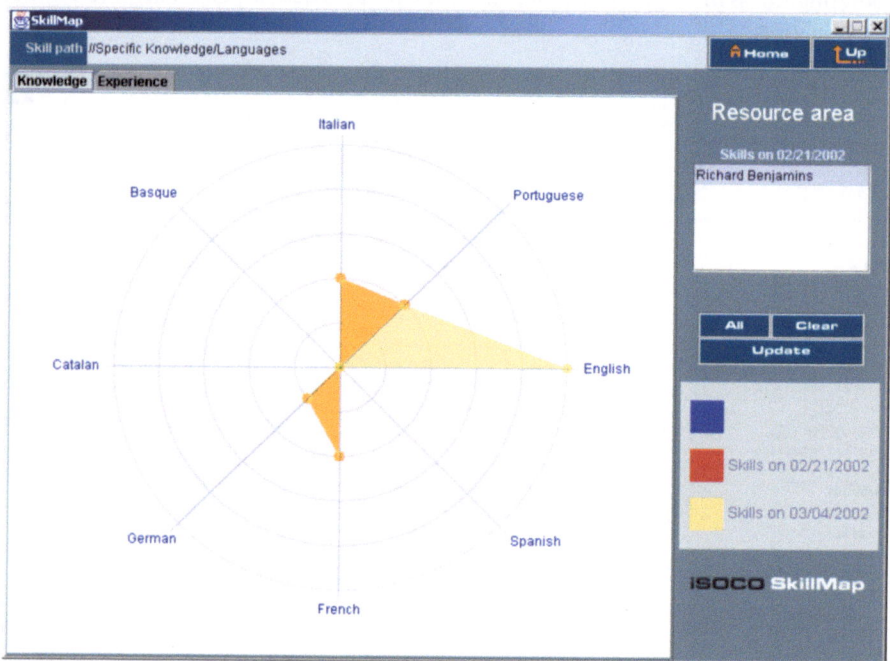

Fig. 3. Graphical visualization of knowledge progress (fictive) of a particular person. There is no progress except for English.

In the same way that projects have requirements (and thus are knowledge buyers), this is also true for profiles (a description of the competencies required to fulfil certain functions in an organization), departments (competencies required to work in a particular department) and the organization as a whole (a high-level characterization of the competencies needed in the organization in order to accomplish its mission). In each of those, one can specify the levels of the skills needed along with their importance.

2.2 The Market Mechanism – Matchmaking

Since we have implemented the approach in a software program, we have created an electronic online marketplace of knowledge. Buyers and sellers can now be brought together through a matchmaking algorithm. We have designed an algorithm able to deal with approximate matches [4] when no perfect matches exist. The algorithm considers the following factors:
- The skills needed versus offered
- The skill level needed versus offered
- The importance of the skill required
- The agents who introduced the skill level. If there are several agents who evaluated a skill of a person, a weighted average is taken based on a hierarchy of permissions (see section on [3.2 Profile-based permissions]): the higher in the hierarchy, the more weight the evaluation of that agent has.

The algorithm can be parameterised on the following points:
- The availability of the sellers (e.g. not assigned to other projects)
- Ignore, prevent or penalize higher skill levels than required
- Consider or ignore the interest of the persons in the skill
- Consider only particular profiles
- Consider or ignore other relevant factors as location, opportunity cost, etc.

Any user with the required permissions can perform this parameterisation through the web-based interface. The factors mentioned above are considered in the current application. However, one could add any constraint useful for a particular organization as long as the needed knowledge is stored somewhere in a corporate database.

The essence of the algorithm can be described as follows. For each skill-level required (to buy), we find all persons having that skill (whatever its level). A person having (to sell) all the skills with the required level will obtain a high ranking. Persons covering fewer skills or inferior levels, have lower ranking. The ranking is based on the contribution of the seller to the buyer's need. The contribution to each required skill is based on the seller's skill level for the required skill, its interest in that skill, and the importance of that skill for the buyer. The matching algorithm considering a single person is represented with the following formulas:

$$V_j = \sum_{i=1}^{n} SW_i \cdot \delta_{ij}$$
(1)

Where
- V_j is the calculated value for each person with respect to all required skills of the buyer.

- *SWi* is the normalized importance (weight) of a skill for the buyer. Normalization is needed for later ranking.
- δij represents the contribution of a person$_j$. to a required skill$_i$.

Normalization means that the sum of all skill weights (*SW*) equals 1:

$$\sum_{i=1}^{n} SWi \ = \ \sum_{i=1}^{n} \frac{\overline{yi}}{Y} \ = \ \frac{\overline{y1} + \overline{y2} + ... + \overline{yn}}{Y} \ = \ \frac{Y}{Y} = 1 \tag{2}$$

Where yi is the importance (weight) of each skill$_i$ required, and Y is a dynamic normalization factor for each sale.

The contribution of a person's skill to the calculated value of that person concerning that required skill is a function of the person's skill level, his interest, and the importance of the skill for the buyer:

$$\delta ij \ = \ f \ (\overline{\lambda ij} , \overline{\mu i} , \overline{\varphi ij}) \tag{3}$$

Where

- $\overline{\lambda ij}$ is the average skill level on skill$_i$ for person$_j$.
- $\overline{\mu i}$ is the average need for the skill$_i$ (in terms of the buyer).
- $\overline{\varphi ij}$ is the average interest that person$_j$ has in skill$_i$.
- f calculates the score of the person in a given skill

Average refers to the fact that there can be multiple sources for the same information. E.g., two project managers can assign different importance to the same skill required for a project. Since the resulting Vj is normalized ($0 \leq Vj \leq 1$), we can sort the results of the matching process. The higher the value of Vj, the more valuable person$_j$ is for the buyer.

Apart from calculating the value for single persons, we can also suggest teams of specific sizes (a group of sellers) whose union of skills satisfy the demand. In order to do this, we need to repeatedly apply the matching process until the team size has been reached, or until all requirements have been fulfilled. On each cycle of the algorithm, which adds a member to the team, a corresponding reduction of the buyer's needs takes place (since part of the needs are now satisfied).

An interesting feature of the algorithm is that it calculates knowledge gaps: explicit representations of the set of skills missing for a particular project, profile, department, etc. Gaps are important indicators that some action needs to be taken.

Propagation of Skills

Skill levels of persons are scored only on the leaf skills, i.e. the terminal skills of the skill hierarchy (OBDC, Java, etc.). Buyers of skills (projects, profiles, etc.) can in addition express their needs in terms of non-terminal skills, i.e. intermediate nodes in the hierarchy (e.g. programming). The reason for this is that sometimes buyers are not interested in specific skills but rather in a range of skills organized in a category.

Because we use higher-level skills to categorize lower-level skills (see Section [The goods – the competencies]), skill levels of the former depend on those of the latter. In order to apply the matching algorithm, a propagation process is needed from the values on low-level skills to higher-level skills. The heuristic underlying the propagation process are the following:

- The parent skill-level is equal to the maximum of the children's skill level if the average of the children is greater than/equal the maximum of the children minus 1
- The parent skill level is equal to the maximum minus 1 of the children's skill level if the average of the children is smaller than the maximum of the children minus 1

The propagation algorithm favours a balanced lower-level skill set over an unbalanced one. In other words, when two persons have the same arithmetical average level concerning children skills of a particular parent skill, then the person having medium levels on all children skills gets a higher score on the parent skill than a person who has some high scores and some low scores on the children skills.

2.3 Beneficiaries of the Market

A combination of a web-based interface, an interactive visualization tool, and an explicit permission management system maximizes optimal use of the tool for a range of different users. The tool is able to visualize knowledge progress of persons (as in Fig. 3), departments and the organization as a whole, as well as knowledge coverage and gaps between skills needed and required, for example with respect to a project (as illustrated in Fig. 4). The permission management system allows for example persons to view and edit their own skills, but prevents viewing the soft skills of others. It also allows managers to edit the skills of people who are under their responsibility. Notice that it is always known who assigned a particular score to a person and when that assignment took place.

Human Resources Managers

The work of human resource departments is facilitated in the following ways:

- Central repository of the skills definition relevant for the organization, enabling easy actualisation
- Reduced maintenance effort of the skill levels due to distributing task to knowledge workers and managers
- Up-to-date access to skill levels and interests of each person along with progression, allowing better planning of personalized training and professional careers.

- Definition and immediate publication of profiles and department requirements on the corporate intranet
- Knowing at all times the knowledge coverage and gaps in the organization, departments and profiles (demand), which, along with the actual knowledge available (offer) allows for a balanced decision concerning hiring versus promoting. Taking informed decisions prevents unnecessary hiring as well as employee frustration
- Knowing with one click what an organization knew more than a year ago

Staffing Department and Project Management
'Finding the right person for the job' is a problem many companies face frequently. In practice this is a hard problem because many factors need to be taken into account, but often the information supporting those factors is not easy available. Skillman alleviates this problem in the following ways:
- Providing easy access to up-to-date information about the knowledge available
- Find an expert for particular skills
- Knowing who is available and who not
- Viewing the requirements (demand) of projects
- Find the person who best matches project requirements
- Find a team of specific size that best matches project requirements
- Consider various constraints in the matching process such as office location, profile, and interests of people
- Calculate and view the knowledge coverage of a particular team for a project
- Provide fact-based information to HR anticipating possible future knowledge gaps

Fig. 4 illustrates the coverage/gap of skills required for a project. It is also possible to select sub teams to see how the coverage changes depending on the presence of particular people (illustrated in Fig. 5).

Knowledge Workers (Including Categories Mentioned Above)
For all people working in an organization, the tool contributes to knowledge management [3] and so-called employee information systems. In particular it provides the following benefits:
- Self management (view, update, add, delete) of own skills and interests
- View progress from a specified date until actual date
- View profile and department requirements
- Calculate gaps between actual competencies and desired ones (e.g. those belonging to a category higher)
- Find experts in particular skills (illustrated in Fig. 6)
- Browse and search the skill hierarchy

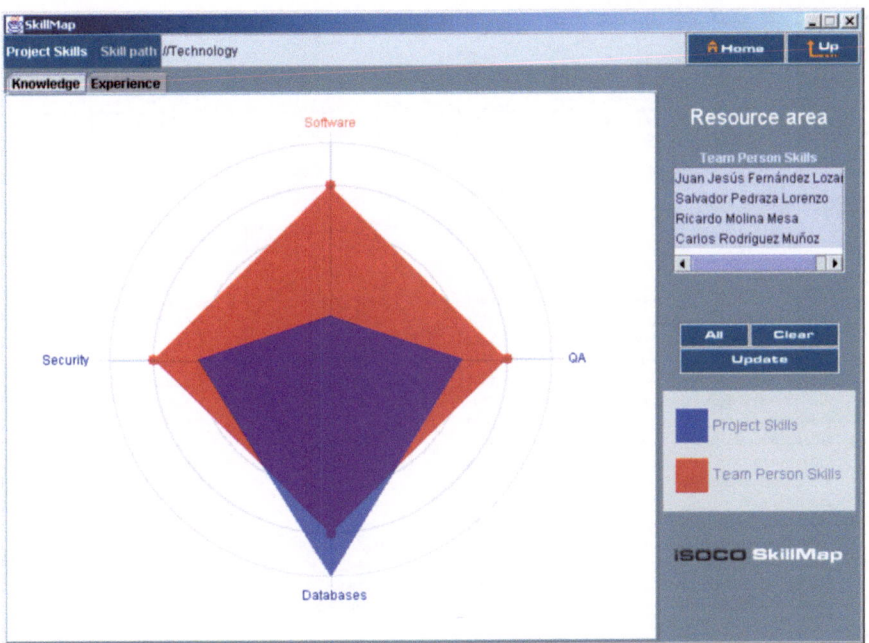

Fig. 4. Knowledge coverage for a particular project. As can be seen, the software part is more than covered, but there are small gaps in database, security and quality assurance knowledge.

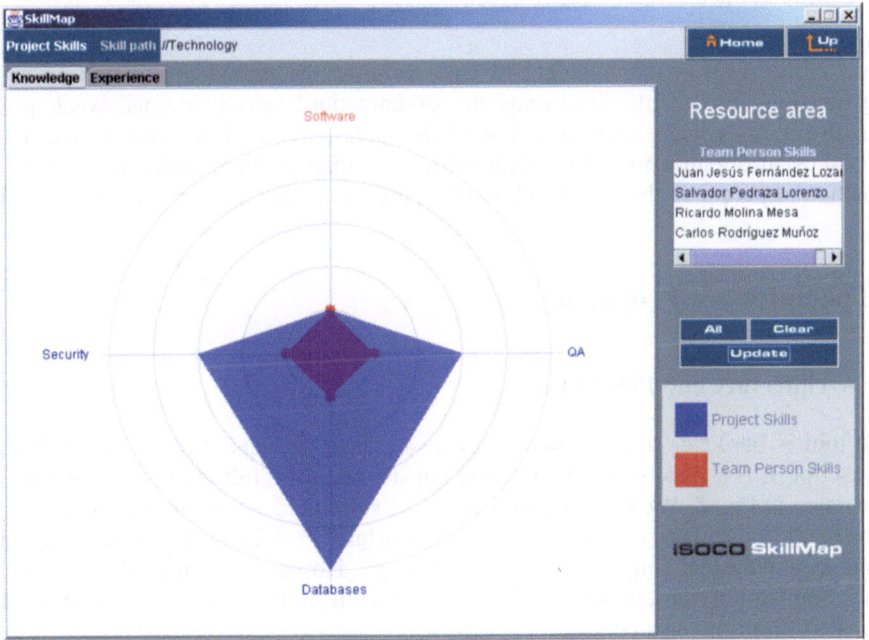

Fig. 5. Knowledge coverage for a particular person of the team of Fig. 4.

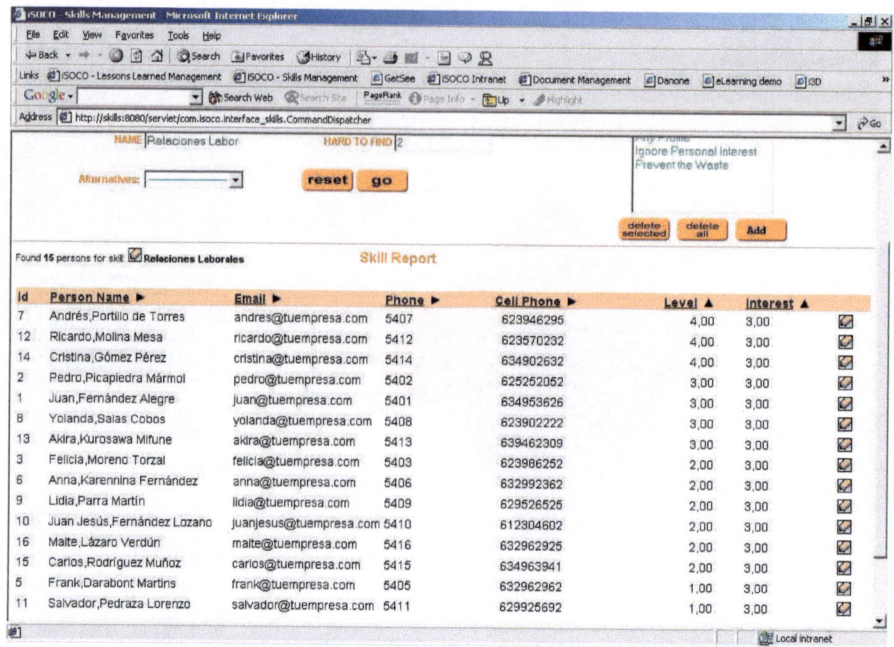

Fig. 6. Ranked list of expert for the HR skill: 'labour relations'.

Top Management

The tool allows top management to easy monitor the knowledge evolution of the organization as a whole. It reveals the organization's strong points, weak points, growth per knowledge area, new knowledge areas, trends, key persons, etc. Fig. 7 illustrates an organizational knowledge coverage map for hard skills. By varying the selection of people in the top right box (Resource area), key persons can be identified.

3 The Software Program

3.1 Architecture and Principles

The tool is based on Java technologies, using Java servlets, JSP, J2EE, JDBC and Javascript. It is a web-based architecture consisting of the following components, and illustrated in Fig. 8. We have used open source software such as the Resin application server (http://www.caucho.com/), the Postgress Object-Relational database management system (http://www.postgresql.org/). However, the tool also works with other application servers and DBMS. The visualization software is based on Java Webstart (http://java.sun.com/products/javawebstart/).

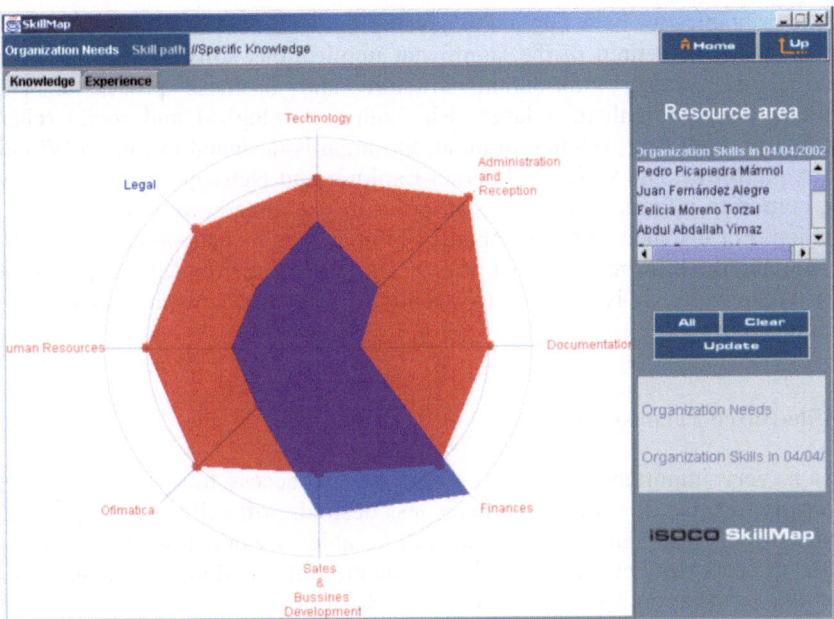

Fig. 7. Organisational knowledge coverage and gaps. The larger (roundish) surface represents skills offered by the employees, the smaller surface represents skills demanded by the organization.

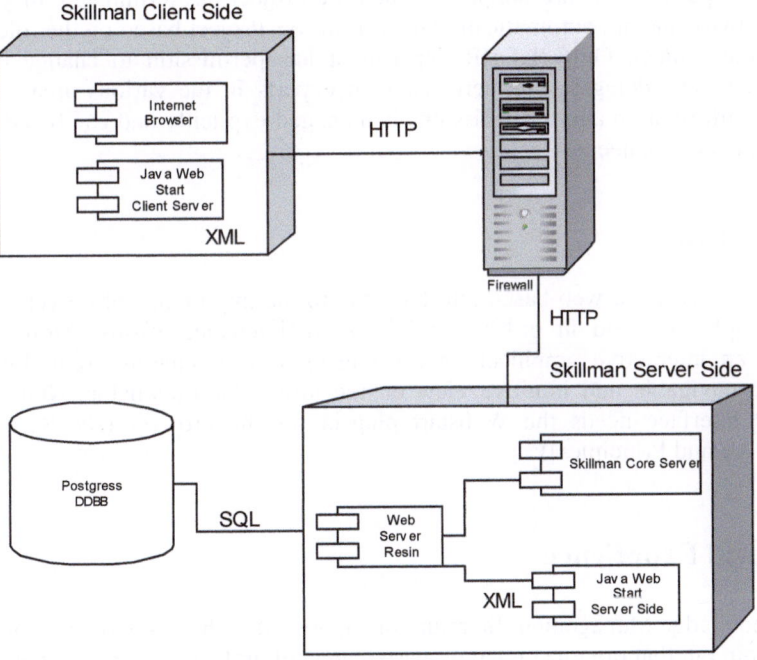

Fig. 8. Architecture of Skillman.

One of the principles we have applied in developing the tool is *non-intrusiveness*. We believe companies are tired of the significant implications software acquisition can have on their existing information structure and business processes. Those implications carry with them a large risk, both technological and social (change management). With this principle in mind, Skillman is designed to run on Windows and Linux platforms, and with MS Internet Explorer and Netscape. It integrates with existing corporate information systems in order to use already available data in the organization. For instance, in our company, Skillman gets its data about persons from the HRMS, and the information about projects and its teams from MS Project. Due to the open architecture, it is possible to integrate with other software such as SAP, PeopleSoft, Meta4, etc.

3.2 Profile-Based Permissions

While it is very important that every employee has access to 'who knows what' concerning hard skills, for soft skills this is less desired. Soft skills often represent an evaluation of personal traits, such as motivation, able to work in teams, capacity to negotiate, openness to ideas, etc. This is confidential information, which should only be accessible to the appropriate people (e.g. HRM).

Another aspect concerns 'who has what permissions?' in the tool. In iSOCO's case, knowledge workers can update their own skills, and view the hard skills of others. Project managers, in addition, can evaluate the skills of the people they are working with. Those permissions are temporal (when the project has terminated, they should be withdrawn), and are automatically taken from MS Project based on the role people have in the project. Only the HR department has permission to change the skill hierarchy, or can delegate this permission to experts in the various areas. All this important information about permissions is managed explicitly and can be adapted to each organization's needs

3.3 User Interface

We have chosen for a web-based interface due to the importance of universal access for all employees, and in order to minimize maintenance efforts. Moreover, we designed an interactive graphical interface using Kiviat diagrams (e.g. Fig. 7) to provide a navigable and intuitive view on the information available. Note that the graphical interface needs the Webstart plug-in for the browser (see Section [3.1 Architecture and Principles]).

4 Practical Experience

In the Knowledge Management literature one reads often that technology alone is not the solution, but that organizational processes and cultural issues are as important. We confirm those findings. In order to successfully roll out the project, the following points have to be taken into account:

- Involve representative people from the organization in the definition of the skills hierarchy (facilitates buy-in)
- Convince people of the importance of the initiative (e.g. by top management involvement and communications)
- Provide basic training concerning the scoring of skill levels. There should be consensus to a certain extent as to when to score a particular level (1-5). Modest people might assign themselves a 3 while being cracks, whereas self-assertive people might put a 5 while performing average. In general this is an unsolvable problem, but a minimal normalization effort has to be carried out. In some cases a workflow protocol might help to solve the problem by having skill-level assignments approved before inclusion in the tool. In any case, if agents give significantly different scores to the same skill, this is an indication that something is wrong. With Skillman, it is possible to detect such issues
- Consider timely actualisation of skills as a criterion for the bonus of salaries
- Show clearly to people how they benefit from the tool. Prevent that it is considered as extra work

Make the HR department leading the implementation of the tool in the organization, which is consistent with the view that such initiatives should be driven by a business pull rather than by a technology push

5 Discussion and Conclusions

As with any decision concerning the acquisition of software products, organizations want to know the expected return of investment. Metrics in knowledge management are not yet advanced enough to give precise answers to this. One of the reasons is that it depends on many factors, such as the type of organization, the existing corporate information systems, the number of employees, its physical distribution, etc. Another reason is that it is very difficult to come up with reliable concrete indicators. It is our experience that best ROI is obtained in knowledge-intensive organizations, such as professional services industry or companies where product innovation is essential due to competitive environment (e.g. pharmaceutical industry, electronic consumer goods, etc.).

Efficiency
- How much time is spent on finding the right person to ask a question?
- How much time is needed to find the right person/team for a particular project?
- How large is the effort to determine what person needs what course?
- What is the damage of wrong allocation of persons to work (counterproductive or non-optimal work)?

Motivational
- What is the 'damage' of wrong allocation of persons to work (frustration)?
- How large is the 'damage' when a new person is hired while an existing employee should have been promoted?

- How much is it worth if employees can view and manage their skills, and calculate knowledge gaps?

Strategic

- How much is it worth to know what persons are key for your business?
- What is the damage if skilled persons leave the company with all their knowledge without knowing what they take with them?
- How much is it worth to know in real time what an organization knows (strong/weak points, trends)?

In the development of Skillman, we adhere to the principle 'sense and respond' as opposed to 'make and sell' [7]. This means that with feedback of actual users we will gradually improve the product. Current feedback has put the following features on our to-do list:

- Generate configurable reports in excel (for reporting)
- Generate printable standard profile descriptions
- Generate printable standard company CVs
- Integrate with applicants information obtained from company's websites (hiring versus promoting decision)
- Intelligent skill updates (e.g. automatically deduce that if a person has been a programmer in a project that used Java, then this person can be assumed to have some knowledge of Java [11])
- Integrate Skillman with a Learning Management System in order to recommend courses based on knowledge gaps and interests.

In this paper we argued that skills management is important for knowledge-based companies. We presented an approach and tool to support this organizational process based on high quality and rich employee profiles. Apart from the proper value of managing those assets, significant added value can be obtained by exploiting the profiles in other applications. The key point to make here relates to *personalization*, meaning to offer different content to people based on their profiles. In the context of intranets of organizations, interesting content to offer based on Skillman profiles, concerns training information including eLearning, internal documents, and external web content.

References

1. Boam, R and Sparrow, P. Designing and Achieving Competency: A Competency-Based Approach to Developing People and Organizations. London: McGraw-Hill, 1992.
2. V. Richard Benjamins, Dieter Fensel and Asuncion Gomez Perez, Knowledge Management through Ontologies. In proceedings of the Second International Conference on Practical Aspects of Knowledge Management (PAKM), 29-30 October, 1998, pp. 5.1-5.12, Basel, Switzerland.
3. V. Richard Benjamins, Knowledge Management in Knowledge-Intensive Organizations. iSOCO white paper (available at http://www.isoco.com/isococom/whitepapers/files/km-88.pdf).

4. Torgeir Dingsøyr, Emil Røyrvik: Skills Management as Knowledge Technology in a Software Consultancy Company. In Proc. of 3rd International Workshop on Learning Software Organizations (LSO'01) September 12 & 13, 2001, Kaiserslautern, Germany.
5. Drew, S.A.W. "Building Knowledge Management into Strategy: Making Sense of a New Perspective," Long Range Planning, February 1999
6. Green, P.C. Building Robust Competencies: Linking Human Resource Systems to Organizational Strategies, San Francisco: Jossey-Bass Publishers, 1999.
7. Stephan H. Haeckel, Adaptive Enterprise: Creating and Leading Sense-And-Respond Organizations. Harvard Business School Press, Boston, Masachusetts.
8. Hebrero, C. Competency-Based HR Management, THE ERICSSON EXPERIENCE,2001. Available at: :
    http://www.andersen.com/resource2.nsf/vAttachLU/HC_competencybasedHR/$File/Com
    petency-Based%20HR%20Management.pdf.
9. Hwang, C. -L. & Kwangsun, Y. (1981). Multiple attribute decision making, methods and applications. In Lecture Notes in Economics and Mathematical Systems, number 186. Springer-Verlag, Berlin, Heidelberg, New York.
10. Merrill Lynch. The Knowledge Web, May 2000.
11. Sure, Y., Maedche, A. and Staab, S: Leveraging Corporate Skill Knowledge - From ProPer to OntoProPer. . Third International Conference on Practical Aspects of Knowledge Management, Basel, Switzerland 2000/01/10.

Knowledge Acquisition and Modeling in Clinical Information Systems: A Case Study

Göran Falkman[1] and Olof Torgersson[2]

[1] Department of Computer Science, University of Skövde,
PO Box 408, SE–541 28 Skövde, Sweden
`goran.falkman@ida.his.se`
[2] Department of Computing Science, Chalmers University of Technology and
Göteborg University, SE–412 96 Göteborg, Sweden
`oloft@cs.chalmers.se`

Abstract. The goal of the MedView project is to develop models, methods, and tools to support clinicians in their daily work and research. MedView is based on a formal declarative model, which constitutes the main governing principle in MedView, not only in the formalization of knowledge, but in visualization models and in the design and implementation of individual tools and the system as a whole as well. Tools are provided for modeling, acquiring, and sharing knowledge, and for visualization and analysis of data.

1 Introduction

In 1995, the MedView project, a joint project with participants from computer science and oral medicine, was initiated. The overall goal of the project is to develop models, methods, and tools to support clinicians in their daily work and research. The central question in MedView is how computing technology can be used to model and manage clinical knowledge in everyday work such that clinicians more systematically can learn from the gathered clinical data.

MedView provides a formalization of clinical examination data and clinical procedures, providing a possibility for recognizing patterns and trends otherwise hidden in the monumental amount of clinical information. MedView is based on a coherent declarative model that constitutes the main governing principle in the project, not only in the formalization of clinical terms and concepts, but in visualization models and in the design and implementation of individual tools and the system as a whole as well.

Several tools have been developed for knowledge formalization, knowledge acquisition, visualization and analysis of data, and knowledge sharing.

MedView is in daily use at several clinics within the Swedish Oral Medicine Network (SOMNET).

The rest of this paper is organized as follows: Section 2 presents the underlying design principles and the declarative model used. Section 3 describes the various knowledge structures used in MedView. In Sect. 4, we describe the tools used for knowledge acquisition. Examples of applications are given in Sect. 5. The paper is concluded in Sect. 6 with a short discussion.

A. Gómez-Pérez and V.R. Benjamins (Eds.): EKAW 2002, LNAI 2473, pp. 96–101, 2002.

$$E \begin{cases} Anamnesis = Common \\ Common = Drug \\ Common = Smoke \\ Drug = Levaxin \\ Smoke = 4 \ cigarettes/day \\ Diagnosis = Diag\text{-}def \\ Diag\text{-}def = Gingival \ lichen \ planus \end{cases}$$

Fig. 1. A definition E defining parts of an examination record in MedView

2   The MedView Approach

2.1   A Formal Foundation

The information stored in traditional paper records is not sufficiently organized and formalized to allow for a general data analysis. MedView addresses the deficiencies of the traditional medical record system by adopting reliable computer science principles with a solid foundation in formal knowledge representation. Basic health care activities and concepts are established and formally defined within SOMNET. The formal foundation provides the necessary means for getting insight into the structure and meaning of medical knowledge [1].

The result is a clear separation between different kinds of knowledge and between different cognitive acts, e.g., between basic examination data and classifications of clinical terms and between the act of gathering knowledge and the act of viewing knowledge. This enables knowledge representations to be tailored to their respective purposes and knowledge management tools to be optimized for each particular act. As a consequence, MedView provides a tool for entering data and several 'viewers' for viewing data in different ways.

2.2   Everyday Tools

A formal foundation is not enough, though. It is equally important that tools are user-friendly, flexible, and extendable by end-users, and rapidly are brought into everyday practice [2]. One of the central design principles of MedView is therefore to provide a transparent framework in which user-centered and flexible tools can be developed, tools which, to a large extent, can be re-configured and extended by the users themselves, without the need of computer experts.

2.3   Declarative Model

The need for closing the gap between the formal foundation and everyday clinical practice [1] motivates a declarative approach: a high abstraction level of tools and interaction models can be maintained without losing the connection with the underlying data and computational models.

The declarative model of MedView is based on the assumption that *definitions* are central tools in all attempts to give a precise and formalized representation of knowledge.

The formal declarative model of MedView is given by a theory of *partial inductive definitions* [3]. Definitions have a logic interpretation, making them suitable for automated reasoning. At the same time, the concept of a definition and the act of defining are simple enough to have obvious intuitive readings.

The conceptual view of a definition is that of a collection of equations. Figure 1 shows a definition, E, defining a small part of an examination record in MedView. In this definition, the term *Anamnesis* is defined by the term *Common*, which in turn is defined by the terms *Drug* and *Smoke* and so on.

2.4   Visualization of Knowledge

Effective presentation of information is an important component in any medical information system, since it can prevent information overload and visually emphasize subtle aspects of clinical processes and data, which otherwise would be hard to discover [4]. Therefore, MedView is designed to take visualization and interaction with knowledge into account right from the start.

The visualization models are based on the underlying declarative model, thereby decreasing the distance between users and visualization [5] and facilitating component-based visualization and integration [6]. Interaction models are provided that allow users to take active part in the various knowledge processes.

3   Knowledge Organization

3.1   Fundamental Knowledge Structures

In MedView, clinical data is seen as definitions of clinical terms. Abstract clinical concepts, e.g., diagnosis, examination, and patient, are given by definitions of collections of specific clinical terms.

For example, the terms *Anamnesis*, *Common*, *Drug*, and *Smoke* are all part of the general *template* defining the concept 'examination'. A concrete instance of a template, an examination record, is given by defining terms like *Drug* and *Smoke* in terms of observed values, e.g., *Levaxin* and *4 cigarettes/day* respectively.

Values for the terms defined in templates are taken from formalized lists of valid values. These *value lists* are given as definitions, and are stored in a knowledge base (KB) along with template definitions and value lists.

Templates and initial value lists are developed by the users themselves using the InterfaceMaker tool (see Sect. 4.2).

3.2   Additional Knowledge Structures

As the KB grows, it becomes increasingly important to be able to group related values into classes in a hierarchical manner. For example, diseases such as Herpes labialis, Herpetic gingivostomatis, and Shingles can be classified into viral diseases. The ability to categorize values into different classes has proven very useful in order to be able to perform more interesting analysis of data.

Value classes are constructed by the users themselves using *class definitions*, which are stored in the KB for future use. The class definitions are definitions in the same sense as template definitions and examination records, and they are expressed in the same format as the examination records. As an example, the following class definition classifies smoking habits into three classes:

$$S_1 \begin{cases} 1 \; cigarettes \; without \; filter/day = \; < 10 \; cigarettes/day \\ 10\text{--}15 \; filter \; cigarettes/day = \; > 10 \; cigarettes/day \\ No = Non\text{-}smoking \end{cases}.$$

To further categorize smokers, a second class definition can be constructed:

$$S_2 \begin{cases} < 10 cigarettes/day = Smoking \\ > 10 cigarettes/day = Smoking \end{cases}.$$

Thus, a complete classification of smoking habits is given by combining S_1 and S_2, i.e., conceptually we form the definition $S = S_1 + S_2$.

In some cases, several clinical terms $t_1, \ldots, t_n$ should be viewed as *specializations* of another term T. For these situations, we use another kind of definition, in which a *generalized term* (T) is defined in terms of its instances $(t_1, \ldots, t_n)$.

4 Knowledge Acquisition

4.1 Formalizing Data

MedView allows domain experts to develop *all* parts of the underlying knowledge representation model without any direct intervention from computer experts and without requiring any programming knowledge.

For example, when the domain experts have agreed upon a formalization of a particular examination protocol and the associated value lists, the formalization is put into a form that can be used in other knowledge-oriented activities using the InterfaceMaker application (IM). Essentially, clinicians use IM to:

- Turn an examination protocol into a template definition providing the general structure of examinations for use by other tools
- Create a textual description of the protocol, consisting of lead-texts and links, used for entering data into the KB (see Sect. 4.2)
- Define initial value lists for all terms defined in a protocol
- Administer the templates used for generating summaries of examination data using natural language generation (see Sect. 5.1).

Thus, using IM, it is possible to both maintain the current set of templates used, and define completely new ones for use in other areas. For instance, MedView could be adopted to dermatology by using IM only.

To keep the value lists complete and harmonized, a tool called MVDManager (MM) has been developed. Using MM, definitions with replacements for incorrect values are defined. MM can also be used for localizing a KB to different languages.

4.2   Entering Data

MedRecords (MR) is the application used to enter data at examinations. In the MedView setting, entering data is the act of creating a definition. Therefore, MR aims to support the act of *defining*, in a precise manner, a medical examination.

MR is best thought of as presenting a template definition i.e., an incomplete definition, to the user. Using value lists, class definitions, free text, and digitized images, the user completes the template by defining the descriptive parameters, e.g., *Occup* and *Born*, in terms of observed values, e.g., *Dentist* and *Sweden*. The result is stored into the KB as a new examination record.

5   Knowledge Application

5.1   Generation of Summaries

The basic viewer is MedSummary (MS). The view of the KB presented by MS is that of a textual summary of one or more examination records using natural language generation. MS uses a summary template definition and a slot-filler definition together with one or more examination records to generate a summary text, which is then presented together with any associated images. By defining different summary templates using IM, the user can experiment with different texts without having any linguistic expertise.

5.2   Knowledge Exploration and Analysis

Using *dynamic queries* [7], a user can explore a data set by manipulating a set of simple query devices, which immediately updates a graphic display of the data set. Dynamic querying has proven very efficient and stimulating for users to interact with.

MedViewer (MV) uses dynamic querying to give users a simple hands-on possibility of exploring data without posing complex queries or learning any particular concepts. The visualizations currently provided by MV are scatter plots, pie charts, bar charts, tables, image browser, and a summary view (generated by MS), but the system is simple to extend with other kinds of visualizations.

The Cube [8] is another analysis tool that uses a dynamic 3D *parallel coordinate plot* [9] to provide an overview of the terms defined in the KB. The Cube was developed to enhance the clinician's ability to intelligibly analyze existing patient material and to allow for pattern recognition and statistical analysis.

On the conceptual level, The Cube is a tool for interactive visualization of the KB in terms of relationships between and within knowledge structures. The Cube itself is modeled using the declarative model of MedView.

5.3   Knowledge Sharing

The clinics participating in MedView maintain local KBs that are regularly added to a central KB shared by all clinics. The WebPhotos application is an early example of a tool for accessing the KB over the Internet. Clinicians also communicate knowledge using summaries created by MS.

6   Discussion

MedView is in daily use at a growing number of clinics within SOMNET. Since 1995, clinical data from over 3000 examinations has been collected into the KB. Clinical practice has indicated that the basic ideas are conceptually appealing to the involved clinicians and that MedView has promoted knowledge sharing within the network.

MedView is rather unique in that it applies a uniform declarative model to all aspects of a clinical information system, from the implementation framework used to the design of the overall system, from fundamental knowledge structures to interaction and visualization models.

The GALEN project [10] has a similar approach in that it provides a uniform representation language for medical terminology and medical concepts together with a common framework for application builders. Compared to GALEN, so far, MedView has focused on the tight coupling between users, visualization, and knowledge structures.

References

[1]   Lucas, P.: Logic engineering in medicine. The Knowledge Engineering Review **10** (1995) 153–179
[2]   Aarts, J.: On articulation and localization—some sociotechnical issues of design, implementation, and evaluation of knowledge-based systems. In Quaglini, S., Barahona, P., Andreassen, S., eds.: Artificial Intelligence in Medicine. Proceedings of the 8th Conference on Artificial Intelligence in Medicine in Europe, AIME 2001, Cascais, Portugal, July 1–4, 2001. Volume 2101 of Lecture Notes in Artificial Intelligence, Springer-Verlag (2001) 16–19
[3]   Hallnäs, L.: Partial inductive definitions. Theoretical Computer Science **87** (1991) 115–142
[4]   Chittaro, L.: Information visualization and its application to medicine. Artificial Intelligence in Medicine **22** (2001) 81–88
[5]   Fechter, J., Grunert, T., Encarnação, L.M., Straßer, W.: User-centered development of medical visualization applications: Flexible interaction through communicating application objects. Computers & Graphics: Special Issue on Medical Visualization **20** (1996) 763–774
[6]   North, C.L., Shneiderman, B.: Snap-together visualization: A user interface for coordinating visualizations via relational schemata. In: Proceedings of Advanced Visual Interfaces 2000. (2000) 128–135
[7]   Ahlberg, C., Shneiderman, B.: Visual information seeking: Tight coupling of dynamic query filters with starfield displays. In: Human Factors in Computing Systems. Proceedings of CHI'94, ACM Press (1994) 313–317
[8]   Falkman, G.: Information visualization in clinical odontology: Multidimensional analysis and interactive data exploration. Artificial Intelligence in Medicine **22** (2001) 133–158
[9]   Inselberg, A.: The plane with parallel coordinates. The Visual Computer **1** (1985) 69–91
[10] Rector, A.L., Nowlan, W.A.: The GALEN project. Computer Methods and Programs in Biomedicine **45** (1993) 75–78

MEGICO: An Intelligent Knowledge Management Methodology

José Luis Maté[1], Luis Felipe Paradela[2], Juan Pazos[1], Alfonso Rodríguez-Patón[1], Andrés Silva[1]

[1]Facultad de Informática, UPM, Campus de Montegancedo s/n, Boadilla del Monte, 28660 Madrid
jlmate@fi.upm.es, jpazos@fi.upm.es, arpaton@fi.upm.es, asilva@fi.upm.es
[2]INAP (Instituto Nacional de Administración Pública), Madrid

Abstract. In this paper, we describe a knowledge management system (KMS) design and construction methodology. For this purpose, section 1 gives a brief introduction that justifies the need for a genuine KMS methodology, like MEGICO. Section 2 very briefly presents MEGICO and section 3 discusses the results and conclusions of its use.

1. Introduction

Looking at the literature on frameworks and methods for KM initiatives that is summarised in [1], added to in [2] and, owing to its importance, Tiwana's roadmap [3], we find that not one of these frameworks or methods is really a methodology as defined by de Hoog [4] and Paradela [2]. This is because, among other things, they do not meet each and every one of the general and specific conditions that de Hoog specified as *necessary* and *sufficient* for any proposal supporting KM initiatives to be considered a genuine methodology. Indeed, most proposals are either descriptive or prescriptive, but not hybrid. And they do not meet the conditions of holism and learning ability, among others. For this reason, we present a methodology that does meet the above conditions, and others specified by Rubenstein-Montano et al. [1]. The methodology is called MEGICO, which is the Spanish abbreviation of Intelligent Knowledge Management Methodology.

2. MEGICO

For obvious reasons of space, we have opted to describe MEGICO using a LISP-type, bracketed linear formula, by means of which all its elements can be reasonably compacted and, based upon their numeration, easily restructured as a tree. Moreover, the description only goes as far as level 3, step, although, in some cases, the methodology can be decomposed down to level 5 [2].

With regard to Phase I, it is evident that there are structural elements that can be completed straightforwardly, such as, Stage I.1.1. Coordinates, for example, or are

A. Gómez-Pérez and V.R. Benjamins (Eds.): EKAW 2002, LNAI 2473, pp. 102-107, 2002.
© Springer-Verlag Berlin Heidelberg 2002

easy to carry out, such as Stage I.2, Contextual Definition, for instance. However, Stage I.3, Definition of the current situation: Feasibility study, calls for a little more attention. Indeed, apart from being difficult to perform, Step I.3.1 Classification of the current situation: Problem analysis and scope is of utmost importance. A problem is unlikely to be able to be solved unless it has been identified and defined beforehand. The question then is as follows. What is the problem? Who has the problem? Why? Where and under what circumstances does it arise? When? How can it be solved? That is, for each particular situation, we will need to clearly answer the six honest-serving men to identify, define and, finally, solve the problematic situation at hand.

Now, let us turn to the stages that are, as we see it, most problematic, namely, problem predefinition and definition. Firstly, it is inconceivable to try to solve a problem unless the problem is felt. Feeling a problem basically involves perceiving a deviation of events with regard to an objective, hence these objectives will have been explicitly and exhaustively established previously in Step I.2.3. Strictly speaking, this predefinition is not final, whence its name. Indeed, it has to be considered as a hypothesis that is questionable until confirmed or refuted by the facts.

On the basis of the information gathered and classified in the respective stage, the Cartesian method is strictly and rigorously applied in the problem definition stage, as follows. Rule of evidence: most problems are not solved because they are poorly defined. It is a well-known fact that a well-defined problem is a problem half-solved. Actually, many problems remain unsolved because the people involved are reticent or refuse to define the problems as they are, perhaps because they foresee what difficulties the alternative to which a proper definition leads entails. Moreover, we often tend to look for a good solution, when, in many cases, the only one that is feasible is a less bad solution. The rule of analysis is then used to, first, completely and exhaustively ascertain all the subproblems and aspects and, secondly, identify the relationship between the identified facts, signs and symptoms, the existing concepts and their relationships. Then, the rule of synthesis is applied to output the conceptual model of the problem, which is the fundamental reference point for the person who has the problem and the person who has to solve the problem. This process of synthesis should avoid any unnecessary assumptions, i.e. assigning an effect to what is merely a possible cause. Finally, the rule of testing is applied to check that nothing has been omitted and nothing is superfluous.

PHASE I. Identification of the Institution and Its Culture:
A. Structural Elements

{STAGE I.1. CO-ORDINATES [STEP I.1.1. Physical Co-ordinates][STEP I.1.2. Financial Co-ordinates][STEP I.1.3. Business Co-ordinates]*} {STAGE I.2. CONTEXTUAL DEFINITION*[STEP I.2.1. Establishment of the Environment][STEP I.2.2. Maturity Level of the Institution as regards KM][STEP I.2.3. Institutional Objectives]*} {STAGE I.3. DEFINITION OF THE CURRENT SITUATION: FEASIBILITY STUDY*[STEP I.3.1. Classification of the Current Situation: Analysis of the Problem and Problem Scope][STEP I.3.2. Impact Analysis and Solution Improvements][STEP I.3.3. Cost-Benefit Analysis]*}*

B. Functional and Representative Elements

<TASKS: Gather all the information required to clearly establish the location of the institution and its self-knowledge, Establish its context and maturity level, Define and prioritise the institution's purposes, ends and objectives, Framework definition><ACTIVITIES: Update all the information, Run surveys, Define the knowledge assets, carry out a knowledge audit and calculate the intellectual worth of the organisation, Analyse surveys, Establish return on investment rates, Calculate indexes and determine the intellectual capital equation><TOOLS: Organisational charts and diagramming, Questionnaires, SWOT matrix, Internet, Documentary management, Audit, Cost-benefit analysis techniques><MODELS AND PROGRAMMES: Institutional ontology, Institutional model, Intellectual capital audit process model>

Phase II, praxiologics or action, is basically, but not exclusively, prescriptive, and its key elements include conceptualisation, the associated conventional knowledge map, the institutional memory and the definition of the knowledge network, with its sources, drains, repositories, etc. All these models and deliverables appear below. This is the phase that demonstrates the flexibility of the methodology. Indeed, depending on the type of KM initiative in question (lessons learned, best practices, global KM system, etc.), the structural and functional elements required will be selected, ignoring the others. For example, if we aim to embark upon a best practices initiative, the task would be confined to conceptualising the problem at hand, activity to defining the state of art and target and so on successively. Accordingly, this phase can be seen as a generator of efficient and adaptable ad hoc methods, which is what makes it a genuine methodology.

PHASE II. Praxiologics: A. Structural Elements

{STAGE II.1. CONCEPTUALISATION[STEP II.1.1. Inventory KM Elements][STEP II.1.2. Bottleneck Analysis][STEP II.1.3. SWOT Analysis]} {STAGE II.2. REFLECTION[STEP II.2.1. Identify Policy Goals][STEP II.2.2. Define and Select Improvements][STEP II.2.3. Define Improvement Models]} {STAGE II.3. KNOWLEDGE CREATION AND DEVELOPMENT[STEP II.3.1. Knowledge Generation][STEP II.3.2. Consolidate Knowledge(][STEP II.3.3. Distribute and Use Knowledge]}

B. Functional and Representative Elements

<TASKS: Classify, monitor and evaluate the performance of the institution or part of the institution, Conceptualise the problem at hand, Define the process of the knowledge>< ACTIVITIES: Define the current state of the art and target, Define knowledge assets policies><TOOLS: Surveys, Questionnaires, Protocol analysis, SWOT matrices, Charts: Ishikawa or fishbone diagrams, Benchmarking, Roadmaps><MODELS AND PROGRAMMES: Effectiveness improvement programmes, Knowledge construction program, Knowledge transfer programmes, Process model and knowledge networks, Hardware, software and legal protection of knowledge><DELIVERIES AND OUTPUT DOCUMENTS: Description of the business situation, Definition of constraints, Definition of alternatives, Results of the use of the referenced methods, Knowledge, infor-

mation maps, etc., Knowledge infrastructure management manual, Corporate memories, KBS, Patents, Copyright, Products, Services, Practical improvements>

Finally, Phase III, implementation, testing and maintenance, is also mainly prescriptive. A variation on the information packaging method (IPM) will be used in this phase, the basic process of which is shown in Figure 1. It is developed in the following four stages. Stage one involves the system architecture and planning. Stage two concerns design and analysis. Stage three addresses technological implementation. Finally, stage four deals with deployment and testing against metrics and users. The spiral represents the infinite cycle between stages 4 and 1, which leads to iterative and incremental improvements.

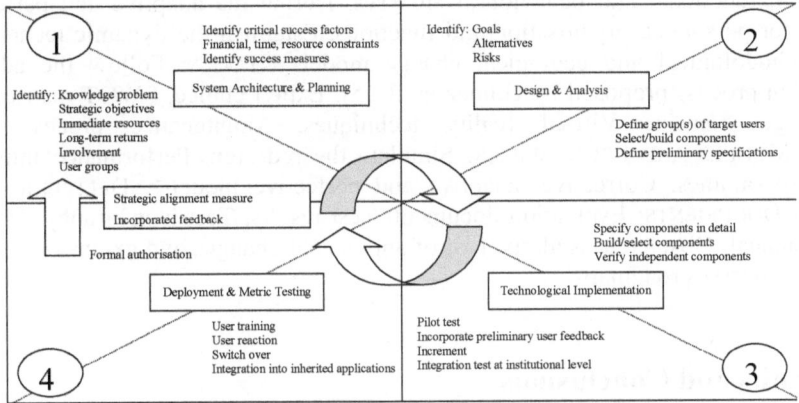

Fig. 1. Information packaging methodology

PHASE III. Implementation or Replacement, Testing and Maintenance:
A. Structural Elements

{*STAGE III.1. DESIGN AND IMPLEMENT TECHNOLOGICAL SUPPORT*[STEP III.1.1. Establish the Technological Infrastructure][STEP III.1.2. Establish the Technological Structure][STEP III.1.3. Define the Technology Replacement Policy]} {*STAGE III.2. PROTECT AND SAFEGUARD KNOWLEDGE*[STEP III.2.1. Identification of Expert Knowledge and Hazards][STEP III.2.2. Safeguarding Expert Knowledge][STEP III.2.3. Protection of Knowledge]} {*STAGE III.3. EVALUATION AND TESTING: DEFINE THE ELEMENTS OF THE EVALUATION*[STEP III.3.1. Establish the Evaluation Criteria][STEP III.3.2. Identify the Assessment Techniques][STEP III.3.3. System Verification and Validation]} {*STAGE III.4. EVALUATION OF KNOWLEDGE TRANSFER*[STEP III.4.1. Definition of Criteria][STEP III.4.2. Establishment of Strengths and Weaknesses][STEP III.4.3. Measurement of Learning Effectiveness]} {*STAGE III.5. IMPLEMENTATION TESTING*[STEP III.5.1. Simulation of the Redesign][STEP III.5.2. White Box Tests][STEP III.5.3. Parallel or Field Testing]} {*STAGE III.6. CORRECTIVE MAINTENANCE*[STEP III.6.1. Identification of Faults and Deficiencies][STEP III.6.2. Analysis of Detected Faults and Deficiencies][STEP III.6.3. Correction of Faults and Rectification of Deficiencies]} {*STAGE III.7. ADAPTIVE MAINTENANCE*[STEP III.7.1. Adaptation to Internal Changes][STEP III.7.2. Adaptation to Changes in the External

Environment][STEP III.7.3. Adaptation to Changes of Location]}{*STAGE III.8. PERFECTIVE MAINTENANCE*[STEP III.8.1. Improved Performance][STEP III.8.2. Extensions][STEP III.8.3. On Demand from Users and Managers]}>

B. Functional and Representative Elements

<TASKS: Evaluate the implementations carried out on an overall and individual basis, Define and implement corrective, adaptive and perfective maintenance><ACTIVITIES: Define the objectives, aspects and assessment techniques, and establish the evaluation method, Identify false manoeuvres, obsoleteness, and faults and deficiencies, Run structural, functional and behavioural analyses, Define the adaptive and perfective models for personnel, organisation and functions, Establish the dynamic technological, methodological and ecological change models><TOOLS: Follow the adapted evaluation process proposed by Gómez et al. [5], Expert choice, SWOT matrices for knowledge transfer, Virtual reality techniques, Maintenance process roadmaps><MODELS AND PROGRAMMES: Simulate the redesign, Performance improvement programmes, Corrective, adaptive and perfective models><DELIVERIES AND OUTPUT DOCUMENTS: Evaluation document, Test results, Test iconography, Maintenance manual, Obsoleteness alerts, List of anticipated changes and extensions, Maintenance processes roadmap>

3. Results and Conclusions

MEGICO has been used as a methodology to carry out over twenty different KM initiatives in different domains, having different scopes and ranges. The most important are summarised in Table 1. The first column in Table 1 contains the organisation promoting or using the initiative. The second column describes the organisation's business area and the third describes the initiative or the type of courses in which it is used.

The following are the findings related to the initiatives carried out using MEGICO:
- Management backing and stakeholder cooperation are essential for the success of the initiative.
- The interaction between the cultural and technological approaches is more intense than it was thought to be and they converge at the organisational level. This interaction affects the entire organisation and leads to changes.
- After applying KM to the methodology itself, as lessons learned from the use of MEGICO, we consider it to be good practice to design specific pathways when MEGICO users are looking for partial initiatives. For example, for the construction of lessons learned systems, they could be offered the part of the methodology they need for this purpose and only this part. This would make MEGICO a partial methodology generator. The same applies for practical improvements and institutional memories, etc.
- Knowledge sharing is more a question of confidence than of financial reward. However, the creation of practice communities and knowledge networks favours sharing.

Table 1. Representative sample of KM initiatives carried out with MEGICO

ORGANISATION	BUSINESS	INITIATIVE
ASAJA	Trade union	Best practices
BBK (Bilbao Savings Bank)	Finances	Design of good practices for its retail banking offices
BBVA (Banco Bilbao Vizcaya Argentaria)	Banking, Finances	Lessons learned systems for corporate banking
La Caixa	Banking, Finances	Institutional memory
COFAGA	Logistics	Institutional memory
Deusto University	Training and R&D	Master
FINSA	Holding Company	Best practices and lessons learned
Iberia	Transport	Ontologies for an institutional memory
INAP (Spanish National Institute of Public Administration)	Public Administration	Master and institutional memory
LANTIK, S.A.	Computing services	Global KM system for the whole institution
Motril Local Administration	Public Administration	Best practices
Technical University of Madrid	Training and R&D	Master, doctorate and artificial intelligence laboratory institutional memory

- It is important, whenever possible, not to develop integrated knowledge architectures, networks and flows in one go. It is much more efficient to do this gradually.
- Finally, a software tool to support MEGICO application was missed in all projects.

Acknowledgements. We would like to thank the CICYT for funding project TIC1998-0741 and all the institutions (which appear in Table 1) that have used or are using the MEGICO methodology. Our thanks also go to Rachel Elliott (CETTICO) for her invaluable help in translating this paper.

References

1. Rubenstein-Montano, B., Liebowitz, J., Buchwalter, J., McCaw, D., Newman, B., Rebeck, K.; A Systems Thinking Framework for Knowledge Management. Decision Support Systems 31 (2001) 5-16
2. Paradela, L. F.: Ph.D. Thesis. UPM (2002) (under review process)
3. Tiwana, A.: The Knowledge Management Toolkit. Prentice Hall PTR, Upper Sadle River, New Jersey (2000)
4. De Hoog, R.: Methodologies for Building Knowledge-Based Systems: Achievements and Prospects. In Liebowitz J. (ed): The Handbook of Applied Expert Systems. CRC Press, Boca Ratón, Florida (1998) 1-1, 1-14
5. Gómez, A.; Juristo, N.; Montes, C., Pazos, J.: "Ingeniería del Conocimiento", Editorial Centro de Estudios Ramón Areces, S.A. Madrid (1997)

A Process Ontology

Stuart Aitken[1] and Jon Curtis[2]

[1] Artificial Intelligence Applications Institute,
University of Edinburgh
stuart@aiai.ed.ac.uk
http://www.aiai.ed.ac.uk
[2] Cycorp Inc., 3721 Executive Center Drive,
Austin, Texas 78731
jonc@cyc.com
http://www.cyc.com

Abstract. This paper describes an ontology for process representation. The ontology provides a vocabulary of classes and relations at a level above the primitive event-instance, object-instance and timepoint description. The design of this ontology balances two main concerns: to provide a concise set of useful abstractions of process, and to provide an adequate formal semantics for these abstractions. The aim of conciseness is to support knowledge authoring - ideally a domain expert should be able to author knowledge in the ontology - providing a sufficiently advanced toolset and interface has been implemented to support this task.

1 Introduction

The Rapid Knowledge Formation project (RKF) [7] aims to develop powerful tools to enable domain experts to author knowledge directly. These tools require knowledge-engineering knowledge in order to function adequately. In addition, the knowledge acquisition process is aided by providing a suitable set of abstractions - in the form of ontology classes and relations - that permit the expert to make complex, and well-founded statements in a concise manner.

This paper describes an ontology for process representation which allows processes to be described purely at the type-level. The semantics of these relations is expressed in terms of more primitive event-to-object relations in the Cyc ontology[6]. A similar semantics in terms of the Process Specification Language (PSL)[9] types and relations has also been developed in the course of this work showing the (relative) independence of the type level and the ground level.

The process ontology aims to provide a concise set of useful abstractions of process which apply across numerous domains. The first domain studied was processes in cell biology, where models were derived from a textbook [1]. Latterly, we are considering military courses of action. The process ontology augments an existing theory of scripted events in Cyc, which is the theory behind the powerful user interface tools developed and tested in RKF.

A. Gómez-Pérez and V.R. Benjamins (Eds.): EKAW 2002, LNAI 2473, pp. 108–113, 2002.
© Springer-Verlag Berlin Heidelberg 2002

The connection between the ontology and the user tools is the subject of Section 2, we then outline the existing Script vocabulary and then present the extensions to it. The theories of participants, conditions and effects and of repeated processes are documented in Section 3. Finally, we consider related work in Section 4, and draw some conclusions in Section 5.

2   The RKF Tools and Ontology

The Cyc knowledge base currently contains more than 100,000 concepts, and 1.4 million axioms and rules [8]. Cyc's knowledge is represented using CycL, a highly expressive language based on second order logic. The Cyc tools developed in the RKF project provide the core functionality of the KRAKEN knowledge-entry system. KRAKEN incorporates powerful natural language tools that allow the user to interact with the system through simple questions and statements in English. The parsing components of the interface use Cyc's lexical and syntactic knowledge to produce intermediate logical representations. The resulting underspecified representation must be 'finalised' to construct valid CycL. This 'finalisation' process proceeds via both syntactic and semantic (knowledge-driven) transformation rules. More details of the NLP components can be found in [8].

The User Interaction Agenda (UIA) provides the following tools:

The *precision suggestor* for placing a concept appropriately in the hierarchy. This tool identifies a small set of possible generalisations and specialisations of a new concept and suggests these to the user.

The *salient descriptor* aims to add a minimal, appropriately general set of relevant assertions about new (or existing, but under-ontologized) concepts. This tool queries the user, in English, for the additional information using general, context-dependent knowledge-acquisition rules. Prompting these queries are knowledge-acquisition rules of the form, *if $P(a)$, it is useful to know $Q(a)$*. Again, the precision suggestor can be used against the output of any salient descriptor interaction, to help ensure that the right level of generality has been achieved.

The *process descriptor* assists the user to enter descriptions of structured event types, or Scripts. A Script is a typical pattern of events that can be expected to re-occur - 'dining in a restaurant' being a well known example. The tool allows the various steps of a process to be defined and ordered, and for the types of actors and roles in the various steps to be identified. The precision suggestor and salient descriptor tools are called upon as necessary.

The relevance of a process ontology becomes all the more evident when one realizes that knowledge creation and refinement is itself a process, describable as a Script in CycL. Thus a rich and inferentially powerful theory of Scripts is potentially useful beyond giving the KRAKEN system the resources to guide the user in defining new processes. With the knowledge that every UIA knowledge-entry session is itself an instantiation of a kind of Script, Cyc will be able to 'follow' the Script, anticipating decision points and user actions, and, overall, more effectively guide knowledge-entry sessions from start to finish, in much the way a genuinely intelligent agent would. Thus one way to interpret the results reported here is to think of them as important stepping stones towards the larger goal of using a process ontology as a core component of knowledge-entry tools, generally.

3   The Process Theory: An Extension of Scripts

This section presents three extensions to the Script theory: Participants, Conditions and Repetition. The Participants theory extends the existing vocabulary for identifying the objects that play a role in a scripted event or a Scene. The Conditions theory is a new theory for specifying the preconditions and effects of a Scene. The Repeated Scripts theory provides the semantics for the repetition of an Event type, within the Process theory. These theories all provide a type-level vocabulary, and are grounded at the instance-level which provides the semantics. As a consequence of the type-level definitions, the problem of identity arises, i.e. which instance plays a given role in an event, given that only its type is specified. Selected ontology relations and their rules are presented to illustrate the approach.

3.1   Participants in Processes

Processes are formalised as Scripts. However, the representation of participants is modified for Processes. Firstly, an explicit count of objects of the given type which play a role in the event must be specified. Secondly, it is necessary to know which objects of that type play a role in a specific event. The new formulation contains the information required for process instances to be created. As the process description is really a specification, we cannot immediately derive a ground instance of the process (a model in terms of event-instances and objects) from it, but can validate a ground model against the type level description.

The relations *actorTypeInScriptCount* and *actorTypeInSceneCount* state the number of things of a given type that play any role in a Script or Scene. These relations have the following rules which conclude with the Cyc relation *relationInstanceExistsCount*, specifying the number of *instances* of *?TYPE* for which *(actors ?EVENT instance)* holds. *actors* is used as the most general predicate relating events and instances, it will be specialised during process modelling.

```
F: (implies (and (actorTypeInScriptCount ?TYPE ?SCRIPT ?INT)
                 (instantiatesScript ?EVENT ?SCRIPT))
            (relationInstanceExistsCount
                 actors ?EVENT ?TYPE ?INT)).
```

The following KE suggestion rules are defined to encode the knowledge acquisition requirements as they apply to Processes. This type of information is important as it drives the suggestion mechanisms of the GUI tools. For a ScriptedEventType, an *actorTypeInScriptCount* is expected, therefore the following rule is defined:

```
F: (implies (isa ?SCRIPT ScriptedEventType)
            (keStrongSuggestion ?SCRIPT
              (thereExists ?TYPE (thereExists ?INT
                (actorTypeInScriptCount ?TYPE ?SCRIPT ?INT))))).
```

Explicit assertions that the object(s) playing a role in one Scene is(are) the same as those in another Scene, or in the Script as a whole, are required. The problem of identifying instances from subevent to subevent arises from the type-level approach where properties of Scenes are stated in the context of Script, but otherwise in isolation from each other. Additional relations are introduced to allow such statements.

3.2   Conditions in Processes

The conditions and effects of scenes are also defined at the type-level. Only Scenes are treated as it is assumed that the conditions of Scripts are derivable from those of the constituent Scenes.

preconditionOfScene holds of a Scene, a predicate, and a specification term. The semantics at the instance level are expressed in terms of the existing Cyc predicate *preconditionFor-PropSit* which holds of an *ELSentence-Assertible* and an *Event*. The predicate and the specification of *preconditionOfScene* determine the *ELSentence-Assertible*. The specification term selects among the objects that have been defined to play a role in the Scene, that is, all objects that are referred to in the conditions must be declared to play a role in the Scene. This is done using the Participant vocabulary.

```
F: (implies (and (preconditionOfScene ?SCENE ?PRED
                    (TypeArgSpec-UnaryFn ?ROLE))
              (isa ?ROLE BinaryRolePredicate)
              (isa ?PRED UnaryPredicate)
              (isa ?SUBEVENT ?SCENE))
    (thereExists ?E (and (?ROLE ?SUBEVENT ?E)
                (preconditionFor-PropSit (?PRED ?E) ?SUBEVENT)))).
```

A Scene may have several preconditions. These are stated independently of each other, and have the interpretation that the conjunction of these *preconditionOfScene* assertions must hold for the event to be executable. The conditions may be unary, binary or ternary relations.

Postconditions are treated in a similar manner to preconditions. Again, establishing identity between the arguments of the pre/postconditions again arises, and additional vocabulary is introduced to allow identity to be asserted.

Planning We have implemented translation procedures that transform the type-level encodings of actions into PDDL and also construct a constraint theory in Cyc [2]. The semantics of the constraint theory are equivalent to those of the PDDL problem definition. Thus we have a dual representation of conditions: a Process semantics which is consistent with Process models, and a constraint semantics which is consistent with the PDDL action encoding. This allows us to call an external planner to perform plan generation when this type of reasoning is required. It is worth noting that the ability to plug in an external planner, though desirable, is not necessary. Cycorp has developed a hierarchical planner within Cyc, currently deployed as a part of their Cyc Secure (TM) product.

3.3   Repetition in Processes

Biological models commonly include processes that are repeated. The number of repetitions may be known, or may be unspecified. Further, repetition may occur until a specific condition is achieved. The key ideas are to define properties of repeated processes, such as termination, and introduce functions that creates a new process (event type) from an existing event type, for example, *(RepeatInOrder ?EVENT ?INT)*. Space prohibits a more detailed presentation.

4   Related Work

The Process ontology is closely related to the Process Specification Language, in terms of both the intended area of application and formal approach. The PSL Core is an instance-level theory of activity which can be mapped to the equivalent event/object relations in Cyc. While the predicates differ, equivalent instance-level models of events can be created.

PSL has several theories which the Process ontology currently lacks. However, PSL does not provide a well defined set of type-level relations for subevent ordering, participants or conditions (fluents in PSL)[1]. Modelling using the core PSL theories must be performed primarily at the event instance level. PSL does define a theory of junctions in processes.

DAML-S [4] contains a process ontology which contains many concepts found in PSL, and in the ontology presented here. For example, types of process include atomic, simple and composite, process parameters (properties) include inputs, outputs and participants and these correspond to roles in our ontology. DAML-S also has preconditions and effects, sequence, split+join and repetition. However, DAML-S currently only defines the names of collections or properties so no detailed comparison is possible.

IDEF3[5] is a process modelling methodology which primarily diagrammatic. Processes, process products, and their connections are represented by a convention of boxes and arrows. The visual presentation is important in the modelling process, and in explaining the model to the managers and employees in an organisation. IDEF3 models have several features which inform the interpretation of the diagrams, including and/or/xor junctions. Processes may have attributes such as triggers which are not shown in the diagram but are documented elsewhere. None of these features have formal semantics. The informality allows a single model to describe many complex phenomena, such as repetition, splits in the flow of processes (junctions) and synchronisation, in a relatively intuitive

---

[1] Many of the type-level relations have no axioms and only a textual definition.

way. Naturally, IDEF3 models cannot be processed by machine without creating an interpretation (explicitly or implicitly). Defining an underlying formal semantics for informal modelling techniques allows the consistency and integrity of the models to be maintained [3]. These practical benefits are important justifications for formalisation in a business context.

5   Conclusions

Through pursuing the type-level approach, we have found there to be a relatively small set of useful abstractions of processes. Consequently, the combination of a type-level vocabulary with the associated knowledge-elicitation rules is a powerful technique for knowledge acquisition. Rather than authoring rules with universally and existentially quantified variables as is required at the event-instance level (a task which, when given to domain experts, certainly requires them to become much more familiar with the logical encoding), the Process Ontology allows a process description to be created incrementally in terms of classes and relations only.

Acknowledgements

This work is sponsored by the Defense Advanced Research Projects Agency (DARPA) under subcontract 00-C-0160-01 with Cycorp on BAA99-35. The U.S. Government is authorised to reproduce and distribute reprints for Governmental purposes notwithstanding any copyright annotation hereon. The views and conclusions contained herein are those of the authors and should not be interpreted as necessarily representing official policies or endorsements, either express or implied, of DARPA, Rome Laboratory or the U.S. Government.

References

1. Alberts, B., Bray, D., Johnson, A., Lewis, J., Raff, M., Roberts, K., and Walter, P. *Essential Cell Biology* Garland Publishing, London, 1998.
2. Aitken S. Process Planning in Cyc: From Scripts and Scenes to Constraints. *Proc. Twentieth Workshop of the UK Planning SIG, PLANSIG 2001*, Ed. Levine, J., December 2001, pp. 257-260.
3. Chen-Burger, Y. and Robertson, D. Formal Support for an Informal Business Modeling Method. *Proc. SEKE 1998*.
4. DAML Web Service Ontology http://www.daml.org/services/
5. *IDEF3 Method Report*, KBSI Inc. http://www.idef.com/idef3.html
6. Lenat, D.B. *Leveraging Cyc for HPKB Intermediate-level Knowledge and Efficient Reasoning* http://www.cyc.com/hpkb/proposal-summary-hpkb.html
7. Rapid Knowledge Formation Project http://reliant.teknowledge.com/RKF/
8. Panton, K., Miraglia, P., Salay, N., Kahlert, R.C., Baxter, D., and Reagan, R. Knowledge Formation and Dialogue using the KRAKEN Toolset. *Proc. IAAI-02*
9. Schlenoff, C., Gruninger, M., Tissot, F., Valois, J., Lubell, J., and Lee, J., *The Process Specification Language (PSL) Overview and Version 1.0 Specification*. NIST Report (NISTIR) 6459, Jan. 1999.

Semantic Commitment for Designing Ontologies: A Proposal

Bruno Bachimont[1], Antoine Isaac[1,2], and Raphaël Troncy[1,3]

[1] Institut National de l'Audiovisuel, Direction de la Recherche
4, Av. de l'Europe - 94366 Bry-sur-Marne
{bbachimont,aisaac,rtroncy}@ina.fr & http://www.ina.fr/
[2] LaLICC, Université de Paris-Sorbonne,
http://www.lalic.paris4.sorbonne.fr
[3] INRIA Rhône-Alpes, Action EXMO,
http://www.inrialpes.fr/exmo

Abstract. The French institute INA is interested in ontologies in order to describe the content of audiovisual documents. Methodologies and tools for building such objects exist, but few propose complete guidelines to help the user to organize the key components of ontologies: subsumption hierarchies. This article proposes to use a methodology introducing a clear semantic commitment to normalize the meaning of the concepts. We have implemented this methodology in an editor, DOE, complementary to other existing tools, and used it to develop several ontologies.

1 Introduction

With the emergence of technical systems which exploit numerical contents, accessing and processing information are evolving at a fair rate. The French institute INA[1] has to manage large multimedia and audio-visual databases, a task that includes allowing an access as efficient as possible to the data stored. INA is thus greatly concerned with indexing – the core of its mission –, which implies dealing with ontologies to create relevant content description of the audio-visual documents.

While trying to use ontologies, one soon has to face the problem of the way they are designed, especially as regards to taxonomy structuration. Indeed, it is acknowledged that the taxonomies of domain concepts are key components of the built ontologies. Consequently, we searched for a methodological approach that gives guidelines to structure taxonomies (Section 2). We claim that none of these methodologies force the ontologist to explicit the real meanings of the concepts and consider thereafter a possible solution, using natural language. We detail the three steps of a methodology proposal (Section 3) and present a tool implementing it. We then conclude and outline further work (Section 4).

---

[1] INA (*Institut National de l'Audiovisuel*) has been archiving TV documents for 45 years and radio documents for 60 years. It stores more than 700 000 hours of broadcast programs (3 000 000 audio-visual documents) and some 2 000 000 images.

A. Gómez-Pérez and V.R. Benjamins (Eds.): EKAW 2002, LNAI 2473, pp. 114–121, 2002.
© Springer-Verlag Berlin Heidelberg 2002

2   Which Methodology for Building Ontologies?

2.1   A Work Still in Progress

Many approaches (for a complete survey, the reader can refer to the OntoWeb Technical RoadMap[2]) have been reported to build ontologies, but few fully detail the steps needed to obtain and structure the taxonomies. For instance, Uschold and Grüninger methodology [7], METHONTOLOGY proposed by the LAI of Madrid [2], or researchers involved in the *On-To-Knowledge* project[3] are rather interested in giving methodological outlines for the whole process of ontology engineering. They focus on the life cycle and the ordering of the general steps to develop these ontologies: identify the purpose of the information system, collect the relevant information for knowledge acquisition, evaluate the results, etc. Obviously, all these tasks are essential according to an "ontological engineering" point of view. However, the conceptualization step, in which the concepts and the relations between them are captured, has to be detailed.

For instance, METHONTOLOGY proposes to build the ontology at the knowledge level using a set of *intermediate representations*. Although the taxonomy is one of these representations, the methodology does not stress on the way to classify the concepts. The methodology introduced in the framework of *On-To-Knowledge* uses lexical pattern matching to extract some subsumption information from the answers given to informal competency questions [3]. It is an original way of considering the problem, but one may wonder whether this helping function could be generally applied. Finally, we may mention Nicola Guarino's taxonomy cleaning method [4], which aims at removing wrong subsumption relation from concept hierarchies thanks to meta-properties defined by logical axioms. It is an interesting approach, yet only applicable after one has already built such a hierarchy: the first move remains to be done by the ontologist alone, which is not satisfying. That is the reason why we are eager to learn about whatever may follow from the merge attempt between this method and METHONTOLOGY [3].

2.2   Requirements for a Methodology Focusing on Natural Language

Among the methodologies evoked, few propose complete guidelines to help the user to organize the hierarchies. We claim here that, finally, none of these methodologies force the ontologist to explicit the real meanings of the concepts in the most natural way: using natural language (NL). Actually, some methodologies recommend using NL to explicit the meaning of the concepts inside comments or through documents surrounding the modeling process, but not in a principled way. The terms used to denote the concepts are still liable to multiple interpretations. This results in possible misunderstandings and consequently bad modeling and use of the ontology. We suggest then to follow an evolved version of methodological guidelines that were first proposed in [1].

---

[2] http://babage.dia.fi.upm.es/ontoweb/wp1/OntoRoadMap/index.html
[3] http://www.ontoknowledge.org

The first problem to face is the under-determination of meaning: every expression in language has its meaning contextually defined, since interpretation may vary according to the context (a specific application). Modeling will thus consist in choosing linguistic labels and associating with them a relevant and non-contextual semantics. The problem is then to determine which kind of semantics and how to use it in a *normalization* effort.

Second, defining a linguistic meaning is not sufficient to specify a system. A usual approach consists in associating a formal semantics with concepts. Formal semantics allows a mathematical modeling of the linguistic meaning as well as of the system behavior. The ontologist needs a semantics formal enough to efficiently specify computations, and yet close enough to the knowledge level to make these computations intelligible.

Finally, an ontology has to introduce knowledge primitives which will be the building blocks for programming a Knowledge-Based System (KBS). From this point of view, a label will be used in rules, or grammars, or inferences, to perform computation. The associated semantics is here a computational or operational one.

To sum up, a knowledge primitive has three semantic descriptions :

a linguistic semantic description that provides a human user with an unambiguous understanding of a term;

a formal semantic description that provides a human user with a mathematical and formal account of the previous level;

a computational description that makes explicit the intended behavior of the computer when handling with this primitive;

The first level is what a human being can understand, the third what a computer can perform, and the second the formal modeling establishing a mapping between the two: how to understand what the KBS is doing, how to specify what it should do.

3   Methodology

The three steps we propose (Fig. 1) consist in a *semantic normalization* of the terms introduced in the ontology, followed by a *formalization* of the meaning of the knowledge primitives obtained and an *operationalization* using knowledge representation languages. The two last steps are not very different from what can be found in other methodologies. The point is the way they are integrated in a process aimed at making ontology development and use easier.

3.1   First Step: Semantic Normalization

The first step of this methodology aims at reaching a semantic agreement about the meaning of the labels used for naming the concepts. Natural language is usually the best access to the knowledge of a domain. In INA, the archivists use a collection of textual documents that are delivered with TV programs. Hence, it

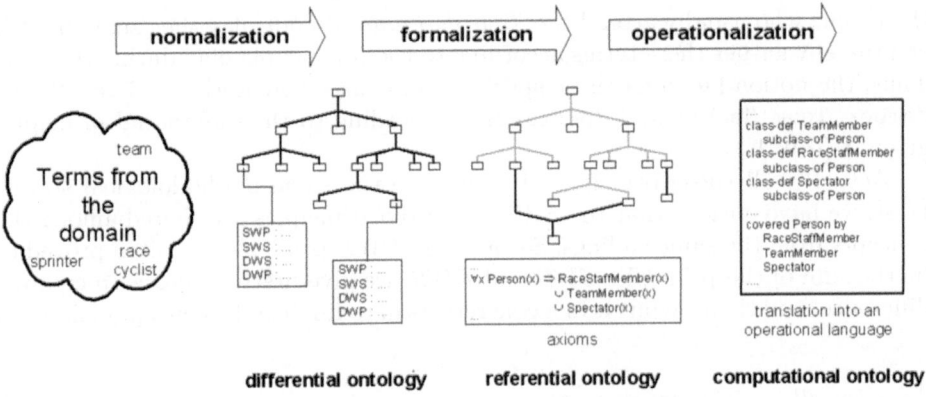

Fig. 1. The 3 steps of the differential methodology for building ontologies

seems natural to look for possible labels, candidates for future primitives, within these documents.

One of our ontologies deals with the field of cycling race, especially the *Tour de France* event. During the analysis of that domain we discovered, for instance, numerous terms referring to human beings who do not play obviously similar roles in a cycling race : `race cyclist`, `spectator`, `team manager`, `reporter`, `race supervisor`, `climber`, `wheeler`, `sprinter`...

After having extracted labels, the ontologist has to specify their meaning clearly, and therefore to use a relevant semantic theory. We are going to build a *differential ontology* which will turn these terms into *notions* based on *differential semantics* ([5]). Practically, the ontologist has to be able to express the similarities and differences of each notion with respect to its neighbors: its parent-notion and its siblings-notions. The result will be a taxonomy of notions, where the meaning of a node is given by the gathering of all similarities and differences attached to the notions found on the way from the root notion (the more generic) to this node.

We propose four principles to render explicit this information:

- The *similarity with parent* principle (or **SWP**): explicits why the notion inherits properties of the one that subsumes it;
- The *similarity with siblings* principle (or **SWS**): gives a semantic axis, a property – assuming exclusive values – allowing to compare the notion with its siblings.
- The *difference with siblings* principle (or **DWS**): precises here the property allowing to distinguish the notion from its siblings;
- The *difference with parent* principle (or **DWP**): explicits the difference allowing to distinguish the notion from its parent;

In the example given above, we can notice that terms like `climber`, `wheeler` and `sprinter` refer to `race cyclists` who are employed by teams. Actually, all the people who usually attend the *Tour de France* do not play the same role. We can thereby gather these terms according to the role people play during the race. Thus, the notion `Person` can be specialized in three new notions – `Race Staff Member`, `Team Member` and `Spectator` – according to the differential principles given in Tab. 1.

Actually, all those principles do not have the same methodological status. First, we have noticed that the *SWP* and *SWS* principles are shared among the concepts from the same siblings. Second, the *DWP* principle has often proved to be the sum of the principles *SWS* and *DWS*: we give firstly a means to create a difference, and then we put it in a concrete form to finalize the concept definition.

⟶ *For all the following notions*
SWP: he is a person
SWS: a property precises why the person is present during the race
⟶ `Race Staff Member`
DWS: he is accredited by the race management
⟶ `Team Member`
DWS: he is employed by a team that takes part in the race
⟶ `Spectator`
DWS: he is neither accredited by the race management, nor employed by a team that
    takes part in the race
⟶ *For all these notions*
DWP: {SWS} + {DWS}

Table 1. The differential principles linked to the concepts directly specializing *Person*

3.2 Second Step: Knowledge Formalization

The ontological tree obtained in the first step allows to disambiguate the notions and to clarify their meanings for a domain-specific application. The transition to extensional semantics aims at linking the notions to a set of referents. The notions become *concepts* behaving as formal primitives and being part of a *referential ontology*. Each concept refers to a set of objects in the domain (its *extension*). Therefore, we can use the operations that exist for sets (*i.e.* union, intersection or complementary) in order to obtain new concepts.

The comparison of extensions allows to define an extensional inheritance relation between concepts: one is subsumed by another if and only if its extension is included in its parent's extension. The subsumption relations of the differential ontology are still true in the referential ontology, but additional nodes may change the tree structure. For instance, `Climber` and `Wheeler` are exclusive notions, but the matching formal concepts can have extensions with common individuals. Typically, the race cyclist `Lance Armstrong` has these two skills.

Hence, we can define in the referential ontology – with a necessary and suffi-cient condition – a new concept `ClimberAndWheeler` to gather such individuals. Multiple inheritance is thereby possible.

Referential semantics allows to introduce new defined concepts but also def-initions for existing concepts imported from the differential ontology. Also, the ontologist has to precise here the arity and domains of the relations. Relation signatures are defined by the means of cartesian product of concepts references. Finally, the ontologist can add some logical axioms in relation to relational alge-bra, part-whole reasoning, composition of relations, exhaustive partitions, etc [6]. For instance, `Race Staff Member`, `Team Member` and `Spectator` form a disjoint coverage of the concept `Person`.

3.3   Third Step: Towards a Computational Ontology

The third and last step of the methodology allows to equip the referential con-cepts with the possible computational operations available in a KBS: this is the *computational ontology*. The system uses an operational knowledge representa-tion language which allows particular inferences. For a language based on the conceptual graph formalism, these inferences are graph operations (joint, projec-tion, etc). For a language based on description logics, these inferences are mainly subsumption tests and classification.

The example below asserts that a `Person`, from the cycling point of view, is either a `Race Staff Member`, a `Team Member` or a `Spectator`. This assertion is written in the DAML+OIL language, an ontology language proposal for the Semantic Web.

```
<daml:Class rdf:about="#Person">
  <daml:disjointUnionOf rdf:parseType="daml:collection">
    <daml:Class rdf:about="#RaceStaffMember"/>
    <daml:Class rdf:about="#TeamMember"/>
    <daml:Class rdf:about="#Spectator"/>
  </daml:disjointUnionOf>
</daml:Class>
```

3.4   Implementing the Methodology: The DOE Editor

DOE[4] (*Differential Ontology Editor*) is a simple prototype that supports the three steps of the methodology detailed above. It is not intended to bring a direct competition with other existing environments (like *Protégé2000*, *OILed*, *OntoEdit* or *WebODE*). Rather, its purpose is to demonstrate by experimenta-tion how taxonomy structuring can benefit from the methodology described in this paper.

During the first step, the ontologist can enter the definition of the notions according to our principles. The tool automatizes partly this task, following the

---

[4] The tool is available for free at `http://opales.ina.fr/public/`.

observations made in Section 3.1. As an illustration, the Fig. 2 shows the interface recalling our **Race Staff Member** example. For the second step, it imports the taxonomies built in the previous step and allows the ontologist to specialize existing concepts and relations, as well as specify the arity and domains of the relations. Here the editor is able to make some consistency checking (propagation of the arity all along the hierarchy – if specified – and inheritance of domains). The last step is implemented by exporting the referential ontology into commonly-used KR languages (DAML-OIL, RDFS). This export mechanism also allows to refine the ontologies built, using the features supported by other editors.

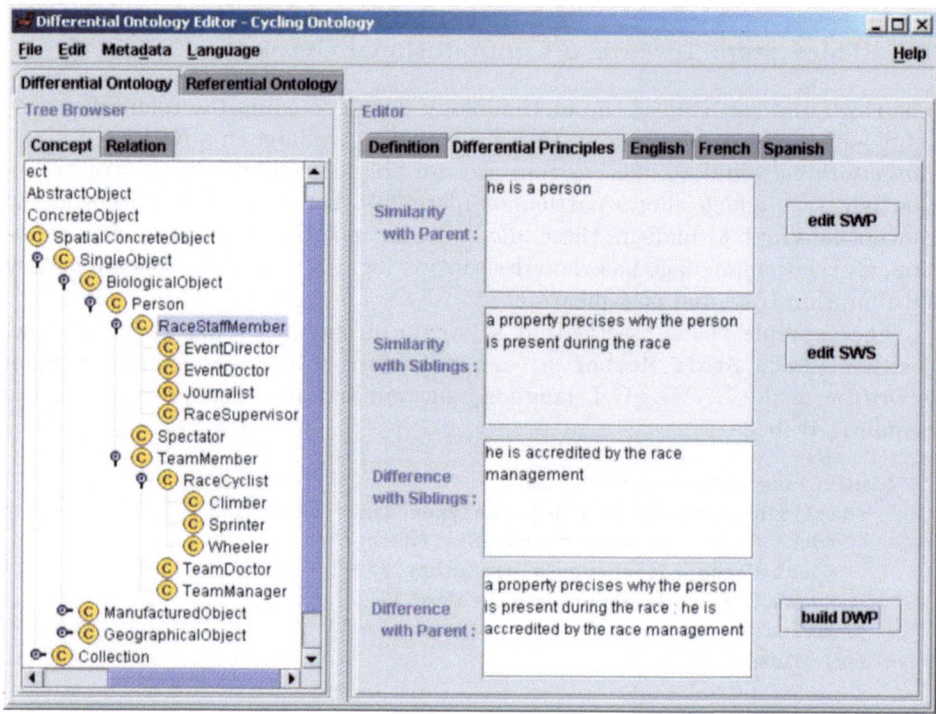

Fig. 2. The differential principles bound to the notion *Race Staff Member* in the *DOE* tool

4 Conclusion and Future Work

We have briefly evoked some methodologies for building ontologies but we have noticed a weakness: nothing forces the ontologist to assign a clear meaning to

concepts, the comments remaining mostly informal. We have proposed guidelines, mainly based on linguistics recommendations (using differential semantics)
to explicit the linguistic meaning of the knowledge primitives of the ontology.
The proposed methodology follows three steps: normalization, formalization and
operationalization. We have implemented this methodology in an edition tool
prototype, *DOE*, and several quite important ontologies have already been built
within it.

For the future, we plan to better integrate our solution in a more complete
ontology engineering process. Prior to the first step of the methodology, we could
use the results of terminological extraction tools to get candidate-concepts and
discover candidate-relations. We should also develop import mechanisms to reuse
ontologies developed with other tools.

References

1. Bouaud, J., Bachimont, B., Charlet, J., Zweigenbaum, P.: Methodological principles
   for structuring an ontology. In *IJCAI-95 Workshop on Basic Ontological Issues in
   Knowledge Sharing*, Montreal, Canada, 1995.
2. Fernández, M., Gómez-Pérez, A. and Juristo, N.: METHONTOLOGY: From Ontological Art Towards Ontological Engineering. In *AAAI97 Spring Symposium Series on
   Ontological Engineering*, 33-40, Stanford, California, 1997.
3. In Gómez-Pérez, A. (editor): Notes for SIG on Enterprise Standard Ontology Environment. Second Ontoweb Meeting, Amsterdam, December 2001.
4. Guarino, N. and Welty, C.: Evaluating Ontological Decisions with OntoClean. In
   Communications of the ACM, 45(**2**): 61-65.
5. Rastier, F., Cavazza, M. and Abeillé, A.: *Sémantique pour l'analyse*. Masson, Paris,
   1994.
6. Staab, S. and Maedche, A.: Ontology Engineering beyond the Modeling of Concepts
   and Relations. In *14th European Conference on Artificial Intelligence (ECAI'00),
   Workshop on Applications of Ontologies and Problem-Solving Methods*, Berlin, Germany, 2000.
7. Uschold, M. and Grüninger, M.: Ontologies: Principles, Methods and Applications.
   Knowledge Engineering Review, (**2**), 93-155, 1996.

User-System Cooperation in Document Annotation Based on Information Extraction

Fabio Ciravegna[1], Alexiei Dingli[1], Daniela Petrelli[2], and Yorick Wilks[1]

[1] Department of Computer Science, University of Sheffield,
Regent Court, 211 Portobello Street, S1 4DP, Sheffield, UK,
{fabio|alexiei|yorick}@dcs.shef.ac.uk
[2] Department of Information Studies, University of Sheffield,
Regent Court, 211 Portobello Street, S1 4DP, Sheffield, UK,
D.Petrelli@shef.ac.uk

Abstract. The process of document annotation for the Semantic Web is complex and time consuming, as it requires a great deal of manual annotation. Information extraction from texts (IE) is a technology used by some very recent systems for reducing the burden of annotation. The integration of IE systems in annotation tools is quite a new development and there is still the necessity of thinking the impact of the IE system on the whole annotation process. In this paper we initially discuss a number of requirements for the use of IE as support for annotation. Then we present and discuss a model of interaction that addresses such issues and Melita, an annotation framework that implements a methodology for active annotation for the Semantic Web based on IE. Finally we present an experiment that quantifies the gain in using IE as support to human annotators.

1. Introduction

The effort behind the Semantic Web (SW) is to add information to web documents in order to access knowledge instead of unstructured material, allowing knowledge to be managed in an automatic way. Much effort has been spent in developing methodologies for enriching documents, mainly requiring manual insertion of annotation. It is reasonable to expect users to manually annotate new documents up to a certain degree, but annotation is a slow time-consuming process that involves high costs. Therefore it is vital for the Semantic Web to produce automatic or semi-automatic methods for document enrichment, either to help in annotating new documents or to extract additional information from existing unannotated or partially annotated documents. Information Extraction from texts (IE) can provide the backbone for such tools. IE is an automatic method for locating important facts in electronic documents. In the SW context, IE can be used for document annotation either in an automatic way (via unsupervised extraction of information) or semi-automatic way (e.g. as support for human annotators in locating relevant facts in documents via information highlighting).
IE is an area of Natural Language Processing with a long history. Its development has been mainly driven by the MUC conferences, a number of competitive exercises

A. Gómez-Pérez and V.R. Benjamins (Eds.): EKAW 2002, LNAI 2473, pp. 122-137, 2002.

supported by Darpa. One of the main issues in IE is the way in which applications are defined. The main constraint in the MUC conferences is that applications are to be developed in a short time (e.g. one month). The MUCs represent a scenario in which the cost of new application is not considered important: by bounding the development time they did not put an upper bound neither to the amount of personnel needed for the application nor to the skills used [1]. As a result, most of the systems were portable by IE expert only.

The Semantic Web represents a completely different scenario where the cost is the issue. The rapid and uncontrolled growth of the Web in the last years is mainly due to the simplicity and effectiveness of HTML. Everyone can make available his/her own pages at nearly no cost (the cost of a PC and a telephone line) with very limited skills (i.e. mainly the ability of using a web editor). If we want the Semantic Web to become the widespread evolution of the current Web we have to provide methodologies with the same type of requirement: portability with limited skills and no (or very limited) cost. The requirement is to be extended to all the tools necessary for building the SW. If IE is to be used for annotation, it must be usable at no cost (exactly as web browsers are free) with limited skills. The kind of IE technologies that require experts in IE can be afforded only by big companies and or big service providers (e.g. search engines companies) and can be used for generic indexing. EaroDAML, [2] is an example of a tool that requires an expert to adapt the system to new applications and that is used for very generic IE for the Web (e.g. named entity recognition). The situation is different in scenarios with distributed agents that provide local services. For example a university department wanting to provide a SW service for their Web pages. In this case they will need to define a specific indexing service themselves. The available budget here is very low and the available skills are quite limited (e.g. a student want-to-be web designer and a system manager). No experts in IE can be envisaged here, nor does the budget allow hiring an expensive external company. In an IE perspective for the SW there is the clear need to allow users with no knowledge of IE to build applications (e.g. specialized annotation services for the set of pages).

Adaptive IE systems (IES) use Machine Learning to learn how to adapt to new applications/domains using only annotated corpora [3] 4][5]. They can be adapted to provide annotations for the SW: they monitor the annotations inserted by the user and learn how to reproduce them. When equivalent cases are encountered, annotations are automatically inserted by the IES and users have just to check them. Some new annotation tools for the Semantic Web are starting including adaptive IE as support to annotation. At the Open University, the MnM annotation tool [6] interfaces with both the UMass IE tools[1] and Sheffield's Amilcare[2]. At the University of Karlsruhe the Ontomat annotizer [7] interfaces with Sheffield's Amilcare. The current methodology of interaction between annotation tool and IES is still quite simplistic, influencing also the way in which users and annotation system interacts. Generally a batch interaction mode is adopted, i.e., the user annotates a batch of texts and the IE tool is trained on the whole batch. Then annotation is started on another batch of texts and the IE system proposes annotations to users when cases similar to those found in the training batches are recognized. Although the use of adaptive IE constitutes quite an

---

[1] www-nlp.cs.umass.edu/software/badger.html
[2] www.dcs.shef.ac.uk/~fabio/Amilcare.html

improvement with respect to the completely manual annotation approach, in our opinion the tremendous potentialities of adaptive IE technologies are not fully exploited. We believe that it is time to consider the way in which the interaction can be organized in order to both maximize effectiveness in the annotation process and minimize the burden of annotating/correcting on the user's side. We expect that such change will also influence the user-annotation tool interaction style by moving from a simplistic user-system interaction to real user-system collaboration[3]. We propose two user-centered criteria as measure of appropriateness of this collaboration: *timeliness* and *intrusiveness* of the IE process. The first shows the ability to react to user annotation: how timely is the system to learn from user annotations. The latter represents the level to which the system bothers the user, because for example it requires CPU time (and therefore stops the user annotation activity) or because it suggests wrong annotations.

Timeliness: when the IE system (IES) is trained on blocks of texts, there is a time gap between the moment in which annotations are inserted by the user and the moment in which they are used by the system for learning. User and system work in strict sequence, one after the other. This sequential scheduling hampers true collaboration. If a batch of texts contains many similar documents, users may spend considerable amount of time in annotating similar documents without receiving feedback from the IES for the simple reason that no learning is scheduled for the moment. The IES is not supportive to the user neither the user effort is very useful, since similar cases are of very little use for the learner because they cannot offer the variety of phenomena that empower learning. The bigger the size of the batch of texts the worse, the problem of lack of timeliness is. A true collaboration implies a (re)training of the system after every annotated text is released by the user. Training can take a considerable amount of CPU time, therefore stop the annotation session for a while. A positive collaboration requires not to constraint the user time to the IES training time (otherwise intrusiveness increases). We believe that an intelligent scheduling is needed to keep timeliness in learning without increasing intrusiveness.

Intrusiveness: the IE system can bother users in a number of ways, for example by proposing annotations generated by unreliable rules (e.g. induced using an insufficient number of cases). A positive collaboration requires to enable users to tune the proactivity of the IE system in order to avoid intrusiveness.

In this paper we present an IE-based annotation methodology for the Semantic Web that takes into account the problems of timeliness and intrusiveness mentioned above. Moreover we quantitatively evaluate the support provided by IE in a simulation of experiment of text annotation.

2. Towards a New Interaction Model

We propose an interaction model that aims at producing a non-intrusive and timely support for users during the annotation process. In this section we describe the way in

---

[3] Collaboration means working together for a common goal, all partners contributing with their own capabilities and skills.

which user and system interact and discuss how such requirements are met by our model.

2.1. User-System Interaction

We split the annotation process into two main phases from the IES point of view: (1) *training* and (2) *active annotation with revision*. In user terms the first corresponds to unassisted annotation, while the latter mainly requires correction of annotations proposed by the IES.

During **training** users annotate texts without any contribution from the IES. Here the IES uses the user annotations to train its learner. During this phase the IES is constantly inducing rules. We can define two sub-phases: (a) *bootstrapping* and (b) *training with verification*. During bootstrapping the only IES task is to learn from the user annotations. This sub-phase can be of different length, depending on the minimum number of examples needed for a minimum of training. During the second sub-phases, the user continues with the unassisted annotation, but the IES behaviour changes, as it uses its induced rules to silently compete with the user in annotating the document. The IES automatically compares its annotations with those inserted by the user and calculates its accuracy. Missing annotations or mistakes are used to retrain the learners. The training phase ends when the IES accuracy reaches the user preferred level of pro-activity. It is therefore possible to move to the next phase: active annotation.

The **active annotation with revision** phase is heavily based on the IES suggestions and the user's main task is correcting and integrating the suggested annotations (i.e. removing and adding annotations). Human actions are inputted back to the IES for retraining. This is the phase where the real system-user cooperation takes place: the system helps the user in annotating; the user feeds back the mistakes

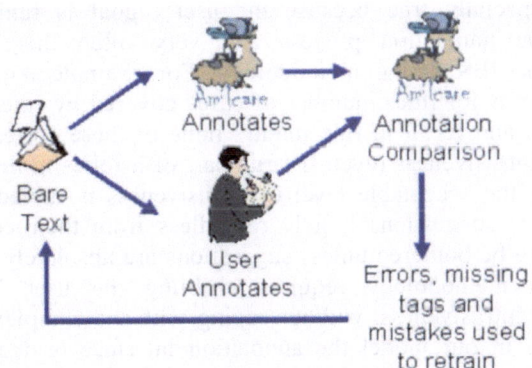

Figure 1. The training with verification sub-phase. In this figure Amilcare is used as example of adaptive IES.

to help the system perform better. In user terms this is where the added value of the IES becomes apparent, because it heavily reduces the amount of annotation to insert manually. This supervision task is much more convenient from both cognition and actions. Correcting annotations is simpler than annotating bare texts, it is less time consuming and it is also likely to be less error prone.

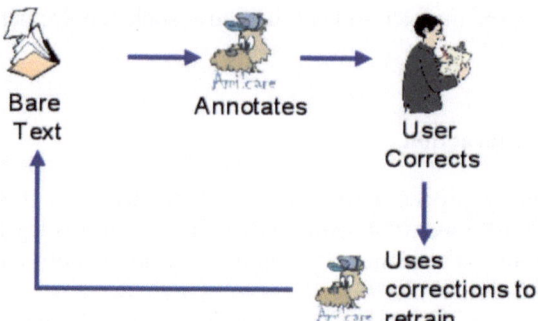

Bare   Annotates
Text

User
Corrects

Uses
corrections to
retrain

Figure 2. The active annotation with revision phase

2.2. Coping with Intrusiveness

The design of the interaction model aims to limit intrusiveness of the IES in a number of ways. First of all the IES does not require any specific annotation interface or any specific adaptation by the user. It integrates in the usual user environment and provides suggestions in a way that is both familiar and intuitive for the user. To some extent users could even ignore that the IES is working for them.

Secondly intrusiveness as a side effect of proactivity is coped with, especially during *active annotation with revision*, when the IES can bother users with unreliable annotations. The requirement here is to enable users to tune the IES behaviour so that the level of suggestions is appropriate. Some IES provide internal tuning methods for balancing features such as precision and recall or the minimum number of cases to be covered in order to accepted a rule for annotation. Such tuning methodologies are designed for IE experts since they require a deep knowledge of the underlying IE system. This is especially true because the user's goal is tuning the level of intrusiveness in the annotation process and very often there is no obvious correspondent in the IES tuning methodology. For example Amilcare allows to modify error thresholds for rules, number of cases covered by rules for acceptance, balance of precision and recall in rule tuning: none of these correspond directly to tuning the level of intrusiveness (even if large part of it relies in the precision/recall balance). Moreover, the acceptable level of intrusiveness is subjective: some users might like to receive suggestions largely regardless from their correctness, while others do not want to be bothered unless suggestions are absolutely reliable. A user-friendly interaction methodology requires enabling the user in selecting the appropriate level of intrusiveness, without coping with the complexity of tuning an adaptive IE system. In our model the annotation interface bridges the qualitative vision of users (e.g. a request to be more/less active or accurate) with the specific IES settings (e.g. change error thresholds), as also suggested in [8]. This is important because the annotation interface is a tool designed for specific user classes and therefore able to elicit tuning requirements by using the correct terminology for the specific context.

Finally the IES training requires CPU time and this can slow down or even stop the user activity. For this reason most of the current systems use a batch mode of training so to limit training to specific moments (e.g. coffee time). As explained above, the batch approach presents timeliness problems. We propose background learning to provide timely support without intrusiveness. If we observe how time is spent in the annotation process (select a document, manually annotate the document, save the annotation), we notice that most of the user time is spent in the manual annotation process. This is the right moment to train the IES in the background without the user noticing it. In principle it is possible to treat every annotation event in the interface as a request to train on a specific example, but this requires the ability to retreat annotations in case of user errors, making the interaction with the IES quite complex. In our approach the IES works in the background with two parallel and asynchronous processes. While the user annotates document $n+1$ the system learns the annotations inserted in document n (i.e. the last annotated). At the same time (i.e. as a separate process) the IES applies the rules induced in the previous learning sessions (i.e. from document 1 to document $n-1$) in order to extract information from document n (either for suggesting annotations during active annotation or in order to silently test its accuracy during unassisted learning). The advantage is that there is no idle time for the user, as the annotation of a document generally requires a great deal more time than training on a single text.

2.3. Coping with Timeliness

Timeliness means just in time learning from previous user annotations. Timeliness is not fully obtained with the above interaction methodology: the IES annotation capability always refers to rules learned by using the entire annotated corpus but the last document. This means that the IES is not able to help when two similar documents are annotated in sequence. From the user point of view such a situation is equivalent to train on batches of two texts. In this respect the collaboration between the system and the user fails in being effective. We believe that timeliness is a matter of perception from the user side, not an absolute feature; therefore the only important matter is that users perceive it. Considering that in many applications the order in which documents are annotated is unimportant, in such cases it is possible to organize the annotation order so to avoid the possibility of presenting similar documents in sequence and therefore to hide the small lack of timeliness. In order to implement such feature we need a measure of similarity of texts from the annotation point of view. The IES can be used to work out such a measure. At the end of each learning session all the induced rules are applied to the unannotated part of the corpus so to identify two main subsets: texts were the available rules fire (i.e. annotations can be added: positive subset) and texts were they do not fire at all (uncovered texts: negative subset). Each text in the positive subset can be associated with a score given by the number of annotations that can be added. The score can be used as an approximation of similarity among texts: inserted annotations mean similarity with respect to the part of the corpus annotated so far, no inserted annotation means actual difference. Such information can be used to make the timeliness more effective: a completely uncovered document is always followed by a fairly covered document. In this way a difference between successive documents is very likely and therefore the probability that similar documents are presented in turn within the batch of two (i.e. the blindness window of the system) is very low. Incidentally this strategy also tackles another major problem in annotation, i.e. user boredom, which can make the user productivity and effectiveness fall proportional to time. Presenting users with radically different documents avoids the boredom that comes from coping with very similar documents in sequence.

In the next section a first implementation of the presented interaction model is presented. We introduce both the IES used (Amilcare) and the annotation interface (Melita). Finally we discuss how the current implementation meets the requirements described.

3. Adaptive IE in Amilcare

The model above requires an adaptive IES to strictly cooperate with the user. In our implementation we have used Amilcare[4]. Amilcare is a tool for adaptive Information Extraction from text (IE) designed for supporting active annotation of documents for the Semantic Web. In its standard version it performs IE by enriching texts with XML annotations, i.e. the system marks the extracted information with XML annotations. In the Semantic Web version in which it is supposed to be interacting with an annotation tool, it actually leaves the text unchanged and it returns the extracted information as a triple <annotation, startPosition, endPosition> so to let the annotation tool decide how to actually annotate the text. The only knowledge required for porting Amilcare to new applications or domains is the ability of manually annotating the information to be extracted in a training corpus. No knowledge of IE is necessary.

Adaptation starts with the definition of a tag-set for annotation possibly organized as an ontology where tags are associated to concepts and relations. Then users have to manually annotate a corpus for training the learner. An annotation interface is to be connected to Amilcare for annotating texts, e.g. using XML-based mark ups. As mentioned Amilcare has been integrated with a number of annotation tools so far, including MnM[6], Ontomat[7]. For example MnM automatically converts the user annotations into XML tags to train the learner. Amilcare's learner induces rules that are able to reproduce such annotation. Amilcare can work in two modes: training, used to adapt to a new application, and extraction, used to actually annotate texts. In both modes, Amilcare first of all preprocesses texts using Annie, the shallow IE system included in the Gate package ([9], www.gate.ac.uk). Annie performs text tokenization (segmenting texts into words), sentence splitting (identifying sentences) part of speech tagging (lexical disambiguation), gazetteer lookup (dictionary lookup) ad Named Entity Recognition (e.g. proper names spotting and classification).

When operating in training mode, Amilcare induces rules for information extraction. The learner is based on $(LP)^2$, a covering algorithm for supervised learning of IE rules based on Lazy-NLP [10] [11]. This is a wrapper induction methodology [12] that, unlike other wrapper induction approaches, uses linguistic information for rule generalization. The learner starts inducing wrapper-like rules that make no use of linguistic information, where rules are sets of conjunctive conditions on adjacent words. Then the linguistic information provided by Annie is as the basis for rule

---

[4] www.dcs.shef.ac.uk/~fabio/Amilcare.html

generalization: conditions on words are substituted with conditions on the linguistic information (e.g. condition matching either the lexical category, or the class provided by the gazetteer, etc. [11]). All the generalizations are tested in parallel and the best k generalizations are kept for IE. The idea is that the linguistic-based generalization is used only when the use of NLP information is reliable or effective. The measure of reliability here is not linguistic correctness (immeasurable by incompetent users), but effectiveness in extracting information using linguistic information as opposed to using shallower approaches. Lazy NLP-based learners learn which is the best strategy for each information/context separately. For example they may decide that using the result of a part of speech tagger is the best strategy for recognizing the speaker in seminar announcements, but not to spot the seminar location. This strategy is quite effective for analysing documents with mixed genres, quite a common situation in web documents [13].

The learner induces two types of rules: tagging rules and correction rules. A tagging rule is composed of a left hand side, containing a pattern of conditions on a connected sequence of words, and a right hand side that is an action inserting an XML tag in the texts[5]. Correction rules correct imprecision, i.e. shift misplaced tags to the correct position. They are learnt from the mistakes made in attempting to re-annotate the training corpus using the induced tagging rules. The output of the training phase is a collection of rules for IE that is associated to the specific scenario. When working in extraction mode, Amilcare receives as input a (collection of) text(s) with the associated scenario (including the rules induced during the training phase). It preprocesses the text(s) by using Annie and then it applies its rules and returns the original text with the added annotations (or just the annotation triples in the SW version).

With Amilcare it is possible to define automatic or semiautomatic services for the SW with limited skills (the ability of annotating the texts) and limited cost (the number of texts to be annotated for training –as we will see- is quite limited). For example the university department mentioned in the introduction could use the student creating the pages to annotate the pages. Amilcare would learn in the background without requiring any specific adaptation except the definition of the annotation set (necessary in any case for defining SW services). This is the reason why some annotation tools include Amilcare as support to annotation.

4. The Melita Framework

Melita is an ontology-based demonstrator for text annotation. The goal of Melita is not to produce a further annotation interface, but a demonstrator of how it is possible to actively interact with the IES in order to meet the requirements of timeliness and tuneable pro-activity mentioned above. Melita's main control panel is depicted in figure 3. It is composed of two main areas:

---

[5] In the SW version no tag is actually inserted in the text; as mentioned a triple <*annotation, startIndex, endPosition*> is returned to the external annotation interface.

130   Fabio Ciravegna et al.

1. The ontology (left) representing the annotations that can be inserted; annotations are associated to concepts and relations. A specific color is associated to each node in the ontology (e.g. "speaker is depicted in blue).
2. The document to be annotated (center-right). Selecting the portion of text with the mouse and then clicking on the node in the ontology insert annotations. Inserted annotations are shown by turning the background of the annotated text portion to the color associated to the node in the hierarchy (e.g. the background of the portion of text representing a speaker becomes blue).

Melita does not differ in appearance from other annotation interfaces such as the Gate annotation tool, or MnM or Ontomat. This is because – as mentioned – it is a demonstrator to show how a typical annotation interface could interact with the IES. The novelty of Melita is the possibility of (1) tuning the IES so to provide the desired level of proactivity and (2) scheduling texts so to provide timeliness in annotation learning. The typical annotation cycle in Melita follows the two-phase cycle based on training and active annotation described in the previous section. Users may not be aware of the difference between the two phases. They just will notice that at some point the annotation system will start suggesting annotations and that they have a way to influence when and with which modalities this will happen.

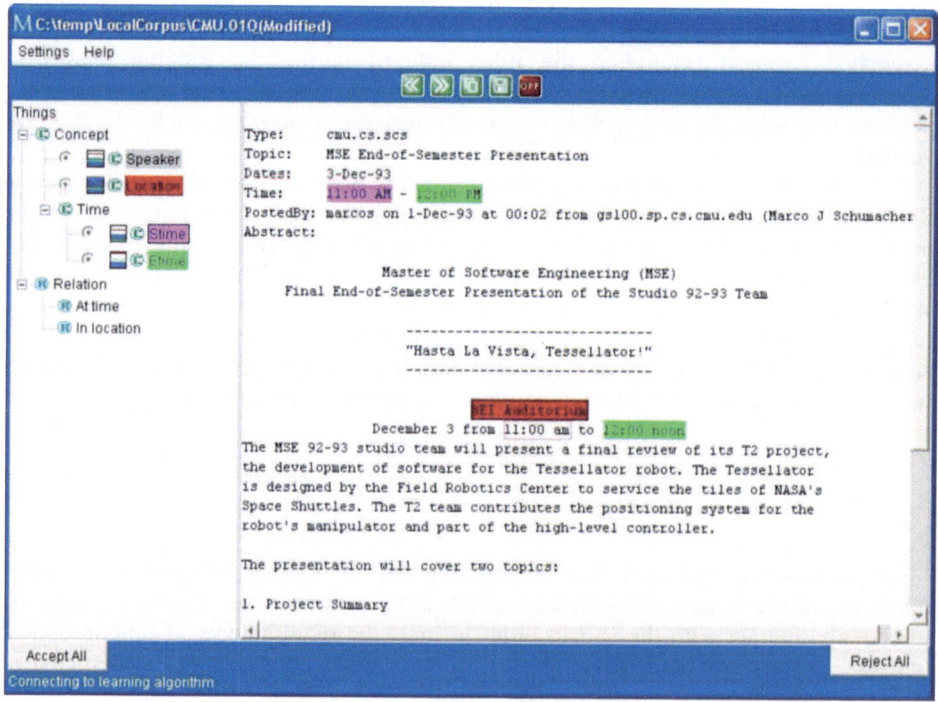

Figure 3: The Melita annotation Interface

4.1. Suggesting Annotations

There are two ways in which Melita can suggest annotations to users, according to the reliability of such suggestions. For suggestions Amilcare is quite sure about, Melita will present them in the document panel in a way similar to the annotations inserted by the user. The background of the text where the information has been found turns into the specific annotation colour (e.g. grey for speaker in figure 3). The difference with respect to the actual user annotations is that a darker border surrounds them in order to be easily spotted for user checking. For example in figure 3 the location "SEI Auditorium" highlighted in red is a reliable Amilcare's suggestion, while "12 PM" is a user defined annotation. In case of suggestions Amilcare is less sure about, they are presented in a different way. The background is left unchanged (white), but a coloured border (the same colour of the potential annotation, e.g. grey for speaker) surrounds the text. For example "11 am" (at the text centre in figure 3) is a suggestion of this type. They are easy to spot by the user, but they are marked as unreliable. A difference in the suggestion's semantics corresponds to the difference in presentation: reliable annotations are supposed to be correct; a user action is required to remove them if they are wrong. Less reliable annotations are supposed to be just suggestions to the user; an action is required to confirm them; otherwise they will not be saved with the text in the end. We believe that both annotation types are useful as they allow to clearly communicating the user what suggestions are to be trusted and which are just a reasonable guess. Reasonable guesses are presented for two reasons: first of all they represent a situation in which the learner requires user feedback: removing such information means a clear message to the learner that the guess is wrong and therefore rules are to be changed. From the user point of view guesses are very often useful because they are often imprecise but nonetheless they tend to correctly identify the area in which such information is present even if the information is not correctly identified (e.g. in "at <time> 3:00</time> pm" the annotation is imprecise – pm should be part of the time – but it is useful to focus the user attention on the place where the correct annotation should go). Note that reliability can vary for different pieces of information. For example a system can become quite reliable in a short time in recognizing some information (e.g. seminar start time) requiring more training examples for others (e.g. speaker). In this case there will be a moment in which the suggested annotations for the time will be reliably inserted (i.e. with coloured background) while the annotations for the speaker will be less reliable (presented with coloured border only).

4.2. Balancing Proactivity

Users must be empowered to customize the strategy above, participating in the definition of what is reliable information and what is not. Also some very unreliable suggestions can be not presented, and – again – we want to empower the user to say which of them are not to be presented. This means that users must be empowered to control proactivity (and therefore intrusivity). In Melita, users can customize the behaviour of the IES, i.e. tuning the IES's level of proactivity, by using a special slidebar (fig.4). It allows to set two thresholds that divide the accuracy space in three areas: the first level decides which is the minimum accuracy the IES must be able to reach in order to start considering annotations as reliable. The second threshold defines the minimum accuracy the system must reach before starting presenting less reliable suggestions. In the example in figure 4 the system will consider reliable (and therefore suggest with coloured background) when the annotation accuracy is greater than 75%. Annotations that do not reach 75% reliability are still suggested (using the coloured border only) if they reach at least 43% of reliability. When accuracy is less than 43% the IES does not suggest at all. There is a general default that can be customised and holds for all the nodes in the ontology and that can be overridden for specific nodes by using the same kind of window. Changing the default for specific annotations (e.g. "speaker") is useful because users can have different feelings about intrusiveness for different kinds of information. Note that users do not need to know in detail what 45% means. They can easily reason from a qualitative point given the current IES behaviour. If the user feels that the IES is not proactive enough, s/he can decide to lower (one of the) two thresholds. If the system is intrusive the user can

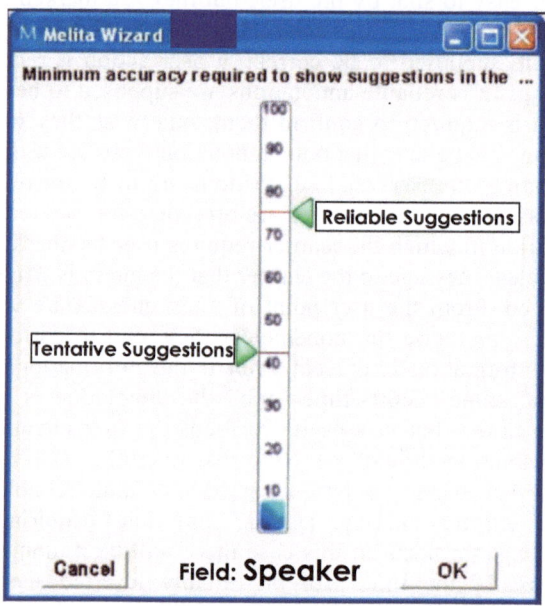

Figure 4. the slidebar to customize intrusiveness

decide to raise them. For turning off all the system suggestions it is just necessary to raise both the thresholds above100%. Moreover the more you move in either direction, the more the effect on the IES will be relevant. It is important that the thresholds are independent because users can have different feeling on intrusiveness for the different suggestion modes. The same slidebar shows also the average accuracy currently reached by the IES in annotating a specific information type: a blue filler mark grows from the bottom (around 10% in figure 4). It represents the distribution of accuracy of the potential suggestions for the specific annotation. Such information can be used in tuning proactivity: less intrusivity=raise a threshold above the average, more proactivity, move a threshold below the average.

5. An Experiment on IE's Effectiveness

We performed a number of experiments for demonstrating how fast the IES converges to an active annotation status and to quantify its contribution to the annotation task, i.e. its ability to suggest correctly. We selected a subset of the Computer Science Jobs announcement corpus, manually annotated by M. E. Califf [14]. This is a corpus used for evaluating adaptive IE algorithms on semi-structured texts [15]. The subtask we selected was to recognise in a set of 250 news posts about job offers for computer scientists: the city, country and state in which the job is offered, the company offering the job, the actual recruiter, the required knowledge about both computer languages and platforms, and the offered salary. We believe that this task can be considered a representative task for the Semantic Web.

In our experiment the annotation in the corpus was used to simulate human annotation. We have evaluated the potential contribution of the IE system at regular intervals during corpus tagging, i.e. after the annotation of 5, 10, 20, 25, 30, 50, 62, 75, 100 and 150 documents (each subset fully including the previous one). Each time we tested the accuracy of the IES on the following 100 texts in the corpus (so when training on 25 texts, the test was performed also on the following 25 texts to be used for training on 50). The ability to suggest on the test corpus was measured in terms of precision and recall. *Recall* represents here an approximation of the probability that the user receives a suggestion in tagging a new document. *Precision* represents the probability that such suggestion is correct. Results are shown in the figure at the end of the paper. On the X-axis the number of documents provided for training is shown. On the Y-axis precision, recall and f-measure[6] are presented.

The maximum support comes in annotating city, country, state and posting date. This is not surprising as they present quite regular fillers. Other experiments on other corpora have shown that an equivalent gain can be obtained also for annotations requiring time expressions as fillers. After training on only 10 texts, the system is potentially able to propose 253 instances of cities (out of 303 present in the corpus), 228 are correct, 22 are wrong, 3 partially correct[7], 72 missing, leading to Precision=90 Recall=75 (see figure 5 and table 1). This is possible because of Amilcare's ability to generalize over both the text context and the gazetteer information provided by Annie, where a list of locations is present. Please note that the recognition of cities, state and country is not a simple Named Entity Recognition task. The system must not only recognise the name of a place, but also recognise that such place is the location of work. There are other locations in the texts that are irrelevant (e.g. in the address of the recruiter) and only the job location must be recognised. This implies the ability to recognise the context in which the location name appears. The same applies to the posting date: there are many other dates in the texts and only the correct one must be identified. The situation is more complex for other fields such as recruiter or company, where 80% F-measure is reached after 100 texts. These annotations are much more difficult to learn than expressions whose filler are either very regular (e.g. time or date expressions) or can be listed in a gazetteer (we did not have a suitable list

---

[6] A balanced average of precision and recall.
[7] Where the proposed and correct annotations partially overlap. They count as half correct in calculating precision and recall.

of companies), because their regularity is much less direct. We performed the same type of analysis on other corpora for adaptive IE, the CMU seminar announcements corpus, where 483 emails are manually annotated with speaker, starting time, ending time and location of seminars (www.isi.edu/~muslea/RISE/) and found analogous results.

Table 1. Amount of training texts needed for reaching at least 75% precision and 50% recall

Tag	Amount of Texts needed for training	Prec	Rec	F-measure
City	10	90	75	82
country	10	81	92	86
state	5	79	87	83
company	100	91	72	86
recruiter	30	81	50	62
language	50	80	59	68
platform	50	77	52	62
salary	5	75	54	62
post_date	5	97	100	98

The above experiments show that the contribution of the IES can be quite high. Reliable annotation can be obtained with limited training, especially when adopting high precision IES configurations. In the case of the job announcement task, our experiments show that it is possible to move from bootstrapping to active annotation after annotating a very limited amount of texts. In table 1 we show the amount of training needed for moving to active annotation for each type of information, given a minimum user requirement of 75% precision. This shows that the IES contribution heavily reduces the burden of manual annotation and that such reduction is particularly relevant and immediate in case of quite regular information (e.g., known location names). In user terms this means that it is possible to focus the activity on annotating more complex pieces of information (e.g. company and recruiter), avoiding to be bothered with easy and repetitive ones (such as locations). With some more training cases the IES is also able to contribute in annotating the complex cases. onclusions and future work

IES can strongly support users in the annotation task, alleviating users from a big deal of the annotation burden. Our experiments show that such help is particular strong and immediate for repetitive or regular cases, allowing focusing the expensive and time-consuming user activity on more complex cases.In our experiment we have quantified such support for an experiment about job announcements. Despite these positive results, we claim that the simple quantitative support is not enough. An interaction methodology between annotation interface, user and IES is necessary in order to reduce intrusivity and maintain timeliness of support. The methodology proposed in this paper addresses such concern, as:

1. It inserts in the usual user environment without imposing particular requirements on the annotation interface used to train the IES (reduced intrusiveness).

2. It maximizes the cooperation between user and IES: users insert annotations in texts as part of their normal work and at the same time they train the IES. The IES in turn simplifies the user work by inserting annotations similar to those inserted by the user in other documents; this collaboration is made timely and effective by the fact that the IES is retrained after each document annotation.

3. The modality in which the IES system suggests new annotations is fully tuneable and therefore easily adaptable to the specific user needs/preferences (intrusiveness is taken under control).

4. It allows to timely train the IES without disrupting the user pace with learning sessions consuming a large amount of CPU time (and therefore either stopping or slowing down the annotation process).

There are two open issues that arise from our experience. On the one hand the effect on the user of excellent IES performances after a small amount of annotation is still to be considered. For example when P=90, R=75 is reached after only 10 texts (as for company in the jobs announcement task), users could be tempted to rely on the IES suggestions only, avoiding any further action apart from correction. This would be bad not only for the quality of document annotation, but also for the IES effectiveness. As a matter of fact, each new annotated document is used for further training. Rules are developed using existing annotations. They are tested on the whole corpus to check against false positives (e.g. the rest of the corpus is considered a set of negative examples). A corpus with a relevant number of missing annotations provides a relevant number of (false) negative examples that disorients the leaner, degrading its effectiveness and therefore producing worse future annotation. The entire dimension of the problem is still to be analysed. We are currently considering applying strategies such as randomly removing annotations in order to test the user attention. On the other hand the time saved by using an IES is still to be quantified. The experiments above seem to suggest a strong reduction of annotation time, but we intend to actually measure the improvement in experiments with real users.

Acknowledgements

This work was carried out within the AKT project (http://www.aktors.org), sponsored by the UK Engineering and Physical Sciences Research Council (grant GR/N15764/01). AKT involves the Universities of Aberdeen, Edinburgh, Sheffield, Southampton and the Open University. Its objectives are to develop technologies to cope with the six main challenges of knowledge management: acquisition, modelling, retrieval/extraction, reuse, publication and maintenance. Thanks to Enrico Motta, Mattia Lanzoni, John Domingue, Steffen Staab and Siegfried Handschuh for a number of useful discussions. Thanks to the Gate group for providing Annie (www.gate.ac.uk) and for help in integrating it into Amilcare.

Bibliography

1. F. Ciravegna, A. Lavelli, G. Satta: 'Bringing information extraction out of the labs: the Pinocchio Environment', in *ECAI2000, Proc. of the 14th European Conference on Artificial Intelligence*, ed., W. Horn, Amsterdam, 2000. IOS Press

2. P. Kogut and W. Holmes: "Applying Information Extraction to Generate DAML Annotations from Web Pages", K-CAP 2001 Workshop Knowledge Markup & Semantic Annotation, Victoria B.C., Canada (2001).

3. M. E. Califf, D. Freitag, N. Kushmerick and I. Muslea (eds.): AAAI-99 Workshop on Machine Learning for Information Extraction, Orlando Florida (1999), http://www.isi.edu/~muslea/RISE/ML4IE/

4. R. Basili, F. Ciravegna, R. Gaizauskas (eds.) ECAI2000 Workshop on Machine Learning for IE, Berlin (2000), www.dcs.shef.ac.uk/~fabio/ecai-workshop.html

5. F. Ciravegna, N. Kushmerick, R. Mooney and I. Muslea (eds.), IJCAI-2001 Workshop on Adaptive Text Extraction and Mining held in conjunction with the 17th International Conference on Artificial Intelligence, Seattle, (2001), http://www.smi.ucd.ie/ATEM2001/

6. M. Vargas-Vera, Enrico Motta, J. Domingue, M. Lanzoni, A. Stutt and F. Ciravegna: "MnM: Ontology driven semi-automatic or automatic support for semantic markup", Proc. of the 13th International Conference on Knowledge Engineering and Knowledge Management, EKAW02, Sigüenza, Spain (2002).

7. S. Handschuh, S. Staab and F. Ciravegna: "S-CREAM - Semi-automatic CREAtion of Metadata", Proc. of the 13th International Conference on Knowledge Engineering and Knowledge Management, EKAW02, Sigüenza, Spain, (2002).

8. F. Ciravegna and D. Petrelli: "User Involvement in Adaptive Information Extraction: Position Paper" in Proceedings of the IJCAI-2001 Workshop on Adaptive Text Extraction and Mining held in conjunction with the 17th International Conference on Artificial Intelligence, Seattle (2001).

9. D. Maynard, V. Tablan, H. Cunningham, C. Ursu, H. Saggion, K. Bontcheva and Y. Wilks: "Architectural Elements of Language Engineering Robustness", Journal of Natural Language Engineering, Special Issue on Robust Methods in Analysis of Natural Language Data, forthcoming in 2002.

10. F. Ciravegna: "Adaptive Information Extraction from Text by Rule Induction and Generalisation" in Proceedings of 17th International Joint Conference on Artificial Intelligence (2001).

11. F. Ciravegna: "(LP)^2, an Adaptive Algorithm for Information Extraction from Web-related Texts" in Proceedings of the IJCAI-2001 Workshop on Adaptive Text Extraction and Mining held in conjunction with the 17th International Conference on Artificial Intelligence (IJCAI-01), Seattle, August, 2001

12. N. Kushmerick, D. Weld and R. Doorenbos: `Wrapper induction for information extraction', Proc. of 15th International Conference on Artificial Intelligence, Japan (1997).

13. F. Ciravegna: "Challenges in Information Extraction from Text for Knowledge Management", IEEE Intelligent Systems and Their Applications, 16-6, November, (2001).

14. M. E. Califf: 'Relational Learning Techniques for Natural Language' IE, *Ph.D. thesis*, Univ. Texas, Austin, (1998), www.cs.utexas.edu/users/mecaliff

15. D. Freitag and N. Kushmerick, `Boosted wrapper induction', in R. Basili, F. Ciravegna, R. Gaizauskas (eds.) *ECAI2000 Workshop on Machine Learning for Information Extraction*, Berlin, 2000, www.dcs.shef.ac.uk/~fabio/ecai-workshop.html.

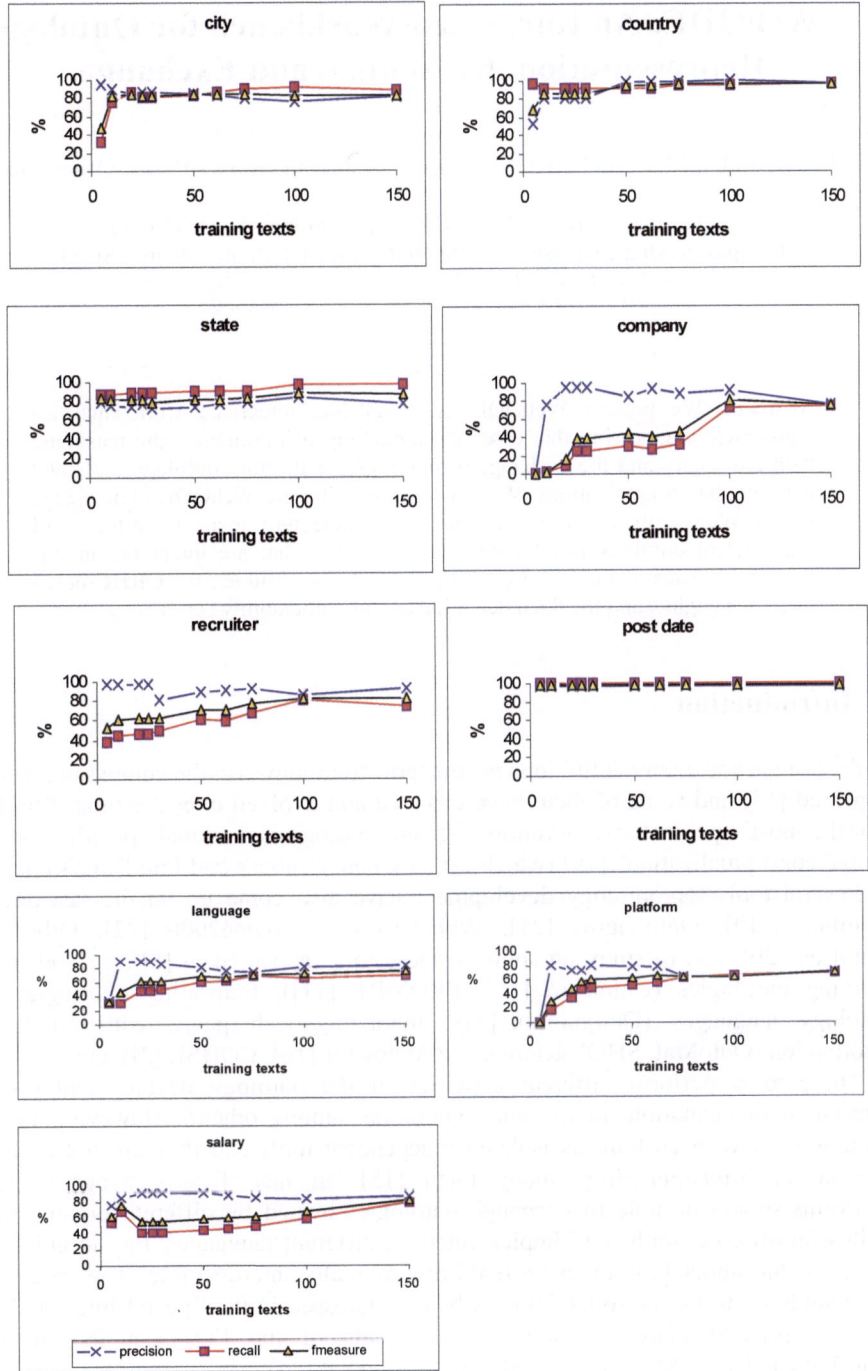

Figure 5. The learning curve for the different information in the job task

WebODE: An Integrated Workbench for Ontology Representation, Reasoning, and Exchange

Óscar Corcho, Mariano Fernández-López, Asunción Gómez-Pérez, Óscar Vicente

Facultad de Informática . Universidad Politécnica de Madrid
Campus de Montegancedo, s/n. 28660 Boadilla del Monte. Madrid. Spain
{ocorcho, mfernandez, asun}@fi.upm.es;
ovicente@delicias.dia.fi.upm.es

Abstract. We present WebODE as a scalable, integrated workbench for ontological engineering that eases the modelling of ontologies, the reasoning with ontologies and the exchange of ontologies with other ontology tools and ontology-based applications. We will first describe the WebODE's knowledge model. We will then describe its extensible architecture, focusing on the set of independent ontology development functionalities that are integrated in this framework, such as the Ontology Editor, the Axiom Builder, the OKBC-based inference engine, and the documentation and interoperability services.

1 Introduction

In the last decade, many definitions for the term "ontology" (in the context of AI) have appeared [15] and some of them have changed and evolved over the time. We think that the most representative definition is: "an ontology is a formal specification of a shared conceptualization" [19] (which extends Tom Gruber's and Pim Borst's ones).

Several tools for ontology development have also come up on the last decade: Ontolingua [9], OntoSaurus [21], WebOnto [7], Protégé2000 [22], OilEd [3], OntoEdit [20], etc. (a study on some of these tools appeared in [8]); and others for merging ontologies (Chimaera [18], PROMPT [11]), translating ontologies into ontology languages (Ontomorph [4]), annotating web pages with ontological information (OntoMat, SHOE Knowledge Annotator [16], COHSE [2]), etc.

These tools perform different activities of the ontology development process (design, implementation, merge and annotation, among others). However, most of these tools have been built as isolated independent tools and they are not normally capable of **interoperating** among them [13]. In fact, heterogeneous ontology platforms should be able to exchange ontologies owned by different organizations, built with different tools, and implemented on different languages; but no guidelines are available about how to make platforms mutually interoperable. The need for a deep study on tools' interoperability is being addressed in the Special Interest Group on Enterprise-Standard Ontology Environments of the European IST network OntoWeb and a survey on these tools can be found at [24].

A. Gómez-Pérez and V.R. Benjamins (Eds.): EKAW 2002, LNAI 2473, pp. 138-153, 2002.

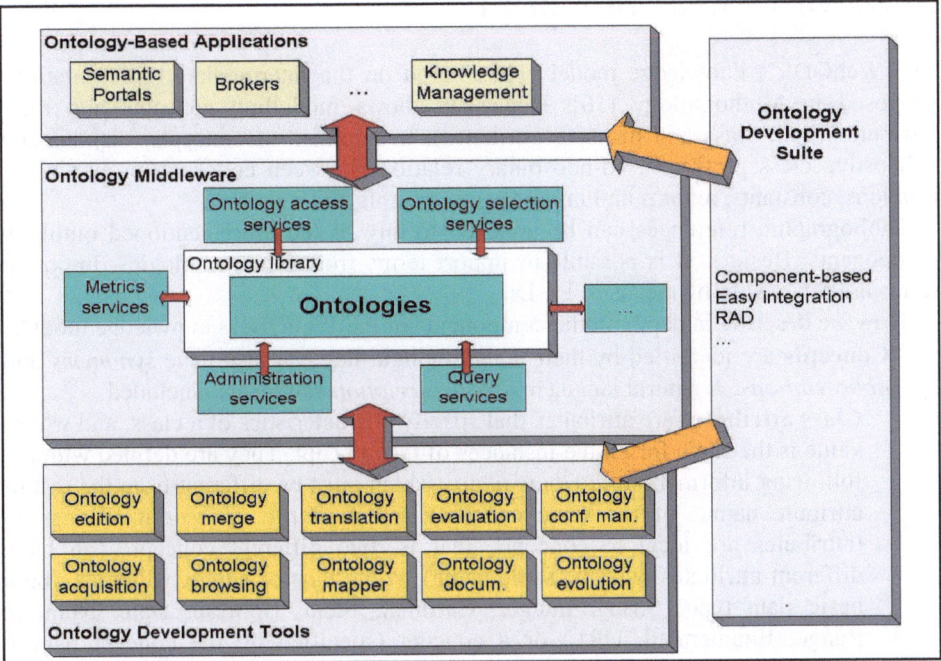

Fig 1. Main modules of an ontological engineering workbench (adapted from [13]).

Except for Protégé2000 [22] and OntoEdit [20], the other tools do not provide an integrated **support for most of the activities of the ontology lifecycle**, nor do they support any existing **methodology** for building ontologies.

Taking into account this situation, in [13] we presented the need for an integrated ontological engineering workbench supporting three groups of activities (see figure 1): (1) ontology development, management and population activities; (2) ontology middleware services to allow the easy used and integration of ontological technology in information systems; and (3) ontology-based applications' development suites to ease the creation of ontology-based applications.

In the context of this framework, we have developed WebODE[1] as a scalable ontological engineering workbench that gives support to most of the ontology development, management and population activities presented in figure 1. It also includes *middleware services* to aid in the integration of ontologies into real-world and Semantic Web applications as well as to provide rapid development tools for applications using ontologies. Finally, WebODE has been created to provide technological support for Methontology [10], an ontology construction methodology. Nevertheless, this fact does not prevent it from being used following other methodologies or no methodological approach at all.

Next sections describe the knowledge model, architecture and main features of WebODE. We will specially focus on the WebODE Axiom Builder (WAB) and the WebODE inference engine.

---

[1] http://webode.dia.fi.upm.es/

2 WebODE's Knowledge Model

The WebODE's knowledge model [1] is based on the intermediate representations proposed in Methontology [10]. Hence, it allows modelling concepts and their attributes (both class and instance attributes), taxonomies of concepts, disjoint and exhaustive class partitions, ad-hoc binary relations between concepts, properties of relations, constants, axioms and instances of concepts and relations.

Bibliographic references can be attached to any of the aforementioned ontology components. Besides, it is possible to import terms from other ontologies. Imported terms are referred to by means of URLs.

Now we describe in depth all the components of the WebODE's knowledge model:

- **Concepts** are identified by their *name*, though they can also have *synonyms* and *abbreviations*. A natural language (NL) *description* can be also included.
  - o **Class attributes** are attributes that specify characteristics of a class, and whose value is the same for all the instances of the concept. They are defined with the following information: *attribute name* (which must be different from the rest of attribute names of the same concept); *name of the concept* it belongs to (attributes are local to concepts, that is, two different concepts can have different attributes with the same name); *value type* or *range*, which can be a basic data type (String, Integer, Cardinal, Float, Boolean, Date, Numeric Range, Enumerated, URL) or a concept (specified by the concept name); *minimum* and *maximum cardinality*, which constrains the number of values that the class attribute may have; and *value(s)*.
    Class attributes can optionally have a *NL description, measurement unit* and *precision* (the last two ones just in case of numeric attributes).
  - o **Instance attributes** are attributes whose value may be different for each instance of the concept. They have the same properties than class attributes and two additional properties, *minimum value* and *maximum value*, which are used in attributes with numeric value types. Values inserted for instance attributes are interpreted as default values for them.
- **Concept groups** are sets of disjoint concepts that are also known as partitions. They are used to create disjoint and exhaustive class partitions. They have a *name*, the *set of concepts* they group together and, optionally, a *NL description*. A concept can belong to several concept groups.
- **Built-in relations** are predefined relations in the WebODE's knowledge model. They are divided into three groups: taxonomy relations between concepts (*subclass-of, not-subclass-of*), taxonomy relations between groups and concepts (*disjoint-subclass-partition, exhaustive-subclass-partition*), and mereology relations between concepts (*transitive-part-of, intransitive-part-of*).
- **Binary ad-hoc relations** between concepts are characterized by their *name*, the *origin* (source) and *destination* (target) concepts, and their *cardinality*, which establishes the number of destination terms of each origin term through the relation. Cardinality can be restricted to 1 (only one destination term) or N (any number of destination terms). Optionally, we can provide their *NL description* and *properties* (they are used to describe algebraic properties of the relation).

- **Constants** are components that have always the same value and can be used in any expression. They are identified by their *name*, and have a *value type*, *value* and *measurement unit*. Its *NL description* can be optionally provided.
- **Axioms** and **rules** are defined by their *name*, an optional *NL description* and a *formal expression* in first order logic (using the syntax provided by WebODE). They will be deeply studied in section 4.2.
- **Properties** are used to describe algebraic properties of ad-hoc relations. They are divided in two groups: *built-in properties* (reflexive, irreflexive, symmetric, asymmetric, antisymmetric and transitive), and *ad-hoc user-defined properties*.
- **Imported terms** are components from other ontologies that are included in another ontology. They are described by their *name* and a URL that includes the *host* and the *ontology name* from which the term is retrieved and the *term name* in that ontology.

Besides, the WebODE's knowledge model supports **views** and **instance sets**. Views are used to highlight specific parts of the ontology. They are analogous to the classical views of database modelling theory.

Concerning instance sets, they make possible to populate a conceptual model for different applications or scenarios, maintaining different, independent instantiations of the same conceptual model in WebODE.

3   WebODE's Architecture

WebODE is built according to a four-tier architecture: client, presentation, business logic, and database tiers. In all these tiers, we have used standard technology. The client tier uses HTML, XML, CSS, JavaScript and Java applets. The presentation tier uses servlets and JSPs. The business logic tier uses Java and RMI-IIOP. Finally, the database tier uses JDBC and Oracle.

We will analyse further the database and business logic tiers, which comprise the "ontology middleware" modules and services from figure 1.

3.1   Database Tier

Currently, WebODE ontologies can be stored in any relational database with JDBC support (WebODE has been tested both in Oracle and MySQL, which gives an idea of the flexibility of this workbench). Its main features are the optimisation of connections to the database (*connection pooling*) and transparent *fault tolerance* capabilities.

Besides, the underlying physical model that represents the WebODE knowledge model has been tuned for obtaining maximum performance.

The database access is abstracted out as an independent service in the platform. In fact, it has been designed as a pluggable component in the architecture. This allows its easy replacement by other modules in charge of data management, such as XML-based databases or RDF-based repositories.

3.2 Business Logic Tier

The business logic tier has been implemented through a proprietary Java and RMI-IIOP based application server called Minerva_LIA. This application server provides an API to create services, which can be added or removed easily with its management console, thus improving the system's flexibility, scalability and integration with third-party solutions, following the latest trends in enterprise middleware.

Minerva_LIA application server's core (built-in) services comprise the basic building blocks for more complex services in WebODE. They are the following: authentication, log, administration, thread management, scheduling and backup.

The other services are plugged on top of the Minerva_LIA application server. In figure 2 we show the structure of all the services used by the WebODE ontology editor. Any of these components can be plugged in or out, so that the whole WebODE workbench and the WebODE ontology editor can be easily personalised.

The core of the WebODE's ontology development services are: the database service (db), the cache, consistency and axiom services, and the ontology access service (ode), which defines an API for accessing WebODE ontologies. One of the main advantages of this architecture is that these services can be accessed remotely from any other application or any other instance of the WebODE workbench.

Finally, the WebODE interoperability services and the ontology documentation service are completely based on the WebODE ontology access API, and the inference engine uses extensively the Prolog exportation service. Other middleware services, such as ODEMerge, ODECatalogue and WebPicker also use the WebODE ontology access API.

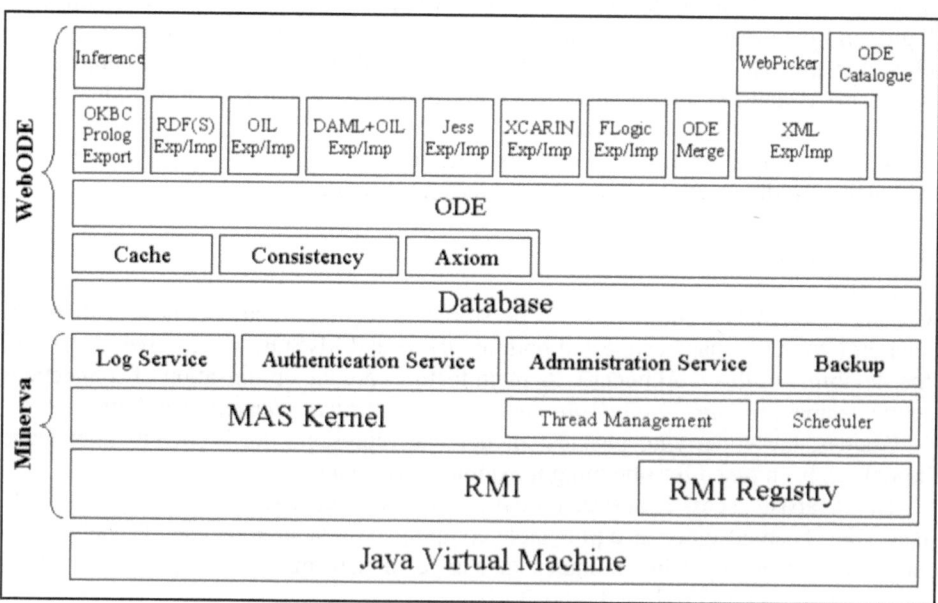

Fig 2. WebODE ontology engineering workbench's architecture.

4 WebODE Ontology Development Services

4.1 Ontology Edition Service

The WebODE Ontology Editor allows the collaborative construction of ontologies at the knowledge level. It provides a default form-based web user interface to create ontologies according to the knowledge model aforementioned. Figure 3 shows the look and feel of the ontology editor, as well as its three main areas. The main user interface components are:

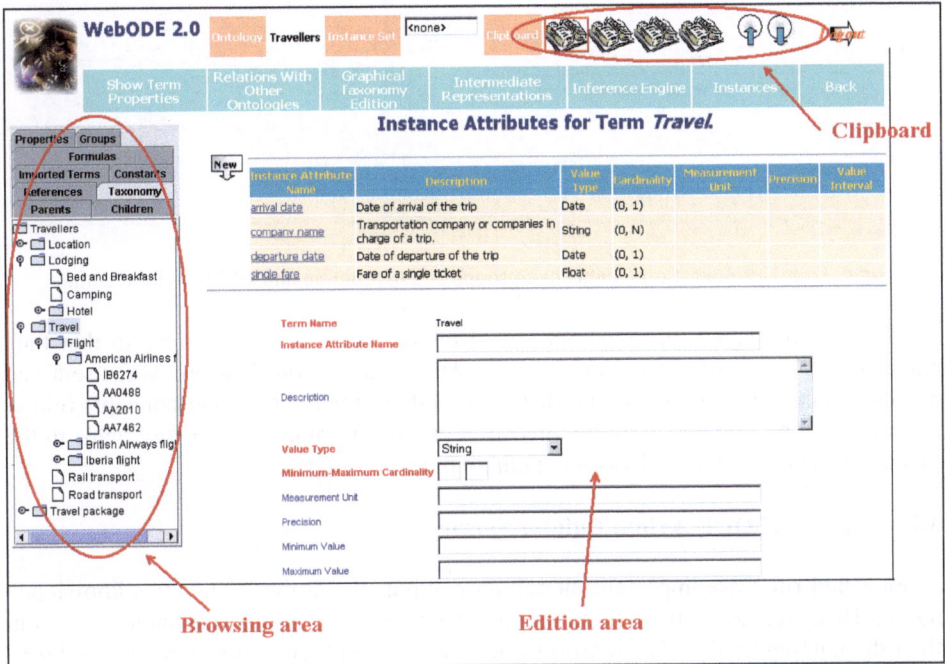

Fig 3. WebODE Ontology Editor

- Browsing area. It allows browsing the whole ontology and provides operations to create new elements and modify or delete the existing ones.
- Clipboard. It allows copying and pasting information easily between forms.
- Edition area. It presents the forms to be filled by the user, according to the component (concept, attribute, relation, etc.) that is being edited.

The WebODE Ontology Editor also includes *OntoDesigner*, a visual tool that aids in the construction of concept taxonomies and ad-hoc relations between concepts.

Concept taxonomies are created with the following set of predefined relations: *subclass of, disjoint decomposition, exhaustive partitions, transitive part of* and *non-transitive part of*. In figure 5 we show a snapshot of OntoDesigner while editing an ontology on the travelling domain.

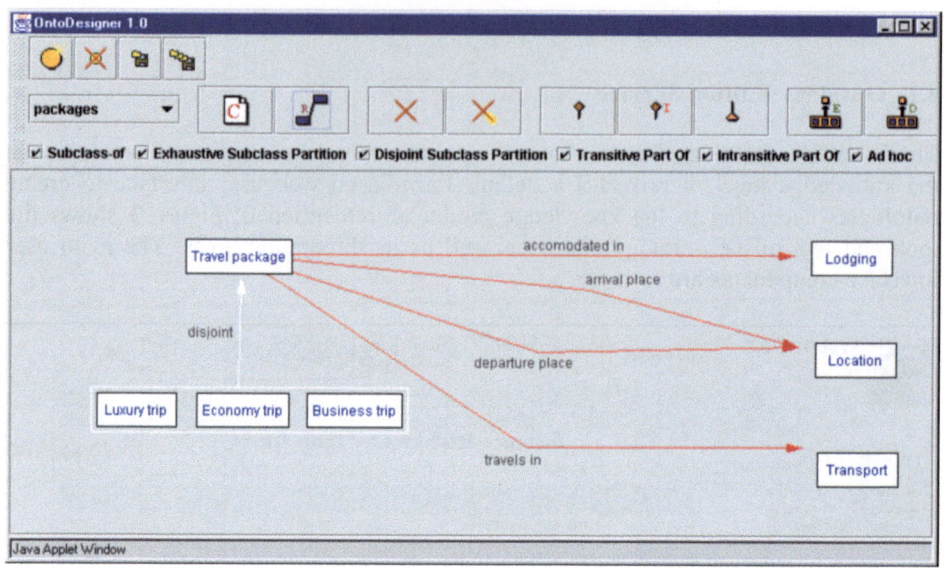

Fig 4. OntoDesigner. Some concepts, groups and taxonomic and ad-hoc relationships.

With OntoDesigner, users can create different views of an ontology, so that they can highlight parts of the ontology, as explained in section 2. Moreover, users can decide whether showing or hiding different kinds of relations among concepts (either predefined or ad-hoc ones), in the sense of a graphical prune. This feature helps in the manual evaluation of the relations contained in an ontology.

4.2 WAB: WebODE Axiom Builder Service

Axioms and rules are important modelling components in the WebODE's knowledge model. However, we noticed that ontology developers did not usually include them in their domain ontologies. The reason for this was twofold: either (a) they did not know the exact syntax they had to use to define axioms and rules; or (b) they found difficulties to write them in a simple HTML form, as WebODE did not provide adequate support for the axiom modelling task.

To solve this problem, we have created WAB (WebODE Axiom Builder). WAB is an axiom and rule editor that is integrated in the WebODE Ontology Editor. It allows creating first order logic axioms and rules using a graphical user interface. It also provides a library of built-in axioms, which can be reused for creating other axioms, rather than building them from scratch.

4.2.1 Axiom Building
We will explain how WAB works using an example. Let us suppose that we want to create the following axiom: "every train that departs from a European location must arrive at another European location". This axiom is written in WebODE as follows:

```
forall(?X,?Y,?Z)  (Train(?X) and
                   Origin(?X,?Y) and EuropeLocation(?Y) and
                   Destination(?X,?Z)
                   -> EuropeLocation(?Z))
```

Figure 5 shows the WAB interface once we have pressed the universal quantification symbol in order to write our axiom. In this sense, this interface helps non-expert users in writing their axioms.

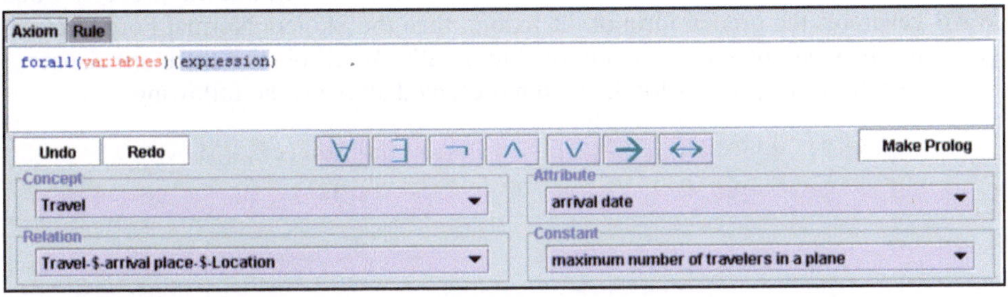

Fig 5. WAB: WebODE Axiom Builder. Well-formed axioms' construction

Figure 6 shows the axiom completed in WAB. In this axiom editor, we can create well-formed expressions in first order logic, using: universal quantification, existential quantification, negation, conjunction, disjunction, implication and biconditional. We can also use those terms that have been already defined in the ontology (concepts, attributes, relations and constants). If we select a concept in the *Concept* drop-down list, shown in figure 4, the attributes and relations that can be applied to this concept appear in the *Attribute* and *Relation* drop-down lists, respectively (including those attributes and relations that are not defined directly in the concept but are inherited in the concept taxonomy). In the example of figure 6, *companyName* is an attribute of concept *MeanOfTransport* and *Destination* is an ad-hoc relation between *MeanOfTransport* and *Location*. This prevents users from entering attributes or relations that cannot be applied to a concept.

WAB also allows users to write directly the axiom expression, without using its facilities for doing it. The following grammar is used in WebODE axioms:

```
axiom ::=        atom | axiom OR axiom | axiom AND axiom | axiom -> axiom | axiom <->
             axiom |
             NOT axiom | FORALL (var_list) axiom | EXISTS (var_list) axiom | ( axiom )
atom ::=     ID ( term_list ) | SUBCLASS ( term_list ) | NOT_SUBCLASS ( term_list ) |
             DISJOINT ( term_list ) | EXHAUSTIVE ( term_list ) | TRANSITIVE ( term_list ) |
             INTRANSITIVE ( term_list ) |
             term > term | term < term | term >= term | term <= term | term = term | ( atom )

term ::= ID | num | ID ( term_list ) | term + term | term - term | term * term | term / term | ( term )
term_list ::= term | term , term_list
var_list ::= ID  | ID , var_list
```

Once the axiom is defined, we must click on the "Make Prolog" button to parse it and ensure that it has been correctly defined. Not only does WAB perform a syntactic check of the axiom, in the sense of testing that it is compliant with the WebODE's axiom grammar. But also it checks that the vocabulary used in the axiom is defined in the ontology, that the ad-hoc relations can be applied between two variables, that the attributes are defined for the concepts to which they are applied, etc.

The final result of this parsing is that the axiom is transformed to Horn clauses, if possible. To perform this transformation, we follow a well-known process. First, WAB generates the prenex form of the axiom; then the Skolem Normal Form; next, it generates the Conjunctive Normal Form and, finally, WAB obtains the Horn clauses.

The result of this process for the axiom presented above is the following:

```
¬Train(x2) ∨ ¬Origin(x2,x1) ∨ ¬Destination(x2,x0) ∨
¬ EuropeLocation(x1) ∨  EuropeLocation(x0)
```

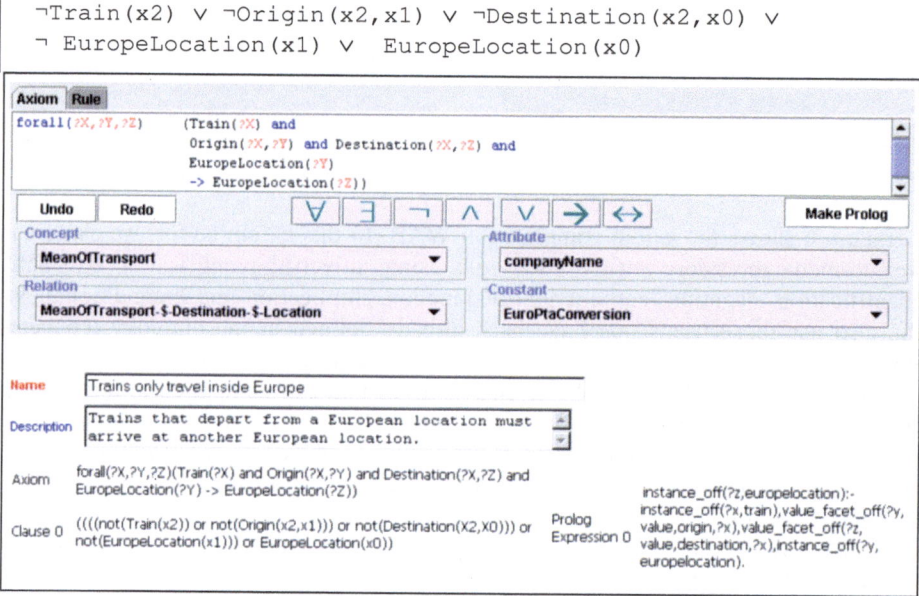

Fig 6. WAB: WebODE Axiom Builder. Axiom transformation into Prolog

For each clause obtained in the previous transformation, WAB creates a Prolog rule, which can be stored in the WebODE database, so that they can be used in the WebODE's Prolog inference engine. In this process, the vocabulary used in the logical expression is also transformed according to the vocabulary provided by the OKBC protocol knowledge representation primitives [5]. As shown below, our example uses the OKBC primitives *instance_of* and *value_facet_of* are used.

```
instance_of(Z,europelocation) :-
        instance_of(X,train),
        value_facet_of(Y,value,origin,X),
        value_facet_of(Z,value,destination,X),
        instance_of(Y,europelocation).
```

4.2.2 Rule Building

The same approach is used for creating rules with WAB. Let's suppose that we want to create a rule that states that "all the trips by ship that depart from Europe are handled by the company Costa Cruises". In this case, we will create the following rule (shown in figure 7):

```
if EuropeLocation(Y) and Origin(X,Y) and Ship(X)
then companyName(X,costaCruises)
```

The syntax of WebODE rules is much simpler than that used for axioms. This eases the modelling of knowledge in the form of "if ... then" structures, which are used in many systems. The following grammar is used for WebODE rules:

```
lhs ::= atom | atom AND lhs

rhs ::= atom

rule ::= IF lhs THEN rhs
```

Hence, the left-hand side of the rule consists of conjunctions of atoms, while the right-hand side of the rule is a single atom.

Once a rule is created, WAB checks both the syntax of the rule and its consistency with the rest of the ontology, and it transforms the rule into Horn clauses. For the example above, we obtain the following Horn clause:

```
¬EuropeLocation(Y) ∨ ¬Origin(X,Y) ∨ ¬Ship(X) ∨
companyName(X,costaCruises)
```

And, consequently, the following Prolog rule, which can be stored in the WebODE database:

```
value_facet_of(costaCruises,value,companyname,X):-
    instance_of(Y,europelocation),
    value_facet_of(Y,value,origin,X),
    instance_of(X,ship).
```

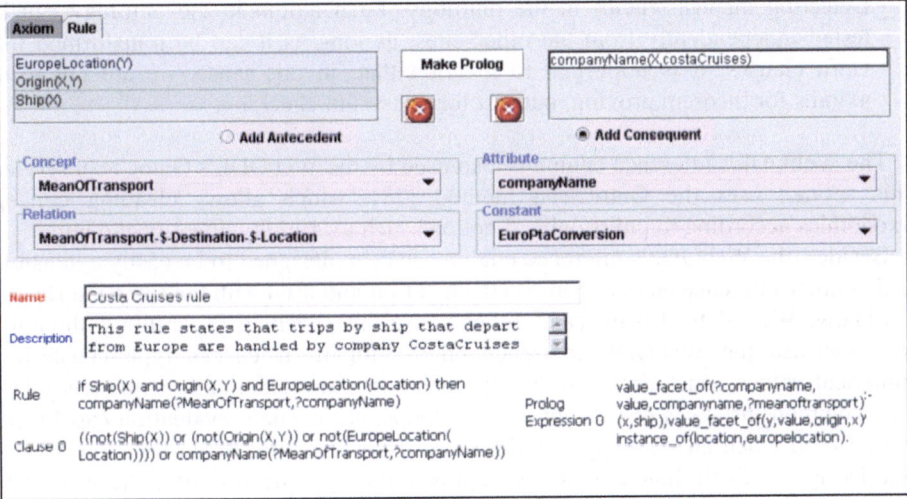

Fig 7. WAB: WebODE Axiom Builder. Rule edition

The transformations of axioms and rules to the OKBC vocabulary are done because the WebODE's inference engine allows working with the primitives defined in OKBC, as we will see in the next section. Moreover, WebODE ontologies are completely translated to Prolog syntax, so that these generated Prolog rules can be used either for checking constraints on the ontology or for generating new information from it. We will see the results of the Prolog translation in section 4.4.

4.3 WebODE's Inference Engine Service

As we have commented in section 4.2, WebODE includes an **OKBC-based inference engine**. This inference engine reasons with a subset of the primitives identified in that protocol [5], and allows using such primitives to query ontologies (currently, WebODE's inference engine makes use of Ciao Prolog [17]).

The following groups of OKBC primitives have been implemented:
- Primitives to query about concept taxonomies and instances: *get-class-instances, get-class-subclasses, get-class-superclasses* and *get-instance-types*.
- Primitives to query about slots: *get-frame-details, get-slots, get-slot-domain, get-slot-type, get-slot-value, get-slot-values, get-slot-values-in-detail, get-slot-facets, get-facet-value* and *get-facet-values*.
- Primitives to check whether a condition holds for a term (class, instance or slot): *individual-p, instance-of-p, member-facet-value-p*, and *member-slot-value-p*.

At present, we are using this inference engine for several purposes:
- Querying about the ontology components, either with these OKBC primitives or with a user-defined Prolog program, as long as it uses these OKBC primitives or the Prolog representation of ontology components, which are presented in section 4.4.
- Asserting new knowledge using the Prolog expressions that correspond to the rules and axioms created with WAB, as explained above.
- Detecting inconsistencies in the ontology. Each axiom in the ontology can be tested independently from the other ones, as long as it can be transformed into Horn clauses. It is important to mention that, in this sense, we are not using axioms for theorem proving, but just for constraint checking.

The WebODE's inference engine is also used by the WebODE's OntoClean service. This service uses the OntoClean method [23], which allows cleaning concept taxonomies according to philosophical notions such as: rigidity, identity and unity.

Besides, the WebODE's inference engine has been designed to be easily extensible, so that other inference engines can be attached to it and used with the same interface.

Finally, WebODE also provides other constraint checking capabilities, though it does not use the WebODE inference engine for it. It checks type constraints, numerical values constraints, cardinality constraints and taxonomic consistency [14] (i.e., common instances of disjoint classes, loops, etc.). These evaluation capabilities can be used when an ontology is built either using the form-based user interface or OntoDesigner. Such functionality is supplied through the use of a Minerva_LIA service, as part of the ontology development and management services.

4.4 WebODE Interoperability Services

Ontologies built using WebODE can be easily integrated in other ontology servers or used in ontology-based applications. Possible choices for interoperability include:

- WebODE's ontology access API, which can be accessed by other applications using RMI, and is completely compliant with the WebODE's knowledge model.
- XML. WebODE ontologies can be exported into and imported from XML, following a well-defined DTD[2] that uses the same knowledge representation vocabulary used for expressing the WebODE knowledge model. Ontologies can be translated completely or on a view or instance-set basis.
- Ontology languages, through the ontology language export/import modules. Currently, WebODE is able to export to and import ontologies from: RDF(S), OIL, DAML + OIL, the XMLization of CARIN and FLogic. If we take into account that the WebODE knowledge model is very expressive [1], we are able to provide high quality translations that preserve most of the original information contained in the ontology and take advantage of most of the modelling characteristics of the target and source languages. As with XML, ontologies can be translated completely or on a view or instance-set basis.
- Jess [12]. WebODE generates all the concepts as Java beans, which contain also information about their attributes and ad-hoc relations. These beans can be easily uploaded in the Jess system. This means that we can use the ontology developed in WebODE inside the Jess system, and develop our own programs in Jess using the ontology components.
- Prolog syntax of OKBC [5]. WebODE provides a subset of the primitives defined in the OKBC protocol. They are expressed in Prolog, as explained in the previous section. Table 1 summarizes the mapping between the WebODE's knowledge model and the Prolog OKBC translation.

WebODE ontology component	*OKBC Prolog representation*
Concept: Travel	**class**: class(travel)
Concept groups	-- (they do not exist in OKBC)
Class attribute: Hotel quality	**own slot**: own-slot-of(quality,hotel)
Instance attribute: Hotel price	**template slot**: template-slot-of(price,hotel)
Subclass-of: Flight is a subclass of Travel	**subclass of**: subclass-of(flight,travel)

Ad-hoc relation:
     the departure place of a
     Travel is a Location
	slot:
	 slot-of(departurePlace,travel)
	 facet-of(type,departurePlace,travel,location)

Constant: average price	**term**: averagePrice
Axiom & rule	**Prolog rule**: cf. section 4.2
Instance: John is a Traveller	**instance**: instance-of(john,traveller)
Property	-- (they do not exist in OKBC)
Imported term: Date	**term**: date

Table 1. Summary of WebODE transformations into OKBC Prolog syntax.

---

[2] http://webode.dia.fi.upm.es/webode/dtd/webode_2_0.dtd

4.5 WebODE's Ontology Documentation Service

WebODE ontologies are automatically documented in different formats: HTML tables representing the Methontology's intermediate representations, HTML concept taxonomies and XML.

Concepts Dictionary for *Travel Ontology*

Concept name	Synonyms	Acronyms	Instances	Class attributes	Instance attributes	Relations
AA7462	--	--	AA7462_Feb08_2002 AA7462_Feb16_2002	--	--	same flight as
American Airlines flight	--	--	--	company	--	--
British Airways flight	--	--	--	company	--	--
Five stars hotel	--	--	--	number of stars	--	--
Flight	--	--	--	--	--	same flight as
Location	--	--	--	--	name size	--
Lodging	--	--	--	--	price of standard room	placed in
Travel	--	--	--	--	arrival date company departure date return fare single fare	arrival place departure place
Travel package	--	--	--	--	age budget final price name number of days travel restrictions	arrival place departure place accomodated in travels in
Two stars hotel	--	--	--	number of stars	--	--

Fig 8. WebODE's documentation service: Concepts Dictionary Intermediate Representation.

Users can decide whether obtaining the documentation of the whole ontology or of parts of it (specific views or instance sets). As an example, figure 8 presents part of the concept dictionary of the *Travel* ontology, which contains its concepts, their class and instance attributes, instances and ad-hoc binary relations.

The HTML documentation service shows the concept taxonomy, the concept attributes and the ad-hoc binary relations between concepts.

5 WebODE Middleware Services

In this section, we present some *middleware* applications that we have built inside the WebODE workbench. They are fully integrated in the middle tier and, as such, run within the Minerva_LIA application server. They use some of the services described in this paper, such as the interoperability services and the inference engine.

- **WebPicker** [6] is a set of wrappers that allow importing standards of classification of products and services in the context of electronic commerce into WebODE (UNSPSC, e-cl@ss and RosettaNet). We are currently extending it to wrap other sources of information, such as Cyc.
- **ODEMerge** performs merging of concepts, attributes and relationships from two different ontologies built for the same domain, according to semantic criteria and resources used for natural language processing.
- **ODECatalogue** is able to generate electronic catalogs from ontologies according to some parameters. The catalogue generation from an ontology assures a correct and rich classification of the different products.

6   Conclusions

In this paper, we have presented the WebODE ontological engineering workbench, whose main contributions are detailed below:

1) **Integrated technological support for many activities of the ontology lifecycle**.

- WebODE supports in an integrated platform many activities of the ontology lifecycle that, until recently, have just been supported by isolated, independent tools. In fact, it does not only support development activities, but also management and support ones, such as documentation, evaluation, merge or integration.
- Additionally, WebODE allows developing ontologies at the knowledge level. Ontology developers do not need worry about building an ontology directly in an implementation language. Later, the contents of the ontology can be automatically translated into several implementation languages.
- First order logic axioms and rules can be more easily created according to the WebODE syntax, using the WebODE Axiom Builder. They are also translated into Prolog syntax, if possible, using some primitives extracted from the OKBC knowledge model. Primitives from the OKBC protocol can be used to send queries about WebODE ontologies with the Prolog inference service.
- Finally, WebODE is not only useful for building ontologies, but also provides a wide range of services for ontology-based applications.

2) **Technological support for ontology development methodologies.**

- WebODE has been built to provide support to a methodology for ontology development: Methontology.
- However, this does not prevent WebODE from being used with another ontology development methodology or without any specific methodological approach.

3) **Ontology interoperability.**

- Interoperability amongst modules and services inside the WebODE workbench. The use of a common API to access WebODE ontologies from any service and the use of XML exportation/importation functionalities allow modules and services interoperate easily.
- Interoperability with other tools and applications. The translation functionalities available in the workbench allow exchanging ontologies with other tools, environments or applications.

This workbench has been successfully used, with different domains and purposes and by different groups of people, in the following projects:

- The European IST project MKBEEM (IST 1999-10589). In this project, B2B and B2C ontologies have been built and reengineered using WebODE.
- The Ontoweb thematic network (IST-2000-29243). We have built the OntoRoadMap application[3] on top of WebODE. It is an ontology-based web application that allows the community to register, browse and search ontologies, methodologies, tools and languages for building ontologies, as well as ontology-

---

[3] http://babage.dia.fi.upm.es/ontoweb/wp1/OntoRoadMap/index.html

based applications in areas like the: semantic web, e-commerce, KM, NLP, III, etc., This application uses an ontology in the domain of ontologies.

- The Spanish CICYT project ContentWeb (TIC2001-2745). In this project, we have created WebPicker for (semi)automatic ontology acquisition from e-commerce standards for the classification of products and services (*UNSPSC*, *RosettaNet* and *e-cl@ss*) and in the domain of leisure activities.
- The Spanish CICYT project on Methodology for Knowledge Management (TIC-980741). We have built using WebODE ontologies that model a few institutions.
- (Onto)²Agent. We have built the Reference Ontology, that asseses ontology-based applications' developers on the most suitable ontology to use in an application.
- Environment Ontology (UPM-AM-9819). In this project, we have built the *Elements* and *Environmental Ions* ontologies, in the domain of chemistry, and have integrated them with existing ontologies, such as the Ontolingua's ontology Standard Units.
- MRO (Ontologies for cataloguing business services). In this project, we have merged heterogeneous electronic catalogues in the domain of office furniture.

In the future we will provide more functions both to the WebODE Ontology Editor and the *middleware* area, such as an ontology translation manager for the WebODE interoperability services, ontology configuration management capabilities, ontology upgrading and semantic annotation services. We will therefore lay the foundations for a more complete implementation of the workbench presented in section 1. We will also focus on the implementation of an ontology development suite that allows a high reusability of ontologies and rapid creation of ontology-based applications. Finally, WebODE services will be soon made available as Semantic Web services.

Acknowledgements

This work is supported by a FPI grant funded by UPM and by the project "ContentWeb: Plataforma tecnológica para la web semántica: ontologías, lenguaje natural y comercio electrónico[4]" (TIC-2001-2745). This work would not have been possible without the help of JC Arpírez, JF Cebrián, R de Diego, M Lama, A López, V López, E Mohedano, JP Pérez and JA Ramos in the implementation and tests of WebODE services, and M Blázquez and JM García-Pinar in the development of ODE.

References

1. Arpírez, J.C.; Corcho, O.; Fernández-López, M.; Gómez-Pérez, A. *WebODE: a scalable ontological engineering workbench*. First International Conference on Knowledge Capture (K-CAP 2001). Victoria, Canada. October, 2001.
2. Bechhofer, S., Goble, C. *Towards Annotation Using DAML+OIL*. KCAP'01 Workshop on Semantic Markup and Annotation. Victoria, Canada. October, 2001.
3. Bechhofer, S.; Horrocks, I; Goble, C.; Stevens, R. *OilEd: a Reason-able Ontology Editor for the Semantic Web*. Proceedings of KI2001, Joint German/Austrian conference on Artificial Intelligence, September 19-21, Vienna. Springer-Verlag LNAI Vol. 2174, pp 396--408. 2001.

---

[4] ContentWeb: Platform for the Semantic Web: ontologies, natural language and e-commerce

4. Chalupsky, H. *OntoMorph: A Translation System for Symbolic Knowledge*. KR-2000. 471-482. 2000.

5. Chaudhri V. K.; Farquhar A.; Fikes R.; Karp P. D.; Rice J. P. *The Generic Frame Protocol 2.0*. Technical Report, Stanford University.1997.

6. Corcho, O.; Gómez-Pérez, A. *WebPicker: Knowledge Extraction from Web Resources*. 6th Intl. Workshop on Applications of Natural Language for Information Systems (NLDB'01). Madrid. June, 2001.

7. Domingue, J. *Tadzebao and Webonto: Discussing, Browsing and Editing Ontologies on the Web*. KAW98. Banff, Canada. 1998.

8. Duineveld, A.; Studer, R.; Weiden, M; Kenepa, B.; Benjamis, R. *WonderTools? A comparative study of ontological engineering tools*. KAW99. Banff. Canada. 1999.

9. Farquhar A., Fikes R., Rice J., *The Ontolingua Server: A Tool for Collaborative Ontology Construction*. 10th Knowledge Acquisition for Knowledge-Based Systems Workshop, Banff, Canada. 1996.

10. Fernández-López, M.; Gómez-Pérez, A.; Pazos, J.; Pazos, A. *Building a Chemical Ontology using methontology and the Ontology Design Environment*. IEEE Intelligent Systems and their applications. #4 (1):37-45. 1999.

11. Fridman, N., Musen, M. *PROMPT: Algorithm and Tool for Automated Ontology Merging and Alignment*. AAAI-2000. Austin, Texas. August, 2000.

12. Friedman-Hill, E.J. *Jess, The Expert System Shell for the Java Platform*. Version 6.1a1 (3 April 2002). http://herzberg.ca.sandia.gov/jess/docs/61/

13. Gómez-Pérez, A. *A proposal of infrastructural needs on the framework of the semantic web for ontology construction and use*. FP6 Programme Consultation Meeting 9. April 27th, 2001.

14. Gómez-Pérez, A. *Evaluation of Ontologies*. International Journal of Intelligent Systems. 16(3). March, 2001.

15. Guarino, N.; Giaretta, P. *Ontologies and Knowledge Bases: Towards a Terminological Clarification*. In N. Mars (ed.) Towards Very Large Knowledge Bases: Knowledge Building and Knowledge Sharing. IOS Press, Amsterdam: 25-32. 1995

16. Heflin, J.; Hendler, J. *A Portrait of the Semantic Web in Action*. IEEE Intelligent Systems, 16(2), 2001.

17. Hermenegildo, M., Bueno, F., Cabeza, D., Carro, M., García, M., López, P., Puebla, G. *The Ciao Logic Programming Environment*. International Conference on Computational Logic (CL2000). July, 2000.

18. McGuinness, D., Fikes, R., Rice, J., Wilder, S. *The Chimaera Ontology Environment*. AAAI-2000. Austin, Texas. August, 2000.

19. Studer, R.; Benjamins, V.R.; Fensel, D. *Knowledge Engineering. Principles and Methods*. IEEE Transactions on Data and Knowledge Engineering, 25(1-2), 1998, pp.161–197.

20. Sure, Y.; Erdmann, M.; Angele, J.; Staab, S.; Studer, R.; Wenke, D. *OntoEdit: Collaborative Ontology Development for the Semantic Web*. International Semantic Web Conference (ISWC02). Sardinia. Italy. June, 2002. LNCS 2342. pp. 221-235.

21. Swartout, B.; Ramesh P.; Knight, K.; Russ, T. *Toward Distributed Use of Large-Scale Ontologies*. AAAI Symposium on Ontological Engineering. Stanford. USA. March, 1997.

22. *Using Protégé-2000 to Edit RDF*. Technical Report. Stanford University. http://www.smi.Stanford.edu/ projects/protege/protege-rdf/protege-rdf.html

23. Welty, C.; Guarino, N. *Supporting Ontological Analysis of Taxonomic Relationships*. Data and Knowledge Engineering. September 2001.

24. A survey on ontology tools. Deliverable D13.IST OntoWeb Thematic Network. May 2002.

Some Ontology Engineering Processes and Their Supporting Technologies

Alan Flett, Mariana Casella dos Santos, and Werner Ceusters

Language and Computing (L&C), Hazenakkerstraat 20A,
9520 Zonnegem, Belgium
Tel: +32 (0)53 62 95 45 Fax: +32 (0)53 62 95 55
{mariana, werner}@landc.be
http://www.landc.be

Abstract. We describe the ontology engineering processes and their
supporting technologies at L&C, a company developing intelligent medical applications based on ontologies. We describe the principal tasks that
the modellers of our ontology have to execute, how they are supported
and guided by some specifically ontology-focused management practices,
and how (semi-)automated technology can also aid in their support and
guidance, so as to produce a higher quality and quantity of ontology
product. The ontology processes include the development of new structures of concepts and relations, the integration of other ontologies and
terminologies, the integration of the ontology to natural language applications, and the reforming of the current ontology's formal structure.
The automated supports we talk about include OntoClean, a principled
methodology for analyzing ontological properties and their constraints.
We finally note how far we think our ontology technology comes to some
proposed desiderata recently given for "enterprise standard" ontology
environments.

1 Introduction

L&C develops intelligent medical applications that process medical language.
This intelligent processing of medical language can either be in the form of understanding prescriptions, performing semantic indexing and information retrieval,
or voice operated medical applications. Typically, these have as a foundation the
knowledge-based resource of an ontology. This ontology, called LinkBase(r), is a
model of various aspects and parts of medicine, including anatomy, pharmaceuticals, occupational risk, and procedures: in short, everything to do with healthcare. It consists of approximately 1,000,000 concepts, 400 link types, 3,000,000
terms, and 3,000,000 links. The other important component in our technological armory as intimated above is language technology. Consequently, integrating
the ontology with the language technology is also an important area for us. But,
it is the ontology development processes that are the focus of this paper. In
the section "Modelling processes" we describe the various ontology development
processes gone through here at L&C. In the section "Ontology management processes and technologies" we describe how our technology supports these various

A. Gómez-Pérez and V.R. Benjamins (Eds.): EKAW 2002, LNAI 2473, pp. 154–165, 2002.

modelling processes. In the section "Future work: intelligent automated support" we describe the future work we will do to help better support these processes using (semi-)automated techniques. The section "Conclusions" concludes our paper.

2   Modelling Processes

The modelling processes are arguably the most critical processes in the company, after perhaps product development, for the success of the company. Medical ontologies are currently perhaps the largest scale domain ontology development tasks today. Medical ontologies arguably have one very complicated system to model (the human body), which has been analyzed and continues to be analyzed in the greatest detail possible; not to mention all the contingent procedures and pharmaceuticals devised over time to repair it. So, it can be claimed with some justification that it is one of the most finely grained, comprehensive, and large, bodies of knowledge (BoKs) in existence (the gene sequencing projects-taken as medical knowledge-reinforcing this somewhat!); several attempts at representing in a formal manner various chapters of the book of medical knowledge have been made over the years including Open GALEN[1], The Digital Anatomist Project[2], MeSH[3], and a swarm of others. So, the modelling processes undertaken herein are large-scale and complex, and bring in to focus many domain ontology development issues. To these we now turn.

2.1   Novel Refinement

Novel refinement is where new modelling primitives and structures/patterns are deemed necessary to either model some previously un-modelled aspect or part of the world (of medicine, in our case). This typically requires the creation of new concepts and relations.

LinkBase(r) content is updated on the basis of information coming from various sources: clinical reports, literature, coding and classification systems, etc. A set of criteria are used to decide whether or not new primitives are required. The main primitives are concepts, terms and relationships.

A new concept is added if at least one of the following criteria is met: i) the concept is explicitly represented in a third party system towards which a mapping from LinkBase(r) has to be maintained; ii) there is at least one language covered by the system that has the possibility to express the candidate concept using one word or token; iii) there are terms that in a given language are polysemous and for which all possible meanings are not yet represented; iv) a newly introduced relationship may lead to reification (hence concepts) that are expressed by terms in at least one language; v) a term is found for which no concept already exists.

---

[1] http://www.opengalen.org/
[2] http://sig.biostr.washington.edu/projects/da/
[3] http://www.nlm.nih.gov/mesh/meshhome.html

A new term is added to an existing concept if at least one of the following criteria is met: i) it is found in relevant documents and is a true synonym of the existing concept; ii) it is a multiword term in which the individual components co-occur significantly; iii) it is a multiword term and the meaning of the term contains more information than the sum of the individual tokens (e.g., "bacterial meningitis" adds to "bacterial" and "meningitis" by specifying the actor-relationship, while in "bacterial cell wall" a part-whole relation is specified).

A new relationship is added when the set of existing relationships is insufficient to capture in detail the semantics of new concepts, or when a literature review reveals new insights with respect to logics on issues such as time, mereology, processes, etc. In addition to these basic primitives, additional elements turned out to be useful. They might provide better quality assurance of the model (e.g., role restrictions), or improved reasoning (e.g., transitivity and compositionality over relationships). Their integration in the system follows (as yet) a less formal path. A paradigmatic case of novel refinement was the introduction of elements of occupational medicine to LinkBase(r). Concepts denoting a "risk" for a disease or condition, or substances and situations considered as "risk factor" to the development of these diseases or conditions, where not yet present in our ontology and couldn't be fully represented with the existing relationships. These concepts, amongst others, as well as new types of relationships to be placed between them, where introduced in Link Base. The result was the creation of a new modelling form where the "risk" of a particular disease is a property of the "risk factor" for this disease, which is then related to the disease itself. Other new concepts involved (e.g., the "exposure to a risk factor") are also completely represented in this new form.

2.2   Integrative Refinement

Integrating content is where ex-L&C ontologies/terminologies are deemed to be interesting or required for our applications. Interesting content consists typically of more specialized information, or have a substantial large quantity of concepts and terms, e.g., Anatomical Therapeutic Chemical (ATC), a classification system for classifying drugs, widely used in Europe. The required contents are necessary for the functioning of L&C's applications, e.g., the International Classification of Diseases (ICD) is currently used in a coding application.

An assumption is that all concepts will already find suitable parents in our ontology. It has two distinguished phases. On the first stage, which is fully automated, the external ontologies/terminologies are stored in an area of Link Base called META ENTITY, with their original style and structure. The concepts from these ontologies/terminologies are compared to the existing terms/concepts in the representation field of Link Base called DOMAIN ENTITY. When an exact match is found a specific relationship is placed between the META concept, from the external ontology/terminology, and the matching existing DOMAIN concept. If an exact match is not found a new DOMAIN concept is created (see novel refinement) in order to be related to the META concept. The second stage of integration includes asserting primitive criteria (e.g., the parent of the concept, necessary relations) and definitional criteria (i.e., necessary and sufficient conditions) to the newly created concepts. It is done by the ontologists in a fully manual procedure or in a semi automated procedure (e.g., if we have many concepts describing cancer, and all are a subclass of the concept "cancer", then we can add a is-a link between all of those cancer concepts and the concept "cancer").

Many obstacles and difficulties can be encountered during the process of integration, and might require the revising of previous modelling structures and patterns (see reflective refinement), or to create new ones (see novel refinement), e.g., during the mapping to OPCS 4 (Office of Population Census and Survey)[4]— a classification of surgical procedures-a terminological problem was encountered. Some terms were considered to be of a different meaning amongst the already integrated terminologies and OPCS 4, while within Link Base's representation field DOMAIN ENTITY a mix of these different meanings was found. The necessity then arose of reclassifying those concepts and stipulating a consensual meaning for them, as well as stipulating new relations between the concepts representing the surgical procedures from OPCS 4 and pre-existing relational DOMAIN concepts, as body parts or specific actions that take place during these procedures).

One of the main problems that we currently face during the mapping process is related to its first stage where an exact match between terms needs to be found.[5] Possible term variations that would still keep the same conceptual meaning (e.g., plural, presence of commas or hyphens, British and American English spelling differences) are not taken into consideration, which results in a large amount of newly created concepts with the same conceptual meaning as pre-existing concepts that must then be aligned. One might believe this problem would have a rather simple solution, but considering the great ambiguity of medical terminology it's difficult not to fall into mistakes of interpretation and consequently false results on our applications if assumptions are made blindly between potentially similar terms (e.g., a concept named "Salivary gland excision" had a different interpretation than a concept named "Excision of salivary gland", the former representing the excision of a structure from the salivary

---

[4] http://www.doh.gov.uk/hes/standard_data/coding_information/opcs/

[5] As a partial solution to this problem a new tool has been developed in the management system, where the paths of relationships are followed to find possible concepts with the same conceptual meaning. Given a certain token, the tool will first find concepts in the ontology that have terms assigned to them where one or more of the words in the token are present. Then it intersects, following existing relationships, the concepts found for each of the words present in the token. This intersection generates as a result a set of concepts, ranked by their relationship's importance, which are probable to have the same meaning as the given token. In order to avoid any wrong assumption the result set of concepts is then analyzed by an Ontologist that validates the alignment or relationship between the given token and the result concept.

gland like a tumour or a cyst, while the later represents the excision of part or the whole of the salivary gland itself).

The process of mapping is evolutionary, and has been progressing to become each time more automated and efficient as a deeper study of the ex-ontologies/terminologies is made before integration and the possible obstacles are foreseen and partially automatically prevented. One example of a more automated approach to mapping is our database integration bean. This bean allows for the mapping of tables and relations, and hence the content, of an external database to the concepts and relations used in LinkBase(r). So, for example, if a concept called "drug type" was mapped to the concept "pharmaceutical" in the LinkBase(r) ontology, we could seamlessly explore the new drug child concepts under "pharmaceutical" as though these concepts were part of the ontology. The clever part is in the method used to find the semantically valid mappings. Here we use an algorithm that uses the terms of the database and the terms of the concepts in the ontology and finds new concepts which might be useful given the database terms. The application has obvious shortcomings, and should be considered as more of a CASE tool to help the developer on the semantic mapping.

Integrating Content to Language Systems L&C's ontology is completely language independent, in the sense that it doesn't make use of any grammatical information from any language. On the other hand, applications based on our ontology can be applied in any European language by the assignment of multilingual terms and lexemes to the modelled and integrated concepts in the DOMAIN ENTITY representation field. During the process of language integration important focus is given to the consensual meaning determined by the modelling representation of the DOMAIN concepts, and only terms used in natural language to express exactly this same meaning can be assigned to these concepts (this is an assumption we make). Time is then spent on careful research of similar terms or literal translations which might have different meanings in their current use. (The main difficulties of the process of language integration are: The absence of a spelling check, due to the lack of reliable medical dictionaries that could be used as a source; The presence of concepts expressed by terms composed by a combination of many words, which leaves room for endless possibilities of combinations (e.g., KIDNEY CANCER can have as terms "kidney malignancy", "renal malignancy", "malignant neoplasm of kidney", "malignant tumor of kidney", "malignant renal neoplasm").

2.3   Reflective Refinement

Reflective refinement is where a review of the current form of the content is made and deemed inadequate somehow, resulting in a partial recasting of some or all of the current content into partially new forms (evolutionary reforming), e.g., the addition of a new relation to a concept, or in a total reforming of some or all current content into new forms (revolutionary reforming), e.g., the deletion of an existing relation to a concept, and the creation of a new (form of) concept. Reflective refinement is different from novel refinement in that it is more concerned with the structure and form of the content, as opposed to simply being a content issue (which is what novel refinement is).

For example, reforming the ontology with the General Ontological Language (GOL) [SHH01] would be a reforming of content. In that methodology (ontology) there are several novel and primitive ontological relations which are at present not in our ontological model of the worlds of healthcare. It is to be expected that some reforming of the current ontology would be necessitated if we were to try and incorporate those new relations and concepts.

Conditions where reflective refinement is needed are amongst others:

1. Discrepancy amongst the meaning of content from different ex-Link Base ontologies/terminologies to be mapped and the meaning of content in Link Base's DOMAIN representation field.
2. Content form organized in a particular field of Link Base where restricted kinds of relationships are allowed and which are not fully appropriate in relation to the new content.
3. Content form that brings errors of assumption by the ontology browser and consequently errors to our applications.
4. Content deemed insufficient for natural language processing.

During the process of adding content we often encounter obstacles related to the actual form of some content. The form can be either insufficient or inappropriate for a complete representation of the new content (e.g., while integrating content related to surgical procedures, the form in which the "surgical approach" (the specific anatomic dissection by which an organ or part is exposed in surgery) content was structured was considered inappropriate to represent the difference between surgical approaches and consequently between the surgical procedures where they take place. The surgical approaches were represented as a STATE (characteristic) of a surgical procedure, what didn't allow us to place an appropriate/valuable relation between them and the body sites involved in the dissection. A revolutionary reforming was then done, where the old modelling form as STATES was abandoned, and the surgical approaches are now modelled as MOTION PROCESSES that have the different body sites as their targets and a specific link to the surgical procedures where they take place). Reflective refinement can be done on a specific part of content, as the example above, or on a whole field of the content involved in relations to various different other fields (e.g., a new form was given to the field that represents the anatomy of the human body on an evolutionary reforming process. For example, there are concepts that should be related to a body part/anatomical site in a representation that expresses a relation either to the totality of that body part or to a smaller part of if (e.g., the concept PANCREATECTOMY represents either an excision of the totality of the pancreas or of a smaller part of it, as the pancreas head or tail). This representation was not possible on our previous approach that considered only the totality of a body part as a target concept to the necessary relationships. Our new approach (as detailed by Hahn in [HSR98]) consists of three possible concepts that can be related to, defined as such by the specific relations between them: the "body part structure", representing the totality or a part of the totality of a body part; the "body part", representing the totality; and the "body part part", representing a part of the totality of a body part (e.g., PANCREAS STRUCTURE, PANCREAS and PANCREAS PART). The concept PANCREATECTOMY is then represented by a relation to the concept PANCREAS STRUCTURE.).

3   Ontology Management Processes and Technologies

The modellers require varied and continuous support for them to be able to model effectively and efficiently execute the previously described processes above. The more automated this goal can be achieved the better. Many ontology-related development issues have as a root the observation that are domain experts with no ontology modelling expertise who do the modelling. This state of affairs has some support to being preferred over having logicians model some domain (it is what Smith et al. [SHH01] call the ontologists credo)—it should be noted that it is to be expected that (ontologically-minded) logicians model upper level ontologies to do with space, time, causality, etc. The problem then, however, is that the kind of modelling required is often of a formality and complexity that takes a lot of getting used to. In the sections that follow we describe some of the technology which we have developed to try and support the ontology development process, where the majority of the ontology modelling work is undertaken by healthcare domain experts (mostly doctors).

3.1   Modelling Editor

The ontology editor, called LinKFactory(r), is a bean-based multiple-windows environment, where there are around 30 specialized beans, which can be linked to each other both intra- and inter-window. All its beans have a drag and drop functionality, and through the bean environment, the user can build user-oriented focussing (e.g., if she clicks on a concept then one of the other beans, a full definition bean will be notified of the event, its parameters, and will display the criteria (necessary conditions) and full definitions (necessary and sufficient conditions)of the concept). There are different scenarios of process focus bean configurations ready-rolled for the user to select in a library. A partial enumeration of the beans we have developed include: link type hierarchy, link type property, concept hierarchy, concept property, concept full definition, translation, bookmark, terminology, query, and so on.

Technical Details LinKFactory(r) stores its data in a relational database (we currently use Oracle). The data is accessed using a functional API which hides the actual structure of the data (some of the API could be described as "knowledge level"). LinKFactory(r) is platform independent (Windows, Solaris, UNIX, and Linux, have all been successfully used) and database vendor independent

(Oracle, Sybase, SqlServer have all been successfully used). The application is written in Java and uses RMI. LinKFactory(r) uses Beans, where each bean has a view of the underlying data structure and can consequently display the relevant views onto the ontology that the modeller wants when performing a certain task. For more detail on the technical aspects of the implementation of LinKFactory(r), see [CMDT01].

3.2   Modeller Support and Guidance

Apart from the automated support the modellers should receive at edit-time, there are also other management issues, such as hierarchical user privileges, modelling guidance and teaching. Our ontology contains about 350 different link types sometimes of subtle semantic difference and a complex and strict interaction between the different elements (concepts, terms, links, definitions). It focuses simultaneously at the medical knowledge and at the linguistic value involved in the content, and quality and consistency of modelling are vital for the success of further inferred knowledge and natural language processing. Consequently the Link Base is of high degree of complexity, which brings difficulties to the ontologists to provide an accurate and consistent modelling of the content. Coaching and quality control management are then important and some mechanisms were developed to support them:

1. "Hierarchical user privileges" is a mechanism in the management system where elements are owned by the users that created them. The users are organized in a hierarchical structure according to their skills and experience. Elements can only be modified by its owner user, or by users at a higher level in the hierarchy. This mechanism prevents content to be changed in a circular/redundant process, prevents content modelled in a correct form to be modified to an incorrect form, and brings up mistakes and problems on the reasoning of the ontologists. It has the problem of relatively hampering the work of very talented new users.

2. "Log files review" is a mechanism of reviewing the actions performed by the users in the management system that are stored in a log file. The review is done either by the user that performed the actions or by another user, and has the purpose of revealing problems and mistakes of all kinds (attention, reasoning, spelling, knowledge) as well as providing a learning opportunity on different modelling techniques, reasoning and style. The files are distributed and checked weekly, in a way that each Ontologist reviews the work of a different Ontologist each week This allows them to get in contact with different aspects of the ontology, and it brings up diversity of point of view.

3. "Restricted action privileges" is a mechanism of the management system by which users are restricted to perform actions that imply substantial changes in the ontology (e.g., joining concepts, creating new link types). Any action can be allowed or restricted to a user according to a decision of the management of the ontology team based on the users skills and experience.

Coaching is an important activity within the ontologists group and it's done either individually, from a more experienced modeller to a new one, or with group lectures and discussions of new issues.

4   Future Work: Intelligent Automated Support

We are currently in the process of implementing a version of OntoClean to help structure the ontology with regards to more rigorous and formal metaphysical ideas. This is the first phase of a rolling development program to beef-up the automated support and modelling capabilities of the ontology technology. We also aim to support our modellers though the completion of as many inferences as is possible axiomatically. That is, we will try and maintain a collection of applicable axioms that formally describe the ontology and make these available to some support algorithm that tries and applies these axioms locally and in a not necessarily complete manner. That is, we are only supporting the user in making the modelling easier and more complete, but we are not interested, at present, with having a complete model.

4.1   OntoClean

OntoClean [GW02, WG01, GW00] is a methodology to guide the development of ontologies with fewer modelling errors. This is achieved by applying meta properties to ontology, which, when expressed of domain properties, constrain the subsumption relation between those so described domain properties. This brings more rigor to the modelling process, resulting in more "clean" ontologies, with the result that categorical errors in modelling are reduced or eliminated. This is a "good thing" per se but can also help when ontologies are attempted to be merged or integrated in some way. Examples of the metaproperties which OntoClean takes careful note of are rigidity, identity, unity, and dependence. The various permutations of having or not having such metaproperties results in a set of type, e.g., type, sortal, category, phased-sortal, etc. These types form a hierarchy and there are various enforceable constraints. For example, if we have concluded that a domain property is a sortal, then it may only subsume further sortals, no non-sortals may be subsumed by it. There are various other useful constraints, and these help to structure and constrain what is permissible a la an observance of the OntoClean methodology. We aim to implement OntoClean in LinKFactory(r), where it will provide online support for modellers, constraining and supporting what they do. One problem, already noted above as being one major problem in supporting modellers, is that they often have no modelling expertise. So, one may be wondering, how does the introduction of even more sophisticated metaphysical ideas supposed to help the average modellers, as opposed to the ontologically sophisticated. Well, the answer we give here (and we think the authors of OntoClean do seem to hint at it) is that the properties they are dealing with are general, and that actually quite simple questions can be asked of the user to ascertain whether or not certain of the metaproperties do in fact hold. So, instead of asking the user "Is this property anti-rigid?", simpler questions can be asked such as "Are there any instances of this property which necessarily must at some time not be of this type?" This question is basically an informal definition of what it means to be anti-rigid, and is perhaps still not the ideal way of acquiring such information. We think this is a valid concern, if we also accept the ontologist's credo and its implications in the real world.

4.2   Axiomatization

Axiomatization of the ontology is an important task, which will help to further specify the interpretation and meaning of the terms in it. It will also facilitate the support of the modellers through both constraining the space of valid modelling and by completing incomplete modelling. This should help to speed up the modelling as well as delivering a higher quality ontology product.

Example Axiomatization We use here the relation ("link" in our parlance) *has-theme* and its contra link *is-theme-of*. For patterns of links and concepts as shown below in Figure 1[6] we may conclude that "bronchial aspirate" is a subclass of "aspirate".

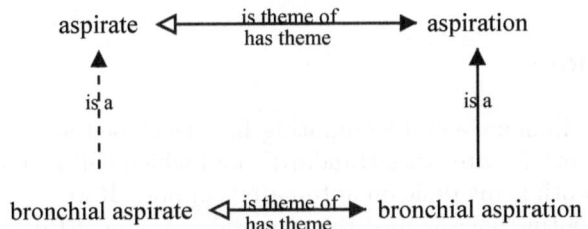

Fig. 1. An example where the inference does hold between the concepts "bronchial aspirate" and "aspirate".

We can generalize this to the axiom:

$$\forall x z (\exists y w$$
$$is - theme - of(x, y) \land is - a(y, w) \land$$
$$is - theme - of(z, w) \land has - theme(w, z))$$
$$\rightarrow is - a(x, z). \tag{1}$$

---

[6] The legend for this figure is as follows. A solid line is told information, whereas a dotted line is deduced information. An arrow means that the link is valid, whereas a circle means that the link is invalid. A filled end-of-line shape means that the top relation is to be read in the direction of it, whereas the bottom relation is to be read in the direction of the hollow end-of-line shape.

Here, based on the axiom new knowledge is inferred about the ontology, that is there should be a link between those two concepts. If instead we happened to be modelling the situation as we se below in Figure 2 then we should actually be stopped from adding a subclass relation between the concepts "supplement" and "drug used for hepatic amebiasis", as not all drugs used for hepatic amebiasis are supplements (that is, supplemental to some other drug). To make the link contra we would need to have, what we call, mutual semantic specificity on the source (domain) and target (range) of the link (relation).

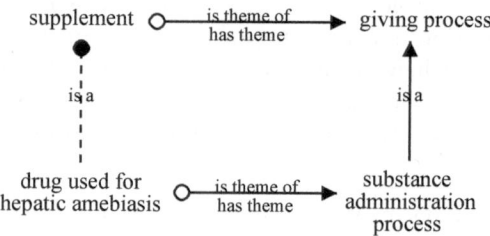

Fig. 2. An example where the inference does not hold between "drug used for hepatic amebiasis" and "supplement".

5   Conclusions

We believe that Language and Computing has developed an ontology develop-ment environment of "enterprise-standard", and which will be improved further by the current work being done on automated support. If we measure what Lan-guage and Computing have against the proposals given in [FB01] for "enterprise-standard" ontology environments, then it is our claim that we at Language and Computing go a long way to satisfying almost all of the desiderata contained therein. Such desiderata included: visualization, modularization, versioning, rea-soning transparency, multitasking (query, browsing, editing, and database like features in general, such as stability, scale), competency, and methodology. We claim that LinKFactory(r) has most of the multitasking desiderata; users can access, edit, and query, the ontology server in a safe manner (over the Internet if need-be). We also claim that LinKFactory(r) has other data-base-like desiderata, as well as mufti-user access; that is, versioning, stability, and scalability. We also claim that we measure up well to the user-interface desiderata of being highly configurable and personalizable; and, in the future, we will have much more in the way of automated support of the modellers, making them more efficient and increasing the quality of the final ontology product.

References

[CMDT01]   Werner Ceusters, Peter Martens, Christoffel Dhaen, and Boris Terzic. Linkfactory: an advanced formal ontology management system. Victoria, Canada, October 2001. K-CAP 2001.

[FB01]   Alan Flett and Mike Brown. Enterprise standard ontology environments. Seattle, USA, 2001. IJCAI. Presented at an ontology workshop at IJCAI 2001.

[GW00]   Nicola Guarino and Chris Welty. A formal ontology of properties. In R. Dieng and O. Corby, editors, *Knowledge Engineering and Knowledge Management: Methods, Models and Tools. 12th International Conference EKAW2000*, pages 97–112. Springer Verlag, 2000.

[GW02]   Nicola Gurino and Chris Welty. Evaluating ontological decisions with ontoclean. *Communications of the ACM*, 45(2):61–65, 2002.

[HSR98]   Udo Hahn, Stefan Schulz, and Martin Romacker. An ontological engineering methodology for part-whole reasoning in medicine. 1998. citeseer.nj.nec.com/hahn98ontological.html.

[SHH01]   Barry Smith, Barbara Heller, and Heinrich Herre. A unified framework for building ontological theories with application and testing in the field of clinical trials (first draft). 2001. http://www.ontology.uni-leipzig.de/.

[WG01]   Chris Welty and Nicola Gurino. Supporting ontological analysis of taxonomic relationships. *Data and Knowledge Engineering*, 39(1):51–74, 2001.

Sweetening Ontologies with DOLCE

Aldo Gangemi, Nicola Guarino, Claudio Masolo,
Alessandro Oltramari, Luc Schneider

ISTC-CNR, Rome/Padua, Italy
gangemi@ip.rm.cnr.it, {Nicola.Guarino, Alessandro.Oltramari,
Claudio.Masolo, Luc.Schneider}@ladseb.pd.cnr.it

Abstract. In this paper we introduce the *DOLCE* upper level ontology, the first module of a Foundational Ontologies Library being developed within the WonderWeb project. *DOLCE* is presented here in an intuitive way; the reader should refer to the project deliverable for a detailed axiomatization. A comparison with *WordNet's* top-level taxonomy of nouns is also provided, which shows how *DOLCE*, used in addition to the *OntoClean* methodology, helps isolating and understanding some major WordNet's semantic limitations. We suggest that such analysis could hopefully lead to an „ontologically sweetened" WordNet, meant to be conceptually more rigorous, cognitively transparent, and efficiently exploitable in several applications.

1 Introduction

In the recent years, we developed a methodology for testing the ontological adequacy of taxonomic links called OntoClean [14, 13], which was used as a tool for a first systematic analysis of WordNet's upper level taxonomy of nouns [6]. The first version of OntoClean was based on an ontology of properties (unary *universals*), characterized by means of meta-properties. We are now complementing OntoClean with an ontology of *particulars* called DOLCE (Descriptive Ontology for Linguistic and Cognitive Engineering), which is presented here in some detail.

DOLCE is the first module of a *Library of Foundational Ontologies* being developed within the WonderWeb project[1]. In contrast with „lightweight" ontologies, which focus on a minimal terminological structure (often just a taxonomy) fitting the needs of a specific community, the main purpose of foundational ontologies is to *negotiate meaning*, either for enabling effective cooperation among multiple artificial agents, or for *establishing consensus* in a mixed society where artificial agents cooperate with human beings. The WonderWeb vision is to have *a library* of such ontologies, reflecting different ontological choices. The idea is to make the rationales and alternatives underlying such choices as explicit as possible, as a result of a careful isolation of the fundamental ontological options and their formal relationships. The library would form a network of different but systematically related modules which the various Semantic Web applications can commit to, according to their ontological assumptions.

---

[1] http://wonderweb.semanticweb.org/deliverables/D17.shtml

A. Gómez-Pérez and V.R. Benjamins (Eds.): EKAW 2002, LNAI 2473, pp. 166-181, 2002.
© Springer-Verlag Berlin Heidelberg 2002

This paper is structured as follows. In the next section we introduce the basic assumptions and distinctions underlying DOLCE; then we discuss some ontological inadequacies of WordNet's taxonomy of nouns, revising and extending the analysis presented in [6]. Finally, we discuss the preliminary results of an alignment work aimed at improving WordNet's overall ontological (and cognitive) adequacy, and facilitate its effective deployment in practical applications.

2 The DOLCE Upper Ontology

According to the vision introduced above, we do *not* intend DOLCE as a candidate for a „universal" standard ontology. Rather, it is intended to act as starting point for comparing and elucidating the relationships with other future modules of the library, and also for clarifying the hidden assumptions underlying existing ontologies or linguistic resources such as WordNet.

As reflected by its acronym, DOLCE has a clear *cognitive bias*, in the sense that it aims at capturing the ontological categories underlying natural language and human commonsense. We believe that such bias is very important for the Semantic Web (especially if we recognize its intrinsic social nature [3]). We do not commit to a strictly referentialist metaphysics related to the intrinsic nature of the world: rather, the categories we introduce here are thought of as cognitive artifacts ultimately depending on human perception, cultural imprints and social conventions (a sort of „cognitive" metaphysics). We draw inspiration here from Searle's notion of „deep background" [18], which represents the set of skills, tendencies and habits shared by humans because of their peculiar biological make up, and their evolved ability to interact with their ecological niches [9]. The consequences of this approach are that our categories are at the so-called *mesoscopic* level, and they do not claim any special robustness against the state of the art in scientific knowledge: they are just *descriptive* notions [21] that assist in making *already formed* conceptualizations explicit. They do not provide therefore a *prescriptive* (or „revisionary" [21, 15]) framework to conceptualize entities. In other words, our categories describe entities in a post-hoc way, reflecting more ore less the surface structure of language and cognition.

DOLCE is an ontology of *particulars*, in the sense that its domain of discourse is restricted to them. The fundamental ontological distinction between *universals* and *particulars* can be informally understood by taking the relation of *instantiation* as a primitive: particulars are entities which have no instances[2]; universals are entities that do have instances. Properties and relations (corresponding to predicates in a logical language) are usually considered as universals. We take the ontology of universals as formally separated from that of particulars. Of course, universals *do* appear in an ontology of particulars, insofar they are used to organize and characterize them: simply, since they are not in the domain of discourse, they are not themselves subject to being organized and characterized (e.g., by means of *metaproperties*). An ontology of unary universals has been presented in [12]. In this paper, we shall occasionally use notions (e.g., rigidity) taken from such work in our meta-language.

---

[2] More exactly, we should say that they *can't* have instances. This coincides with saying that they have no instances, if we include *possibilia* (possible instances) among instances.

2.1 Enduring and Perduring Entities

DOLCE is based on a fundamental distinction between *enduring* and *perduring* entities, i.e. between what philosophers usually call *continuants* and *occurrents* [19], a distinction still strongly debated both in the philosophical literature [22] and within ontology standardization initiatives[3]. Again, we must emphasise that this distinction is motivated by our cognitive bias: we do not commit to the fact that both these kinds of entity „really exist", and we are indeed sympathetic with the recent proposal made by Peter Simons, that enduring entities can be seen as equivalence classes of perduring entities, as the result of some kind of abstraction mechanism [20].

The difference between enduring and perduring entities (which we shall also call *endurants* and *perdurants*) is related to their behavior in time. Endurants are *wholly* present (i.e., all their proper parts are present) at any time they are present. Perdurants, on the other hand, just extend in time by accumulating different temporal parts, so that, at any time they are present, they are only *partially* present, in the sense that some of their proper temporal parts (e.g., their previous or future phases) may be not present. E.g., the piece of paper you are reading now is wholly present, while some temporal parts of your reading are not present any more. Philosophers say that endurants are entities that *are in time*, while lacking however temporal parts (so to speak, all their parts flow with them in time). Perdurants, on the other hand, are entities that *happen in time*, and can have temporal parts (all their parts are fixed in time)[4].

Hence endurants and perdurants can be characterised by whether or not they can exhibit change in time. Endurants can „genuinely" change in time, in the sense that the very same endurant as a whole can have incompatible properties at different times; perdurants cannot change in this sense, since none of their parts keeps its identity in time. To see this, suppose that an endurant has a property at a time *t*, and a different, incompatible property at time *t'*: in both cases we refer to the whole object, without picking up any particular part. On the other hand, when we say that a perdurant has a property at *t*, and an incompatible property at *t'*, there are always two different parts exhibiting the two properties.

The main relation between endurants and perdurants is that of *participation*: an endurant „lives" in time by *participating* in a perdurant. For example, a person, which is an endurant, may participate in a discussion, which is a perdurant. A person's life is also a perdurant, in which a person participates throughout its all duration.

In the following, we shall take the term *occurrence* as synonym of *perdurant*. We prefer this choice to the more common *occurrent*, which we reserve for denoting a type (a *universal*), whose instances are occurrences (*particulars*).

---

[3] See for instance the extensive debate about the „3D" vs. the „4D" approach at suo.ieee.org, or the SNAP/SPAN opposition sketched at ontology.buffalo.edu/bfo.

[4] Time-snapshots of perdurants (i.e., in our time structure, perdurants whose temporal location is atomic, and which lack therefore proper temporal parts) are a limit case in this distinction. We consider them as perdurants since we assume that their temporal location is fixed (a time-snapshot at a different time would be a different time-snapshot).

2.2 DOLCE's Top Categories

The taxonomy of the most basic categories of particulars assumed in DOLCE is depicted in Figure 1. They are considered as rigid properties, according to the Onto-Clean methodology that stresses the importance of focusing on these properties first. Some examples of „leaf" categories instances are illustrated in Table 1.

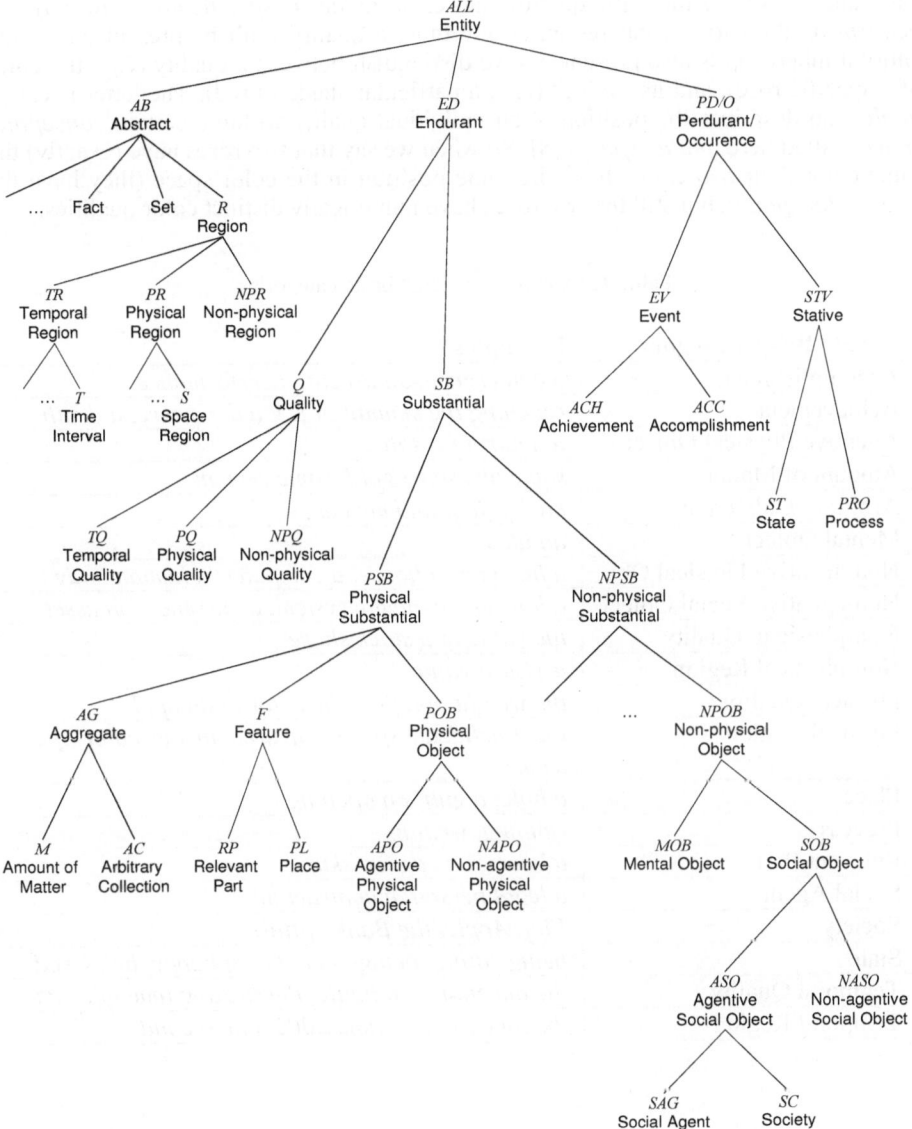

Fig. 1. Taxonomy of DOLCE basic categories.

Qualities and quality regions. Qualities can be seen as the basic entities we can perceive or measure: shapes, colors, sizes, sounds, smells, as well as masses, lengths, electrical charges… The term 'Quality' is often used as a synonymous of 'property', but this is not the case in DOLCE: qualities are particulars, properties are universals. Qualities *inhere* to entities: every entity (including qualities themselves) comes with certain qualities, which exist exactly as long as the entity exists. Within a certain ontology, we assume that these qualities belong to a finite set of *quality types* (like color, size, smell, etc.), and are characteristic for (*inhere in*) specific individuals: no two particulars can have the same quality, and each quality is *specifically constantly dependent* on the entity it inheres in: at any time, a quality can't be present unless the entity it inheres in is also present. So we distinguish between a quality (e.g., the color of a specific rose), and its „value" (e.g., a particular shade of red). The latter is called *quale*, and describes the position of an individual quality within a certain *conceptual space* (called here *quality space*) [8]. So when we say that two roses have (exactly) the same color their *two* colors have the same position in the color space (they have the same *color quale*), but still the two roses have numerically distinct color qualities.

Table 1. Examples of „leaf" basic categories.

„Leaf" Basic Category	Examples
Accomplishment	*a conference, an ascent, a performance*
Achievement	*reaching the summit of K2, a departure, a death*
Agentive Physical Object	*a natural person*
Amount of Matter	*some air, some gold, some cement*
Arbitrary Collection	*my left foot and my car*
Mental Object	*an idea*
Non-agentive Physical Obj.	*a hammer, a house, a computer, a human body*
Non-agentive Social Object	*a law, an economic system, a currency, an asset*
Non-physical Quality	*the value of a stock share*
Non-physical Region	*a 1Euro value*
Physical Quality	*the weight of a pen, the color of an apple*
Physical Region	*the Euclidean space, an area in the color spectrum*
Place	*a hole, a gulf, an opening*
Process	*running, writing*
Relevant Part	*a bump, an edge, a skin*
Social Agent	*a legal person, a contractant*
Society	*Fiat, Apple, the Bank of Italy*
State	*being sitting, being open, being happy, being red*
Temporal Quality	*the duration of a battle, the starting time of a race*
Temporal Region	*the time axis, 22 june 2002, one second*

This distinction between qualities and qualia is inspired by [10] and the so-called *trope theory* [1] (with some differences that can't be discussed here[5]). Its intuitive rationale is mainly due to the fact that natural language – in certain constructs – often seems to make a similar distinction. For instance, when we say „the color of the rose turned from red to brown in one week" or „the room's temperature is increasing" we are not speaking of a certain shade of red, or a specific thermodynamic status, but of something else that changes its properties in time while keeping its identity. This is why we assume that *qualities are endurants*.

On the other hand, when we say that „red is opposite to green" or „red is close to brown" we are not speaking of qualities, but rather of regions within quality spaces. The specific shade of red of our rose – its color quale – is therefore a point (or an atom, mereologically speaking) in the color space.

Each quality type has an associated quality space with a specific structure. For example, lengths are usually associated to a metric linear space, and colors to a topological 2D space. The structure of these spaces reflects our perceptual and cognitive bias.

In this approach, we can explain the relation existing between 'red' intended as an adjective (as in „this rose is red") and 'red' intended as a noun (as in „red is a color") (Figure 2): the rose is red because its color is located in the red region within the color space (more exactly, its color quale is a part of that region). Moreover, we can explain the difference between „this rose is red" and „the color of this rose is red" by interpreting „red" as synonymous of *red object* in the first case, and of *red color* in the latter case.

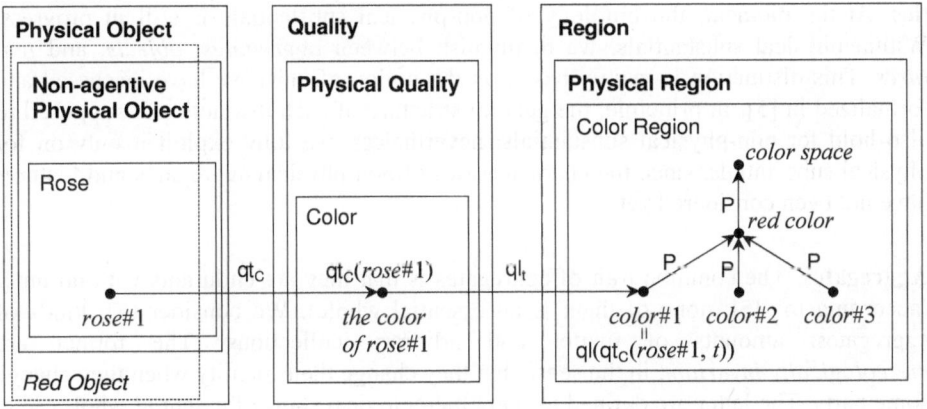

Fig. 2. Qualities and quality regions.

---

[5] An important difference is that standard trope theories explain a qualitative change in terms of a substitution of tropes (an old trope disappears and a new one is created). We assume instead that qualities are a sort of „enduring tropes".

In our ontology, space and time are considered as quality types like color, weight, etc. The spatial (temporal) individual quality of an entity is called *spatial* (*temporal*) *location*, while its quale is called *spatial* (*temporal*) *region*. For example, the spatial location of a physical object is just one of its individual qualities: it belongs to the quality type *space*, and its quale is a region in the geometric space. Similarly for the temporal location of an occurrence, whose quale is a region in the temporal space. This allows an homogeneous approach that remains neutral about the properties of the geometric/temporal space adopted (for instance, one may assume a circular time).

Concerning the inherence relation, we distinguish between *direct* and *indirect* quality inherence. So *temporal qualities* are those that directly inhere to occurrences, and *physical qualities* are those that directly inhere physical entities (physical entities, in turn, are those having a direct spatial location). Then, for example, occurrences have physical qualities only indirectly, insofar these qualities directly inhere to their participants.

Substantials. Roughly, we see substantials as stable aggregates of qualities: they are endurants that can have qualities, but are not themselves qualities. Most of such aggregations are cognitive artifacts, resulting from the tendency humans have to partition their environment around „islands of stability" that have enough permanence and features to be used as pervading frameworks of reference [21]. The term „substantial" is inspired to the Aristotelian notion of *substance*, but is indeed more general than the latter, which is closer to our notion of *object* (see below).

Substantials form the main branch of our taxonomy. We distinguish between *physical* and *non-physical substantials*, according to whether they have direct spatial qualities. At the moment, the ontology of non-physical substantials is still in progress. Within physical substantials, we distinguish between *aggregates*, *objects*, and *features*. This distinction is mainly based on the notion of unity we have discussed and formalized in [5]. In principle, the general structure of such distinction is supposed to also hold for non-physical substantials: nevertheless, we fully exploit it only on for physical substantials, since the characteristics of non-physical aggregates and features have not been considered yet.

Aggregates. The common trait of aggregates is that they are endurants with no unity (according to **[5]**, none of them is an essential whole). We consider two kinds of aggregates: amounts of matter and arbitrary collections. The former are *mereologically invariant*, in the sense that they change their identity when they change some parts. The latter are defined as mere mereological sums of essential wholes (e.g. objects, see below) which are not themselves essential wholes (like the sum of a person's nose and a computer keyboard). They are essentially mereologically pseudo-invariant, in the sense that they change their identity when a member[6] is changed, while a change in the non essential parts of a member is allowed. We may have called these arbitrary collections 'groups', or perhaps 'sets'; but we prefer to use 'set' for abstract entities, and 'group' for something having an intrinsic unity.

---

[6] We assume here that a member is a special part of a collection, see [5].

Objects. The main characteristic of objects is that they are endurants with unity. They have no *common* unity criterion, however, as different subtypes of objects may have different unity criteria. Differently from aggregates, (most) objects are admitted to change some of their parts while keeping their identity: they can have therefore *temporary parts*. Often objects (indeed, all endurants) are considered as ontologically independent from occurrences (discussed below). However, if we admit that every object has a life, it is hard to exclude a mutual specific constant dependence between the two. Nevertheless, we may still use the notion of dependence to (weakly) characterize objects as being not specifically constantly dependent *on other objects*.

Features. Typical examples of features are „parasitic entities" such as holes, bumps, surfaces, or stains, which are (in most cases) specifically constantly dependent on physical objects[7] (their hosts). All features are essential wholes, but no common unity criterion may exist for all of them. However, typical features have a topological unity, as they are singular entities. Features may be *relevant parts* of their host, like a bump or an edge, or *places* like a hole in a piece of cheese, the underneath of a table, the front of a house, which are not parts of their host. We include within features also boundaries, which may be conceptualized in various ways, and are not discussed here.

It may be interesting to note that we do not consider body parts like heads or hands as features: the reason is that we assume that a hand can be detached from its host (differently from a hole or a bump), and we assume that in this case it retains its identity. Should we reject this assumption, then body parts would be features (relevant parts).

Non-physical substantials and the agentive/non-agentive distinction. Physical objects that have *intentionality* (the capability of heading for/dealing with objects or states of the world, see [18]) are called *Agentive*, those which do not are called *Non-agentive*. In general, the former are *constituted* by the latter: human persons are constituted by organisms, robots are constituted by machinaries, and so on (constitution is taken here as a primitive relation, which is axiomatized in [17]). Among non-agentive physical objects we have *ordinary objects* like houses, organs, pieces of wood, etc. *Non-physical Objects* are divided into *Mental* and *Social* according to whether they are „produced" by a single agent or recognized by a community of agents. In the first case we say that *mental objects* (like an idea) are specifically dependent on *agentive physical objects*, while in the second case we need to further distinguish between *Agentive* and *Non-agentive social objects*. Examples of the former category are *social agents* like the president of United States or a top manager of Microsoft, conceived as „reified roles" depending on agentive physical objects (certain persons) only in a *generic* way, as the role may survive a replacement of the person. Social agents are *not* constituted by agentive physical objects (although they depend on them), while they can constitute *societies*, like the CNR, Microsoft, etc. *Non-Agentive Social Objects* like laws, shares, peace treaties ecc. are generically

---

[7] In some cases, features are just *generically* dependent on their host, in the sense that *some* (suitable) object must exist whenever the feature exists: think for instance of a whirlpool: if it is a feature, what is its host?

dependent on societies, which are therefore the „conditio sine qua non" of their ontological status.

Occurrences. Occurrences comprise what are variously called events, processes, phenomena, activities and states. They can have temporal parts or spatial parts. For instance, the first movement of (the execution of) a symphony is a temporal part of it. On the other side, the play performed by the left side of the orchestra is a spatial part. In both cases, these parts are occurrences themselves. We assume that objects can't be parts of occurrences, but rather they *participate* in them.

An ontology of occurrences has to take into account two basic aspects: *change* and *homeomericity.*

The first one concerns a naive view of our everyday experience of the world: for instance, if we see a ship standing still on the sea for an hour, we'll say that «the ship hasn't changed its position for an hour»; on the other side, if during the same interval we see the ship navigating from the harbor to an oil platform, we'll say «the ship has been moving for an hour». In the latter example, the detection of a movement implies that we are talking about a *dynamic occurrence*, while in the former we are speaking about a *stationary* occurrence.

The second aspect has been extensively discussed in [2]: intuitively, we can say that an occurrence is homeomeric if and only if all its temporal parts can be described *in the same way* used for the whole occurrence. Every temporal part of „John sitting here" for an hour is still a „sitting here of John". But if we consider "the complete ascent of Everest by Messner", there are no parts of such event which constitute a complete ascent of Everest by Messner. In linguistic as well as in philosophical terminology, the notion of the „*homeomericity*" of an occurrence is often introduced with respect to a property characteristic of (or *exemplified by*) the occurrent itself. If such property holds for all the temporal parts of the occurrence, then the occurrence is homeomeric. In our axiomatization, this presupposes a finite list of occurrence-types which have to be "declared" in advance. An occurrence-type is *stative* or *eventive* according to whether or not it holds of the mereological sum of two of its instances. For instance, a *sitting* occurrence is stative since the sum of two sittings is still a sitting occurrence. Within stative occurrences, we distinguish between *states* and *processes* according to whether the corresponding types hold of every part of their instances: so *sitting* is a state, while *running* is a process, since there may be (very short) temporal parts of a running that are not themselves runnings.

Finally, eventive occurrences (*events*) are called *achievements* if they are atomic, otherwise they are *accomplishments.*

3   Ontological Problems in WordNet

Let us see now how the ontology we introduced, together with the general principles of the OntoClean methodology, can be of help in analyzing the ontological structure of WordNet[8]. We believe that such analysis is important, as the number of applications

---

[8] We refer here to WordNet 1.6 (see [6] for a partial overview on the top-level structure)

where WordNet is being used more as an ontology than just as a lexical resource seems to be growing more and more. To be used as an ontology, however, some of WordNet's lexical links need to be re-interpreted as semantic links, connecting together intended meaning of words, according to our own conceptualizations. One of such links is the hyponym/hypernym relation, which corresponds in many cases to the usual subsumption (or IS_A) relation between concepts. An early attempt at exploring the semantic and ontological problems lying behind this correspondence is described in [11]. Let us extend now such discussion in the light of the DOLCE ontology.

Confusion between concepts and individuals. The first critical problem we found in WordNet was the confusion between concepts and individuals. For instance, if we look at the hyponyms of the „unique beginner" Event, we'll find the synset Fall - an individual - whose gloss is „the lapse of mankind into sinfulness because of the sin of Adam and Eve", together with conceptual hyponyms such as Social_Event, and Miracle.[9] Under Territorial_Dominion we find Macao and Palestine together with Trust_Territory. The latter synset, defined as "a dependent country, administered by a country under the supervision of United Nations", denotes a general kind of country, rather than a specific country as those preceding it. If we go deeper in the taxonomy, we find many other examples of this sort. For instance, the hyponyms of Composer are a mixture of concepts and instances: there are classes corresponding to different special fields, such as Contrapuntist, or Songwriter, and examples of famous musicians of the past, such as Bach, and Beethoven.

Under Martial_Art, whose top hypernym is Act, we find Karate, and Kung Fu, but these synsets do not stand for concepts, they represent individuals, namely particular examples of martial arts.

If we look through Organization, under the branch whose root is Group, we find conceptual hyponyms such as Company, Alliance, Federation, Committee, together with instances like Irish_Republican_Army, Red Cross, and so on.

We face here a general problem: the concept/individual confusion is nothing but the product of an „expressivity lack". In fact, if there was an INSTANCE-OF relation, we could distinguish between a concept-to-concept relation (subsumption) and an individual-to-concept one (instantiation).

Confusion between object-level and meta-level: the case of Abstraction. The synset Abstraction_1 seems to include both object-level concepts, such as Set, Time, and Space, and meta-level concepts such as Attribute and Relation. From the corresponding gloss, an abstraction „is a general concept formed by extracting common features from specific examples". An abstraction seems therefore intended as a psychological process of generalization, in accordance to Locke's position ([16], p.211). This meaning seems to fit the latter group of terms (Attribute, Relation, and possibly some hyponyms of Quantity), but not the former. Moreover, it is quite natural to consider attributes and relations as meta-level concepts, while set, time, and space, seem to belong to the object domain.

---

[9] In the text body, we usually do not report all the synonyms of a synset (or their numeration), but only the most meaningful ones.

OntoClean constraints violations. A core aspect of OntoClean is the analysis of subsumption constraints induced by the identity, rigidity, and unity meta-properties. In our analysis, we only found rigidity violations. We suspect that there are two reasons why we didn't observe other kinds of violation: on one hand, we limited our analysis to the consistency of lower levels against the upper level, where the criteria of identity and unity are very general; on the other hand, WordNet tends, notoriously, to multiply senses, so the chances of conflict are relatively limited.

The most common violation we have registered is bound to the distinction between roles and types. A role cannot subsume a type. Let's see an important clarifying example.

In its first sense, Person (which we consider as a type) is subsumed by two different concepts, Organism and Causal_Agent. Organism can be conceived as a type, while Causal_Agent as a formal role. The first subsumption relationship is correct, while the second one shows a rigidity violation. We propose therefore to drop it.

Someone could argue that every person is necessarily a causal agent, since 'agentivity' (capability of performing actions) is an essential property of persons. Causal_Agent should therefore be intended as a synonym of 'intentional agent', and considered as rigid. But, in this case, it would have only hyponyms denoting things that are (essentially) causal agents, including animals, spiritual beings, the personified Fate, and so on.

Unfortunately, this is not what happens in WordNet: Agent, one of Causal_Agent hyponyms, is defined as: "an active and efficient cause; capable of producing a certain effect; (the research uncovered new disease agents)". Causal_Agent subsumes roles such as Germicide, Vasoconstrictor, Antifungal. Instances of these concepts are not causal agents essentially. This means that considering Causal_Agent as rigid would introduce further inconsistencies.

These considerations allow us to add a pragmatic guideline to our methodology: when deciding about the formal meta-property to attach to a certain concept, it is useful to look at all its children.

Missing polysemy detection. WordNet is said to recognize most of the conventional senses of a word (obviously not all the possible contextual senses[10]). Nonetheless, there are cases where relevant polysemy has not been detected. Such a case emerges in two modalities: the first is multiple hyperonymy, the second is sense gap. Here we show an example of the first.

Multiple hyperonymy is not widespread in WordNet nouns (about 900 synsets) and it is often used appropriately, as in Surgical_Knife, which has two hyperonyms: Surgical_Instrument and Knife_1. In this case, Surgical_Instrument is a role, then there is no conflict in specializing from Knife_1 (which is a type) to Surgical_Knife (which is a role). But there are cases of multiple and incompatible identity criteria, as in Law, which has the two hyperonyms Legal_Document and Rule. According to DOLCE, we consider Legal_Document as subsumed by Non-Agentive Physical Object, and Rule as subsumed by Non-Agentive Social Object. So the two categories are disjoint. Con-

---

[10] By the way, contextual polysemy does not usually affect the category of the sense of a word, but its so-called *connotation*.

sequently, this multiple hyperonymy generates a logical incoherence, which could not be detected without an explicitly axiomatized upper-level.

Moreover, this is a case of *systematic polysemy*, since a legal document is the physical support for a law. The relation axioms in DOLCE help detecting systematic polysemy, which is a major source for building domain *core* ontologies [7].

Heterogeneous levels of generality. Going down the lower layers of WordNet's top level, we register a certain 'heterogeneity' in their intuitive level of generality. For example, among the hyponyms of Entity there are types such as Physical_Object, and roles such as Subject. The latter is defined as „something (a person or object or scene) selected by an artist or photographer for graphic representation", and has no hyponyms (indeed, almost any entity can be an instance of Subject, but none is necessarily a subject)[11].

For Animal (subsumed by Life_Form) this heterogeneity becomes clearer. Together with classes such as Chordate, Larva, Fictional_Animal, etc., we find out more specific concepts, such as Work_Animal, Domestic_Animal, Mate_3, Captive, Prey, etc. We are induced to consider the formers as types, while the latters as roles.

Although problematic on the side of ontological distinctions among event-classes, the hyponyms of Phenomenon_1 represent another meaningful example of heterogeneity. At the same taxonomic level there are „reasonably" general synsets like Natural_Phenomenon and Process together with a specific concept like Consequence, which could be modeled as anti-rigid (every event can be a consequence of the occurring of a previous event, but we could assume that this is not the essential characteristic of the event itself).

In short, intuitively some synsets sound too specific when compared to their siblings. Look at them from the formal point of view we are developing, we can pinpoint their "different generality" by means of the distinction between types and roles.

4 Mapping WordNet into DOLCE

Let us consider now the results of integrating the WordNet top concepts into our upper level. According to the OntoClean methodology, we have concentrated first on the so-called *backbone taxonomy*, which only includes the rigid properties. Formal and material roles have been therefore excluded from this preliminary work.

Comparing WordNet's unique beginners with our ontological categories, it becomes evident that some notions are very heterogeneous: for example, Entity looks like a "catch-all" class containing concepts hardly classifiable elsewhere, like Anticipation, Imaginary_Place, Inessential, etc. Such synsets have only a few children and these have been already excluded in our analysis.

Some examples of our merging work are sketched in Table 2. Some problems encountered for each category are discussed below.

---

[11] We can draw similar observations for relation_1 and set_5 with respect to abstraction_1, etc.

Table 2. Mapping WordNet into DOLCE (some examples).

Aggregate	**Quality**
Amount of matter	position$place
body_substance	time_interval$interval
chemical_element	chromatic_color
mixture	…
compound$chemical_compound	**Occurrence**
mass_5	**State**
fluid_1	condition$status
Arbitrary collection	cognitive_state
…	existence
Physical Object	death_4
Non-agentive	degree
body_of_water$water	medium_4
landdry_landearth$…	relationship_1
body$organic_structure	relationship_2
artifact$artefact*	conflict
biological_group	…
kingdom	**Process**
collection	decrement_2
Body	increment
blackbody$full_radiator	shaping
body_5	activity_1
universe$existence$nature$creation	chelation
…	execution
Agentive	activity_1
life_form$organism$being$…	…
citizenry	**Accomplishment**
sainthood	accomplishment$achievement
ethnic group	…
Social Object	**Abstract**
Non-agentive	**Region**
rule$prescript	space_1
law	time_1
…	time_interval$interval
circuit_5	chromatic_color
Agentive	…
social_group	statement_1
…	proposition
Feature	…
Relevant Part	symbol
edge_3	set_5
skin_4	…
paring$parings	
…	
Place	
opening_3	
excavation$hole_in_the_ground	

4.1 Aggregates, Objects, and Features

Entity is a very confused synset. A lot of its hyponyms have to be "rejected": in fact there are roles (Causal_Agent, Subject_4), unclear synsets (Location[12]) and so on. This Unique Beginner maps partly to our Aggregate and partly to our Object category. Some hyponyms of Physical_Object are mapped to our top concept Feature.

By removing roles like Arrangement and Straggle, Group$grouping appears to include Agentive Social Object (social group, ethnic group), Non-agentive Social Object (circuit), Agentive Physical Object (citizenry) and Non-agentive Physical Object (biological group, kingdom; collection).

Possession_1 is a role, and it includes both roles and types. In our opinion, the synsets marked as types (Asset, Liability, etc.) should be moved towards lower levels of the ontology, since their meanings seem to deal more with a specific domain - the economic one - than with a set of general concepts (except some concepts that can be mapped to Mental Object, such as Own_Right). This means that the remainder branch has also to be eliminated from the top level, because of its overall anti-rigidity (the peculiarity of roles).

4.2 Abstracts and Qualities

ABSTRACTION_1 is the most heterogeneous unique beginner: it contains abstracts such as Set_5, quality regions such as Chromatic_Color, qualities (mostly from the synset Attribute) and a hybrid concept (Relation_1) that contains social objects, concrete entities (as Substance_4[13]), and even meta-level categories. Each child synset has been mapped appropriately.

Psychological_feature contains both mental objects (Cognition[14]) and events (Feeling_1). We consider Motivation as a material role, so to be added to lower levels of the taxonomy of mental objects.

The classification of qualities deals mainly with adjectives. This paper focuses on the WordNet database of nouns; nevertheless our treatment of qualities foreshadows a semantic organization of the database of adjectives too, which is a current desideratum in the WordNet community (see [4], p. 66).

4.3 Occurences

Event_1, Phenomenon_1, State_1 and Act_1 are the Unique Beginners of those branches of WordNet denoting occurrences. In particular, the hyponyms of State_1 seem to fit well with our state category, as the children of Process (a subordinate of Phenomenon). For the time being, we restrict the mapping of our accomplishment category to the homonymous synset of WordNet. Event_1 is too heterogeneous to be

---

[12] Referring to Location, we find roles (There, Here, Home, Base, Whereabouts), instances (Earth), and geometric concepts like Line, Point, etc.).

[13] „The stuff of which an object consists".

[14] „The psychological result of perception, and learning and reasoning".

clearly partitioned in terms of our approach: to a great extent, however, its hyponyms could be added to lower levels of the taxonomy of occurrences.

5   Conclusions

We are confident that foundational ontologies will eventually improve communication among agents in most cases of information exchange: information retrieval and extraction, semantic web services, software requirement analysis and unified modeling process, control knowledge, etc. In fact, foundational ontologies can act as a *reference* for agents to commit to certain theories, as a set of formal *guidelines* for domain modeling, and as a *tool* for making heterogeneous ontologies interoperate or merge. According to the needs, an upper level ontology can be used either in a light version, for computationally intensive applications, or as an off-the-shelf fully axiomatized theory, to be consulted as a reference source for more sporadic meaning negotiation purposes. That is why we intended DOLCE to be as detailed and rigorous as possible, and yet we plan to release a light-weight version.

In the light of this vision, we have started using DOLCE (or one of its preliminary versions) in several projects, either as a tool or a set of guidelines, with substantial results in the creation of well-founded and useful ontologies (by the way, there is still no benchmark or testbed for ontology quality, since there is small agreement on the criteria to adopt, and we are suggesting some of them …).

The WordNet experiment is one of the research applications of DOLCE, already presented in several contexts, which seems promising in bridging one of the multidisciplinary gaps in ontological engineering, between the domain of lexical technologies, and that of conceptual modelling.

6   Acknowledgements

We would like to thank Stefano Borgo for the fruitful discussions and comments on the earlier version of this paper. This work was jointly supported by the Eureka Project IKF (E!2235, Information and Knowledge Fusion), the IST Project 2001-33052 *WonderWeb* (Ontology Infrastructure for the Semantic Web) and the National project TICCA (Cognitive Technologies for Communication and Cooperation with Artificial Agents).

References

1.   Campbell, K.: Abstract Particulars. Basil Blackwell, Oxford. (1990)
2.   Casati, R. and Varzi, A. (eds.): Events. Dartmouth, Aldershots, USA (1996)
3.   Castelfranchi, C.: Information Agents: The Social Nature of Information and the Role for Trust. In: M. Klusch and F. Zambonelli (eds.), Cooperative Information Agents V, 5th International Workshop, CIA 2001. Springer, Modena, Italy (2001) 208-210

4.   Fellbaum, C. (ed.) WordNet - An Electronic Lexical Database. MIT Press (1998)

5.   Gangemi, A., Guarino, N., Masolo, C., and Oltramari, A.: Understanding top-level onto-logical distinctions. In Proceedings of IJCAI-01 Workshop on Ontologies and Information Sharing. Seattle, USA, AAAI Press (2001) 26-33

6.   Gangemi, A., Guarino, N., and Oltramari, A.: Conceptual Analysis of Lexical Taxono-mies: The Case of WordNet Top-Level. In: C. Welty and S. Barry (eds.), Formal Ontology in Information Systems. Proceedings of FOIS2001. ACM Press (2001) 285-296

7.   Gangemi, A., Pisanelli, D. M., and Steve, G.: Understanding Systematic Conceptual Structures in Polysemous Medical Terms. In Proceedings of AMIA Annual Symposium (2000)

8.   Gärdenfors, P.: Conceptual Spaces: the Geometry of Thought. MIT Press, Cambridge, Massachussetts (2000)

9.   Gibson, J. J.: The Theory of Affordances. In: R. E. Shaw and J. Bransford (eds.), Perceiv-ing, Acting and Knowing. LEA, Hillsdale (1977)

10. Goodman, N.: The Structure of Appearance. Harvard University Press, Cambridge MA. (1951)

11. Guarino, N.: Some Ontological Principles for Designing Upper Level Lexical Resources. In: A. Rubio, N. Gallardo, R. Castro and A. Tejada (eds.), Proceedings of First Interna-tional Conference on Language Resources and Evaluation. ELRA - European Language Resources Association, Granada, Spain (1998) 527-534

12. Guarino, N. and Welty, C.: A Formal Ontology of Properties. In: R. Dieng and O. Corby (eds.), Knowledge Engineering and Knowledge Management: Methods, Models and Tools. 12th International Conference, EKAW2000. Springer Verlag, France (2000) 97-112

13. Guarino, N. and Welty, C.: Evaluating Ontological Decisions with OntoClean. Communi-cations of the ACM, **45**(2) (2002) 61-65

14. Guarino, N. and Welty, C.: Identity and subsumption. In: R. Green, C. Bean and S. Myaeng (eds.), The Semantics of Relationships: an Interdisciplinary Perspective. Kluwer (in press) (2002)

15. Loux, M. J.: Metaphysics, a Contemporary Introduction. Routledge (1998)

16. Lowe, E. J.: The possibility of metaphysics. Clarendon Press, Oxford (1998)

17. Masolo, C., Gangemi, A., Guarino, N., Oltramari, A., and Schneider, L.: WonderWeb Deliverable D17: The WonderWeb Library of Foundational Ontologies. (2002)

18. Searle, J.: Intentionality. Cambridge University Press, Cambridge (1983)

19. Simons, P.: Parts: a Study in Ontology. Clarendon Press, Oxford (1987)

20. Simons, P.: How to Exist at a Time When You Have No Temporal Parts. The Monist, **83**(3) (2000) 419-436

21. Strawson, P. F.: Individuals. An Essay in Descriptive Metaphysics. Routledge, London and New York (1959)

22. Varzi: Foreword to the special issue on temporal parts. The Monist, **83**(3) (2000)

Turning Lead into Gold?
Feeding a Formal Knowledge Base with
Informal Conceptual Knowledge

Udo Hahn[1] and Stefan Schulz[2]

[1] Text Knowledge Engineering Lab
Universität Freiburg, Werthmannplatz 1, D-79085 Freiburg
[2] Abteilung Medizinische Informatik
Universitätsklinikum Freiburg, Stefan-Meier-Str. 26, D-79104 Freiburg

Abstract. We describe an ontology engineering methodology by which conceptual knowledge is extracted from an informal medical thesaurus (UMLS) and
automatically converted into a formal description logics system. Our approach
consists of four steps: concept definitions are automatically generated from the
UMLS source, integrity checking of taxonomic and partonomic hierarchies is
performed by the terminological classifier, cycles and inconsistencies are eliminated, and incremental refinement of the evolving knowledge base is performed
by a domain expert. We report on experiments with a knowledge base composed
of 164,000 concepts and 76,000 relations.

1   Introduction

Unlike many other disciplines, medicine has a long standing tradition in assembling
and structuring its knowledge, e.g, disease taxonomies, medical procedures, anatomical terms, etc., in a wide variety of medical terminologies, thesauri and classification
systems. These efforts are typically restricted to the provision of broader and narrower terms, related terms or (quasi-)synonymous terms. This is most evident in the
UMLS, the *Unified Medical Language System* [15, 14], an umbrella system which
covers more than 60 medical thesauri and classifications (e.g., MeSH, ICD, SNOMED,
Digital Anatomist). Two components of the UMLS are of special interest for knowledge
engineering, *viz.*

1. The **UMLS SN** (Semantic Network) forms the upper ontology and consists of 134
   semantic types linked by 54 types of semantic relations, which makes a total of
   7,473 edges,
2. The **UMLS Metathesaurus** contains 776,940 concepts in its 2002 version, each of
   them being assigned to one or more types of the UMLS SN. These concepts are
   tightly linked by the semantic relations given by the UMLS SN. There is a total of
   10,147,419 semantic links between Metathesaurus concepts, most of them inherited
   from the sources, some added by the UMLS developers. The vast majority of these
   links introduce thesaurus-like broader/narrower relationships.

A. Gómez-Pérez and V.R. Benjamins (Eds.): EKAW 2002, LNAI 2473, pp. 182–196, 2002.
© Springer-Verlag Berlin Heidelberg 2002

Both, the UMLS SN and the Metathesaurus, form a huge semantic network. Its semantics is shallow and entirely intuitive, which is due to the fact that their usage was primarily intended for humans as a backbone for various forms of health-related knowledge management. Given the size, the evolutionary diversity and inherent heterogeneity of the UMLS, there is no surprise that the lack of a formal semantic foundation leads to inconsistencies, circular definitions, etc. [2]. This may not cause utterly severe problems when humans are in the loop and its use is limited to disease or procedure encoding, accountancy or document retrieval tasks. However, anticipating its use for more knowledge-intensive applications such as natural language understanding of medical narratives [7] those shortcomings might lead to an impasse.

As a consequence, formal models for dealing with medical knowledge have been proposed, using representation mechanisms based on conceptual graphs, semantic networks or description logics [3, 13, 19, 29, 5]. Not surprisingly, there is a price to be paid for more expressiveness and formal rigor, *viz.* increasing modeling efforts and, hence, increasing maintenance costs [17]. Operational systems making full use of this rigid approach, especially those which employ high-end knowledge representation languages, are usually restricted to rather small subdomains. The most comprehensive of these sources we know of is the GRAIL-encoded GALEN knowledge base which covers up to 9,800 concepts [19]. The limited coverage then hampers their routine usage, an issue which is always highly rewarded in the medical informatics community.

The knowledge bases developed within the framework of the above-mentioned terminological systems have almost all been designed from scratch – without making systematic use of the large body of knowledge contained in those medical terminologies. An intriguing approach would be to join the massive *coverage* offered by informal medical terminologies with the high level of *expressiveness* and *reasoning capabilities* supported by rigid knowledge representation systems in order to develop formally solid medical knowledge bases on a larger scale. In the paper, we describe such a knowledge engineering methodology. The resulting medical ontology will form the domain knowledge backbone of MEDSYNDIKATE, a system for the automatic acquisition of factual and evaluative knowledge from medical finding reports [7, 6].

2   Reasoning Along Part-Whole Hierarchies

Medical ontologies are typically organized around taxonomic (*is-a* relation) and partonomic (*part-of* relation) knowledge. Hence, medical knowledge representation efforts have to take account of both hierarchy types and the reasoning patterns they imply. Partonomic knowledge has been an issue within diverse areas ranging from philosophy (mereology), data modeling for database systems and object-oriented programming, to knowledge representation proper in the field of artificial intelligence. Major strands of this work are discussed by Artale et al. [1] under the heading of object-centered representation approaches. This also includes the description logic (DL) paradigm to which we subscribe in our work, too.

From our application domain, the need arises to have formally solid inference mechanisms for taxonomic (generalization hierarchies), as well as partonomic reasoning (part-whole hierarchies) available within a uniform representation model. We also require an inference engine which performs this style of advanced reasoning on large data sets ($\gg$ 10,000 items). Hence, we consider KL-ONE-type descriptions logics [31], at the formal representation level, and LOOM's classification-based inference machine [11, 12], at the system level, the most convenient match of our requirements and the current state of the art in terminological reasoning.

Unlike generalization-based reasoning in concept taxonomies, no fully conclusive mechanism exists up to now for reasoning along part-whole hierarchies. In the description logics community several language extensions have been proposed which provide special constructors for part-whole reasoning [19, 10]. This seems a reasonable way to proceed as long as the transitivity property of a relation can be assumed, in general. In the medical [8] as well as commonsense domains [4, 30], however, various exceptions exist such that the transitivity of *part-of* relations cannot be granted, in general. Hence, both the expression of regular transitive use, as well as exception handling for nontransitive *part-of* relations have to be taken into consideration. Even a more pressing issue is the phenomenon of the propagation of properties across part-of hierarchies, often referred to as 'inheritance across transitive roles' (e.g., *inflammation-of* ∘ *part-of* → *inflammation-of*) [18]. Especially with biomedical knowledge this reasoning pattern cannot be generalized.

Motivated by previous informal approaches [22, 24], we formalized a model of partonomic reasoning [8] that meets the above requirements and also does not exceed the expressiveness of the well-understood, parsimonious concept language $\mathcal{ALC}$[31].[1] Our proposal is centered around a particular data structure for partonomic reasoning, so-called *SEP triplets* (cf. Figure 1). They define a characteristic pattern of *is-a* hierarchies which support the emulation of inferences typical of transitive *part-of* relations. In this formalism, the relation *anatomical-part-of* describes the partitive relation between physical parts of an organism.

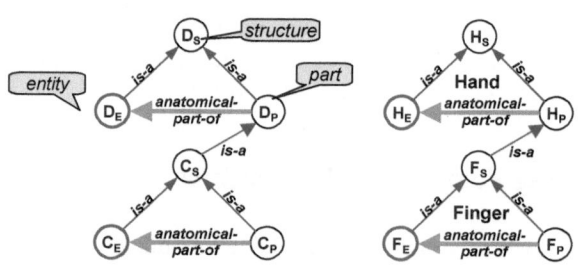

Fig. 1. SEP Triplets: Partitive Relations within Taxonomies

A triplet consists, first of all, of a composite 'structure' concept, the so-called **S-node** (e.g., *Hand-Structure*, H_S). Each *Structure* concept subsumes directly an anatomical *Entity* concept, on the one hand, and a common subsumer of anything that is a part

---

[1] $\mathcal{ALC}$ allows for the construction of hierarchies of concepts and relations, where $\sqsubseteq$ denotes subsumption and $\doteq$ definitional equivalence. Existential ($\exists$) and universal ($\forall$) quantification, negation ($\neg$), disjunction ($\sqcap$) and conjunction ($\sqcup$) are supported. Role filler constraints (e.g., typing by C) are linked to the relation name R by a dot, $\exists R.C$.

of that entity concept, on the other hand. These two concepts are called **E-node** and **P-node**, e.g., *Hand* (H_E) and *Hand-Part* (H_P), respectively.

Whereas E-nodes denote the anatomical concepts proper to be modelled in our domain, S-nodes and P-nodes constitute representational artifacts required for the formal reconstruction of systematic patterns of partonomic reasoning. More precisely, a P-node is the common subsumer of those concepts that have their role *anatomical-part-of* filled by the corresponding E-node concept, as an existential condition. For example, *Hand-Part* subsumes those concepts all instances of which have a *Hand* as a necessary whole. As an additional constraint, E-nodes and P-nodes can be modelled as mutually disjoint. This is a useful assumption for most concepts standing for singleton objects, where parts and wholes cannot be of the same type (a red blood cell cannot be part of yet another red blood cell). On the contrary, masses and collections can have parts and wholes of the same type, e.g., a tissue can be part of another tissue. A reconstruction of some basic anatomical relations in terms of SEP triplets is illustrated in Figure 2.

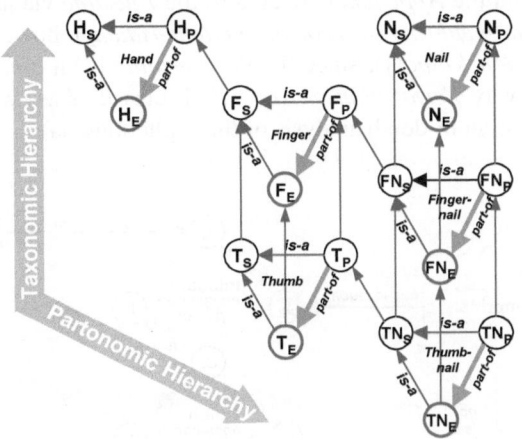

Fig. 2. SEP Triplet Model of a Partonomic Hierarchy

The reconstruction of the relation *anatomical-part-of* by taxonomic reasoning proceeds as follows. Let us assume that C_E and D_E denote E-nodes, C_S and D_S denote the S-nodes that subsume C_E and D_E, respectively, and C_P and D_P denote the P-nodes related to C_E and D_E, respectively, via the role *anatomical-part-of* (cf. Figure 1). These conventions can be captured by the following terminological expressions:

$$C_E \sqsubseteq C_S \sqsubseteq D_P \sqsubseteq D_S \qquad (1)$$

$$D_E \sqsubseteq D_S \qquad (2)$$

The P-node is defined as follows (here with the disjointness constraint between D_E and D_P, i.e., no instance of D can be *anatomical-part-of* any other instance of D):

$$D_P \doteq D_S \sqcap \neg D_E \sqcap \exists anatomical\text{-}part\text{-}of.D_E \qquad (3)$$

Since C_E is subsumed by D_P (according to (1)), we infer that the relation *anatomical-part-of* holds between C_E and D_E, too:

$$C_E \sqsubseteq \exists anatomical\text{-}part\text{-}of.D_E \tag{4}$$

An extension of this encoding scheme which allows additional reasoning about *has-part* in a similar way, is proposed in [26], though it has not been considered in the knowledge base described in this paper.

The encoding of concept hierarchies in terms of SEP triplets allows the knowledge engineer to switch the transitivity property of part-whole relations off and on, dependent on whether the E-node or the S-node, respectively, is addressed as the target concept for a conceptual relation. In the first case, the propagation of roles across part-whole hierarchies is disabled, in the second case it is enabled. As an example (cf. Figure 3), *Enteritis* is defined as *has-location Intestine$_E$*. The range of the relation *has-location* is restricted to the E-node of *Intestine*. This precludes, e.g., the classification of *Appendicitis* as *Enteritis* though the *Appendix* is related to the *Intestine* via an *anatomical-part-of* relation. *Glomerulonephritis* (*has-location Glomerulum$_S$*), however, is classified as *Nephritis* (*has-location Kidney$_S$*), since the *Glomerulum* is an *anatomical-part-of* the *Kidney*. In the same way, *Perforation-of-Appendix* is classified as *Intestinal-Perforation* (cf. Hahn et al. [8] for an in-depth analysis of these phenomena).

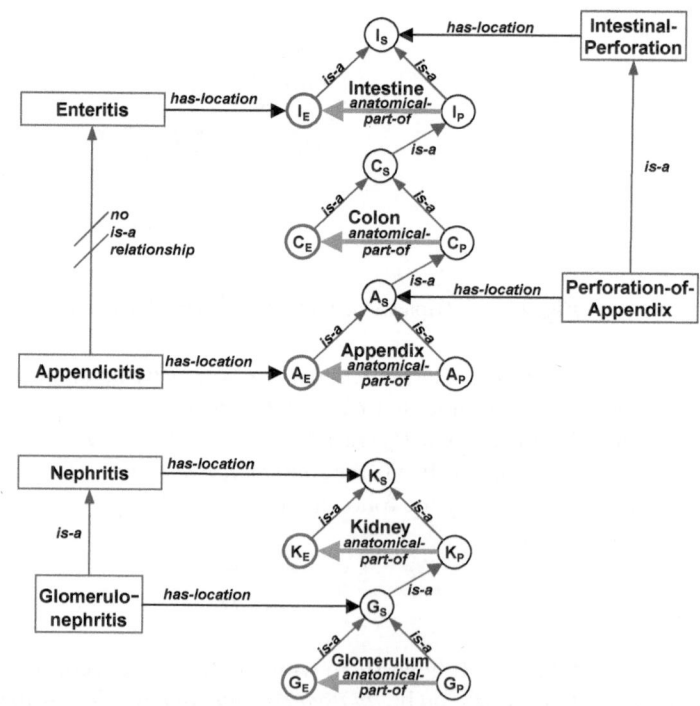

Fig. 3. Enabling/Disabling Transitivity in a SEP-Encoded Partonomy

3   Knowledge Import and Refinement

Our goal is to extract conceptual knowledge from two major subdomains of the UMLS, *viz.* anatomy and pathology, in order to construct a formally sound knowledge base using a terminological knowledge representation language. This task will be divided into four steps: (1) automatic generation of terminological expressions, (2) automatic consistency checking by a terminological classifier, (3) manual restitution of formal consistency in case of inconsistencies, and, finally, (4) manual curation and refinement of the formal representation structures. These four steps are illustrated by the workflow diagram depicted in Figure 4.

Step 1: Automatic Generation of Terminological Expressions. Sources for concepts and relations were the 1999 release of the UMLS SN and the UMLS metathesaurus. Figure 5 exhibits the semantic links between two UMLS CUIs (concept unique identifier),[2] These tables, available as ASCII files, were imported into a Microsoft Access relational database and manipulated using SQL embedded in the VBA programming language. For each CUI in the *mrrel* subset its alphanumeric code was substituted by the English preferred term.

After manual remodeling of the top-level concepts of the UMLS SN (in variable depth, according to the target domain) we extracted, from a total of 85,899 concepts, 38,059 anatomy and 50,087 pathology concepts from the metathesaurus. The criterion for the inclusion into one of these sets is the assignment to predefined semantic types. Also, 2,247 concepts were found to be included in both sets, anatomy and pathology. Since we wanted to keep the two subdomains strictly disjoint, we maintained these overlapping concepts duplicated, and prefixed all concepts by *ana-* or *pat-* according to their respective subdomain. This can be justified by the observation that these hybrid concepts exhibit, indeed, multiple meanings. For instance, *tumor* has the meaning of a malignant disease on the one hand, and of an anatomical structure on the other hand.

As target structures for the anatomy domain we chose SEP triplets. These are expressed in the terminological language LOOM which we had previously extended by a special *deftriplet* macro (cf. Table 1 for an example).

Only UMLS-supplied *part-of*, *has-part* and *is-a* relation attributes were considered for the construction of taxonomic and partonomic hierarchies (cf. Figure 4). Hence, for each anatomy concept one SEP triplet was created. The result is a mixed *is-a* and *part-whole* hierarchy a straightforward example of which is depicted in Figure 2.

For the pathology domain, we treated *CHD* (child) and *RN* (narrower relation) from the UMLS as indicating taxonomic (*is-a*) links. No part-whole relations were considered, since this category does not apply to the pathology domain. Furthermore, for all anatomy concepts contained in the definitional statements of pathology concepts the S-node is the default concept to which they are linked, thus enabling the propagation of roles across the part-whole hierarchy.

---

[2] As a convention in UMLS, any two CUIs must be connected by at least a shallow relation (in Figure 5, CHiID relations in the column REL are assumed between CUIs). Shallow relations may be refined in the column RELA, if a thesaurus is available which contains more specific information. Some CUIs are linked either by *part-of* or *is-a*. In any case, the source thesaurus for the relations and the CUIs involved is specified in the columns X and Y (e.g., MeSH 1999, SNOMED International 1998).

UMLS relation	number of links	Step 1 — Automatic generation of Loom definitions, augmented by P-Loom language elements ;;; = comment line	Step 2 — Submission to Loom classifier. Validation for formal consistency by Loom	Step 3 — Manual restitution of formal consistency	Step 4 — Manual rectification and refinement of the resulting knowledge base
Anatomy Concepts Linked to Anatomy Concepts					
sibling_of	267.218	;;; SIB			add negations in order to express taxonomic or partitive disjointness
child_of	59.808	;;; CHDRN			include related concepts into :is-primitive or :part-of clause where plausible
narrower_term	24.223	;;; CHDRN			
isa	9.755	:is-primitive	check for definitional cycles	remove taxonomic parent concepts	substitute of primitive links by non-primitive ones where possible
location_of	4.803	;;; LOCATION_OF			include related concepts into :has-part clause where plausible
has_location	4.803	;;; HAS_LOCATION			include related concepts into :part-of clause, where plausible
has_part	4.321				check whether this part is mandatory (under "real-anatomy" assumption)
has_conceptual_part	126	:has-part			
part_of	4.321		1. check for partonomic cycles 2. check for disjointness between E and P node	1. remove partonomic or taxonomic parent concepts 2. redefine triplet as single concept	check for plausibility and completeness
conceptual_part_of	126	:part-of			
parent	59.808	;;; PARRB			include related concepts into :has-part clause where plausible
broader_term	24.223	;;; PARRB			
inverse_isa	9,755	<do nothing>			
associated_with	14				
mapped_from	2.643				
other_relation	10.908				
qualified_by	1.864				
allowed_qualifier	1.864				
mapped_to	2643				
<other named relations>	11.886	(:some x)	check for inherited constraints	remove constraints	remove or add constraints
Pathology Concepts Linked to Pathology Concepts					
sibling_of	457.542	;;; SIB			add negations in order to express taxonomic disjointness
child_of	72.426	:is-primitive	check for definitional cycles	remove parent concepts	substitute primitive links by non-primitive ones whenever possible
narrower_term	26.972				
isa	3.635				
inverse_isa	3.635	<do nothing>			
associated_with	13.902				
mapped_to	15.024				
mapped_from	15.024				
part_of	1				
has_part	1				
parent	72.426				
broader_term	28.972				
other_relation	25.796				
qualified_by	6.255				
allowed_qualifier	6.255				
<other named relations>	4.162	(:some x)	check for inherited constraints	remove constraints	remove or add constraints
Pathology Concepts Linked to Anatomy Concepts					
CUlpat = CUlana	2.247	(:some has_anatomic_correlate)			plausibility check of concept "duplication" (assignment to both domains)
<missing>		<do nothing>			add pathology-anatomy links
associated_with	2.314	(:some associated_with <anatomy_concept> S)		check for consistency	render links complete, link to E-node instead of S-node when role propagation has to be disabled
has_location	9,230	(:some has_location <anatomy_concept> S)			
<other>		<do nothing>			

Fig. 4. Workflow Diagram for the Construction of a LOOM Knowledge Base from the UMLS

As a fundamental assumption, all roles generated in this process were considered as being existentially quantified. This means that any relation r (*part-of*, *has-location*, etc.) which holds between two concepts, A and B, is mapped to a role $R.B$ which is a necessary condition in the definition of the concept A. All conceptual constraints for a concept definition are mapped to a conjunction of constraints.

CUI1	REL	CUI2	RELA	x	y
C0005847	CHD	C0014261	part_of	MSH99	MSH99
C0005847	CHD	C0014261		CSP98	CSP98
C0005847	CHD	C0025962	isa	MSH99	MSH99
C0005847	CHD	C0026844	part_of	MSH99	MSH99
C0005847	CHD	C0026844		CSP98	CSP98
C0005847	CHD	C0034052		SNMI98	SNMI98
C0005847	CHD	C0035330	isa	MSH99	MSH99
C0005847	CHD	C0042366	part_of	MSH99	MSH99
C0005847	CHD	C0042367	part_of	MSH99	MSH99
C0005847	CHD	C0042367		SNM2	SNM2
C0005847	CHD	C0042449	isa	MSH99	MSH99

Fig. 5. Semantic Relations in the UMLS Metathesaurus

In both subdomains, shallow relations such as the extremely frequent *sibling* relation (*SIB*) were included as comments into the code to provide heuristic guidance for the subsequent manual refinement phase.

Step 2: Automatic Consistency Checking by the LOOM **Classifier.** The import of UMLS anatomy concepts resulted in 38,059 *deftriplet* expressions for anatomical concepts and 50,087 *defconcept* expressions for pathological concepts. Each *deftriplet* was expanded into three *defconcept* (S-, E-, and P-nodes), and two *defrelation* (*anatomical-part-of-x*, *inv-anatomical-part-of-x*) expressions, summing up to 114,177 concepts. This yielded (together with the concepts from the UMLS SN) a total of 240,764 definitory LOOM expressions.

From 38,059 anatomy triplets, 1,219 *deftriplet* statements contained a *:has-part* clause followed by a list of a variable number of triplets, with more than one argument in 823 cases (average cardinality: 3.3). 4,043 *deftriplet* statements contained a *:part-of* clause, only in 332 cases followed by more than one argument (average cardinality: 1.1). The resulting knowledge base was then submitted to the terminological classifier and checked for terminological cycles and consistency. In the anatomy subdomain, one terminological cycle and 2,328 inconsistent concepts were found, in the pathology subdomain 355 terminological cycles though not a single inconsistent concept were determined (cf. Table 2).

Step 3: Manual Restitution of Consistency. The inconsistencies in the anatomy part of the knowledge base identified by the classifier could all be traced back to the simultaneous linkage of two triplets by both *is-a* and *part of* links, an encoding that raises

```
(deftriplet Heart
    :is-primitive Hollow-Viscus
    :has-part (:p-and
        Fibrous-Skeleton-Of-Heart
        Wall-Of-Heart
        Cavity-Of-Heart
        Left-Side-Of-Heart
        Right-Side-Of-Heart
        Aortic-Valve
        Pulmonary-valve ))
```

Table 1. Generated Triplets in LOOM Format

|| Anatomy	Pathology
Triplets defconcept	38,059	—
statements	114,177	50,087
cycles	1	355
inconsistencies	2,328	0

Table 2. Classification Results

a conflict due to the disjointness required for corresponding P- and E-nodes we used as a default (cf. expression (3)). In most of these cases the affected parents belonged to a class of concepts that obviously cannot be appropriately modeled as SEP triplets, e.g., *Subdivision-Of-Ascending-Aorta* or *Organ-Part*. The meaning of each of these concepts almost paraphrases that of a P-node, so that the violation of the SEP-internal disjointness condition could be accounted for by substituting the triplets involved with simple LOOM concepts, by matching them with already existing P-nodes, or by disabling *is-a* or *part-of* links.

In the pathology part of the knowledge base, we expected a large number of terminological cycles to occur, simply as a consequence of interpreting the extremely weak *narrower term* and *child* relations in terms of taxonomic subsumption (*is-a*). Bearing in mind the size of the knowledge base, we consider 355 cycles a tolerable number. Those cycles were primarily due to very similar concepts, e.g., *Arteriosclerosis* vs. *Atherosclerosis*, *Amaurosis* vs. *Blindness*, and residual categories ("other", "NOS" = *not otherwise specified*). These were directly inherited from the source terminologies and are notoriously difficult to interpret out of their definitional context, e.g., *Other-Malignant-Neoplasm-of-Skin* vs. *Malignant-Neoplasm-of-Skin-NOS*. In many cases the decision which relations could be maintained and which relations had to be eliminated was taken arbitrarily, since in biomedical terminology often no consensus can be achieved on the exact meaning of terms. As the result of the analysis we obtained a negative list which consisted of 630 concept pairs. In a subsequent extraction cycle we incorporated this list in the automated construction of the LOOM concept definitions and, with these new constraints, a fully consistent knowledge base was generated.

Step 4: Manual Rectification and Refinement of the Knowledge Base. To set up this high-volume knowledge base including the aforementioned working steps required three months of work for a single person, in total. The fourth step – when performed for the whole knowledge base – is very time-consuming and requires broad and in-depth medical expertise. Random samples from both subdomains were analyzed by the second author, a domain expert. The data we here supply refer to the analysis of two random samples of each 100 anatomy and 100 pathology concepts. This took one person about a single month. From the experience we gained in the anatomy and pathology subdomains so far, the following workflow can be derived:

– *Checking the correctness of the taxonomic and partonomic hierarchies.* Taxonomic and partonomic links are manually added or removed. Primitive subsumption is substituted by non-primitive one whenever possible. This is a crucial point, because the automatically generated hierarchies contain only information about the parent concepts and necessary conditions. As an example, the automatically generated definition of *Dermatitis* includes the information that it is an *Inflammation*, and that the role *has-location* must be filled by the concept *Skin*. An *Inflammation* that *has-location Skin*, however, cannot automatically be classified as *Dermatitis*.

Results: In the *anatomy* sample, only 76 concepts out of 100 could be unequivocally classified as belonging to 'canonical' anatomy. (The remainder, e.g., *ana-Phalanx-of-Supernumerary-Digit-of-Hand*, referring to pathological anatomy was immediately excluded from analysis.) Besides the assignment to the UMLS semantic types, only 27 (direct) taxonomic links were found. 83 UMLS relations (mostly *child* or *narrower* relations) were manually upgraded to taxonomic links. 12 (direct) *part-of* and 19 *has-part* relations were found. Four *part-of* relations and one *has-part* relation had to be removed, since we considered them as implausible. 51 UMLS relations (mostly *child* or *narrower* relations) were manually upgraded to *part-of* relations, and 94 UMLS relations (mostly *parent* or *broader* relations) were upgraded to *has-part* relations. After this workup and upgrade of shallow UMLS relations to semantically more specific relations, the sample was checked for completeness again. As a result, 14 *is-a* and 37 *part-of* relations were still considered missing.

In the *pathology* sample, the assignment to the pathology subdomain was considered plausible for 99 of 100 concepts. A total of 15 false *is-a* relations was identified in 12 concept definitions. 24 *is-a* relations were found to be missing.

- *Check of the* :has-part *arguments assuming 'real anatomy'*. In the UMLS sources *part-of* and *has-part* relations are considered as symmetric. According to our transformation rules, the attachment of a role *has-anatomical-part* to an E-node B_E, with its range restricted to A_E, implies the existence of a concept A for the definition of a concept B. On the other hand, the classification of A_E as being subsumed by the P-node B_P, the latter being defined via the role *anatomical-part-of* restricted to B_E, implies the existence of B_E given the existence of A_E. These constraints do not always conform to 'real' anatomy, i.e., anatomical concepts that may exhibit pathological modifications. Figure 6 (left) sketches a concept A that is necessarily *anatomical-part-of* a concept B, but whose existence is not required for the definition of B. This is typical of the results of surgical interventions, e.g., a large intestine without an appendix, or an oral cavity without teeth, etc.

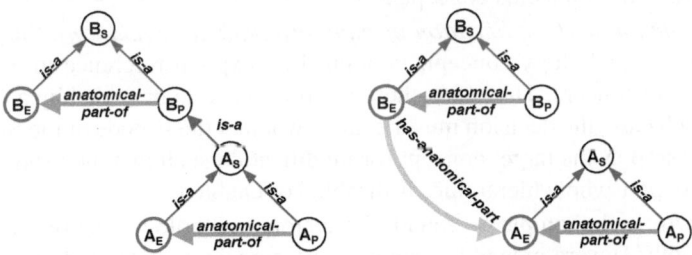

Fig. 6. Patterns for Part-whole Reasoning Using SEP triplets

Results: All 112 *has-part* relations obtained by the automatic import and the manual workup of our sample were checked. The analysis revealed that more than half of them (62) should be eliminated in order not to obviate a coherent classification of pathologically modified anatomical objects. For instance, maintaining *has-anatomical-part.Thumb* as an existential restriction in the definition of *Hand* would disallow to classify as *Hand* all those that have no thumb due to congenital or acquired abnormalities.[3] As an example, most instances of *Ileum* do not contain a *Meckel's Diverticulum*, whereas all instances of *Meckel's Diverticulum* are necessarily *anatomical-part-of Ileum*. Many surgical interventions that remove anatomical structures (appendix, gallbladder, etc.), produce similar patterns. In our formalism, this corresponds to a single taxonomic link between an S-node and a P-node (cf. Figure 6, left part). The contrary is also possible (cf. Figure 6, right part): the definition of A_E does not imply that the role *anatomical-part-of* be filled by B_E, but B_E does imply that the inverse role be filled by A_E. As an example, a *Lymph-node* necessarily contains *Lymph-follicles*, but there exist *Lymph-follicles* that are not part of a *Lymph-node*. This pattern is typical of the mereological relation between macroscopic (countable) objects, such as organs, and multiple uniform microscopic objects.

– *Analysis of the sibling relations and defining concepts as being disjoint.* In UMLS, the *SIB* relation links concepts that share the same parent in a taxonomic or partonomic hierarchy. Pairs of sibling concepts may have common descendants or not. If not, they constitute the root of two disjoint subtrees. In a taxonomic hierarchy, this means that one concept implies the negation of the other (e.g., a benignant tumor cannot be a malignant one, *et vice versa*). In a partitive hierarchy, this can be interpreted as spatial disjointness, *viz.* one concept does not spatially overlap with another one. As an example, *Esophagus* and *Duodenum* are spatially disjoint, whereas *Stomach* and *Duodenum* are not (they share a common transition structure, called *Pylorus*), such as all neighbor structures that have a surface or region in common. Spatial disjointness can be modeled so that the definition of the S-node of the concept A implies the negation of the S-node of the concept B [27].
Results: We found on the average 6.8 siblings per concept in the anatomy domain, 8.8 in the pathology domain. So far, the analysis of sibling relations has been performed only for the anatomy domain. From a total of 521 sibling relations, 9 were identified as *is-a*, 14 as *part-of*, and 17 as *has-part*, whereas 404 referred to topologically disconnected concepts.

– *Completion and modification of anatomy–pathology relations.* Surprisingly, only very few pathology concepts contained an explicit reference to a corresponding anatomy concept. Therefore, these relations have to be added by a domain expert. In each case, the decision must be made whether the E-node or the S-node has to be addressed as the target concept for modification such that the propagation of roles across part-whole hierarchies is disabled or enabled.
Results: In the sample we found 522 anatomy-pathology relations, from which 358 (i.e., 69%!) were judged incorrect by the domain experts. In 36 cases an adequate

---

[3] In Table 1 the concepts marked by *italics*, *viz.* *Aortic-valve* and *Pulmonary-valve* should be eliminated from the *:has-part* list, because the anatomical entities they denote may be missing in certain cases as a result of congenital malformations, inflammatory processes or surgical interventions.

anatomy-pathology relation was missing. All 164 *has-location* roles were analyzed as to whether they were to be filled by an S-node or an E-node of an anatomical triplet. In 153 cases, the S-node (which allows propagation across the part-whole hierarchy) was considered to be adequate, in 11 cases the E-node was preferred. The analysis of the 100 pathology concepts revealed that only 17 were to be linked with an anatomy concept. In 15 cases, the default linkage to the S-node was considered to be correct, in one case the linkage to the E-node was preferred, in another case the linkage was considered to be false.

The high number of implausible constraints points to the lightweight semantics of *has-location* links in the UMLS sources. While we interpreted them in terms of a conjunction for the import routine, a disjunctive meaning seems to prevail implicitly in many definitions of top-level concepts such as *Tuberculosis*. In this example, we find all anatomical concepts that can be affected by this disease linked by *has-location*. All these constraints (e.g., *has-location Urinary-Tract*) are inherited to subconcepts such as *Tuberculosis-of-Bronchus*. A thorough analysis of the top-level pathology concepts is necessary, and conjunctions of constraints will have to be substituted by disjunctions where necessary.

4   Discussion and Conclusions

In medicine, domain knowledge has to be supplied on a larger scale. Instead of developing sophisticated medical knowledge bases from scratch, we here propose a 'conservative' approach — reuse existing large-scale resources, but refine the data from these resources so that advanced representational requirements imposed by more expressive knowledge representation languages are met. The resulting knowledge bases can then be used for sophisticated applications requiring formally sound medical reasoning such as text understanding.

The benefits and problems of converting conceptual knowledge from semantically weak specifications to a rigorous knowledge representation formalism have been described by Pisanelli et al. [16]. They extracted knowledge from the UMLS semantic network, as well as from parts of the metathesaurus and converted it into a description logics system. Spackman & Campbell [28] describe how the SNOMED nomenclature evolves from a multi-axial coding system into a formally founded ontology. Their general goal is to avoid ambiguous or semantically invalid representations of composite concepts. However, both approaches do not provide a special reasoning mechanism for partonomic relations.

Within the formal framework of GALEN, a fragment of the Read Thesaurus was translated into *Grail*, a knowledge representation system also based on description logics [20]. In a cross-validation study it was checked, on the one hand, whether the definitions contained in the Read Thesaurus were logically consistent and, on the other hand, whether the *Grail* domain model was rich enough to encode them. Although *Grail* comes with a special-purpose reasoning mechanism dedicated to partonomies, the adaptation was limited to simple generic hierarchies as only these structure the Read Thesaurus.

The developers of VOXEL-MAN [23], a multimedia tutoring systems for anatomy, and of the Digital Anatomist (UWDA), an anatomical semantic network [21], have both emphasized partitive hierarchies though at an informal level. Whereas in VOXEL-MAN a fine-grained ontology of partonomic relations is sketched that accounts for various part-whole relations found in the anatomy domain, the UWDA developers restrict themselves to a small set of relations leading to a precise separation between partonomic and taxonomic hierarchies. They excel with a high granularity of description and a broad coverage.

Our approach tries to combine the broad coverage and fine-grained concept descriptions of the UWDA with the formal rigor of description logics. Additionally, we enhance the imported knowledge with part-whole specific reasoning capabilities indispensable in the medical domain, though this has already been described as a hard problem for terminological languages [9].

It remains to be seen whether conservative structural extensions of a stable language platform are able to carry over to the many varieties of partonomic reasoning and different part-whole relations, or whether newly designed operators or other fundamental language extensions are needed. In the medical domain, at least, where the restriction to one subrelation of *part-of,* viz. *anatomical-part-of,* is sufficient, a relatively simple "data structure" extension like the SEP triplets yields already adequate results, without the necessity to resort to profound extensions of the terminological language. We have evidence that the triplet mechanism we here propose can be straightforwardly extended to cover mereotopological and (limited) spatial reasoning, as well [27, 25].

Our study shows that it is relatively straightforward to restitute consistency of the UMLS knowledge base, but it is nearly impossible to reach a high degree of both adequacy and completeness due to the huge amount of manual work required. Restituting adequacy should, however, not be primarily taken as eliminating obvious 'errors' contained in the UMLS sources, but rather as making choices between alternative conceptualizations of medical term whose meaning differs slightly due to the heterogeneity of the knowledge sources. Another aspect is the need of rectification of concept definitions which have become incorrect due to rigid axiomatic assumptions driving the automated export procedure (e.g., the conjunctive reading of defining attributes), which is not true in all cases, and, thus, necessarily requires individual manual specification.

A realistic scenario may consist in the manual elimination of obviously inadequate statements, followed by the completion of the concept definitions focused on a specific subdomain of interest. In these repetitive manual refinement cycles we found the implications of using the terminological classifier, the inference engine which computes subsumption relations, of utmost importance and of outstanding heuristic value. Hence, the knowledge refinement cycles are truly semi-automatic, fed by medical expertise on the side of the human knowledge engineer, but also driven by the reasoning system which makes explicit the consequences of (im)proper concept definitions.

References

[1] Alessandro Artale, Enrico Franconi, Nicola Guarino, and Luca Pazzi. Part-whole relations in object-centered systems: An overview. *Data & Knowledge Engineering,* 20(3):347–383, 1996.

[2] James J. Cimino. Distributed cognition and knowledge-based controlled medical terminologies. *Artificial Intelligence in Medicine,* 12(1):153–168, 1998.

[3] James J. Cimino, Paul D. Clayton, George Hripsack, and Stephen B. Johnson. Knowledge-based approaches to the maintenance of a large controlled medical terminology. *Journal of the American Medical Informatics Association,* 1(1):35–50, 1994.

[4] D. Alan Cruse. On the transitivity of the part-whole relation. *Journal of Linguistics,* 15:29–38, 1979.

[5] Aldo Gangemi, Domenico M. Pisanelli, and Geri Steve. An overview of the ONION project: Applying ontologies to the integration of medical terminologies. *Data & Knowledge Engineering,* 31(2):183–220, 1999.

[6] Udo Hahn, Martin Romacker, and Stefan Schulz. Discourse structures in medical reports – watch out! The generation of referentially coherent and valid text knowledge bases in the MEDSYNDIKATE system. *International Journal of Medical Informatics,* 53(1):1–28, 1999.

[7] Udo Hahn, Martin Romacker, and Stefan Schulz. How knowledge drives understanding: Matching medical ontologies with the needs of medical language processing. *Artificial Intelligence in Medicine,* 15(1):25–51, 1999.

[8] Udo Hahn, Stefan Schulz, and Martin Romacker. Part-whole reasoning: A case study in medical ontology engineering. *IEEE Intelligent Systems & Their Applications,* 14(5):59–67, 1999.

[9] Ira J. Haimowitz, Ramesh S. Patil, and Peter Szolovits. Representing medical knowledge in a terminological language is difficult. In R. A. Greenes, editor, *SCAMC'88 – Proceedings of the 12th Annual Symposium on Computer Applications in Medical Care,* pages 101–105. Washington, D.C.: IEEE Computer Society Press, 1988.

[10] Ian Horrocks and Ulrike Sattler. A description logic with transitive and inverse roles and role hierarchies. *Journal of Logic and Computation,* 9(3):385–410, 1999.

[11] Robert MacGregor and Raymond Bates. The LOOM knowledge representation language. Technical Report RS-87-188, Information Sciences Institute, University of Southern California, 1987.

[12] Robert M. MacGregor. A description classifier for the predicate calculus. In *AAAI'94 – Proceedings of the 12th National Conference on Artificial Intelligence,* volume 1, pages 213–220. Seattle, WA, USA, July 31 - August 4, 1994. Menlo Park, CA: AAAI Press & MIT Press, 1994.

[13] Eric Mays, Robert Weida, Robert Dionne, Meir Laker, Brian White, Chihong Liang, and Frank J. Oles. Scalable and expressive medical terminologies. In J. J. Cimino, editor, *AMIA'96 – Proceedings of the 1996 AMIA Annual Fall Symposium (formerly SCAMC). Beyond the Superhighway: Exploiting the Internet with Medical Informatics,* pages 259–263. Washington, D.C., October 26-30, 1996. Philadelphia, PA: Hanley & Belfus, 1996.

[14] Alexa T. McCray. The nature of lexical knowledge. *Methods of Information in Medicine,* 37(4/5):353–360, 1998.

[15] Alexa T. McCray and Stuart J. Nelson. The representation of meaning in the UMLS. *Methods of Information in Medicine,* 34(1/2):193–201, 1995.

[16] Domenico M. Pisanelli, Aldo Gangemi, and Geri Steve. An ontological analysis of the UMLS metathesaurus. In C. G. Chute, editor, *AMIA'98 – Proceedings of the 1998 AMIA Annual Fall Symposium. A Paradigm Shift in Health Care Information Systems: Clinical Infrastructures for the 21st Century,* pages 810–814. Orlando, FL, November 7-11, 1998. Philadelphia, PA: Hanley & Belfus, 1998.

[17] Alan L. Rector. Clinical terminology: Why is it so hard? *Methods of Information in Medicine,* 38:147–157, 1999.

[18] Alan L. Rector. Analysis of propagation along transitive roles: Formalisation of the galen experience with medical ontologies. In I. Horrocks and Tessaris S., editors, *DL02 - 2002 International Workshop on Description Logics, Toulouse, France,* 2002. Published as CEUR Workshop Proceedings (CEUR-WS.org) via http://CEUR-WS.org/Vol-53/.

[19] Alan L. Rector, Sean Bechhofer, Carole A. Goble, Ian Horrocks, W. Anthony Nowlan, and W. Danny Solomon. The GRAIL concept modelling language for medical terminology. *Artificial Intelligence in Medicine*, 9:139–171, 1997.

[20] Jeremy E. Rogers, Colin Price, Alan Rector, W. Daniel Solomon, and Nick Smeijko. Validating clinical terminology structures: Integration and cross-validation of READ THESAURUS and GALEN. In C. G. Chute, editor, *AMIA'98 – Proceedings of the 1998 AMIA Annual Fall Symposium. A Paradigm Shift in Health Care Information Systems: Clinical Infrastructures for the 21st Century*, pages 845–849. Orlando, FL, November 7-11, 1998. Philadelphia, PA: Hanley & Belfus, 1998.

[21] Cornelius Rosse, José Leonardo V. Mejino, Bharath R. Modayur, Rex Jakobovits, Kevin P. Hinshaw, and James F. Brinkley. Motivation and organizational principles for anatomical knowledge representation: The DIGITAL ANATOMIST symbolic knowledge base. *Journal of the American Medical Informatics Association*, 5(1):17–40, 1998.

[22] James G. Schmolze and William S. Mark. The NIKL experience. *Computational Intelligence*, 6(1):48–69, 1991.

[23] Rainer Schubert and Karl-Heinz Höhne. Partonomies for interactive explorable 3D-models of anatomy. In C. G. Chute, editor, *AMIA'98 – Proceedings of the 1998 AMIA Annual Fall Symposium. A Paradigm Shift in Health Care Information Systems: Clinical Infrastructures for the 21st Century*, pages 433–437. Orlando, FL, November 7-11, 1998. Philadelphia, PA: Hanley & Belfus, 1998.

[24] Erich B. Schulz, Colin Price, and Philip J. B. Brown. Symbolic anatomic knowledge representation in the Read Codes Version 3: Structure and application. *Journal of the American Medical Informatics Association*, 4(1):38–48, 1997.

[25] Stefan Schulz and Udo Hahn. Mereotopological reasoning about parts and (w)holes in bio-ontologies. In Chris Welty and Barry Smith, editors, *Formal Ontology in Information Systems. Collected Papers from the 2nd International Conference*, pages 210–221. Ogunquit, Maine, USA, October 17-19, 2001. New York, NY: ACM Press, 2001.

[26] Stefan Schulz and Udo Hahn. Necessary parts and wholes in bio-ontologies. In D. Fensel, F. Giunchiglia, D. McGuinness, and M.-A. Williams, editors, *Principles of Knowledge Representation and Reasoning. Proceedings of the 8th International Conference – KR 2002*, pages 387–394. Toulouse, France, April 22-25, 2002. San Francisco, CA: Morgan Kaufmann, 2002.

[27] Stefan Schulz, Udo Hahn, and Martin Romacker. Modeling anatomical spatial relations with description logics. In J. M. Overhage, editor, *AMIA 2000 – Proceedings of the Annual Symposium of the American Medical Informatics Association. Converging Information, Technology, and Health Care*, pages 779–783. Los Angeles, CA, November 4-8, 2000. Philadelphia, PA: Hanley & Belfus, 2000.

[28] Kent A. Spackman and Keith E. Campbell. Compositional concept representation using SNOMED: Towards further convergence of clinical terminologies. In C. G. Chute, editor, *AMIA'98 – Proceedings of the 1998 AMIA Annual Fall Symposium. A Paradigm Shift in Health Care Information Systems: Clinical Infrastructures for the 21st Century*, pages 740–744. Orlando, FL, November 7-11, 1998. Philadelphia, PA: Hanley & Belfus, 1998.

[29] Françoise Volot, M. Joubert, and Marius Fieschi. Review of biomedical knowledge and data representation with Conceptual Graphs. *Methods of Information in Medicine*, 37(1):86–96, 1998.

[30] Morton Winston, Roger Chaffin, and Douglas J. Herrmann. A taxonomy of part-whole relationships. *Cognitive Science*, 11:417–444, 1987.

[31] William A. Woods and James G. Schmolze. The KL-ONE family. *Computers & Mathematics with Applications*, 23(2/5):133–177, 1992.

Ontology Versioning and Change Detection on the Web

Michel Klein[1], Dieter Fensel[1], Atanas Kiryakov[2], and Damyan Ognyanov[2]

[1] Vrije Universiteit Amsterdam
De Boelelaan 1081a, 1081 HV Amsterdam, the Netherlands
{michel.klein|dieter}@cs.vu.nl
[2] OntoText Lab., Sirma AI Ltd.
38A Hristo Botev blvd., Sofia 1000, Bulgaria
{naso|damyan}@sirma.bg

Abstract. To effectively use ontologies on the Web, it is essential that changes in ontologies are managed well. This paper analyzes the topic of ontology versioning in the context of the Web by looking at the characteristics of the version relation between ontologies and at the identification of online ontologies. Then, it describes the design of a web-based system that helps users to manage changes in ontologies. The system helps to keep different versions of web-based ontologies interoperable, by maintaining not only the transformations between ontologies, but also the conceptual relation between concepts in different versions. The system allows ontology engineers to compare versions of ontology and to specify these conceptual relations. For the visualization of differences, it uses an adaptable rule-based mechanism that finds and classifies changes in RDF-based ontologies.

1 The Web Needs Change Management for Ontologies

The envisaged next generation of the Web (called Semantic Web [6]) will consist of data defined and linked in such a way that it can be used for more effective discovery, automation, integration, and reuse across various applications[1]. In this vision, ontologies have an important role in defining and relating concepts that are used to describe data on the web. However, the distributed and dynamic character of the web will cause that many versions and variants of ontologies will arise. Ontologies are often developed by several persons and continue to evolve over time. Moreover, domain changes, adaptations to different tasks, or changes in the conceptualization might cause modifications of the ontology. This will likely cause incompatibilities in the applications and ontologies that refer to them and will give wrong interpretations to data or make data inaccessible [14].

To form a real Semantic *Web*, it is necessary that the knowledge that is represented in the different versions of ontologies is interoperable. It is therefore important to create links between ontology versions that specify how the knowledge in the different versions of the ontologies is related. These links can be used to re-interpret data and knowledge under different versions of ontologies.

---

[1] http://www.w3.org/2001/sw/Activity

A. Gómez-Pérez and V.R. Benjamins (Eds.): EKAW 2002, LNAI 2473, pp. 197–212, 2002.
© Springer-Verlag Berlin Heidelberg 2002

In this paper, we present various elements of a methodology for ontology versioning. We describe a method to specify relations between versions of ontologies and we also propose an identification scheme for ontologies. We then present a web-based system that supports the user in specifying the relations between ontology versions. The system, called OntoView, can also be used store ontologies and to provide a transparent interface to different versions. The goal of this system is not to provide a central registry for ontologies, but to allow ontology engineers to store their versions and variants of ontologies and relate them to other (possibly remote) ontologies. The resulting mapping relations between versions can also be exported and used outside the system.

The rest of the paper is organized as follows. In the next section, we analyze the characteristics of the relation between different versions of ontologies. Section 3 contains a discussion of ontology identification and proposes a identification scheme for ontologies. In section 4, we give an overview of the versioning support system and describe its the main functions. Section 5 describes the main feature of the system: comparing ontologies. In that section, we explain the mechanism we used to find changes in RDF-based ontologies and present some of the rules that we used to encode change types. We discuss some open issues in section 6, and we conclude the paper in section 7.

2   Characteristics of a Version Relation

There are three important aspects to discuss when considering an version relation between ontologies. First, this is **the difference between version relations and conceptual relations inside an ontology**.

Ontologies usually consist of a set of class (or concept) definitions, property definitions and axioms about them. The classes, properties and axioms are related to each other and together form a model of a part of the world. A change constitutes a new version of the ontology and also a *version relation* between the definitions of concepts and properties in the original version of the ontology and those in the new version.[2]

The relations between concepts inside an ontology, e.g. between class A and class B, are thus fundamentally different from the version relations between two versions of a concept, e.g. between class $A_{1.0}$ and class $A_{2.0}$. In the first case, the relation is a purely conceptual relation in the domain of interest; in the second case, however, the relation describes meta-information about the change of the concept.

Nevertheless, two versions of a concept still have *some* conceptual relation. In other words, although the update relation itself is not a conceptual relation, the participating versions of a concept (e.g. $A_{1.0}$ and $A_{2.0}$) do have a particular conceptual (logical) relation to each other.

Altogether, we distinguish the following properties of an version relation:

- **transformation** or **actual change**: a specification of what has actually changed in an ontological definition, specified by a set of change operations (cf. [1]), e.g., change of a restriction on a property, addition of a class, removal of a property, etc.;
- **conceptual relation**: the relation between constructs in the two versions of the ontology, e.g., specified by equivalence relations, subsumption relations, or logical rules;

---

[2] Except for removals and additions of classes and properties, of course.

- descriptive meta-data like **date, author**, and **intention** of the update: this describes the when, who and why of the change;
- **scope**: a description of the context in which the update is valid. In its simplest form, this might consist of the date when the change is valid in the real world, conform to *valid date* in temporal databases [18] (in this terminology, the "date" in the descriptive meta-data is called *transaction date*). More extensive descriptions of the scope, in various degrees of formality, are also possible.

A well-designed ontology change specification mechanism should take all these characteristics into account.

Another issue to discuss about ontology updates is the **possible discrepancy between changes in the specification and changes the conceptualization**. We have seen that an ontology is a *specification* of a *conceptualization*. The actual specification of concepts and properties is thus a *specific representation* of the conceptualization: the same concepts could also have been specified differently. Hence, a change in the specification does not necessarily coincide with a change in the conceptualization [14], and changes in the specification of an ontology are not per definition ontological changes.

For example, there are changes in the definition of a concept which are not meant to change the concept itself: attaching a slot "fuel-type" to a class "Car". Both class-definitions still refer to the same ontological concept, but in the second version it is described more extensively. Theoretically, the other way around is also possible: a concept could change without a change in its specification. However, this usually means that the concept is badly modelled.

It is important to distinguish changes in ontologies that affect the conceptualization from changes that don't. In [19] the following terms are used to make this distinction:

- **conceptual change**: a change in the way a domain is interpreted (conceptualized), which results in different ontological concepts or different relations between those concepts;
- **explication change**: a change in the way the conceptualization is specified, without changing the conceptualization itself.

It is important to notice that it is not possible to determine automatically whether a change is a conceptual change or a explication change. This requires insight in the conceptualization, and is basically a decision of the ontology engineer. However, heuristics can be applied to suggest the effects of changes. We will discuss that later on.

A third, somewhat different, aspect of an update is the **packaging of changes**, i.e., the way in which updates are applied to an ontology. This is an important practical issue for the development of an ontology change management system.

We can distinguish two different dimensions with respect to the packaging of the change specification. One dimension is the *granularity* of the specification: this can be either the level of a single "definition" or the level of a "file" as a whole.

The second dimension is the *method* of specification. There are several methods thinkable:

- a "transformation specification": an update specified by a list of change operations (e.g., add A, change B, delete C);

- a "replacement": an update specified by replacing the old version of a concept or an ontology with a new version; this is an implicit change specification;
- a "mapping": an update specified as a mapping between the original ontology and another one. Although this is not a update in the regular sense, an explicit mapping to another ontology can be considered as an update to the viewpoint of that ontology.

This gives several possible change specifications. For example, a change can be specified individually, as a mapping between one specific definition in one ontology and another definition in another ontology, but it can also be done at a file level, by defining the transformation of the ontology.

Notice that the packaging methods are not equivalent, i.e., they do not give the same information about the update relation. It is clear that the mapping provides a conceptual relation between versions of concepts, something that is not specified in a transformation.

3   Ontology Identification on the Web

Identification of versions of ontologies is very important. Ontologies describe a consensual view on a part of the world and function as reference for that specific conceptualization. Therefore, they should have a unique and stable identification. A human, agent or system that conforms to a specific ontology, should be able to refer to it unambiguously. We will now discuss the major issues of ontology identification on the Web, and outline an identification mechanism.

3.1   Identity of Ontologies

The first question that has to be answered when we want to identify versions of an ontology on the web is: what is the identity of an ontology? This is not as trivial as it seems. For example, one could ask whether an update of a natural language description changes the identity of an ontology. If one regards a specific *specification* of a conceptualization as an essential characteristic of an ontology, then every modification to that specification forms a new version of the ontology. In that case, the descriptions specify different concepts, which are *per definition* not equal.

Looking at this from another perspective, one might regard an ontology primarily as a conceptualization, which is represented as complete as possible in a specification. In this case one could argue that an update to a natural language description of a concept is not a conceptual change, but just a more precise description of the same conceptualization. This would be an example of an explication change: the specification is changed, but the concept that is described remains the same.

In this philosophical debate, we take the following (practical) position. We assume that an ontology is represented in a file on the web. Every change that results in a different character representation of the ontology constitutes a revision. In case the logical definitions are not changed, it is the responsibility of the author of the revision to decide whether this revision is conceptual change and thus forms an new conceptualization with its own identity, or just an change in the representation of the same conceptualization.

If we relate this to the distinction between conceptual changes and explication changes, this means that whenever there has been a conceptual change in an ontology, it gets a new identifier. In case of explication changes, the ontology keeps the same identifier if and only if these changes were non-logical changes (thus, changes in the natural language description). This is summarized in table 1. Again, note that it is up to the ontology engineer to decide whether a change is a conceptual change or not.

	logical	non-logical
conceptual	new	new
explication	new	unchanged

Table 1. Change types and their effect on the identity of an ontology.

3.2 Identification on the Web

The second question is: how does this relate to web resources and their identity? To answer this question, we have look at identification mechanisms on the web (i.e. URIs, URNs and URLs) and see how we can use them for the identification of the "entities" in our domain (i.e., the entities in the domain of ontology versions, e.g. a conceptualization, a revision, a specification).

Things on the web are called "resources" in the W3C[3]-terminology. According to the definition of Uniform Resource Identifiers (URI's) (defined in [5]), "a resource can be anything that has identity". In [7] is stated: "a 'resource' is a conceptual entity (a little like a Platonic ideal)". Both definitions comprise our idea of an ontology. Hence, an ontology can be regarded as a resource. An URI, which "is a compact string of characters for identifying an abstract or physical resource" [5] can be used to identify the resources. Notice that URI's provide a general identification mechanisms, as opposed to Uniform Resource Locators (URL's), which are bound to the *location* of a resource.

Usually, the XML Namespace mechanism [8] is used for the identification of web-based ontologies. This means that an ontology is identified by a URI. In practice, people tend to use a URL for this. In other words, they couple the identity of an ontology with the location of the ontology file on the web. The important step in our proposed method is to separate the identity of ontologies completely from the identity of files on the web that specify the ontology. In other words, the class of ontology resources should be distinguished from the class of file resources. As we have seen above, a revision — which is normally specified in a new file — *may* constitute a new ontology, but this is no automatism. Every revision is a new file resource and gets a new file identifier, but does not automatically get a new ontology identifier. If a change does not constitute a

---

[3] The standardization body for the World Wide Web

conceptual change, the new version gets a new location, but does not get a new identifier. For example, the location of an ontology can change from "../example/1.0/rev0" to "../example/1.0/rev1", while the identifier is still "../example/1.0".

3.3   Baseline of an Identification Method

When we take into account all these considerations, we propose an identification method that is based on the following points:

- a distinction between three classes of resources:
  1. files;
  2. ontologies;
  3. lines of backward compatible ontologies.
- a change in a file results in a new file identifier;
- the use of a URL for the file identification;
- a change in the conceptualization or in the logical definition results in a new ontology identifier, but a non-logical explication change doesn't;
- a separate URI for ontology identification with a two level numbering scheme:
  - minor numbers for backward compatible modifications (an ontology-URI ending with a minor number identifies a specific ontology);
  - major numbers for incompatible changes (an ontology-URI ending with a major number identifies a line of backward compatible ontologies);
- individual concepts or relations, whose identifier only differs in minor number, are assumed to be equivalent;
- ontologies are referred to by an ontology URI with the according major revision number and the *minimal extra commitment*, i.e., the lowest necessary minor revision number.

The ideas behind these points are the following. As already pointed out in the beginning of this section, the distinction between ontology identity and file identity has the advantage that file changes and location changes (e.g., copy of an ontology) can be isolated from ontological changes. By using a separate URI, it is possible to encode all the information in it that is necessary for our usage, and it also prevents confusion with URL's that specify a location.

The distinction between individual ontologies on the one hand and lines of backward compatible ontologies on the other hand, provides a simple way to indicate a very general type of compatibility, likewise the "BACKWARD-COMPATIBLE-WITH" field in SHOE [13]. The distinction we make is also in line with the idea of "levels of generality", which is discussed in [7]. Applications can conclude directly — without formal analysis or deduction steps — that a version can be validly used on data sources with the same major number and a equal or lower minor number. To achieve a maximal backward compatibility, we also propose that not the minor number of the newest revision is specified in a data source, but the minimal addition to the base version that is used by this data source. For example, suppose an ontology with concepts A, B and C. Version 1.1 added a concept D and version 1.2 added concept E. Then a data source data only relies on concepts A, C and D, would specify its commitment only to version 1.1, although there is already a version 1.2 available. We adopted this idea from software-program library versioning, as described in [10].

An interesting point for discussion is whether it would be possible to specify the *real* ontological commitment, instead of only the necessary extra commitment. In our example, this would mean that the data sources specifies that it relies on exactly A, C and D. This would require a different type of identification.

The point that states that individual concepts with a identifier that only differs in minor number are considered to be equivalent, is necessary to actually enable the backward compatibility. By default, all resources on the web with a different identifier are considered to different. This statement allows the creation of a stand-alone ontology revision, which has concepts that are equal to a previous version.

4   OntoView: Support for Ontology Versioning

Up to now, we discussed two theoretical aspects of ontology versioning: the characteristics of a version relation and the identification of ontologies. Based on this, we will now describe a system that provides support for the versioning of online ontologies. The main function of the system is to help a user to manage changes in ontologies and keep ontology versions as much interoperable as possible. It does that by comparing versions of ontologies and highlighting the differences. It then allows the users to specify the conceptual relation between the different versions of concepts. This function is described more extensively in the next section.

It also able to store ontologies and to provide a transparent interface to arbitrary versions of ontologies. To achieve this, the system maintains an internal specification of the relation between the different variants of ontologies, with the aspects that were defined in section 2: it keeps track of the **meta-data**, the **conceptual relations** between constructs in the ontologies and the **transformations** between them.

OntoView is inspired by the Concurrent Versioning System CVS [4], which is used in software development to allow collaborative development of source code. The first implementation is also based on CVS and its web-interface CVSWeb[4]. However, during the ongoing development of the system, we are gradually shifting to a complete new implementation that will be build on a solid storage system for ontologies, e.g., Sesame[5].

The ideas underlying the versioning system are not depending on a specific ontology language. However, the implementation of specific parts of the system assume RDF based languages, for example the mechanism to detect changes. In the remainder of this article, we will use DAML+OIL[6] [11,12] and RDF Schema (RDFS) [9] as ontology languages. These two languages are widely considered as basis for future ontology languages for the Web.

Besides the ontology comparison feature — which will be described in detail in the next section — the system has the following functions:

---

[4] Available from `http://stud.fh-heilbronn.de/~zeller/cgi/cvsweb.cgi/`

[5] A demo is available at `http://sesame.aidministrator.nl`

[6] Available from `http://www.daml.org/language/`

- **Reading changes and ontologies.** OntoView will accept changes and ontologies via several methods. Currently, ontologies can be read in as a whole, either by providing a URL or by uploading them to the system. The user has to specify whether the provided ontology is new or that it should be considered as an update to an already known ontology. In the first case, the user also has to provide a "location" for the ontology in the hierarchical structure of the OntoView system.

  Then, the user is guided through a short process in which he is asked to supply the meta-data of the version (as far as this can not be derived automatically, such as the date and user), to characterize the types of the changes (see below in section 5), and to decide about the identifier of the ontology.

  In the future, OntoView will also accept changes by reading in transformations, mapping ontologies, and updates to individual definitions. These update methods provides the system with different information than the method described above. For that reason, this also requires an adaptation of the process in which the user gives additional information.

- **Identification.** OntoView uses the namespace mechanism with URIs for ontology identification, separated from the location of the ontology file. Depending on the compatibility effects of the type of change (see table 1), it assigns a new identifier or it keeps the previous one.

  OntoView supports two ways of persistent and unique identification of web-based ontologies. First, it can in itself guarantee the uniqueness and persistency of namespaces that start with "http://ontoview.org/", because the system is located at the domain `ontoview.org`. Second, because the location and identification of ontologies are not necessarily coupled, it can also store ontologies with arbitrary namespaces. In this case, the ontology engineer is responsible for guaranteeing the uniqueness. The ontologies with arbitrary namespaces are not directly retrievable by their namespace, but can be accessed via a search function.

- **Analyzing effects of changes.** Changes in ontologies do not only affect the data and applications that use them, but they can also have unintended, unexpected and unforeseeable consequences in the ontology itself [16].

  OntoView provides some basic support for the analysis of these effects. First, on request it can also highlight the places in the ontology where conceptually changed concepts or properties are used. For example, if a property "hasChild" is changed, it will highlight the definition of the class "Mother", which uses the property "hasChild". In the future, this function should also exploit the transitivity of properties to show the propagation of possible changes through the ontology.

  Further, we expect to extend the system with a reasoner to automatically verify the changes and the specified conceptual relations between versions. For example, we could couple the system with FaCT [3] and exploit the Description Logic semantics of DAML+OIL to check the consistency of the ontology and look for unexpected implied relations.

- **Exporting changes.** The main advantage of storing the conceptual relations between versions of concepts and properties is the ability to use these relations for the re-interpretation of data and other ontologies that use the changed ontology. To facilitate this, OntoView can export differences between ontologies as separate mapping ontologies, which can be used as adapters for data sources or other ontologies. The mappings are created on basis of conceptual information that is attached to the update relation.

Mapping ontologies are separate ontologies that import definitions from two other (versions of) ontologies and relates these definitions conceptually to each other. They only provide a partial mapping, because not all changes can be specified conceptually, e.g. complicated changes like splits of concepts, or deletions. The definitions are imported by the namespace mechanism. This mechanism allows RDF-based ontologies to refer to definitions in other ontologies, by connecting the URI (identifier) of an other ontology with a symbolic name. The exported mapping ontologies are represented with the standard constructs of the ontology langauge.

The meta-data about the ontology update is specified as a set of properties of the conceptual relations themselves. In RDF Schema and DAML+OIL, this meant that we also have to re-ify the mapping statements. For this purpose, we defined an RDFS "meta-schema" that specifies the classes and properties that are used to attach the meta-information about an update to the mapping statements. Due to space restrictions, we cannot show it here.

This method has two advantages. First, when specified over re-ified statements, the meta-data does not interfere with the actual ontological knowledge, as would be the case when meta-data is specified as characteristics of classes and properties. Second, because the meta-data is data about the *mappings themselves*, agents or systems that understand the meta-data can use this to decide which mappings are applicable in a specific context and which are not.

In the future, it should also be possible to export *transformations* between two versions of an ontology. A transformation is a complete specification of all the change operations. This can be used to re-execute changes and to update ontologies that have some overlap with the versioned ontology in exactly the same way as the original one. However, transformations facilitates data re-interpretations only to a very small extent. A mapping ontology provides better re-interpretation, because it also captures human knowledge about the relations.

5   Comparing Ontologies

One of the central features of OntoView is the ability to compare ontologies at a structural level. The comparison function is inspired by UNIX `diff`, but the implementation is quite different. Standard `diff` compares file version at line-level, highlighting the lines that textually differ in two versions. OntoView, in contrast, compares version of ontologies at a *structural* level, showing which definitions of ontological concepts or properties are changed. An example of such a graphical comparison of two versions of a DAML+OIL ontology is depicted in Figure 1.[7]

5.1   Types of Change

The comparison function distinguishes between the following types of change:

---

[7] This example is based on fictive changes to the DAML+OIL example ontology, available from `http://www.daml.org/2001/03/daml+oil-ex.daml`.

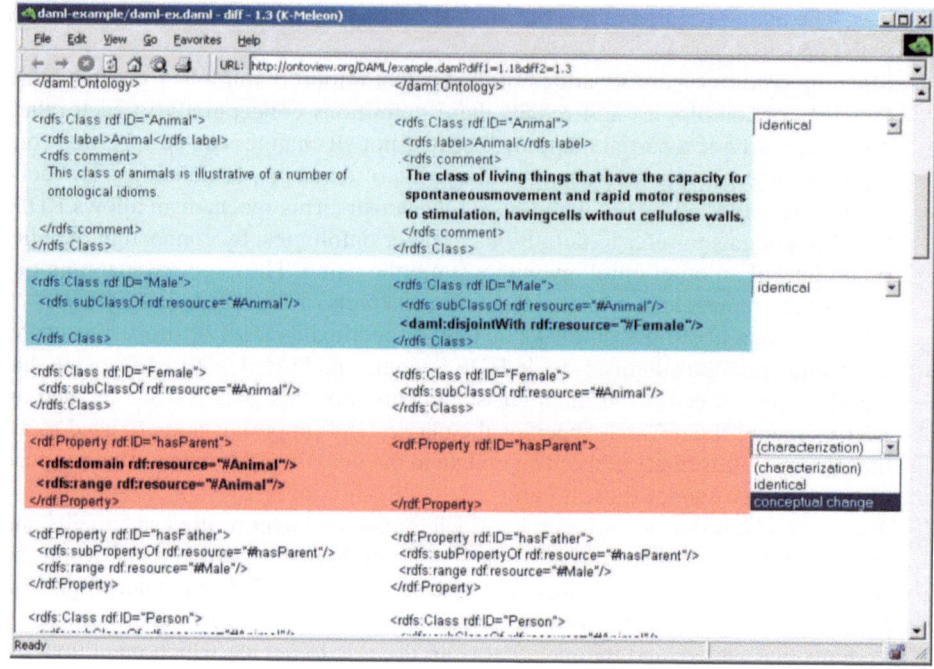

Fig. 1. Comparing two ontologies

- Non-logical change, e.g. in a natural language description. In DAML+OIL, this are changes in the rdfs:label of an concept or property, or in a comment inside a definition. An example is the first highlighted change in Figure 1 (class "Animal').
- Logical definition change. This is a change in the definition of a concept or property that affects its formal semantics. Examples of such changes are alterations of subClassOf, domain, or range statements. Additions or deletions of local property restrictions in a class are also logical changes. The second and third change in the figure is (class "Male" and property "hasParent") are examples of such changes. Note that there are also logical changes that do not affect the semantics
- Identifier change. This is the case when a concept or property is given a new identifier, i.e. a renaming.
- Addition of definitions.
- Deletion of definitions.

Each type of change is highlighted in a different color, and the actually changed lines are printed in boldface.

Most of these changes can be detected completely automatically, except for the identifier change, because this change is not distinguishable from a subsequent deletion and addition of a simple definition. In this case, the system uses the location of the definition in the file as a heuristic to determine whether it is an identifier change or not.

It is a deliberate choice not to show all changes, but only the ones which we think that are of interest to the ontology modeler. This choice is explained in the next paragraphs, together with the mechanism that we use to detect and classify changes. Experimental validation should show whether this list of change types is sufficient.

5.2 Detecting Changes

There are two main problems with the detection of changes in ontologies. The first problem is the abstraction level at which changes should be detected. Abstraction is necessary to distinguish between changes in the representation that affect the meaning, and those that don't influence the meaning. It is often possible to represent the same ontological definition in different ways. For example, in RDF Schema, there are several ways to define a class:

```
<rdfs:Class rdf:ID="ExampleClass"/>
```

or:

```
<rdf:Description rdf:ID="ExampleClass">
  <rdf:type rdf:resource="...org/2000/01/rdf-schema#Class"/>
</rdf:Description>
```

Both are valid ways to define a class and have exactly the same meaning. Such a change in the representation would not change the ontology. Thus, detecting changes in the *representation* alone is not sufficient.

However abstracting too far can also be a problem: considering the *logical meaning* only is not enough. In [2] is shown that different sets of ontological definitions can yield the same set of logical axioms. Although the logical meaning is not changed in such cases, the ontology definitely is. Finding the right level of abstraction is thus important.

Second, even when we found the correct level of abstraction for change detection, the conceptual implication of such a change is not yet clear. Because of the difference between conceptual changes and explication changes (as described in section 2), it is not possible to derive the conceptual consequence of a change completely on basis of the visible change only (i.e., the changes in the definitions of concepts and properties). Heuristics can be used to suggest conceptual consequences, but the intention of the engineer determines the actual conceptual relation between versions of concepts.

In the next two sections, we explain the algorithm that we used to compare ontologies at the correct abstraction level, and how users can specify the conceptual implication of changes.

5.3 Rules for Changes

The algorithm uses the fact that the RDF data model [15] underlies a number of popular ontology languages, including RDF Schema and DAML+OIL. The RDF data model basically consists of triples of the form `<subject, predicate, object>`, which can be linked by using the object of one triple as the subject of another. There are several syntaxes available for RDF statement, but they all boil down to the same data model. An set of related RDF statements can be represented as a graph with nodes and edges. For example, consider the following DAML+OIL definition of a class "Person".

```
<daml:Class rdf:ID="Person">
  <rdfs:subClassOf rdf:resource="#Animal"/>
  <rdfs:subClassOf>
    <daml:Restriction>
      <daml:onProperty rdf:resource="#hasParent"/>
      <daml:toClass rdf:resource="#Person"/>
    </daml:Restriction>
  </rdfs:subClassOf>
</daml:Class>
```

When interpreted as a DAML+OIL definition, it states that a "Person" is a kind of "Animal" and that the instances of its hasParent relation should be of type "Person". However, for our algorithm, we are first of all interested in the RDF interpretation of it. That is, we only look at the triples that are specified, ignoring the DAML+OIL meaning of the statements. Interpreted as RDF, the above definition results in the following set of triples:

subject	predicate	object
Person	rdf:type	daml:Class
Person	rdfs:subClassOf	Animal
Person	rdfs:subClassOf	*anon-resource*
anon-resource	rdf:type	daml:Restriction
anon-resource	daml:onProperty	hasParent
anon-resource	daml:toClass	Person

This triple set is depicted as a graph in Figure 2. In this figure, the nodes are resources that function as subject or object of statements, whereas the arrows represent properties.

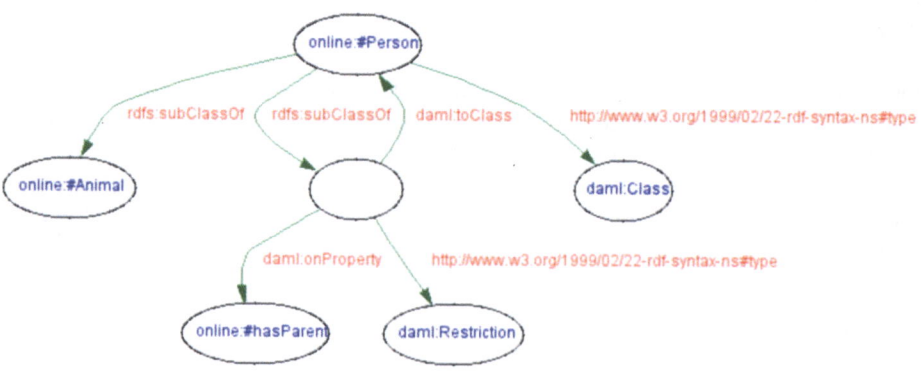

Fig. 2. An RDF graph of a DAML class definition.

The algorithm that we developed to detect changes is the following. We first split the document at the first level of the XML document. This groups the statements by their intended "definition". The definitions are then parsed into RDF triples, which results in a set of small graphs. Each of these graphs represent a specific definition of a concept or a property, and each graph can be identified with the identifier of the concept or the property that it represents.

Then, we locate for each graph in the new version the corresponding graph in the previous version of the ontology. Those sets of graphs are then checked according to a number of rules. Those rules specify the "required" changes in the triples set (i.e., the graph) for a specific type of change, as described in section 5.1.

The rules have the following format:

```
IF exist:old
      <A, Y, Z>*
    exist:new
      <X, Y, Z>*
    not-exist:new
      <X, Y, Z>*
THEN change-type A
```

They specify a set of triples that should exists in one specific version, and a set that should not exists in another version (or the other way around) to signal a specific type of change. With this rule mechanism, we were able to specify almost types of change (except the identifier change).

For example, a rule to specify a change in the property type looks as follows:

```
IF exist:old
      <X, rdf:type, rdf:#Property>
      <X, rdf:type, daml:#UniqueProperty>
    exist:new
      <X, rdf:type, rdf:#Property>
    not-exist:new
      <X, rdf:type, daml:#UniqueProperty>
THEN logicalChange.propertytype X
```

The rules are specific for a particular RDF-based ontology language (in this case DAML+OIL), because they encode the interpretation of the semantics of the language for which they are intended. For another language other rules would have been necessary to specify other differences in interpretation. The semantics of the language are thus encoded in the rules. For example, the last example not looks at changes in values of predicates (as the first does), but at a change in the type of property. This is a change that is related to the specific semantics of DAML+OIL.

Also, notice that the mechanism relies on the "materialization" of all `rdf:type` statements that are encoded in the ontology. In other words, the closure of the RDF triples according to the used ontology language has to be computed. For example, the rules in example rule above depend on the existence of a statement `<X,rdf:type,rdf:#Property>`. However, this statement can only be derived using the semantics of the `rdfs:subPropertyOf` statement, which — informally spoken[8] — says that if a property is an instance of type X, then it is also an instance of the supertypes of X. The application of the rules thus has to be preceded by the materialization of

---

[8] The precise semantics of RDF Schema are still under discussion.

the superclass- and superproperty hierarchies in the ontology. For this materialization, the entailment and closure rules in the RDF Model Theory[9] can be used.

5.4 Specifying the Conceptual Implication of Changes

The comparison function also allows the user to *characterize* the conceptual implication of the changes. For the first three types of changes that were listed in section 5.1, the user is given the option to label them either as "identical" (i.e., the change is an explication change), or as "conceptual change", using the drop-down list next to the definition (Figure 1). In the latter case, the user can specify the conceptual relation between the two version of the concept. For example, the change in the definition of "hasParent" could by characterized with the relation $hasParent_{1.1}$ subPropertyOf $hasParent_{1.3}$.

More complicated changes, such as deletions, splits of concepts, replacements etcetera, require additional characterizations that specify how the new change should be interpreted. We will developed this in the future.

6   Discussion

There are a few other issues and choices about the design of the system that we want to discuss. First, we purposely do not provide support for finding mappings between arbitrary ontologies. The intention of our system is to provide users with a system to manage versions of ontologies and maintain their relations. Finding the relations is a different task. However, it might be possible to incorporate this function in a future version of the system, e.g. by interfacing it with a ontology mapping tool.

We did not yet specify the way in which the "scope" of the mapping is described. The "scope" will have several dimensions, of which "time" is only one. This is something what still has to be done. Without such a specification, it is difficult to assess the validness of a conceptual relation between concepts in different versions. We can assume that such a relation is at least valid between two successive versions, but we do not know whether such mapping is allowed to "propagate" via other mappings to other ontologies. Research on this is necessary.

A situation in which versioning support is also necessary is the collaborative development of an ontology [17]. We think that OntoView is also useful in this situation, especially because all the conceptual implications of versions have to be characterized individually by users. This integrates the conflict resolution in the update procedure. That is, because users specify the conceptual relation of their changes with the previous version while specifying the update, it is not necessary to resolve conflict between definitions afterwards. Every version of the definition has its own identifier and is conceptually related to the other versions.

A side remark about the use of a versioning system for collaborative ontology development is that this gives an evolutionary way of ontology building. Each person can have its own conceptualization, which is conceptually linked to the conceptualizations

---

[9] http://www.w3.org/TR/rdf-mt/

of others. In this sense, the combination of versions and adaptations in itself forms a *shared* conceptualization of a domain.

Finally, we want to mention that the system is still under construction. In section 4 we extensively depicted the foreseen functionality of OntoView. However, as became clear of some of the descriptions, not everything is already realized. The basis functions are implemented, but a number of more advanced functions are still being developed.

7 Summary and Conclusion

When ontologies are used in a distributed and dynamic context, versioning support is essential ingredient to maintain interoperability. In this paper we have analyzed the versioning relation, described its aspects, proposed an identification mechanism and finally depicted a system that helps users to manage changes in online ontologies.

We described how this systems supports helps users to compare ontologies, and what the problems and challenges are. We presented a algorithm to perform a comparison for RDF-based ontologies. This algorithm doesn't operate on the representation of the ontology, but on the data model that is underlying the representation. By grouping the RDF-triples per definition, we still retained the necessary representational knowledge. We also explained how ontology engineers have to specify the conceptual implication of changes. This honors the fact that it is not possible to derive all conceptual implications of changes automatically, because this requires insight in the conceptualization.

The analysis of a versioning relation between ontologies revealed several dimensions of it. In the system that we described, all these dimensions are maintained separately: the descriptive **meta-data**, the **conceptual relations** between constructs in the ontologies, and the **transformations** between the ontologies themselves. This multi-dimensional specification allows both complete transformations of ontology representations and partial data re-interpretations, which help interoperability. The conceptual differences can be exported and used stand alone, for example to adapt data sources and ontologies.

The important step in the identification method that we proposed is to separate the identity of ontologies completely from the identity of files that contain the specification of the ontology. This allows to distinguish identity changing revisions from explication changes. Moreover, we distinguish backward compatible revisions from incompatible revisions.

The described versioning methodology and the system is not yet finished and have to be developed further. Moreover, validation in a realistic setting is needed. However, we believe that the things that we presented can help to manage changes in ontologies, which will be an essential requirement for the interoperability of evolving ontologies on the web.

References

1. J. Banerjee, W. Kim, H.-J. Kim, and H. F. Korth. Semantics and Implementation of Schema Evolution in Object-Oriented Databases. *SIGMOD Record (Proc. Conf. on Management of Data)*, 16(3):311–322, May 1987.

2. S. Bechhofer, C. Goble, and I. Horrocks. DAML+OIL is not enough. In *Proceedings of the International Semantic Web Working Symposium (SWWS)*, Stanford University, California, USA, July 30 – Aug. 1, 2001.

3. S. Bechhofer, I. Horrocks, P. F. Patel-Schneider, and S. Tessaris. A proposal for a description logic interface. In P. Lambrix, A. Borgida, M. Lenzerini, R. Möller, and P. Patel-Schneider, editors, *Proceedings of the International Workshop on Description Logics (DL'99)*, pages 33–36, Linköping, Sweden, July 30 – Aug. 1 1999.

4. B. Berliner. CVS II: Parallelizing software development. In USENIX Association, editor, *Proceedings of the Winter 1990 USENIX Conference*, pages 341–352, Washington, DC, USA, Jan. 22–26, 1990. USENIX.

5. T. Berners-Lee, R. Fielding, and L. Masinter. RFC 2396: Uniform Resource Identifiers (URI): Generic syntax, Aug. 1998. Status: DRAFT STANDARD.

6. T. Berners-Lee, J. Hendler, and O. Lassila. The semantic web. *Scientific American*, 284(5):34–43, May 2001.

7. T. Berners-Lee. Generic resources, 1996. Design Issues.

8. T. Bray, D. Hollander, and A. Layman. Namespaces in XML. http://www.w3.org/TR/REC-xml-names/, Jan. 1999.

9. D. Brickley and R. V. Guha. Resource Description Framework (RDF) Schema Specification 1.0. Candidate recommendation, World Wide Web Consortium, Mar. 2000.

10. D. J. Brown and K. Runge. Library interface versioning in solaris and linux. In *Proceedings of the 4th Annual Linux Showcase and Conference*, Atlanta, Georgia, Oct., 10–14 2000.

11. D. Fensel, I. Horrocks, F. van Harmelen, S. Decker, M. Erdmann, and M. Klein. OIL in a nutshell. In R. Dieng and O. Corby, editors, *Knowledge Engineering and Knowledge Management; Methods, Models and Tools, Proceedings of the 12th International Conference EKAW 2000*, number 1937 in LNCS, pages 1–16, Juan-les-Pins, France, Oct. 2–6, 2000. Springer-Verlag.

12. D. Fensel and M. A. Musen. The semantic web: A new brain for humanity. *IEEE Intelligent Systems*, 16(2), 2001.

13. J. Heflin and J. Hendler. Dynamic ontologies on the web. In *Proceedings of the Seventeenth National Conference on Artificial Intelligence (AAAI-2000)*, pages 443–449. AAAI/MIT Press, Menlo Park, CA, 2000.

14. M. Klein and D. Fensel. Ontology versioning for the Semantic Web. In *Proceedings of the International Semantic Web Working Symposium (SWWS)*, pages 75 – 91, Stanford University, California, USA, July 30 – Aug. 1, 2001.

15. O. Lassila and R. R. Swick. Resource Description Framework (RDF): Model and Syntax Specification. Recommendation, World Wide Web Consortium, Feb. 1999. See http://www.w3.org/TR/REC-rdf-syntax/.

16. D. L. McGuinness, R. Fikes, J. Rice, and S. Wilder. An environment for merging and testing large ontologies. In A. G. Cohn, F. Giunchiglia, and B. Selman, editors, *KR2000: Principles of Knowledge Representation and Reasoning*, pages 483–493, San Francisco, 2000. Morgan Kaufmann.

17. H. S. Pinto and J. ao Pavão Martins. Evolving ontologies in distributed and dynamic settings. In *Proceedings of the Eighth International Conference on Principles of Knowledge Representation and Reasoning (KR2002)*, Toulouse, France, Apr. 22–25, 2002.

18. J. F. Roddick. A survey of schema versioning issues for database systems. *Information and Software Technology*, 37(7):383–393, 1995.

19. P. R. S. Visser, D. M. Jones, T. J. M. Bench-Capon, and M. J. R. Shave. An analysis of ontological mismatches: Heterogeneity versus interoperability. In *AAAI 1997 Spring Symposium on Ontological Engineering*, Stanford, USA, 1997.

Hozo: An Environment for Building/Using Ontologies Based on a Fundamental Consideration of "Role" and "Relationship"

Kouji Kozaki, Yoshinobu Kitamura, Mitsuru Ikeda, and Riichiro Mizoguchi

The Institute of Scientific and Industrial Research, Osaka University
8-1 Mihogaoka, Ibaraki, Osaka, 567 -0047 Japan
Tel: +81-6-6879-8416, Fax: +81-6-6879-2123,
{kozaki,kita,ikeda,miz}@ei.sanken.osaka-u.ac.jp

Abstract. We have developed an environment for building/using ontologies, named Hozo, based on both of a fundamental consideration of an ontological theory and a methodology of building an ontology. Since Hozo is based on an ontological theory of a role-concept, it can distinguish concepts dependent on particular contexts from so-called basic concepts and contribute to building reusable ontologies.

Introduction

Building an ontology requires a clear understanding of what can be concepts with what relations to others. Although several tools for building ontologies have been developed to date, few of them were based on enough consideration of an ontological theory. We argue that a fundamental consideration of these ontological theories is needed to develop an environment for developing an ontology. We discuss mainly "role concept" and "relationship", and consider how these ontologically important concepts should be treated in our environment. On the basis of the consideration we have developed an environment for building and using ontologies, named "Hozo". This paper presents an outline of the functionality of Hozo. The next section discusses a *role-concept* and *a relation concept* in Hozo. Section 3 outlines the architecture of Hozo. Section 4 presents the implementation of Hozo and examples of its use. Next we discuss conclusions and some future work.

A Consideration of "Role" and "Relation"

What Is a Role? : Basic Concept, Role Concept, and Role Holder

John Sowa introduces the *firstness* and the *secondness* of concepts [Sowa 95]. The former is roughly defined as a concept which can be defined without mentioning other concepts. Examples include ion, a man, a tree, etc. The latter is roughly defined as a concept which cannot be defined without mentioning other concepts. Examples

A. Gómez-Pérez and V.R. Benjamins (Eds.): EKAW 2002, LNAI 2473, pp. 213-218, 2002.

include wife, husband, student, child, etc. We call concepts of the *secondness* type except artifacts ***role-concepts*** in this paper. Based on his theory, we identified three categories for a concept. That is, a *basic concept*, a *role-concept*, and a *role holder*.

A ***role-concept*** represents a role which a thing plays in a specific context and it is defined with other concepts. On the other hand, a ***basic concept*** does not need other concepts for being defined. An entity of the basic concept that plays a role such as husband role or wife role is called a ***role holder***. For example in "a bicycle", its wheel plays the role as a front wheel ("a front wheel role") or a role that steers its body ("a steering role"), which is defined as a *role-concept*. A wheel that plays these roles is called "a front wheel" and "a steering wheel", respectively, which are *role holders*.

Dependency Analysis of Role-Concepts

There are various roles dependent on the whole,□a relation, a task or a domain, and roles in artifacts, and so on. For building an ontology, it is important to discriminate among a role concept, a role holder and a basic concept. To give a guideline for such discrimination, we organized domain concepts which role concepts dependent on. In this paper we extracted 5 top-level categories and about 300 domain concepts from technical documents about oil-refinery plant operation [Mizoguchi 00]. Those top-level categories are as follows:

- **Device**: components of the plant.
- **Target object**: objects which a device targets in processing.
- **Attribute**: attributes of devices or target objects.
- **Domain activity**: behaviors and functions of devices.
- **Condition/Feature vocabulary**: vocabulary of condition and feature of devices or objects.

We do not claim the concepts listed in Table 1 are exhaustive. However, we carefully analyzed our domain, oil-refinery plant operation, and came up with domain concepts which role concepts dependent on from each categories, and classified them into 27 concepts in all. Although they might look domain dependent, the authors believe the dependency on the oil refinery domain is small, which is partially demonstrated by the concepts which are not from the oil-refinery plant domain.

Target object
- *functions which the object receive:*
  e.g.) remained ingredient, combustion gas, reflux object, exhaust gas drinking water
- *a name of the whole device which has the object as input/output:*
  e.g.) decomposition device material Cradiatowater
- *a name of place (a part of a device):*
  e.g.) side reflux, top reflux
- *roles dependent on functions of the object:*
  e.g.) cooling medium, solvent medium, diluting medium, catalyst (catalytic agent), cleaner (cleaning material)
- *roles against a device:*
  e.g.) input object, output object, raw materials
- *time (temporal ?) position in a production process:*
  e.g.) intermediate product, finished product

Device
- *its physical relationship with other devices (structure):*
  e.g.) pre flash drum, front wheel, rear wheel
- *functions which the device has:*
  e.g.) heating furnace Cdrawpump, steering wheel, stay bar
- *a name of the device which it is attached to:*
  e.g.) bypass valve, radiator hose
- *target attribute for its function:*
  e.g.) liquid level control valve
- *target object for its function:*
  e.g.) crude dram, off-gas compressor
- *way of achievement which was applied to the device:*
  e.g.) atmospheric-pressure distillation device, reduced-pressure distillation device

(a)   (b)

Table 1. The domain concepts which role concepts dependent on. (part)

Relation Concept and Wholeness Concept

There are two ways of conceptualizing a thing. Consider a "brothers" and a "brotherhood". "The Smith brothers" is a conceptualization as a *concept*, on the other hand "brotherhood between Bob and Tom" is conceptualized as a *relation*. On the basis of the observations that most of the things are composed of parts and that those parts are connected by a specific relation to form the whole, we introduced **"wholeness concept"** and **"relation concept"**. The former is a conceptualization of the whole and the latter is that of the relation. In the above example, the "brothers" is a *wholeness concept* and the "brotherhood" is a *relation concept*. Because a *wholeness concept* and a *relation concept* are different conceptualizations derived from the same thing, they correspond to each other. Theoretically, every thing that is a composite of parts can be conceptualized in both perspectives as a *wholeness concept* and a *relation concept*.

Hozo

We have developed an environment, named "Hozo[1]", for building/using ontologies based on fundamental ontological theories. "Hozo" is composed of "Ontology Editor", "Onto-Studio" and "Ontology Server"(Fig.1). The ontology and the resulting model are available in different formats (Lisp, Text, XML/DTD,DAML+OIL) that make it portable and reusable.

Ontology Editor provides users with a graphical interface, through which they can browse and modify ontologies by simple mouse operations. It treats "role concept" and "relation" on the basis of fundamental consideration discussed in section 2 [Kozaki 00]. This interface consists of the following four parts (Fig.2):

1. *Is-a* **hierarchy browser** displays the ontology in a hierarchical structure according to only *is-a* relations between concepts.

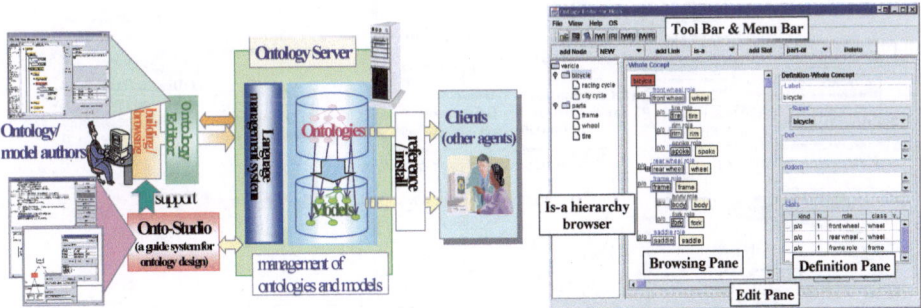

Fig. 1. The architecture of Hozo   **Fig. 2.** A snapshot of Ontology Editor

---

[1] "Ho" is a Japanese word and means unchanged truth, laws or rules in Japanese, and we represent "ontologies" by the word. "Zo" means to build in Japanese.

2. **Edit panel** is composed of a *browsing panel* and a *definition panel*. The former displays the concept graphically, and the latter allows users define a selected concept in the *is-a* hierarchy browser.

3. **Menu bar** is used for selecting tools

4. **Tool bar** is used for selecting commands

Onto-Studio is based on a method of building ontologies, named AFM (Activity-First Method) [Mizoguchi 95]. It helps users design an ontology from technical documents. Figure.3 shows the skeletal building process of ontologies using Onto-Studio. It consists of 4 phases and 12 steps. The followings outline these 4 phases.

1. *Extraction of task-units*: In this phase, users extract **task-units** which contain only one process from technical documents which are written in natural language.
   (1) Divide technical documents into small **blocks** to extract vocabulary easier.
   (2) Extract **task-units** which contain only one process from these blocks.
   (3) Make each task-unit a flow chart which is called **concrete task-flow**.

2. *Organization of task-activities*: In this phase, users specify input/output of task-activities and organize task-activities.
   (4) Conceptualize **task-activities** from verbs in task-units.
   (5) Organize task-activities in an *is-a* hierarchy.
   (6) Define role-concepts, called **task-activity roles**, which appear in input/output of these task-activities.

3. *Analysis of task- structure*: In this phase, users analyze flow of task-activities, specify flow of objects from input to output, and define task-context-roles.
   (7) Generalize concrete task-flows to obtain **general task-flows**.
   (8) Describe **object-flows**, which clearly express relations between inputs and outputs of task-activities, in the general task-flows obtained above.
   (9) Define **task-context roles** on the basis of these object-flows. By task-context roles, we mean role-concepts dependent on the whole process of a task.
   (10) Extract **domain terms** which play the task-context role.

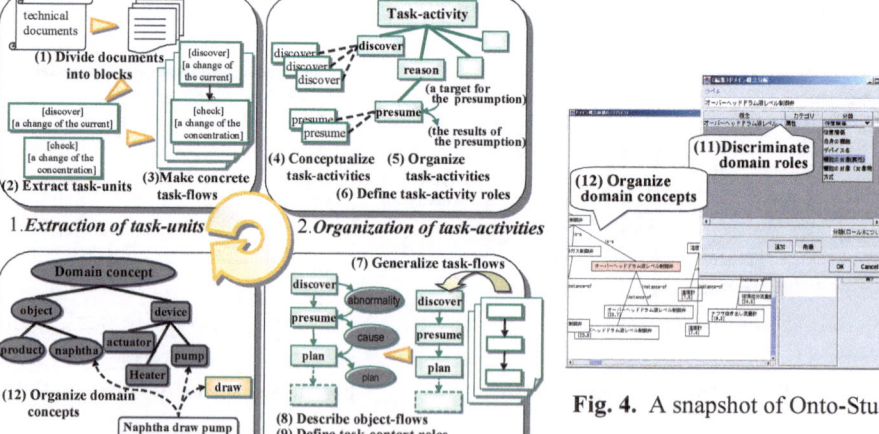

Fig. 3. The building process of ontologies using Onto-Studio.

Fig. 4. A snapshot of Onto-Studio

4. ***Organization of domain concepts***: In this phase, users organize domain concepts extracted in phase 3.
    (11) Discriminate between roles dependent on domain concepts and basic concepts.
    (12) Organize domain concepts in an *is-a* hierarchy.
In practice these steps are not done in a water fall manner. Users can go back and forth during the process. In each step Onto-Studio provides users with graphical interfaces to help them perform suggested procedures. For example, Figure.4 shows a window to help users discriminate domain roles from basic concepts.

Implementation and Application

The current version of Ontology Editor has been implemented in Java2 (JDK1.3) and been used for five years not only by our lab members but also by some researchers outside [Jin 99, Inaba 00, Barros 01,Kitamura 01].

    Here we give more detail of the plant ontology [Mizoguchi 00]. The plant model contains a remarkable fact that multiple names are used to denote the same entity. Let us take an example shown in Fig.5 in which two controllers exist: Level controller (LC29) and flow controller (FC29). Both controllers use the same control valve (VFC29) as an actuator. The control valve VFC29 is called by a different name depending on which controller the operator focuses on. In Hozo, this example is represented that the basic concept "control valve" plays multiple roles depending on the context (Fig.6).

    Role concept analysis and its use in helping users extract role concept from a set of domain concepts have been investigated on the basis of our experience in the development of a plant ontology described above. In order to see the performance of Onto-Studio, we restructured the plant ontology from the same technical documents we used at the first time. As a result, we extracted 355 task-units and restructured a task ontology which is consists of 36 task-activities. Based on the task ontology, we obtained 5 general task-flows and extracted 356 domain concepts. A domain ontology consists 190 basic concepts which were discriminated from the role concepts. As a consequence of this restructuring, we identified about 20 errors in role concept extraction in the original ontology. This result suggests that Onto-Studio can provide a good support in building an ontology.

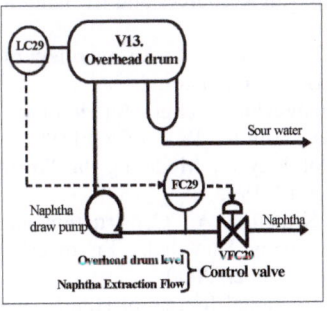

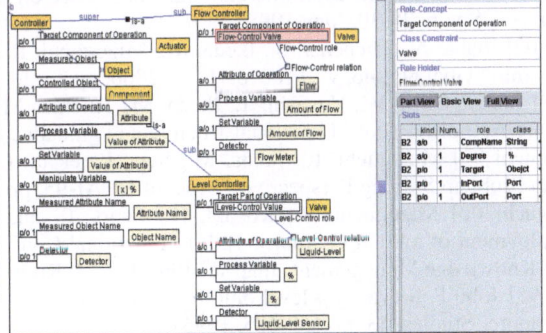

Fig.5. Cascaded control of LC and FC

Fig.6. A snapshot of the plant ontology definition about *Controller*

Conclusion and Future Work

We discussed an environment for ontology development, Hozo, concentrating mainly on how its Hozo treats *role-concepts* and *wholeness/relation concepts*. Several ontology development environments have been already developed. Hozo is similar to them in that sense, but is different from them in some respects:

1. Clear discrimination among a ***role-concept*** (husband role), a ***role-holder*** (husband) and a ***basic concept*** (man) is done to treat "Role" properly.

2. Management of the correspondence between a ***wholeness concept*** and a ***relation concept***.

3. A guide system for building an ontology based on task/domain role concept.

We have identified some room to improve Hozo through its extensive use. The following is the summary of the extension:

- Ontological organization of various role-concepts.

- Augmentation of the axiom definition and the language.

- Gradable support functions according to a user's level of skill.

- Improvement of Onto-Studio by applying in more practical examples.

References

[Barros 01] Barros, B., Mizoguchi, R., et al.: A Platform for Collaboration Analysis in CSCL: An ontological approach, Proceedings of AIED01, San Antonio, Texas, May 19-23 2001

[Kitamura 01] Kitamura, Y., Sano, T., Namba, K. and Mizoguchi, R.: A Functional Concept Ontology and Its Application to Automatic Identification of Functional Structures, Advanced Engineering Informatics (Artificial Intelligence in Engineering), to appear, 2002.

[Kozaki 00] Kozaki, K., et al: Development of an Environment for Building Ontologies which is based on a Fundamental Consideration of "Relationship" and "Role":PKAW2000, pp.205-221, Sydney, Australia, December, 2000

[Guarino 98] Guarino, N.: Some Ontological Principles for Designing Upper Level Lexical Resources. Proc. of the First International Conference on Lexical Resources and Evaluation, Granada, Spain, 28-30, May 1998.

[Inaba 00] Inaba, A., Thepchai, S., Ikeda, M., Mizoguchi, R., and Toyoda, J.: An overview of "Learning Goal Ontology", Proc. of ECAI2000, pp.23-30, Berlin, Germany, 2000

[Jin 99] Jin, L., Chen, W., Hayashi, Y., Ikeda, M., Riichiro Mizoguchi, R., et al. :An Ontology-Aware Authoring Tool - Functionalstructure and guidance generation -, Proc. of AIED'99

[Mizoguchi 95] Mizoguchi, R., Ikeda, M., Seta, K. et al.: Ontology for Modeling the World from Problem Solving Perspectives, Proc. of IJCAI-95, pp. 1-12, 1995.

[Mizoguchi 00] Mizoguchi, R., Kozaki, K., Sano, T., and Kitamura, Y.: Construction and Deployment of a Plant Ontology, 12th International Conference on Knowledge Engineering and Knowledge Management, Juan-les-Pins, French Riviera, October, 2000.

[Sowa 95] John F. Sowa: Top-level ontological categories, International Journal of Human and Computer Studies, 43, pp.669-685, 1995

An Ontology-Driven Approach to Web Site Generation and Maintenance

Yuangui Lei, Enrico Motta, and John Domingue

Knowledge Media Institute
The Open University
Walton Hall, MK7 6AA
{y.lei, e.motta, j.b.domingue}@open.ac.uk

Abstract. Building and maintaining a data-intensive web site is costly and time-consuming and a number of approaches have addressed this problem using a model-based methodology. This paper presents IIPS (Intelligent Information Presentation System), a system that uses an ontology-driven approach to site generation and management. IIPS provides a suite of visual tools, which make it possible to model a data-intensive web site at a conceptual level, using site, interface and domain ontologies. As a result, the site designer can focus on the conceptual structure of the target web site and associated resources, independently of its realization. IIPS also provides explicit mapping mechanisms, which make it possible to generate quickly site implementations from the conceptual model. IIPS improves over existing model-based approaches to web design, by providing knowledge-level support for all aspects of web design, including site and resource specification, presentation and domain data.

1 Introduction

As the web is becoming the major computing platform for sharing data, the need to develop sophisticated data-driven applications to exploit the Internet is increasing in domains such as knowledge portals, electronic commerce, digital libraries, and distance learning. Nevertheless, web application development and maintenance remain costly and time-consuming. To address this problem, many researchers have proposed the use of model-based methodologies to try and simplify the whole process of generation and maintenance of data-intensive web applications [1,2,3,4].

These approaches typically separate the specification of the web site from the domain data. However, most of them, e.g. [1,2], only provide methodological guidance to define site models, rather than explicit conceptual modelling support. Moreover they do not support automatic site generation. As a result, developers still need to do a lot of work to realise site specifications and to integrate these with domain data. Some approaches do provide knowledge-level support for site modelling, e.g. WebML [3] and OntoWebber [4], however they fail to model user interface issues, such as page layouts and graphic user interfaces.

In this paper we describe an Intelligent Information Presentation System (IIPS), which improves over existing approaches to web site generation and maintenance.

A. Gómez-Pérez and V.R. Benjamins (Eds.): EKAW 2002, LNAI 2473, pp. 219-234, 2002.

IIPS uses an ontology-driven approach to site generation and management: it provides a suite of visual tools, which make it possible to model a data-intensive web site at a conceptual level, using site, interface and domain ontologies. The site ontology models the navigational structure and the compositional structure of a generic data-intensive web site, the interface ontology models web-based user interfaces and the domain ontology specifies the data relevant to the site. Thus, the site designer can focus on the conceptual structure of the target web site and associated resources, independently of its realisation. IIPS also provides explicit mapping mechanisms, which make it possible to generate quickly site implementations from the conceptual model. An important advantage of this approach is that by exploiting the conceptual, explicitly represented specifications of the web site and the interfaces, IIPS is able to reason about these, e.g., in order to customise presentations in an intelligent way for different types of users and devices.

The paper is organized as follows: section 2 presents an overview of the IIPS system; section 3 describes the IIPS ontologies; section 4 introduces automatic site generation through ontology mapping; section 5 illustrates some initial ideas about how IIPS can exploit the ontological specifications to generate smart, customised interfaces; section 6 discusses the IIPS solution to site maintenance; section 7 describes the initial prototype implementation of IIPS. Finally, sections 8 and 9 compare and contrast IIPS with other relevant approaches and discuss future work.

2 Overview of the IIPS System

Fig. 1 shows the framework of IIPS. As shown in the figure, IIPS accepts a domain ontology as input, and produces a data-intensive web site. The IIPS approach is based on the following methods:

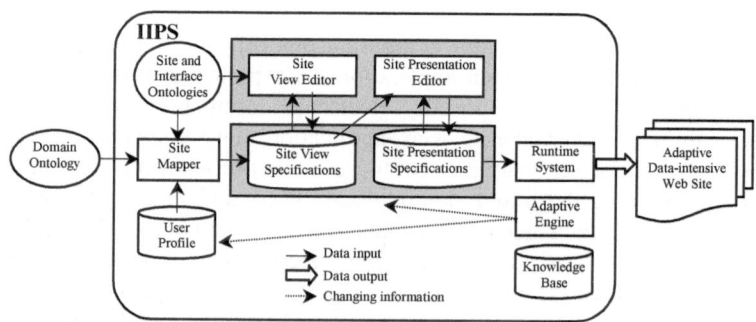

Fig. 1. IIPS Framework

- *Ontology-driven site generation and maintenance.* IIPS defines a set of ontologies to model data-intensive web sites, and uses a domain ontology to drive the target web site generation and maintenance. To create data-intensive web sites with IIPS, developers only need to provide a domain ontology to describe the domain data structure, and the system will generate default web site specifications automatically through mapping. The main advantage of this approach is that developers, especially domain experts, can focus on developing the domain ontology, checking the consistency of the domain ontology, and developing the conceptual structure of the target web site and associated resources.

- *Use of declarative site specifications* to facilitate tool construction and maintenance. The declarative nature of a site model offers many potential benefits over traditional hard-coded site specifications. First, it facilitates the construction of tools to assist developers at design-time, and end-users at run-time, for the declarative model provides a common representation which can be reasoned about [5]. Second, it supports rapid prototyping and iterative development. Developers can construct prototype systems rapidly based on the default system generated by mapping. Finally, it allows a measure of tool independence, so that a site could be reengineered using a different tool set.

- *Use of RDF as the underlying knowledge representing language* to represent ontologies, site specifications, and target web sites. Resource Description Framework (RDF) [6] is a foundation for processing metadata, which provides interoperability between applications that exchange machine-understandable information on the Web. RDF schema [7] provides a mechanism to define particular vocabularies for RDF documents. However, it is not powerful enough to describe the constraints on and relationships among ontologies. At the moment, we use RDF schema to represent the basics of the site ontology, the interface ontology and domain ontologies, and exploit OCML [8] to describe constraints and relationships. We use RDF statements to describe site specifications and annotate target web sites. Later we will consider using DAML+OIL [9] or OWL [10] as the underlying language to represent ontologies.

- *Separation of presentations from site contents.* IIPS uses a *site view specification* to describe the navigational structure, the compositional structure, and contents of a web site, and uses *a presentation specification* to describe presentation instructions, including layouts and visual appearances. This approach separates presentation from site view specification completely. As a result, one site view can be rendered according to different presentation instructions, thus creating totally different presentations.

- *Provision of a set of graphic tools* to support site generation and management. The tools suite of IIPS consists of *a site mapper* to generate default site specifications automatically; *a site editor* to allow developers to edit the site views and presentations manually, and to allow end users to customize site views; *a runtime system* to render site specifications to a web site; *an adaptive engine* to provide adaptive interfaces to end users; and *an ontology editor* to allow users to edit and extend ontologies.

3 Modelling of Web Site

3.1 Site Ontology

The site ontology is defined to model the navigational structure and the compositional structure of a data-intensive web site on the basis of pre-existing site modelling approaches. It conceptualizes a generic data-intensive web site at an implementation independent level, and makes use of the user interface ontology to model the user interfaces of a data-intensive web site. Fig. 2 provides an overview of the site ontology:

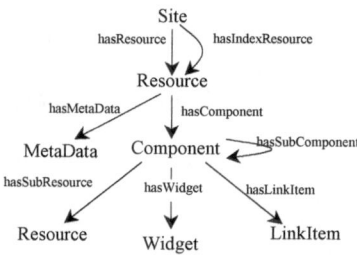

Fig. 2. Overview of the Site Ontology

- The class *Site* models a web site as a logical collection of resources. It has slots *hasResource* and *hasIndexResource*. The slot *hasResource* specifies resources a web site contains. The slot *hasIndexResource* describes the entry point of a web site that helps users to navigate through.
- The class *Resource* models web resources such as web pages and Java applets. It contains a slot *component* that describes contents of a resource, and a slot *hasMetadata*. To model typical resources which appear in data-intensive web sites, IIPS defines a series of resource primitives, which are shown in table 1.
- The class *Component* models contents of resources. It consists of slots: *hasSubResource* that specifies resources that may appear in a component, *hasSubComponent* that describes sub-components, and *hasWidget* and *hasLinkItem* that describe widgets and hyperlink items. IIPS defines five component primitives to model typical types of contents that can be used to compose resources. Details are shown in table 1.
- The class *Widget* models basic interface elements that can present any kind of information at a conceptual level. It is an abstract class to describe widgets. IIPS defines three primitives to model abstract widgets as shown in table 1.
- The class *LinkItem* models contents that have an associated hyperlink. It has three slots: *hasAssociatedResourceURI* to specify associated resource, *hasParameter* to filter the resource content, and *output* to present prompt information.

- The class *DataItem* describes domain data in the site ontology and the interface ontology. It has two subclasses: *ClassItem* and *SlotItem*. The class *ClassItem* describes domain class entities. The class *SlotItem* models domain properties or slots.
- The class *MetaData* models metadata for resources.

Table 1. Primitives of resources, components, and widgets

Class Name			Description	Slot List
Resource			Modelling web resources.	• hasComponent • hasMetaData
	IndexResource		Serving as an entry point of a web site	• hasNavigationComponent
	IndexedResource		Presenting indexed information about a set of instances of domain entities	• hasIndexComponent
	DatalistResource		Presenting detailed information about a set of instances of domain entities	• hasDataComponent • hasLinkItem • hasParameter
	Knowledgeacquisition Resource		Allowing end users to input facts about domain entities	• hasKaComponent
	SearchResource		Allowing end users to make queries	• hasSearchComponent • hasDataComponent
Component			Modelling contents of composing resources	• hasSubResource • hasSubComponent • hasWidget
	InputComponent			
		KaComponent	Modelling contents to allow users to input facts about domain entities	• hasClassItem • hasKaCommand
		SearchComponent	Modelling contents to allow users to make queries	• hasClassItem • hasSearckKey • hasSearchCommand
	OutputComponent			
		NavigationComponent	Modelling contents of presenting navigation information	• hasLinkitem
		IndexComponent	Modelling contents of presenting indexed instances of domain entities	• hasLinkItem • hasIndexKey
		DataComponent	Modelling contents of displaying detailed information about a set of domain instances	• hasClassItem
Widget			Modelling basic interface elements	
	Input		Modelling widgets allowing users to input facts	• hasSlotItem • hasDefaultValue • hasInputType • hasStyle
	Output		Describing widgets presenting information	• hasOutputType • hasValue
	Command		Modelling widgets allowing user to invoke a task	• hasTask

3.2 Interface Ontology

Since more and more web sites employ complex graphic user interfaces to facilitate interactions with end users, it is no longer adequate to focus only on data content and navigation structure as many approaches do. User interfaces should be modeled to conceptualize interface design knowledge and provide an explicit interface knowledge base for interface generation.

The interface ontology in IIPS defines four classes to model web-based user interfaces: *Presentation, Template, Layout,* and *Container,* and a series of *mapping rules* to provide presentation guidelines for user interface generation. The *presentation* class defines presentations for interface elements. It has a slot *dataResourceURI* to specify a resource object that a presentation will work on, a slot *layout* and a slot *template*. Class *Layout* models ways to construct a presentation. Class *Template* is defined to facilitate reusing presentations. It has a sub class *WidgetTemplate* to model templates to render conceptual widgets. The *Container* class models interface elements which hold other interface elements, such as windows, forms, dialogs, and panels. The *mapping rules* define a set of rules for mapping data types to widgets. For example, Boolean data can be mapped to a check box, a radio-button, or a text output.

3.3 An Example

To illustrate the usage of IIPS site ontologies to model a data-intensive web site, we use the web site of the Knowledge Media Institute at the Open University (http://kmi.open.ac.uk) as a data-intensive web site example. As a site instance, the KMi web site contains an index page and a list of resources to present information. Fig. 3 shows a fragment of RDF statements describing the KMi web site (The namespace prefix 'so' refers to the namespace of IIPS site ontologies: xmlns:so="http://kmi.open.ac.uk/ylei/iips/siteontology/").

```
<rdf:Description rdf:about="http://kmi.open.ac.uk">
  <rdf:type rdf:resource="http://kmi.open.ac.uk/ylei/iips/siteontology#Site" />
  <so:IndexResource rdf:resource="http://kmi.open.ac.uk/home-f.cfm"/>
  <so:Resource>
   <rdf:Bag>
     <rdf:li rdf:resource="http://kmi.open.ac.uk/people/members.html"/>
     <rdf:li rdf:resource="http://kmi.open.ac.uk/people/affiliate.html"/>
   </rdf:Bag>
   ...
  </so:Resource>
</rdf:Description>
```

Fig. 3. Specifications describing the KMi web site

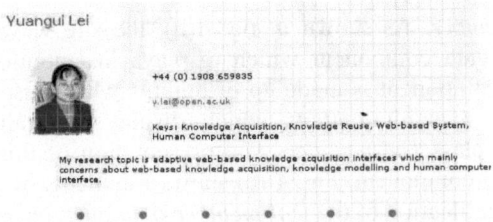

Fig. 4(a). Screenshot of the KMi-member page

```
<rdf:Description rdf:about="http://kmi.open.ac.uk/members.htm">
  <rdf:type rdf:resource="http://kmi.open.ac.uk/ylei/iips/siteontology#Resource"/>
  <so:Component rdf:resource="http://kmi.open.ac.uk/viewspec/components/kmi-member-dataComponent"/>
</rdf:Description>

<rdf:Description rdf:about="http://kmi.open.ac.uk/viewspec/components/kmi-member-dataComponent">
  <rdf:type rdf:resource="http://kmi.open.ac.uk/ylei/iips/siteontology#DataComponent"/>
  <so:ClassItem rdf:resource="http://kmi.open.ac.uk/kmi-ontology/kmi-member" />
  <so:Output>
    <rdf:Description rdf:about="http://kmi.open.ac.uk/images/bullet">
      <so:OutputType>image</so:OutputType>
      <so:Value>http://kmi.open.ac.uk/img/text/b-bullet.gif</so:Value>
    </rdf:Description>
  </so:Output>
  <so:DynamicOutput>
    <rdf:Description rdf:about="http://kmi.open.ac.uk/viewspec/slotentities/kmi-member-name">
      <rdf:type rdf:resource="http://kmi.open.ac.uk/ylei/iips/siteOntology#DynamicOutput"/>
      <so:OutputType>text</so:OutputType>
      <so:SlotItem rdf:resource="http://kmi.open.ac.uk/kmi-ontology/ kmi-member-name" />
    </rdf:Description>
  </so:DynamicOutput>
  ...
</rdf:Description>
```

Fig. 4(b). The site view specification of the *kmi-member page*

```
<rdf:Description rdf:about="http://kmi.open.ac.uk/presentationspec/presentation/kmi-member-dataComponent-presentation">
<rdf:type rdf:resource="http://kmi.open.ac.uk/ylei/iips/siteontology#Presentation"/>
<so:Container rdf:resource="http://kmi.open.ac.uk/presentationspec/container/dataContainer" />
<so:DataResourceURI>http://kmi.open.ac.uk/viewspec/components/kmi-member-dataComponent </so:DataResourceURI>
<so:Layout>
<rdf:Description rdf:about="http://kmi.open.ac.uk/presentationspec/layout/kmi-member-data-component">
  <rdf:type rdf:resource="http://kmi.open.ac.uk/ylei/iips/siteontology#Layout"/>
  <so:Presentation>
    <rdf:Description rdf:about="http://kmi.open.ac.uk/presentationspec/presentation/kmi-member-name">
      <so:DataResourceURI>http://kmi.open.ac.uk/viewspec/slotentities/kmi-member-name</so:DataResourceURI>
      <so:Template rdf:resource="http://kmi.open.ac.uk/presentationspec/template/larger-blue-text" />
    </rdf:Description>
  </so:Presentation>
  ...
</rdf:Description>
</so:Layout>
</rdf:Description>
```

Fig. 4(c). The presentation specification of the *data component of kmi-member*. The dataResourceURI property specifies the data component as the resource object that the presentation will work on

To illustrate how to describe web pages presenting information about domain entities, we use *kmi-member* as an entity example. Fig. 4(a) shows the screenshot of the kmi-member web page. This page is made up components to display instantiations of the class *kmi-member*. As shown in fig. 4(b), the site view specification of this page contains one data component which displays instantiations of the class *kmi-member*. The data component is made up of outputs which display prompt messages for each slot, and dynamic outputs which display the value of slots of each instantiation of the class *kmi-member*. The presentation of this page is constructed from that of the data component. Fig. 4 (c) shows fragments of code appearing in the site presentation specification of the *kmi-member data component*.

4 Automatic Site Generation through Ontology Mapping

The idea of using a domain ontology to drive software generation is not new. Researchers in the knowledge acquisition area have developed several knowledge acquisition meta-tools, such as DASH [11], Protégé 2000 [12], and Knote [13], which use a domain ontology to drive the knowledge acquisition tool generation. The major advantage of this methodology is that developers, especially domain experts, can specify software tools readily, and that a pre-existing ontology can be used as the basis for the specifications.

IIPS uses the same methodology in driving data-intensive web site generation. Unlike approaches mentioned above where tool specification and implementation are tightly coupled together, IIPS defines a set of comprehensive ontologies to model the target software – data-intensive web sites explicitly, and conceptualizes a target web site at a high level without being concerned about the implementation. As a result, the target web site can be rendered in different ways.

The automatic site generation mainly involves site mapping, which is responsible for generating site specifications through mapping a domain ontology to the site ontology. IIPS uses relationships among the classes defined in a domain ontology to drive the design of the structure and content of the target web site. It makes use of the following site mapping rules to generate site specifications:

- IIPS can identify the top nodes of the domain ontology, and map them to an index resource, which serves as the entry point of the target web site.
- Each class, which needs to be instantiated during the run time of the target web site, is mapped to a series of resources. These resources include a data list resource which presents instances, an indexed resource which displays index information about a set of instances, a search resource which contains search-components to allow users to make a query, and a knowledge-acquisition resource which enables users to input facts about the class.
- The process of instantiating a knowledge-acquisition component involves scanning properties (slots) of the given class, and mapping properties to widgets according to mapping rules defined in the interface ontology. Each slot is mapped to an input widget to allow users to enter data, and an output widget to present a prompt message. In addition, command widgets, which are associated with knowledge acquisition tasks, are needed in the knowledge-acquisition component.
- The search component instantiation process is similar to the knowledge acquisition component. The difference lies in its command widget, which is associated with a search task.

The default site specification generated by ontology mapping contains conceptual structures and contents. The run-time system of IIPS can create default interfaces and presentations for them.

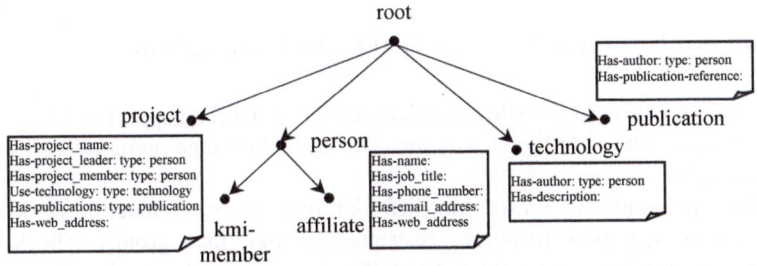

Fig. 5. Sample Ontology

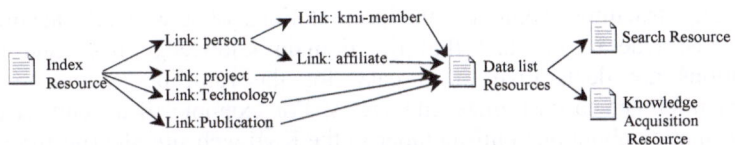

Fig. 6. The site structure generated for the sample ontology by site mapping

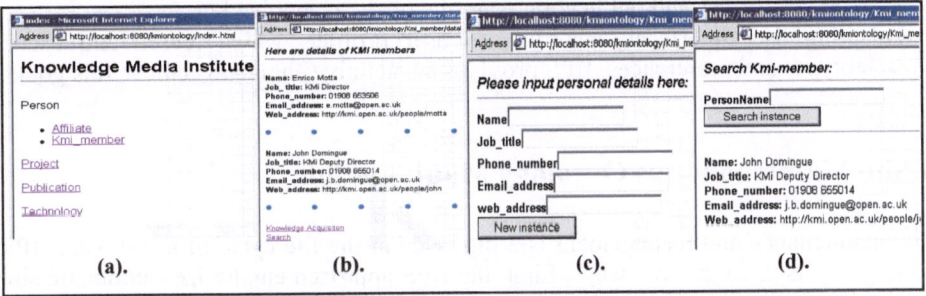

Fig. 7. Screenshots of web pages generated by the IIPS prototype system from the sample ontology. Figure (a) shows the index page. Figure (b), (c) and (d) show the data list page, the knowledge acquisition page, and search page of class *kmi-member*

Fig. 5 shows a sample ontology to illustrate the automatic site generation. There are six domain class entities. The class *person* has sub-classes *kmi-member* and *affiliate*. Fig. 6 shows the default site structure generated by the IIPS site mapper through ontology mapping.

In this example, the index resource contains five hyperlink items. The general class *person* is mapped to a foldable hyperlink item that contains further hyperlinks. Each of the other classes is mapped to a series of resources, including a data list resource, a search resource, and a knowledge acquisition resource. Users can access these resources through accessing data list resources of each class entity. Fig. 7 shows screenshots of web pages generated by the IIPS prototype system from the sample ontology.

5 Intelligent Support for User Interface Generation

The declarative nature of the site specifications gives IIPS a capability to reason about user interfaces. The intelligent support for user interface generation happens in following cases:

- Creating different site views for different user groups. General users can only browse and customize resources restricted to their user groups. The knowledge acquisition resources are hidden from the site view. Advanced users can browse and customize pages, and input facts to the knowledge base. The developers and webmasters have the highest access to the target web site. They can browse and edit every site view, and create new user groups.
- Customizing structures, contents, and presentations of a web site according to users' needs. Due to the fact that the domain knowledge base and the site specifications are declarative, it is easy for the run-time system to exploit intelligent inference to customize site views. For example, if an end user wants more information about one kmi-member in the KMi web site, the run-time system can create a new web page through reasoning about the site view specification and the domain knowledge base. The new web page contains hyperlinks to all of the web resources about this person, including his or her home page, kmi-member page, project pages and publication pages he or she is involved in.
- Adapting user interfaces according to user profiles, which record end users' stereotypes and preferences. IIPS provides an adaptive engine to achieve this goal.

6 Site Maintenance as Ontology Manipulation

Site maintenance and management is a big issue in the life cycle of a web site. IIPS addresses this issue in three ways. First, the IIPS approach emphasizes automatic site generation from a domain ontology because it can relieve developers of developing a web site from scratch, and help them to focus on the work of developing domain ontologies. Second, the IIPS approach provides visual facilities to support developers to edit the site content and presentation manually. Finally, the IIPS approach supports automatic web site re-engineering after the domain ontology has been changed without loss of the customization information made by developers during the site editing process. Because the site specifications are declarative, the automatic site re-engineering only changes information about domain entities.

In IIPS, site maintenance can be achieved not only at the content level but also at the site specification level. At the content level, IIPS provides knowledge acquisition forms to allow end users to make contributions to knowledge bases. At the site specification level, IIPS provides a site view editor to edit structure and content of a web site, and a site presentation editor to edit interfaces and presentations. The purpose of these editors is two-fold. First, they provide facilities for developers to edit the target web sites. Developers can utilize them to extend the site ontology through inheriting concepts in the site ontology, e.g. developers can define new types of data component to specify how the data component looks exactly. Second, they also support end users in customizing the site views restricted to their group. End users cannot change the web site, but they can choose information they are interested in and filter the irrelevant information.

7 Prototyping

Fig. 8 shows the major components of IIPS system. It is made up of three major components: *a knowledge warehouse, a suite of support tools*, and *a runtime system* to render the site specifications to target web sites.

The *knowledge warehouse* hosts ontologies, domain knowledge bases, site specifications, and user profiles. It serves as data repository for data represented in RDF schema and RDF statements. The *support tools* provide design-time support as well as run-time support. The *run-time system* is responsible for reading the site specifications, generating target web sites, and invoking the *adaptive engine* to provide on-line adaptive interfaces.

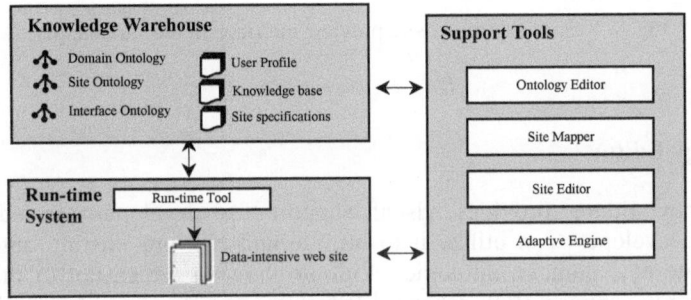

Fig. 8. Major components of the IIPS prototype system

7.1 Site Mapper

The Site Mapper is responsible for creating default site specifications through mapping the domain ontology to the site ontology. It provides facilities for developers to customize the domain ontology, preview default site views, and build default site specifications.

Customizing a domain ontology means specifying and refining domain data structures on the basis of a domain ontology. It involves selecting classes from the domain hierarchy structure, and selecting slots for each selected class. Customizing a domain ontology doesn't mean changing the domain ontology. It will not result in losing slots for classes. For example, if we only choose the class *kmi-member* and the class *affiliate*, and don't choose the class *person*, the class *kmi-member* and *affiliate* will keep all their inherited slots with them, and will not lose any information.

To illustrate the site mapping result clearly, we use the sample ontology shown in Fig. 5 as a domain ontology to drive the site generation. Fig. 9 shows the screenshot of the site preview interface. The left frame shows the site view structure, which is displayed in tree style. Each node represents a resource, the relationship between a child and a parent is hyperlink. The right frame displays detail information about the selected resource node, including its declarative contents and preview.

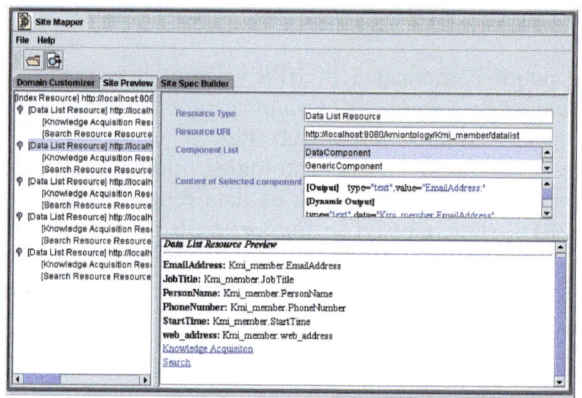

Fig. 9. Screenshot of the site preview interface in the site mapper

7.2 Ontology Editor

The Ontology Editor provides visual support for developers to edit domain ontologies. Developers can utilize it to browse and edit pre-existing ontologies, as well as create new domain ontologies. Fig. 10 shows a screenshot of the ontology editor. It mainly supports RDF schema [7] format, and also provides mechanisms to translate ontology representation between RDF schema and OCML [8]. Ontology files can be saved as both RDF Schema and OCML format. Although the definition of a class is separated from property definitions, the IIPS ontology editor provides a very straightforward way to allow users to edit classes and properties together. It provides a *class tree tab* to facilitate class editing, and a *property tree tab* to help users to concentrate on property definitions. Class editing and property editing are not separate in the ontology editor. Users can select properties for classes during the process of editing classes. At the same time, they also can achieve this by selecting domain classes for a property during the process of editing properties.

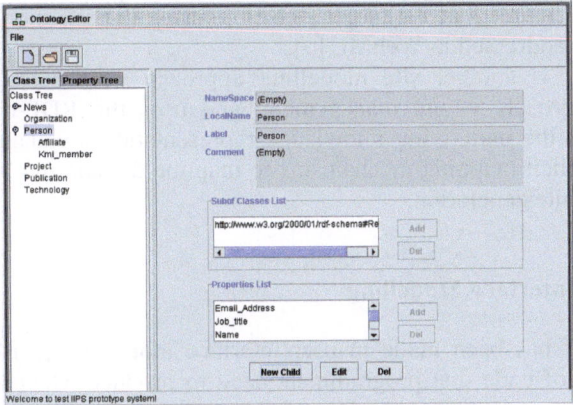

Fig. 10. A screenshot of the ontology editor

Besides the site mapper and the ontology editor, we have worked out an initial run-time system, which is responsible for reading site specifications and creating dynamic web pages. Fig. 7 shows screenshots of web pages generated by the initial run-time system.

8 Related Work

The work on IIPS brings efforts from four areas together: data-intensive web site modelling, user interface modelling, software tool generation from ontologies, and the application of RDF to web engineering.

Related Work on Data-Intensive Web Site Modelling

Recently, research towards modelling of data-intensive web applications has been intensified due to the fact that the processes of web application development from scratch and web application maintenance are inefficient, time-consuming, and costly. Many modelling approaches have been proposed to tackle this problem [1,2,3,4]. Closest to our approach is the work on WebML [3]. It provides explicit site models, and supports automatic site generation. It make uses of a *structural model* to express domain data structure, a *composition* model to specify contents to composite a hypertext, a n*avigation model, a presentation model* to describe the layout and presentation, and a p*ersonalization model* to specify the features and personalization requirements of users and user groups. However, our approach models a web site much more thoroughly than WebML [3] because it models user interfaces explicitly. WebML [3] does provide a presentation model to express the layout and graphic appearance of pages. However, it only concerns the look and feel of web pages. We argue that the user interface is more than presentation which emphasizes presenting information rather than user-interface interactions. Furthermore, we emphasize the importance of the semantics of the target web site during the site modelling process, which has not been addressed in WebML [3].

OntoWebber [4] is another site modelling approach similar to IIPS. It is an ontology-based approach to site management, and uses the RDF-based language DAML+OIL [9] as the underlying knowledge representation language. However, it fails to provide explicit mapping mechanisms to map the domain model with the site model to automate site generation.

Related Work on Interface Modelling

A substantial effort has been made in user interface modelling [5,14,15] to try to reduce the amount of code that programmers need to produce when creating a user interface. However, most approaches have failed to become widespread due to the fact that these approaches tightly couple user interface definition with the user interface implementation, and thus lack the flexibility to be rendered in different ways.

UIML [14] and XIML [15] are recent approaches proposed to address the problem of authoring user interfaces for multiple platforms. These two languages are both declarative, appliance-independent, and generic. However they do not separate the application model from the user interface model completely.

XSL [16] addresses this problem very well. It is a language for expressing stylesheets that describe how to present an XML document. The XSL approach is domain independent. However, it focuses on the presentation of the source data. That is to say, it emphasizes presenting information rather than user-interface interactions. IIPS concerns not only the presentation of the source data, but also user interfaces, such as interface mapping rules between a data type and a user control object.

Related Work on Software Generation from Ontology

The feasibility of ontology-driven software generation has been demonstrated in the knowledge acquisition area, where various ontology-driven knowledge acquisition metatools have been developed [11,12,13]. IIPS distinguishes itself from these tools in that the target system is completely different. IIPS aims to generate a data-intensive web site. Unlike the approaches mentioned above, IIPS provides an explicit ontology to describe the target system and support ontology mapping, and conceptualizes a target web site at a high level without being concerned with the implementation. Thus, the IIPS approach is much more generic.

Related Work on Applying RDF to Web Engineering

XWMF [17] aims to create a machine-understandable web sites through exploiting RDF to model web application and its content. It provides a generic web engineering schemata and RDF as the basic vocabulary to model a web application. However, it does not provide a set of explicit models to describe web sites, therefore it is very different from the IIPS approach, although they address similar goals of creating machine-understandable web applications.

SEAL [18] and SEAL-II [19] aim to build and manage semantic web portals on the basis of ontologies. However, they mainly focus on semantic browsing, semantic-based ranking, semantic querying, and information contribution from end users, rather than on web site modelling and automatic site generation. They do not provide explicit site models, or the mapping approach to automatic site generation, and are thus quite different from IIPS.

RSS [20], which stands for RDF (or Rich) Site Summary, is a lightweight metadata description and syndication format. It provides a vocabulary to describe a "channel" consisting of URL-retrievable items. Each item consists of a title, link, and brief description. It models a web site in a very simple way.

9 Conclusions

In this paper, we have presented IIPS, an intelligent information presentation system that uses an ontology-driven approach to drive the generation and maintenance processes of data-intensive web sites. IIPS distinguishes itself from pre-existing data-intensive web site modelling approaches in several ways. First, it provides comprehensive ontologies to model data-intensive web sites, with an emphasis on user interface modelling that has been missing in other approaches. Second, it supports automatic site generation, as well as providing a suite of visual tools to support manual management and maintenance. Finally, it provides intelligent support for user interface generation.

An initial prototype system of IIPS has been completed, including a site mapper, an ontology editor, and an initial run-time system. Future work will focus on the site editor to allow developers to edit site views and presentations and allow end users to customize a web site, and the adaptive engine to provide adaptive user interfaces for target web sites.

Acknowledgements

We would like to thank Murray Altheim and Arthur Stutt for their insightful comments on earlier drafts of this paper.

References

1. Franca Garzotto, Paolo Paolini and Daniel Schwabe, HDM--a model-based approach to hypertext application design, ACM Trans. Inf. Syst. 11, 1 (Jan. 1993), Pages 1 – 26.
2. T. Isakowitz, E.A. Stohr and P. Balasubramaninan, RMM: A Methodology for Structured Hypermedia Design, Communications of the ACM, August 1995.
3. Stefano Ceri, Piero Fratenali, Aldo Bongio, Web Modelling Language (WebML): a modelling language for designing Web sites, www9 Conference, Amsterdam, May 2000.

4. Yuhui Jin, Stefan Decker, Gio Wiederhold, OntoWebber: Model-Driven Ontology-Based Web site Management, Semantic Web Workshop, Stanford, California, July 2001.
5. P.Szekely, P.Sukaviriya, P.Castells, J.Muthukumarasamy,and E.Salcher, Declarative interface models for user interface construction tools: the MASTERMIND approach, In Proc. EHCI'95, 1995.
6. Resource Description Framework (RDF) Model and Syntax, W3C Proposed Recommendation, http://www.w3.org/TR/PR-rdf-syntax/.
7. Resource Description Framework (RDF) Schema Specification 1.0, W3C Candidate Recommendation, http://www.w3.org/TR/rdf-schema/.
8. Motta E., Reusable Components of Knowledge Modelling: Case Studies in Parametric Design Problem Solving, IOS Press, Amsterdam, 1999.
9. Ian Horrocks, Frank van Harmelen, Peter Patel-Schneider, Tim Berners-Lee, Dan Brickley, Dan Connolly, Mike Dean, Stefan Decker, Dieter Fensel, Pat Hayes, Jeff Heflin, Jim Hendler, Ora Lassila, Deb McGuinness, Lynn Andrea Stein, DAML+OIL, http://www.daml.org/2001/03/daml+oil-index, 2001.
10. Jeff Heflin, Raphael Volz, and Jonathan Dale, Requirements for a Web Ontology Language, W3C Working Draft, 7 March 2002, http://www.w3.org/TR/2002/WD-webont-req-20020307/.
11. Henrik Eriksson, Angel R. Puerta, and Mark A. Musen, Generation of Knowledge-Acquisition Tools from Domain Ontologies, Int. J. Human-Computer Studies (1994) 41, 425-453.
12. William E.Grosso, Henrick Eriksson. Ray W. Fergerson, Johh H. Gennari, Samson W. Tu, and Mark A. Musen, Knowledge Modelling at the Millennium, In Proc. the 12th International Workshop on Knowledge Acquisition, Modelling and Management (KAW'99) Banff, Canada, October 1999, http://smiweb.stanford.edu/pubs/SMI_Abstracts/SMI-1999-0801.html.
13. Enrico Motta, Simon Buckingham Shum, and John Domingue, Ontology-driven document enrichment: principles, tools and applications, Int. J. Human-Computer Studies (2000) 52, 1071-1109.
14. Marc Abrams, Constantinos Phanouriou, Alan L. Batongbacal, Stephen M. Williams, Jonathan E. Shuster, UIML: An Appliance-Independent XML User Interface Language, WWW8 Conference Paper, Toronto Convention Centre, Toronto, Canada, May 11-14, 1999.
15. Angel Puerta and Jacob Eisenstein, XIML: A Common Representation for Interaction Data, in Proceedings of the 7th international conference on Intelligent user interfaces, pp. 214-215, 2002.
16. Sharon Adler, Anders Berglund, Jeff Caruso, Stephen Deach, Tony Graham, Paul Grosso, Eduardo Gutentag, Alex Milowski, Scott Parnell, Jeremy Richman, Steve Zilles, Extensible Stylesheet Language (XSL) Verson 1.0, 2001, http://www.w3.org/TR/xsl/.
17. Reinhold Klapsing, Gustaf Neumann, Wolfram Conen: Semantics in Web Engineering: Applying the Resource Description Framework, IEEE MultiMedia Journal, Vol. 8, No. 2, April-June, 2001.
18. Nenad Stojanovic, Alexander Maedche, Setffen Staab, Rudi Studer, SEAL-A Framework for Developing SEmantic PortALs, K-Cap 2001 - First International Conference on Knowledge Capture, Oct. 21-23, 2001, Victoria, B.C., Canada.
19. Hotho, A., Maedche, A., Staab, S., & Studer, R., SEAL-II — the soft spot between richly structured and unstructured knowledge. Journal of Universal Computer Science, vol. 7, no. 7 (2001), 566-590.
20. Gabe Beged-Dov, Dan Brickley, Rael Dornfest, Ian Davis, Leigh Dodds, Jonhathan Eisenzopt, David Galbraith, R.V. Guha, Ken MacLeod, Eric Miller, Aaron Swartz, and Eric van der Vlist, RDF Site Summary (RSS) 1.0, http://groups.yahoo.com/group/rss-dev/files/specification.html, 2000.

MAFRA — A MApping FRAmework for Distributed Ontologies

Alexander Maedche[1], Boris Motik[1], Nuno Silva[1,2], and Raphael Volz[1]

[1] Forschungszentrum Informatik at the Univ. Karlsruhe,
D-76131 Karlsruhe, Germany
http://www.fzi.de/WIM
{maedche,motik,silva,volz}@fzi.de
[2] ISEP Instituto Superior de Engenharia,
Instituto Politecnico do Porto, Portugal
http://www.dei.isep.ipp.pt

Abstract. Ontologies as means for conceptualizing and structuring domain knowledge within a community of interest are seen as a key to realize the Semantic Web vision. However, the decentralized nature of the Web makes achieving this consensus across communities difficult, thus, hampering efficient knowledge sharing between them. In order to balance the autonomy of each community with the need for interoperability, mapping mechanisms between distributed ontologies in the Semantic Web are required. In this paper we present MAFRA, an interactive, incremental and dynamic framework for mapping distributed ontologies.

1 Introduction

The current WWW is a great success with respect to the amount of stored documents and the number of users. However, the ever-increasing amount information on the Web places a heavy burden of accessing, extracting, interpreting and maintaining information on the human users of Web. Tim Berners-Lee, the inventor of the WWW, coined the vision of Semantic Web, providing means for annotation of Web resources with machine-processable metadata providing them with background knowledge and meaning (see [2]). Ontologies as means for conceptualizing and structuring domain knowledge are seen as the key to enabling the fulfillment of the Semantic Web vision.

However, the de-centralized nature of the Web makes indeed inevitable that communities will use their own ontologies to describe their data. In this vision, ontologies are themselves distributed and the key point is the mediation between distributed data using mappings between ontologies [16]. Thus, complex mappings and reasoning about those mappings are necessary for comparing and combining ontologies, and for integrating data described using different ontologies. Existing information integration systems and approaches (e.g., TSIMMIS [6], Information Manifold [8], Infomaster[1], MOMIS[2], Xyleme [3]) are "centralized" systems of mediation between users and dis

---

[1] http://infomaster.stanford.edu/infomaster-info.html
[2] http://sparc20.ing.unimo.it/Momis/
[3] http://www.xyleme.com

A. Gómez-Pérez and V.R. Benjamins (Eds.): EKAW 2002, LNAI 2473, pp. 235–250, 2002.

tributed data sources, which exploit mappings between a single mediated schema and schemas of data sources. Those mappings are typically modelled as views (over the mediated schema in the local-as-view approach, or over the sources schemas in the global-as-view approach) which are expressed using languages having a formal semantics. For scaling up to the Web, the "centralized" approach of mediation is probably not flexible enough, and distributed systems of mediation are more appropriate.

Building on this idea and on existing work, we introduce MAFRA, an Ontology MApping FRAmework (MAFRA) for distributed ontologies in the Semantic Web. Within MAFRA we provide an approach and conceptual framework that provides a generic view onto the overall distributed mapping process. In particular, in this paper we focus on representation and execution aspects of mappings. However, the proposed framework offers support in all parts of the ontology mapping life-cycle.

Organization of this paper. In section 2 we introduce the underlying conceptual architecture of MAFRA. In section 3 we focus on mapping representation and present the current status of our semantic bridging ontology and discuss its features. Section 4 presents the realized mapping implementation within KAON - an ontology and Semantic Web application framework[4]. Before we conclude a short discussion of related and future work is given in section 5.

2   Conceptual Framework

An ontology mapping process, as defined in [14], is the set of activities required to transform instances of a source ontology into instances of a target ontology. By studying the process and analyzing different approaches from the literature we observed a set of commonalities and assembled them into the MAFRA conceptual framework, outlined in Figure 1. The framework consists of five horizontal modules describing the phases that we consider fundamental and distinct in a mapping process. Four vertical components run along the entire mapping process, interacting with horizontal modules.

2.1   Horizontal Dimension of MAFRA

Within the horizontal dimension, we identified following five modules:

Lift & Normalization. This module focuses on raising all data to be mapped onto the same representation level, coping with syntactical, structural and language heterogeneity [19]. Both ontologies must be normalized to a uniform representation, in our case RDF(S), thus eliminating syntax differences and making semantics differences between the source and the target ontology more apparent [14]. This lift process is not further elaborated in this paper - we shall simply assume that the source and target ontologies are already represented in RDF-Schema with their instances in RDF. Also one essential step of this first phase is normalization. Three distinct ordered tasks are performed in our approach: *(i)* tokenization of the entities, *(ii)* elimination of resulting stop words and *(iii)* expansion of acronyms. The result is a list of normalized lexica.

---

[4] http://kaon.semanticweb.org

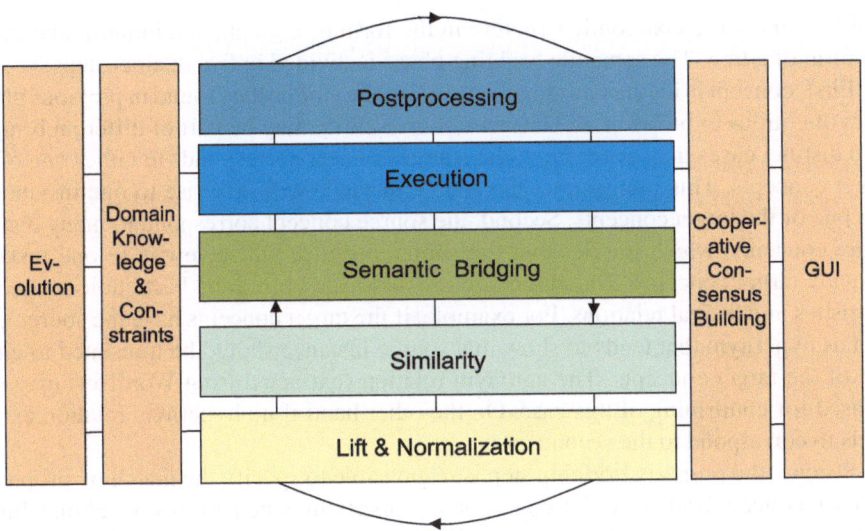

Fig. 1. Conceptual Architecture

Similarity. This module establishes similarities between entities from the source and target ontology, thus, it supports mapping discovery. Several different similarity measures have been proposed in literature [14, 3, 5, 10, 1].

We adopted a multi-strategy process (similar to [5]), that calculates similarities between ontology entities using different algorithms. The first strategy focuses on acquiring a *lexical similarity* between each entity in source entity with each and all entities in target entity. For that WordNet and an altered Resnik algorithm [15] are used. Subsequently, a next step calculates the so called *property similarity*, that is responsible to acquire the similarity between concepts based on their properties, either attributes or relations. The *bottom-up similarity* intends to propagate the similarity (or dissimilarity) from lower parts of the taxonomy to the upper concepts. It uses the property similarity as input and propagates the values to the top. This similarity gives a good overall view of similarity between taxonomies. Complementarily, the *top-down similarity* propagates similarities from top to bottom, and assumes special relevance when top level concepts have a higher or lower similarity. A detailed description and an evaluation of our similarity measures and the overall discovery module is provided in a companion paper [17].

Semantic Bridging. Based on the similarities computed in the previously described phase, the semantic bridging phase is responsible for establishing correspondence between entities from the source and target ontology. It intends to specify bridges between entities in a way that each instance represented according to the source ontology is translated into the most similar instance described according to the target ontology. This simple principle motivate our approach in semantic bridge specification following the evidence that RDFS ontologies normally rely and exploit the underlying OO part of

RDFS, namely the taxonomic structure in the form of a graph, and in particular cases, the form of a tree. The semantic bridging phase is divided in five distinct steps:

First, concept bridging chooses according to the similarities found in previous phase, pairs of entities to be bridged. The same source entity may be part of different bridges. Two distinct cases may arise: First, the source concept corresponds to either one of the target concepts. This implies that the source instance will give rise to one instance of just one of the target concepts. Second, the source concept correspond to many distinct target concepts, which implies that the source instance will give rise to one instance of many target concepts. The automatic process tries to find the best choice based on heuristics and lexical relations. For example, if the target concepts have the source concept as hypernym that tends to show that source instance should be translated to either one of the target concepts. The antonym relation (extracted from WordNet) may also be used for confirming of this case. On the other hand if no hypernym relation exist it tends to correspond to the second case.

Second, the property bridging step is responsible to specify the matching properties for each concept bridge. As for concepts, a property may be part of several matchings, which implies the same two cases previously mentioned for concepts. Therefore, the same strategy may be used in here. It is important to emphasize that properties in our approach are of two types, distinguishing between attributes and relations. If source and target properties are of different types the transformation specification information is required, where the domain expert is asked to supply this information.

Third, the inferencing step focus in endowing the mapping with bridges for concepts that do not have a specific counterpart target concept. In fact, a source concept c_s^1 may not always have a target concept counterpart c_t^1. However, if a match exists between the source concept c_s^0 (a super concept of c_s^1) and c_t^0, than an implicit similarity exists between c_s^1 and c_s^0.

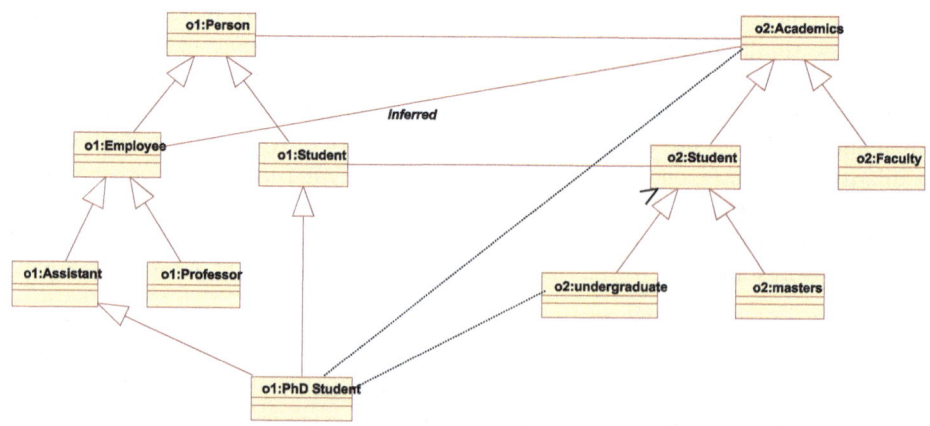

Fig. 2. Inferring best possible bridge

This scenario is depicted in Figure 2. Even if the concept EMPLOYEE has no direct counterpart in the target ontology, instances of this concept should be translated into

ACADEMICS instances. This can be automatically inferred because EMPLOYEE is sub concept of PERSON, which in turn is bridged with ACADEMICS. However this is not always a straight forward solution because ambiguity arises in some situations. To infer a bridge to PHD_STUDENT concept is one of such situations. This concept is sub concept of two concepts, which means that any instance of PHD_STUDENT is also an instance of both EMPLOYEE and STUDENT. However, such qualification do not exists in target ontology. In this situations we use available domain knowledge, namely the exploitation of previous mappings where such concepts were bridged. However, for the moment this decision is up to the domain expert. Inferred bridges are always sub bridges of some higher bridge and should not state the target entity. In this example, the process creates an inferred bridge that relies on between PERSON and ACADEMICS to execute the translation. This is called encapsulation in the OO paradigm.

Fourth, the refinement step intends to improve quality of bridges between a source concept and sub concepts of target concepts. In fact this is a complementary procedure of the similarity phase. Besides this step is optional, it becomes important if a good mapping quality is necessary.

Fifth, the transformation specification step intends to associate a transformation procedure to the translation, in a way that source instance may be translated into target instances. This task may be automatized in some extend, specially in well known situations, which can be acquired through experience. However this task is fundamentally a domain expert step. There are two main issues that are extremely dependent on the domain expert: *(i)* the alternative bridge conditions specification arising in concept bridging and property bridging, and *(ii)* the specification of mapping between different types of properties.

Execution. This module actually transforms instances from the source ontology into target ontology by evaluating the semantic bridges defined earlier. In general two distinct modes of operation are possible, namely offline (static, one-time transformation) and online (dynamic, continuous mapping between source and the target) execution. A description of our offline execution engine is provided in section 4.

Post-processing. The post-processing component takes the results of the execution module to check and improve the quality of the transformation results. The most challenging task of post-processing is establishing object identity - recognizing that two instances represent the same real-world object [7]. The post-processing process is not further elaborated in this paper.

2.2   Vertical Dimension of MAFRA

The vertical dimension of MAFRA contains modules that interact with horizontal modules during the overall mapping process. Following four modules have been identified. However, we will only focus on the GUI component in this paper.

Evolution. This aspect focuses on keeping semantic bridges obtained by the "Semantic Bridge" module, which must be kept in synchrony with the changes in the source and target ontologies. We refer the interested reader to [18] where we describe a user-driven ontology evolution strategy.

Cooperative Consensus Building. The cooperative consensus building aspect is responsible for establishing a consensus on semantic bridges between two communities participating in the mapping process. This is a requirement as one has to choose frequently from multiple, alternatively possible mappings .The amount of human involvement required to achieve consensus may be reduced by automating the mapping process as much as possible.

Domain Constraints and Background Knowledge. The quality of similarity computation and semantic bridging may be dramatically improved by introducing background knowledge and domain constraints, e.g. by using glossaries to help identify synonyms or by using lexical ontologies, such as WordNet or domain-specific thesauri, to identify similar concepts.

Graphical User Interface. Mapping is a difficult and time consuming process, which is not less difficult than building an ontology itself, i.e. deep understanding of both conceptualizations required on human side, thus extensive graphical support must be given and it is a separate issue how this can be achieved in an optimal way. The graphical user interfaces (GUI) is further elaborated in section 4.

3   Semantic Bridging

As mentioned in subsection 2.1, the role of the semantic bridging component is to semantically relate entities from the source and target ontologies. A role of a semantic bridge is to encapsulate all necessary information to transform instances of one source ontology entity to instances of one target ontology entity.

3.1   Dimensions of Semantic Bridges

The nature of semantic bridges may be understood by considering different dimensions, each describing one particular aspect of a semantic bridge. By analyzing ontologies used on the Semantic Web, we identified following five dimensions of semantic bridges:

- Entity dimension: Semantic bridges may relate the ontology entities *(i)* concepts (modeling classes of objects from the real world), *(ii)* relations (modeling relationships between objects in the real world), and, *(iii)* attributes (modeling simple properties of objects in the real world) and *(iv)* extensional patterns (modeling the content of the instances).
- Cardinality dimension: This dimension determines the number of ontology entities at both sides of the semantic bridge, ranging from $1 : 1$ to $m : n$. However, we have found that in most cases $m : n$ is not a common requirement, so $1 : n$ and $m : 1$ suffice. Even when $m : n$ are encountered, often they may be decomposed into m $1 : n$ bridges.
- Structural dimension: This dimension reflects the way how elementary bridges may be combined into more complex bridges. We distinguish between the following different relations that may hold between bridges:

- **Specialization** allows a bridge to reuse definitions from another bridge and provide additional information (e.g. a bridge relating Employee concepts from two ontologies may be a specialization of a more general bridge relating Person concepts),
- **Abstraction** is a variation of the type of the super-classes. When this attribute is set, the specified bridge should not be executed independently, but only as super-class of another.
- **Composition** relation between to bridges specifies that a bridge is composed of other bridges,
- **Alternatives** relation between bridges specifies a set of mutually exclusive bridges.
- Constraint dimension: The constraint dimension permits to control the execution of a semantic bridge. It reflects relevant constraints applied during the execution phase to instances from the source ontology. Constraints act as conditions that must hold in order the transformation procedures is applied onto the instances of the source ontology, e.g. the bridge evaluate only if the value of the source instance matches a certain pattern.
- Transformation dimension: This dimension reflects how instances of the source ontology are transformed during the mapping process. Transformations assume different complexity and variety depending on the ontologies being bridged.

3.2   Semantic Bridging Ontology (SBO)

Within our approach four different types of relations between entities, a particular semantic bridge exists. A specification of all available semantic bridges, organized in a taxonomy, is a semantic bridging ontology (SBO). To actually relate the source and target ontology, the mapping process creates an instance of SBO containing semantic bridge instances, each encapsulating all necessary information to transform instances of one source entity to instances of the target entity. Figure 3 describes the most important entities of the semantic bridging ontology. We refer to the five, previously described semantic bridge dimensions:

- Three basic types of entities are considered: Concepts, Relations and Attributes,
- The class SEMANTIC BRIDGE is the most generic bridge, it defines the relations to source and target entities. It is specialized according to the entity type and according to cardinality. Though, there are many combinations of entity types and cardinality bridges that are not explicitly specified, it is important to mention that they can be easily specialized from more general bridges.
- The class SERVICE represents a class used to reference resources that are responsible to connect to, or describe transformations. This class is intended to be used to describe these transformations resources. Because services are normally external to the execution engine, it is required to describe some fundamental characteristics like name, interface (number and type of arguments) and location. Argument and its sub classes Arg and ArgArray permits to describes these characteristics in a simple and direct form.

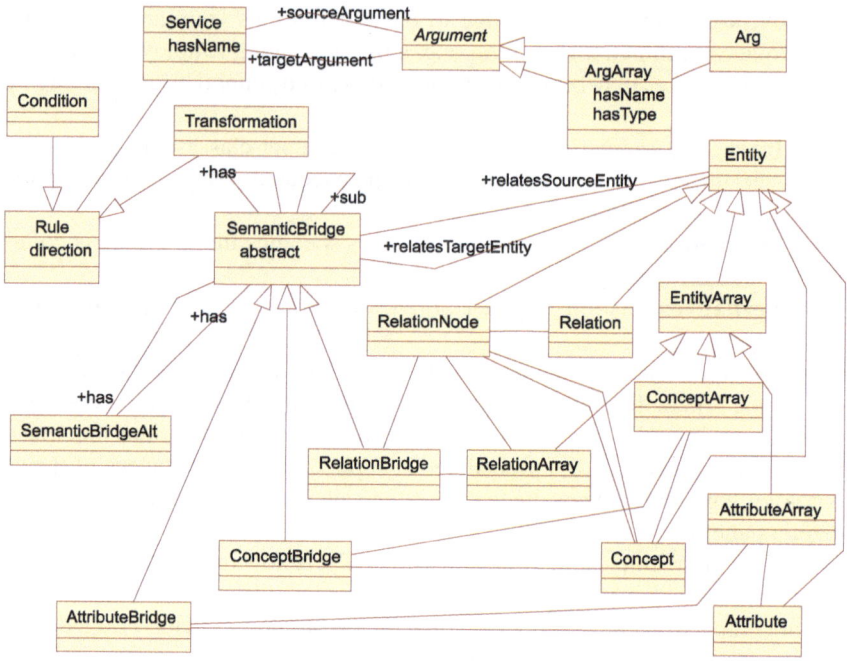

Fig. 3. Bridging Ontology view in UML

- RULE is the general class for constraints and transformation-relevant information, which provides a relation to the service class.
- The class TRANSFORMATION is mandatory in each semantic bridge except if the semantic bridge is set as abstract. It uses the inService relation to link to the transformation procedure, and any execution engine and function specific attributes in order to specify extra requirements;
- The class CONDITION represents the conditions that should be verified in order to execute the semantic bridge. Condition is operationally similar to transformation in the sense that it must specify all the extra requirements for the function that test the conditions. Because any semantic bridge may have a condition, it allows to control complex transformations according to both the schema and instances data, specially in combination with SemanticBridgeAlt and the Composition constructs.
- The COMPOSITION modelling primitive identified above is supported by the has-Bridge relation in the SEMANTICBRIDGE class. It has no cardinality limit nor type constraint which allows any semantic bridge to aggregate many different bridges. Those semantic bridges are then called one by one, and processed in the context of the former.
- The ALTERNATIVE modelling primitive is supported by the SemanticBridgeAlt class. It groups several mutual exclusive semantic bridges. The execution parser

checks each of the bridges condition rules and the first bridge which conditions hold is executed while the others are discarded.

In the following, we will describe how the semantic bridging ontology has been represented so it may be used within Semantic Web applications.

SBO represented in DAML+OIL. DAML+OIL[5] has been choosen to represent the semantic bridge ontology[6]. DAML+OIL builds on and extends RDF-Schema and provides a formal semantics for it. One of the goals in specifying the semantic bridge ontology was to maintain and exploit the existent constructs and minimize extra constructs, which would maximize as much as possible the acceptance and understanding by general Semantic Web tools.

3.3   Example

Let us consider Figure 4 where a small part of two different ontologies are represented. The ontology on the left side (o1) describes the structure of royal families and associated individuals. These concepts are combined with events, both individual events (birth date and death date) and family events (marriages and divorces). The ontology on the right side (o2), characterizes individuals using a very simple approach. It is mainly restricted in representing if the individual is either a Man or a Woman. The goal of this example is to specify a mapping between the source and target ontology, using the developed semantic bridge ontology). A mapping structure represented according to SBO tends to arrange bridges in a hierarchical way.

First, the mapping must define the two ontologies being mapped. Additionally, one may specify top-level semantic bridges which serve as entry points for the translation, even if there are not mandatory. In this case the translation engine starts executing the "Individual-Individual" bridge.

```
<Mapping rdf:ID="mapping">
    <relatesSourceOntology rdf:resource="&o1;"/>
    <relatesTargetOntology rdf:resource="&o2;"/>
    <hasBridge rdf:resource="#Individual-Individual"/>
</Mapping>
```

Notice that the target ontology intends to create instances of either WOMAN or MAN, but not of INDIVIDUAL. In object oriented terminology the INDIVIDUAL concept is said to be abstract. It is therefore required to state that this concept bridge should not be used to create instances, but serve just as support to sub bridges, like it happens in object oriented paradigm. SBO uses the abstract property in these circumstances. If no abstract property is specified or if it is set to FALSE, then the concept bridge is considered as non-abstract.

It is now necessary to set the alternative between INDIVIDUAL and either WOMAN or MAN. This situation is specified by a SemanticBridgeAlt. In this case the alternatives are two ConceptBridge's: "Individual-Woman" and "Individual-Man". Bridges may be numerically ordered which can useful if the last bridge has no specified condition. Both rdf:_n like syntax and the one presented are allowed to specify the order.

---

[5] http://www.daml.org/2001/03/daml+oil-index.html
[6] The SBO ontology is available online at http://kaon.semanticweb.org/2002/04/SBO.daml

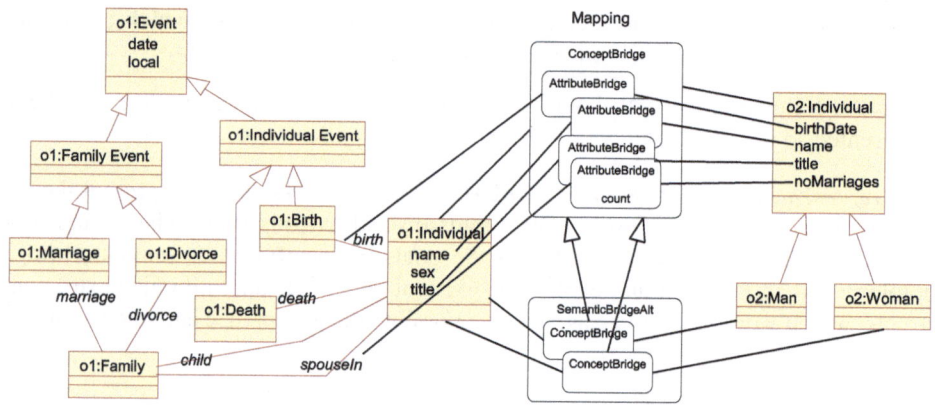

Fig. 4. UML representation of two small ontologies

```
<SemanticBridgeAlt rdf:ID="ManOrWoman">
    <hasBridge><Seq ordinal="1"><bridge rdf:resource="#Individual-Woman"/></Seq>
    </hasBridge>
    <hasBridge><Seq ordinal="2"><bridge rdf:resource="#Individual-Man"/></Seq>
    </hasBridge>
</SemanticBridgeAlt>
```

The alternative ConceptBridge's are presented next: "Individual-Woman" and "Individual-Man".

```
<ConceptBridge rdf:ID="Individual-Woman">
    <subBridgeOf rdf:resource="#Individual-Individual"/>
    <relatesSourceEntity rdf:resource="#Individual"/>
    <relatesTargetEntity rdf:resource="#Woman"/>
    <whenVerifiedCondition rdf:resource="#isFemale"/>
</ConceptBridge>

<ConceptBridge rdf:ID="Individual-Man">
    <subBridgeOf rdf:resource="#Individual-Individual"/>
    <relatesSourceEntity rdf:resource="#Individual"/>
    <relatesTargetEntity rdf:resource="#Man"/>
</ConceptBridge>
```

Both bridges rely on the "Individual-Individual" bridge to translate MAN and WOMAN inherited attributes from INDIVIDUAL. Hence, both are specified as sub-bridges of "Individual-Individual" concept bridge. Additionally, "Individual-Woman" concept bridge specifies the whenVerifiedCondition property to "isFemale". As remarked bellow, this condition is responsible to test if the individual is of feminine sex. If the condition is verified the bridge is executed. Otherwise, and because the condition is tested in the context of a SemanticBridgeAlt, the next concept bridge in the alternative is processed. The next concept bridge in the alternative is "Individual-Man" which has no associated condition, and therefore it is unconditionally executed.

Respecting the translation process, consider that an INDIVIDUAL instance is to be translated. The translation engine seeks for bridges relating INDIVIDUAL to any target ontology entity. Three are found, but one of them is abstract and is therefore rejected. The other two are both defined in the context of a SemanticBridgeAlt. The SemanticBridgeAlt choosing/exclusion process starts. One of the bridges (or eventually none if none of the associated conditions is verified) is selected. The concept bridge must then create a target instance which will serve as context for complementary bridges.

Complementary attribute bridges are in this example simple 1:1 attribute bridges, relating one attribute from o1 to an attribute in the target ontology, through the associated transformation.

```
<AttributeBridge rdf:ID="name-name">
    <relatesSourceEntity rdf:resource="#name"/>
    <relatesTargetEntity rdf:resource="#name"/>
    <accordingToTransformation rdf:resource="#copyName"/>
</AttributeBridge>

<Transformation rdf:ID="copyName">
    <mapSourceArgument>
        <MapArg><from rdf:resource="#name"/><to>sourceString</to></MapArg>
    </mapSourceArgument>
    <mapTargetArgument>
        <MapArg><from>targetString</from><to rdf:resource="#name"/></MapArg>
    </mapTargetArgument>
    <inService>CopyString</inService>
</Transformation>
```

Concerning the transformation, it intends to map between the bridge entities and the transformation service arguments. This mapping specification varies according to the service be requested, either in type, cardinality and used tags. For example, the "copyName" transformation specifies the "CopyString" service to be called. This service expects to receive a source argument called "sourceString" and the output is named "targetString". The transformation maps "sourceString" with the attribute "o1:Individual.name" and "targetString" to the "o2:Individual.name". "title-title" attribute bridge is very similar to the previous and is not be presented.

In contrast, "marriages" attribute bridges are slightly different from previous ones. Notice that the source entity is not an attribute but a relation to another concept. Normally an AttributeBridge would not be correctly applied. However, since this is a very common mapping pattern the translation engine allows to process the relation as an attribute. That could eventually be a problem if the translation service expects an attribute. However, the "CountRelations" service expects a relation which is the case of "spouseIn" and therefore no problem occurs.

```
<AttributeBridge rdf:ID="mariages">
    <relatesSourceEntity rdf:resource="#spouseIn"/>
    <relatesTargetEntity rdf:resource="#noMariages"/>
    <accordingToTransformation rdf:resource="#countSpouses"/>
</AttributeBridge>

<Transformation rdf:ID="countSpouses"> <putServiceArgument>
        <MapArg><from>relation</from><to rdf:resource="#spouseIn"/></MapArg>
    </putServiceArgument>
    <mapTargetArgument>
        <MapArg><from>count</from><to rdf:resource="#noMariages"/></MapArg>
    </mapTargetArgument>
    <inService>CountRelations</inService>
</Transformation>
```

```
<AttributeBridge rdf:ID="birth-birthDate">
    <relatesSourceEntity rdf:resource="#birth"/>
    <relatesTargetEntity rdf:resource="#birthDate"/>
    <accordingToTransformation rdf:resource="#Birth"/>
</AttributeBridge>

<Transformation rdf:ID="Birth">
    <putServiceArgument>
        <MapArg><from>1</from><to rdf:resource="#birth"/></MapArg>
    </putServiceArgument>
    <putServiceArgument>
        <MapArg><from>2</from><to rdf:resource="#date"/></MapArg>
    </putServiceArgument>
    <mapTargetArgument>
        <MapArg><from>targetString</from><to rdf:resource="#birthDate"/></MapArg>
    </mapTargetArgument>
    <inService>RoyalDate</inService>
</Transformation>
```

Finally, the "isFemale" condition is considered. This condition is responsible to verify if an instance of an individual is of feminine sex. In this case the pattern refers to the fact that the value of sex attribute has value "F". Normally, the services applied in a condition return a boolean value. However, this constraint would depend on the translation engine once it is possible to create a table of correspondences between boolean types and other types. For example, it would be reasonable to consider a true result if the service returns a set of entities or false if it return a empty set.

```
<Condition rdf:ID="isFemale">
    <putServiceArgument>
        <MapArg><from>1</from><to rdf:resource="#sex"/></MapArg>
    </putServiceArgument>
    <putServiceArgument>
        <MapArg><from>pattern</from><to>F</to></MapArg>
    </putServiceArgument>
    <inService>CascadeAndMatch</inService>
</Condition>
```

4   Implementation

MAFRA is currently under development within the KAON Ontology and Semantic Web Framework[7]. For the moment we achieved the implementation of four modules of MAFRA: The automatic similarity discovery module, the semantic bridging representation, the graphical user interface and the execution engine.

A screen-shot of the user interface for mapping specification is presented in Figure 5. In this example two ontologies have been opened side by side, and in between an instance of the semantic bridging ontology is created using a simplified user interface.

The developed mapping tool represents the domain expert interface with the similarity and semantic bridging modules, and the possibility to interact within the mapping process. The user participation is fundamental and must be promoted. We adopted a tree view similar to the most common ontology editors. The mapping tool defines two tree views for the ontologies being mapped (in the left and in the right) and a central tree view representing the mapping. Bridges are manipulated through drag and drop actions. Entities from ontologies are dragged and dropped in a bridge and are stored either in

---

[7] http://kaon.semanticweb.org

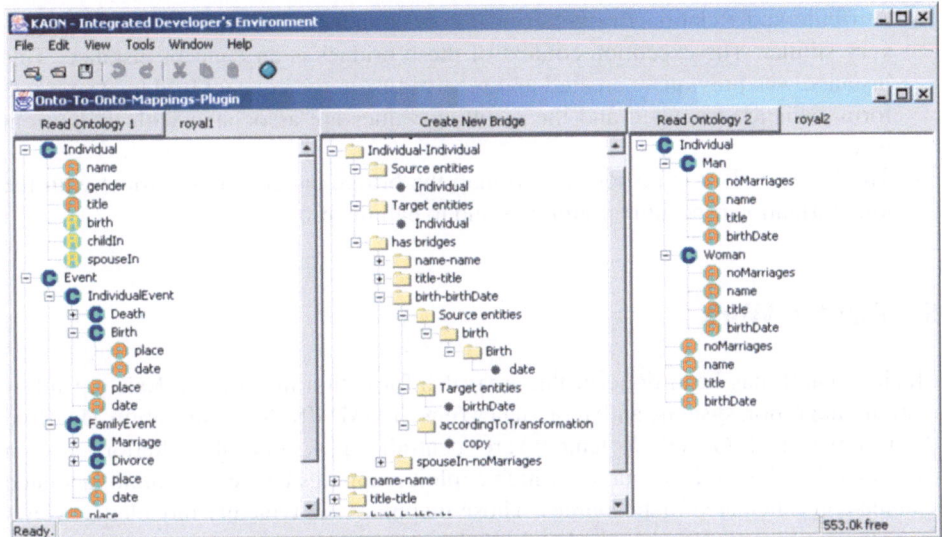

Fig. 5. Creating Mappings Using KAON Tools

the source or target entities folder. The same happens when specifying the mappings between bridges parameters and services arguments. For the moment it is not possible to edit transformation and condition procedures. They are read/parsed into the interface through a menu command.

The execution engine has been implemented in Java, exploiting the features of KAON, and it represents the first step of out efforts in developing a general translation engine for SBO instances. The execution engine uses a mapping instance, which is an instantiation of the SBO, and a set of source ontology instances. The transformation engine parses the mapping into the KAON ontology model and executes it. The process runs for each concept instance that have an associated concept bridge. The internal structure of the execution engine resemble very much the semantic bridge ontology model. A class is defined for some of the major components of the SBO which implement the functionally described in section 3:

- The mapping class is responsible to read source instances and call the associated bridge, if any. However, as described before, a source instance may have multiple associated bridges which implies the mapping checks it and call the alternative bridge instead.
- The AlternativeBridge class is responsible to try the execution of each of its composing bridge, one after another until one of them is executed.
- The ConceptBridge class encompasses all the information related to the instance, and it encodes the necessary functionality to to carry out the task. Mostly, the ConceptBridge class has four ordered tasks: *(i)* check if the whenVerifiedCondition holds; if it holds *(ii)* create an empty target instance, *(iii)* call the subBridge's bridges (concept and attribute bridge) if some exists, and *(iv)* call the hasBridge's bridges.

- Attribute and Relation Bridge, even if conceptually different their functioning is very similar. The execution context of these bridges is an concept instance. This instance was previously created and received from the concept bridge. The transformations are executed and the resulting values are associated with the current instance.
- The Service class is responsible to map the bridge parameters (entities) with the transformation procedure arguments and to call the procedures.

5   Related Work

Much research has been done in the area of information integration. Existing information integration systems and approaches (e.g., TSIMMIS [6], Information Manifold [8], Infomaster[8], MOMIS[9], Xyleme [10]) are "centralized" systems of mediation between users and distributed data sources, which exploit mappings between a single mediated schema and schemas of data sources. Those mappings are typically modeled as views (over the mediated schema in the local-as-view approach, or over the sources schemas in the global-as-view approach) which are expressed using languages having a formal semantics. For scaling up to the Web, the "centralized" approach of mediation is probably not flexible enough, and distributed systems of mediation are more appropriate.

Furthermore, mapping approaches can mainly be distinguished along the following three categories: discovery, [14, 3, 5, 10, 1], mapping representation [9, 1, 11, 13] and execution [4, 11]. However, none of the proposed solutions has really encompassed the overall mapping process specially considering the evolution and consensus building of semantic bridges. Having this in mind, we have introduced the Ontology MApping FRAmework (MAFRA) as a basis for managing and executing mapping between distributed ontologies in the Semantic Web. Within MAFRA we provide an approach and conceptual framework that provides a generic view and figure onto the overall mapping process. In this paper we have set a specific focus on the semantic bridging phase corresponding to the mapping representation category. The approaches which resemble our approach more closely are [13] and [12]. Basically, our work has been motivated by the work done in [13], where an ontology has been specified for the translation between the domain-knowledge-base components and problem-solving-method components. The approach that comes nearest to ours has been described in [12]. They describe an approach for integrating vocabularies including means for mapping discovery and representing mappings with a focus on B2B applications (product catalogues) has been described. In contrast to our work, the RDFT ontology describes a set of core bridges to *(i)* lift XML tags to the RDF model and *(ii)* to define bridges between RDF(S) classes and properties and to *(iii)* translate transformation results back to XML. In the paper [12] it remains unclear, how execution specific information in the form of our constraint and transformation dimension is attached to the bridges.

---

[8] http://infomaster.stanford.edu/infomaster-info.html

[9] http://sparc20.ing.unimo.it/Momis/

[10] http://www.xyleme.com

6 Conclusion and Future Work

Ontologies may used for achieving a common consensus within a user community about conceptualizing, structuring and sharing domain knowledge. Based on the application scenario provided by Ontologging we have motivated that it is unrealistic to assume that one single ontology for different communities of users is realistic in real-world applications. We argue that decentralization has been one of the key elements for the scalability of the World Wide Web and its underlying applications. In order to balance the autonomy of each community with the need for interoperability, mapping mechanisms between ontologies have been proposed. In this paper we presented the Ontology Mapping Framework (MAFRA) supporting the interactive, incremental and dynamic ontology mapping process in the context of the Semantic Web. In this paper a specific focus has been set on the semantic bridging phase where we have provided a detailed description of a semantic bridge meta-ontology, that is instantiated when mapping between two domain ontologies.

In the future much work remains to be done. First, depending on the domain ontologies, data sources, application scenarios, user participation, capabilities and other factors further semantic bridges may be necessary. For example, procedural mechanisms may complement the taxonomy of semantic bridges. Thus, we consider the semantic bridging ontology as evolving. Second, considering the mapping process as a consensus building process of two communities, we will on the basis of our technological infrastructure KAON, perform an experiment how multi-user mapping may be efficiently supported. Third, we will develop an integrated LIFT tool that allows to lift several existing data representations including relational databases, XML-Schema, DTDs onto the same data model. Executing a dynamic mapping process keeping the autonomy of the different input data will be a challenging task.

Acknowledgements. Research for this paper was financed by European Commission, IST, project "Ontologging" (IST-2000-28293) and by Marie Curie Fellowship on Semantic Web Technologies. Special thanks to Gabor Nagypal for fruitful discussions on defining the semantic bridging ontology and Oliver Fodor for stimulating discussions on the lift component and cooperative mapping. Thanks to the students Frank Westerhausen and Zoltan Varady who did the implementation work for the graphical user interface and the static transformation engine.

References

[1] S. Bergamaschi, S. Castano, D. Beneventano, and M. Vincini. Semantic integration of heterogeneous information sources. In *Special Issue on Intelligent Information Integration, Data & Knowledge Engineering*, volume 36, pages 215–249. Elsevier Science B.V., 2001.

[2] T. Berners-Lee. *Weaving the Web*. Harper, San Francisco, 1999.

[3] W. Cohen. The whirl approach to data integration. *IEEE Intelligent Systems*, pages 1320 1324, 1998.

[4] T. Critchlow, M. Ganesh, and R. Musick. Automatic generation of warehouse mediators using an ontology engine. In *Proceedings of the 5 th International Workshop on Knowledge Representation meets Databases (KRDB'98)*, 1998.

[5] A. Doan, J. Madhavan, P. Domingos, and A. Halevy. Learning to map between ontologies on the semantic web. In *Proceedings of the World-Wide Web Conference (WWW-2002)*, 2002.

[6] J. Hammer, H. Garcia-Molina, K. Ireland, Y. Papakonstantinou, J. Ullman, and J. Widom. Information Translation, Mediation, and Mosaic-Based Browsing in the TSIMMIS System. In *Exhibits Program of the Proceedings of the ACM SIGMOD International Conference on Management of Data, page 483, San Jose, California, June 1995.*, 1995.

[7] S. Khoshafian and G. Copeland. Object identity. In *Proceedings of the 1st ACM OOPSLA conference, Portland, Oregon, September 1986.*, 1985.

[8] Alon Y. Levy, Anand Rajaraman, and Joann J. Ordille. Querying Heterogeneous Information Sources Using Source Descriptions. In *Proceedings of VLDB-96, 1996*, 1996.

[9] J. Madhavan, P. A. Bernstein, and E. Rahm. Generic schema matching with cupid. In *Proceedings of the 27th International Conferences on Very Large Databases*, pages 49–58, 2001.

[10] A. Maedche and S. Staab. Computing Similarities between Ontologies. In *Proceedings of the 13th European Conference on Knowledge Engineering and Knowledge Management EKAW-2002, Madrid, Spain*, 2002.

[11] P. Mitra, G. Wiederhold, and M. Kersten. A graph-oriented model for articulation of ontology interdependencies. In *Proceedings of Conference on Extending Database Technology (EDBT 2000)*. Konstanz, Germany, 2000.

[12] B. Omelayenko. Integrating Vocabularies: Discovering and Representing Vocabulary Maps. In *Proceedings of the First International Semantic Web Conference (ISWC-2002), Sardinia, Italy, June 9-12, 2002.*, 2002.

[13] J. Y. Park, J. H. Gennari, and M. A. Musen. Mappings for reuse in knowledge-based systems. In *Technical Report, SMI-97-0697, Stanford University*, 1997.

[14] E. Rahm and P. Bernstein. A survey of approaches to automatic schema matching. *VLDB Journal*, 10(4):334–350, 2001.

[15] P. Resnik. Semantic similarity in a taxonomy: An information-based measure and its application to problems of ambiguity in natural language. *Journal of Artificial Intelligence*, 11(11):95–130, 1999.

[16] M.C. Rousset. Standardization of a web ontology language. *IEEE Intelligent Systems, March/April 2002*, 2002.

[17] N. Silva. Discovering Mappings between Distributed Ontologies. In *Internal Report, University of Karlsruhe, July 2002.*, 2002.

[18] L. Stojanovic, A. Maedche, B. Motik, and N. Stojanovic. User-Driven Ontology Evolution. In *Proceedings of the 13th European Conference on Knowledge Engineering and Knowledge Management EKAW-2002, Madrid, Spain*, 2002.

[19] P.R.S. Visser, D.M. Jones, T.J.M. Bench-Capon, and M.J.R. Shave. An analysis of ontology mismatches: Heterogeneity versus interoperability. In *AAAI 1997 Spring Symposium on Ontological Engineering, Stanford CA., USA*, pages 164–72, 1997.

Measuring Similarity between Ontologies

Alexander Maedche[1] and Steffen Staab[2,3]

[1] FZI - Research Center for Information Technologies at the University of Karlsruhe,
Haid-und-Neu-Str. 10-14, D-76131 Karlsruhe, Germany
http://www.fzi.de/WIM
[2] Institute AIFB, Univ. Karlsruhe,
D-76128 Karlsruhe, Germany
http://www.aifb.uni-karlsruhe.de/WBS
[3] Ontoprise GmbH,
76131 Karlsruhe, Germany
http://www.ontoprise.de

Abstract. Ontologies now play an important role for many knowledge-intensive applications for which they provide a source of precisely defined terms. However, with their wide-spread usage there come problems concerning their proliferation. Ontology engineers or users frequently have a core ontology that they use, e.g., for browsing or querying data, but they need to extend it with, adapt it to, or compare it with the large set of other ontologies. For the task of detecting and retrieving relevant ontologies, one needs means for measuring the similarity between ontologies. We present a set of ontology similarity measures and a multiple-phase empirical evaluation.

1   Introduction

A core purpose for the use of ontologies is the exchange of data not only at a common syntactic, but also at a shared semantic level. Especially on the WWW more and more ontologies are constructed and used, beginning to replace the old-fashioned ways of exchanging business data via standardized comma-separated formats by standards that adhere to semantic specifications given through ontologies. Thus, in the near future more and more ontologies will be made available on the WWW. With this upswing and beginning widespread usage of ontologies, however, new problems are incurred. Ontology engineers or users frequently have a core ontology that they use, e.g., for browsing or querying data, but they need to extend it with, adapt it to, or compare it with the large set of other ontologies. For the task of detecting and retrieving relevant ontologies, one needs means for measuring the similarity between ontologies on a canonical scale (e.g., the reals in $[0, 1]$).

So, how may we measure the similarity of ontologies or of ontology parts? One could make use of the formal structures of ontologies and try at the unification of ontologies or ontology parts (which is essentially subgraph matching). The drawback here would be that all real-world ontologies that we know of do not only specify its conceptualization by logical structures, but to a large extent also by reference to terms that are grounded through human natural language use. For instance, modeling that MAN

A. Gómez-Pérez and V.R. Benjamins (Eds.): EKAW 2002, LNAI 2473, pp. 251–263, 2002.
© Springer-Verlag Berlin Heidelberg 2002

and WOMAN are subordinates of PERSON suffices for many purposes even without any further differentiae. Two ontologies that contain these parts agree on their semantics only to a small extent by formal means, but to a larger extent by reference to common terminology. Furthermore, missing structures need not be problematic. For instance, if one ontology comes with concepts referred to by VEHICLE, CAR, SPORTSWAGON and the other with VEHICLE and SPORTSWAGON only, the semantic exchange of data may still be rather easy, even though the second ontology lacks the two taxonomic links from VEHICLE to CAR and to SPORTSWAGON.

Looking at these requirements, we have found a lack of comprehensive methodological inventory to measure similarity between real-world ontologies, as well as practical, reproducable experiences with measuring similarity between ontologies. Firstly, this paper is about introducing the necessary inventory. We break down the overall task and propose a set of measures that capture the similarity of ontologies at two different levels, the lexical and the conceptual. In general our similarity measures describe the extent to which one ontology specification is covered by the other — and *vice versa*. Secondly, this paper is about providing some practical experiences and results with the proposed measures. Five subjects, four novices and one ontology engineering expert, have modeled ontologies in three different phases about a commonly well-known domain given some additional background knowledge in form of domain texts. The ontologies generated by the different subjects then served as input to an empirical evaluation study of our similarity measuring framework.

In the following, we first prepare the ground for our proposal and our empirical evaluation study by formally specifying the ontology structure and its semantic we refer to subsequently. In the two sections thereafter, we propose measures for describing the similarity of different ontology parts at the lexical and conceptual level. In Section 5, we describe the empirical evaluation study and the results we achieved there, before we relate to other research and conclude the paper with an outlook on future challenges.

2   A Two-Layer View of Ontologies

In order to compare two ontologies and measure similarity between them (or between parts of them), one may consider different semiotic levels. The two levels that we can focus on (abstracting from an actual application) are: First, at the lexical level we may investigate how terms are used to convey meanings. Second, at the conceptual level we may investigate what conceptual relations exist between the terms.[1] For this investigation we define a simple notion of ontology and some auxiliary functions in six steps.

Definition 1 (Concept Language). *Our simple concept language is defined starting from atomic concepts and roles. Concepts are unary predicates and roles are binary predicates over a domain $\mathcal{U}$, with individuals being the elements of $\mathcal{U}$. Correspondingly, an interpretation $\mathcal{I}$ of the language is a function that assigns to each concept symbol (taken from the set $\mathcal{A}$) a subset of the domain $\mathcal{U}$, $\mathcal{I} : \mathcal{A} \mapsto 2^{\mathcal{U}}$, to each role symbol (taken from the set $\mathcal{P}$) a binary relation of $\mathcal{U}$, $\mathcal{I} : \mathcal{P} \mapsto 2^{\mathcal{U} \times \mathcal{U}}$. Concept terms and role*

---

[1] Further studies could look at the pragmatic and the social level and try find out about the application of terms in concrete applications and social contexts.

terms are defined inductively with terminological axioms and using operators. C and D denote concept terms, R and S denote roles.

Concept Forming Operator

Syntax	Semantics
C_{atom}	$\{d \in \mathcal{U}^{\mathcal{I}} \mid C_{atom} \text{ atomic}, d \in \mathcal{I}(C_{atom})\}$
$C \sqcap D$	$C^{\mathcal{I}} \cap D^{\mathcal{I}}$
$\forall R.C$	$\{d \in \mathcal{U}^{\mathcal{I}} \mid \forall e (d,e) \in R^{\mathcal{I}} \Rightarrow e \in C^{\mathcal{I}}\}$

Role Forming Operators

Syntax	Semantics
R_{atom}	$\{(d,e) \in \mathcal{U}^{\mathcal{I}} \times \mathcal{U}^{\mathcal{I}} \mid R_{atom} \text{ atomic}, (d,e) \in \mathcal{I}(R_{atom})\}$
$R \sqcap S$	$R^{\mathcal{I}} \cap S^{\mathcal{I}}$
$C \times D$	$\{(d,e) \in C^{\mathcal{I}} \times D^{\mathcal{I}}\}$

Terminological Axioms

Axiom	Semantics	Axiom	Semantics
$D \doteq C$	$D^{\mathcal{I}} = C^{\mathcal{I}}$	$D \sqsubseteq C$	$D^{\mathcal{I}} \subseteq C^{\mathcal{I}}$
$S \doteq R$	$S^{\mathcal{I}} = R^{\mathcal{I}}$	$S \sqsubseteq R$	$S^{\mathcal{I}} \subseteq R^{\mathcal{I}}$

Definition 2 (Lexicon). *The lexicon consists of a set of terms (lexical entries) for concepts, $\mathcal{L}^c$, and a set of terms for relations, $\mathcal{L}^r$. Their union is the lexicon $\mathcal{L} := \mathcal{L}^c \cup \mathcal{L}^r$.*

Definition 3 (Reference Function). *The reference functions $\mathcal{F}, \mathcal{G}$, with $\mathcal{F} : 2^{\mathcal{L}^c} \mapsto 2^{\mathcal{A}}$ and $\mathcal{G} : 2^{\mathcal{L}^s} \mapsto 2^{\mathcal{P}}$. $\mathcal{F}$ and $\mathcal{G}$ link sets of lexical entries[2] $\{L_i\} \subset \mathcal{L}$ to the set of concepts and relations they refer to, respectively. In general, one lexical entry may refer to several concepts or relations and one concept or relation may be refered to by several lexical entries. Their inverses are $\mathcal{F}^{-1}$ and $\mathcal{G}^{-1}$.*

We distinguish between terms and concept/relation symbols, because we want to allow for the explicit expression of ambiguities. For instance, one term like "bank" may refer to two concept symbols, viz. BANK-1 being a subconcept of FURNITURE and BANK-2 being a subconcept of COMPANY. Expressing this by disjunction (e.g., BANK $\doteq$ BANK-1 $\sqcup$ BANK-2) would be logically equivalent, but it would conflate two ontological states, viz. "bank" being an ambiguous natural language term and BANK-1 being a construed symbol for precise logical denotation.

Definition 4 (Core Ontology). *A core ontology $\mathcal{O}$ is a tuple $(\mathcal{A}, \mathcal{P}, \mathcal{D}, \mathcal{L}, \mathcal{F}, \mathcal{G})$, which consists of a set of concept symbols $\mathcal{A}$, a set of relation symbols $\mathcal{P}$, a set of statements $\mathcal{D}$ in the concept language defined above, a lexicon $\mathcal{L}$ and two reference functions $\mathcal{F}, \mathcal{G}$.*

Definition 5 (Concept Hierarchy). *The concept hierarchy $\mathcal{H}$ is defined by*
$$\mathcal{H} := \{(C,D) \mid C, D \in \mathcal{A} \wedge C^{\mathcal{I}} \subseteq D^{\mathcal{I}}\}$$

---

[2] The reference functions are defined on sets of lexical entries (instead of single entities) in order to allow for a more compact description of formulae later on.

Definition 6 (Domain/Range). *Domain ($d(R)$) and range ($r(R)$) of a relation R are defined by $\{d|\exists e(d, e) \in R^\mathcal{I}\}$ and $\{e|\exists d(d, e) \in R^\mathcal{I}\}$, respectively.*

In the following sections we propose and use methods for measuring similarity of ontologies based on the lexical and the conceptual level of ontologies.

3 Lexical Comparison Level

The *edit distance* formulated by Levenshtein [5] is a well-established method for weighting the difference between two strings. It measures the minimum number of token insertions, deletions, and substitutions required to transform one string into another using a dynamic programming algorithm. For example, the edit distance, ed, between the two lexical entries "TopHotel" and "Top_Hotel" equals 1, ed("TopHotel", "Top_Hotel") = 1, because one insertion operation changes the string "TopHotel" into "Top_Hotel".

Based on Levenshtein's edit distance we propose a *lexical similarity measure* for strings, the String Matching (SM), which compares two lexical entries L_i, L_j:

$$\mathrm{SM}(L_i, L_j) := \max\left(0, \frac{\min(|L_i|, |L_j|) - \mathrm{ed}(L_i, L_j)}{\min(|L_i|, |L_j|)}\right) \in [0, 1].$$

SM returns a degree of similarity between 0 and 1, where 1 stands for perfect match and zero for bad match. It considers the number of changes that must be made to change one string into the other and weighs the number of these changes against the length of the shortest string of these two. In our example from above, we compute SM("TopHotel", "Top_Hotel") = $\frac{7}{8}$. In order to provide a summarizing figure for the lexical level of two sign systems, e.g. for the lexica referring to concepts $\mathcal{L}_1^c, \mathcal{L}_2^c$ of two ontologies $\mathcal{O}_1, \mathcal{O}_2$, we compare two sets $\mathcal{L}_1, \mathcal{L}_2$ returning the averaged String Matching $\overline{\mathrm{SM}}(\mathcal{L}_1, \mathcal{L}_2)$:

$$\overline{\mathrm{SM}}(\mathcal{L}_1, \mathcal{L}_2) := \frac{1}{|\mathcal{L}_1|} \sum_{L_i \in \mathcal{L}_1} \max_{L_j \in \mathcal{L}_2} \mathrm{SM}(L_i, L_j).$$

$\overline{\mathrm{SM}}(\mathcal{L}_1, \mathcal{L}_2)$ is an asymmetric measure that determines the extent to which the lexical level of a sign system $\mathcal{L}_1$ (the target) is covered by the one of a second sign system $\mathcal{L}_2$ (the source). Obviously, $\overline{\mathrm{SM}}(\mathcal{L}_1, \mathcal{L}_2)$ may be quite different from $\overline{\mathrm{SM}}(\mathcal{L}_2, \mathcal{L}_1)$. E.g., when $\mathcal{L}_2$ contains all the strings of $\mathcal{L}_1$, but also plenty of others, then $\overline{\mathrm{SM}}(\mathcal{L}_1, \mathcal{L}_2) = 1$, but $\overline{\mathrm{SM}}(\mathcal{L}_2, \mathcal{L}_1)$ may approach zero. Compared to the relative number of hits,

$$\mathrm{RelHit}(\mathcal{L}_1, \mathcal{L}_2) := \frac{|\mathcal{L}_1 \cap \mathcal{L}_2|}{|\mathcal{L}_1|},$$

$\overline{\mathrm{SM}}$ diminishes the influence of string pseudo-differences in different ontologies, such as use vs. not-use of underscores or hyphens, use of singular vs. plural, or use of additional markup characters. Of course, SM may sometimes be deceptive, when two strings resemble each other though they there is no meaningful relationship between them, e.g. "power" and "tower". In our case study, however, we have found that in spite of this added "noise" SM may be very helpful for proposing good matches of strings.

4   Conceptual Comparison Level

At the conceptual level we may compare semantic structures of ontologies $\mathcal{O}_1, \mathcal{O}_2$, that vary for concepts $\mathcal{A}_1, \mathcal{A}_2$. In our model the conceptual structures are constituted by $\mathcal{H}_1, \mathcal{H}_2$ and $\mathcal{P}_1, \mathcal{P}_2$.

4.1   Comparing Taxonomies $\mathcal{H}_1, \mathcal{H}_2$

Though there has been a long discussion in the literature about comparing the similarity of two concepts in a common taxonomy (cf. Section 6), we have not found any discussion about *comparing two taxonomies.*

We start by determining the extent to which two taxonomies as seen from two particularly identified concepts compare. More precisely, we assume that we have one lexical entry $L \in \mathcal{L}_1^c \cap \mathcal{L}_2^c$ that refers via $\mathcal{F}_1$ and $\mathcal{F}_2$ to two concepts C_1, C_2 from two different taxonomies $\mathcal{H}_1, \mathcal{H}_2$. The intensional semantics of C_1 (C_2) may be seen to be constituted by the *semantic cotopy* (SC) of C_1 (C_2), i.e. all its super- and subconcepts:

$$\mathrm{SC}(C_i, \mathcal{H}) := \{C_j \in \mathcal{A} | \mathcal{H}(C_i, C_j) \vee \mathcal{H}(C_j, C_i)\}.$$

SC is overloaded to process sets of concepts, too.

$$\mathrm{SC}(\{C_1, \ldots, C_n\}, \mathcal{H}) := \bigcup_{i := 1 \ldots n} \mathrm{SC}(C_i, \mathcal{H}).$$

The taxonomic overlap (TO) between $\mathcal{H}_1$ and $\mathcal{H}_2$ as seen from the concepts referred to by L may then be computed by following $\mathcal{F}_1^{-1}$ and $\mathcal{F}_2^{-1}$ back to the common lexicon.

$$\mathrm{TO}'(L, \mathcal{O}_1, \mathcal{O}_2) := \frac{|\mathcal{F}_1^{-1}(\mathrm{SC}(\mathcal{F}(\{L\}), \mathcal{H}_1)) \cap \mathcal{F}_2^{-1}(\mathrm{SC}(\mathcal{F}(\{L\}), \mathcal{H}_2))|}{|\mathcal{F}_1^{-1}(\mathrm{SC}(\mathcal{F}(\{L\}), \mathcal{H}_1)) \cup \mathcal{F}_2^{-1}(\mathrm{SC}(\mathcal{F}(\{L\}), \mathcal{H}_2))|}$$

Averaging over all lexical entries we may thus compute a semantic similarity for the two given hierarchies.

In addition, however, we must consider the case where a lexical entry L is in $\mathcal{L}_1^c$, but not in $\mathcal{L}_2^c$. Then, the simplest assumption is that the L is simply missing from $\mathcal{L}_2^c$, but when comparing the two hierarchies the optimistic taxonomic approximation is the one that searches for the maximum overlap given a fictive membership of L to $\mathcal{L}_2^c$ by

$$\mathrm{TO}''(L, \mathcal{O}_1, \mathcal{O}_2) := \max_{C \in \mathcal{C}_2} \left\{ \frac{|\mathcal{F}_1^{-1}(\mathrm{SC}(\mathcal{F}(\{L\}), \mathcal{H}_1)) \cap \mathcal{F}_2^{-1}(\mathrm{SC}(C), \mathcal{H}_2)|}{|\mathcal{F}_1^{-1}(\mathrm{SC}(\mathcal{F}(\{L\}), \mathcal{H}_1)) \cup \mathcal{F}_2^{-1}(\mathrm{SC}(C), \mathcal{H}_2)|} \right\}$$

Given these premises the averaged similarity $\overline{\mathrm{TO}}$ between two taxonomics $(\mathcal{H}_1, \mathcal{H}_2)$ of ontologies $(\mathcal{O}_1, \mathcal{O}_2)$ may then be defined by:

$$\overline{\mathrm{TO}}(\mathcal{O}_1, \mathcal{O}_2) := \frac{1}{|\mathcal{L}_1^c|} \sum_{L \in \mathcal{L}_1^c} \mathrm{TO}(L, \mathcal{O}_1, \mathcal{O}_2), \text{ with}$$

$$\mathrm{TO}(L, \mathcal{O}_1, \mathcal{O}_2) := \begin{cases} \mathrm{TO}'(L, \mathcal{O}_1, \mathcal{O}_2) & \text{if } L \in \mathcal{L}_2^c \\ \mathrm{TO}''(L, \mathcal{O}_1, \mathcal{O}_2) & \text{if } L \notin \mathcal{L}_2^c \end{cases}$$

Example: A partial example for comparing taxonomies is given in Figure 1: The taxonomic overlap TO′("hotel", $\mathcal{H}_1, \mathcal{H}_2$) is determined by $\mathcal{F}_1^{-1}(\text{SC}(\mathcal{F}(\{\text{"hotel"}\}), \mathcal{H}_1)) = \{\text{"hotel"}, \text{"accomodation"}\}$ and $\mathcal{F}_2^{-1}(\text{SC}(\mathcal{F}(\{\text{"hotel"}\}), \mathcal{H}_2)) = \{\text{"wellness hotel"}, \text{"hotel"}\}$ resulting in TO′("hotel", $\mathcal{H}_1, \mathcal{H}_2) = \frac{1}{3}$ as input to $\overline{\text{TO}}$.

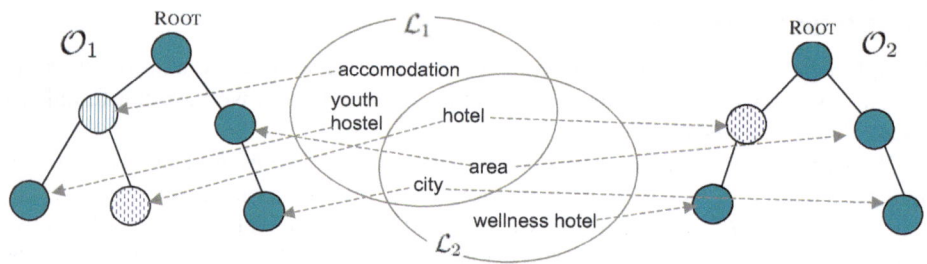

Fig. 1. Two Example Ontologies $\mathcal{O}_1, \mathcal{O}_2$

When we consider the lexical entry "accomodation", which is only in $\mathcal{L}_1^c$, we compute the taxonomic overlap as follows: We compute for the lexical entry "accomodation" $\mathcal{F}_1^{-1}(\text{SC}(\mathcal{F}(\{\text{"accomodation"}\}), \mathcal{H}_1)) = \{\text{"youth hostel"}, \text{"accomodation"}, \text{"hotel"}\}$. The concept referred to by "hotel" in $\mathcal{A}_2$ yields the best match resulting in $\mathcal{F}_2^{-1}(\text{SC}(\mathcal{F}(\{\text{"hotel"}\}))) = \{\text{"wellness hotel"}, \text{"hotel"}\}$ and, thus, TO″("accomodation", $\mathcal{H}_1, \mathcal{H}_2) = \frac{1}{4}$.

The reader may note several properties of $\overline{\text{TO}}$: First, $\overline{\text{TO}}$ is asymmetric. While TO′ is a symmetrical measure, TO″ is asymmetric, because depending on coverage it may be very easy to integrate one taxonomy into another one, but it may be very difficult to do it the other way around. Second, for ease of presentation of the basic principles we have given here a shortened definition. The longer version specially considers the (minority of) cases, where one lexical entry refers to several concepts. The longer version does not consider the semantic cotopies of all referred concepts for computing TO, but only those that eventually optimize TO. Third, obviously $\overline{\text{TO}}$ becomes meaningless when $\mathcal{L}_1^c$ and $\mathcal{L}_2^c$ are disjoint. The more $\mathcal{L}_1^c$ and $\mathcal{L}_2^c$ overlap (or are made to overlap, e.g. through a syntactic merge), the better $\overline{\text{TO}}$ may focus on existing hierarchical structures and not on optimistic estimations of adding a new lexical entry to $\mathcal{L}_2^c$.

4.2 Comparing Relations $\mathcal{P}_1, \mathcal{P}_2$

At the lexical level a relation R_1 is referred to by a lexical entry L_1. At the conceptual level it specifies a pair $(C_1, D_1), C_1, D_1 \in \mathcal{C}$ describing the concept C_1 that the relation belongs to and its range restriction D_1.

We determine the accuracy that two relations match, RO (relation overlap), based on the geometric mean value of how similar their domain and range concepts are. The geometric mean reflects the intuition that if either domain or range concepts utterly fail to match, the matching accuracy converges against 0, whereas the arithmetic mean value might still turn out a value of 0.5.

The similarity between two concepts (the concept match CM) may be computed by considering their semantic cotopy. However, the measures derived from complete cotopies underestimate the place of concepts in the taxonomy. For instance, the semantic cotopy of the concept corresponding to "hotel" in $\mathcal{L}_2$ (Figure 1) is identical to the semantic cotopy of the one corresponding to "wellness hotel". Hence, for the purpose of similarity of concepts (rather than taxonomies), we define the upwards cotopy (UC) as follows:

$$\mathrm{UC}(C_i, \mathcal{H}) := \{C_j \in \mathcal{A} | \mathcal{H}(C_i, C_j)\}.$$

Based on the definition of the upwards cotopy (UC) the concept match (CM) is then defined in analogy to TO':

$$\mathrm{CM}(C_1, \mathcal{O}_1, C_2, \mathcal{O}_2) := \frac{|\mathcal{F}_1^{-1}(\mathrm{UC}(C_1, \mathcal{H}_1)) \cap \mathcal{F}_2^{-1}(\mathrm{UC}(C_2, \mathcal{H}_2))|}{|\mathcal{F}_1^{-1}(\mathrm{UC}(C_1, \mathcal{H}_1)) \cup \mathcal{F}_2^{-1}(\mathrm{UC}(C_2, \mathcal{H}_2))|}.$$

Then RO′ of relations R_1, R_2 may be defined by:

$$\mathrm{RO}'(R_1, \mathcal{O}_1, R_2, \mathcal{O}_2) := \sqrt{\mathrm{CM}(\mathrm{d}(R_1), \mathcal{O}_1, \mathrm{d}(R_2), \mathcal{O}_2) \cdot \mathrm{CM}(\mathrm{r}(R_1), \mathcal{O}_1, \mathrm{r}(R_2), \mathcal{O}_1)}.$$

In order to take reference by $L \in \mathcal{L}_1^r, L \in \mathcal{L}_2^r$ into account:

$$\mathrm{RO}''(L, \mathcal{O}_1, \mathcal{O}_2) := \frac{1}{|\mathcal{G}_1(\{L\})|} \sum_{R_1 \in \mathcal{G}_1(\{L\})} \max_{R_2 \in \mathcal{G}_2(\{L\})} \{\mathrm{RO}'(R_1, \mathcal{O}_1, R_2, \mathcal{O}_2)\}$$

Some lexical entries only refer to relations in $\mathcal{P}_1$:

$$\mathrm{RO}'''(L, \mathcal{O}_1, \mathcal{O}_2) := \frac{1}{|\mathcal{G}_1(\{L\})|} \sum_{R_1 \in \mathcal{G}_1(\{L\})} \max_{R_2 \in \mathcal{P}_2} \{\mathrm{RO}'(R_1, \mathcal{O}_1, R_2, \mathcal{O}_2)\}$$

Combined we have for $L \in \mathcal{L}_1^r$:

$$\mathrm{RO}(L, \mathcal{O}_1, \mathcal{O}_2) := \begin{cases} \mathrm{RO}''(L, \mathcal{O}_1, \mathcal{O}_2) & \text{if } L \in \mathcal{L}_2^r \\ \mathrm{RO}'''(L, \mathcal{O}_1, \mathcal{O}_2) & \text{if } L \notin \mathcal{L}_2^r \end{cases}$$

The averaged relation overlap $\overline{\mathrm{RO}}$ is then defined by:

$$\overline{\mathrm{RO}}(\mathcal{O}_1, \mathcal{O}_2) := \frac{1}{|\mathcal{L}_1^r|} \sum_{L \in \mathcal{L}_1^r} \mathrm{RO}(L, \mathcal{O}_1, \mathcal{O}_2).$$

Example. We take Figure 1 as an example setting for computing RO. We assume one relation R_1 in $\mathcal{O}_1$, referenced by "located at" and specifying the domain and range corresponding to ("hotel", "area"). In $\mathcal{O}_2$, the same lexical entry may refer to R_2, with domain and range corresponding to ("hotel", "city"). Computing CM for the concepts referred to by "hotel" in $\mathcal{O}_1$ and $\mathcal{O}_2$ results in $\frac{1}{2}$. The CM between the concepts referred to by "area" in $\mathcal{O}_1$ and "city" in $\mathcal{O}_2$ also returns $\frac{1}{2}$. Thus, the RO' for the lexical entry "located at" boils down to $\sqrt{\frac{1}{2} \cdot \frac{1}{2}} = 0.5$ as input to $\overline{RO}$.

The reader may note two major characteristics of $\overline{RO}$. First, it depends on the agreement of the lexica and the taxonomies of $\mathcal{O}_1$ and $\mathcal{O}_2$. Without reasonable agreement, $\overline{RO}$ may not reach high values of similarity. Second, $\overline{RO}$ is also asymmetric reflecting the coverage of relations of the first by the second ontology.

5   Empirical Evaluation

In this section we present a case study that has been carried out in a seminar on ontology engineering at our institute. We have pursued two main objectives with our evaluation study: *(i)* we wanted to determine the quality of our measures and evaluate them on actual data, and, *(ii)*, we wanted to investigate and get an intuition about how similar ontologies about the same domain are that have been modeled by different persons.

5.1   Evaluation Study

The experiment was carried out with four subjects, viz. undergraduates in industrial engineering. The modeling expertise of the subjects was limited. Before actual modeling, they received 3 hours training in ontology engineering in general and 3 hours in using our ontology engineering workbench. Furthermore, they were acquainted with the purpose of the ontology, viz. as an ontology for information extraction and semantic search. Our study required from each of them the building of ontologies in the tourism domain using their background knowledge and using web pages from a WWW site about touristic offers, e.g. hotels with various attractions or cultural events. Our objective was an overall cross-comparison of ontologies, but we also wanted to test the appropriateness of single measures, To avoid error chaining, we therefore performed the evaluation in three phases (resulting in $4 \cdot 3 = 12$ ontologies). Furthermore, an expert ontology engineer (subject 0) modeled a "gold standard" for the task (a 13th ontology).

Phase I: A small top level structure was given to the subjects.[3] Based on this top level and the available knowledge sources, the subjects had to model a *complete* tourism domain ontology. To keep the ontologies within comparable ranges, the students were required to model around 300 concepts and 80 relations.

Phase II: The second phase was geared to produce results for $\overline{TO}$, while avoiding the uncertainties of lexical disagreement. Therefore, the subjects were given 310 lexical entries (for concepts) from the gold standard and the top level structure described before.

---

[3] It contained four concepts referred to by "thing", "material", "intangible", and "situation".

Then everyone of them had to, first, model the taxonomy for concepts referred to by the 310 lexical entries and, second, model about 80 relations.

Phase III: The last phase was defined to control $\overline{RO}$ in absence of "noise" from different taxonomies and lexica. There the taxonomy (from the gold standard) was given. It consisted of 310 lexical entries, $\mathcal{L}^c$, and a set of 310 corresponding concepts, $\mathcal{A}$, taxonomically related by $\mathcal{H}$. The subjects had to model about 80 relations.

5.2 Lexical Comparison Level

The phase I-ontologies described above are used for general cross-comparison, including the lexical level. The pairwise string matching ($\overline{SM}$, cf. Section 3) of the five lexica referring to concepts and relations, respectively, returned the results depicted in Table 1.

Results: The results for computing $\overline{SM}(\mathcal{L}_1^c, \mathcal{L}_2^c)$ of matching lexical entries referring to concepts vary between 0.38 and 0.65 with an average of 0.45. Comparing lexical entries referring to relations $\overline{SM}(\mathcal{L}_1^s, \mathcal{L}_2^s)$ results in values between 0.16 and 0.53 with an average of 0.36. Several typical, though not necessarily good, pairs for which high string match values were computed are shown in Table 2. RelHit($\mathcal{L}_1^c, \mathcal{L}_2^c$) ranged between 20 to 25%, *i.e.* this percentage of lexical entries referring to concepts matched exactly. For lexical entries referring to relations the results were much worse, *viz.* between 10 to 15%.

	Subject			
$i \backslash j$ 0	1	2	3	4
0 -	0.51,0.35	0.53,0.21	0.46,0.39	0.5,0.29
1 0.43,0.52 -		0.65,0.43	0.43,0.53	0.39,0.41
2 0.42,0.24	0.54,0.37 -		0.36,0.24	0.4,0.2
3 0.38,0.47	0.43,0.45	0.38,0.28 -		0.38,0.36
4 0.46,0.38	0.41,0.5	0.48,0.16	0.43,0.39 -	

Table 1. $\overline{SM}(\mathcal{L}_i^c, \mathcal{L}_j^c)$, $\overline{SM}(\mathcal{L}_i^s, \mathcal{L}_j^s)$ for phase I-ontologies.

Interpretation: Analysing the figures we find that human subjects have a considerable higher agreement on lexical entries referring to concepts than on ones referring to relations. Investigating the auxiliary measures we have found that SM values above 0.75 in general retrieve meaningful matches — in spite of few pitfalls (cf. Table 2).

5.3 Conceptual Comparison Level

At the conceptual level we may compare semantic structures of ontologies $\mathcal{O}_1, \mathcal{O}_2$, that vary for concepts $\mathcal{A}_1, \mathcal{A}_2$. We use the ontologies of phase I, II, and III for evaluating our measures introduced in Section 4.

L_1	L_2	$SM(L1, L2)$
Sehenswuerdigkeit [seesight]	Sehenswürdigkeit [seesight]	0.875
Verkehrsmittel [vehicle]	Luftverkehrsmittel [air vehicle]	0.71
Zelt [tent]	Zeit [time]	0.75
Anzahl_Betten [number_beds]	hat_Anzahl_Betten [has_number_beds]	0.77

Table 2. Typical string matches

Results: Table 3 presents the results we have obtained for the phase I-ontologies using the similarity measures taxonomy overlap ($\overline{TO}$) and relation overlap ($\overline{RO}$). The reader may note that these ontologies have been built without any previous assumptions about the lexica $\mathcal{L}_1$ and $\mathcal{L}_2$, thus their similarity values are well below those of later phases where the lexica for concepts were predefined.

		Subject			
$i\backslash j$	0	1	2	3	4
0	-	0.33,0.35	0.31,0.25	0.32,0.5	0.29,0.28
1	0.35,0.15	-	0.4,0.41	0.34,0.03	0.28,0.15
2	0.28,0.12	0.36,0.25	-	0.25,0.04	0.24,0.15
3	0.36,0.4	0.31,0.32	0.24,0.04	-	0.26,0.03
4	0.38,0.29	0.31,0.21	0.32,0.2	0.32,0.26	-

Table 3. $\overline{TO}(\mathcal{O}_i, \mathcal{O}_j)$, $\overline{RO}(\mathcal{O}_i, \mathcal{O}_j)$ for phase I-ontologies.

Table 4 depicts the similarity measures computed for phase II-ontologies. Values for $\overline{TO}$ range between 0.47 and 0.87, the average $\overline{TO}$ over all 20 cross-comparisons results in 0.56. $\overline{RO}$ yields values from 0.34 to 0.82 with an average of 0.47.

		Subject			
$i\backslash j$	0	1	2	3	4
0	-	0.57,0.5	0.54,0.47	0.54,0.48	0.59,0.39
1	0.57,0.44	-	0.86,0.78	0.48,0.45	0.55,0.35
2	0.54,0.46	0.87,0.82	-	0.46,0.46	0.58,0.35
3	0.54,0.44	0.48,0.5	0.46,0.47	-	0.47,0.34
4	0.58,0.4	0.55,0.45	0.57,0.45	0.47,0.35	-

Table 4. $\overline{TO}(\mathcal{O}_i, \mathcal{O}_j)$, $\overline{RO}(\mathcal{O}_i, \mathcal{O}_j)$ for phase II-ontologies.

Interpretation: The figures indicate that subjects tend to agree or disagree on taxonomies irrespective of the amount of material being predefined. In fact, correlation between $\overline{\text{TO}}$ values of phase I- and phase II- ontologies support this indication, because correlation is 0.58 — distinctly positive — for the ontologies with and without predefined lexica. Furthermore, we may conjecture that comparison between $\overline{\text{TO}}$ values (in order to select the best) remains meaningful even with a restricted overlap of lexica.

Results: Table 5 depicts the similarity measures computed for phase III-ontologies, where only $\overline{\text{RO}}$ has been computed, because the taxonomy was predefined. $\overline{\text{RO}}$ here ranges between 0.23 and 0.71, the average $\overline{\text{RO}}$ over all 20 cross-comparisons achieving 0.5.

	Subject				
$i\backslash j$	0	1	2	3	4
0	-	0.61	0.38	0.51	0.54
1	0.69	-	0.56	0.57	0.55
2	0.4	0.49	-	0.35	0.23
3	0.67	0.71	0.5	-	0.57
4	0.45	0.44	0.3	0.41	-

Table 5. $\overline{\text{RO}}(\mathcal{O}_i, \mathcal{O}_j)$ for phase III-ontologies.

Interpretation: The correlation of $\overline{\text{RO}}$ values between phases I and II computes to 0.34, between phases I and III to 0.27, and between phases II and III to 0.16. In general, higher $\overline{\text{RO}}$ values are reached without a predefined taxonomy — this reflects the observation that subjects found it easy to use a predefined lexicon, but extremely difficult to continue modeling given a predefined taxonomy.

Overall, we may conjecture that the engineers' use of their lexicon correlates rather strongly with their conceptual model and *vice versa*. The similarity measures for subject 3 ontologies with subject 4 ontologies result in very low values at the lexical and at the conceptual level. In contrast, subject 1 ontologies reach high similarity values with subject 2 ontologies at all levels.

6 Related Work

Similarity measures for ontological structures have been widely researched, e.g. in cognitive science, databases [9], software engineering[11], and AI (e.g., [8, 1, 4, 3]). Though this research covers many wide areas and application possibilities, most of it has restricted its attention to the determination of similarity of lexicon, concepts, and relations *within one ontology*.

The nearest to our comparison *between two ontologies* come [2, 3] and [13]. [2] introduces several similarity measures in order to locate a new complex concept into an existing ontology by similarity rather than by logic subsumption. Bisson restricts the attention to the conceptual comparison level. In contrast to our work the new concept is described in terms of the existing ontology. Furthermore, he does not distinguish relations into taxonomic relations and other ones, thus ignoring the semantics of inheritance. [13] compute description compatibility in order to answer queries that are formulated with a conceptual structure that is different from the one of the information system. In contrast to our approach their measures depend to a very large extent on a shared ontology that mediates between locally extended ontologies. Their algorithm also seems less suited to evaluate similarities of sets of lexical entries, taxonomies, and other relations.

Dieng & Hug [3] compare concept lattices in order to find out about the common location of two concepts in a merged ontology using several measures taking also advantage of the lattice. Again, however, their concerns are different from ours as they do not determine similarities of ontologies.

Research in the area of schema integration has been carried out since the beginning of the 1980s. Schema comparison analyzes and compares schema in order to determine correspondences and comes therefore near to our approach. However, their purpose is the alignment of pairs of tables or concepts [9] and often restricted to string and data type similarities.

Finally, so-called pathfinder networks [10] began in 1981 as an attempt to develop a network model for proximity data. They use use multidimensional scaling techniques. This statistical techniques transforms the concept network relationships into inter-point distances in a space of minimal dimensionality. In this space different similarity operations are performed. In contrast to our work, however, pathfinder networks do not focus on "real-world ontologies" including a lexical layer.

7 Conclusion

We have considered ontologies as two-layered systems, consisting of a lexical and a conceptual layer. Based on this core ontology model a methodological inventory to measure similarity between ontologies with each other based on the notions of lexicon $\mathcal{L}$, reference functions $\mathcal{F}, \mathcal{G}$ and semantic cotopy (SC, UC) has been described. Then, we have performed a three-phase empirical evaluation study to see how our measures perform in isolation and in combination. With our investigation we have created a methodological baseline and collected some empirical experiences.

Our measures may be applied in different application fields. First, we are currently working on an "ontology search engine" that will use the proposed measures as a basis retrieving ontologies based a user-defined core ontology that matches against available ontologies. Classical evaluation measures like precision and recall from the information retrieval community will serve as input for a quality-based evaluation of the proposed measures. Second, in [7] we describe how the measures presented in this paper may be extended for the instance level. Based on these instance-based similarity measures we provide means for computing a hierarchical clustering of ontology-based instances. Preliminary evaluation studies of applying the instance-based similarity measures within a clustering algorithm have shown promising results. Third, the measures proposed within this paper have shown to be very useful for supporting the discovery of mappings between two ontologies (see [6]). Fourth, such applications scenarios will become important for integrating existing ontologies into an ontology engineering process or for facilitating collaborative ontology engineering (cf. [12]).

Acknowledgements. Research for this paper was partially funded by the EU IST projects Bizon (IST-2001-33506) and SWAP (IST-2001-34103).

References

[1] E. Agirre and G. Rigau. Word sense disambiguation using conceptual density. In *Proc. of COLING-96*, 1996.

[2] G. Bisson. Learning in FOL with a similarity measure. In *Proc. of AAAI-1992*, pages 82–87, 1992.

[3] R. Dieng and S. Hug. Comparison of personal ontologies represented through conceptual graphs. In *Proceedings of ECAI 1998*, pages 341–345, 1998.

[4] E. Hovy. Combining and standardizing large-scale, practical ontologies for machine translation and other uses. In *Proc. of the First Int. Conf. on Language Resources and Evaluation (LREC)*, 1998.

[5] I. V. Levenshtein. Binary Codes capable of correcting deletions, insertions, and reversals. *Cybernetics and Control Theory*, 10(8):707–710, 1966.

[6] A. Maedche, B. Motik, N. Silva, and R. Volz. MAFRA – A MApping FRamework for Distributed Ontologies. In *Proceedings of the 13th European Conference on Knowledge Engineering and Knowledge Management EKAW-2002, Madrid, Spain*, 2002.

[7] A. Maedche and V. Zacharias. Clustering Ontology-based Metadata in the Semantic Web. In *Proceedings of the Joint Conferences 13th European Conference on Machine Learning (ECML'02) and 6th European Conference on Principles and Practice of Knowledge Discovery in Databases (PKDD'02), Springer, LNAI, Finland, Helsinki*, 2002.

[8] R. Rada, H. Mili, E. Bicknell, and M. Blettner. Development and application of a metric on semantic nets. *IEEE Transactions on Systems, Man, and Cybernetics*, 19(1), 1989.

[9] E. Rahm and P. Bernstein. A survey of approaches to automatic schema matching. *VLDB Journal*, 10(4):334–350, 2001.

[10] R. W. Schvanefeldt. *Pathfinder Associative Networks: Studies in Knowledge Organization.* Ablex Publishing Corporation, Norwood, New Jersey, 1989.

[11] G. Spanoudakis and P. Constantopoulos. Similarity for analogical software reuse: A computational model. In *Proc. of ECAI-1994*, pages 18–22, 1994.

[12] Y. Sure, M. Erdmann, J. Angele, S. Staab, R. Studer, and D. Wenke. Ontoedit: Collaborative ontology development for the semantic web. In *Proceedings of the 1st International Semantic Web Conference (ISWC2002), June 9-12th, 2002, Sardinia, Italia*, LNCS 2342, pages 221–235. Springer, 2002.

[13] P. Weinstein and W. Birmingham. Comparing concepts in differentiated ontologies. In *Proc. of KAW-99*, 1999.

Ontology-Mediated Business Integration

Borys Omelayenko

Division of Mathematics and Computer Science
Vrije Universiteit, De Boelelaan 1081, 1081hv,
Amsterdam, the Netherlands
borys@cs.vu.nl

Abstract. Traditional database- or XML-mediated business integration approaches use inexpressive mediating models of database schemas or XML trees, and a number of validation tasks need to be solved with ad-hoc programming techniques. We propose an architecture for an ontology-based business integration service relying on a composite mediating ontology constructed from several business, a temporal, and a mapping ontologies. The architecture allows using inference over these ontologies to perform various validations tasks.

1 The Need for Expressive Mediating Models

Current state-of-the-art business integration services are based on XML-mediated frameworks that utilize a tree-based model of XML documents and have to replace database-mediated approaches. XML provides natural means to represent the part-of hierarchy of labelled data strings that simplifies the document transformation process. Such an approach is adopted by the leading business integration toolkits BizTalk[1] and CapeStudio.[2]

Ontologies provide much richer modelling means with classes and properties organized into is-a hierarchies and enriched with axioms and relations processable with inference. They are promised to be the panacea for numerous integration problems in both traditional and Semantic Web contexts. However, quite often ontologies are used as simple or structured vocabularies and in this role they do not provide any substantial benefits comparing to existing techniques, besides getting some flavor coming with modern terminology.

Constructing a shared domain ontology from scratch is a difficult task suffering the knowledge acquisition bottleneck. However, a number of specific parts of the business integration domain have been carefully modelled within several standardization initiatives driving by large consortiums. We used the following standardized models:

WSDL The Web Service Description Language[3] specifying internet interface to specific company's ERP systems. Web-services are described in WSDL

---

[1] http://www.BizTalk.org
[2] http://www.capeclear.com/products/capestudio
[3] http://www.w3.org/TR/wsdl

A. Gómez-Pérez and V.R. Benjamins (Eds.): EKAW 2002, LNAI 2473, pp. 264–269, 2002.

with **Types** and **Port Types** that refer to XML Schemas of the messages (i.e. documents) and events at which these messages occur.[4]

PSL Process Specification Language[5] ontology defines classes for activities, timepoints, occurrences of activities, and a number of temporal relations between them (a timepoint **before** another timepoint, an object **participates_in**. an activity at a timepoint, etc.) as well as **objects** that possess no temporal properties.

ebXML (Electronic Business with XML[6]) specifies **Collaborations** of companies playing certain **Roles** in **Activities** communicating via **BusinessTransactions**.

These models describe large pieces of knowledge in the supporting documents, which need to be explicitly formalized and integrated in a single ontology.

The objective of the mediating service is to produce all the messages, expected by the companies linked to the service, with attached filled-in XML documents by requesting and parsing input messages and attached documents. Straightforwardly, the mediator needs to possess a collection of XSLT [1] scripts translating the XML documents via a mediating set of documents or a database. This approach is efficient under the following assumptions:

- Event sequences produced by ERP systems of different companies are similar with frequent one-to-one correspondences between the pairs of events.
- Each document has a counterpart to be translated to, or there exists well-specified dependency between the documents.

These two assumptions hamper scalability of the approach and prevent new companies from participating in the collaborations. One-to-one correspondence between events or documents occurs not that often. The companies playing different roles within procurement chains produce and expect different documents at different points in time. It is quite common that an acknowledgement for a purchase order request is required by one ERP system and not generated by the other one [2]. And even common documents like product catalogs tend to represent different compulsory information in addition to the common kernel.

Moreover, each document is not more than a collection of properties of several domain objects grouped together for a certain specific operation. E.g. a purchase order does not specify the products, nor the supplier. Instead, it refers to some property of a product (e.g. description and price, while other properties of the product, like weight, are available via separate requests) and to some property of the supplier (e.g. supplier name, skipping its bank information).

The mediation service needs to reconstruct the objects by parsing these references and partial information obtained from different documents. Nowadays

---

[4] WSDL also defines instance messages as instances of **Types** and their binding to document transmitting protocols that lays outside the focus of present paper. Here we treat web services as collections of events and XML documents transferred in accordance to these events.

[5] http://www.mel.nist.gov/psl/

[6] http://www.ebXML.org

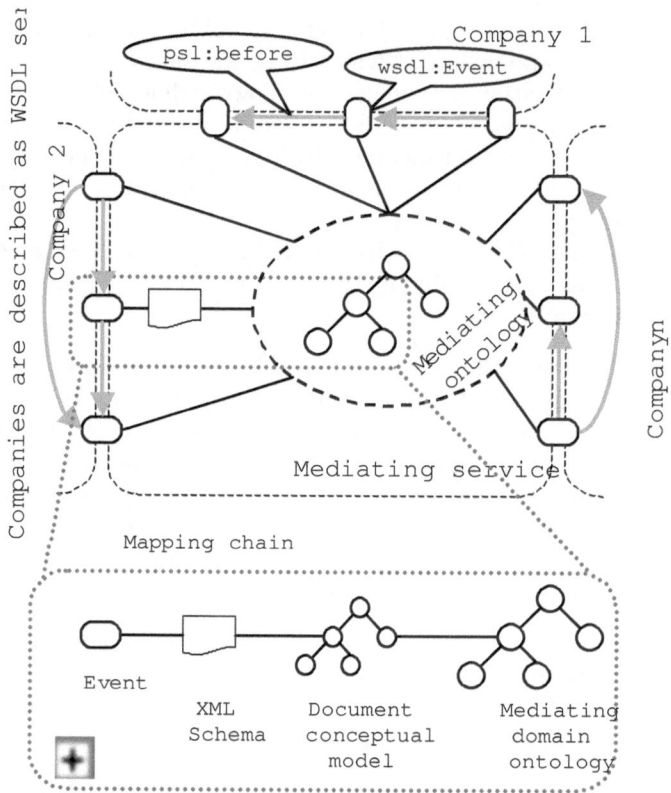

Fig. 1. The architecture of the mediating service. Several companies are represented as web services and their messages and attached documents are linked to the mediating service via the mediating ontology. Each link magnified in the figure as a mapping chain contains models for XML serializations of messages that are then mapped to their conceptual models, that are in turn mapped to the mediating ontology

it is done at the mediating databases or XML documents. These models are inexpressive and contain the data structures with just a few relations and cannot represent the objects directly. As a result the objects are represented indirectly as collections of strings. Representing and validating domain relations and axioms over indirectly presented objects require lots of ad-hoc programming.

We need to reconstruct and explicitly represent domain objects, relations and axioms to reason about them to perform really scalable and efficient integration.

2   Constructing the Mediating Ontology

The mediating service architecture presented in Figure 1 envisages several companies presented as WSDL-described web services. Each service expects or produces XML documents included into the messages occurring at certain events. The order of the events is specified according to a temporal ontology as illustrated with the psl:before relation in the figure.[7] The mediating service contains the mediating domain ontology specifying all the domain objects used by the companies in their documents. Each of the events produced by each of the services is mapped to the mediating ontology via a mapping chain magnified in the figure.

Each mapping chain includes several conceptual models:

- Mediating domain ontology.
- Conceptual models for the objects as detailed as they are specified at the XML Schemas for the documents.
- A model for particular XML document serialization (i.e. XML elements and attributes) needed to link the conceptual models to actual XML serializations.

The main assumption concerning usability of our approach is that *in the procurement domain the differences between document serializations are much bigger than between implicit conceptual models of the objects described in the documents.* For example, the cXML and xCBL serializations for a product catalog do not have a single XML tag with the same name, while they still specify more-or-less the same information (see [3] for some discussion and a sample).

Let us sketch the models used within each mapping chain magnified in the figure and their inter-relationships.

A model of XML document serialization consists of the classes representing XML elements, XML attributes, and the values of enumerated of fixed XML attributes. These are needed, e.g. to specify that attribute id identifies different objects if being attached to different elements. This ontology specifies all the knowledge needed to understand the input and fill in the output XML documents.

All the classes that possess temporal semantics are defined as subclasses of the classes from the **PSL ontology**. Then PSL temporal axioms are used to validate temporal constraints (e.g. specifying that a product should be mentioned in an invoice psl:before it gets mentioned in a delivery request).

WSDL contains two concepts important for our service: wsdl:Events and wsdl:Messages. Events naturally possess temporal semantics and are defined as subclasses of the psl:timepoint class, while messages stand for documents (psl:objects).

It is not realistic to assume the companies participating in the integration to provide well-elaborated ontologies for their documents, it is also not realistic to assume an individual at the mediating company being able to produce and maintain them.

However, there is a specific XML Schema for the documents attached to each WSDL message. Well-designed XML Schema contains lots of knowledge about the objects being described in the document, e.g. most of the part-of relations. It

---

[7] There might exist explicitly specified workflows behind the events. However, we do not discuss workflow integration in this paper.

is possible to automatically construct a preliminary object's conceptual model from XML DTDs or Schemas [4]. Well-defined XML Schemas for documents form the main source of information for performing conceptual modelling. These automatically derived models are then slightly updated by the user and aligned to the temporal and domain ontologies, that require less effort than constructing them from scratch.

Actual **models of the objects described in the documents** are created by the user by placing the classes from the automatically derived models in the right places in the hierarchy of domain classes from the mediating ontology. By doing this the user applies the relations and semantics of the domain classes to the objects mentioned in the documents.

The mediating ontology represents all the objects that can appear during the integration process: Partners, Product Descriptions, Vocabularies like UNSPSC[8] product codes. The mediating ontology holds all the domain-specific and temporal constraints. Physical objects are represented as instances of the classes of the mediating ontology.

The mediating ontology is not constructed from the scratch but from the specific conceptual models coming with the documents. The mediator needs to constantly update the mediating ontology if a new company requires some specific objects or attributes that haven't yet been incorporated.

Mapping ontology specifies the constructs needed to map XML models to specific document models and to the mediating model. We developed the RDFT ontology [5] based on the CWM (Common Warehouse Modelling) architecture for a mapping ontology [6]. RDFT contains all the basic primitives connecting classes and properties (like `rdft:Class2Class` and `rdft:Property2Property` bridges) with some modifications specific to our domain (like `rdft:Event2Event` bridges).

In addition to document integration we need to support **business collaborations** by mapping all the messages supporting all the transactions performed within a group of companies. Hence, we align ebXML classes standing for documents, activities, events, transactions, and collaborations to the corresponding PSL classes.

The language to represent all these conceptual models should be widely acceptable and allow easy integration with other XML-related standards. We choose RDF Schema [7], a recent W3C standard to represent the models. RDF Schema has limited expressive power to be regarded as an ontology language, e.g. it does not provide any means to represent axioms. We use Prolog to represent them and to inference over the models. Until now we succeeded to represent the models in RDF Schemas and the inference tasks in Prolog. We will consider the upcoming Web ontology language OWL[9] as a replacement when it will be available and there will be a need for that.

---

[8] www.unspsc.org
[9] http://www.w3.org/2001/sw/WebOnt/

3   Inference Tasks

The main outcome of the above-mentioned models is the emerging ability to perform inference to solve a number of labor-consuming programming tasks. Some of these tasks are:

- Checking completeness of the integration, i.e. verifying whether all the values required in the target documents are mapped via the conceptual models and compulsory attributes and elements of the source XML documents.
- Checking whether all the source documents needed to construct the target document can be queried before the target document is required, and the responses can be collected within acceptable deadlines to produce the target document in time.
- Checking consistency of the maps, i.e. finding duplicating data transformation chains.
- Verifying temporal consistency according to the business rules, such as the time period allocated by a supplier to receive payment confirmation must be longer than the period allocated by a buyer to issue the payment.

A number of questions remain open: (i) Whether it is realistic to require conceptual modelling for the objects presented in the documents? (ii) Is it possible to keep the mediating ontology sufficient for instance data transformation and minimal the same time, and whether it is possible to do it with a high degree of automation? They should be answered from both theoretical and practical points of view.

Acknowledgements. The author would like to thank Hans Akkermans, Dieter Fensel, and Michel Klein for their discussions and comments.

References

[1] Clark, J.: XSL Transformations (XSLT). Technical report, W3C Recommendation, November 16 (1999)
[2] Bussler, C.: B2B Protocol Standards and their Role in Semantic B2B Integration Engines. Bulletin of the Technical Committee on Data Engineering **24** (2001) 3–11
[3] Omelayenko, B., Fensel, D.: An Analysis of B2B Catalogue Integration problems: Content and Document Integration. In: Proceedings of the International Conference on Enterprise Information Systems (ICEIS-2001), Setubal, Portugal (2001) 945–952
[4] Mello, R., Heuser, C.: A Rule-Based Conversion of a DTD to a Conceptual Schema. In Kunii, H., Jojodia, S., Solvberg, A., eds.: Conceptual Modeling - ER'2001. Number 2224 in LNCS, Yokohama, Japan, Springer (2001) 133–148
[5] Omelayenko, B.: RDFT: A Mapping Meta-Ontology for Business Integration. In: Proceedings of the Workshop on Knowledge Transformation for the Semantic for the Semantic Web at the 15th European Conference on Artificial Intelligence (KTSW-2002), Lyon, France (2002) 77–84
[6] CWM: Common Warehouse Model Specification. Technical report, Object Management Group (2001)
[7] Brickley, D., Guha, R.: Resource Description Framework (RDF) Schema Specification 1.0. Technical report, W3C Candidate Recommendation, March 27 (2000)

Representation of Ontologies for Information Integration

Chantal Reynaud[1,2] and Brigitte Safar[1]

[1] University of Paris Sud-CNRS (LRI), INRIA (Futurs),
LRI, Building 490, 91405 Orsay Cedex, France
{cr, safar}@lri.fr
http://www.lri.fr/~cr
[2] University of Paris-X, Nanterre,
200 Avenue de la République, 92001, Nanterre Cedex, France

Abstract. An information integration system provides a uniform query interface to a collection of autonomous and distributed sources, connected to each other thanks to a global mediated schema, called domain ontology. The problem addressed in the paper is how to represent such an ontology into CARIN-$\mathcal{ALN}$, a formalism combining classes and rules. We focus on the choices for representing classes, properties and constraints using the characteristics of the formalism. We also propose a method in two steps for representing a domain ontology in the framework of a mediator. The first step is directed by the formalism and the functionalities of the mediator. The second step is an optimization phase guided by the way functionalities of the mediator are implemented.

1 Introduction

The rapid growth of information available online has raised the need for developing information integration systems. An information integration system provides a uniform query interface to a collection of autonomous and heterogeneous sources. It frees the users from having to find the relevant information sources, interact with each source in isolation using a particular interface, and manually combine data from the multiple sources.

Substantial work has been made in information integration leading to develop systems such as TSIMMIS [5], the Information Manifold [9], Infomaster [3], or PICSEL [6]. These systems are based on the specification of a single global mediated schema describing a domain of interest, called domain ontology, and on a set of source descriptions expressing how the content of each source available to the system is related to the domain of interest. Languages used to describe the ontology, the queries and the contents of the sources are key elements in all these systems. They need to be as expressive as possible but they also must be able to efficiently address the reformulation process of a query posed on the mediated schema into queries against the source schemas. However, in all these systems, techniques guiding ontology representation have not been considered.

A. Gómez-Pérez and V.R. Benjamins (Eds.): EKAW 2002, LNAI 2473, pp. 270–284, 2002.

The problem addressed in this paper is how to encode/represent an ontology into a given formalism combining classes and rules in the framework of the mediator PICSEL [1]. CARIN-$\mathcal{ALN}$ [6] is the formalism that we have used. It provides the knowledge engineer a framework being both a source of constraints and a guide for building the ontology. Given this framework, our aim, in this paper, is to describe the construction process of an ontology. We want to focus on ontology representation, distinguishing representation from modelisation. Modelisation is the identification of knowledge while representation considers knowledge as already identified and studies the representation formalisms offering the best tradeoff expressiveness/efficiency. The focus of our work is on the choices for representing classes, properties and constraints using the characteristics of the formalism.

The logical formalism CARIN-$\mathcal{ALN}$ [10] benefits from combining the expressive powers of datalog rules (function-free Horn rules) and the $\mathcal{ALN}$ Description Logics (DL). Horn rules are a natural representation language and are attractive because they are a tractable subset of first order logic for which several efficient inference procedures have been developed. DL are a family of representation languages that have been designed especially to model rich hierarchies of classes of objects. The hybrid language, CARIN-$\mathcal{ALN}$, significantly benefits from the expressive power of the two formalisms while maintaining the decidability of query answering and providing sound and complete reasoning services. So, limitations have been imposed for computational reasons on the ontology representation.

The recent explosion of interest in the World Wide Web has fuelled interest in ontologies. In particular, it has been predicted that ontologies, capturing consensual knowledge and including a vocabulary of terms, with a precised and formal specification of their meaning, will play a key role in the Semantic Web. An ontology is a key component to express metadata about web resources and to enable the processing and sharing of knowledge between programs on the Web. This has led to new research work to facilitate content description and semantic interoperability. In particular, the realization of the Semantic Web is underway with the development of new content-based markup languages such as OIL [4] or DAML [8] having a well-defined formal semantics, providing efficient reasoning support and enabling the manipulation of complex taxonomic and logical relations between entities on the Web. Our contribution is closed to works in ontologies developped in the Semantic Web area. However, in contrast to these works, we are interesting in the representation process itself, the language being given. Moreover, our work is complementary to work developed in the Knowledge Engineering area that emphasizes modelling. These works look for techniques or methods to find the good concepts or the good relations. They propose methods or techniques to build ontologies from analysis of accessible corpus (textual [1] [11], semi-structured or structured [7] documents) or reuse techniques [2]. Such approaches could have been used to build the model of the ontology that we have to represent.

---

[1] PICSEL is supported by FranceTelecom under contract number 97 1B 378.

The contributions of the work presented in this paper, are twofold. The first one is to provide guidelines to represent an ontology in CARIN-$\mathcal{ALN}$, a formalism combining classes and rules, in the framework of a mediator. The second one is to propose a method for representing a domain ontology in information integration. Ontology representation is viewed as a two-step process. The first step is guided by the language and the functionalities of the mediator. The second step, which aims at refining and optimizing the representation obtained in the first step, is guided by the way the functionalities of the mediator are implemented.

The paper is organized as follows. In section 2, we present the information integration problem and describe the mediator approach which is the approach followed in PICSEL. Section 3 presents the representation languages used. The two-step representation process of an ontology is described in sections 4 and 5. We conclude in section 6. The examples in the paper are coming from the tourism products domain, which is a real case that we have considered, in collaboration with the Web travel agent Degriftour.

2   Information Integration and Mediator Approach

Information integration provides easy access to multiple, distributed, heterogeneous and autonomous information sources that may contain relevant and complementary information. Indeed, users do not want to handle heterogeneity. Their aim is to query a multitude of sources as a centralized and homogeneous system. Thus, specific querying tools over various sources are needed to give users the illusion that they interrogate a centralized and homogeneous information system while preserving the autonomy of each information source. A mediator architecture is a solution to design such information integration systems. We give a description of such architecture in Figure 1.

Information sources underlying a mediator system are autonomous and preexisting sources, which were created independently. A domain ontology plays the role of a single global mediated schema. Descriptions of source contents are expressed as views over the mediated schema. These source descriptions, also called mappings because they model the correspondence between the mediated schema and the schemas of the data sources, play a central role in the query answering process. Users pose queries in terms of the domain ontology rather than directly in terms of the source schemas. That way, a user query that is formulated on a domain ontology is translated by the data integration system into a set of queries against local schemas using the source descriptions. Then the queries are executed against the data sources through wrappers in order to get the answers to the user query.

The existing mediator-based information integration systems can be distinguished depending on the type of mappings between the mediated schema and the schemas of the sources. There are two main approaches for modelling interschemas correspondence:Global As Views (GAV) and Local As Views (LAV). The GAV approach has been the first one to be proposed and comes from the

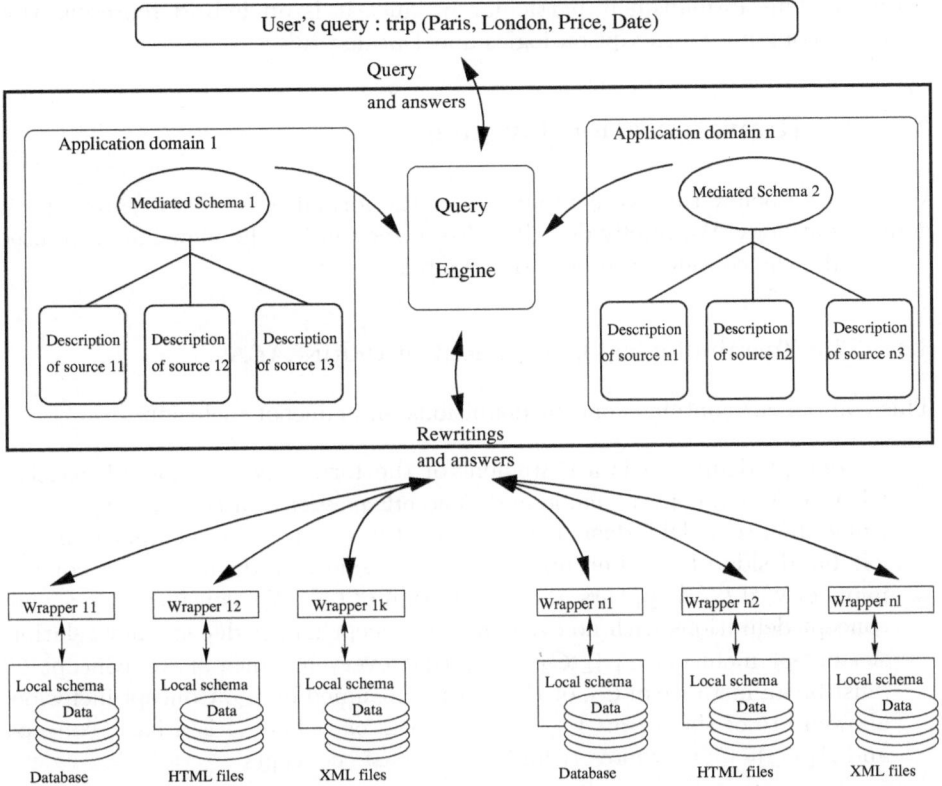

User's query : trip (Paris, London, Price, Date)

Fig. 1. Summary of the different kinds of knowledge in the ontology and indication of the processes which exploit them in shaded areas

Federated Databases world. The mediated schema is defined in function of the schemas of the sources to integrate, i.e., each relation of the mediated schema is defined as a view on the relations of the source schemas. In that case, query rewriting algorithms are very efficient because query reformulation simply consists of replacing each atom of the query by its definition in terms of the relations of the source schemas. However, it leads to update the mediated schema whenever any of the sources changes or when new sources are added. The LAV approach is dual and has opposite advantages and drawbacks. Its consists of describing the contents of the sources in function of the mediated schema. In such a case, adding new sources is quite straightforward because each source is defined independently of each other. However the algorithms to rewrite a domain level query into a source level query involves testing containment of views, which is computationnally expensive.

The work described in this paper has been made in the setting of the PICSEL mediator which follows a LAV approach. It differs from existing mediator systems by CARIN, the logical formalism usable in the system to express the domain ontology. This formalism is particular because it is an hybrid representation language combining description logics and Datalog rules.

3   The Representation Language

We describe below the two components of the formalism used to represent the domain ontology. We briefly describe also in section 3.3 the view language used to describe the content of information sources.

3.1   The Terminological Component of CARIN-$\mathcal{ALN}$

This component contains concept definitions and concept inclusions.

- A concept definition is a statement of the form $CN :=$ ConceptExpression, where CN is a concept name and ConceptExpression is a concept expression, using the $\mathcal{ALN}$ DL. Basic concepts are those which do not appear in any left hand side of a definition. A concept name CN depends on a concept name CN' if CN' appears in the definition of CN. We consider only acyclic concept definitions with no cycle in the concept names dependency relation.
- A concept inclusion $C_1 \sqsubseteq C_2$ states that every instance of the concept C_1 must be an instance of C_2, or that C_1 is subsumed by C_2. Concept inclusions allowed are of the form: $A \sqsubseteq$ ConceptExpression, where A is a basic concept, and $A_1 \sqcap A_2 \sqsubseteq \bot$, where A_1 and A_2 are basic concepts.

$\mathcal{ALN}$ contains the DL constructors of *conjunction* ($C_1 \sqcap C_2$), *value restriction* ($\forall$R C) which represents the set of elements in relation by R only with elements of the concept C, *number restrictions* ($\geq$ n R) (respectively ($\leq$ n R)), which represent the set of elements in relation by R with at most, (respectively at least), n distinct elements, and *negation* ($\neg$) (restricted to basic concepts only).

3.2   The Deductive Component of CARIN-$\mathcal{ALN}$

The deductive component of a CARIN knowledge base contains:

- A set of rules that are logical sentences of the form $p_1(\bar{X}_1, \bar{Y}_1) \wedge \ldots \wedge p_n(\bar{X}_n, \bar{Y}_n) \to q(\bar{X})$, where $\bar{X} = \bar{X}_1 \cup \ldots \cup \bar{X}_n$ and $\bar{Y} = \bar{Y}_1 \cup \ldots \cup \bar{Y}_n$ are variable vectors. These rules allow to define relations q (of any arity) in function of other predicates $p_1, p_2, ..., p_n$. The variables of $\bar{X}_i$, distinct from the variables of $\bar{Y}$, are considered to be existentially quantified. The base relations are those which do not appear in any consequent of rules. Some base relations, unary relations, are expressions of concepts, others, binary relations, are expressions of roles in the terminological component.
- A set of integrity constraints: $p_1(\bar{Y}_1) \wedge \ldots \wedge p_m(\bar{Y}_m) \to \bot$, where p_i are n-ary relations.

3.3 The Description of the Sources Content

The content of each information source $\mathcal{S}$ is represented with the vocabulary $\mathcal{V}_S$ composed of as many local relations v_i as domain relations whose instances can be found in the source $\mathcal{S}$. These local relations are called views. The description of the content of a source $\mathcal{S}$ in terms of its views contains:

- a set $\mathcal{I}_s$ of logical implications $v_i(x) \to p(x)$. These implications establish a link between each view and the domain relation p whose instances can be found in the source $\mathcal{S}$.
- a set $\mathcal{C}_s$ of constraints on the instances of the form: $v \sqsubseteq C$, where C is a concept expression, or $l_1(\bar{X}_1) \wedge \cdots \wedge l_n(\bar{X}_n) \to \bot$, where each $l_i(\bar{X}_i)$ is either a view $v_i(\bar{X}_i)$, either the negation of a view (at most one negation of a view per constraint).

Example 1 Let $\mathcal{S}_1$ be a source providing instances of Hotels located in the Mediterranean:

$\mathcal{I}_{s_1}$: $v_{11}(x) \to$ Hotel(x) $v_{12}(x, y) \to$ located(x, y)
$\mathcal{C}_{s_1}$: $v_{11}(x) \sqsubseteq (\forall$located InMediterranean$)$
    $v_{12}(x, y) \wedge \neg v_{11}(x) \to \bot$

4 Representation Directed by the Language

The expressive power of CARIN-$\mathcal{ALN}$ is very rich and offers multiple choices for representing a domain ontology. We give here the solutions that we adopted. Our strategy was to favour the terminological component, and to use the deductive part of the formalism only to circonvent its limits. Indeed, the designer is guided during all the representation process by a classifier which automatically classifies the concepts in the terminological part considering their definition. The resulting hierarchy can be visualized. This is a good help and no equivalent reasoning service can be provided by the deductive component of the language.

4.1 Knowledge Represented in the Terminological Component

Representing a domain ontology means to supply descriptions of object classes and descriptions of links among classes. In data modeling, each class is defined through its relations with other classes: classes which generalize it and classes related through domain-specific properties. Properties are of two kinds. There are properties that a user would like to precise when querying the system or when describing the content of a source. There are also properties necessary to structure and organize the classes between each other. For example, assAccomodationPlace allows to relate a Lodging to an AccomodationPlace. This link is important because the choice criteria of users may concern characteristics of the accomodation place (address, category, equipments) where the lodging is located. Either specific properties or the set of necessary and sufficient properties that an entity must satisfy to belong to a class are given.

During the representation phase, classes of objects have been represented by unary relations, called concepts. Links among classes and properties have been represented by binary relations, called roles, and with DL constructors of value restriction ($\forall$) and of number restrictions ($\geq$, $\leq$). In DL, a role is not defined in function of the concepts that are related. One may use assService as a role for Product, AccomodationPlace or Resort as well. In our work, we chose to use identical names for roles when the concepts are related with a generalization/specialization link and distinct names otherwise to eliminate ambiguities. In example 2, we have illustrations of various statements. Example 2.a is a definition of the concept Product which has a unique price, a unique beginning date, it may have associated amenities or equipments. Example 2.b is the definition of SportActivity, an activity whose associated nature is a sport. Product and SportActivity are both defined concepts. Example 2.c is an illustration of the inclusion of the basic concept CulturalEquipment (not explicitly defined) into the concept Equipment.

Example 2

a. (Product := (≥ 1 assPrice) $\sqcap$ (≤ 1 assPrice) $\sqcap$ ($\forall$assPrice Number)
   $\sqcap$ (≥ 1 assDepDate)$\sqcap$ (≤ 1 assDepDate)$\sqcap$ ($\forall$assDepDate Date)
   $\sqcap$ ($\forall$assProdAmenity Amenity) $\sqcap$ ($\forall$assProdEquipment Equipment))
b. (SportActivity :=   Activity $\sqcap$ ($\forall$assActivityNature Sport))
c. (CulturalEquipment $\sqsubseteq$ Equipment)

For efficiency reasons, CARIN-$\mathcal{ALN}$ does not allow existential quantification. To overcome this lack, we use multiple specialized roles. So, to define that a FamilialResort is a resort with a nursery and a doctor, two distinct roles assNursery and assMedicalAssistance have been introduced while the unique assEquipment role name would have been enough if it would be possible to use it in existential sentences: ($\exists$ assEquipment Nursery) and ($\exists$ assEquipment Doctor), where Nursery and Doctor are two disjoint concepts.

Example 3 (FamilialResort := Resort $\sqcap$ (≥ 1 assNursery) $\sqcap$ ($\forall$assNursery Nursery) $\sqcap$ (≥ 1 assMedicalAssistance) $\sqcap$ ($\forall$assMedicalAssistance Doctor))

The concept hierarchy built by the classifier is a guide to detect anomalies and then make modifications or to discover concepts having common roles. For example, the concept Lodging comes from factorizing the common roles of the concepts Room and Flat. These two concepts inherit roles associated to the general concept Lodging and they only retain their specific roles.

Moreover, thanks to the inclusion mechanism, a concept can be defined as a specialization of another one, without additional specification. Multiple view points can be represented. For example, the concept Boat can be defined as being both a MeansOfTransport and an AccomodationPlace. That way, whole hierarchies have been built grouping concepts with no explicit properties. This facility is used when the name of the concepts is clear enough, not ambiguous and then sufficient to be understandable by a user.

Not defined concepts (basic concepts) are the only concepts that can appear in disjunctions. Example 4 specifies that a cultural equipment can not be a sport equipment.

Example 4   CulturalEquipment ⊓ SportEquipment ⊑ ⊥

One can also express typing constraints on roles using the constructor of value restriction. In example 2.a, the restriction (∀assDepDate Date) specifies that the role assDepDate relates elements of type Product only to elements of type Date.

4.2   The Use of Rules

The use of rules is sometimes a necessity (case 1 to 4) to circonvent the limits of the terminological part. Sometimes rules allow easy writing (case 5).

- Case 1. To express relations that are neither unary nor binary. The rule R_1 defines a return flight as a 4-ary relation R-Flight. A return flight is characterized by a departure city (denoted by the first variable $D\text{-}City$ in the consequent of the rule), a departure date ($D\text{-}Date1$), an arrival city ($A\text{-}City$), a return date ($D\text{-}Date2$). The possible combinations of a flight to and back a given destination obey some constraints that are expressed by the conditions in the antecedent of the rule.
  R_1 : Flight(f1) ∧ depCity(f1, D-City) ∧ arrCity(f1, A-City) ∧ depDate(f1, D-Date1) ∧ Flight(f2) ∧ depCity(f2, A-City) ∧ arrCity(f2, D-City) ∧ depDate(f2, D-Date2) ∧ prior(D-Date1, D-Date2)
  → R-Flight(D-City, D-Date1, A-City, D-Date2).
- Case2. To build a disjunctive definition of a relationship. The rules R_2 and R_3 express that a product for young people (ForYoung) is a product either with at most one associated service or with cheap services. Such relation can not be defined in the terminological component because of the absence of the constructor OR.
  R_2 : Product (x) ∧ (≤ 1 assServiceProduct) → ForYoung(x)
  R_3 : Product (x) ∧ assServiceProduct(x,y) ∧ Cheap(y) → ForYoung(x)
- Case 3. To express non exclusive constraints. The value restriction constructor (∀R C) allows to express constraints on the domain of the concepts in relation with other ones, but theses constraints are exclusive. Then, in the following definition, "WithMountainSite := Place ⊓ (∀practicableSport MountainSport)" the value restriction says that all practicable sports in a WithMountainSite are MountainSport. That eliminates Swimming or Tennis. If we want to represent that we can go skiing or swimming in a WithMountainSite providing a swimming pool, one must use rules. Practicable sports in a site can be defined as depending both of physical characteristics of this site (cf. R_4 and R_5) and of its sport equipments (cf. R_6).
  R_4: WithMountainSite(l) ∧ MountainSport(s) → practicableSport(l, s).
  R_5 : WithBeachSite(l) ∧ WaterSport(s) → practicableSport(l, s).
  R_6: WithSwimmingPoolSite(l) ∧ Swimming(s) → practicableSport(l, s).
- Case 4. To express an inverse relation. In the terminological component, concept definitions are acyclic and roles are oriented relations. For example, the role assSite denotes a binary relation, in the terminological component, between one AccomodationPlace and the Site where it is situated. To define the inverse relationship, we use a rule (cf. R_7).
  R_7 : AccomodationPlace(r) ∧ assSite(r, l) ∧ Site(l) → beingSituated(l,r).

- Case 5. To express a link corresponding to multiple combined roles in the terminological part. For example, the rule R_8 allows to derive the predicate assLodgingResort which links directly Lodging to the name of the ski resort where its AccomodationPlace is situated.

  R_8 : Lodging(l) $\land$ assAccomodationPlace(l,r) $\land$ assAccomodationPlaceResort(r, st) $\land$ SkiResort(st) $\land$ assName(st,n) $\rightarrow$ assLodgingResort(l,n).

4.3 The Use of Integrity Constraints

Constraints different from disjunctive constraints between basic concepts (not defined) must be represented as integrity constraints.

- Constraints conveying functional dependencies.

  The following constraint expresses that a phone number is specific to a unique accomodation place.

Example 5 phoneNumber(x_1,y) $\land$ AccomodationPlace(x_1) $\land$ phoneNumber(x_2,y) $\land$ AccomodationPlace(x_2) $\land$ $x_1 \neq x_2 \rightarrow \bot$

- Typing constraints on predicate arguments

  Typing constraints are of the form:

  $P(\bar{X}) \land \neg C_i(x_i) \rightarrow \bot$, with $\bar{X} = (x_1, x_2, ..., x_i, ...x_n)$. They allow to define the domain of values (set of elements of C_i) of each element x_i of the relation P. Then, according to example 6, the relation assAmenity always establishes a link with an amenity.

Example 6 assAmenity(x,y) $\land \neg$ Amenity(y) $\rightarrow \bot$

Typing constraints can replace a value restriction in a definition statement. When a role is used in the definition of several concepts, with the same value restriction (ex: ($\forall$assAmenity Amenity)), a constraint avoids the repetition of the value restriction in each definition. When the value restrictions are different, the concept that appears in the constraint must be a concept that generalizes all the restricted concepts. In such case, however, the constraint is not equivalent to the value restrictions which are more precise. These ones are preserved but the constraint is also useful. It will be applied if no more precise restriction is specified (cf. example 7).

Example 7
(HotelRoom := Room $\sqcap$ ($\forall$assAccomodationPlace Hotel))
(BoatCabin := Room $\sqcap$ ($\forall$assAccomodationPlace Boat))

The first concept that generalizes both Hotel and Boat is AccomodationPlace. We can then write the following constraint:

  assAccomodationPlace(x,y) $\land \neg$ AccomodationPlace(y) $\rightarrow \bot$.

This constraint will hold each time the assAccomodationPlace role is used in a concept definition statement with no value restrictions.

• Exclusive constraints between ordinary predicates.

These constraints are of the form: $p_1(\bar{X}_1) \wedge ... \wedge p_n(\bar{X}_n) \rightarrow \bot$. They enable to express semantic constraints relative to the application domain. That way, the example 8.a says that there is no direct flight between two conflictual countries. Exclusive constraints are also useful for exception treatments. In example 7, BoatCabin is defined as a specialization of the concept room and then, inherits all its properties, in particular its amenities. The constraint in example 8.b states that Terrace is an exception because it is not an amenity for BoatCabin.

Example 8

a. Country(p_1) $\wedge$ Country(p_2) $\wedge$ inConflict(p_1,p_2) $\wedge$ LinkingTransport(t, p_1,p_2)
   $\wedge$ NonStopFlight(t) $\rightarrow \bot$
b. BoatCabin(l) $\wedge$ assAmenityRoom(l, p) $\wedge$ Terrace(p) $\rightarrow \bot$

At the end of the first step of the representation process, we obtain an initial operational version of the ontology composed of about 200 concepts and 300 roles. This ontology adheres to the constraints of the langage and to the model of the ontology prior built. Its content has been defined during the modelisation phase and enriched in this first representation step according to the functionalities of the mediator, for which, we ignore, at this step, how they will be implemented.

5   Expanded and Optimized Representation

The representation that we obtained in precedent section is directly usable as a support for the interface guiding query expression and, also by the engine to compute query plans. We describe now, how this ontology has then been expanded and optimized by considering the use of the knowledge in the implemention of these two functionalities.

5.1   Expansion for Query Expression

The ontology provides the users with all the terms of a domain, elementary concepts and associated roles, allowing them to express a lot of queries relative to complex concepts. The objective of the interface is to help to build queries, and to avoid manipulating the query language. So, the approach consists in providing predefined queries relative to frequently searched topics (SunnyTrip, ShortBreak, and so on.) to users. These topics are complex concepts combining elementary tourism products in the ontology, for example an arrangement by which Transport and Accomodation can be purchased by a tourist at an-all inclusive price. Each topic is represented by a predicate defined by a rule (cf. example 9). The body of the rule is a conjunction of concepts and roles in the terminological component and, possibly of ordinary predicates defined by rules.

Example 9

InclusiveTour(t) $\wedge$ assLodging(t,l) $\wedge$ Lodging(l) $\wedge$ assAccomodationPlace(l, a) $\wedge$ AccomodationPlace(a) $\wedge$ situatedIn(a, s) $\wedge$ SunnySite(s) $\rightarrow$ SunnyTrip(t, s)

InclusiveTour, Lodging, AccomodationPlace, SunnySite are concepts.
assLodging, assAccomodationPlace, situatedIn are role names.

As soon as a topic is selected, the interface exploits the body of the rule defining the corresponding predicate. It proposes to the user to specialize the concepts included in the body of the rule, using the concept hierarchy, or to introduce new properties for these concepts, using the associated roles. Each choice affects automatically the initial query.

Such an approach led to list all the most searched topics and to expand the initial ontology with corresponding predicates.

5.2 Optimization for Query Rewriting

Computing query plans involves, in a first stage, rewriting user queries in terms of views on the sources. The rewriting possibilities are: immediate rewriting by a view, replacing an ordinary predicate by the body of the different rules which define it, replacing a terminological concept by its definition (and the definition is recursively replaced until the basic concepts are obtained).Then the engine builds all possible regroupings of concepts and of roles which can be rewriten by a view. This last mechanism is costly. In the worst case, query expansion is exponential in the size of terminological expressions appearing in the query. As a result, the more the definitions are composed of roles and of value restrictions, the more the expansion process is costly. As the model of the ontology is very detailed, the number of roles characterising each concept is very high. Representing all these roles leads to inefficiency.

Roles are essential when building the ontology because the classifier classifies a new concept according to its roles. Roles are also very useful for the user because they can help in understanding the meaning of concepts in the ontology and support the interface for query expression. On the other hand, roles are not all useful to compute query plans. So, we decided to optimize the representation of the ontology, so as to limit the size of the expansions (and then of the number of possible rewritings).

Concepts on the top of the hierarchy are generic and abstract concepts (Product, Site, LeisureActivity, Equipment, Amenity, AccomodationPlace, and so on.). On the opposite, queries are about very concrete objects. A user does no search an instance of a tourism product but an instance of a Lodging or of a Transport, for example, with some properties. This way, roles of an abstract concept are used only because their specializations inherit them. Moreover, all the roles are not useful to compute query plans. For example, when a user is looking for renting an apartment in a skiing resort located in Haute-Savoie in France, what is important for the engine is to find sources providing instances of such accomodations with the particularities of being in a skiing resort located in Haute-Savoie. As all tourism products, apartment rentals have, for example, a price but it is useless to consider all the roles shared by all tourism products in the rewriting process in terms of views on the sources.

Our approach is then to use the following heuristics: all the root concepts of the different hierarchies of the ontology will become not defined concepts in the optimized ontology, like their son concepts when they only depend on not defined root concepts (initially not defined in the ontology or after the application of the heuristics). Consequently, the concepts which are sons of root concepts and which only depend on not defined root concepts, become also not defined. Their role relate root (generic) concepts in the hierarchy. They correspond to properties structuring the ontology (example: assAccomodationPlace linking Lodging to AccomodationPlace). Once the heuristics has been applied, such properties will not appear any more except in the definitions of specialized concepts.

On the other hand, concept definitions may be very useful for the query engine when they allow to detect disjunctions between concepts. So, in example 10, the two defined concepts, HotelRoom and GuestHouseRoom, are considered as disjoint by the engine because the value restrictions in their definitions involved Hotel and GuestHouse, two concepts defined as being disjoint in the terminology. In such a case, the role assAccomodationPlace is essential in the two definitions.

Example 10
(HotelRoom := Room ⊓ (∀assAccomodationPlace Hotel))
(GuestHouseRoom := Room ⊓ (∀assAccomodationPlace GuestHouse))

All these constatations led us to structure in a better way the ontology, with two objectives: to preserve its whole richness and to maintain the efficiency of the query engine. Considering that the classifier is not used any more once the ontology has been built, we chose not to maintain in the ontology the roles of initially defined concepts, transformed in not defined concepts during the optimization process and to represent them with typing constraints. They are always accessible for query expression and for the description of the sources. The user can access to them. Nevertheless, they are not exploited in the expansion step any more.

This new representation, which is a simplification of the original one (it is not equivalent), allows us to obtain a hierarchy in which a lot of concepts have no definition. They are described by simple inclusion statements. Defined concepts appear most generally at the bottom of the hierarchy (cf. example 11). Thanks to this new structuration, the cost of the query plans becomes acceptable.

Example 11 In the new hierarchy, the concepts Product, Lodging, Room have no definition any more and concepts HotelRoom, GuestHouseRoom, BoatCabin are defined as specialized concepts of Room (cf. example 10).
   Room ⊑ Lodging ⊑ Product

Table 1 summarizes the different categories of knowledge represented in the ontology and the processes which exploit them (shaded areas in the table). Currently, this new organization gives good results but additionnal tests are necessary to give a quantitative measure of the benefits. Moreover, the optimization phase can most likely be improved. This work must be considered as the result of a first optimization work on an ontology.

Table 1. Summary of the different kinds of knowledge in the ontology and indication of the processes which exploit them in shaded areas

Representation Structures		Nature of the represented knowledge	Query Plan computing		Interface
			Rewriting	Verification	
Terminological Component	Concept definition	Defined concepts	▓		▓
	Concept inclusion	Basic concepts	▓		▓
	Disjunction of concepts	Disjunctions between basic concepts	▓		▓
Deductive Component	Integrity constraint	Functional dependencies		▓	▓
		Typing constraints on predicate arguments		▓	▓
		Semantic constraints		▓	
	Rules	n-ary relations (n>2)	▓		▓
		Disjunctions	▓		▓
		Short cuts of roles	▓		▓
		« Non exclusives » constraints	▓		▓
		Inverse relations	▓		▓
		Predefined queries	▓		▓

6   Conclusion

In this paper, we described the representation process of an ontology in the setting of a mediator. Two steps have been distinguished. The first one has aimed at building a first operational version of an ontology according to a model prior built and also according to constraints inherent to the representation language CARIN-$\mathcal{ALN}$. We described how this first step has been developped to build an ontology of a real application domain, the tourism products domain. The second step uses the current version of the ontology to compute query plans and to support a user interface. This second step led to refine the representation of the ontology by adding new predicates useful for the interface and also by reorganizing the knowledge. Our aim was to preserve the whole richness of the model but also to obtain an efficient system. An organisation of knowledge based on the way this knowledge is used in the application has appeared as a good solution.

The representation process, often considered as a simple translation one, appears here to be a complex process for which few methodological guidelines exist. This paper must be viewed as a contribution towards such guidelines. We address them to future ontology designers having to build an ontology for a mediator. However, in spite of the explicitation and of the description of the process to represent an ontology in the setting of our project, building an ontology remains a difficult and very time consuming task. This problem is an important scientific problem for the development of mediators.

A second contribution of the paper is to illustrate the role of rules in ontology languages. An important focus in PICSEL was the complexity of the reasoning. For this reason, we considered a formalism maintaining the decidability of query answering. The limitations that we have imposed for computational reasons by using $\mathcal{ALN}$, a rather restricted description logics, has not been an obstacle for a modeling point of view. Thanks to the expressive power of datalog rules, the limits of $\mathcal{ALN}$ expressions have been overstepped. Moreover, predicates appearing in a consequent of a rule have been very useful for describing the content of sources or for query expression because they allow easy writing.

Acknowledgments

We would like to thank M.-C. Rousset for many fruitful discussions and F. Goasdoue who implemented the query engine and has allowed us the optimization of the ontology.

References

1. Aussenac N., Biebow B. and Sulzman B. Revisiting Ontology Design:A method Based on Corpus Analysis, In *Proceedings of EKAW,* 172-188, 2000.
2. Clark P., Thompson J., Holmback H. and Duncan L. Exploiting Thesaurus-Based Semantic net for Knowledge-Based Search, In *Proceedings of AAAI,* 988-995, 2000.
3. Duschka O. and Genesereth M. Query planning in Infomaster, In *Proceedings of the ACM Symposium on Applied Computing,* San Jose, USA, 1997.
4. Fensel D., Horrocks I. Van Harmele F., Deckers S., Erdmann M. and Klein M. OIL in a nutshell, In *ECAI Workshop Notes - Applications of Ontologies and Problem-Solving Methods,* 4.1 - 4.12, 2000.
5. Garcia-Molina H., Papakonstantinou Y., Quass D., Rajarama A., Sagivy Y., Ullman J. and Widom J. The TSIMMIS project: Integration of heterogeneous information sources, In *Journal Intelligent Information Systems,* 8(2), 117-132, 1997.
6. Goasdoue F., Lattes V. and Rousset M.-C. The Use of CARIN Language and Algorithms for Information Integration: the PICSEL Project. In *International Journal of Cooperative Information Systems,* Vol. 9, n°4, pp. 383-401, 2000.
7. Goasdoue F. and Reynaud C. Modeling Information Sources for Information Integration, In *Proceedings of EKAW,* 121-138, 1999.
8. Hendler J. and McGuinnes D.L. The DARPA agent markup language, In *IEEE Intelligent Systems,* 6(15), 72-73, 2000.
9. Levy A., Rajarama A. and Ordille J. Querying heterogeneous information sources using source descriptions, In *Proceedings of the Int. Conf. On Very Large Data Bases (VLDB),* 251-262, 1996.

10. Levy A. and Rousset M.-C. Combining Horn rules and Description Logics in CARIN. In *Artificial Intelligence*, $n°104$, pp. 165-209, 1998.
11. Maedche A. and Staab S. Mining Ontologies from Text, In *Proceedings of EKAW*, 189-202, 2000.

User-Driven Ontology Evolution Management

Ljiljana Stojanovic[1], Alexander Maedche[1], Boris Motik[1], Nenad Stojanovic[2]

[1] FZI - Research Center for Information Technologies at the University of Karlsruhe,
Haid-und-Neu-Str. 10-14, D-76131 Karlsruhe, Germany
{Ljiljana.Stojanovic,Alexander.Maedche,Boris.Motik}@fzi.de
[2] Institute AIFB, University of Karlsruhe,
76128 Karlsruhe, Germany
nst@aifb.uni-karlsruhe.de

Abstract. With rising importance of knowledge interchange, many industrial and academic applications have adopted ontologies as their conceptual backbone. However, industrial and academic environments are very dynamic, thus inducing changes to application requirements. To fulfill these changes, often the underlying ontology must be evolved as well. As ontologies grow in size, the complexity of change management increases, thus requiring a well-structured ontology evolution process. In this paper we identify a possible six-phase evolution process and focus on providing the user with capabilities to control and customize it. We introduce the concept of an evolution strategy encapsulating policy for evolution with respect to user's requirements.

1 Introduction

With rising importance of knowledge interchange, many industrial and academic applications have adopted ontologies as their conceptual backbone. However, business dynamics and changes in the operating environment often give rise to continuous changes to application requirements, that may be fulfilled only by changing the underlying ontologies [16]. This is especially true for WWW and Semantic Web applications [2], that are based on heterogeneous and highly distributed information resources and therefore need efficient mechanisms to cope with changes in the environment.

Ontology evolution is the timely adaptation of an ontology to changed business requirements, to trends in ontology instances and patterns of usage of the ontology-based application, as well as the consistent management/propagation of these changes to dependent elements. A modification in one part of the ontology may generate subtle inconsistencies in other parts of the same ontology, in the ontology-based instances as well as in depending ontologies and applications [11]. This variety of causes and consequences of the ontology changes makes ontology evolution a very complex operation that should be considered as both, an organizational and a technical process [22]. It requires a careful analysis of the types of the ontology changes [13] that can trigger evolution as well as the environment in which the whole ontology evolution process is realized [25].

A. Gómez-Pérez and V.R. Benjamins (Eds.): EKAW 2002, LNAI 2473, pp. 285–300, 2002.
© Springer-Verlag Berlin Heidelberg 2002

Although evolution over time is an essential requirement for successful application of ontologies [6], methods and tools to support this complex task completely are missing. This level of ontology management is necessary not only for the initial development [8] and maintenance of ontologies, but is essential during deployment, when scalability, availability, reliability and performance are absolutely critical [17].

In this paper we analyze ontology evolution requirements and present a novel, process-oriented approach that fulfils them. We specifically focus on the problem that the ontology has to remain consistent under complex changes during evolution. As for some changes there may be several different consistent states of the ontology, we introduce the notion of an evolution strategy allowing the user to customize the process according to her needs. Consequently, the user can transfer the ontology in the desired consistent state. Finally, we substantiate our discussion on ontology evolution by presenting its current implementation within KAON[1] framework.

The paper is organized as follows: Section 2 identifies the requirements for the ontology evolution and derives an ontology evolution process that fulfils them. Section 3 explores the complexity of the semantics of change problem and introduces different evolution strategies that allow user to control and to customize the evolution process. As a proof of the concept, section 4 contains a short description how ontology evolution been implemented. After a discussion of related work, concluding remarks outline some future work.

2 Ontology Evolution Requirements

Based on our experience in building ontologies and using them in several applications [25], we have formulated the following set of design requirements for ontology evolution:

- It has to enable resolving the given ontology changes [7] and to ensure the consistency of the underlying ontology and all dependent artifacts [24];
- It should be supervised allowing the user to manage changes more easily [28];
- It should offer advice to user for continual ontology refinement [19].

The first requirement is an essential one for any ontology evolution approach – after applying a change to a consistent ontology, the ontology should remain in consistent state. The second requirement complements the first one by presenting the user with information needed to control changes and make appropriate decisions. The last one states that potential changes improving the ontology may be discovered semi-automatically from ontology-based data and through analysis of user's behavior.

More careful analysis of these requirements (e.g. the changes have to be captured, analyzed, applied and validated by the user) implies the necessity to consider the ontology evolution problem as a composition of several subproblems realized in a determined sequence. This sequence of activities, resolving ontology changes in a composite way, is called the ontology evolution process. Consequently, the system, i.e. software, which copes with the ontology evolution problem has to be process-

---

[1] http://kaon.semanticweb.org

based, following currently the most popular programming paradigm in the business software development.

2.1 Resolving Changes While Keeping Consistency

Consistency requirement states that after applying and resolving changes in an ontology already in a consistent state[2], the ontology, its instances and dependent ontologies/applications must remain in (another) consistent state. This requirement encompasses two crucial aspects of the ontology evolution: enabling resolution of changes and maintenance the consistency of the system, and may be realized through following four phases as shown in Figure 1.

Change Representation. To resolve changes, they have to be identified and represented in a suitable format [13, 20]. Elementary changes in the ontology are derived from our ontology definition given in [25] specifying fine-grained changes that can be performed in the course of ontology evolution. However, this granularity of ontology evolution changes is not always appropriate. Often, intent of the changes may be expressed on a higher level. For example, the may need to generate a common superconcept sc of two concepts c_1 and c_2. He may bring the ontology into desired state through successive application of a list of elementary changes, such as 'Add_concept sc', 'Delete_SubConceptOf relation from c_1 to its current parent', 'Add_SubConceptOf relation from c_1 to sc', 'Delete_SubConceptOf relation from c_2 to its current parent' and 'Add_SubConceptOf relation from c_2 to sc'. However, this has significant drawbacks:

- There is an impedance mismatch between the intent of the request and the way the intent is achieved. It is required to create a superconcept of two concepts, but one needs to translate this operation into five separate steps, making the whole process error prone.
- A lot of unnecessary changes may be performed if each change is applied alone. For example, removing sub-concept-of relation from c_1 may introduce changes to property instantiations that should be reversed when assign sub-concept-of relation from c_1 to sc.

To avoid these drawbacks, it should be possible to express changes on a more coarse level, with the intent of change directly visible. Composite changes, representing a group of elementary changes applied together, are shown in the table 1.

Above mentioned changes are represented as instances of an evolution ontology – a special ontology which explicitly represents semantic information about ontology entities, changes in the ontology and mechanisms to discover and resolve changes. Detailed discussion of this ontology is out of scope of this paper and is given in [13].

---

[2] A consistent state of an ontology is the state in which all constraints, which are defined on the structure and content of an ontology are satisfied. An example of the structural constraints is the need to define the domain and the range for each relation in the ontology. Content constraints are related to the axioms in the ontology.

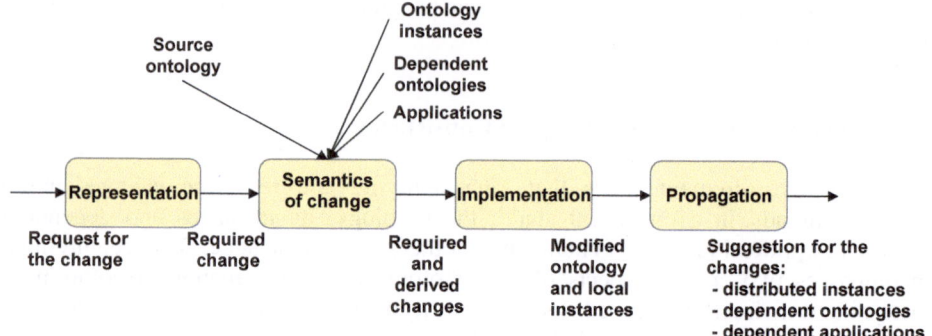

Figure 1. Four Elementary Phases of Ontology Evolution Process

Table 1. Composite changes in the ontology

Composite change	Description
Merge concepts	Replace several concepts with one and aggregate all instances.
Extract subconcepts	Split a concept into several subconcepts and distribute properties among them.
Extract superconcept	Create a common superconcept for a set of unrelated concepts and transfer common properties to it.
Extract related concept	Extract related information into a new concept and relate it to the original concept.
Shallow concept copy	Duplicate a concept with all its properties.
Deep concept copy	Recursively apply shallow copy to all subconcepts of a concept.
Pull up properties	Move properties from a subconcept to a superconcept.
Pull down properties	Move properties from a superconcept to a subconcept.
Move properties	Move properties from one concept to another concept.
Shallow property copy	Duplicate a property with same domain and range.
Deep property copy	Recursively apply shallow copy to all subproperties of a property.
Move Instance	Moves an instance from one concept to another.

Semantics of Change. Application of an elementary change in the ontology can induce inconsistencies in other parts of the ontology. We distinguish syntax and semantic inconsistency. Syntax inconsistency arises when undefined entities at the ontology or instance level are used or ontology model constraints are invalidated. Semantic inconsistency arises when meaning of an entity is changed due to changes performed in the ontology [29].

For example, removal of a concept which is the only element of domain set for some property results in syntax inconsistency [9]. Resolving that problem is treated as a request for a new change in the ontology, which can induce new problems that cause new changes and so on. Therefore, one change can potentially trigger other changes and so on. If an ontology is large, it may be difficult to fully comprehend the extent and meaning of each induced change. The task of 'semantics of change' phase is to enable resolution of induced changes in a systematic manner, ensuring consistency of the whole ontology. To help in better understanding of effects of each change, this phase should contribute maximum transparency providing detailed insight into each change being performed. Some mechanisms used in this phase are described in the section 3.

In the course of evolution, actual meaning of concepts often shifts to better represent the structure of the real world. While some shifts of concept meaning are performed explicitly, a meaning of a concept can sometimes shift implicitly through changes in other parts of the ontology. For example, consider an ontology describing a relationship between jaguars and persons. In this ontology the meaning of the concept *Jaguar* is clear through the existence of the property *eats* that links *Jaguar*s and *Person*s – it is obvious that concept *Jaguar* stands for an animal from the feline family. For any reason one may delete the concept *Person*, which may result in the removal of the property *eats* as well. After the change is performed, the semantics of concept *Jaguar* is not clear any more – is it a Jaguar cat or a Jaguar car? These kinds of ambiguities can be eliminated in several ways. The simplest solution is by introducing a superconcept *Animal* before the change is performed. However, if the ontology is large, such issues may be easily overlooked because it is very hard to keep the complete ontology structure in mind at once.

This problem can be avoided using a richer description [13] determining semantic role of ontology entities. By attaching meta-information about e.g. essential properties of a concept [29], deeper knowledge about concept meaning is provided. Moreover, semantic ambiguities of ontology entities may be resolved through additional documentation, such as who is the author of an entity, what is the purpose of introducing an entity etc. Contrary to meta-information determining the semantic role of ontology entities, "documentation" meta-information cannot be used for formal consistency checking.

Change Implementation. In order to avoid performing undesired changes, before applying a change to the ontology, a list of all implications to the ontology should be generated and presented to the user [28]. He should be able to comprehend the list and approve or cancel the change. When the changes are approved, they are performed by successively resolving changes from the list. If changes are cancelled, the ontology should remain intact. This is more elaborated in description of implementation in section 4.

Change Propagation. When the ontology is modified, ontology instances need to be changed to preserve consistency with the ontology [9]. This can be performed in three steps. If the instances are on the Web they are collected in the knowledge base [14]. In the second step, modification of instances is performed according to the changes in the ontology [23]. In the last step "out-of-date" instances on the Web are replaced with corresponding "up-to-date" instances.

Ontologies often reuse and extend other ontologies. Therefore, an ontology update might also corrupt ontologies that depend on the modified ontology and consequently, all artifacts that are based on these ontologies. This problem can be solved by recursive applying the ontology evolution process on these ontologies.

When an ontology is changed, applications based on the changed ontology may not work correctly. An ontology evolution system has to recognize which change in the ontology can affect the functionality of dependent applications [10, 21] and to react correspondingly. More information about possible problems in this phase and ways for solving them are given in [24].

2.2 User's Management of Changes

There are numerous circumstances where it may be desired to reverse the effects of ontology evolution, to name just a few:

- The ontology engineer may fail to understand the actual effect of the change and approve the change that shouldn't be performed.
- It may be desired to change the ontology for experimental purposes.
- When working on an ontology collaboratively, different ontology engineers may have different ideas about how the ontology should be changed.

In order to enable recovering from these situations, we introduce the validation phase in the ontology evolution process (see Figure 2). It enables validation of performed changes and undoing them at user's request. It is important to note that reversibility means undoing all effects of some change, which may not be the same as simply requesting an inverse change manually. For example, if a concept is deleted from a concept hierarchy, its subconcepts will need to be either deleted as well, attached to the root concept, or attached to the parent of the deleted concept. Reversing such a change is not equal to recreating the deleted concept – one needs, also, to revert the concept hierarchy into original state.

The problem of reversibility is typically solved by creating evolution logs. An evolution log tracks information about each change in the system, allowing to reconstruct the sequence of changes leading to current state of the ontology. With each change evolution logs additionally associate following information [13]:
- Meta-information such as change description, cost of change, time of change, cause of the change etc.,
- Identity of the change author.

2.3 Continual Improvement

In ontology evolution we may distinguish two types of changes: top-down and bottom-up, whose generation is part of the "capturing phase" in the ontology evolution process. Top-down changes are explicit changes, driven, for example, by top-manager who want to adapt the system to new requirements and can be easily realized by an ontology evolution system. However, some changes in the domain are implicit, reflected in the behavior of the system and can be discovered only through analysis of its behavior. For example, if a customer group doesn't contain members for a longer period of time, it may mean that it can be removed. This second type of change mined from the set of ontology instances are called bottom-up changes.

Another source of bottom-up changes is the structure of the ontology itself [19]. Indeed, the previously described "validation phase" results in an ontology which may be in a consistent state, but contains some redundant entities or can be better structured with respect to the domain. For example, multiple users may be working on different parts of an ontology without enough communication. They may be deleting subconcepts of a common concepts at different points in time to fulfill their immediate needs. As a result, it may happen that only one subconcept is left. Since classification with only one subclass beats the original purpose of classification, we consider such ontology to have a suboptimal structure. Moreover, based on heuristics and/or data mining algorithms [12], suggestions for changes that refine ontology structure may be induced by analysis of patterns of ontology usage. By tracking when concept has last been retrieved by a query, it may be possible to discover that some concepts are out of date and should be deleted or updated. To aid users in detecting such situations, we investigated the possibilities of applying the self-adaptive systems principles and proactively make suggestions for *ontology refinements* – changes to the ontology with the goal of improving ontology structure, making the ontology easier to understand and cheaper to modify.

2.4 The Overall Ontology Evolution Process

Complete ontology process derived from our discussion of ontology evolution requirements is presented in Figure 2. It has a cyclic structure, since validation of realized changes may (automatically) induce new changes in order to obtain model consistency or to satisfy users' expectations. The first requirement from section 2 for ontology consistency results in phases 2 to 5, the second requirement for user supervision results in phase 6 and the third requirement for continual ontology refinement results in phase 1.

3 Evolution Strategy

As mentioned, the role of "semantics of change" phase in ontology evolution process if to figure out which elementary changes need to be performed for one change request, e.g. deletion of a concept. If this were left to the user, evolution process would be too error-prone and time consuming – it is unrealistic to expect that humans will be able to comprehend entire ontology and interdependencies in it [28]. This requirement is especially hard to fulfill if the rationale behind domain conceptualization is ambiguous or if the user does not have the experience. There are many ways to achieve consistency after a change request. For example, when a concept from the middle of the hierarchy is being deleted, all subconcepts may either be deleted or reconnected to other concepts. If subconcepts are preserved, then properties of the deleted concept may be propagated, its instances distributed, etc. Thus, for each change in the ontology, it is possible to generate different sets of additional changes, leading to different final consistent states. Most of existing systems for the ontology development [22] provide only one possibility for realizing a change and this is usually the simplest one. For example, the deletion of a concept always causes the deletion of all its subconcepts.

Thus, to resolve a change, the evolution process needs to determine answers at many *resolution points* – branch points during change resolution where taking a different path will produce different results. Each possible answer at each resolution point is an *elementary evolution strategy*. Common policy consisting of a set of elementary evolution strategies, each giving an answer for one resolution point, is an *evolution strategy* and is used to customize the ontology evolution process. Thus, an evolution strategy unambiguously defines the way how elementary changes will be resolved [3]. Typically a particular evolution strategy is chosen by the user at the start of the ontology evolution process.

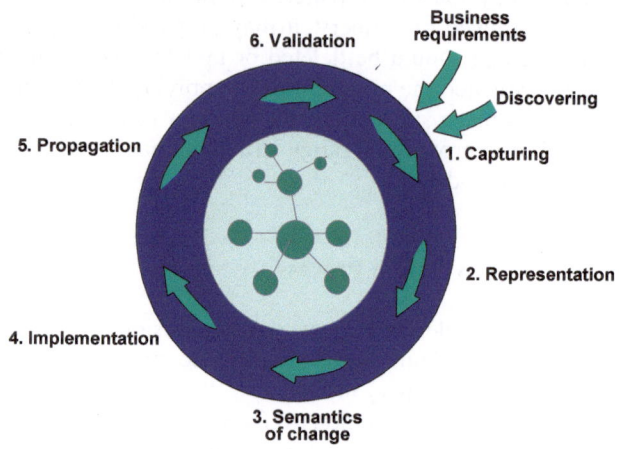

Figure 2. Ontology Evolution Process

To derive the set of resolution points within an evolution strategy, we started by considering types of changes that may be applied to an ontology. Next we analyzed what consequences can each change have on the ontology with respect to its definition [25] and dependencies between ontology entities. We isolated changes that can provoke syntax inconsistencies and, consequently, cannot be applied. For example, "Add_SubConceptOf" change is not allowed if it causes an inheritance hierarchy cycles. Further, we identified that some changes can generate the need for subsequent changes, some of them offering different ways of resolution. For each particular resolution way we defined an elementary evolution strategy. For each elementary change we defined an algorithm containing resolution points encountered during change resolution. Each resolution point represents a branching point, and each elementary evolution strategy represents one possible branch. The choice of exactly one elementary evolution strategy for each possible resolution point forms an evolution strategy.

3.1 Evolution Strategy Example

Let us explain our approach through an example of deleting a concept C embedded in a complex concept hierarchy. In order to keep the ontology in a consistent state, following resolution points may be observed:

- what to do with orphaned subconcepts of C;
- what to do with properties that subconcepts of C inherit from C's parents;

- what to do with all properties whose domain is C;
- what to do with the properties whose range is C;
- what to do with instances of C;
- what to do with instances of other concepts having relations with instances of C.

For each of these resolution points, there is a set of elementary evolution strategies defining possible options. E.g., in case of the first resolution point, as illustrated in Figure 3, orphaned subconcepts of C may be:

- connected to the parent concept(s) of C;
- connected to the root concept of the hierarchy;
- deleted as well.

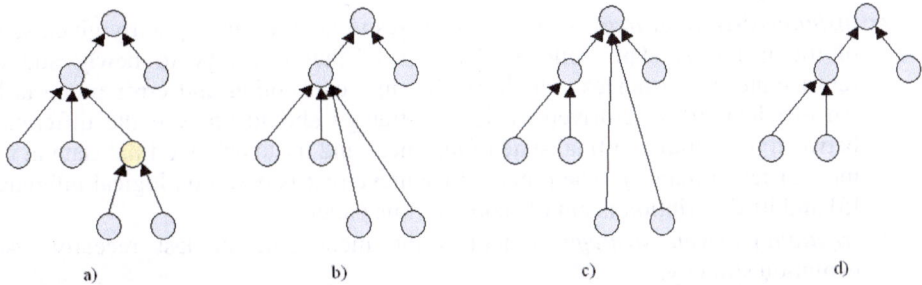

a)   b)   c)   d)

Figure 3. Resolution Points for Deleting Concept C: a) Original ontology; b) Connection to the parent concept; c) Connection to the root concept; d) Deletion of the subconcepts

Similarly we may elicit remaining elementary strategies for all mentioned resolution points. The part of the algorithm for deletion of a concept with corresponding resolution points and available elementary evolution strategies is given in Figure 4.

3.2 Advanced Evolution Strategies

In real business the choice of how a change (e.g. deletion of a concept) should be resolved may be based on characteristics of the final state of the ontology (e.g. make depth of hierarchy as small as possible) or on characteristics of the process for resolving changes itself (e.g. incur minimal cost of changes).

In order to enable such customization of the ontology evolution process, the user may choose an *advanced evolution strategy*. It represents a mechanism to priorities and arbitrate among different evolution strategies available in a particular situation, relieving the user of choosing elementary evolution strategies individually.

Advanced evolution strategy automatically combines available elementary evolution strategies to satisfy user's criteria. We have identified the following set of advanced evolution strategies:

- ***structure-driven strategy*** – resolves changes according to criteria based on the structure of the resulting ontology, e.g. the number of levels in concept hierarchy. This strategy follows the requirements of the real-word ontology-based applications, e.g. MEDLINE[3]. MEDLINE requires a weekly update, usually involving only supplementary concept records. However, concept hierarchy is updated annually. This kind of changes is performed by keeping the hierarchy minimal, because it alleviates, according to the authors of MEDLINE, the understanding of the conceptualization.

- *process-driven strategy* – resolves changes according to process of changes itself, for example optimized per cost[4] of the process or per a number of steps involved[5]. Determining what has to be change and how to change it requires a deep understanding of how the ontology entities interact one with another. We cannot expect that the user spends time explaining the reasons for all performed changes and their ordering. One strategy enabling that the user can easily follow and understand sequences of the changes is to perform the minimal number of the updates.

- *instance-driven strategy* – resolves changes to achieve an explicitly given state of the instances. This relieves the user of the necessary to newly add or redistribute the instances, which can be time consuming and error prone task. An efficient instance-driven evolution strategy should analyze the difference between the initial and final state of instances and try to achieve final state in the most efficient manner. The process to achieve that is based on logical inference [5] and its description is out of scope for this paper.

- *frequency-driven strategy* – applies the most used or last recently used evolution strategy.

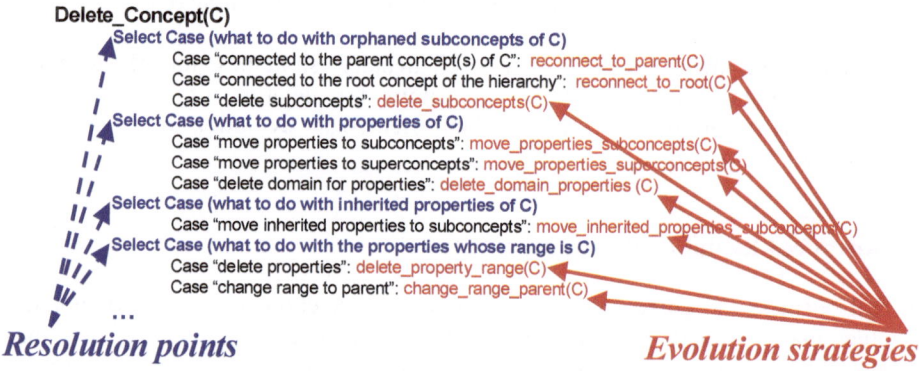

Figure 4. Algorithm for Concept Deletion

---

4 Implementation

The Karlsruhe Ontology and Semantic Web framework (KAON) has been developed at the University of Karlsruhe. It is used as a basis for several ontology-enabled research and industry projects. It's primary goal is to establish a platform needed to apply Semantic Web technologies to e-commerce scenarios, knowledge management, automatic generation of Web portals, E-Learning etc. The simplified conceptual architecture of KAON emphasizing points of interest related to ontology evolution is presented in Figure 5.

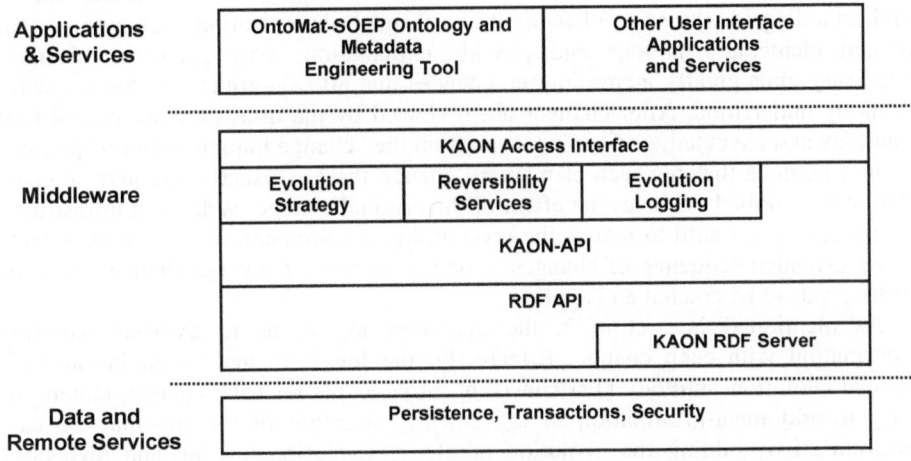

Figure 5. Conceptual KAON Architecture with Respect to Ontology Evolution

Roughly, KAON components can be divided into three layers:

- Applications and Services Layer realizes UI applications and provides interfaces to non-human agents. Among many applications realized, OntoMat-SOEP provides ontology and metadata engineering capabilities. It realizes many requirements related to ontology evolution and is described next in more detail.
- KAON API as part of the Middleware Layer is the focal point of KAON architecture since it realizes the model[6] of ontology based applications. The bulk of requirements related to ontology evolution is realized in this layer and is described in the next section.
- Data and Remote Services Layer provides data storage facilities. This layer also realizes concurrency and transactional atomicity of updates. Further elaboration of this layer is out of scope for this paper.

---

[6] The term model refers to the model component of the Model-View-Controller architectural pattern.

4.1 Ontology Evolution in KAON API

Before the ontology evolution process is started, a particular evolution strategy must be selected. Changes to the ontology are performed by assembling elementary and composite changes into a sequence. However, before the ontology is actually updated, this sequence is passed to the present evolution strategy to perform the steps described in section 3 in the "semantics of change" phase, resulting in an extended sequence of changes. To ensure atomicity of updates, either all or no change from the extended sequence of changes should succeed, so validity of change sequence is checked before any updates are actually performed. Transparency is realized by presenting the extended sequence of changed to the user for approval. To further aid the understanding of why some changes are performed, the evolution strategy may group related elementary actions and provide explanations why particular change is necessary, thus greatly increasing the chances that all side-effects of changes will be properly understood. After changes are reviewed by the user, they are passed to the ontology and executed, performing steps from the "change implementation" phase.

It is obvious that for each elementary change there is exactly one inverse change that, when applied, reverses the effect of the original change. With such infrastructure in place, it is not hard to realize the reversibility requirement: to reverse the effect of some extended sequence of changes, a new sequence of inverse changes in reverse order needs to be created and applied.

As mentioned in section 2, the evolution log needs to associate additional information with each change. Effectively, the log is treated as an instance of a special evolution ontology [13] consisting of concepts for each change, making it is easy to add meta-information to log entries. Structure of the log may be easily customized by editing the evolution ontology. Evolution logging and reversibility services are provided as special services of KAON API, allowing different applications reuse these powerful features. E.g., actions performed in one application may be easily reverted in another.

4.2 Ontology Evolution in KAON Applications

As mentioned in the previous section, ontology evolution is primarily realized through KAON API. However, UI applications provide human-computer interaction for evolution, whose primary role is to present change information in an orderly way, allowing easy spotting of potential problems. Also, any application that changes the ontology must realize the reversibility requirement in its user interface as well. Currently evolution requirements are realized within the OntoMat-SOEP ontology and metadata engineering tool, as follows:

- As shown in left part of Figure 6, users may set up the desired evolution strategy which consists of four resolution points. For each resolution point the user must choose appropriate elementary evolution strategy.
- Before changes are performed, their impact is reported to the user (the right part of Figure 6). Presentation of changes follows the progressive disclosure principle: related changes are grouped together and organized in a tree-like form. The user initially sees only the general description of changes. If he is

interested in details, he can expand the tree and view complete information. He may cancel the operation before it is actually performed.

- An unlimited undo-redo function is provided. Although is this function by large the responsibility of the KAON API, the user interface is responsible for restoring the visual context after an undo operation.

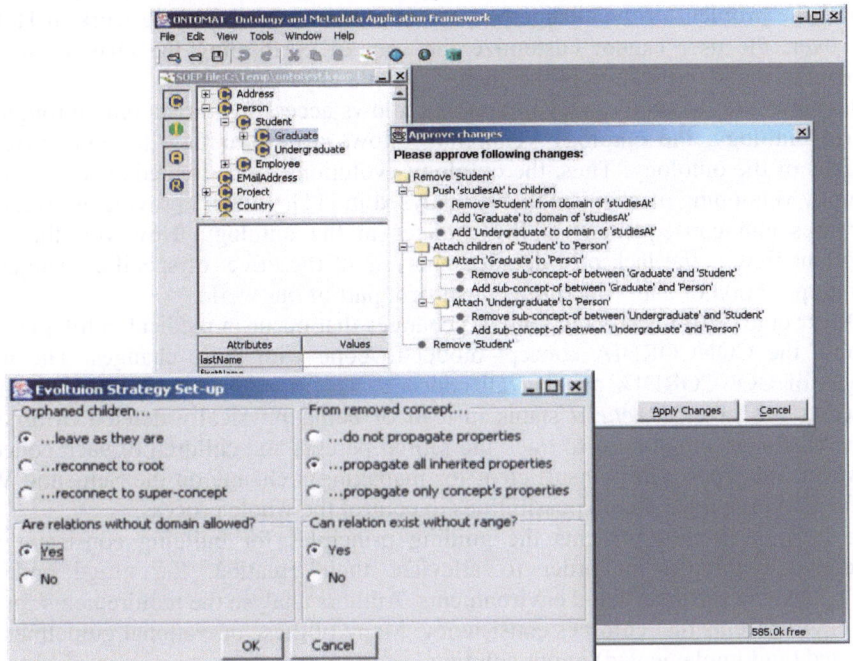

Figure 6. Ontology Evolution in KAON framework: Evolution Strategy Set-up and Ontology Evolution User Interface in OntoMat-SOEP

A sample screenshot of OntoMat-SOEP is given in Figure 6. In this scenario, the user requested to remove *Student* concept. The evolution strategy decided to push property *studiesAt* of that concept to children. By opening a node in the tree, the user can see what changes will actually be performed. Hence, the change information can be viewed at different levels of granularity. Similarly, the strategy decided that children of the concept will be attached to parent of the deleted concept. For each child a detailed list elementary changes needed to achieve that is presented.

5 Related Work

In the last decade there has been very active research in the area of ontology engineering. The majority of researches in this area are focused on construction issues. However, coping with the changes and providing maintenance facilities require a different approach. We cannot say that there exist commonly agreed methodologies and guidelines for ontology evolution. Thus, there are very few approaches investigating the problems of changing in the ontologies.

Heflin [9] points out that ontologies on the Web will need to evolve and he provides a new formal definition of ontologies for the use in dynamic, distributed environments. Although good design may prevent many ontological errors, some errors will not be realized until the ontology is put into use. However, this problem as well as the problem of the change propagation are not treated in the work of Heflin. Moreover, the user cannot customize the way of performing the change and the problem of the identification of the change is not analysed.

In contrast to the ontology evolution that allows access to all data only through the newest ontology, the ontology versioning allows access to data through different versions of the ontology. Thus, the ontology evolution can be treated as a part of the ontology versioning mechanism that is analysed in [11]. Authors provide an overview of causes and consequences of the changes in the ontology. However, the most important flaw is the lack of a detailed analysis of the effect of specific changes on the interpretation of data which is a constituent part of our work.

Oliver et al. [20] discuss the kinds of changes that occur in medical ontologies and propose the CONCORDIA concept model to cope with these changes. The main aspects of CONCORDIA are that all concepts have a permanent unique identifier. Concepts are given a *retired* status instead of being physically deleted. Moreover special links are maintained to track the retired parents and children of each concept. However, this approach is insufficient for managing a change on the Semantic Web especially while there are no possibilities to control the whole process.

In [16] the author presents the guiding principles for building consistent and principled ontologies in order to alleviate their creation, the usage and the maintenance in the distributed environments. Authors analyse the requirements for the tool environments that enforces consistency. Many of these operational guidelines are included (and implemented) in our solution.

[29] presents an extended ontology knowledge model that represents semantic information about concepts explicitly. However, this enriched semantic is not used for supporting evolution problems, but to describe what is known by agents in a multi-agent system.

Other research communities also have influenced our work. The problem of schema evolution and schema versioning support has been extensively studied in relational and database papers ([1], [21]). In [18] authors discuss the differences that steam from different knowledge models and different usage paradigms. Moreover, research in ontology evolution can also benefit from the many years of research in knowledge-based system evolution [3, 15]. The script-based knowledge evolution [28] that identifies typical sequences of changes to knowledge base and represents them in a form of scripts, is similar to our approach. In contrast to the knowledge-scripts that allow the tool to understand the consequences of each change, we go step further by allowing the user to control how to complete the overall modification and by suggesting the changes that could improve the ontology.

6 Conclusion

In this paper we presented a novel approach for dealing with ontology changes. The approach is based on a six-phase evolution process, which systematically analyses the causes and the consequences of the changes and ensures the consistency of the ontology and depending artifacts after resolving these changes. In order to enable the user to obtain the ontology most suitable to her needs, we specifically focus on the possibilities to customize the ontology evolution process. We identify two means to do that: (i) to enable the user to set up one of predefined or advanced evolution strategies that are used for resolving the changes and (ii) to suggest the user to generate some change, implied by the analysis of the structure of the ontology, ontology instances or user behaviors in the underlying ontology-based applications.

Although our implementation is in an early phase and therefore the real evaluation is missing, we made some experiments with one of our ontology-based applications, particular the AIFB portal [25]. Comparison of time needed to resolve "per-hand" initiated change, shows the real necessity for the methodological support for the ontology evolution, even for the very experienced ontology engineers. Moreover, the detailed analysis of the possibility to use our approach in the case of highly-distributed Web applications, such MEDLINE, shows many benefits of the presented approach for the large-scale ontologies and motivates further research in that direction.

References

1. J. Banerjee, W. Kim, H.J. Kim, H. Korth, Semantics and implementation of schema evolution in object-oriented databases, In proceedings of the Annual Conference on Management of Data, pp- 211-322, ACM SIGMOD, May 1997.
2. T. Berners-Lee, *XML 2000 – Semantic Web talk*, 2000, http//www.w3.org/2000/Talks/1206-xml2k-tbl/slide10-0.html, 2000.
3. P. Breche, M. Wörner, *How to remove a class in an ODBS*, In ADBS'95, 2nd International Conference on Application Database, Santa Clara, California, 1995
4. A. Bultman, J. Kuipers and F. van Harmelen, *Maintenance of KBS's by domain experts: The Holy Grail in Practice*, Lecture Notes in AI, IEA/AIE'00, 2000.
5. S. Decker, M. Erdmann, D. Fensel and R. Studer, *Ontobroker: Ontology based access to distributed and semi-structured information*, Meersman, R. et al. (Eds.), Database Semantics: Semantic Issues in Multimedia Systems, pp. 351–369. Kluwer Academic Publisher, 1999.
6. D. Fensel, *Ontologies: Dynamics Networks of Meaning*, In Proceedings of the the 1st Semantic web working symposium, Stanford, CA, USA, July 30th-August 1st, 2001.
7. E. Franconi, F. Grandi, and F. Mandreoli, *A semantic approach for schema evolution and versioning in object-oriented databases*, Proc. CL2000, 2000.
8. A. Gomez-Perez, *Ontological engineering: A state of the art*, Expert Update, 2(3):33-43, Autumn 1999.
9. J. Heflin, *Towards the Semantic Web: Knowledge Representation in a Dynamic, Distributed Environment*, Ph.D. Thesis, University of Maryland, College Park. 2001.
10. W. Hürsch, *Maintaining consistency and behaviour of object-oriented systems during evolution*, In Proc. of the ACM Conference on Object-Oriented Programming, Systems, Languages and Applications (OOPSLA '97), Vol.32 No. 10, pp1-21, 1997.

11. M. Klein and D. Fensel, *Ontology versioning for the Semantic Web*, Proc. International Semantic Web Working Symposium, USA, July 30 - August 1, 2001.

12. A. Maedche and S. Staab, *Ontology Learning for the Semantic Web*, IEEE Intelligent Systems, 16(2), March/April 2001. Special Issue on Semantic Web, 2001.

13. A. Maedche, L. Stojanovic, R. Studer, R. Volz: *Managing Multiple Ontologies and Ontology Evolution in Ontologging*, In Proceedings of the Conference on Intelligent Information Processing, World Computer Congress 2002, Montreal, Canada, 2002.

14. A. Maedche, M. Ehrig, S. Handschuh, L. Stojanovic, R. Volz, *Ontology-Focused Crawling on Documents and Relational Metadata*, In Proceedings of the Eleventh International World Wide Web Conference WWW-2002, (Poster), Hawaii, 2002.

15. T. Menzis, Knowledge maintenance: The state of the art. The Knowledge Engineering Review, 10(2), 1998.

16. D. McGuinness, Conceptual Modeling for Distributed Ontology Environments, In the Proceedings of the ICCS 2000, August 14-18, Darmstadt, Germany , 2000.

17. D. McGuinness, R. Fikes, J. Rice, and S. Wilder, *An environment for merging and testing large ontologies*, In Proceedings of KR-2000. principle of Knowledge Representation and Reasoning. Morgan-Kaufman, 2000.

18. N. F. Noy, M. Klein, Ontology Evolution: Not the Same as Schema Evolution, SMI technical report SMI-2002-0926, 2002.

19. N. F. Noy, D. McGuinness, *Ontology Development 101: A Guide to creating your first Ontology*, Stanford Knowledge Systems Laboratory Technical Report KSL-01-05 and Stanford Medical Informatics Technical Report SMI-2001-0880, March 2001

20. D. E. Oliver, Y. Shahar, M. A. Musen, and E. H. Shortliffe, *Representation of change in controlled medical terminologies*, AI in Medicine,15(1):53–76, 1999.

21. J.F. Roddick, *A Survey of Schema Versioning Issues for Database Systems*, Information and Software Technology, 37(7):383-393, 1996.

22. S. Staab, H.-P. Schnurr, R. Studer and Y. Sure, *Knowledge Processes and Ontologies*, IEEE Intelligent Systems. 16(1), Jan./Feb. 2001. Special Issue on Knowledge Management, 2001.

23. L. Stojanovic, N. Stojanovic and R. Volz, *Migrating data-intensive Web Sites into the Semantic Web*, In Proceedings of the ACM Symposium on Applied Computing SAC, 2002.

24. L. Stojanovic, N. Stojanovic, S. Handschuh, *Evolution of the Metadata in the Ontology-based Knowledge Management Systems*, In Proceedings of Experience Management 2002, Berlin, 2002.

25. N. Stojanovic, A. Maedche, S. Staab, R. Studer and Y. Sure, *SEAL — A Framework for Developing SEmantic PortALs*, ACM K-CAP 2001. October, Vancouver, 2001.

26. N. Stojanovic, L. Stojanovic, *Searching for the Knowledge in the Semantic Web*, The 15th International FLAIRS Conference, Pensacola, Florida, May 14-16, 2002.

27. N. Stojanovic, L. Stojanovic: *Evolution in the ontology-based knowledge management system*. In Proceedings of the European Conference on Information Systems - ECIS 2002, Gdańsk, Poland, 2002.

28. M. Tallis, Y. Gil, *Designing Scripts to Guide Users in Modifying Knowledge-based Systems*, AAAI/IAAI 1999: 242-249

29. V.A.M. Tamma, T.J.M Bench-Capon, A conceptual model to facilitate knowledge sharing in multi-agent systems, In Proceedings of the OAS 2001. Montreal, pp. 69-76, 2001.

Attribute Meta-properties for Formal Ontological Analysis

Valentina Tamma and Trevor J.M. Bench Capon

Department of Computer Science, University of Liverpool,
Chadwick Building, Liverpool L69 7ZF, UK,
{valli, tbc}@csc.liv.ac.uk

Abstract. Formal ontological analysis is a methodology that uses ideas
from philosophy in order to guide the process of building ontologies with
a correct and as untangled a structure as possible.
This paper presents an ontology model that aims to facilitate formal
ontological analysis, by providing a set of *meta-properties* which characterise the behaviour of concept properties in a concept definition, to
provide a richer semantics of the concept. We describe concepts in terms
of their attributes (characterising features) and we also describe the
role played by these features in the concept definition: whether they are
prototypical or exceptional; whether they are permitted to change over
time, and if so, how often this happens; how likely is a concept to show
these features, etc. We show that these meta-properties, besides enriching concept descriptions, can be used to determine whether the notions
of *identity* and *rigidity* hold, thus supporting in part the OntoClean [31]
methodology.

1 Introduction

Many current applications such as e-commerce and the semantic web rely on
the ability of different resources or agents to interoperate with each other and
with users. In some cases, interoperation becomes quite complex, because agents
may have been independently developed, and so the assumption that agents use
the same communication language and the same terminology in a consistent
way cannot be made. When dealing with independently developed agents, their
interoperability with humans and others depends on their ability to understand
each other.

Ontologies are an explicit, formal specification of a shared conceptualisation,
where *a 'conceptualisation' refers to an abstract model of some phenomenon in
the world by having identified the relevant concepts of that phenomenon. 'Explicit' means that the type of concepts used, and the constraints on their use
are explicitly defined. · 'Formal' refers to the fact that the ontology should be
machine-readable. 'Shared' reflects the notion that an ontology captures consensual knowledge, that is it is not private to some individual, but accepted by a
group* [27]. That is, ontologies provide a formally defined specification of the
meaning of those terms that are used by agents to interoperate.

A. Gómez-Pérez and V.R. Benjamins (Eds.): EKAW 2002, LNAI 2473, pp. 301–316, 2002.

Agents can differ in their understanding of the world surrounding them, in their goals, and their capabilities, but they can still interoperate in order to perform a task, provided they can reach agreement on a shared understanding, mainly obtained by reconciling the differences. This kind of reconciliation might be accomplished by *merging* the ontologies to which the agents refer, that is, by building a single ontology that is the merged version of the different ontologies, which often cover similar or overlapping domains [4].

Ontology merging starts with the attempt to find the places in which the source ontologies overlap [18], that is the coalescence of two semantically identical terms in different ontologies so that they can be referred to by the same name in the resulting ontology. This is the only step of the merge process which is relevant to the scope of this article. The coalescence of terms in diverse ontologies has to be accomplished despite heterogeneous agent ontologies and heterogeneity has to be reconciled in order to share knowledge. Defining the different types of heterogeneity is out of the scope of this article, although we recognise that it can hinder attempts to coalesce terms, especially when it is the semantics that is heterogeneous. Ontology or semantic heterogeneity occurs when different ontological assumptions about overlapping domains are made [30].

The ontologies involved in the merging process, be they heterogeneous or not, are usually assumed to be either built according to some kind of engineering methodology, such as Methontology [3], or their ontology taxonomic structures are validated according to some methodology such as OntoClean [31]. Both methodologies aim to ensure that the ontology obtained after applying them is correct, that it does not contain cycles or recursive definitions, and it has a taxonomic structure that is as untangled as possible.

Methontology and OntoClean are complementary methodologies in that the former provides the guidelines for building or re engineering ontologies, whereas the latter can be used either in the validation step (when ontologies are engineered or restructured) or simultaneously with the ontology construction (when ontologies are built from scratch). These two methodologies are currently undergoing an integration process [2] as part of the activities of the OntoWeb special interest group on Enterprise-standards Ontology Environments (SIG's home page: http://delicias.dia.fi.upm.es/ontoweb/sig-tools/index.html).

Methodologies to obtain well-built ontologies, however, are not sufficient to support a semi-automatic coalescence process. In fact we cannot recognise whether two concepts (that can be heterogeneous) are similar, only on the basis of the terms denoting them, the relationships with other terms, and their descriptions, but we need to have a full understanding of the concepts. As noted by McGuinness [17], an explicit representation of the semantics of terms would be a step towards understanding whether two concepts are similar. It emerges that the current ontology models are not expressive enough to provide such an explicit representation. Even when heavyweight ontologies are used (that is, concepts described in terms of attributes, linked by relations, organised into an Is-a relationship and constrained by axioms), their expressiveness does not allow a full account of the semantics of the concepts described. The ontology model we present in this paper is enriched by attribute meta-properties which account for the behaviour of attributes in the concept definition.

This paper is organised as follows: Section 2 presents the OntoClean methodology and the notions of formal ontological analysis, while Section 3 introduces our proposal for an ontology model encompassing a set of meta-properties for attributes which are then discussed in the following subsections. This ontology model was also presented in [29]: in this paper we do not discuss any implementation issues and we concentrate on the meta-properties, clarifying the relationship with the concept meta-properties used in OntoClean and the role attribute meta-properties play in associating senses to concepts. Section 4 discusses the attribute meta-properties and relates them with two notions (identity and rigidity) of formal ontological analysis and with roles. Finally, Section 5 draws conclusions.

2   Identity, Unity, Essence, and Dependence and Their Use in OntoClean

OntoClean [31] is a methodology to perform a *formal ontological analysis* on taxonomies in order to verify which formal meta-properties hold, thus making clear and explicit the modelling assumptions made while designing the ontologies. The clarification and explication of the modelling assumptions is a necessary step in evaluating ontologies, since it permits knowledge engineers to detect and reconcile ontological conflicts that may affect one or more ontologies. Ontological conflicts may become apparent when two ontologies are compared in order to coalesce terms, and they reveal cases of ontological heterogeneity. For example, two well known ontologies [1] (Wordnet [19] and Panglos [11]), present the following conflict: one models Physical Object as subconcept of Amount of matter wheres the other models Amount of matter as subconcept of Physical object. This is a case of ontology heterogeneity due to different modelling of the concepts. Such ontological conflicts need to be detected and resolved if terms are to be coalesced.

OntoClean is firmly based on the philosophical notions of *identity, unity, essence (rigidity),* and *dependence.* The attribute meta-properties we present in this paper are related to these notions, and we discuss them below.

Identity: Identity is the logical relation of numerical sameness, in which a thing stands only to itself. Based on the idea that everything is what it is and not another thing, philosophy has tried for a long time to identify the criteria which allow a thing to be identified for what it is even when it is cognised in two different forms, by two different descriptions and/or at two different times [32, 9]. This comprises both aspects of finding constitutive criteria (which features a thing must have in order to be what it is), and of finding re-identification criteria (which features a thing has to have in order to be recognised as itself by a cognitive agent).

---

[1] Strictly speaking, neither Wordnet nor Panglos are ontologies. However, they are often used and referred to as ontologies.

OntoClean does not make any difference between identity and re-identification, but we believe that these are distinct, although equally important aspects of identity. It happens to be the case the fingerprints are unique to individuals. This means that, in the actual world, fingerprints can serve as re-identification criteria. But it is possible that everyone had the same fingerprints: in such a possible world, fingerprints would not provide re-identification criteria. Moreover, fingerprints cannot be used to discover identity across possible worlds, and cannot be a criterion *constitutive* of such identity.

Although the problem of *identifying* what features an entity should have in order to be what it is and recognised as such has been central to philosophy, it has not had the same impact in conceptual modelling and more generally AI. The ability to identify individuals is central to the modelling process; more precisely, it is not the mere problem of identifying an entity in the world that is central to the ontological representation of the world, but the ability to *re-identify an entity in all its possible forms*, or more formally, *re-identification in all possible worlds*. That is, the problem is related to distinguishing a specific instance of a concept from its siblings on the basis of certain *characteristic properties* which are unique and intrinsic to *that instance*. Intrinsic properties are usually modelled as *attributes*.

Identity is, of course inherently time dependent, since time gives rise to a particular system of possible worlds where it is highly likely that the same instance of a concept exhibits different features This problem is known as *identity through change*: an instance of a concept may remain the same while exhibiting different properties at different instants of time. Therefore it becomes important to understand not only which features or properties can change and which cannot [31], but also, we add, the situations that can trigger such changes.

Identity is an absolute notion (whereas re-identification is not), although we recognise that applying identity to certain concepts, such as those representing artifacts, is not always straightforward.

Unity: the notion of *unity* is often included in a more generalised notion of identity, although these two notions are different. While identity aims to characterise what is unique for an entity of the world when considered as a whole, the goal of unity is that of *distinguishing the* parts *of an instance from the rest of the world by means of a* unifying relation *that binds them together (not involving anything else)* [31]. For example, the question 'Is this my car?' represents a problem of identity, whereas the question 'Is the steering wheel part of my car?' is a problem of unity. Also the notion of unity is affected by the notion of time; for example, can the parts of an instance be different at different instants of time?

Essence: The notion of *essence* is strictly related to the notion of *necessity* [10]. An *essential property* is a property that is necessary for an object, that is, a property that is true in every possible world [15]. Based on the notion of *essence*, Guarino and colleagues [8] have introduced the notion of *rigidity*. A rigid property is a property that is necessary to all instances in any instant of time, that is a property ϕ such that: $\Box(\forall x,\ t\phi(x,\ t) \rightarrow \Box\forall t'\ \phi(x,\ t'))$. For this formula, and in the remainder of this paper, we use the modal notions of *necessity* $\Box$ and *possibility* $\diamond$ quantified over possible worlds (in Kripke's semantics [13]), meaning that the extension of predicates concerns what exists in any possible world. We use these operators according to the following meanings: $\Box\ \phi$ means that ϕ holds in *all* possible worlds $\diamond\ \phi$ means that ϕ is possible, i.e. that ϕ holds in *at least* one possible world, which might be accessible from the actual world. Rigidity strictly depends on the notions of *time* and *modality* [29]; this point is further elaborated in Section 4.2. It is important,however, not to confuse modal necessity with temporal permanence. Modal necessity means that the property is true in every possible world. Time is undoubtedly one partition of these worlds, but temporal permanence means that the property is true in that world (time), with no information concerning the other possible worlds, and this might happen by pure chance. For example, fingerprints are temporally permanent, but might differ in other possible worlds.

Dependence: In OntoClean [31], the notion of dependence is considered related to concept properties. In this context, dependence permits us to distinguish between *extrinsic* and *intrinsic* properties based on whether they depend on objects other than the one they are ascribed to or not.

In order to establish which of these meta-properties hold, OntoClean is supported by a description logic based system that can help knowledge engineers to assign the meta-properties to concepts and to verify the taxonomic structure on the grounds of the modelling methodology. In this paper we focus our attention on the process of assigning the meta-properties. OntoClean guides knowledge engineers in this process by asking them to answer some questions such as "Does the property carry identity". Knowledge engineers can answer yes, no or unsure, in this latter case more specific questions can be asked, such as "Are instances of the property countable?".

The OntoClean methodology depends on the knowledge engineer's understanding of the ontologies being analysed and can thus be problematic if used to evaluate independently designed ontologies. Moreover, OntoClean does not take into account the structure of concept definitions, as it does not consider the characteristic features (or *attributes*) that might have been used to define concepts. This work proposes an enriched ontology model whose aim is to complement the OntoClean methodology, by providing an additional way to determine meta-properties to concepts. In our proposal we describe concepts in terms of their attributes, which are in turn described not only in terms of their structural features (such as range, domain, cardinality etc.), but also in terms of their meta-properties, which describe the contribution given by the attributes to the concept definition. We describe the enriched ontology model and the meta-properties for attributes in the next sections.

3   Enriched Ontology Model

The ontology conceptual model [2] we propose comprises *concepts, attributes, relations*, and *instances*. We do not consider here axioms. Concepts represent the entities of the domain and the tasks we want to model in the ontology. Concepts are described in terms of defining properties, which are represented by associating an *attribute* with either a single value or a set of values. Concepts are organised into an Is-a hierarchy, so that a concept attributes and their values are inherited by subconcepts. Multiple inheritance is permitted, so attributes and their values can be inherited from multiple parents. The values associated with an attribute can be restricted in order to provide a more specific definition of a concept [14].

Attributes can be described in terms of their structural characteristics, such as the concepts that they are defining, their allowed values, the type of the values (string, integer, etc.), and the maximum and minimum values (if attributes are numeric). Attributes can also be described in term of the following meta-properties:

- *Attribute's behaviour over time*: The meta-properties *Mutability, Mutability Frequency, Event Mutability* and *Reversible Mutability* provide a better description of attributes by characterising their behaviour over time, that is, whether they are allowed to change their value during the concept lifetime (*Mutability*); and how often the change occurs (*Mutability Frequency*); whether the change is reversible (*Reversible Mutability*); and what triggers change (*Event Mutability*);
- *Modality*: this meta-property is a qualitative description of the degree of inheritability of a concept property by its subconcepts;
- *Prototypes* and *Exceptions*: the meta-properties *Prototypical* and *Exceptional* aim to describe properties that are prototypical for a concept, that is the properties that obtain for the *prototypical* (from a cognitive viewpoint, following Rosch [21]) instances of a concept. Exceptions are those properties which can be ascribed to a concept although being highly unusual;
- *Inheritance* and *Distinction*: *inherited* meta-properties regard those properties that hold because inherited from an ancestor concept, although they may be overruled in the more specific concept in order to accommodate inheritance with exceptions. *Distinguishing* properties are those that permit us to distinguish among siblings of a same concept. In other words a distinguishing property ϕ is a property such that $\Diamond \exists x\ \phi(x)\ \land\ \Diamond \exists x\ \neg\phi(x)$, that is there is possibly something for which the property ϕ holds, and there is possibly something for which the property does not hold, and these are neither tautological nor vacuous [31]. Distinguishing properties can lead to disjoint concepts in the ontology's taxonomic structure.

---

[2] by conceptual model we mean the knowledge engineer's evolving conception of the domain knowledge. It is the knowledge that actually determines the construction of a formal knowledge base. A conceptual model is an intermediate design construct, a template to begin to constrain and codify human skill, it is neither formal nor directly executable on a computer [16]

These meta-properties provide means to distinguish between *necessary* and *sufficient* conditions for class membership. Indeed, the modality meta-property and those describing the behaviour over time permit the identification of essential (or rigid) properties and necessary properties are those that are essential to all instances of a concept. Prototypical properties are good candidates to identify sufficient conditions, as discussed in Section 3.3.

Relations between concepts are supported by the model as are instances. Finally, the ontology model supports roles. Concepts are also used to represent *roles*, which can be thought of describing the *part played* by a concept in a context, (a more complete discussion on roles is postponed to Section 4.3). Roles are described in terms of their context, and the formal role relationship holds, that is, roles are related to concepts by a 'Role-of' relations.

This ontology model has been used to model a medical condition *Disseminated Intravascular Coagulation* (DIC) [28], whose evolution depends on the changes over time of its symptoms. This ontology model is proving quite promising since it permits physicians to fully capture the changes in the attribute values, how these affect the hierarchy formed by the different types of DIC, and to make explicit most of the modelling assumptions. However, its use is not restricted to medical domains.

This ontology model enriches the traditional model proposed initially by Gruber [6], in that it permits the characterisation of the properties of a concept. From this viewpoint it should be considered more expressive. The solution of adding information characterising concept properties is a controversial one. Indeed, any number of meta-properties could be used to characterise attribute's behaviour. Here we focused our attention on those meta-properties that support formal ontological analysis.

Although we do realise that often it is not true that 'more is better', this work claims that an ontology model which include this type of property characterisation is helpful to deal with ontology heterogeneity problems in two ways. On the one hand the model complements the set of formal ontological properties proposed in [31], and can guide in assigning them to concepts in a way which depends on concept definitions in terms of attributes. This is particularly useful when knowledge engineers need to assign formal properties to ontologies they have not designed.

Additionally, this conceptual model for ontologies facilitates a better understanding of the concepts' semantics. Currently ontology merging is performed by hand based on the expertise of the knowledge engineers and on the ontology documentation. Even in this case the ontology model we propose can prove useful by providing a characterisation of the properties, which can help to identify semantically related terms. The following subsections describe all the meta-properties for attributes except Inheritance and Distinction (which are trivial) in more detail:

3.1   Behaviour over Time

The meta-properties which model the behaviour of the attributes over time are:

- *Mutability*, which models the liability of a concept property to change. A property is mutable if it can change during the concept's lifetime;
- *Mutability Frequency*, which models the frequency with which a property can change in a concept description;
- *Event Mutability*, which models the reasons why a property may change;
- *Reversible Mutability*, which models reversible changes of the property.

These meta-properties describe the behaviour of *fluents* over time, where the term *fluent* is borrowed from situation calculus to denote a property of the world that can change over time. Modelling the behaviour of fluents corresponds to modelling the changes in properties that are permitted in a concept's description without changing the essence of the concept.

Fluents are used to characterise time dependency in processes. Hence, here and in [28] we take the view that changes in concept properties can be modelled as *processes* [25].

Describing the behaviour over time also involves distinguishing properties whose change is *reversible* from those whose change is *irreversible*.

Property changes over time are caused either by the natural passage of time or are triggered by specific event occurrences, and so, they need to be represented by a suitable temporal framework that permits us to reason with time and events. In [29] we chose *Event Calculus* [12] to accommodate the representation of changes. Event calculus deals with local event and time periods and provides the ability to reason about change in properties caused by a specific event and also the ability to reason with incomplete information.

We mentioned above that processes model changes in concept properties (which correspond to changes in the values associated with attributes). Processes can be described in terms of their starting and ending points and of the changes that happen in between. We can distinguish between *continuous* and *discrete changes*, the former describing incremental changes that take place continuously while the latter describe changes occurring in discrete steps called *events*. Analogously we can define *continuous properties* as those changing regularly over time, such as the age of a person, versus *discrete properties* which are characterised by an event which causes the property to change. If a property mutability frequency is *regular* (that is it changes regularly), then the process is continuous, if it is *volatile* the process is discrete, and if it changes *once only* in the concept's lifetime, then the process is considered discrete and the triggering event is set equal to *time-point*=T.

Any regular occurrence over time can be, however, expressed in form of an event, since most of the forms of reasoning for continuous properties require discrete approximations. Therefore in the ontology model we present here, continuous properties are thought of as discrete properties where the event triggering the change in property is the passing of time from the instant t to the instant t'. Events are always thought of as *point events*, and we consider *durational events* (events which have a duration) as being a collection of *point events* in which the property whose mutability is modelled by the set of meta-properties hold as long as the event lasts.

3.2   Modality: Weighing the Validity of Attribute Properties

The term modality is used to express the way in which a statement is true or false, which permits us to establish whether a statement constitutes a *necessary truth* and to distinguish necessity from possibility [13]. The term can be extended to qualitatively measure the way in which a statement is true by trying to estimate the number of possible worlds in which such a truth holds. This is the view we take, by denoting the degree of confidence that we can associate with the property holding in a given world with the meta-property *modality*. This notion is analogous to the *rankings* defined by Goldszmidt and Pearl [5]: *Each world is ranked by a non-negative integer κ representing the degree of surprise associated with finding such a world* (in which the property does not hold).

Here we use the term modality to denote the degree of surprise in finding a world where the property P holding for a concept C does not hold for one of its subconcepts C'. The additional semantics encompassed in this meta-property is important to account for statements that have different degrees of credibility. Indeed there is a difference in asserting facts such as "Cats are pets" and "All felines are pets", the former is generally more believable than the latter, for which many more counterexamples can be found. The ability to distinguish facts whose truth holds in more or less possible worlds is important in order to find which facts are true in *every* possible world and therefore constitute *necessary truth*, which permits us to establish *rigidity*.

Furthermore, the ability to evaluate the degree of confidence in a property describing a concept is also related to the problem of reasoning with ontologies obtained by merging. In such a case, mismatches can arise if a concept inherits conflicting properties. In order to be able to reason with these conflicts some assumptions have to be made, concerning on how likely it is that a certain property holds. In case of conflict the property degree of credibility can be used to apply some forms of non monotonic reasoning or belief revision. For example, we could rank the possible alternatives on the grounds of the degree of credibility following an approach similar to the one presented in [5].

3.3   Prototypes, Exceptions, and Concepts

A full understanding of a concept includes not only the set of properties generally recognised as describing a typical instance of the concept, but also the known exceptions. In this way, we partially follow the cognitive view of prototypes and graded structures, which is also reflected by the information modelled in the meta-property *modality*. In this view all cognitive categories show gradients of membership which describe how well a particular subclass fits people's idea or image of the category to which the subclass belong [21]. Prototypes are the subconcepts which best represent a category, while exceptions are those which are considered exceptional although still belonging to the category.

Prototypes show all the sufficient conditions for class membership. For example, let us consider the biological category *mammal*: a *monotreme* (a mammal who does not give birth to live young) is an example of an exception with respect to the property of giving birth to live young. Prototypes depend on the context; there is no universal prototype but there are several prototypes depending on the context, therefore a prototype for the category *mammal* could be *cat* if the context taken is that of *animals that can play the role of pets* but it is *lion* if the assumed context is *animals that can play the role of circus animals*.

The context is in part determined by the task for which the ontology is built, even in those cases where the ontology is intended to be task neutral, because of the *interaction problem* [1]. Thus, attributes considered prototypical are very likely to differ in ontologies constructed for different tasks.

The ability to distinguish between prototypes and exceptions helps to determine which properties are necessary and sufficient conditions for concept membership. In fact a property which is prototypical and that is also inherited by all the subconcepts becomes a natural candidate for a necessary condition. Prototypes, therefore, permit the identification of the subconcepts that best fit the cognitive category represented by the concept *in the specific context given by the ontology*. On the other hand, by describing which properties are exceptional, we provide a better description of the membership criteria in that it permits us to determine which properties, although rarely holding for that concept, are still possible properties describing the cognitive category.

Prototypes and exceptions can prove useful in dealing with conflicts arising from ontology merging. When no specific information is made available about a concept and it inherits conflicting properties, then we can assume that the prototypical properties hold for it.

In the ontology model presented above the context can be partially described by the roles applicable to the concept for which prototypical and exceptional properties are modelled. Ontologies typically presuppose context and this feature is a major source of difficulty when merging them, since information about context is not always made explicit.

4   Discussion

The ontology model presented in previous section could be implemented in any kind of ontology representation formalisms. In [29] we presented an implementation of the ontology model above in a frame-based representation formalism, and so attributes were described by associating values to slots, and their structural description and meta-properties were modelled by the slot's facets.

By adding the meta-properties to the ontology model, we provide an explicit representation of the attributes' behaviour over time, their prototypicality and exceptionality, and their degree of applicability to subconcepts. This explicit representation may be used to support and complement the OntoClean methodology [31], in that they can help in determining which meta-properties hold for concepts, as we will illustrate in the sub-sections of this section.

Furthermore, the enriched ontology model we propose forces knowledge engineers to make ontological commitments, that is the agreement as to the meaning of the terms used to describe a domain [7] explicit. The extent of knowledge shared depends on the extent of the different agents' ontological commitment made explicit. Real situations are information-rich events, whose context is so rich that, as it has been argued by Searle [23], it can never be fully specified. When dealing with real situations one makes many assumptions about meaning and context [22], and these are rarely formalised. But when dealing with ontologies these assumptions must be formalised since they are part of the ontological commitments that have to be made explicit. Enriching the semantics of the attribute descriptions with things such as the behaviour of attributes over time or how properties are shared by the subconcepts makes some important assumptions explicit.

The enriched semantics helps to recognise and reconcile cases of ontology heterogeneity. By adding information on the attributes we are also aiming to measure the similarity between concepts more precisely and to disambiguate between concepts that *seem* similar while they are not. Indeed, two concepts are to be considered similar if they have similar names, if they are described by similar attributes and *if these attributes show the same behaviour in the concept description* [28].

A possible drawback of enriching the ontology model is that knowledge engineers are required a deeper analysis of a domain. We realise that it makes the process of building an ontology even more time consuming but we believe that a more precise ontological characterisation of the domain at least balances the increased complexity of the task. Indeed, in order to include the attribute meta-properties to the ontology model, knowledge engineers need to have a full understanding not only of the concept they are describing, but also of the context in which the concept is used. Arguably, they need such knowledge if they are to perform the modelling task thoroughly.

The evaluation of the price to pay for this enriched expressiveness and of the kind of reasoning inferences permitted by this model are strictly dependent on the domain and the task at hand. We can imagine that the automatic coalescence of terms might require more sophisticated inferences whose cost we cannot evaluate *a priori*. In some other cases, the simple matching between properties' charactersiations might help in establishing or ruling out the possiblity of semantic relatedness. For example, if two concepts are described by the same properties but with different characterisations, this might indicate that the concepts have been conceptualised differently.

4.1 Identity

The idea of modelling the permitted changes for a property is strictly related to the philosophical notion of *identity*. The meta-properties modelling the behaviour over time are, thus, relevant for establishing the *identity* of concepts [31], since the proposed ontology model addresses the problem of modelling identity when time is involved, namely *identity through change*, which is based on the common sense notion that an individual may remain the same while showing different properties at different times [10]. The knowledge model we propose explicitly distinguishes the properties that can change from those which can-

312 Valentina Tamma and Trevor J.M. Bench Capon

not, and describes the changes in properties that an individual can be subjected to, while still being recognised as an instance of a certain concept. Properties that do not change over time are those that are good candidates to become re-identification criteria.

Prototypical and exceptional properties and the modality meta-properties describing how the property is inherited in the hierarchy can all contribute to determine what are the necessary and sufficient conditions for class membership. Necessary and sufficient conditions are ultimately the conditions that permit us to define the properties constitutive of identity and to distinguish them from those that permit re-identification.

In order to find suitable identity criteria (which permit to identify a concept), knowledge engineer should look at *essential properties*, that is those properties which hold for an individual in every possible circumstance in which the individual exists. It is important to note that essential properties should also be intrinsic if they are to be used to determine identity.

Also inheritance and distinction contribute to identify identity criteria, in that identity criteria have to be looked for among the distinguishing properties.

4.2 Essence and Rigidity

Identity through change is also relevant to determine *rigidity*, which derives from the notion of *essence* we defined in Section 2. There we defined a *rigid property* as *a property that is essential to* all *its instances*.

In [29] and in [28] we have related the notion of *rigidity* to those of *time* and *modality*; and, by including in our ontology model a meta-property *modality* and those concerning the behaviour over time, we can precisely identify rigidity in the subset of the set of possible worlds. Indeed, since an ontology defines a vocabulary, we can restrict ourselves to the set of possible worlds which is defined as the set of maximal descriptions obtainable using the vocabulary defined by the ontology [20]. By characterising the rigidity of a property in this subset of possible worlds we aim to provide knowledge engineers the means to reach a better understanding of the *necessary* and *sufficient* conditions for the class membership. However, this does not mean that the rigidity of a property depends on any account of whether the property is used to determine class membership or not. That is, the final aim is to try to separate the properties constitutive of identity from those that permit re-identification. Under the assumption of restricting the discourse to this set of possible worlds, *rigid properties* are those properties which are inherited by all subconcepts, and thus which have a certain degree of belief associated with the meta-property *modality* and that cannot change in time.

It is important to note that, although in [29] we have modelled this information as a facet which can take value in the set {*All, Almost all, Most, Possible, A Few, Almost none, None*}, the choice of such a set is totally arbitrary, and it is intended only as an example of a possible way to represent this meta-property. Alternatively, knowledge engineers should be able to associate with this meta-property either a probability value, if they know the probability with which the property is inherited by subconcepts, or a degree of belief (such as a κ-value, as in [5], which depends on an ϵ whose value can be changed according to the knowledge available, thus causing the κ function to change), if the probability function is not available.

4.3 Roles Dependence on Identity and Rigidity

Rigidity is not only central in order to distinguish necessary truth but also to distinguish *roles* from concepts.

A definition of role that makes use of the formal meta-properties and includes also the definition given by Sowa [24] is provided by Guarino and Welty. In [31] they define a role as: ' *the properties expressing the* part *played by one entity in an event, often exemplifying a particular relationship between two or more entities. All roles are* anti-rigid *and* dependent... *A property ϕ is said to be anti-rigid if it is not essential to* all *its instances, i.e.* $\Box(\forall x,\ t\phi(x,\ t)\ \rightarrow\ \Diamond\exists\ t'\ \neg\ \phi(x,t'))...$ *A property ϕ is* (externally) dependent *on a property ψ if, for all its instances x, necessarily some instance of ψ must exist, which is not a part nor a constituent of x, i.e.* $\forall x \Box(\phi(x)\ \rightarrow\ \exists y\psi(y)\ \wedge\ \neg P(y,x)\ \wedge\ \neg C(y,x))$ ', where $P(y,x)$ denotes that y is a *part* of x while $C(y,x)$ denotes that y is a *constituent* of x. In other words a concept is a role if its individuals stand in relation to other individuals, and they can enter or leave the extension of the concept without losing their identity. From this definition it emerges that the ability to recognise whether rigidity holds for some property ϕ is essential in order to distinguish whether ϕ is a role.

Roles may be 'naturally' determined when social context is taken into account, and the social context determines the way in which a role is acquired and relinquished. For example, the role of *President of the country* is relinquished differently depending on the context provided by the country. So, for example, in Italy the role may be acquired and relinquished only once in the lifetime of an individual, whereas if the country is the United Sates, the role can be acquired and relinquished twice, because a president can be re-elected. Social conventions may also determine that once a role is acquired it cannot be relinquished at all. For example, the role *Priest* in a catholic context is relinquished only with the death of the person playing the role. The ability to distinguish roles gives also a deeper understanding of the possible contexts in which a concept can be used. Recognising a role can be equivalent to defining a context, and the notion of context is the basis on which prototypes and exceptions are defined.

In [26] Steimann compares the different characteristics that have been associated in the literature with roles. From this comparison it emerges that the notion of role is inherently temporal, and roles are acquired and relinquished dependent on either time or a specific event. For example the object *person* acquires the role *teenager* if the person is between 13 and 19 years old, whereas a person becomes *student* when they enroll for a degree course. Moreover, from the list of features in [26] it follows that many of the characteristics of roles are time or event related, such as: an object may acquire and abandon roles dynamically, may play different roles simultaneously, or may play the same role several time, simultaneously, and the sequence in which roles may be acquired and relinquished can be subjected to restrictions. Indeed, what distinguishes a role from a concept, in the modelling process, is that a role holds during a specific span of time in which some property holds. For example, the role 'Student' is applicable only if the property of being registered to a university holds. Therefore, the meta-properties that model the behaviour over time permits the representation of the acquisition and relinquishment of a role.

For the aforementioned reasons, ways of representing roles must be supported by some kind of explicit representation of time and events. Indeed the proposed model provides a way to model roles as fluents; moreover, by modelling the reason for which a property change, we provide knowledge engineers the ability to model the events that constrain the acquisition or the relinquishment of a role.

5   Conclusions

Sharing ontologies independently developed is a burning issue that needs to be resolved. This paper presents a set of meta-properties describing concept's characteristic features (attributes) that can be used to support both the process of building correct ontologies (by complementing and supporting the formal ontological analysis performed by the OntoClean methodology [31]) and the disambiguation of cases of ontology heterogeneity. Formal ontological analysis is usually demanding to perform and we believe that the set of meta-properties for attributes we propose can support knowledge engineers in determining the meta-properties holding for the concepts by forcing them to make the ontological commitments explicit.

The meta-properties we propose, namely Mutability, Mutability Frequency, Reversible Mutability, Event Mutability, Modality, Prototypicality, Exceptionality, Inheritance and Distinction encompass semantic information aiming to characterise the behaviour of properties in the concept description. We have argued that such a precise characterisation can help to disambiguate among concepts that only seem similar, and in turn can support mappings across the structure of multiple shared ontologies that we have devised as alternative to the current approaches to knowledge sharing. We claim that this characterisation of the concept properties is also very important in order to provide a precise specification of the semantics of the concepts. Such characterisation is essential if we want to perform a formal ontological analysis, in which knowledge engineers can precisely determine which formal tools they can use in order to build an ontology which has a taxonomy that is clean and not very tangled.

The novelty of this characterisation is that it explicitly represents the behaviour of attributes over time by describing the permitted changes in a property used to describe a concept. It also explicitly represents the class membership mechanism by associating with each attribute (represented in a slot) a qualitative quantifier representing how properties are inherited by subconcepts. Finally, the model does not only describe the prototypical properties holding for a concept but also the exceptional ones. By providing this explicit characterisation, we are asking knowledge engineers to make more hidden assumptions explicit, thus providing a better understanding not only of the domain in general, but also of the role a concept plays in describing a specific domain.

Acknowledgements

We wish to express our gratitude to Asunción Gómez-Pérez for the many discussions and valuable comments on the PhD thesis from which this paper is derived. We have also benefitted from the discussion with Mariano Fernández López and we would like to thank him for his thought provoking comments. The PhD presented in this paper was funded by BT plc.

References

[1] T. Bylander and B. Chandrasekaran. Generic tasks in knowledge-based reasoning: The right level of abstraction for knowledge acquisition. In B. gaines and J. Boose, editors, *Knowledge acquisition for knowledge bases*, volume 1, pages 65–77. Academic Press, London, 1988.

[2] M. Fernández-López, A. Gómez-Pérez, and N. Guarino. The methontology & ontoClean merge. Technical report, OntoWeb special interest group on Enterprise-standards Ontology Environments, 2001.

[3] M. Fernández-López, A. Gómez-Pérez, A. Pazos-Sierra, and J. Pazos-Sierra. Building a chemical ontology using METHONTOLOGY and the ontology design environment. *IEEE Intelligent Systems and their applications*, January/February:37–46, 1999.

[4] N. Fridman Noy and M.A. Musen. SMART: Automated support for ontology merging and alignment. In *Proceedings of the 12th Workshop on Knowledge Acquisition, Modeling and Management (KAW)*, Banff, Alberta, Canada, 1999. University of Calgary.

[5] M. Goldszmidt and J. Pearl. Qualitative probabilisties for default reasoning, belief revision, and causal modelling. *Artificial Intelligence*, 84(1-2):57–112, 1996.

[6] T. R. Gruber. A translation approach to portable ontology specifications. *Knowledge Acquisition*, 5(2):199–220, 1993.

[7] N. Guarino. Formal ontologies and information systems. In N. Guarino, editor, *Proceedings of FOIS'98*, Amsterdam, 1998. IOS Press.

[8] N. Guarino, M. Carrara, and P. Giaretta. An ontology of meta-level-categories. In *Principles of Knowledge representation and reasoning: Proceedings of the fourth international conference (KR94)*, pages 270–280, San Mateo, CA, 1994. Morgan Kaufmann.

[9] E. Hirsch. *The concept of identity*. Oxford University Press, New York, 1982.

[10] I. Kant. *Critique of pure reason*. St. Martin's press, New York, 1965. Translation by N. Kemp Smith from *Kritik der reinen Vernunft*, 1787.

[11] K. Knight and S. Luk. Building a large knowledge base for machine translation. In *Proceedings of the American Association of Artificial Intelligence Conference, AAAI-94*, Seattle, WA, 1994.

[12] R. Kowalski and M. Sergot. A logic-based calculus of events. *New Generation Computing*, 4:67–95, 1986.

316   Valentina Tamma and Trevor J.M. Bench Capon

[13] S.A. Kripke. *Naming and necessity*. Harvard University Press, Cambridge, Massachusetts, USA, 1980.

[14] O. Lassila and D. McGuinness. The role of frame-based representation on the semantic web. *Electronic Transactions on Artificial Intelligence (ETAI) Journal: area The Semantic Web*, To appear, 2001.

[15] E.J. Lowe. *Kinds of being. A study of individuation, identity and the logic of sortal terms*. Basil Blackwell, Oxford, UK, 1989.

[16] G.F. Luger. *Artificial intelligence. Structures and strategies for complex problem solving*. Addison Wesley-Pearson Education, Harlow, England, fourth edition, 2002.

[17] D.L. McGuinness. Conceptual modelling for distributed ontology environments. In B. Ganter and G.W. Mineau, editors, *Proceedings of the Eighth International Conference on Conceptual Structures Logical, Linguistic, and Computational Issues (ICCS 2000)*, volume LNAI 1867, 2000.

[18] D.L. McGuinness, R.E. Fikes, J. Rice, and S. Wilder. An environment for merging and testing large ontologies. In A.G. Cohn, F. Giunchiglia, and B. Selman, editors, *Principles of Knowledge Representation and Reasoning. Proceedings of the seventh international conference (KR'2000)*, pages 483–493, San Francisco, CA, 2000. Morgan Kaufmann.

[19] G.A. Miller, R. Beckwith, C. Fellbaum, D. Gross, and K. Miller. Introduction to wordnet: An on line lexical database. Technical report, Cognitive Science Laboratory, Princeton University, 1993.

[20] A. Plantiga. *The nature of necessity*. Clarendon Library of logic and philosophy. Clarendon Press, New York, 1989.

[21] E.H. Rosch. Cognitive representations of semantic categories. *Journal of Experimental Psychology: General*, 104:192–233, 1975.

[22] E.H. Rosch. Reclaiming concepts. *Journal of Consciousness Studies*, 6(11-12):61–77, 1999.

[23] J.R. Searle. *Intentionality*. Cambridge University Press, Cambridge, 1983.

[24] J.F. Sowa. *Conceptual Structures: Information Processing in Mind and Machine*. Addison-Wesley, Reading, MA, 1984.

[25] J.F. Sowa. *Knowledge Representation: Logical, Philosophical, and Computational Foundations*. Brooks Cole Publishing Co., Pacific Grove, CA, 2000.

[26] F. Steimann. On the representation of roles in object-oriented and conceptual modelling. *Data and Knowledge Engineering*, 35:83–106, 2000.

[27] R. Studer, V.R. Benjamins, and D. Fensel. Knowledge engineering, principles and methods. *Data and Knowledge Engineering*, 25(1-2):161–197, 1998.

[28] V. Tamma. *An ontology model supporting multiple ontologies for knowledge sharing*. PhD thesis, University of Liverpool, 2002.

[29] V.A.M. Tamma and T.J.M. Bench-Capon. An enriched knowledge model for formal ontological analysis. In C. Welty and B. Smith, editors, *Proceedings of the international conference on formal ontology and information systems (FOIS'01)*, New York, 2001. ACM press.

[30] P.R.S. Visser, D.M. Jones, T.J.M. Bench-Capon, and M.J.R. Shave. Assessing heterogeneity by classifying ontology mismatches. In N. Guarino, editor, *Formal Ontology in Information Systems. Proceedings FOIS'98, Trento, Italy*, pages 148–182. IOS Press, 1998.

[31] C. Welty and N. Guarino. Supporting ontological analysis of taxonomical relationships. *Data and knowledge engineering*, 39(1):51–74, 2001.

[32] D. Wiggins. *Identity and Spatio-Temporal continuity*. Basil Blackwell, Oxford, 1967.

Managing Reference: Ensuring Referential Integrity of Ontologies for the Semantic Web

Harith Alani, Srinandan Dasmahapatra, Nicholas Gibbins, Hugh Glaser,
Steve Harris, Yannis Kalfoglou, Kieron O'Hara, and Nigel Shadbolt*

Intelligence, Agents and Multimedia Group (IAM),
Department of Electronics and Computer Science,
University of Southampton,
Southampton SO17 1BJ,
UK
{ha,sd,nmg,hg,swh,y.kalfoglou,kmo,nrs}@ecs.soton.ac.uk

Abstract. The diversity and distributed nature of the resources available in the semantic web poses significant challenges when these are used to help automatically build an ontology. One persistent and pervasive problem is that of the resolution or elimination of coreference that arises when more than one identifier is used to refer to the same resource. Tackling this problem is crucial for the referential integrity, and subsequently the quality of results, of any ontology-based knowledge service. We have built a coreference management service to be used alongside the population and maintenance of an ontology. An ontology based knowledge service that identifies communities of practice (CoPs) is also used to maintain the heuristics used in the coreference management system. This approach is currently being applied in a large scale experiment harvesting resources from various UK computer science departments with the aim of building a large, generic web-accessible ontology.

1 Introduction

In the context of the Semantic Web ([5]), ontologies are a key technology, providing formalisms in which to express metaknowledge about content and resources. Such formalisms will facilitate the knowledge-based enrichment or annotation of such content and resources. This in turn will allow reasoning over annotations. Reasoning will permit the presentation of content and resources to the users that need them, when they need them. This will facilitate the provision of a range of intelligent Web services ([21]). These services could include, for instance, content-based discovery of knowledge sources, natural language querying, or e-marketplaces.

As these services become increasingly prevalent, ontologies will become more important, and ubiquitous. They will increase in scale, and the issue of *ontology engineering* will become evermore important, as distributed teams (some of

---

* The names of the authors appear in alphabetical order.

A. Gómez-Pérez and V.R. Benjamins (Eds.): EKAW 2002, LNAI 2473, pp. 317–334, 2002.
© Springer-Verlag Berlin Heidelberg 2002

whose members will not be experienced in knowledge representation) begin to put them together. Furthermore, we would expect to see the increasing prevalence of ontology *merging*, where a single ontology is created from the union of two or more ontologies. For example, an interdisciplinary ontology may be created from merging ontologies covering the different disciplines, or a topic-specific ontology may be made usable by merging it with a large general purpose ontology. Finally, such resources carry maintenance costs, particularly in fast evolving domains; the merging of new bodies of information with the old ontology must become more or less routine if ontologies' shelf-lives are to be of acceptable length.

It has been suggested [11] that ontology development lifecycle management policies need to be understood in this context. Thus merging, and other associated tasks such as documenting the rationale for the particular design and structure of an ontology or configuration management, need to be written explicitly into lifecycles. In other words, ontology builders should *start* from the assumption that their work will be merged with that of others and in various ways reused.

However, merging ontologies carries with it obvious risks. The fact that ontologies can be expected to have a distributed etiology implies that the coordination of ontology development will be hard, even with the use of the lifecycle policies suggested in [11] or the benefits of any emerging web/ontology standards. In particular, the uses of terms cannot be expected to be consistent across merged ontologies. Indeed, intra-ontological context can cause reference problems. [20] reports such difficulties in e-commerce ontologies: "systematic treatment was required ... to separate terms like *steamers* under clothing appliances from *steamers* under kitchen appliances." The problem is made more acute in ontologies since the standard techniques for coreference resolution from computational linguistics are deprived of the cues they require to work in the context of ontology structure merging [4].

As part of the Advanced Knowledge Technologies project [2], we have developed an ontology for experimental use, including merging of a number of databases and other resources in the field of computer science. The problem of maintaining referential integrity was an immediate challenge, and the domain has provided us with an opportunity to investigate the issue. A combination of approaches to maintaining referential integrity has been used, in a series of steps starting from general defeasible heuristics for initial disambiguation, through to the application of advanced heuristic services to refine the picture.

We will propose a systematic protocol to assess and flag potential mismatches between semantic intent and encoded content that might affect the reliability of the system. In this paper, we shall focus our attention on the problem of multiple identifiers for the same referent represented in a populated ontology.

We can only assume that our methodology cannot but be circular — we can only rely on the knowledge-based system, in particular the populated ontology itself, to inform us of indicators of referential profligacy. Our procedure will start with the most local features of the representation — the actual realisation of the identifier in terms of characters — and move to more global features of how the classes to which instances belong are related. At each step we shall identify a hypothetical relation that the instances might satisfy and cluster the set of individuals by this relation. We then apply the less local information from the ontology in order to further fine-grain the clusters. At each stage, the grain-size of the referential cohorts can be tuned depending on the nature of the decision processes that such a choice might affect.

Obviously the issue of referential ambiguity and integrity is not a new one, and we review a variety of approaches in section 2. Section 3 discusses our own approach in detail, setting out methods for ontology population (section 3.1), clustering candidate sets of coreferences (section 3.2), and the application of general and more knowledge-based heuristics (section 3.3). The experimental investigation and validation of our approach is discussed in section 4.

2   Work and Issues Related to Referential Integrity

2.1   Referential Integrity and Coreference

The problem of reference has been recognised for centuries — indeed much understanding of classical texts depends on knowing whether two names denote the same person. Thus the great Roman orator, statesman, and man of letters, born in Arpinum, Latium in 143BC is known as Cicero but in much writing he is referred to as Tully. Classical texts are full of references to people who just happen to share the same name and often the same occupation. Thus there are two individuals Marcus Porcius Cato one a great grandson to the other and both of whom were Roman statesmen and writers. Despite conventions arising to distinguish between them 'Cato the Elder' also known as 'Cato the Censor' is still a source of potential referential confusion with 'the Younger Cato of Utica'. These examples have not just fueled an industry in the philosophy of language but illustrate the perennial problem of ensuring that expressions refer to the appropriate objects.

Referential integrity is the database-related practice of ensuring implied relationships are enforced, thereby protecting users from the consequences of their own non-omniscience; we have taken the term, in the context of ontologies, to mean the managing of reference so that the domain is sufficiently understood to allow reasoning about underlying objects to go ahead unhindered by referential confusions.

We have already mentioned the difficulty of different areas in the same ontology providing different contexts for class names to be repeated (steamers). It is obvious that merging ontologies will increase opportunities for clashes as the authors will be ignorant of each others' work and naming conventions. The problem is not restricted to naming; relations will throw up the same confusions. For example, if *Boose* is the author of a book published by Springer in 1999, and *Gaines* is the author of a book published by Springer in 1999, is it the same book?

There are a number of related issues here, but we will focus on the problem of *coreference*. Coreference is the problem that arises when two names refer to the same thing: *IJHCS* and *Int.J.Hum.Comp.Studs*; *Shadbolt*, nigel_shadbolt and *Shadbotl*. Heuristics and memories of previous confusions will be of value, but would need to be very sensitive — for instance, it may be that the system takes *Shadbotl* to be an orthographic variant of *Shadbolt*, whereas it may actually be referring to an obscure Aztec god.

This is a particular problem for the semantic web. Firstly coreference, while not introducing the arguably greater error of conflating two different individuals, will still lead to a lack of efficiency and ability to draw the full set of conclusions if unnoticed; a serious problem if ontologies are to be the workhorses of the Web.

Secondly, coreference must be expected to be endemic on the Semantic Web. Entities (resources) are referred to by Uniform Resource Identifiers (URIs; [28]), human-readable strings. These URIs are names, which denote a set of equivalent instances of a resource – mirrored webpages, for example (this redundancy provides a degree of robustness to a distributed system such as the Semantic Web). Semantic Web resources are not necessarily digital artifacts like web pages which can be retrieved by resolving the URI which names that resource; URIs can also denote resources which are physical entities, such as people or organisations. Languages such as the Resource Description Framework (RDF) ([18] are then used to make statements about the resources denoted by these URIs.

While the semantics of the URIs used as names by the Semantic Web require that identical names must refer to the same entity, they do not require that those names be unique. So URIs should not suffer the Cato problem but will frequently face the Cicero=Tully dilemma. Consequently, two data sources on the Semantic Web may contain statements which refer to the same resource, but by different URIs. As URIs need not denote digital objects, it is not always possible to resolve them and determine if two URIs are coreferent by comparing the objects that they denote. In fact, it is current common practice for Semantic Web agents to treat URIs as opaque symbols and to ignore any retrieval semantics which might otherwise be associated with them (for example, the structure of an `http` URI gives the necessary means for an agent to be able to retrieve the object indicated by that URI).

Because the names used by one agent need not be used by another, it may not be possible to directly combine knowledge from different agents, and so knowledge from one agent must be transformed into a form based on the names used by a different agent. The cost of performing inference across the knowledge of more than one agent must now also include the cost of identifying any coreferent names and subsequently rewriting them in a common form.

Another issue is that of anonymous resources: these are the RDF equivalent of using an existentially quantified variable. Anonymity can be treated as a form of name scoping, in which an agent maintains a local scope for the names it uses in order to avoid collisions with the names used by other agents. When a reasoning service needs to use information from a source which does not externally publish the identifiers it uses, it typically makes the assumption that all existentially quantified variables refer to different entities. In RDF, this is accomplished by assigning a unique *generated identifier* or *genid* to each occurrence of an anonymous resource. In doing so, the RDF processor has transformed a source which has attempted to avoid the issue of name uniqueness (by not using names) into one which is guaranteed to use a different unique name to denote an anonymous resource each time one is mentioned. Thus the web is full of potential referential conundrums.

2.2   Traditional Knowledge-Based Systems

As we have noted, the problems that we have set out above as relating to the semantic web are hardly new. The general response in artificial intelligence, for example in the area of knowledge-based systems, is to use a *unique name assumption* [25], whereby there is a 1-1 correspondence between names and domain objects. This is a simplifying assumption that vastly reduces computational complexity, rendering the issue of coreference trivial.

However, this simplifying assumption ignores the problems of scale that the semantic web and the giant datasets that it is intended to handle will throw up. Even a reasonably-sized KBS would have a small cohort of builders, generally not distributed over space, and so the effort of ensuring the unique name assumption holds is minute compared to any attempt to enforce it over the virtual, geographical and temporal range of the web.

Hence it is unlikely that the AI solution to coreference identification problems, neat though it is, will export. This was reflected in the decision not to introduce the unique name assumption into the DAML+OIL language that is intended to represent ontologies on the web. Instead roundabout locutions such as the `daml:sameIndividualAs` and `daml:equivalentTo` relations have been introduced into the language.

2.3   Databases

Similar problems also crop up in database research, for example with the merging of relational and object-oriented databases, or with varying formats from different vendors. If a table contains two instances of *John Smith*, then the question arises whether these are two John Smiths or one. In an OOD, each Smith (if two there be) would have his own object identity, but in a relational database the problem is generally addressed by adding object identifiers (OIDs) dynamically; generating these can cause difficulties, such as hotspots in the DB caused by repeated calls for OIDs that result in timeouts, and create requirements such as the need to have a flexible enough design not to be dependent on any particular storage medium. Alternatively, large Universally Unique Identifiers (UUIDs) can be created, at some cost of space. Problems such as coreference can be eliminated by using UUIDs behind the scenes to, in effect, reinstate the unique names assumption. However, this device does not remove the need to check that coreference has been eliminated after all. Jagadish and Qian ([15])review a variety of tradeoffs between the approaches taken to these and other referential problems in object-oriented and relational databases.

In database technologies the merging of databases often relies on a mediation layer between the heterogeneous structures. There are different approaches to creating this extra layer. One method is to create a common data model, but for the reasons already reviewed such an approach would be impractical over the global expanse of the semantic web. Another would be to specify matching rules translating directly between source and target; this again is likely to be impractical for very large resources because this type of approach, as noted, in effect leave it up to the user to spot instances of coreference.

Another possibility is the use of query languages and mediators that can answer questions about an information source, generally based on a relational algebra and calculus ([7]). Such languages can either take the form of direct extensions to relational formalisms [9], or define operators similar to functions in Frame Programming Languages ([13]). For example, Abiteboul and Kanellakis ([1]) use OIDs as powerful primitives for the database query language IQL; OIDs are used to represent data structures, to manipulate sets and to express computable queries. Jagadish and Qian ([15]) on the other hand integrate declarative global specifications of constraints, including referential integrity, into an OOD, to attempt to allow both efficiency of representation and localised processing for specific applications.

The difficulty, as ever, is to produce referential integrity without too much of a burden on the user. The problem is arguably more acute in the semantic web world, as ontologies are generally more complex and larger than database schemas. Moreover, database approaches to the problem of ensuring referential integrity when merging or addressing multiple resources still tend to be dominated by syntactic rather than semantic considerations ([12]).

2.4   Resource Merging Tools and Techniques

There has been a good deal of research into explicit tools and techniques for ontology merging. Interesting approaches include, among others, Ontomorph, Chimaera, and PROMPT. OntoMorph ([6]) provides two mechanisms for translating different forms of symbolically represented knowledge: "(a) syntactic rewriting via pattern-directed rewrite rules that allow concise specification of sentence-level transformations based on pattern-matching, and (b) semantic rewriting which modulates syntactic rewriting via (partial) semantic models and logical inference supported by an integrated knowledge representation system." Onto-Morph can be viewed as a set of rewrite rules coupled with heuristics and a description logic classifier to check subsumption dependencies. Chimaera ([20]), based on Ontolingua ([10]), offers support to the user by diagnosing areas of the source ontologies where coverage or correctness may be affected by a lack of referential integrity, based on heuristics such as similarities of class names. Currently the only relations reported that Chimaera has supported are subclass/superclass relations, and the set of heuristics is fairly limited, but even so experiments have shown that, despite the restricted palette, it has a wide range of application.

As it turns out, the merging of individuals, the main focus of this paper, is not currently supported, but that is flagged in future work.

PROMPT ([12]) has a broader ambition, to provide the user with support — recall that both OntoMorph and Chimaera are diagnostic tools which leave the decision as to what to do up to the user. The potential size of ontologies entails that reducing the amount of input that the user has to produce, whether creative or routine, is essential, and the AKT approach follows that line (section 3). PROMPT supports a propose-and-revise cycle of actions. It first creates an initial list of matches between the source ontologies, like Chimaera, based on class names. It then suggests a remedial operation (the user can override this or specify his own operation in an editing environment), and then PROMPT can perform the selected/defined operation, execute additional changes consistent with the operation, and determine a new set of conflicts (suggesting more solutions to start the cycle once again).

In each of these cases, we should note that the heuristics in use are not particularly sophisticated, and yet are shown by experiments to be effective ([20], [12]); this indicates that our own set of initial heuristics is likely to make a real difference to large ontologies (section 3.2). Moreover, we also use the ontology's structure itself to determine potential referential problems at a later step (section 3.3). The systems currently in existence actually rely quite heavily on the user's input; it is likely that as ontologies become more ubiquitous more of these operations will have to be automated. The research problem will be improving the trade-off between accuracy and the conservation of human resources.

Our own approach resembles in spirit approaches that facilitate semantic interoperability of heterogeneous resources (e.g. legacy software components) by extracting metadata from the components themselves or user assumptions ([14], [31]). Extracting the information implicit in the resources themselves, and providing explicit models of their mutual constraints, is the key to understanding the interoperability constraints.

3   A Stepwise Process in Identifying Coreferences

To tackle the problem of identifying coreferences, we devised a stepwise process which begins by populating the ontology with instances and ends with coreferences detection. In essence, this relies on the simple idea that references are first deemed to be similar enough to be considered co-referent by using different indicators of similarity, and a final decision process to integrate these measures of similarity. The process is illustrated in figure 1. Step 1 on the left-hand side is the ontology population step. This task is (semi-) automatic and described in section 3.1 below. The centre of the figure demonstrates step 2 which produces two sets of clusters of potential instance duplicates[1]. The string-based clusters are created using soft string similarity measures, while the generic clusters are

---

[1] For the sake of clarity we use the term duplicates when we refer to coreferences in this step as this is more commonly used when dealing with database-like structures.

produced by applying a set of generic heuristics. Step 2 is described in more detail in section 3.2.

The third step in our approach makes use of the notion of *communities of practice* (COPs)where the connections between the instances clustered in previous steps are analysed. The degree of overlap between the connection trends is used as a duplication indicator. More about this step in section 3.3.

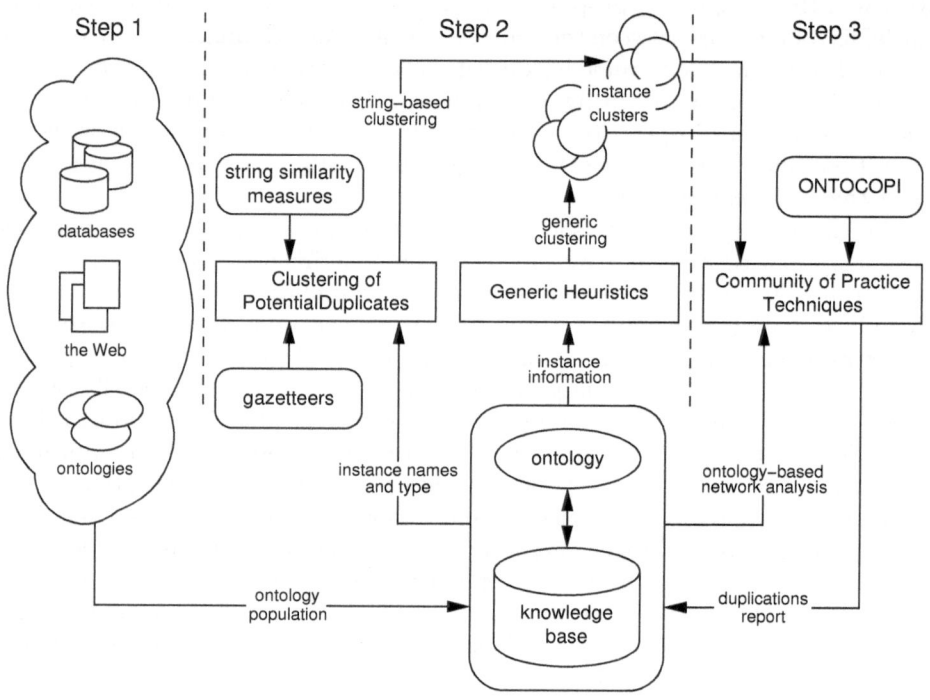

Fig. 1. A stepwise process for identifying coreferences.

3.1   Populating the Ontology

In this section we present the procedure for the initial population of the ontology from structured sources such as legacy databases. This process consists of four parts: a) mapping entity types to classes and attributes and relationships to their equivalent properties in the ontology (a discussion of this is beyond the scope of this paper; we encourage the reader to consult [24] for a review of approaches) b) assigning identifiers to strong entities, c) assigning identifiers to weak entities and d) constructing the resulting expressions.

A strong entity is one which possesses a primary key which uniquely identifies it, and so one to which we can assign a unique identifier without introducing coreference problems. We construct such identifiers by concatenating the name of the table which holds the entity set and the values of the attributes that constitute the primary key, and appending them to the identifier that denotes the database. We have no such uniqueness guarantees for weak entities, which do not possess a primary key, and so we generate a different identifier (a genid) for each weak entity that we encounter. We choose this approach over that of referring to weak entities by anonymous means (such as RDF's anonymous resource mechanism) because the later steps in our process need identifiers to be able to refer to coreferents.

Finally, we construct an description for each entity (both strong and weak) in a straightforward way by collecting together their attribute values and relations and rewriting them using corresponding properties from the ontology that were identified in the mapping stage.

3.2   Clustering Duplicates and Applying Heuristics

Before we proceed to describe the clustering methods we use and how they inform our heuristics we briefly discuss approaches that have been common in the Semantic Web community when faced with coreference (or duplicate) identification. There have been two broadly defined tasks: (a) identification of coreferent names, and (b) elimination of such coreference by rewriting statements from one or more sources such that any names which occur in those statements are replaced by the equivalent names used in another source, if such exist. One approach to the problem of identifying coreferences, the Semantic Web community argues, would be to create a centralised service by which data sources can provide a mapping from their names to those used by another source, but this has two key problems: consistency and latency issues involved in the maintenance of such a dictionary, and the inability to establish equivalence of anonymous resources by the simple fact that anonymous resources have no name.

A quite different approach is to use an ontology to guide the design of heuristic rules that will be used to identify coreferences or duplicates. For example, if two data sources declare that two resources with different URIs that represent people have the same social security number, and it is known from the ontology that a social security number can only be used by one person, it can be deduced that the two URIs refer to the same person. The social security number property of a person is an *identifying property* which has a uniqueness constraint such that distinct resources must have different values for that property[2]. A rule that uses an identifying property to infer that two URIs are coreferential is sound because of this uniqueness constraint.

However, this approach requires knowledge of the domain to specify which property is the identifying one. In addition, these might be comparatively rare and searching for them in an unfamiliar ontology is time consuming and error prone. To tackle this, we adopt a more generic view of using the underlying

---

[2] In DAML terms, identifying properties are subclasses of either
`daml:UnambiguousProperty` or `daml:UniqueProperty`.

ontological structures as a basis for defining the heuristic rules. To design these heuristics though, we need to cluster the ontology into sets of potential duplicates. It is to this process that we now turn.

We shall define a set of relations $I_i \subseteq N \times N$ by some procedures indexed by i to induce a clustering of N, *i.e.* we may define a set of subsets of N, wherein names are pairwise related by I_i within each of the subsets. We shall refer to this process as *parallel clustering*, where for each class defined in the ontology, we identify pairs of instances of the class that are similar based on two different criteria. In one we rely on the information encoded in the ontology which we assign to the instances as tuples of attribute-value pairs, thus identifying an instance with the values of all its attributes. In the other we assume that the name given to the instance may be sufficient for its identification[3].

The first clustering method indiscriminately takes all the information in the ontology and for each instance n of a class as input, producing a set of instances of the same class that are related to it, as determined by some procedure indexed by i. Here i could include a thresholding criterion based on the method used for clustering and the degree of slack required of knowledge processes downstream. It is this indifference to the preferential semantics of the attributes that prompts us to call this branch of the parallel clustering "generic" which is reflected in the superscript on I. However, there do exist such generic procedures to be rewritten in terms of rules, like decision trees ([23]), which can be used to ascribe semantics to the clusters that are hidden by our protocol.

We use this clustering method to inform the design of our generic heuristics. For example, a person instance in an underlying academic ontology might also have attributes such as telephone number, postal address, project membership and papers published. These are then used alongside email address mentioned above in the rule for identifying properties and we use the thresholding criterion to identify duplicates. In doing so, we make this procedure (almost) domain-independent as no knowledge of the underlying ontology is required upfront. Domain knowledge is only introduced in the thresholding criterion that the engineer is invited to apply to the generic protocol applied to any ontology.

The second clustering method groups elements using a different relational criterion. In the first instance, this is a simple string-matching criterion, using a dynamic programming algorithm (for example, [29]) to align name strings relative to each other. For instance, we could have two strings n and n' to be related nI_in' by procedure indexed by i which determines how far the strings have to be in terms of the Levenstein string-edit distance (the sum of insertions, deletions and substitutions) [19] [4]. This string-based matching can be supplemented

---

[3] This assumption is akin to Kripke's arguments for names as rigid designators ([17]), identifying the same referent in all possible worlds. In this case, the possible worlds are distinguished by values of the attributes.
[4] The use of edit-string distances for strings of 4-letter nucleotide alphabets is common in bioinformatics, in which case the intended "semantics" lies in the identification of the corresponding amino-acid sequences.

by a domain-dependent gazetteer for identifying common variants of names of objects.

The intuition behind using this two-fold clustering is the observation that due to legacy issues in populating ontologies, there might be *no overlap* between the attribute values of the same individual represented in the knowledge base.

We now have two sets of clusters each of which can now be explored by methods that heavily draw upon the information in the knowledge base to suggest reasons to the user/engineer as to why identifiers may have a common referent. The task of the steps outlined thus far has been to reduce the computational load of these more computationally intensive processes. These methods though, are not foolproof. Since we treat the underlying ontology as a "black box" we might get an overlap below the threshold criterion defined for identifying duplicates but still the objects are duplicates because the attributes that don't match are contextually equivalent. That is, the attributes do not match and cannot be detected with the clustering methods described here, but the context in which these attributes are defined and the way their objects are connected to each other might reveal potential duplicates. In particular, preliminary experiments with this service has thrown up possible guidelines for ontology population that will carry over much more of the context of knowledge capture to aid this process of determining reference. To further explore this dimension in searching for duplicates we need a mechanism which will allow us to reason about the context in which an object and its attributes are defined, and more crucially, how these are connected. Such a mechanism is described in the following section and is based on the notion of communities of practice.

3.3   Using Communities of Practice to Check for Duplicates

In this section, we shall use the relationships registered in the ontology to specify the appropriate relations by which we can either further refine the set of potentially coreferent identifiers, or at least to register the names in the knowledge base with the appropriate relational tags. The procedures adopted can be distinguished from those in section 3.2 in two ways. First, we can look at the classes and relationships that are specific to the domain under consideration and use domain knowledge to structure further analyses. Secondly, we consider the extension of the relationships by composing relationships R, R' between instances represented in the ontology. We compose $n_1 R n$ and $n R' n_2$ to define $n_1 R_n^* n_2$ where R_n^* is a combined relation indexed by the intermediate object n (transitivity is not taken for granted).

ONTOCOPI is an Ontology-based Community of Practice Identifier ([3]), which applies Ontology-based Network Analysis ([3],[22]) to locate the community of practice (CoP) of a given instance. CoPs are informal groups of individuals sharing an interest, task, or a problem ([30]). Here we use ONTOCOPI to produce CoPs for the instances in a given set of potential duplicates $N_k^{(p)s}$ (see 3.2) obtained by the gazetteer and string-based clustering performed on the class of People. For each element from the set of people we define the CoP of person n as the set of people who share a sufficient amount of indirect shared information. This was formulated and described in [22] as a natural number indexed map from the set of people in the ontology to its power set (the set of its subsets, the set of CoPs) obtained by evaluating a graph-traversal algorithm with paths of K edges, each of which is a graphical representation of relations in the ontology.

The degree of overlap between the CoPs can be calculated as a measure of their similarity. If the similarity of two sets is higher than a given threshold (CoP similarity measure) then the two instances in question are regarded as duplicates and are assumed to be the same individual.

The approach of CoP comparison to locate duplication is bound to fail in certain cases. For example, if there are two people with the same surname, and same attributes and similar values for these attributes, that is happen to work in the same environment, on the same projects, and in the same teams, then the two people will have highly overlapping CoPs in which case they will most likely be considered identical. A tactic to help avoid these situations is to assemble sets of heuristics that check for functionally discriminating attributes. In the domain of academic institutions illustrated here one would be if both these names appear as authors on the same paper, which would then set them apart.[5] However, these heuristics might have only limited coverage. For example, in the data set we were considering we did not find any such cases among our 13000 instances. Another more problematic situation is when two people instances are actual duplicates, but are hard to identify by our approach due to the lack of sufficient knowledge about one or both instance, e.g. a person's instance with only a name and title. However, one might say that such instances offer little of value for knowledge services.

The CoPs calculated by ONTOCOPI are generic in the sense that all ontology relationships can be taken into account regardless of their type. This reduces the method to yet another clustering tool when divested of its people and activity-related semantics. Relationships can be selected and weighted as required to put more emphasis on certain relationships while reducing the effect of others. This is desirable if certain relationships are known to lead to coreference identification more than others. For example co-authorship and project membership could be regarded as stronger indications of possible duplication than conference attendance and department membership. The analyses presented here have focused on people as the main class of interest in managing coreference. When viewed as a clustering technique relying on general network enalysis, this method is no less applicable in domains where the objects of interest our duplicate instances of projects, papers, journals, etc.

---

[5] From the mid-eighties, the area of physics called conformal field theory had a number of such instances – A. B. and Al. B. Zamolodchikov and to a less frequent extent V. S. and Vl. S. Dotsenko from the Landau Institute in Moscow and E. and H. Verlinde from Utrecht would have a number of coincident values for these slots.

3.4   Example

We applied the approach described in this paper on a small set of of People instances in our ontology to identify duplicates, using the a threshold of 80% for all measures. The generic clustering technique compared the attribute values of all instances and found no similarities because the selected instances either had very few attribute values to compare, or the values were different, which resulted in very low generic measure values, and therefore no clusters were created.

Instance	ID	Weight
Shadbolt	genid46405	
O'Hara	ECS_02831	10.202
Crow	genid46409	2.0
Shadbolt	ECS_02686	1.825
Löckenhoff	genid46696	1.565
Fensel	genid46692	1.565
Studer	genid46688	1.565
Shadbolt	genid46673	1.565
Shadbolt	genid46651	1.565
Scutt	genid46638	1.565
Motta	genid46621	1.565
Shadbolt	genid46625	1.565
Shadbolt	genid46606	1.565
Stutt	genid46602	1.565
Zdrahal	genid46598	1.565
Motta	genid46594	1.565
Reichgelt	genid46581	1.565
Shadbolt	genid46577	1.565
Hallam	genid46553	1.565
Major	genid46549	1.565

(a)

Instance	ID	Weight
Shadbolt	genid46478	
O'Hara	ECS_02831	10.202
Schreiber	genid46474	2.0
Shadbolt	genid46482	2.0
Shadbolt	ECS_02686	1.825
Löckenhoff	genid46696	1.565
Fensel	genid46692	1.565
Studer	genid46688	1.565
Shadbolt	genid46673	1.565
Shadbolt	genid46651	1.565
Scutt	genid46638	1.565
Motta	genid46621	1.565
Shadbolt	genid46625	1.565
Shadbolt	genid46606	1.565
Stutt	genid46602	1.565
Zdrahal	genid46598	1.565
Motta	genid46594	1.565
Reichgelt	genid46581	1.565
Shadbolt	genid46577	1.565
Hallam	genid46553	1.565

(b)

Instance	ID	Weight
Shadbolt	genid46625	
O'Hara	ECS_02831	10.202
Motta	genid46621	2.0
Shadbolt	ECS_02686	1.825
Löckenhoff	genid46696	1.565
Fensel	genid46692	1.565
Studer	genid46688	1.565
Shadbolt	genid46673	1.565
Shadbolt	genid46651	1.565
Scutt	genid46638	1.565
Shadbolt	genid46606	1.565
Stutt	genid46602	1.565
Zdrahal	genid46598	1.565
Motta	genid46594	1.565
Reichgelt	genid46581	1.565
Shadbolt	genid46577	1.565
Hallam	genid46553	1.565
Major	genid46549	1.565
Shadbolt	genid46536	1.565
Stutt	genid46532	1.565

(c)

Fig. 2. ONTOCOPI in action: Communities of Practice for three instances: (a) N.R.Shadbolt (b) NR.Shadbolt (c) N.Shadbolt.

The String Similarity Measure create two small clusters. The first cluster contained the three person instances N.R.Shadbolt, NR.Shadbolt, and N.Shadbolt, with $(11/12) * 100\% = 91.6\%$ and $(10/12) * 100 = 83\%$ string similarity of the second and third string respectively relative to the first[6], while the second cluster contained A.Brown and P.Brown with a string similarity of 85%.

The final stage is to compare the CoPs of the instances in each cluster. The CoPs in figure 2 were computed in ONTOCOPI for the three instances of *Shadbolt* in the first cluster using the automatic relation setting and a link threshold of 4 (i.e. looking for paths of 4 edges or fewer). The left column in the figure shows the name of the instance, the column in the middle displays the system's generated unique ID, and the right column displays the CoP values as calculated by ONTOCOPI. Only the first 20 entries in each CoP will be considered. It can be seen that there are only 3 instances in CoP (a) that are not in (b), and 3 in (b) that are not in (a). The similarity of the two CoPs can be measured as $(34/40) * 100\% = 85\%$, and 90% is the similarity of (a) to (c). Because these COP-similarity values are above or equal to the 80% threshold set earlier, the three *Shadbolt* instances in question will be regarded as duplicates.

---

[6] String Similarity = 1- the ratio of the Levenstein string distance and the total string length.

Instance	ID	Weight
Brown	ECS_00114	
White	ECS_00029	18.552
Beeby	ECS_01705	14.281
Al-Hashimi	ECS_02635	13.63
Currie	ECS_00015	10.446
Electronics Sys...	Electronics E...	7.455
Ross	ECS_00028	7.404
Brignell	ECS_00117	6.674
Grabham	ECS_02155	5.878
Zwolinski	ECS_00017	5.85
James	ECS_02646	4.802
Schmitz	ECS_02694	3.724
Williams	ECS_00332	3.667
Alhoseyni-Alm...	ECS_01664	3.293
Papakostas	ECS_01586	3.293
Kilic	ECS_01747	3.095
Chappell	ECS_02756	3.071
Gonciari	ECS_02793	2.746
Varea	ECS_02709	2.746
Glynne-Jones	ECS_02154	2.702

(a)

Instance	ID	Weight
Brown	ECS_02783	
Hall	ECS_01650	22.135
Shadbolt	ECS_02686	16.987
De Roure	ECS_00047	16.343
Jennings	ECS_02355	16.033
Carr	ECS_00060	14.278
Lewis	ECS_00048	13.788
Davis	ECS_00046	13.286
Harnad	ECS_00101	12.989
Intelligence, Ag...	Intelligence,...	11.183
Crowder	ECS_01768	10.44
Luck	ECS_02839	10.126
Hill	ECS_00386	9.473
Heath	ECS_00385	9.454
Dobie	ECS_00381	8.812
Wills	ECS_00395	8.475
Moreau	ECS_00395	8.391
Elliott	ECS_02337	7.844
Hitchcock	ECS_00387	6.943
O'Hara	ECS_02831	6.866

(b)

Fig. 3. ONTOCOPI in action: Communities of Practice for two instances: (a) A.Brown and (b) P.Brown.

If the similarity between CoPs is low, then no duplication will be reported. Figure 3 presents the output of ONTOCOPI for the two *Browns* in the second cluster. After calculating the CoPs of both instances, no overlap was found, and hence the two Browns will be regarded as names of different people.

4   Experimental Deployment

The work reported in this paper is part of the UK funded Advanced Knowledge Technologies (AKT) Interdisciplinary Research Collaboration (IRC)). This is a six year programme of research begun in October 2000 between five UK Universities - Aberdeen, Edinburgh, Sheffield, the OU and Southampton. One of the goals of the project is to demonstrate the sorts of knowledge intensive technologies that might be deployed on the web to support knowledge management. A number of broad problem opportunity areas have been identified as offering contexts in which to demonstrate these technologies. Unsurprisingly one of these was the use of our own methods to help organise and facilitate the knowledge management practices within our own IRC.

Given the central role our IRC was advocating for ontologies within the semantic web the decision was taken to build a reference ontology for the AKT project. This has evolved over the past 18 months and there is now a sustained effort to populate it with instances from the participating parts of all five of the partner sites. It was agreed that Southampton would be the first site to populate the reference ontology and much of the work reported in this paper arose out of that effort. During the first phase of ontology instantiation something in the order of 18000 instances were included. The primary objects of interest in the AKT ontology include people, publications, projects, research interests meeting events. A phase of automatic coreference management reduced this number by around 6000. The more knowledge intensive phase exploiting communities of practice eliminates another less quantitatively substantial but nevertheless important set of duplicates - those relating to personnel with large publication outputs.

We quickly recognised that there was a need for services that were constantly running to check for changes in the entities held in our various resources - for example our publications database, a database of personnel, and the projects announced and described in particular areas of the Departmental intranet. The question was how far could these methods scale and would some of our services become even more useful if applied to larger instantiated ontologies.

The aim is to populate the AKT reference ontology with instances from each partner site. Since each site has very different resources that hold the information we are interested in we have adopted two main harvesting strategies. The first develops extraction scripts for each site to extract content of the type required for the reference ontology. Often, as might be expected, these are PERL scripts and varieties of relational database query templates. The second approach uses the maintained web sites of each partner as the primary resource. A visual scripting language tool DOME has been developed [27] that is trained on the prototypical page structure of the various partners' web pages. Thus each site has a set of pages that describe or enumerates its staff. Although the structure and format is different for each site it is a relatively straightforward process to train DOME to extract the content and realise it as canonical RDF that maps directly to our ontology.

The daily updates provided by these scripts are already being published on our AKT intranet. The design and implmentation of this referential integrity acrchitecture has allowed us to specify the protocols by which harvesting of data is conducted, which allows a more controlled management of the knowledge repository. We are exploring the scalability of this service.

Our reference ontology can serve not just for the Departments involved in AKT but also the wider UK Computer Science community. There are already bodies in existence that would very much like to have available via a set of annotated web pages the sort of information that our ontology embodies. Examples include current UK computer science faculty, declared areas of research interest, or currently active projects etc. This real time harvesting supplemented by an ontology reference checking service may provide a much better snapshot of actual reality than the *mandraulic* process currently in operation where Departments are asked to submit this same information in a variety of formats for all sorts of purposes. If a community ontology has perceived value one can enter a virtuous spiral where the community begins to use it as *the* reference model to help annotate their own content making subsequent harvesting easier.

The other advantage of the large scale deployment we hope to see and will certainly have for the AKT partners is the provision of a variety of other knowledge services that use these populated ontologies. An obvious example is to extend the COP analysis across various partner sites to see what sorts of inter institutional COPs emerge. This helps us understand the research landscape and the current and shifting patterns of cooperation and intellectual influence [3].

5   Conclusions

We have described a methodology for helping with the management of referential integrity and applied to medium scale ontologies. We advocated a mixture of statistical, string based and AI methods involving human mediation only at the point of key decisions regarding the collapse or otherwise of referential duplicates. Populating ontologies of a reasonable size is required if we are to run many of the knowledge services imagined in the vision being advocated for the Semantic Web.

Automatic methods that harvest content from the web with respect to any reference ontology are bound to be promiscuous, potentially generating thousands of duplicates in only medium sized contexts. It is important that automatic methods of the sort described here perform much of the initial pruning. Thereafter, we advocate the use of knowledge intensive methods to present analyses to help effect decisions about whether to collapse or keep entities distinct.

There are assumptions that some may question in this work. One is the extent to which reference ontologies will be useful at all. In previous work some of the authors have presented a system, APECKS, developed by Tennison [26] where the emphasis was on the collaborative construction of ontologies and in which the expectation was that the class structures and attributes of the ontologies themselves were the objects of debate. APECKS takes a different line to most ontology servers, in that it is designed for use by domain experts, possibly in the absence of a knowledge engineer, and its aim is to foster and support debate about domain ontologies. To that end, it does not enforce ideals of consistency or correctness, and instead allows different conceptualisations of a domain to coexist. Under this view the ontologies would be rather different between users and maintaining different ontologies for different users could be as important as using agreed common reference ontologies across users. However, the issue of populating these idiosyncratic ontologies with instances still arises. Indeed the problem of referential integrity becomes one that literally has to be re-run for each variant.

The content of real value in an ontology that is built and maintained by an organisation or community are objects such as people, projects, products, processes and publications. These objects are typically comprised of many attributes and relations. They may be described from multiple perspectives in different resources on the web. It is important to determine whether these objects are distinct or the same. We think that the methods outlined here are well suited to supporting the increasingly complex detective work of establishing referential identity. We have detailed how we hope to demonstrate the utility of these services in a community wide knowledge harvesting and publication activity mediated via a reference ontology.

Acknowledgements

This work is supported under the Advanced Knowledge Technologies (AKT) Interdisciplinary Research Collaboration (IRC), which is sponsored by the UK Engineering and Physical Sciences Research Council under grant number GR/N15764/01. The AKT IRC comprises the Universities of Aberdeen, Edinburgh, Sheffield, Southampton and the Open University. The views and conclusions contained herein are those of the authors and should not be intepreted as necessarily representing official policies or endorsements, either expressed or implied, of the EPSRC or any other member of the AKT IRC.

References

1. S. Abiteboul and P. Kanellakis. Object identity as a query primitive. In *Proceedings of the International Conference on Management of Data, ACM SIGMOD, Portland, OR, USA*, 1989.
2. AKT. The akt manifesto. Technical report, 2001. http://www.aktors.org/publications/Manifesto.doc
3. H. Alani, K. O'Hara, and N. Shadbolt. ONTOCOPI: Methods and tools for identifying communities of practice. In *Proceedings of the 2002 IFIP World Computer Congress, Montreal, Canada*, August 2002.
4. A. Bagga. Evaluation of coreferences and coreference resolution systems. In *Proceedings of the First Language Resource and Evaluation Conference*, may 1998.
5. T. Berners-Lee, HendlerJ., and O. Lassila. The semantic web. *Scientific American*, may 2001.
6. H. Chalupksy. OntoMorph: A Translation System for Symbolic Knowledge. In *Proceedings of the 17th International Conference on Knowledge Representation and Reasoning (KR-2000), Colorado, USA*, April 2000.
7. E.F. Codd. Relational completeness of data base sublanguages. In RustinR., editor, *Database Systems*. Prentice-Hall, 1972.
8. DARPA. DARPA Agent Markup Langugage. Technical report, DARPA, mar 2001.
9. U. Dayal. Queries and views in an object-oriented data model. In R. Hull, R. Morrison, and D. Stemple, editors, *Database Programming Languages: Proceedings of the 2nd International Workshop*. Morgan Kaufmann, 1989.
10. A. Farquhar, R. Fikes, W. Pratt, and J. Rice. The Ontolingua Server: a Tool for Collaborative Ontology Construction. In *proceedings of the 10th Knowledge Acquisition Workshop, KAW'96,Banff,Canada*, November 1996. Also available as KSL-TR-96-26.
11. M. Fernandez-Lopez, A. Gomez-Perez, and M-D. Rojas-Amaya. Ontology's crossed life cycles. In *Proceedings of the 12th International Conference on Knowledge Engineering and Knowledge Management (EKAW'00), Juan-les-Pins, France*, pages 65–79. Springer, 2000.
12. N. Fridman-Noy and M. Musen. PROMPT: Algorithm and Tool for Automated Ontology Merging and Alignment. In *Proceedings of the 17th National Conference on Artificial Intelligence, (AAAI'00), Austin, TX, USA*, July 2000.
13. G. Gardarin, F. Machuca, and P. Pucheral. Ofl: A functional execution model for object query languages. In N.J. Carey and A.S. Schneider, editors, *Proceedings of the 1995 ACM SIGMOD International Conference on Management of Data, San Jose, California, USA*, pages 59–70. ACM Press, may 1995.
14. S. Heiler, R.J. Miller, and V. Vintrone. Using metadata to address problems of semantic interoperability in large object systems. In *Proceedings of the First IEEE Metadata Conference, Silver Spring, Maryland, USA*, 1996.

15. H. Jagadish and X. Qian. Integrity maintenance in an object-oriented database. In *Proceedings of the 18th International Conference on Very Large Databases, Vancouver, Canada*, pages 469–481, August 1992.

16. G. Kappel and M. Schrefl. Local referential integrity. In *Proceedings of the International Conference on Conceptual Modeling / the Entity Relationship Approach*, pages 41–61, 1992.

17. S.A. Kripke. *Naming and Necessity*. Oxford: BasilBlackwell, 1980.

18. O. Lassila and R. Swick. Resource Description Framework(RDF) Model and Syntax Specification. W3c recommendation, W3C, feb 1999.

19. V.I. Levenstein. Binary codes capable of correcting deletions, insertions and reversals. *Cybernetics Control Theory*, 10:707–710, 1966.

20. D. McGuinness, R. Fikes, J. Rice, and S. Wilder. An Environment for Merging and Testing Large Ontologies. In *Proceedings of the 17th International Conference on Principles of Knowledge Representation and Reasoning (KR-2000), Colorado, USA*, April 2000.

21. E. Motta, S. Buckingham-Shum, and J. Domingue. Ontology-driven document enrichment: principles, tools and applications. *International Journal of Human-Computer Studies*, (52):1071–1109, 2000.

22. K. O'Hara, H. Alani, and N. Shadbolt. Identifying Communities of Practice: Analysing Ontologies as Networks to Support Community Recognition. In *Proceedings of the 2002 IFIP World Computer Congress, Montreal, Canada*, August 2002.

23. J.R. Quinlan. Induction of decision trees. *Machine Learning*, 1:81–106, 1986.

24. A. Rahm and A. Bernstein. A survey of approaches to automatic schema matching. *The Very Large Databases Journal*, 10(4):334–350, 2001.

25. R. Reiter. Equality and domain closure in first order data bases. *Journal of the Association of Computing Machinery*, 27:235–249, 1980.

26. J. Tennison, K. O'Hara and N. Shadbolt APECKS: Using and Evaluating a Tool for Ontology Construction with Internal and External KA Support. *International Journal of Human-Computer Studies, In Press*

27. T. Leonard and H. Glaser Large scale acquisition and maintenance from the web without source access Workshop 4, Knowledge Markup and Semantic Annotation, K-CAP 2001

28. Sollins,K. and Masinter,L. Functional Requirements for Uniform Resource Names. RFC 1737.

29. R.A. Wagner and M.J. Fischer. The string-to-string correction problem. *Journal of the ACM*, 21:168–173, 1974.

30. E. Wenger. *Communities of Practice: The Key to Knowledge Strategy*. Cambridge University Press, 1998.

31. I-Y. Yao, K-T. Ko, R. Neches, and R. MacGregor. Semantic interoperability scripting and measurements. In *Proceedings of the Working Conference on Complex and Dynamic Systems Architecture, Brisbane, Australia*, 2001.

Alice: Assisting Online Shoppers through Ontologies and Novel Interface Metaphors

John Domingue[1], Maria Martins[1*], Jaicheng Tan[1], Arthur Stutt[1], and Helgi Pertusson[2**]

[1]The Knowledge Media Institute
The Open University, Milton Keynes, UK
Tel: +44 1908 655014, Fax: -3169
{J.B.Domingue, J.Tan, A.Stutt}@open.ac.uk
http://kmi.open.ac.uk/
[2]Innn Inc., Laugavegur 26, 101 Reykjavik, Iceland
http://www.innn.com/

Abstract. In this paper we describe some results of the Alice project. Alice is an ontology based e-commerce project which aims to support online users in the task of shopping. Ontologies describing customers, products, typical shopping tasks and the external context form the basis for the Alice architecture. We also exploit two novel interface metaphors originally developed for navigating databases: the Guides metaphor and Dynamic Queries. The Guides metaphor was developed at Apple to reduce the cognitive load on learners navigating a large hypermedia database. Within Alice we use the Guides metaphor to allow online shoppers to classify themselves. We discuss the link between Alice Guides and Kozinet's notion of e-tribes or Virtual Communities of Consumption. Our second interface metaphor Dynamic Queries (coupled with Starfield displays) allow users to very quickly find relevant items by displaying the results of queries, posed via specialised slider widgets, within 100 milliseconds. We have constructed a tool, Quiver, which constructs Dynamic Query interfaces on-the-fly as the result of queries to knowledge models stored on the Alice server.

Introduction

Currently shopping on the internet is not always a pleasant experience. Navigating websites with thousands of products by browsing virtual aisles or by keyword search is time consuming and often frustrating. Each aisle will typically contain hundreds of items that are hard to differentiate. The shopper has to rely on a product's name and sometimes on a small accompanying picture. Neither of which are particularly descriptive. Keyword searches over generic product types (e.g. flour) will often return hundreds of irrelevant items (e.g. wholemeal flour bread). Online shopping websites

---

* Current contact details: Business School, The University of Gloucestershire, Cheltenham, UK
Email: mmartins@glos.ac.uk
** Current contact details: cTarget Inc., Brautarholt 1, 105 Reykjavik, Iceland.
Email: hp@ctarget.com

A. Gómez-Pérez and V.R. Benjamins (Eds.): EKAW 2002, LNAI 2473, pp. 335-351, 2002.
© Springer-Verlag Berlin Heidelberg 2002

also contain a lot of irrelevant information related to new types of products or reduced items.

Contrast the above with the local 'corner shop' which was prevalent in villages in England in the 1950s. Of course there are a variety of differences between a corner shop and an online shopping site. These include the fact that one is physical and the other virtual. Also corner shops sometimes have a better layout. Nether the less we believe that one of the key differences to the customer's shopping experience was due to the fact that the shop had a human agent, the shopkeeper, who used his or her knowledge to *personalise* the interaction. Typically, the shopkeeper would know which products were currently in stock and products that could easily be obtained. Additionally, the shopkeeper understood the relationships between the products, for example, when one product could be substituted for another (out of stock product), or how one product complemented another (e.g. a particular cheese and wine combination). Regular customers would also benefit from the fact that their personal tastes and preferences, their current situation (e.g. number of dependents), and their previous purchases were known to the shopkeeper. The shopkeeper was also able to relate desired products to the local context including the surrounding geography and community and the resident culture and events.

The overall goal of the Alice project is to make the experience of online shopping seem more like visiting a local corner shop than browsing or searching long lists. In the rest of this paper we will describe some of the results of the project structured in the following fashion. In the next section of the paper we describe the Alice approach. We then illustrate the approach through a short scenario. The subsequent two sections describe the architecture of the system and an interface for detecting the patterns of behaviour of online customers. Finally, a discussion section, linking the Alice approach to a notion of e-tribes, is followed by some conclusions.

Approach

The Alice framework is based on the use of ontologies for representing knowledge related to online shopping. An ontology [13] is an explicit representation of a view of a domain of discourse (a conceptualisation) usually composed of a set of concepts and relationships. Over the last few years the use of ontologies has become relatively popular, for example a web search for ontology will now return more that 64,000 web pages [14]. Moreover, ontologies are widely deployed within the knowledge acquisition and modelling communities, have been successfully used in a variety of web based applications (e.g. [7]) and form one of the cornerstones of the semantic web [3]. Within Alice we use five ontologies to create a personalised online shopping experience. The five ontologies are:

- *Products* – this ontology describes the main attributes of products, for example, how a product is used, its components, complementary products and a product's geographic origin.
- *Shopping Tasks* – this ontology represents typical shopping tasks, for example a monthly shop for household essentials and shopping for an evening meal.
- *External Context* – appropriate items from the local context are described within this ontology. For example, relevant local social events, groups, and small businesses.

- *Customer* – this ontology represents the main attributes of a customer including his or her shopping and browsing histories.
- *Alice Media* – this ontology maps between the other four ontologies and relevant web resources.

The first four ontologies to a greater or lesser degree reflect the four categories of knowledge used by a local corner shopkeeper. Our definition of a product borrows from the product ontology available on the ontolingua server. Specifically, we use the relations list-price, has-model-number and has-special-discount.

In contrast with the other four ontologies, modelling customers within a formal representation is particularly problematic. This is for a number of reasons. Firstly, there is no definitive knowledge source for classifying customers' according to their shopping behaviour. There exist many competing marketing and economic models of consumer behaviour, but none of these give a 'foolproof' account of why and when humans purchase goods. Second, a customers' behaviour will vary depending on his or her current situation, for example, buying a single urgently needed item vs. buying goods for a week, or having a personal cash flow problem until the next salary payment. Major life events, such as having a baby, will also dramatically affect behaviour.

Determining a customer's current state is also non trivial. Two options are to infer the customer's state from their interactions or to explicitly ask the customer. The former option is prone to error because the individual user interactions - selecting hyperlinks or options from menus – contains little informational content. Whilst accurate the latter option has to be carefully applied because customers are, in general, unwilling to spend significant amounts of time on any task that does not have an immediate benefit.

An additional factor linked to the above is that it is imperative that any online system only offers pertinent advice. Offering a customer advice based on an incorrect model would result in the system being quickly discarded.

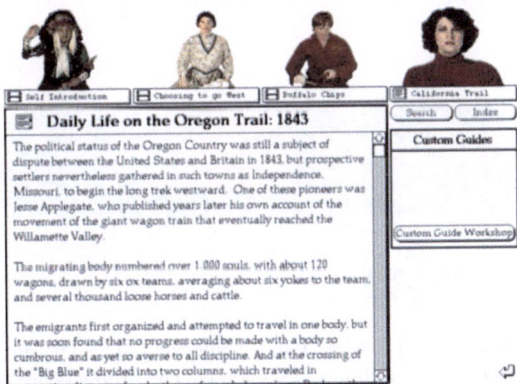

Fig. 1. A screen snapshot of the Guides system (taken from http://www.abbedon.com/ project/guides.html with permission (copyright 1990 Apple Computer)). The first three Guides above explain early American history from the perspective of: a native American, a female settler, and a frontiersman. The last icon represents the system Guide who gave overview information.

Our approach within the Alice project has been to use the Guides metaphor [8, 18, 26] as a mechanism to allow customers to classifying themselves. Guides were produced at Apple in the late 1980s as an interface for an educational hypermedia database depicting early American history. The Guides who were characters drawn from this period, delivered stories from specific viewpoints. Each story consisted of a series of video clips. A screen snapshot of the Guides system can be seen in Fig. 1. Four Guides are shown at the top of the screen. The first three deliver stories on early American history from the viewpoint of a native American, a female settler and a frontiersman. The icon on the far right represents the system Guide who delivered overview information.

Within Alice we decided to use the Guides metaphor to enable customers to state their shopping preferences. We shall give an overview of our implementation using a short scenario.

A Scenario

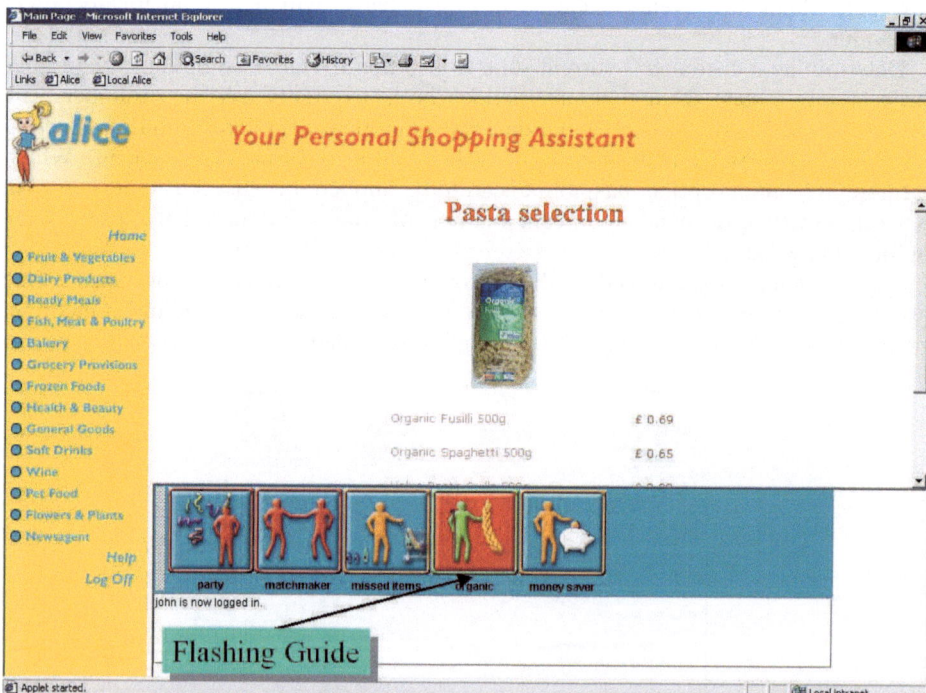

Fig. 2. A screen snapshot of the Alice Guides interface. The left panel contains a standard navigation bar as found in most online supermarkets. The products are shown in the large pane in the centre of the browser. The Guides interface is shown in the bottom panel. The customer is browsing a selection of pastas and the *Organic Guide* is indicating that it would like to start a dialogue by blinking red.

In the following scenario an online shopper is looking to buy some pasta within a fictional 'Alice Supermarket'. A screen snapshot from the shopper's web browser is shown in Fig. 2. The navigation menu on the left and the product display area in the centre of the window are similar to those found in most online supermarkets. The Alice Guides interface is contained in the panel at the bottom. The shopper has selected five Guides to go shopping with:

 Party Guide – this Guide assumes that the task for the session is to buy products for a party. The Guide prompts with related offers (e.g. the free loan of wine glasses), recipes and local services (e.g. marquee hire).

 Matchmaker Guide – this Guide matches products that are purchased to similar or complementary products. For example, it would match pasta with bottled pesto sauce.

 Missing Items Guide – we have found that shoppers will sometimes forget to select the 'Add to Basket' button and consequently fail to purchase a desired product. When the customer goes to the checkout this Guide collects a list of items that the customer browsed in detail but did not add to his or her basket.

 Organic Guide – when appropriate this Guide recommends organic versions of goods that are being viewed.

 Money Saver Guide – this Guide informs the shopper of any offers or promotional items which are related to the currently viewed item.

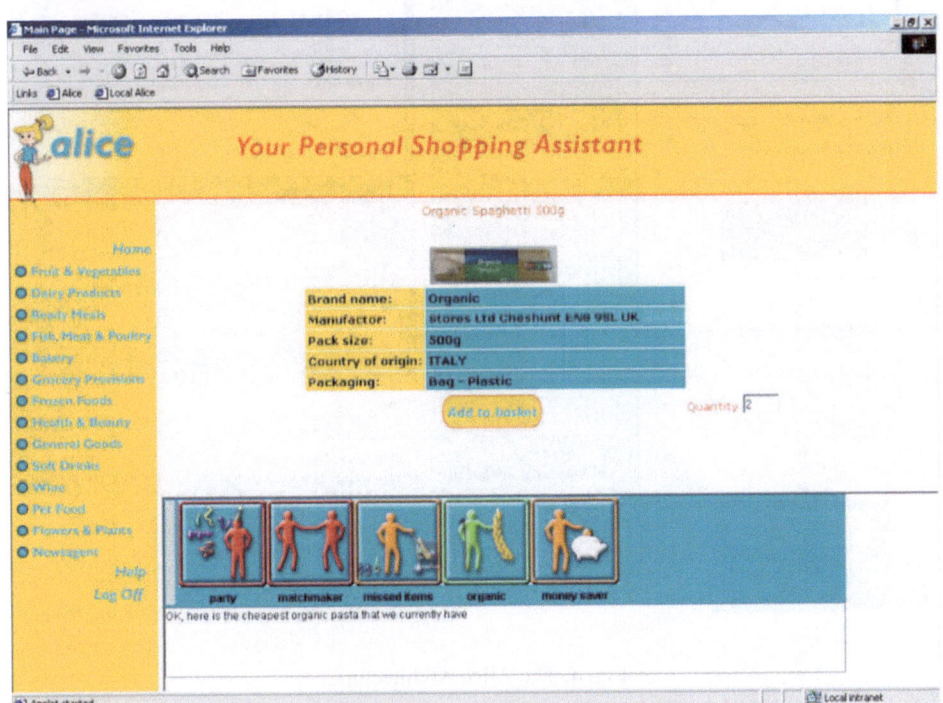

Fig. 3. A screen snapshot just after the *Organic Guide* has displayed the cheapest organic pasta.

340   John Domingue et al.

In Fig. 2 the shopper is browsing the pasta section of the online store. The *Organic Guide* indicates that it has something to contribute by blinking red a number of times (the Guide's normal colour is blue). The shopper is free to ignore the Guide and to carry on browsing but she elects to see what the Guide has to say and selects the *Organic Guide* icon. The *Organic Guide* offers the cheapest organic pasta. The shopper agrees and the display changes to Fig. 3. Note that hundreds of potential items (a well known online store we checked has over a hundred different pastas) have been narrowed to one in precisely two mouse clicks. The shopper decides to buy 2 packets.

The key design feature of the Alice Guides is that the customer selects them. This means that they reflect the customer's own perspective of themselves (e.g. rich, ethical) and therefore the customer will be tolerant of any inappropriate suggestions made. Also, depending on the current situation the customer can chose to temporarily ignore certain Guides, for example, the *Money Saver Guide* when shopping for a specific luxurious item.

The Alice Architecture

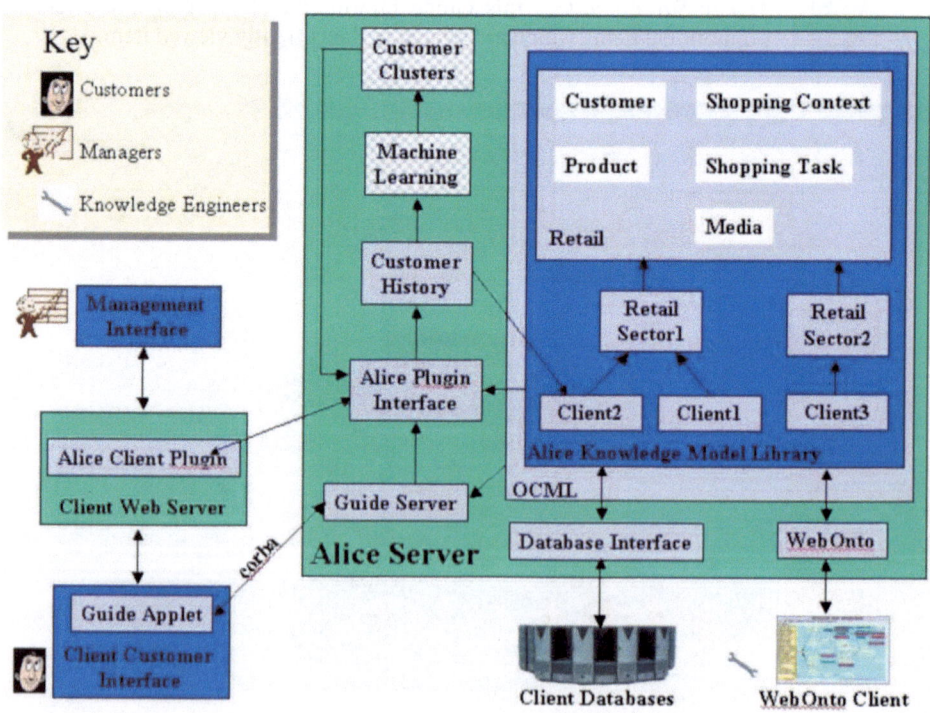

Fig. 4. The Alice Architecture.

The Alice architecture is composed of a server and several specific clients. One of the overriding goals when conceiving the system was that it should be easy to incorporate into an existing online infrastructure. Consequently, the Alice server was designed to sit alongside an existing web server. The architecture is shown in Fig. 4. The Alice server contains a library of ontologies implemented in OCML [22]. OCML, which can be conceived as an 'Operational Ontolingua' has been used in over a dozen knowledge management and knowledge modelling projects within our lab (e.g. [23]). Knowledge modelling in OCML is supported by a library of reusable definitions, which is structured according to the basic categories of the OCML modelling framework: task, method, domain and application [22]. The library also relies on a number of base ontologies, which provide definitions for basic modelling concepts, such as numbers, sets, relations, tasks, methods, and roles. Export mechanisms exist from OCML to Ontolingua [13], XML [34], RDF [33], and GXL [15].

The ontologies are split into three levels: retail, retail sector and client. At the retail level there are the five ontologies described earlier. Each of these five ontologies contain definitions which are applicable across the whole retail industry. Below is the retail sector level where definitions applicable to specific retail sectors are stored. For example, for childrens' toys important attributes would be age-range and educational value.

The client level knowledge models represent specific companies. These models would contain mappings from the generic Alice models to the existing corporate resources. For example, to the company's database schemas. The client specific models are also used to link to the client web server via the *Alice Client Plugin* module. This module communicates with the *Alice Plugin Interface* via a set of HTTP like messages. The server responds with a message that is either plain text, HTML, a list or a set of attribute value pairs. The number and type of messages is set by an XML based configuration file. An implementation of the plugin module exists in PHP and future implementations are planned for Java, Perl and active server pages.

The customer's interactions with the web based interface are sent via the *Alice Plugin Interface* to a customer history. The customer history is used in two ways. Firstly, the products browsed and purchased are asserted as facts within the company's specific knowledge model and are used to trigger a customer's Guides. The customer history is also used by a module which clusters the history according to customer and product attributes. The results are fed through to a manager's interface allowing a company's sales and marketing departments to discover new relationships between products and new clusters of customer behaviour. When appropriate new knowledge gleaned from the results of clustering will be used to create new Guides. This module is under construction and will be based on an unsupervised clustering technique [4].

The knowledge models are created and maintained using WebOnto [6]. In addition to its use in over a dozen projects within our lab WebOnto has been available as a public service since autumn 1999. The public library contains over a hundred models and has just over 150 registered users. In a comparative evaluation of several knowledge modelling tools WebOnto was evaluated very favourably, in particular being judged as the most user-friendly and as the one requiring the shortest learning curve [11].

```
(def-guide-trigger (amount-trigger party-guide)
 "Check that the customer buys the required amount of food
 for a party"
 (current-customer ?customer)
 (user-name ?customer ?user-name)
 (has-profile ?customer ?profile)
 (has-history ?customer ?customer-history)
 (party-number-of-guests ?profile ?n)
 (last-item-bought ?customer-history ?item)
 (item-name ?item ?item-name)
 (amount-too-low ?item ?n)
 :action
 (low-amount-for-party ?user-name ?item-name ?n))
```

Fig. 5. The definition of an amount trigger for the party Guide.

The Guide module contains the server part of the Guide system which is implemented on top of the OCML forward chaining system. Guides have a set of associated triggers and actions. Triggers enable a Guide to be activated when certain conditions occur. The definition of a trigger contains a set of clauses and an action. When the clauses match the contents of the current knowledge base the action is invoked. An example trigger, amount-trigger, for the party Guide is shown in Fig. 5. Amount-trigger invokes the low-amount-for-party action if the customer buys insufficient quantity of a product to satisfy the specified number of guests at a party. Actions provide a high level mechanism for defining how a Guide will interact with a customer.

The Guide Applet sits within the supermarket's existing online shopping interface. Communication between the Guide server and the Guide applet is via a CORBA interface. The main types of messages defined including logging in, and adding, removing and alerting Guides. The underlying infrastructures for the server and client, Xanalys LispWorks™ and Java v.1.4, and have inbuilt CORBA interfaces.

The Manager's Interface

Once the Alice system has been installed within a company managers will need to analyse customers' browsing and shopping behaviours in order to identify new types of products and customer characteristics. These characteristics may then lead to changes to the website including the design and creation of new Guides. From a marketing perspective, following the Pareto rule of 80-20, the overall goal of any analysis is to determine the significant attributes with respect to the 20% of customers who purchase the 80% of products. For example, 16% of US beer drinkers account for 88% of annual consumption [17].

Within Alice we have created a visual query tool, Quiver, to support the analysis of shopping behaviour through the Alice ontologies. Quiver couples Dynamic Query and Starfield like interfaces [1, 30] to our ontology server. Dynamic queries and starfield displays were developed within the Human Computer Interaction Lab at the University of Maryland in the early 1990s. A number of control widgets – sliders, checkboxes and buttons – generate queries in real time to a database. The results of each query is presented in a specialised two dimensional graphical display, termed a starfield display, within 100 milliseconds. The tight coupling of the widgets generating database queries to the graphical display enables users to quickly navigate large data stores. Quiver, creates a two dimensional graphical display and coupled sliders from a query to a knowledge model held on the Alice server.

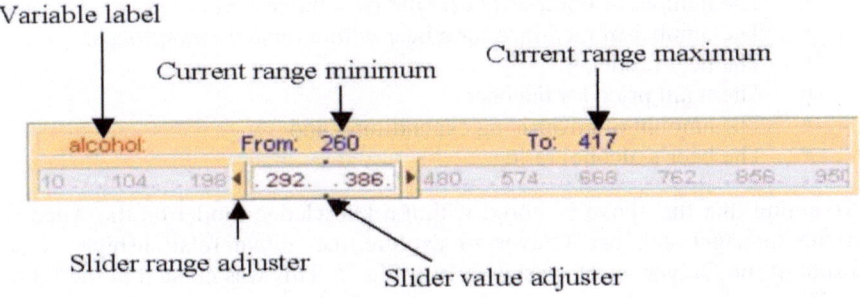

Fig. 6. An annotated screen snapshot of the Quiver slider for the variable 'alcohol'. The slider filters the graphical display area to only show those items whose alcohol rating is between 260 and 417.

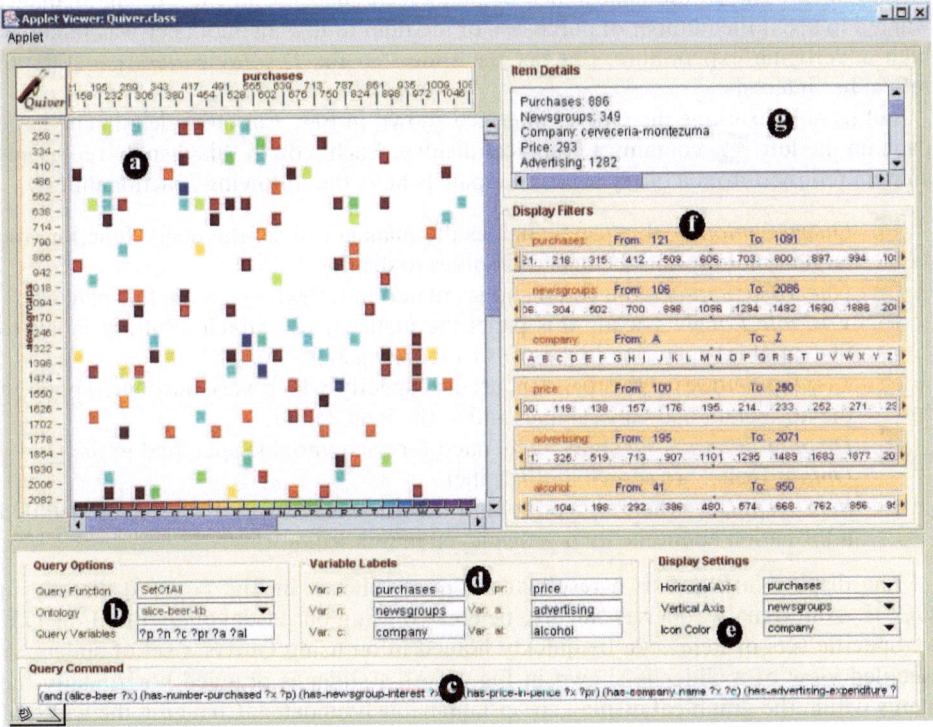

Fig. 7. A screen snapshot of Quiver displaying items from a beer knowledge base. The full query which generated this snapshot is shown in Fig. 8.

We shall now describe Quiver through a mini scenario. Imagine that a manager responsible for the marketing of wines and spirits has decided to investigate the possible influences on the sales of bottled beer over the last week. In particular, she wants to explore the relationships between:

- The number of bottles of beer sold over the last week,
- The number of mentions for a beer within related newsgroups,
- The beer producer,
- The retail price for the beer,
- The amount of advertising expenditure, and
- The beer's alcohol rating.

Assuming that the above is stored within a knowledge model on the Alice server then the manager can use Quiver to explore the above relationships. A screen snapshot of the Quiver interface shown is in Fig. 7. This was created in the following way. First the manager selected the query function SetOfAll, the ontology alice-beer-kb and specified the query variables (?p ?n ?c ?pr ?a ?al) using the *Query Options* panel (b). Then using the *Variable Labels* panel (d) new names (purchases, newsgroups, company, price, advertising and alcohol) were given to the variables. The query was then entered into *Query Command* panel (c). The display then took on the appearance of the screen snapshot in Fig. 7. The manager wanted to see if the number of purchases of medium to low alcohol beer was linked to high advertising expenditure. She set the sliders in the *Display Filters* panel (f) to reflect her interests.

Let us now examine the Quiver interface shown in Fig. 7 in more detail. The large pane on the left, (a), contains a graphical display. Each icon in this display represents an item returned from a query. The other panels have the following functionalities:

(b) *Query Options* – this panel enables the manager to set the query function, the target ontology and the query variables to display.
(c) *Query Command* – the command is entered in OCML syntax in this panel.
(d) *Variable Labels* – using this panel the manager can attach arbitrary labels to the variables specified in the *Query Options* panel.
(e) *Display Settings* – this panel is used to specify which variables correspond to the horizontal and vertical axes and to the icon colour.
(f) *Display Filters* – the sliders generated for each variable specified in the *Query Options* panel are shown in this panel.
    Item Details – when an icon within the graphical display is selected detailed information about the item is displayed in this window.

The display in Fig. 7 is a result of the query shown in Fig. 8 posed directly in OCML. Additionally, queries can also be created using our visual query tool Lois [7].

Specific sets of items can be quickly homed in on using Quiver's set of sliders. A detailed view of a slider is shown in Fig. 6. As a slider is dragged horizontally the items within the graphical display are instantaneously updated. Changing the width of a slider - using the slider's range adjusters - changes the range of data covered.

```
(setofall '(?p ?n ?c ?pr ?a ?al)
   '(and (alice-beer ?x) (has-number-purchased ?x ?p)
         (has-newsgroup-interest ?x ?n)
         (has-price-in-pence ?x ?pr)
         (has-company-name ?x ?c)
         (has-advertising-expenditure ?x ?a)
         (has-alcoholic-rating ?x ?al)))
```

Fig. 8. The OCML query which generated the display shown in Fig. 7.

Discussion

The Guides metaphor was created to resolve the tension between providing flexible routes through a hypermedia database and not placing an undue cognitive load on the user by offering a large selection of links. Although each Guide provided a fixed path through the database, flexibility was still supported through the choice of Guides.

Within the Alice framework Guides provide a mechanism for customers to classify themselves. The first time a customer logs onto an Alice enhanced shopping site she will be assigned a number of Guides by default. When the shopper feels the need she will be able to add or delete her current Guides. Because it is the customer who says 'this is who I am' they will feel an ownership of their characterisation and consequently be more tolerant of any mismatches between their preferences and the recommended products.

We envisage that Guides will be designed by a company's sales department and broadly fall into the categories of knowledge that we stated our corner shopkeeper would use, namely, customer, products, shopping tasks and external context.

Guides in Alice form a bridge between the formal knowledge models and the individual user. We also want to argue that Alice Guides can help in the formation and support of online communities.

According to Rheingold, the Web encourages the growth of virtual communities of various kinds [28]. Rheingold's perspective has been the subject of a great deal of criticism on philosophical and political grounds. Although Rheingold attempts to answer these criticisms in a new chapter in the latest edition of his book, there are still critics such as Dreyfus [10]. Dreyfus suggests that Rheingold's *electronic agora* is in fact 'dangerously distopian' since its participants can remain anonymous and are not exposed to the real-world risk associated with the vulnerabilities of embodiment. Despite these criticisms there is no doubt that such communities do exist. Furthermore, the communities of interest to e-commerce are less open to the sorts of philosophical criticisms deployed by Dreyfus and others—real-world risk and the inability to make public commitments are largely irrelevant to a community centred around an interest in communicating, say, about the music of Bob Dylan.

While many e-commerce sites attempt to foster virtual communities through, for example, their facilities for the publication of consumer reviews of products, their approach is half-hearted at best since they remain attached to a form of marketing which is directed at the individual consumer. Kozinets [17] calls this *database marketing*, and suggests that the marketer (or e-store) bases efforts to influence consumer behaviour on the incorrect assumption of a one-way relationship between active seller and passive buyer. Of the two main forms of personalization (see below) *contented-based filtering* is the most individualistic with information technology being used essentially to track and make inferences about what consumers have purchased in the past. Although *collaborative filtering* tries to make inferences about what is relevant for a particular consumer based on some measure of similarity with other consumers it remains essentially oriented to individuals. Indeed, the choice of the term *personalization* suggests an individualistic approach to the relationship between seller and buyer.

Another approach is possible and may be more relevant to virtual communities. Kozinets [17] defines *Virtual Communities of Consumption* as "affiliative groups whose online interactions are based upon shared enthusiasm for, and knowledge of, a specific consumption activity or related group of activities" (p. 254). He mentions Barbie doll collectors, X-Files fans and wine lovers. Kozinets stresses that the consumption of a particular product is only part of what is important to members of these groups. Of equal importance is knowledge of various kinds, for example, knowledge about a product and its context, knowledge of a community's cultural norms and knowledge of its specialized language. In addition the identity of the community member may be more or less defined in terms of the consumption of the particular cultural or commercial product. According to Kozinets types of group members can be defined in terms of two axes: the degree of self-centrality of the consumption activity and the degree of social ties to a community. From this perspective *devotees* (who identify closely with the product but less so with the group) and *insiders* (who identify strongly with both) are most significant to the marketer. Thus it is not only important to determine the community that a consumer belongs to, it is also important to determine the correct type of community member. Kozinets mentions three characteristics of community-based as opposed to individualistic consumers: (1) they are more proactive; (2) they are more influenced by the community they belong to; and (3) they can provide valuable, multi-faceted information to marketers. He concludes that marketers "must provide community members with the raw materials they need to construct a meaningful community" (p. 264).

While in the long run, some hybrid of individualistic and community based marketing will prove to be more attractive to many e-commerce sites, we have emphasized the latter in the Alice project. If we take each of Kozinets' three points in turn we can indicate to what extent Alice can (or could in future) comply with them:

Consumers are proactive. In Alice we provide a default set of Guides but allow the consumer to select their own. Their selection reflects their self-assessment of themselves as consumers or in Kozinets' terms as members of particular e-tribes. While many of the Guides act as critics of or assistants with the consumer's interaction with Alice (e.g., Matchmaker, Missing Item) others can be seen as system components knowledgeable about the characteristics of particular communities (e.g., Organic, Money Saver). For instance, the Organic Guides allow consumers to express the activist tendencies associated with these communities. In future versions of the system we might include more awareness of meta-categories of community member such as devotee and insider. We might also provide the means for communication between consumers and stores, for example, in the form of a complaints procedure. More also needs to be done to allow community members to creatively review and criticize products, policies and marketing strategies perhaps through some form of Web log. In addition, since Alice is part of the Semantic Web, intelligent, ontologically-guided searches could be instigated for additional consumer reviews, buying Guides and so on.

Consumers are communal. As well as the community-oriented Guides discussed above Guides could also be used as an interface for building communities. A future version of our Guides will be linked to an instant messaging server such as Jabber [20]. A 'Seek Soulmates' Guide would attempt to establish chat or email sessions with other online customers who employ a similar set of Guides. In addition, the Quiver tool could be adapted to identify, visualize and provide the means of contacting individuals both for managers and other consumers. While many consumers would find such a tool overly sophisticated, the kind of technology-savvy community member identified by Rheingold would have little trouble. As we have said we also intend to use clustering to "notice" new communities and create new (community) Guides based on these. By so doing we would go a long way towards the provision of raw materials for constructing communities demanded by Kozinets.

Community-based consumers provide valuable information to marketers. In addition to the usual information about products bought, items viewed and ratings given to products, the e-tribe aware e-store should be able to derive what Kozinets calls a "cultural profile" of its consumers. According to Kozinets this would lead to a more detailed picture of the interests of the community (or, indeed, communities) the consumer belongs to, which could be used to assess "interconnections between seemingly disparate forms of consumption" and to see where "consumers are focussing their attention" (p. 260). He singles out insiders and devotees as important here. While Alice does not currently provide such a facility for marketers, the Quiver tool coupled with customer histories and clustering might form the basis for a more multi-faceted approach to understanding consumers in the future. We might also extend the learning abilities of Guides (so that they could track the individuals they interact with and learn from them) and create a new tier of system component which can notice significant patterns in the combination of Guides employed.

Related Work

The Alice Guides are a particular approach to personalization. Jakob Nielsen defines personalization as:

> "...to serve up individualized pages to the user based on some form of model of that user's needs." [24]

Other approaches to personalization include content based and collaborative filtering. Content-based filtering recommends items based on their similarity to what the customer has bought in the past. An example of this approach is the Intelligent Personalised TV Guides [5].

Collaborative filtering makes recommendations based on the preferences of customers from the same group. Users are compared based on how similar their ratings are, and they are recommended items favoured by other people with similar interests. A well known example of collaborative filtering is www.amazon.com. ALEXA (http://www.alexa.com) is a web browser that recommends related links based in part on other people's web surfing habits.

The main problem in some types of business is the lack of information about customers' habits. Customers do not want to fill forms about themselves, unless they can clearly see the advantage of doing so (for instance, credit card companies often offer a prize draw for filling in a survey). Thus, it is difficult to fully understand their shopping behaviour. An alternative approach is to use Knowledge Discovery and Data Mining techniques on retailer's databases [1, 16]. In Alice, we intend to use an unsupervised clustering technique based on [4], to cluster customers according to their buying patterns (i.e. their shopping baskets). Alice will then extract rules encoding the consumption patterns. A similar approach was adopted by Lawrence, et. al [19] to identify groups of shoppers with similar spending histories.

Stereotypes [29] assume that facts about people are not statistically independent. This suggests that facts can be clustered into groups that frequently co-occur. Thus, a user model built with stereotypes adds a whole cluster of user facts at once, as soon as some evidence that is known to be a predictor of the cluster is observed. Therefore, it might be possible to make predictions about the behaviour of users on the basis of an amount of evidence – which can be acquired before an action is performed. The role of these predictions is to provide a basis for an action until specific knowledge becomes available.

Let us now examine initiatives related to the development of shareable product data. ISO 10303 (STEP) is an International Standard for product data representation and exchange which has existed since 1994. The development of STEP was initiated and is still driven by industry's need for technologies that enable application systems to exchange and share data about technical products. A STEP model is not however the same as an ontology - STEP definitions tend to be semantically weak. An overview of the problems in precisely capturing semantics within STEP models are discussed in [21].

A five level hierarchical categorisation of products is contained in the United Nation Standard Products and Services Codes (UN/SPSC) taxonomy. This structure however has no attributes. The Universal Content Extended Classification (UCEC) is an extension of UN/SPSC, developed by ContentEurope.com S.A. and now managed by The Electronic Commerce Code Management Association (ECCMA), has over 12,000 categories of products but again there are no attributes. A classification of a number of content standards including a number of product and e-business standards can be found at [9]

Although, visualization is considered relatively important by the ontology and e-commerce community (visualization is stated as a key issue for a proposed Internet Services Operating System [27] from the OntoWeb industrial applications special interest group), the number of visualization systems targeted at ontology based tools are relatively few. The most popular visualization used for browsing ontologies is the folder based tree views supplied as part of Java. A notable exception is Jambalaya [32], an application of the SHRIMP visualization framework [31] to view knowledge models in Protégé [25].

Conclusions

Alice is an example of a semantic web [3] e-commerce application. One of the main problems that the semantic web aims to solve is that of information overload. By indexing web resources with a formal representation items of interest can be found from their semantics. Although a lot of work is under way in creating the semantic web (see for example, [12]) most of this work focuses on infrastructure issues. Within the Alice project we have focused on how interface metaphors can augment semantic web technology to aid in user interaction within an e-commerce context. In this paper we have described two metaphors that we currently use: Dynamic Queries and Guides.

Quiver couples knowledge modelling technology to highly interactive navigation mechanisms through its on-the-fly dynamic query interface generation. Combining the strengths of ontology based queries and dynamic queries will benefit both knowledge engineers developing knowledge systems and end users looking for relationships in large volumes of data. Moreover, we expect that as the semantic web grows tools like Quiver that can present semantic data in a form that non computer specialists can understand will become ubiquitous.

The Alice Guides form a bridge between online communities of users and semantically enriched web resources. We believe that a community-based approach to marketing coupled with tribalized Guides begin to provide an online approximation of the old style community shop which we mentioned in our introduction. It is paradoxical that this particular type of store may be disappearing from the real world just as it is beginning to materialize in cyberspace.

Acknowledgements

This work was sponsored by INNN (www.innn.com) and by the Advanced Knowledge Technologies (AKT) project. AKT is an Interdisciplinary Research Collaboration (IRC), which is sponsored by the UK Engineering and Physical Sciences Research Council under grant number GR/N15764/01. The AKT IRC comprises the Universities of Aberdeen, Edinburgh, Sheffield, Southampton and The Open University.

The Alice graphic design work was carried out by Harriett Cornish.

The authors are grateful to feedback received on versions of this paper from Simon Buckingham Shum, Marc Eisenstadt and Paul Mulholland.

Reference

1. Agrawal, R., Mannila, H., Srikant., R., Toivonen, H. and Verkamo, A. I. (1996). Fast discovery of association rules. In Fayyad, U. et al. Eds. Advances in Knowledge Discovery and Data Mining. MIT Press, Cambridge.

2. Ahlberg, C., Williamson, C., and Shneiderman, B., (1992) Dynamic queries for information exploration: An implementation and evaluation, Proceedings of ACM CHI'92: Human Factors in Computing Systems, pp. 619-626.
3. Berners-Lee T., Hendler J., and Lassila O. (2001) The Semantic Web, Scientific American, May, 2001.
4. Cheeseman, P. and Stutz, J. (1996) Bayesian Classification (AutoClass): Theory and Results. In Fayyad, M. et al. (editors), Advances in knowledge discovery and data mining. MIT Press.
5. Cotter, P. and Smyth, B. (2001) PTV: Intelligent Personalised TV Guides. Smart Media Institute, Dep. of Computer Science, University College Dublin (available at http://www.ptv.ie).
6. Domingue, J. (1998) Tadzebao and WebOnto: Discussing, Browsing, and Editing Ontologies on the Web. In B. Gaines and M. Musen (editors), Proceedings of the 11th Knowledge Acquisition for Knowledge-Based Systems Workshop, April 18th-23th, Banff, Canada, (available at http://kmi.open.ac.uk/people/domingue/banff98-paper/domingue.html).
7. Domingue, J. and Motta, E. (2000) Planet-Onto: From News Publishing to Integrated Knowledge Management Support. IEEE Intelligent Systems Special Issue on "Knowledge Management and Knowledge Distribution over the Internet", pp. 26-32, May/June, 2000.
8. Don, A., Oren, T. and Laurel, B. (1991) Guides 3.0, Proceedings of ACM CHI'91 Conference, New Orleans, LA, April 27th-May 2nd, pp. 44-448.
9. Martin Dörr, Nicola Guarino, Mariano Fernández López, Ellen Schulten Milena Stefanova, Austin Tate. State of the Art in Content Standards. OntoWeb (available at http://www.ontoweb.org/download/deliverables/D3.1.pdf.)
10. Dreyfus, H. L. (2001) On the Internet. Routledge: London.
11. Duineveld, A., Stoter, R., Weiden, M., Kenepa, B., and Benjamins, V. R. (200) Wondertools? A comparative study of ontological engineering tools. International Journal of Human Computer Studies, 52(5), pp. 1111-1133.
12. Fensel D. and Musen, M. (2001) Special Issue on The Semantic Web. IEEE Intelligent Systems, March/April, 16(2).
13. Gruber, T. R. (1993) A Translation Approach to Portable Ontology Specifications. Knowledge Acquisition, 5(2).
14. Gruninger, M. and Lee, J. (2002) Ontology Applications and Design. Communications of the ACM Vol. 45, No. 2, pp. 39-41 February, 2002.
15. Holt, R., Schürr, A., Sim, S. E., and Winter, A. (2001) GXL (1.0) Document Type Definition, Dagstuhl Edition, February 14, 2001, (available at http://www.gupro.de/GXL/).
16. Jain, A.K.; M.N.Murty; P.J.Flynn. Data Clustering: A Review. ACM Computing Surveys, Vol. 31, N.3, 1999.
17. Kozinets, R. V. (1999) E-Tribalized marketing?: The Strategic Implications of Virtual Communities of Consumption. European Management Journal, 17(3), pp. 252-264.
18. Laurel, B., Oren, T. and Don, A. (1990) Issues in Multimedia Interface Design: Media Integration and Interface Agents, CHI '90 Conference Proceedings, Seattle, WA, pp. 133-139, April 1-5, 1990.
19. Lawrence, R. D., Almasi, G. S., Kotlyar, V., Viveros, M. S., and Duri, S. S. (2001) Personalization of Supermarket product recommendations. Data Mining and Knowledge Discovery, 5, pp. 11-32.
20. Lee, S. and Smelser, T. (2002) Jabber Programming, Hungry Minds.
21. Metzger, F. (1996) The Challenge of Capturing the Semantics of STEP Data Models Precisely, Workshop on Product Knowledge Sharing for Integrated Enterprises, held in conjunction with the First International Conference on Practical Aspects of Knowledge Management, October 30-31, Basel, Switzerland, (available at http://www.ladseb.pd.cnr.it/infor/Ontology/BaselPapers/Metzger.pdf).
22. Motta, E. (1999) Reusable Components for Knowledge Models. IOS Press, Amsterdam.

23. Motta, E., Buckingham Shum, S. and Domingue, J. (2001) Ontology-Driven Document Enrichment: Principles, Tools and Applications. International Journal of Human Computer Studies, 52(5), pp. 1071-1109, 2000.
24. Nielsen, J. (1998) Personalization is Over-rated. Alertbox, October 4, 1998, (available at www.useit.com/alertbox/981004.html).
25. Noy, N. F., Sintek, M., Decker, S., Crubezy, M., Fergerson, R. W. and Musen, M. A. (2001) Creating Semantic Web Contents with Protege-2000. IEEE Intelligent Systems 16(2) pp. 60-71, 2001.
26. Oren, T., Salomon, G., Kreitman, K., and Don, A. (1990) Guides: Characterizing the Interface. In Laurel, B. cd., The Art of Human-Computer Interface Design, Reading, MA Addison-Wesley, pp. 367-381.
27. Persidis, A. (2001) The Working Group on Web Services Integration White Paper, ONT-SIG4-WG2-P1, June 20, 2001 (available at http://www.cs.vu.nl/~maksym/sig4/papers/SIG4_wp.doc).
28. Rheingold, H. (2000) The Virtual Community: Homesteading on the Electronic Frontier. Revised edition. MIT Press: Cambridge, MA.
29. Rich, E. (1985) Stereotypes and User Modeling. In User's model in Dialog Systems Kobsa, A. and W. Wahlster (eds.). Spring-Verlag.
30. Shneiderman, B. (1994) Dynamic queries for visual information seeking, IEEE Software 11, 6 pp. 70-77.
31. Storey, M.-A. D., Fracchia, F.D. and Müller, H. A. (1999) Customizing A Fisheye View Algorithm to Preserve the Mental Map. Journal of Visual Languages and Computing, 10, pp. 245-267, 1999.
32. Storey, M.-A. D., Musen, M. A., Silva, J., Best, C., Ernst, N., Fergerson, R. W. and Noy, F. (2001) Jambalaya: Interactive visualization to enhance ontology authoring and knowledge acquisition in Protégé Workshop on Interactive Tools for Knowledge Capture, held in conjunction with KCAP'01, The First International Conference on Knowledge Capture. Victoria, British Columbia, Canada, October 21-23, 2001.
33. W3C. (1999) Resource Description Framework, (RDF) Model and Syntax Specification, W3C Recommendation 22 February 1999 (available at http://www.w3.org/TR/REC-rdf-syntax/).
34. W3C (2000) Extensible Markup Language (XML) 1.0 (Second Edition), October, 2000, (available at http://www.w3.org/TR/2000/REC-xml-20001006).

Acquiring Configuration Knowledge Bases in the Semantic Web Using UML

Alexander Felfernig[1], Gerhard Friedrich[1], Dietmar Jannach[1], Markus Stumptner[2], and Markus Zanker[1]

[1] Institut für Wirtschaftsinformatik und Anwendungssysteme, Produktionsinformatik,
Universitätsstrasse 65-67, A-9020 Klagenfurt, Austria,
{felfernig,friedrich,jannach,zanker}@ifit.uni-klu.ac.at
[2] University of South Australia, Advanced Computing Research Centre,
5095 Mawson Lakes (Adelaide), SA, Australia
mst@cs.unisa.edu.au.

Abstract. The Semantic Web will provide the conceptual infrastructure to allow new forms of business application integration. This paper outlines our approach for integrating Web-based sales systems for highly complex customizable products and services (configuration systems) making use of descriptive representation formalisms of the Semantic Web. The evolving trend towards highly specialized solution providers cooperatively offering configurable products and services to their customers requires the extension of current (standalone) configuration technology with capabilities of knowledge sharing and distributed configuration problem solving. On the one hand, a standardized representation language is needed in order to tackle the challenges imposed by heterogeneous representation formalisms of state-of-the-art configuration environments (e.g. description logic or predicate logic based configurators), on the other hand it is important to integrate the development and maintenance of configuration systems into industrial software development processes. We show how to support both goals by demonstrating the applicability of the Unified Modeling Language (UML) for configuration knowledge acquisition and by providing a set of rules for transforming UML models into configuration knowledge bases specified by languages such as OIL or DAML+OIL which represent the foundation for potential future description standards for Web services.

1 Introduction

There is an increasing demand for applications providing solutions for configuration tasks in various domains (e.g. telecommunications industry, automotive industry, or financial services) resulting in a set of corresponding configurator implementations (e.g. [2, 11, 13, 22]). Informally, configuration can be seen as a special kind of design activity [16], where the configured product is built from a predefined set of component types and attributes, which are composed conforming to a set of corresponding constraints.

Triggered by the trend towards highly specialized solution providers cooperatively offering configurable products and services, joint configuration by a set of business partners is becoming a key application of knowledge-based configuration systems. The

A. Gómez-Pérez and V.R. Benjamins (Eds.): EKAW 2002, LNAI 2473, pp. 352–357, 2002.

configuration of virtual private networks (VPNs) [9] or the configuration of enterprise network solutions are application examples for distributed configuration processes. In the EC-funded research project CAWICOMS[1] the paradigm of Web services is adopted to accomplish this form of business application integration [8]. In order to realize a dynamic matchmaking between service requestors and service providers, configuration services are represented as Web services describing the capabilities of potentially cooperating configuration systems. Currently developed declarative languages (e.g., DAML-S[2]) for semantically describing the capabilities of a Web-service are based on DAML+OIL, that is why we show how the concepts needed for describing configuration knowledge can be represented using semantic markup languages such as OIL [10] or DAML+OIL [20].

The Unified Modeling Language (UML) [15] is a widely adopted modeling language in industrial software development. Based on our experience in building configuration knowledge bases using UML [5], we show how to effectively support the construction of Semantic Web configuration knowledge bases using UML as a knowledge acquisition frontend. The approach presented in this paper enhances the application of Software Engineering techniques to knowledge-based systems by providing a UML-based knowledge acquisition frontend for configuration systems. Vice versa, reasoning support for Semantic Web ontology languages can be exploited for checking the consistency of UML configuration models. The resulting configuration knowledge bases enable knowledge interchange between heterogenous configuration environments as well as distributed configuration problem solving in different supply chain settings.

The paper is organized as follows. In Section 2 we discuss the representative concepts for configuration knowledge bases and in Section 3 we give a description logic based definition of a configuration task as basis for the translation of UML configuration models into a corresponding OIL-based representation.

2   Configuration Knowledge Representation

Knowledge-based configuration systems build on a configuration model, that represents the generic product structure. The representations concepts for modeling generic product structures are defined in the de facto standard configuration ontologies [5, 18] that are based on Ontolingua [12] and represent a synthesis of resource-based [13], function-based, connection-based [14], and structure-based [19] configuration approaches:

- **Component types.** Component types represent the basic building blocks a final product can be built of. They are characterized by attributes.
- **Generalization hierarchies.** Component types with a similar structure are arranged in generalization hierarchies.
- **Part-whole relationships.** Part-whole relationships between component types state the range of subparts an aggregate consists of.

---

[1] CAWICOMS is the acronym for Customer-Adaptive Web Interface for the Configuration of products and services with Multiple Suppliers (EC-funded project IST-1999-10688).

[2] See http://www.daml.org/services for reference.

- **Compatibilities and requirements.** Some types of components must not be used together within the same configuration, i.e. they are incompatible. In other cases, the existence of one component of a specific type requires the existence of another specific component within the configuration.
- **Resource constraints.** Parts of a configuration task can be seen as a resource balancing task, where some of the component types produce some resources and others are consumers.
- **Port connections.** In some cases the product topology - i.e., exactly how the components are interconnected - is of interest in the final configuration. The concept of a *port* is used for this purpose.
- **Constraints.** The basic structure of the product is modeled using the aforementioned modeling concepts. In addition, constraints which are related to technical restrictions and economic factors can be expressed on the product model.

In the Knowledge Acquisition Workbench of the CAWICOMS Project graphical representation concepts of the Unified Modeling Language (UML) [15] are used to allow the domain expert acquiring and maintaining the configuration models. In order to allow the refinement of the basic meta-model with domain-specific modeling concepts, UML provides the concept of *profiles* - the configuration domain specific modeling concepts are the constituting elements of a UML *configuration profile* which can be used for building configuration models.

UML profiles can be compared with ontologies discussed in the AI literature. UML *stereotypes* are used to further classify UML meta-model elements (e.g. classes, associations, dependencies). Stereotypes are the basic means to define domain-specific modeling concepts for profiles (e.g. for the configuration profile).

3   Translation of UML Configuration Models into OIL

In the following we give a description logic based definition of a configuration task [6] and present some example rules to automatically translate UML configuration models into a corresponding OIL representation. The definition is based on a schema S=($\mathcal{CN}$, $\mathcal{RN}$, $\mathcal{IN}$) of disjoint sets of names for concepts, roles, and individuals [3], where $\mathcal{RN}$ is a disjunctive union of roles and features.

Definition 1 (Configuration task): In general we assume a configuration task is described by a triple $(DD, SRS, CLANG)$. DD represents the domain description of the configurable product and SRS specifies the particular system requirements defining an individual configuration task instance. $CLANG$ comprises a set of concepts $C_{Config} \subseteq \mathcal{CN}$ and a set of roles $R_{Config} \subseteq \mathcal{RN}$ which serve as a configuration language for the description of actual configurations. A configuration knowledge base KB = $DD \cup SRS$ is constituted of sentences in a description language. □

In addition we require that roles in $CLANG$ are defined over the domains given in C_{Config}, i.e. $range(R_i) = CDom$ and $dom(R_i) = CDom$ must hold for each role $R_i \in R_{Config}$, where $CDom \doteq \bigsqcup_{C_i \in C_{config}} C_i$. We impose this restriction in order to assure that a configuration result only contains individuals and relations with corresponding definitions in C_{Config} and R_{Config}.

Based on this definition, a corresponding configuration result (solution) is defined as follows [6], where the semantics of description terms are given using an interpretation $\mathcal{I} = \langle \Delta^{\mathcal{I}}, (\cdot)^{\mathcal{I}} \rangle$, where $\Delta^{\mathcal{I}}$ is a domain of values and $(\cdot)^{\mathcal{I}}$ is a mapping from concept descriptions to subsets of $\Delta^{\mathcal{I}}$ and from role descriptions to sets of 2-tuples over $\Delta^{\mathcal{I}}$.

Definition 2 (Valid configuration): Let $\mathcal{I} = \langle \Delta^{\mathcal{I}}, (\cdot)^{\mathcal{I}} \rangle$ be a model of a configuration knowledge base KB, $CLANG = C_{config} \cup R_{config}$ a configuration language, and $CONF = COMPS \cup ROLES$ a description of a configuration. $COMPS$ is a set of tuples $\langle C_i, INDIVS_{C_i} \rangle$ for every $C_i \in C_{config}$, where $INDIVS_{C_i} = \{ci_1, \ldots, ci_{n_i}\} = C_i^{\mathcal{I}}$ is the set of individuals of concept C_i. These individuals identify components in an actual configuration. $ROLES$ is a set of tuples $\langle R_j, TUPLES_{R_j} \rangle$ for every $R_j \in R_{config}$ where $TUPLES_{R_j} = \{\langle rj_1, sj_1 \rangle, \ldots, \langle rj_{m_j}, sj_{m_j} \rangle\} = R_j^{\mathcal{I}}$ is the set of tuples of role R_j defining the relation of components in an actual configuration.□

The automatic derivation of an OIL-based configuration knowledge base requires a clear definition of the semantics of the used UML modeling concepts. The semantics of UML configuration models are given by a set of corresponding translation rules. The resulting knowledge base restricts the set of possible configurations, i.e. enumerates the possible instance models which strictly correspond to the UML class diagram defining the product structure. For obvious space restrictions only the translation rule for part-whole relationships is shown:

Part-whole relationships are important model properties in the configuration domain. In [1, 17, 18] it is pointed out that part-whole relationships have quite variable semantics depending on the regarded application domain. In most configuration environments, a part-whole relationship is described by the two basic roles *partof* and *haspart*. In the following these two basic roles are introduced. Multiplicities used to describe a part-whole relationship denote how many parts the aggregate can consist of and between how many aggregates a part can be shared if the aggregation is non-composite.

Rule (Part-whole relationships): Let w and p be component types in a graphical UML representation, where p is a part of w and ub_p is the upper bound, lb_p the lower bound of the multiplicity of the part, and ub_w is the upper bound, lb_w the lower bound of the multiplicity of the whole. Furthermore let *w-of-p* and *p-of-w* denote the names of the roles of the part-whole relationship between w and p, where *w-of-p* denotes the role connecting the part with the whole and *p-of-w* denotes the role connecting the whole with the part, i.e., *p-of-w* $\sqsubseteq$ *haspart*, *w-of-p* $\sqsubseteq$ $Partof_{mode}$, where $Partof_{mode} \in \{partof_{composite}, partof_{shared}\}$. The roles $partof_{composite}$ and $partof_{shared}$ are assumed to be disjoint, where $partof_{composite} \sqsubseteq partof$ and $partof_{shared} \sqsubseteq partof$. DD is extended with

    class-def p.

    class-def w.

    slot-def *w-of-p* subslot-of $Partof_{mode}$ inverse *p-of-w* domain p range w.

slot-def p-of-w subslot-of *haspart* inverse w-of-p domain w range p.
p: slot-constraint w-of-p min-cardinality lb_w w.
p: slot-constraint w-of-p max-cardinality ub_w w.
w: slot-constraint p-of-w min-cardinality lb_p p.
w: slot-constraint p-of-w max-cardinality ub_p p. □

Remark: The semantics of *shared* part-whole relationships ($partof_{shared} \sqsubseteq partof$) are defined by simply restricting the upper bound and the lower bound of the corresponding roles. In addition the following restriction must hold for each concept using partof relationships:

$(((slot\text{-}constraint\, partof_{composite}\; cardinality\; 1\; top)\; and\; (slot\text{-}constraint\, partof_{shared}\; cardinality\; 0\; top))\; or\; (slot\text{-}constraint\, partof_{composite}\; cardinality\; 0\; top)).$

This restriction denotes the fact that a component which is connected to a whole via composite relationship must not be connected to any other component. □

For further details, an example and the complete set of translation rules see the long version of this paper [7].

4   Conclusions

The application of the modeling concepts presented in this paper has its limits when building configuration knowledge bases - in some domains there exist complex constraints that do not have an intuitive graphical representation. Happily, (with some minor restrictions discussed in [6]) we are able to represent such constraints using languages such as OIL or DAML+OIL. UML itself has an integrated constraint language (Object Constraint Language - OCL [21]) which allows the formulation of constraints on object structures. The translation of OCL constraints into representations of Semantic Web ontology languages is the subject of future work, a translation into a predicate logic based representation of a configuration problem has already been discussed in [4]. The current version of our prototype workbench supports the generation of OIL-based configuration knowledge bases from UML models which are built using the modeling concepts presented in this paper, i.e. concepts for designing the product structure and concepts for defining basic constraints (e.g. *requires*) on the product structure.

References

[1] A. Artale, E. Franconi, N. Guarino, and L. Pazzi. Part-Whole Relations in Object-Centered Systems: An Overview. *Data & Knowledge Engineering*, 20(3):347–383, 1996.

[2] V.E. Barker, D.E. O'Connor, J.D. Bachant, and E. Soloway. Expert systems for configuration at Digital: XCON and beyond. *Communications of the ACM*, 32(3):298–318, 1989.

[3] A. Borgida. On the relative expressive power of description logics and predicate calculus. *Artificial Intelligence*, 82:353–367, 1996.

[4] A. Felfernig, G. Friedrich, and D. Jannach. Generating product configuration knowledge bases from precise domain extended UML models. In *Proceedings of the 12th International Conference on Software Engineering and Knowledge Engineering (SEKE'2000)*, pages 284–293, Chicago, USA, 2000.

[5] A. Felfernig, G. Friedrich, and D. Jannach. UML as domain specific language for the construction of knowledge-based configuration systems. *International Journal of Software Engineering and Knowledge Engineering (IJSEKE)*, 10(4):449–469, 2000.

[6] A. Felfernig, G. Friedrich, D. Jannach, M. Stumptner, and M. Zanker. A Joint Foundation for Configuration in the Semantic Web. *Proceedings of the Workshop on Configuration (ECAI'2002)*, 2001.

[7] A. Felfernig, G. Friedrich, D. Jannach, M. Stumptner, and M. Zanker. Transforming UML domain descriptions into Configuration Knowledge Bases for the Semantic Web. Lyon, France, 2002.

[8] A. Felfernig, G. Friedrich, D. Jannach, and M. Zanker. Semantic Configuration Web Services in the CAWICOMS Project. Sardinia, Italy, 2002.

[9] A. Felfernig, G. Friedrich, D. Jannach, and M. Zanker. Web-based Configuration of Virtual Private Networks with Multiple Suppliers. Cambridge, UK, 2002. Kluwer Academic Publisher.

[10] D. Fensel, F. vanHarmelen, I. Horrocks, D. McGuinness, and P.F. Patel-Schneider. OIL: An Ontology Infrastructure for the Semantic Web. *IEEE Intelligent Systems*, 16(2):38–45, 2001.

[11] G. Fleischanderl, G. Friedrich, A. Haselböck, H. Schreiner, and M. Stumptner. Configuring Large Systems Using Generative Constraint Satisfaction. *IEEE Intelligent Systems*, 13(4):59–68, 1998.

[12] T. Gruber. Ontolingua: A mechanism to support portable ontologies. *Technical Report KSL 91-66*, 1992.

[13] E.W. Jüngst M. Heinrich. A resource-based paradigm for the configuring of technical systems from modular components. In *Proceedings of the 7th IEEE Conference on AI applications (CAIA)*, pages 257–264, Miami, FL, USA, 1991.

[14] S. Mittal and F. Frayman. Towards a Generic Model of Configuration Tasks. In *Proceedings 11th International Joint Conf. on Artificial Intelligence*, pages 1395–1401, Detroit, MI, 1989.

[15] J. Rumbaugh, I. Jacobson, and G. Booch. *The Unified Modeling Language Reference Manual*. Addison-Wesley, 1998.

[16] D. Sabin and R. Weigel. Product Configuration Frameworks - A Survey. In B. Faltings and E. Freuder, editors, *IEEE Intelligent Systems, Special Issue on Configuration*, volume 13, pages 50–58. IEEE, 1998.

[17] U. Sattler. Description Logics for the Representation of Aggregated Objects. In *Proceedings of the 14th European Conference on Artificial Intelligence (ECAI 2000)*, pages 239–243, Berlin, Germany, 2000.

[18] T. Soininen, J. Tiihonen, T. Männistö, and R. Sulonen. Towards a General Ontology of Configuration. *AI Engineering Design Analysis and Manufacturing Journal, Special Issue: Configuration Design*, 12(4):357–372, 1998.

[19] M. Stumptner. An overview of knowledge-based configuration. *AI Communications*, 10(2), June, 1997.

[20] F. vanHarmelen, P.F. Patel-Schneider, and I. Horrocks. A Model-Theoretic Semantics for DAML+OIL. *www.daml.org*, March 2001.

[21] J. Warmer and A. Kleppe. *The Object Constraint Language - Precise Modeling with UML*. Addison Wesley Object Technology Series, 1999.

[22] J.R. Wright, E. Weixelbaum, G.T. Vesonder, K.E. Brown, S.R. Palmer, J.I. Berman, and H.H. Moore. A Knowledge-Based Configurator that supports Sales, Engineering, and Manufacturing at AT&T Network Systems. *AI Magazine*, 14(3):69–80, 1993.

S-CREAM — Semi-automatic CREAtion of Metadata

Siegfried Handschuh[1], Steffen Staab[1], and Fabio Ciravegna[2]

[1] AIFB, University of Karlsruhe
{sha,sst}@aifb.uni-karlsruhe.de,
http://www.aifb.uni-karlsruhe.de/WBS
[2] Department of Computer Science , University of Sheffield,
F.Ciravegna@dcs.shef.ac.uk,
http://www.dcs.shef.ac.uk/~fabio

Abstract. Richly interlinked, machine-understandable data constitute the basis for the Semantic Web. We provide a framework, S-CREAM, that allows for creation of metadata and is trainable for a specific domain. Annotating web documents is one of the major techniques for creating metadata on the web. The implementation of S-CREAM, OntoMat-Annotizer supports now the semi-automatic annotation of web pages. This semi-automatic annotation is based on the information extraction component Amilcare. OntoMat-Annotizer extract with the help of Amilcare knowledge structure from web pages through the use of knowledge extraction rules. These rules are the result of a learning-cycle based on already annotated pages.

1 Introduction

The Semantic Web builds on metadata describing the contents of Web pages. In particular, the Semantic Web requires relational metadata, i.e. metadata that describe how resource descriptions instantiate class definitions and how they are semantically interlinked by properties. To support the construction of relational metadata, we have provided an annotation [14] and authoring [15] framework (CREAM — manually CREAting Metadata) and a tool (OntoMat-Annotizer) that implements this framework. Nevertheless, providing plenty of relational metadata by annotation, i.e. conceptual mark-up of text passages, remained a laborious task.

Though there existed the high-level idea that wrappers and information extraction components could be used to facilitate the work [8, 14], a full-fledged integration that dealt with all the conceptual difficulties was still lacking. Therefore, we have developed S-CREAM (Semi-automatic CREAtion of Metadata), an annotation framework that integrates a learnable information extraction component (viz. Amilcare [1]).

Amilcare is a system that learns information extraction rules from manually marked-up input. S-CREAM aligns conceptual markup, which defines relational metadata, (such as provided through OntoMat-Annotizer) with semantic and indicative tagging (such as produced by Amilcare).

A. Gómez-Pérez and V.R. Benjamins (Eds.): EKAW 2002, LNAI 2473, pp. 358–372, 2002.
© Springer-Verlag Berlin Heidelberg 2002

There two major type of problems that we had to solve for this purpose:

1. When comparing the desired relational metadata from manual markup and the semantic tagging provided by information extraction systems, one recognizes that the output of this type of systems is underspecified for the purpose of the Semantic Web. In particular, the nesting of relationships between different types of concept instances is undefined and, hence, more comprehensive graph structures may not be produced (further elaboration in Section 4). In order to overcome this problem, we introduce a new processing component, viz. a lightweight module for discourse representation (Section 5).
2. Semantic tags do not correspond one-to-one to the conceptual description (Section 5 and 6).
   - Semantic tags may have to be turned into various conceptual markup, e.g., as concept instances, attribute instances, or relationship instances.
   - For successful learning, Amilcare sometimes needs further indicative tags (e.g., syntactic tags) that do not correspond to any entity in a given ontology, but that may only be exploited within the learning cycle.

In the remainder of the paper, we will first describe the existing frameworks, viz. CREAM (Section 2) and Amilcare (3). Second, we will focus on the integration problems (Section 4–5). Third, we will describe a usage scenario (Section 6). Eventually, we will discuss related works and conclude.

2 CREAM/OntoMat-Annotizer

CREAM is an annotation and authoring framework suited for the easy and comfortable creation of relational metadata. OntoMat-Annotizer is its concrete implementation. Before we sketch some of the capabilities of CREAM/OntoMat-Annotizer, we first describe its assumptions on its output representation and some terminology we use subsequently.

We elaborate the terminology here because many of the terms that are used with regard to metadata creation tools carry several, ambiguous connotations that imply conceptually important differences:

- **Ontology**: An ontology is a formal, explicit specification of a shared conceptualization of a domain of interest [13]. In our case it is constituted by statements expressing definitions of DAML+OIL classes and properties [11].
- **Annotations**: An annotation in our context is a set of instantiations attached to an HTML document. We distinguish (i) instantiations of DAML+ OIL classes, (ii) instantiated properties from one class instance to a datatype instance — henceforth called attribute instance (of the class instance), and (iii) instantiated properties from one class instance to another class instance — henceforth called relationship instance.

Class instances have unique URIs, e.g. like 'urn:rdf:936694d5ca907974-ea16565de20c997a-0'.[1] They frequently come with attribute instances, such as a human-readable label like 'Dobbertin'.

- **Metadata**: Metadata are data about data. In our context the annotations are metadata about the HTML documents.
- **Relational Metadata**: We use the term relational metadata to denote the annotations that contain relationship instances.

  Often, the term "annotation" is used to mean something like "private or shared note", "comment" or "Dublin Core metadata". This alternative meaning of annotation may be emulated in our approach by modelling these notes with attribute instances. For instance, a comment note "I like this paper" would be related to the URL of the paper via an attribute instance 'has-Comment'.

  In contrast, relational metadata also contain statements like: The hotel "Zwei Linden" is located in the city "Dobbertin"., *i.e.* relational metadata contain relationships between class instances rather than only textual notes.

Figure 1 illustrates our use of the terms "ontology", "annotation" and "relational metadata". It depicts some part of a tourism ontology.[2] Furthermore it shows the homepage of the Hotel "Zwei Linden"(http://www.all-in-all.de/english/1142.htm) annotated in RDF. For the hotel there is a instances denoted by corresponding URI (urn:rdf:947794d5ca907974ea16565de21c998a-0). In addition, there is a relationship instance between the hotel and the city (Table 1(a))).

3   Amilcare

Amilcare is a tool for adaptive Information Extraction from text (IE) designed for supporting active annotation of documents for Knowledge Management (KM). It performs IE by enriching texts with XML annotations, i.e. the system marks the extracted information with XML annotations. The only knowledge required for porting Amilcare to new applications or domains is the ability of manually annotating the information to be extracted in a training corpus. No knowledge of Human Language technology is necessary. Adaptation starts with the definition of a tagset for annotation. Then users have to manually annotate a corpus for training the learner. As will be later explained in detail, OntoMat-Annotizer may be also used as the annotation interface to annotate texts in a user friendly manner. OntoMat-Annotizer provides user annotations as XML tags to train the learner. Amilcare's learner induces rules that are able to reproduce the text annotation.

Amilcare can work in two modes: **training**, used to adapt to a new application, and **extraction**, used to actually annotate texts.

---

[1] In the OntoMat-Annotizer implementation we create the URIs with the createUniqueResource method of the RDF-API

[2] currently only available in German at
http://ontobroker.semanticweb.org/ontos/compontos/tourism_I1.daml

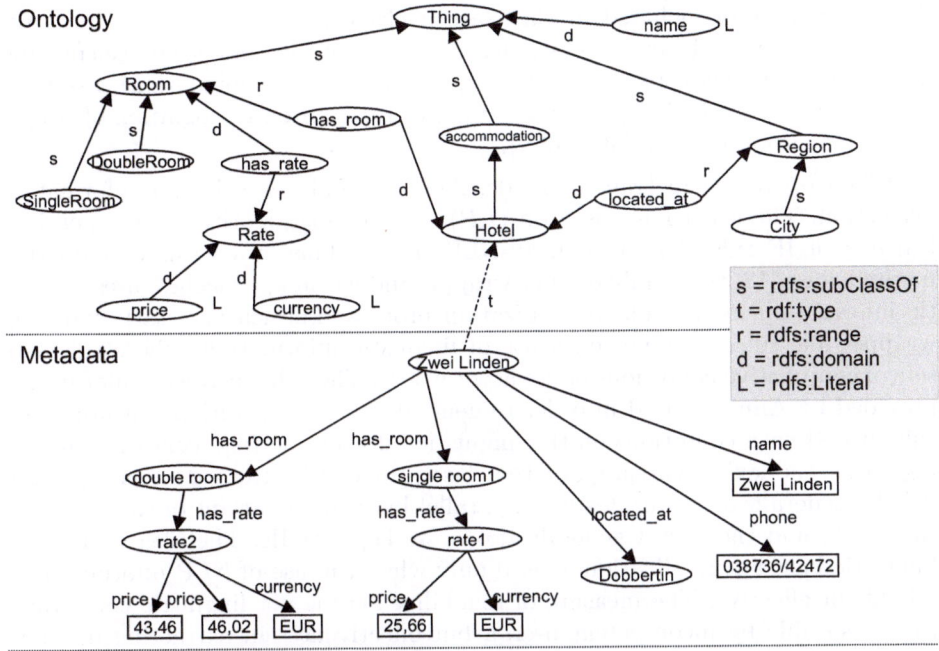

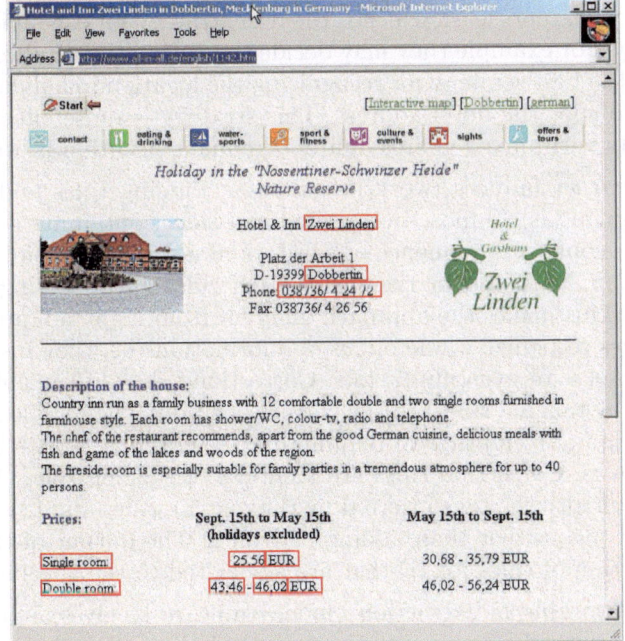

Fig. 1. Annotation example

In both modes, Amilcare first of all preprocesses texts using Annie, the shallow IE system included in the Gate package ([21], www.gate.ac.uk). Annie performs text tokenization (segmenting texts into words), sentence splitting (identifying sentences) part of speech tagging (lexical disambiguation), gazetteer lookup (dictionary lookup) and named entity recognition (recognition of people and organization names, dates, etc.).

When operating in training mode, Amilcare induces rules for information extraction. The learner is based on $(LP)^2$, a covering algorithm for supervised learning of IE rules based on Lazy-NLP [1] [3]. This is a wrapper induction methodology [18] that, unlike other wrapper induction approaches, uses linguistic information in the rule generalization process. The learner starts inducing wrapper-like rules that make no use of linguistic information, where rules are sets of conjunctive conditions on adjacent words. Then the linguistic information provided by Annie is used in order to generalize rules: conditions on words are substituted with conditions on the linguistic information (e.g. condition matching either the lexical category, or the class provided by the gazetteer, etc. [3]). All the generalizations are tested in parallel by using a variant of the AQ algorithm [22] and the best k generalizations are kept for IE. The idea is that the linguistic-based generalization is used only when the use of NLP information is reliable or effective. The measure of reliability here is not linguistic correctness (immeasurable by incompetent users), but effectiveness in extracting information using linguistic information as opposed to using shallower approaches. Lazy NLP-based learners learn which is the best strategy for each information/context separately. For example they may decide that using the result of a part of speech tagger is the best strategy for recognizing the location in holiday advertisements, but not to spot the hotel address. This strategy is quite effective for analyzing documents with mixed genres, quite a common situation in web documents [2].

The learner induces two types of rules: tagging rules and correction rules. A tagging rule is composed of a left hand side, containing a pattern of conditions on a connected sequence of words, and a right hand side that is an action inserting an XML tag in the texts. Each rule inserts a single XML tag, e.g. <hotel>. This makes the approach different from many adaptive IE algorithms, whose rules recognize whole pieces of information (i.e. they insert both <hotel> and </hotel>, or even multi slots. Correction rules shift misplaced annotations (inserted by tagging rules) to the correct position. They are learnt from the mistakes made in attempting to re-annotate the training corpus using the induced tagging rules. Correction rules are identical to tagging rules, but (1) their patterns match also the tags inserted by the tagging rules and (2) their actions shift misplaced tags rather than adding new ones. The output of the training phase is a collection of rules for IE that are associated to the specific scenario.

When working in extraction mode, Amilcare receives as input a (collection of) text(s) with the associated scenario (including the rules induced during the training phase). It preprocesses the text(s) by using Annie and then it applies its rules and returns the original text with the added annotations (Table 1(b)). The Gate annotation schema is used for annotation [21].

Amilcare is designed to accommodate the needs of different user types. While naive users can build new applications without delving into the complexity of Human Language Technology, IE experts are provided with a number of facilities for tuning the final application. Induced rules can be inspected, monitored and edited to obtain some additional accuracy, if needed. The interface also allows balancing precision (P) and recall (R). The system is run on an annotated unseen corpus and users are presented with statistics on accuracy, together with details on correct matches and mistakes (using the MUCscorer [7] and an internal tool). Retuning the P&R balance does not generally require major retraining. Facilities for inspecting the effect of different P&R balances are provided. Although the current interface for balancing P&R is designed for IE experts, we have plans for enabling also naive users [4].

4   Synthesizing S-CREAM

In order to synthesize S-CREAM out of the existing frameworks CREAM and Amilcare, we consider their core processes in terms of input and output, as well as the process of the yet undefined S-CREAM. Figure 2 surveys the three processes.

The first process is indicated by a circled M. It is manual annotation and authoring of metadata, which turns a document into relational metadata that corresponds to the given ontology (as sketched in Section 2 and described in detail in [15]) For instance, an annotator may use OntoMat-Annotizer to describe that on the homepage of hotel "Zwei Linden" (cf. Figure 1) the relationships listed in Table 1(a) show up.

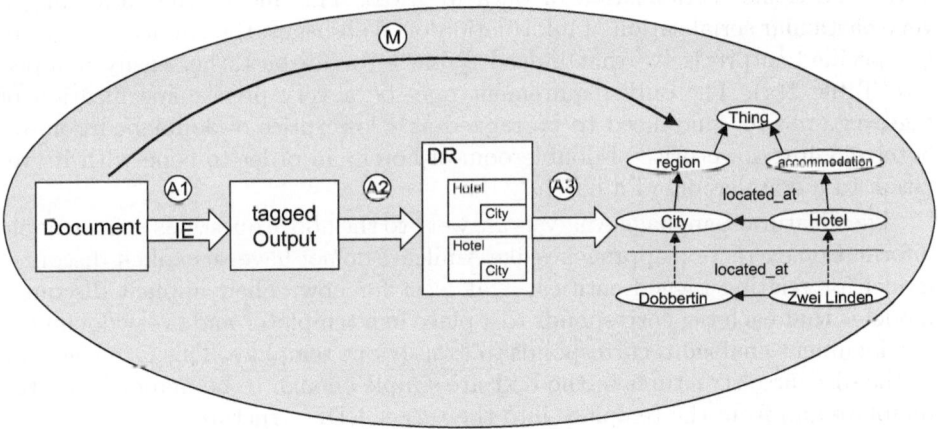

Fig. 2. Two Ways to the Target: Manual and Automatic Annotation

The second process is indicated by a circled A1. It is information extraction, e.g. provided by Amilcare [1], which digests a document and produces either a XML tagged document or a list of XML tagged text snippets (cf. Table 1(b)).

364   Siegfried Handschuh, Steffen Staab, and Fabio Ciravegna

Table 1. Comparison of Output: Manual OntoMat-Annotizer versus Amilcare

Zwei Linden INSTOF Hotel	`<hotel>Zwei Linden</hotel>`
Zwei Linden is LOCATED_AT Dobbertin	
Dobbertin INSTOF City	`<city>Dobbertin</city>`
Zwei Linden HAS_ROOM single_room_1	
single_room_1 INSTOF Single_Room	`<singleroom>Single room</singleroom>`
single_room_1 HAS_RATE rate2	
rate2 INSTOF Rate	
rate2PRICE 25,66	`<price>25,66</price>`
rate2CURRENCY EUR	`<currency>EUR</currency>`
Zwei Linden HAS_ROOM double_room_3	
double_room_3 INSTOF Double_Room	`<doubleroom>Double room</doubleroom>`
double_room_3 HAS_RATE rate4	
rate4 INSTOF Rate	
rate4PRICE 43,46	`<lowerprice>43,46</lowerprice>`
rate4PRICE 46,02	`<upperprice>46,02</upperprice>`
rate4CURRENCY EUR	`<currency>EUR</currency>`
...	...
(a) OntoMat-Annotizer	(b) Amilcare

The obvious questions that come up at this point are: Is the result of Table 1(b) equivalent to the one in Table 1(a)? How can Table 1(b) be turned into the result of Table 1(a)? The latter is a requirement for the Semantic Web.

The "Semantic Web answer" to this is: The difference between Table 1(a) and Table 1(b) is analogous to the difference between an RDF structure and a very particular serialization of data in XML. This means that assuming a very particular serialization of information on Web pages, the Amilcare tags can be specified so precisely[3] that indeed Table 1(b) can be rather easily mapped into Table 1(a). The only requirement may be a very precise specification of tags, e.g. "43,46" may need to be tagged as <lowerprice-of-doublebedroom-of-hotel>43,46</lowerprice-of-doubleroom-of-hotel> in order to cope with its relation to a doubleroom of a hotel.

The "Natural Language Analysis answer" to the above questions is: Learnable information extraction approaches like Amilcare do not have an explicit discourse model for relating tagged entities — at least for now. Their implicit discourse model is that each tag corresponds to a place in a template[4] and every document (or document analogon) corresponds to exactly one template. This is fine as long as the discourse structures in the text are simple enough to be mapped into the template and from the template into the target RDF structure.

In practice, however, the assumption that the underlying graph structures/ discourse structures are quite similar, often does not hold. Then the direct map-

---

[3] We abstract here from the problem of correctly tagging a piece of text.
[4] A template is like a single tuple in an unnormalized relational database table, where all or several entries may have null values.

ping from XML tagged output to target RDF structure becomes awkward and difficult to do.

The third process given in Figure 2 is indicated by the composition of A1, A2 and A3. It bridges from the tagged output of the information extraction system to the target graph structures via an explicit discourse representation. Our discourse representation is based on a very lightweight version of Centering [12, 23] and explained in the next section.

5   Discourse Representation (DR)

The principal task of discourse representation is to describe coherence between different sentences. The core idea is that during the interpretation of a text (or, more general, a document), there is always a logical description (e.g., a RDF(S) graph) of the content that has been read so far. The current sentence updates this logical description by:

1. **Introducing new discourse referents**: I.e. introducing new entities. E.g., finding the term 'Hotel & Inn "Zwei Linden" '(cf. Figure 1) to denote a new object .
2. **Resolving anaphora**: I.e. describing denotational equivalence between different entities in the text. E.g. 'Hotel & Inn "Zwei Linden" ' and 'Country inn' refers to the same object.
3. **Establishing new logical relationships**: I.e. relating the two objects referred to by 'Hotel & Inn "Zwei Linden" ' and 'Dobbertin' via LOCATEDAT.

The problem with information extraction output is that it is not clear what constitutes a new discourse entity. Though information extraction may provide some typing (e.g. <city>Dobbertin</city>), it does not describe whether this constitutes an attribute value (of another entity) or an entity of its own. Neither do information extraction systems like Amilcare treat coherence between different pieces of tagged text.

Grosz & Sidner [12] devised *centering* as a theory of text structures that separate text into segments that are coherent to each other. The principal idea of the centering model is to express fixed constraints as well as "soft" rules which guide the reference resolution process. The fixed constraints denote what objects are available at all for resolving anaphora and establishing new logical inter-sentential relationships, while soft rules give a preference ordering to these possible antecedents. The main data structure of the centering model is a list of *forward-looking centers*, $C_f(U_k)$ for each utterance U_k. The forward-looking centers $C_f(U_k)$ constitutes a ranked list of what is available and what is preferred for *resolving anaphora* and for *establishing new logical relationships* with previous sentences.

The centering model allows for relating a given entity in utterance U_k to one of the forward-looking centers, $C_f(U_{k-1})$. For instance, when reading "The chef of the restaurant" in Figure 1 the centering model allows relationships with "Country inn", but not with "Dobbertin".

The drawback of the centering model is that, first, it has only been devised for full text and not for semi-structured text such as appears in Figure 1 and, second, it often needs more syntactic information than shallow information extraction can provide.

Therefore, we use only an *extremely lightweight*, "degraded" version of *centering*, where we formulate the rules on an *ad hoc* basis as needed by the annotation task. The underlying ideas of the degrading are that S-CREAM is intended to work in restricted, though adaptable, domains. It is not even necessary to have a complete model, because we analyze only a very small part of the text. For instance, we analyze only the part about hotels with rooms, prices, addresses and hotel facilities. Note that thereby, hotel facilities are found in full texts rather than tables and not every type of hotel facility is known beforehand.

We specify the discourse model by logical rules, the effects of which we illustrate in the following paragraphs. Thereby, we use the same inferencing mechanisms that we have already exploited for supporting annotation [15], viz. Ontobroker [5].

As our baseline model, we assume the "single template strategy", viz. only one type of tag, e.g. <hotel>, is determined to really introduce a new discourse referent. Every other pair of tag name and tag value is attached to this entity as an attribute filled by the tag value. E.g. "Zwei Linden" is recognized as an instance of Hotel, every other entity (like "Dobbertin", etc.) is attached to this instance resulting in a very shallow discourse representation by logical facts illustrated in Table 2(a).[5] This is probably the shallowest discourse representation possible at all, because it does not include ordering constraints or other soft constraints. However, it is already adequate to map some of the relations in the discourse namespace ("dr:") to relations in the target space, thus resulting in Table 2(b). However, given this restricted tag set, not every relation can be detected.

For more complex models, we may also include ordering information (e.g. simply by augmenting the discourse representation tuples given in Table 2 by numbers; this may be modelled as 4-arity predicates in F-Logic used by Ontobroker) and a set of rules that maps the discourse representation into the target structure integrating

- rules to only attach instances where they are allowed to become attached (e.g., prices are only attached where they are allowed)
- rules to attach tag values to the nearest preceding, conceptually possible entity (thus, prices for single and double room may be distinguished without further ado).
- rules to create a new complex object when two simple ones are adjacent, e.g., to create a rate when it founds adjacent number and currencies

The centering model describes preferences between competing rules. Further information that could be included is, e.g., adjacency information, etc. Thus, one

---

[5] Results have been selected to be comparable with Table 1.

Table 2. Template Strategy

Zwei Linden DR:INSTOF Hotel	Zwei Linden INSTOF Hotel
Zwei Linden DR:CITY Dobbertin	Zwei Linden is LOCATED_AT Dobbertin
	Dobbertin INSTOF City
Zwei Linden DR:SINGLE_ROOM single room	Zwei Linden HAS_ROOM single_room1
	single_room1 INSTOF Single_Room
Zwei Linden DR:PRICE 25,66	
Zwei Linden DR:CURRENCY EUR	
Zwei Linden DR:DOUBLE_ROOM double_room	Zwei Linden HAS_ROOM double_room1
	double_room1 INSTOF Double_Room
Zwei Linden DR:PRICE 43,46	
Zwei Linden DR:PRICE 46,02	
Zwei Linden DR:CURRENCY EUR	

(a) Discourse Representation	(b) Simple Target Graph Structure

may produce Table 1(a) out of the discourse representation from a numbered Table 2(a).

The strategy that we follow here is to make simple things simple and complex tasks possible. The experienced user will be able to handcraft logical rules in order to define the discourse model to his needs. The standard user, will only exploit the simple template strategy. When the resulting graph structures are simple enough to allow for the latter strategy and a simple mapping, the mapping can also be defined by directly aligning relevant concepts and relations by drag and drop, while in the general case one must write logical rules.

6   Usage Scenario

This section describe a usage scenario. The first step is the project definition. A domain ontology can be the basis for the annotation of different types of documents. Likewise a certain kind of documents can be annotated in reference to different ontologies. Therefore a project defines the combination of a domain ontology (e.g. about tourism) with a certain text type (e.g. hotel homepages). Further the user have do define which part of the ontology is relevant for the learning task, e.g. which attributes of the several concepts will be used for tagging the corpus. The mapping of the Ontology to the Amilcare tags works as follows:

- concepts: concepts are mapped by the name of the concept, e.g. the concept with the name "Hotel" results in a <hotel> tag.
- inheritance: the concepts of the ontology represents a hierarchical structure. To emulate the different levels of conceptualization OntoMat-Annotizer allows to map a concept in multiple tags, e.g. the concept "Hotel" in <company>, <accommodation>, and <hotel>.
- attributes: The mapping of attributes to tags is a tradeoff between an specific and a general naming. The specific naming ease the mapping to the

ontology concepts but at the same time it results in more complex extraction rules. These rules are less general and less robust. For example a specific naming of the attribute "phone" would result in tags like <hotel_phone>, <room_phone>, and <person_phone> in comparison to the general tag <phone>. Therefore the user have to decide for every attribute the adequate accuracy of the naming, because it influences the learning results.

After the definition of the project parameters one needs a corpus, a set of certain type of documents, e.g. hotel homepages.

If there exist already enough annotated documents in the web the user can perform a crawl with OntoMat-Annotizer and collect the necessary documents. The crawl can be limited here to documents which are annotated with the desired ontology. If necessary the ontology sub-set and the mapping to the Amilcare tags must be re-adjusted according to the existing annotations in the crawled documents. Afterwards the desired type of document must be checked still manually.

If there are no annotated documents, one can produce the necessary corpus with OntoMat-Annotizer themselves. The user have to collect and annotate documents of a certain type by the sub-set of the ontology that is chosen in the project definition phase. The document are annotated by OntoMat-Annotizer with RDF facts. These facts are linked by an XPointer description to the annotated text part. Because Amilcare needs as a corpus XML tagged files, these RDF annotations will be transformed into corresponding XML tags according to the mapping done in the project definition. Only these tags are used to train. Other Tags like HTML tags will be used as contextual information.

The learning phase is executed by Amilcare, which is embedded as a plugin into OntoMat-Annotizer. Amilcare processes each document of the corpus and generates extraction rules as described in section 3. After the training Amilcare stores the annotation rules in a certain file which belongs to the project.

Now it is possible to use the induced rules for semi-automatic annotation. Based on the rules the Amilcare plugin produces XML annotation results (cf. A1 in Figure 2). Here a mapping (A2) is done from OntoMat-Annotizer from the flat markup to the conceptual markup in order to create new RDF facts (A3). These mapping is undertaken by the discourse representation (cf. section 5).

These mapping results in several automatic generated proposals for the RDF annotation of the document. The user can interact with these annotation proposals in three different ways of automation: (i) a highlighting of the annotation candidates or (ii) interactive suggestion of each annotation or (iii) a first full automatic annotation of the document and a later refinement by the user.

highlighting mode: The user opens a document he would like to annotate in the OntoMat-Annotizer document editor. Then the highlighting mode marks all annotation candidates by a colored underline. The user can decide on his own if he uses this hint for an annotation or not.

interactive mode: This mode is for the individual document processing. The interactive suggestion is a step-by-step process. Every possible annotation candidate is suggested to the user and he can refuse, accept or change the suggestion in a dialog window.

automatic mode: The fully automatic approach is useful if there is a bunch of documents that needs to be annotated, so it can be done in batch mode. All selected documents are annotated automatically.

7   Related Work

S-CREAM can be compared along fourth dimensions: First, it is a framework for mark-up in the Semantic Web. Second, it may be considered as a particular knowledge acquisition framework vaguely similar to Protégé-2000[9]. Third, it is certainly an annotation framework, though with a different focus than ones like Annotea [17]. Fourth, it produces semantic mark-up with support of information extraction.

7.1   Knowledge Markup in the Semantic Web

We know of three major systems that intensively use knowledge markup in the Semantic Web, viz. SHOE [16], Ontobroker [5] and WebKB [20]. All three of them rely on knowledge in HTML pages. They all start with providing manual mark-up by editors. However, our experiences (cf. [8]) have shown that text-editing knowledge mark-up yields extremely poor results, viz. syntactic mistakes, improper references, and all the problems sketched in the scenario section.

The approaches from this line of research that are closest to *S-CREAM* is the *SHOE Knowledge Annotator*[6] and the WebKB annotation tool.

The SHOE Knowledge Annotator is a Java program that allows users to mark-up webpages with the SHOE ontology. The SHOE system [19] defines additional tags that can be embedded in the body of HTML pages. The SHOE Knowledge Annotator is rather a little helper (like our earlier OntoPad [10], [5]) than a full fledged annotation environment.

WebKB uses conceptual graphs for representing the semantic content of Web documents. It embeds conceptual graph statements into HTML pages. Essentially they offer a Web-based template like interface like knowledge acquisition frameworks described next.

7.2   Comparison with Knowledge Acquisition Frameworks

The S-CREAM framework allows for creating class and property instances to populate HTML pages. Thus it has a target roughly similar to the instance acquisition phase in the Protégé-2000 framework [9] (the latter needs to be distinguished from the ontology editing capabilities of Protégé). The obvious difference between S-CREAM and Protégé is that the latter does not (and has not intended

---

[6] http://www.cs.umd.edu/projects/plus/SHOE/KnowledgeAnnotator.html

to) support the particular Web setting, *viz.* managing and displaying Web pages — not to mention Web page authoring. From Protégé we have adopted the principle of a meta ontology that allows to distinguish between different ways that classes and properties are treated.

7.3   Comparison with Annotation Frameworks

There are a number of — even commercial — annotation tools like ThirdVoice[7], Yawas [6], CritLink [25] and Annotea (Amaya) [17]. These tools all share the idea of creating a kind of user comment about Web pages. The term "annotation" in these frameworks is understood as a remark to an existing document. For instance, a user of these tools might attach a note like "A really nice hotel!" to the name "Zwei Linden" on the Web page. In S-CREAM we would design a corresponding ontology that would allow to type the comment (an unlinked fact) "A really nice hotel" into an attribute instance belonging to an instance of the class comment with a unique XPointer at "Zwei Linden".

Annotea actually goes one step further. It allows to rely on an RDF schema as a kind of template that is filled by the annotator. For instance, Annotea users may use a schema for Dublin Core and fill the author-slot of a particular document with a name. This annotation, however, is again restricted to attribute instances. The user may also decide to use complex RDF descriptions instead of simple strings for filling such a template. However, no further help is provided by Amaya for syntactically correct statements with proper references.

7.4   Semantic Markup with Support from Information Extraction

The only other system we know that produce semantic markup with support from information extraction is the annotation tool cited in [24]. It uses information extraction components (Marmot, Badger and Crystal) from the University of Massachusetts at Amherst (UMass). It allows the semi-automatic population of an ontology with metadata. We assume that this approach is more laborious than to use Amilcare for information extraction, e.g. they had to define their own verbs, nouns and abbreviations in order to apply Marmot for a domain. Also, they have not dealt with relational metadata or authoring concerns so far.

8   Conclusion

CREAM is a comprehensive framework for creating annotations, relational metadata in particular — the foundation of the future Semantic Web. The new version of S-CREAM presented here supports metadata creation with the help of information extraction in addition to all the other nice features of CREAM, like comprises inference services, crawler, document management system, ontology guidance/fact browser, document editors/viewers, and a meta ontology.

---

[7] http://www.thirdvoice.com

OntoMat is the reference implementation of the S-CREAM framework. It is Java-based and provides a plugin interface for extensions for further advancements, e.g. collaborative metadata creation or integrated ontology editing and evolution. The plugin interface has already been used by third parties, e.g. for creating annotation for Microsoft Word^{TM} documents. Along similar lines, we are now investigating how different tools may be brought together, e.g. to allow for the creation of relational metadata in PDF, SVG, or SMIL with OntoMat.

References

[1] Fabio Ciravegna. Adaptive Information Extraction from Text by Rule Induction and Generalisation. In *Proceedings of the 17th International Joint Conference on Artificial Intelligence (IJCAI)e*, Seattle, Usa, August 2001.

[2] Fabio Ciravegna. Challenges in Information Extraction from Text for Knowledge Management. *IEEE Intelligent Systems and Their Applications*, 16(6):88–90, 2001.

[3] Fabio Ciravegna. (LP)^2, an Adaptive Algorithm for Information Extraction from Web-related Texts. In *Proceedings of the IJCAI-2001 Workshop on Adaptive Text Extraction and Mining held in conjunction with 17th International Joint Conference on Artificial Intelligence (IJCAI)*, Seattle, Usa, August 2001.

[4] Fabio Ciravegna and Daniela Petrelli. User Involvement in Adaptive Information Extraction: Position Paper. In *Proceedings of the IJCAI-2001 Workshop on Adaptive Text Extraction and Mining held in conjunction with 17th International Joint Conference on Artificial Intelligence (IJCAI)*, Seattle, Usa, August 2001.

[5] S. Decker, M. Erdmann, D. Fensel, and R. Studer. Ontobroker: Ontology Based Access to Distributed and Semi-Structured Information. In R. Meersman et al., editors, *Database Semantics: Semantic Issues in Multimedia Systems*, pages 351–369. Kluwer Academic Publisher, 1999.

[6] L. Denoue and L. Vignollet. An annotation tool for Web browsers and its applications to information retrieval. In *In Proceedings of RIAO2000*, Paris, April 2000. http://www.univ-savoie.fr/labos/syscom/Laurent.Denoue/riao2000.doc.

[7] Aaron Douthat. The message understanding conference scoring software user's manual. In *7th Message Understanding Conference Proceedings, MUC-7*, 1998. http://www.itl.nist.gov/iaui/894.02/related_projects/muc/.

[8] M. Erdmann, A. Maedche, H.-P. Schnurr, and Steffen Staab. From Manual to Semi-automatic Semantic Annotation: About Ontology-based Text Annotation Tools. In *P. Buitelaar & K. Hasida (eds). Proceedings of the COLING 2000 Workshop on Semantic Annotation and Intelligent Content*, Luxembourg, August 2000.

[9] H. Eriksson, R. Fergerson, Y. Shahar, and M. Musen. Automatic generation of ontology editors. In *Proceedings of the 12th Banff Knowledge Acquisition Workshop, Banff, Alberta, Canada*, 1999.

[10] D. Fensel, J. Angele, S. Decker, M. Erdmann, H.-P. Schnurr, S. Staab, R. Studer, and Andreas Witt. On2broker: Semantic-based access to information sources at the WWW. In *In Proceedings of the World Conference on the WWW and Internet (WebNet 99), Honolulu, Hawaii, USA*, 1999.

[11] Reference description of the DAML+OIL (March 2001) ontology markup language, March 2001. http://www.daml.org/2001/03/reference.html.

372   Siegfried Handschuh, Steffen Staab, and Fabio Ciravegna

[12] B. J. Grosz and C. L. Sidner. Attention, intentions, and the structure of discourse. *Computational Linguistics*, 12(3):175204, 1986.
[13] T. R. Gruber. A Translation Approach to Portable Ontology Specifications. *Knowledge Acquisition*, 6(2):199–221, 1993.
[14] S. Handschuh, S. Staab, and A. Maedche. CREAM — Creating relational metadata with a component-based, ontology driven framework. In *In Proceedings of K-Cap 2001*, Victoria, BC, Canada, October 2001.
[15] Siegfried Handschuh and Steffen Staab. Authoring and Annotation of Web Pages in CREAM. In *Proceeding of the WWW2002 - Eleventh International World Wide Web Conferenceb (to appear)*, Hawaii, USA, May 2002.
[16] J. Heflin and J. Hendler. Searching the Web with SHOE. In *Artificial Intelligence for Web Search. Papers from the AAAI Workshop. WS-00-01*, pages 35–40. AAAI Press, 2000.
[17] J. Kahan, M. Koivunen, E. Prud'Hommeaux, and R. Swick. Annotea: An Open RDF Infrastructure for Shared Web Annotations. In *Proc. of the WWW10 International Conference. Hong Kong*, 2001.
[18] Nicholas Kushmerick. Wrapper induction for information extraction. In *Proceedings of the 15th International Joint Conference on Artificial Intelligence (IJCAI)*, 1997.
[19] S. Luke, L. Spector, D. Rager, and J. Hendler. Ontology-based Web Agents. In *Proceedings of First International Conference on Autonomous Agents*, 1997.
[20] P. Martin and P. Eklund. Embedding Knowledge in Web Documents. In *Proceedings of the 8th Int. World Wide Web Conf. (WWW'8), Toronto, May 1999*, pages 1403–1419. Elsevier Science B.V., 1999.
[21] Diana Maynard, Valentin Tablan, Hamish Cunningham, Cristian Ursu, Horacio Saggion, Kalina Bontcheva, and Yorick Wilks. Architectural Elements of Language Engineering Robustness. *Journal of Natural Language Engineering – Special Issue on Robust Methods in Analysis of Natural Language Data*, 2002. forthcoming.
[22] R.S. Mickalski, I. Mozetic, J. Hong, and H. Lavrack. The multi purpose incremental learning system AQ15 and its testing application to three medical domains. In *Proceedings of the 5th National Conference on Artificial Intelligence*, Philadelphia, USA, 1986.
[23] M. Strube and U. Hahn. Functional Centering — Grounding Referential Coherence in Information Structure. *Computational Linguistics*, 25(3):309–344, 1999.
[24] M. Vargas-Vera, E. Motta, J. Domingue, S. Buckingham Shum, and M. Lanzoni. Knowledge Extraction by using an Ontology-based Annotation Tool. In *K-CAP 2001 workshop on Knowledge Markup and Semantic Annotation*, Victoria, BC, Canada, October 2001.
[25] Ka-Ping Yee. CritLink: Better Hyperlinks for the WWW, 1998. http://crit.org/~ping/ht98.html.

Tracking Changes in RDF(S) Repositories

Damyan Ognyanov, Atanas Kiryakov

OntoText Lab, Sirma AI EOOD, 38A Chr. Botev blvd, 1000 Sofia, Bulgaria
{damyan, naso}@sirma.bg

Abstract. The real-world knowledge management applications require features such as versioning and fine-grained access control. Each of them raises the issue of tracking the changes in a knowledge base. Important part of the research presented is the definition of a formal model for tracking changes in graph-based data models. It was used in the ontology middleware module developed under the On-To-Knowledge project as an extension of the Sesame RDF(S) repository. This paper is further development of the results reported in [5].

1. Introduction

The following features are considered critical for development, management, maintenance, and use of middle-size and big knowledge bases:

- Versioning (tracking changes) of knowledge bases;

- Access control (security) system;

- Meta-information for knowledge bases.

These three aspects are tightly interrelated among each other as depicted on the following scheme. The dependencies are explained in the corresponding sections.

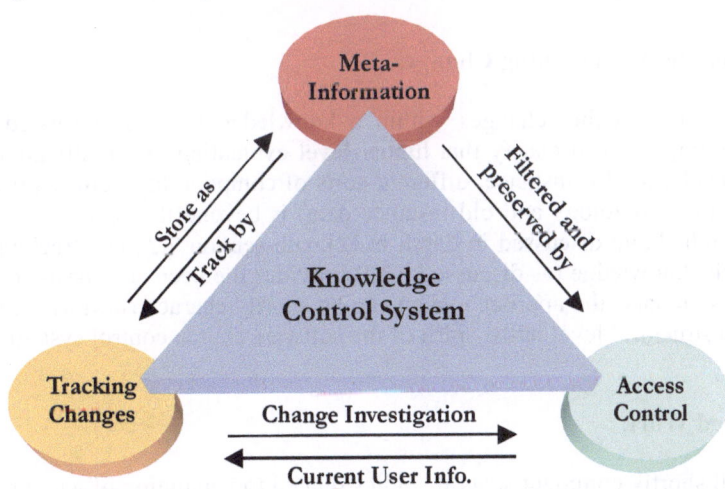

A. Gómez-Pérez and V.R. Benjamins (Eds.): EKAW 2002, LNAI 2473, pp. 373-378, 2002.
© Springer-Verlag Berlin Heidelberg 2002

The composition of the three functions above represents a Knowledge Control System (KCS) that provides the knowledge engineers with the same level of control and manageability of the knowledge in the process of its development and maintenance as the source control systems (such as CVS) provide for the software. From the perspective of the end-user applications, KCS can be seen as equivalent to the database security, change tracking and auditing systems. Our KCS is carefully designed to support these two distinct use cases.

The work presented here was carried as part of the On-To-Knowledge project. The design and implementation of the change tracking within the ontology middleware module presented here is an extension of the Sesame architecture (see [1]). Earlier stage of this research is presented in bigger details in [5] where the reader can find more about the Access control system (security), which is out of the scope of this paper.

In the rest of this introductory section we define better the scope of our research and the terminology used. Section 2 is dedicated to the model and principles for tracking changes in RDF(S) repositories. The implementation approach of is presented in Section 3. A short conclusion follows in the last section.

1.1.   Ontologies Vs. Knowledge Bases

A number of justifications in the terminology are necessary. An almost trivial but very important question is "What the KM tools support: ontologies, data, knowledge, or knowledge bases?" Due to the lack of space we are no going in to comment this basic notions here. A simple   and correct answer is "All of this". The ontology middleware module extends the Sesame RDF(S) repository that affects the management of both ontologies and instance data in a pretty much unified fashion.

For the purpose of compliance with Sesame, here the term repository is used to denote a compact body of knowledge that could be used, manipulated, and referred as a whole. Such may contain (or host) both ontological assertions and instance data.

1.2.   Versioning Vs. Tracking Changes

The problem for tracking changes within a knowledge base is addressed in this section. It is important to clarify that higher-level evaluation or classification of the updates (considering, for instance, different sorts of compatibility between two states or between a new ontology and old instance data) is beyond the scope of this work. Those are studied and discussed in depth in [2], sub-section 2.2. The tracking of the changes in the knowledge (as discussed here) provides the necessary basis for further analysis. In summary, the approach taken can be shortly characterized as "versioning of RDF on a structural level in the spirit of the software source control systems".

1.3.   Related Work

Here we will shortly comment several studies related to versioning of a complex data objects. Although some of the sources discuss similar problems there is not one addressing ontology evolution and version management in a fashion allowing granularity down to the level of statements (or similar constructs) and capturing of the interactive changes in knowledge repositories such as assertions and retractions.

Database schema evolution and the tasks related to keeping schema and data consistent to each other can be recognized as a very similar problem. A detailed and pretty formal study on this problem can be found in [3, 4] – it presents an approach allowing the different sorts of modifications of the schema to be expressed within suitable description logic.

2.   Versioning Model for RDF(S) Repositories

A model for tracking of changes, versioning, and meta-information for RDF(S) repositories is proposed, i.e. (i) the knowledge representation paradigm supported is RDF(S) and (ii) what is being tracked are repositories – independently from the fact if they contain ontologies, instance data, or both. The decision to support tracking of changes, versioning, and meta-information for RDF(S) repositories has a number of consequences and requires more decisions to be taken. The most important principles are presented in the next paragraphs.

VPR1: The RDF statement is the smallest directly manageable piece of knowledge.

Each repository, formally speaking, is a set of RDF statements (i.e. triples) – these are the smallest separately manageable pieces of knowledge. There exist arguments that the resources and the literals are the smallest entities – it is true, however they cannot be manipulated independently – they always appear as a part of a triple. To summarize, there is no way to add, remove, or update (the description of) a resource without also changing some statements, while the opposite does not hold.

VPR2: An RDF statement cannot be changed – it can only be added and removed.

As far as the statements are nothing more than triples, changing one of the constituents, just converts it into another triple. It is because there is nothing else but the constituents to determine the identity of the triple, which is an abstract entity being fully defined by them. Let us take for instance the statement `ST1=<A, PR1, B>` and suppose B is a resource, i.e. an URI of resource. Then ST1 is nothing more but a triple of the URIs of A, PR1, and B – if one of those get changed it will be already pointing to a different resource that may or may not have something in common with the first one. For example, if the URI of A was `http://x.y.z/o1#A` and it get changed to `http://x.y.z/o1#C` then the statement `ST2=<C,PR1,B>` will be a completely different statement.

Further, if the resource pointed by an URI gets changed two cases could be distinguished:

- The resource is changed but its meta-description in RDF is not. Such changes are outside the scope of the problem for tracking changes in formally represented knowledge, and particularly in RDF(S) repositories.
- The description of the resource is changed – it can happen iff a statement including this resource get changed, i.e. added or removed. In such case, there is another

statement affected, but the one that just bears the URI of the same resource does not.

There could be an argument, that when the object of a triple is a literal and it gets changed, this is still the same triple. However, if there is for instance statement <A, R, "abc"> and it changes to <A, R, "cba">, the graph representation shows that it is just a different arc because the new literal is a new node and there could be other statements (say, <B, P, "abc">) still connected to the old one.

As a consequence here comes the next princple:

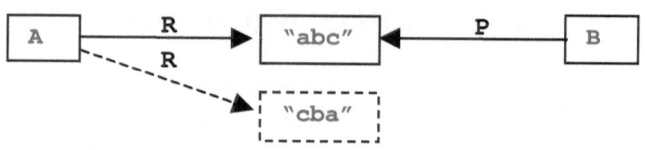

VPR3: *The two basic types of updates in a repository are addition and removal of a statement*

In other words, those are the events that necessarily have to be tracked by a tracking system. It is obvious that more event types such as replacement or simultaneous addition of a number of statements may also be considered as relevant for an RDF(S) repository change tracking system. However, those can all be seen as composite events that can be modeled via sequences of additions and removals. As far as there is no doubt that the solution proposed should allow for tracking of composite events (say, via post-processing of the sequence of the simple ones), we are not going to enumerate or specify them here.

VPR4: *Each update turns the repository into a new state*

Formally, a state of the repository is determined by the set of statements that are explicitly asserted. As far as each update is changing the set of statements, it is also turning the repository into another state. A tracking system should be able to address and manage all the states of a repository.

2.1.   History, Passing through Equivalent States

The history of changes in the repository could be defined as sequence of states, as well, as a sequence of updates. It has to be mentioned that in the history, there could be a number of equivalent states. It is just a question of perspective do we consider those as one and the same state or as equivalent ones. Both perspectives bear some advantages for some applications. We accepted that there could be equivalent states in the history of a repository, but they are still managed as distinct entities.

2.2.   Versions Are Labeled States of the Repository

Some of the states of the repository could be pointed out as versions. Such could be any state, without any formal criteria and requirements – it completely depends on the user's or application's needs and desires. Once defined to be a version, the state becomes a first class entity for which additional knowledge could be supported.

3.   Implementation Approach

For each repository, there is an *update counter* (UC) – an integer variable that increases its value each time when the repository is updated. Let us call each separate value of the UC *update identifier, UID*. Then for each statement in the repository the UIDs when it was added and removed are known – these values determine the "lifetime" of the statement. It is also the case that each state of the repository is identified by the corresponding UID. For each state it is straightforward to find the set of statements that determine it – those that were "alive" at the UID of the state being examined.

The approach could be demonstrated with the sample repository KB1 and its "history". The repository is represented as a graph where the lifetime of the statements is given separated with semicolons after the property names. The history is presented via events in format: `UID:nn {add|remove} <subj, pred, obj>`

```
History:
UID:1 add <A, r1, B>
UID:2 add <E, r1, D>
UID:3 add <E, r3, B>
UID:4 add <D, r3, A>
UID:5 add <C, r2, D>
UID:6 add <A, r2, E>
UID:7 add <C, r2, E>
UID:8 remove <A, r2, E>
UID:9 add <B, r2, C>
UID:10 remove <E, r3, B>
UID:11 remove <B, r2, C>
UID:12 remove <C, r2, E>
UID:13 remove <C, r2, D>
UID:14 remove <E, r1, D>
UID:15 remove <A, r1, B>
UID:16 remove <D, r3, A>
```

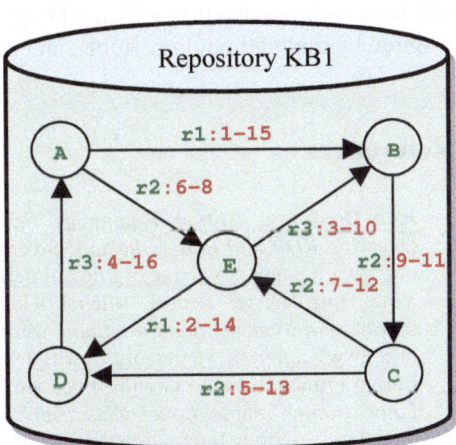

Here follow two "snapshots" of states of the repository respectively for UIDs 2 and 8

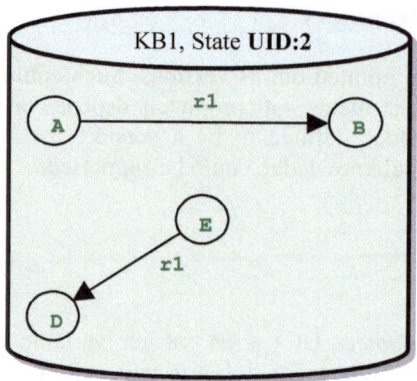 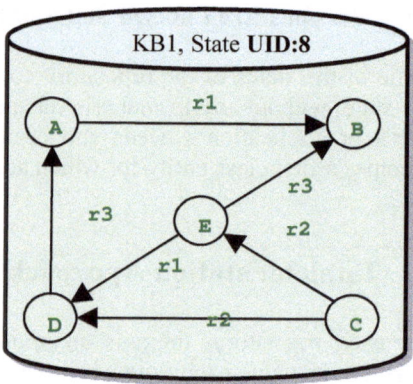

It is an interesting question how we handle in the above model, multiple additions and removals of one and the same statement, which in a sense periodically appears and disappears form the repository. We undertake the approach to consider them as separate statements, because of reasons similar to those presented for the support of distinguishable equivalent statements.

4.   Conclusion and Future Work

The ontology middleware, part of which is the tracking changes module presented still have to prove itself in real-world applications. At this stage it is work in progress inspired by the methodology, tools, and case studies of the On-To-Knowledge project.

References

1. Jeen Broekstra, Arjohn Kampman. *Sesame: A generic Architecture for Storing and Querying RDF and RDF Schema.* Deliverable 9, On-To-Knowledge project, October 2001. http://www.ontoknowledge.org/downl/del10.pdf
2. Ying Ding, Dieter Fensel, Michel Klein, Borys Omelayenko. *Ontology management: survey, requirements and directions.* Deliverable 4, On-To-Knowledge project, June 2001. http://www.ontoknowledge.org/downl/del4.pdf
3. Enrico Franconi, Fabio Grandi, Federica Mandreoli. *Schema Evolution and Versioning: a Logical and Computational Characterization.* In "Database schema evolution and meta-modeling" - Ninth International Workshop on Foundations of Models and Languages for Data and Objects, Schloss Dagstuhl, Germany, Sept.18-21, 2000. LNCS 2065, pp 85-99
4. Enrico Franconi, Fabio Grandi, Federica Mandreoli. *A Semantic Approach for Schema Evolution and Versioning of OODB.* Proceedings of the 2000 International Workshop on Description Logics (DL2000), Aachen, Germany, August 17-19, 2000. pp 99-112
5. Atanas Kiryakov, Kiril Iv. Simov, Damyan Ognyanov. *Ontology Middleware: Analysis and Design.* Deliverable 38, On-To-Knowledge project, March 2002.
6. W3C; Ora Lassila, Ralph R. Swick, eds. *Resource Description Framework (RDF) Model and Syntax Specification.* http://www.w3.org/TR/1999/REC-rdf-syntax-19990222/

MnM: Ontology Driven Semi-automatic and Automatic Support for Semantic Markup

Maria Vargas-Vera[1], Enrico Motta [1], John Domingue [1], Mattia Lanzoni [1],
Arthur Stutt [1], and Fabio Ciravegna [2]

[1] Knowledge Media Institute
The Open University
Walton Hall, Milton Keynes, MK7 6AA, UK
{m.vargas-vera; e.motta; j.b.domingue; m.lanzoni;
a.stutt}@open.ac.uk

[2] Department of Computer Science,
University of Sheffield
Regent Court, 211PortobelloStreet,
Sheffield S1 4DP, UK
f.ciravegna@dcs.shef.ac.uk

Abstract. An important precondition for realizing the goal of a semantic web is the ability to annotate web resources with semantic information. In order to carry out this task, users need appropriate representation languages, ontologies, and support tools. In this paper we present MnM, an annotation tool which provides both automated and semi-automated support for annotating web pages with semantic contents. MnM integrates a web browser with an ontology editor and provides open APIs to link to ontology servers and for integrating information extraction tools. MnM can be seen as an early example of the next generation of ontology editors, being web-based, oriented to semantic markup and providing mechanisms for large-scale automatic markup of web pages.

1 Introduction

An important pre-condition for realizing the goal of the semantic web is the ability to annotate web resources with semantic information. In order to carry out this task, users need appropriate *knowledge representation languages*, *ontologies*, and *support tools*. The knowledge representation language provides the semantic interlingua for expressing knowledge precisely. RDF ([14], [20]) and RDFS [2] provide the basic framework for expressing metadata on the web, while current developments in web-based knowledge representation, such as DAML+OIL (reference description of the daml+oil can be found at http://www.daml.org/2001/03/reference.html) and the language that will be proposed by the WebOnt group (http://www.w3.org), are building on the RDF base framework to provide more sophisticated knowledge representation support. Ontologies [12] provide the mechanism to support interoperability at a conceptual level. In a nutshell, the idea of interoperating agents able to exchange information and carrying out complex problem solving on the web is based on the assump-

A. Gómez-Pérez and V.R. Benjamins (Eds.): EKAW 2002, LNAI 2473, pp. 379-391, 2002.

tion that these agents will share common, explicitly defined, generic conceptualizations. These are typically models of a particular area, such as product catalogues, or taxonomies of medical conditions, although ontologies can also be used to support the specification of reasoning services ([23], [25], [11]), thus allowing not only 'static' interoperability through shared domain conceptualizations, but also 'dynamic' interoperability through the explicit publication of competence specifications, which can be reasoned about to determine whether a particular web service is appropriate for a particular task.

Ontologies and representation languages provide the basic semantic tools to construct the semantic web. Obviously a lot more is needed; in particular, tool support is needed to facilitate the development of semantic resources, given a particular ontology and representation language. This problem is not a new one, knowledge engineers early on realized that one of the main obstacles to the development of intelligent, knowledge-based systems was the so-called *knowledge acquisition bottleneck* [10]. In a nutshell, the problem is how to acquire and represent knowledge, so that this knowledge can be effectively used by a reasoning system. Although the problem is not a new one, the context provided by the semantic web introduces new aspects to the problem, with respect to the nature of the knowledge and the type of users.

Nature of the knowledge. Traditional knowledge acquisition was concerned with knowledge for problem solving. Semantic markup will primarily focus on ontology population, a far easier knowledge acquisition task.

Type of users. Knowledge-based systems are normally written by skilled knowledge engineers. On the web, it is likely that semantic marking up will become a common activity, carried out by content providers who are not necessarily skilled knowledge engineers. This means that more emphasis will have to be put on facilitating semantic markup by 'ordinary' web users (people who are neither experts in language technologies nor 'power knowledge engineers'). In particular, automated knowledge extraction technologies are likely to play an ever increasing important role, as a crucial technology to tackle the semantic web version of the knowledge acquisition bottleneck.

In this paper we present *MnM*, an annotation tool which provides both automated and semi-automated support for marking up web pages with semantic contents. MnM integrates a web browser with an ontology editor and provides open APIs to link to ontology servers and for integrating information extraction tools. MnM can be seen as an early example of the next generation of ontology editors, being web-based, oriented to semantic markup and providing mechanisms for large-scale automatic markup of web pages.

The rest of the paper is organized as follows: in the next section we will show the process model underlying the design of the tool. Section 3 will show an example of the tool in use. Finally sections 4 and 5 discuss related work and re-state the main tenets and results from our research.

2   Process Model

Within this work we have focused on creating a *generic process model* for developing semantically enriched web content. The component tools which are used in MnM are ontology servers, Information Extraction (IE) tools and   augmented web browsers. During our initial work in this area we found that either the existing tools did not directly support the creation of semantic web content or the mapping between the tasks to be carried out and the toolset was non-trivial. Hence, within MnM, we adopted a *generic process model,* which can be easily understood by web developers who are not necessarily expert ontology engineers or human language technology experts.

Another key feature of our process model is that it is generic with respect to the specific ontology server and IE technologies used.

There are five main activities supported by MnM:

- *Browse.* A specific set of knowledge components is chosen from a library of knowledge models on an ontology server.
- *Markup.* The chosen set of knowledge components is selected to form the basis of an IE mechanism. A corpus of documents are manually marked up.
- *Learn.* A learning algorithm is run over the marked up corpus to learn the extraction rules.
- *Test.* The IE mechanism is run over a test corpus to assess its precision and recall measures.
- *Extract.* An IE mechanism is selected and run over a set of documents

We will now provide more details of each of the above activities in turn.

Browse
In this activity the user browses a library of knowledge models which sit on a web based ontology server. The user can see an overview of the existing models and can select which one to focus on (i.e., which ontology to use to initiate the markup process). Within a selected ontology the user can browse the existing items - for example the classes. Items within an ontology can be selected as the starting point for selecting an IE mechanism. More specifically, the selected class forms the basis for a template which will eventually be matched against a corpus of documents and instantiated in the extraction activity.

Mark-Up
The activity of semantic tagging refers to the activity of annotating text documents (written in plain ASCII or HTML) with a set of tags defined in the ontology, in particular we work with a hand-crafted KMi ontology (ontology describing the knowledge Media Institute- KMi).

MnM provides means to browse the event hierarchy (defined in the KMi ontology). In this hierarchy each event is a class and the annotation component extracts the set of possible tags from the slots defined in each class.

Once a class has been selected a training corpus of manually marked up pages needs to be created. Here the user views appropriate documents within MnM's built-in web browser and annotates segments of text using the tags based on the class's slot as given in the ontology (i.e., ontology driven mark-up). As the text is selected MnM inserts the relevant SGML/XML tags into the document.

Learning

MnM integrates web browsing, ontology browsing and IE development. It does not have a built-in IE tool but provides a plug-in interface which allows the integration of IE tools easily.

In a previous version of our MnM we integrated Marmot, Badger and Crystal from the University of Massachusetts [26] and our own NLP components (i.e., OCML preprocessor). A full description of this version can be found in ([28], [29]). However, in this paper we will concentrate on the recent integration work that we have carried out with Amilcare, a tool for adaptive information extraction [3].

Amilcare is designed to support active annotation of documents. It performs IE by enriching texts with XML annotations. To use Amilcare in a new domain the user simply has to manually annotate a training set of documents. No knowledge of Natural Language Technologies is necessary.

Amilcare is designed to accommodate the needs of different user types. While naïve users can build new applications without delving into the complexity of Human Language Technology, IE experts are provided with a number of facilities for tuning the final application. Induced rules can be inspected, monitored and edited to obtain some additional accuracy, if required. The interface also allows precision (P) and recall (R) to be balanced. The system can be run on an annotated unseen corpus and users are presented with statistics on accuracy, together with details on correct matches and mistakes. Retuning the P&R balance does not generally require major retraining, facilities for inspecting the effect of different P&R balances are provided. Although the current interface for balancing P&R is designed for IE experts, a future version will provide support for naïve users [6].

At the start of the learning phase Amilcare preprocesses texts using Annie, the shallow IE system included in the Gate package ([22], www.gate.ac.uk). Annie performs text tokenization (segmenting texts into words), sentence splitting (identifying sentences) part of speech tagging (lexical disambiguation), gazetteer lookup (dictionary lookup), named entity recognition (recognition of people and organization names, dates, etc.). Amilcare then induces rules for information extraction. The learning system is based on LP^2, a covering algorithm for supervised learning of IE rules based on Lazy-NLP ([3], [4]). This is a wrapper induction methodology [19] that, unlike other wrapper induction approaches, uses linguistic information in the rule generalization process. The learning system starts inducing wrapper-like rules that make no use of linguistic information, where rules are sets of conjunctive conditions on adjacent words. Then the linguistic information provided by Annie is used in order to create generalized rules: conditions on words are substituted with conditions on the linguistic information (e.g. condition matching on either the lexical category, or the class provided by the gazetteer, etc. Examples of rules and deep description of the (LP^2) algorithm can be found in [4].

All the generalizations are tested in parallel by using a variant of the AQ algorithm [24] and the best -generalizations are kept for IE. The idea is that the linguistic-based generalization is deployed only when the use of NLP information is reliable or effective. The measure of reliability here is not linguistic correctness, but effectiveness in extracting information using linguistic information as opposed to using shallower approaches. Lazy NLP-based systems learn which is the best strategy for each information/context separately. For example they may decide that using the result of a part of speech tagger is the best strategy for recognizing the speaker in seminar announcements, but not to spot the seminar location. This strategy is quite effective for analyzing documents with mixed genres, a common situation in web documents [5].

The learning system induces two types of rules: tagging rules and correction rules. A tagging rule is composed of a left hand side, containing a pattern of conditions on a connected sequence of words, and a right hand side that is an action inserting an XML tag in the texts. Correction rules shift misplaced annotations (inserted by tagging rules) to the correct position. These are learnt from the errors found whilst attempting to re-annotate the training corpus using the induced tagging rules.

Correction rules are identical to tagging rules, but (1) their patterns also match the tags inserted by the tagging rules and (2) their actions shift misplaced tags rather than adding new ones. The output of the training phase is a collection of rules for IE that are associated with the specific scenario (domain).

Amilcare has been tested on Italian and English but it is easily extendible to cover other languages. It requires to connect a preprocessor for the target language (such as Annie is) including at least a tokenizer and possibly a part of speech tagger and morphological analyzer.

Testing

MnM provides two mechanisms for selecting a test corpus and distinguish this from a training corpora. The user can manually select training and test corpora and these can be in the form of local files or on the web. In addition, it is also possible to simply select a corpus (either locally or on the web) and let the system create test and training corpora randomly.

Extraction

After the training phase Amilcare has a library of induced rules which can be used to extract information from texts.

When working in extraction mode, Amilcare receives as input a (collection of) text(s) with the associated scenario – scenario is the set of tags that the user will insert in the training corpora- (including the rules induced during the training phase). It preprocesses the text(s) by using Annie and then it applies its rules and returns the original text with the added annotations. The Gate annotation schema is used for annotation [22]. Annotation schemas provides means to define types of annotations in Gate. Gate uses the XML schema language supported by W3C for these definitions. However, Gate version 2 supports annotations in SGML/XML.

Once that is done the information extracted is presented to the user for approval. Then the extracted information is sent to the ontology server which will populate the selected ontology.

During the population step the IE mechanism fills predefined slots associated with an extraction template. Each template consists of slots of a particular class as defined in the selected ontology, for instance, the class visiting-a-place-or-people has the slots: visitor, place, etc. More detail about the population phase is given in the following section.

Our goal is to automatically fill as many slots as possible. However, some of the slots may still require manual intervention. There are several reasons for this problem:

- there is information that is not contained in the text,
- none of the rules from our IE libraries match with the sentence that might provide the information (incomplete set of rules). This means that the learning phase needs to be tuned.

The extracted information is also validated using the ontology. This is possible because each slot in each class of the ontology has a type associated with it. Therefore, extracted information which does not match the type definition of the slot in the ontology can be highlighted as incorrect.

Currently our system had been trained using an archive of 200 stories that we had collected in KMi. The training phase was performed using typical examples of stories belonging to each of the different type of events defined in the ontology. We obtained precision 95% and recall 90% using Amilcare on KMi stories.

3   Example

We will now explain the process model we described earlier by walking through a specific extraction example. The domain of our example is a web based news letter, KMi Planet [8], that has been running in our lab for five years. The Planet front page, individual story and archive views are generated automatically from stories which are submitted by email or through a web based form. Over the years we have extended Planet to include semantic retrieval, smart layout and personalization services ([9], [17]). Whilst we were happy with the functionality that these services provided we were concerned that the knowledge base was maintained by hand. We have therefore selected this domain to apply MnM. Figure 1 shows the KMi Planet front page.

The Planet services are implemented within the akt-kmi-planet-kb knowledge base/model which sits on our public knowledge model server (at http://webonto.open.ac.uk - see [7] for a description). This knowledge base builds on a dozen ontologies describing domains such as our lab, events, organisations and technologies.

Figures 2-5 show a user setting up an IE mechanism for extracting Planet stories about visits to KMi. In figure 2 we can see that MnM consists of three main windows. The window on the right is an augmented web browser. The windows on the left form a mini ontology browser: the top window displaying a high level view and the bottom window displaying detailed structure. Figures 2 and 3 show the initial steps in creating the visit story IE mechanism. In figure 2 the user is looking at a portion of the 200 stories in the story archive. The left top panel shows all the knowledge models on the server (shown in the left panel). The user selects akt-kmi-planet-kb and notes from the documentation that it implements the latest Planet knowledge services. Opening akt-kmi-planet-kb displays all of the classes within the knowledge base – note that the majority of the classes are inherited from the ontologies used by akt-kmi-planet-kb.

Figure 3 shows the class "visiting-a-place-or-people" from the event hierarchy within the akt-kmi-planet-kb. The names of the slots are used in the markup phase during the annotation process.

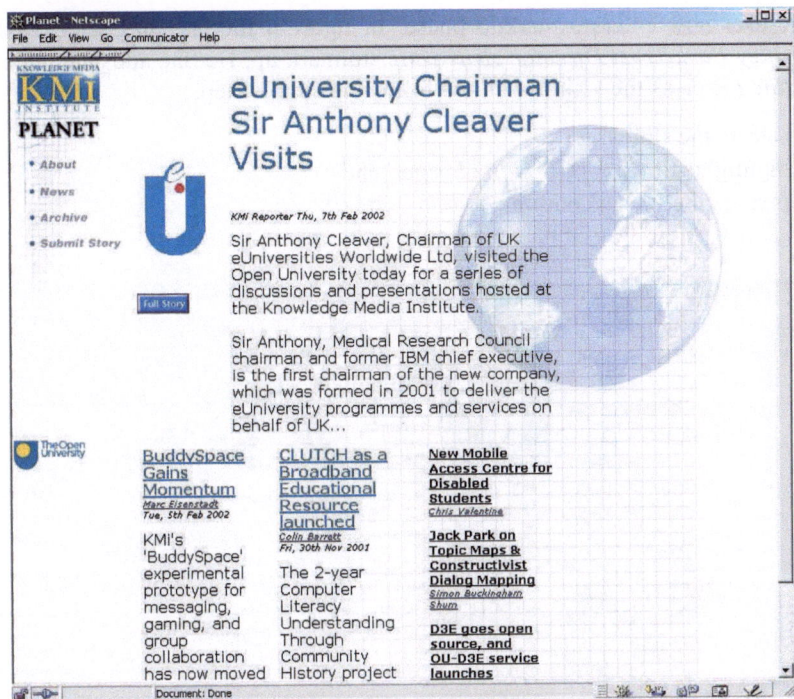

Fig. 1. A screen snapshot of the KMi Planet front page

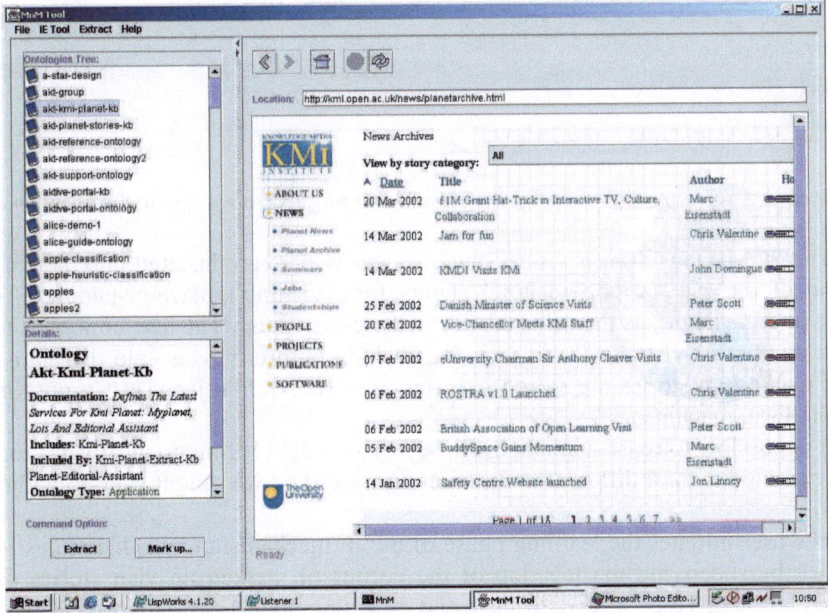

Fig. 2. A screen snapshot showing a user browsing the library of knowledge models held on the WebOnto server

The user now enters a markup phase. In figure 4 the user has selected the story *"Bletchley Park Trust Director visits KMi"* to mark up. He/She adds an entry to mark *Christine Large* as the visitor with the following simple steps:

- selects the slot visitor,
- highlights the text *"Christine Large"* and
- presses the 'Insert' button.

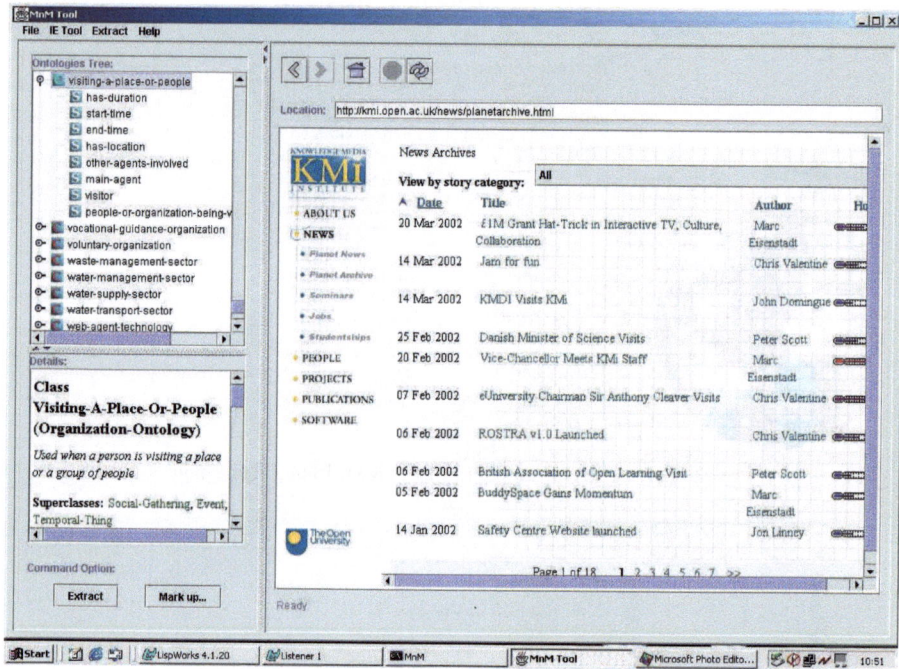

Fig. 3. A screen snapshot showing the class visiting-a-place-or-people in the event hierarchy

The SGML tags <vapop_visitor> and </vapop_visitor> are inserted into the page. The name of the tag ''vapop_visitor'' stands for ''visiting-a-place-or-people'' (vapop) class and ''visitor'' is the selected slot in the class vapop. The user continues to mark up a number of visit stories in a similar fashion before moving into the learn phase. The marked up stories are stored in a directory (c:\AKTProject\TestCorpus\visiting\) on the local machine.

It is possible to reuse annotated stories. This might be important if we want to use the training set for a different extraction purpose (i.e., we might want to add/remove tags).

The user initiates the learning phase of the IE mechanism to produce rules for visit stories by specifying the location of the corpus of marked up visit stories (held in c:\AKTProject\TestCorpus\visiting\) and selecting the 'Learn' button. This causes Amilcare to start up – the Amilcare status window can be seen in figure 4. At this stage Amilcare learns rules for the event "visiting-a-place-or-people".

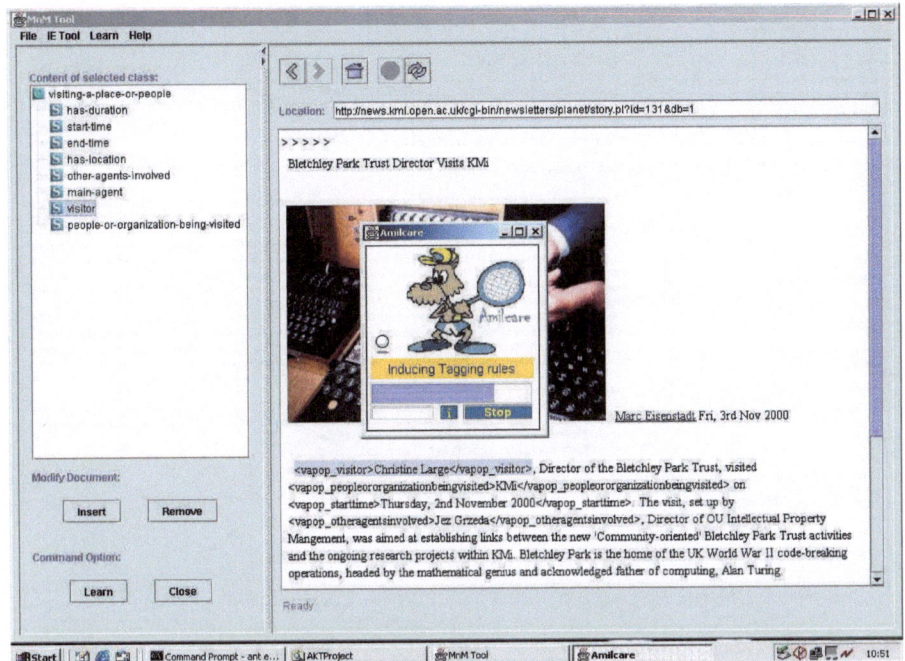

Fig. 4. A screen snapshot showing a marked up KMi Planet story and Amilcare

During the extraction phase the user selects a set of rules and the input set of documents. The input set can either be a directory on the local disk or a URL pointing to a directory of documents. In our example the user has selected a local directory containing a set of planet stories. In figure 5 below Amilcare has finished extracting instances from the input set and the user is checking the created instances. In the top left panel the user has selected the third extracted item. The bottom left panel shows the instance slot values extracted and the web browser on the right shows the source KMi Planet story with the matched text segments highlighted. This view enables the user to quickly determine if the extracted data is correct.

4   Related Work

A number of annotation tools for producing semantic markup exist. The most interesting of these are Annotea [16]; SHOE Knowledge Annotator [15]; the COHSE annotator [1]; AeroDAML [18]; and, OntoMat, a tool being developed using the CREAM annotation framework [13]. A commercial version of OntoMat is available as OntoAnnotate (http://www.ontoprise.de/com/co_produ_tool2.htm).

Annotea provides RDF-based markup but it does not support information extraction nor is it linked to an ontology server. It does, however, have an annotation server which makes annotations publicly available. SHOE Knowledge Annotator allows users to mark up pages in SHOE guided by ontologies available locally or via a URL.

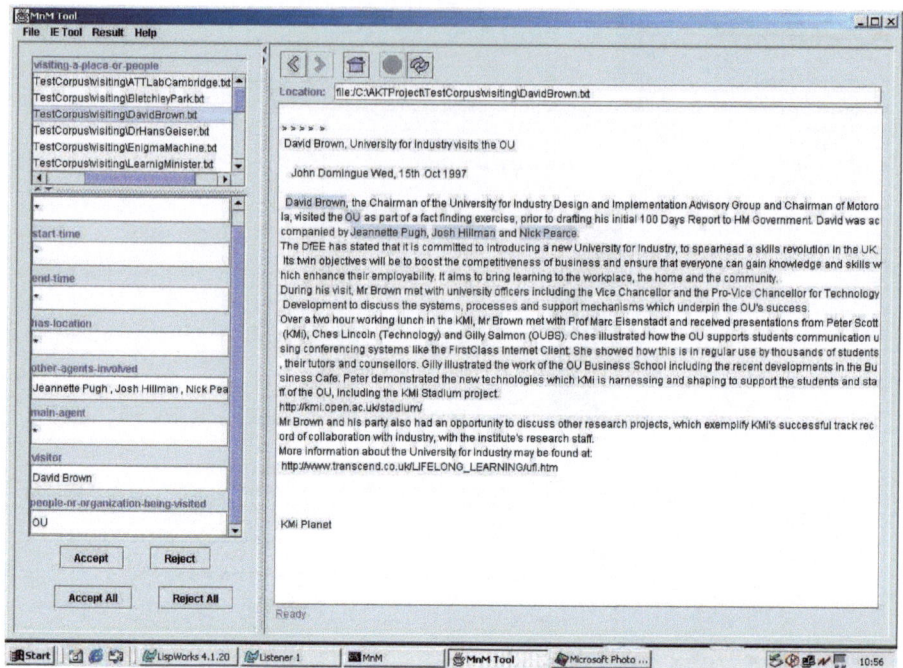

Fig. 5. A screen snapshot showing the result of the extraction phase

These marked up pages can be reasoned about by SHOE-aware tools such as SHOE Search. The COHSE annotator uses an ontology server to mark up pages in DAML+OIL. The results can be saved as RDF. AeroDAML is available as a web page. The user simply enters a URL and the system automatically returns DAML annotations on a web page using a predefined ontology based on WordNet.

Of the systems listed above, OntoMat is closest to MnM both in spirit and in functionality. Both can provide some form of automated extraction. However, while MnM makes it possible to access ontology servers through APIs, such as OKBC, and also to access ontologies specified in a markup format, such as RDF and DAML+OIL, OntoMat only provides the latter functionality. In contrast with OntoMat, MnM can handle multiple ontologies at the same time, which makes it very easy to switch from one to another, and also allows inherited definitions to be displayed for ontology editing and browsing. On the other hand, OntoMat can store pages annotated in DAML+OIL using OntoBroker as an annotation server. It also provides crawlers which can search the Web for marked up pages for addition to its internal knowledge base.

While both MnM and OntoMat are very similar they illustrate a slight difference of emphasis in providing tools for the Semantic Web. While OntoMat adopts the philosophy that the markup which indicates the knowledge content of a web resources should be included as part of that resource, MnM's annotations are stored both as markup on a page and as items in a knowledge base held on the WebOnto combined ontology and knowledge base server.

5   Conclusions

In this paper we have described MnM, an ontology-based annotation tool which provides both automated and semi-automated support for annotating web pages with semantic contents. The first prototype of the system has now been completed and tested with both Amilcare and the UMass set of tools. The early results are encouraging in terms of the quality and robustness of our current implementation, however, there is clearly a lot more work needed to make this technology easy to use for our target user base (people who are neither experts in language technologies nor 'power knowledge engineers'). In particular, all the activities associated with automated markup tend to be very sensitive to the quality of markup and to the appropriateness of the chosen corpora. Amilcare already attempts to address some of these issues through its adaptive mechanisms, however, more work is needed in this area. In addition, we also plan to do more work on the user interface, in particular with respect to the integration of markup, ontology browsing and the 'semantic navigation' of web pages. Currently, ontology and web browsing are integrated with respect to contents annotation, but ontologies do not inform the web browsing component of MnM directly. Our vision for the semantic web is one in which new forms of 'conceptual navigation' will emerge, where association between resources will be semantic as well as hypertextual. We plan to experiment with these ideas and extend the interface of MnM to support novel, markup-driven forms of web browsing, as well as the standard HTML based ones.

Acknowledgements

This work was funded by the Advanced Knowledge Technologies (AKT) Interdisciplinary Research Collaboration (IRC), which is sponsored by the UK Engineering and Physical Sciences Research Council under grant number GR/N15764/01. The AKT IRC comprises the Universities of Aberdeen, Edinburgh, Sheffield, Southampton and the Open University. The authors would like to thank Maruf Hasan and Simon Buckingham Shum for their invaluable help in reviewing the first draft of this paper.

References

1. S. Bechhofer and C. Goble: Towards Annotation Using DAML+OIL. First   International Conference on Knowledge Capture (K-CAP 2001). Workshop   on Semantic Markup and Annotation. Victoria, B.C., Canada. October 2001.
2. D. Brickley, and R. Guha: Resource Description Framework(RDF) Schema Specification 1.0. Candidate recommendation, World Wide Web Consortium, 2000. URL: http://www.w3.org/TR/2000/CR-rdf-schema-20000327.
3. F. Ciravegna: Adaptive Information Extraction from Text by Rule Induction and Generalisation, Proc. of 17th International Joint Conference on Artificial Intelligence   (IJCAI 2001), Seattle, August 2001.

4. F. Ciravegna: LP^2 an Adaptive Algorithm for Information Extraction from Web-related Texts. Proc. of the IJCAI-2001 Workshop on Adaptive Text Extraction and Mining held in conjunction with the 17th International Conference on Artificial Intelligence (IJCAI-01), August, 2001.
5. F. Ciravegna: Challenges in Information Extraction from Text for Knowledge Management in IEEE Intelligent Systems and Their Applications, November 2001, (Trend and Controversies).
6. F. Ciravegna and D. Petrelli: User Involvement in Adaptive Information Extraction: Position Paper in Proceedings of the IJCAI-2001 Workshop on Adaptive Text Extraction and Mining held in conjunction with the 17th International Conference on Artificial Intelligence (IJCAI-01), August, 2001.
7. J. Domingue: Tadzebao and WebOnto: Discussing, Browsing, and Editing Ontologies on the Web. Proceedings of the 11th Banff Knowledge Acquisition Workshop, Banff, Alberta, Canada, April 18-23, 1998.
8. J. Domingue and P. Scott: KMi Planet: A Web Based News Server. Asia Pacific Computer Human Interaction Conference (APCHI'98), Shonan Village Center, Hayama-machi, Kanagawa, Japan, 15-17 July, 1998.
9. J. Domingue and E. Motta: Planet-Onto: From News Publishing to Integrated Knowledge Management Support. IEEE Intelligent Systems Special Issue on "Knowledge Management and Knowledge Distribution over the Internet", May/June, 2000, pp. 26-32. (ISSN 1094-7167).
10. E. A. Feigenbaum: The art of artificial intelligence 1: Themes and case studies of knowl edge engineering. Technical report, Pub. no. STAN-SC-77-621, Stanford University, Department of Computer Science, 1977.
11. D. Fensel. and E. Motta: Structured Development of Problem Solving Methods. Transactions on Knowledge and Data Engineering 13(6):9131-932, 2001.
12. T. R. Gruber: A Translation Approach to Portable Ontology Specifications.Knowledge Adquisition 5(2), 199-220, 1993.
13. S. Handschuh and S. Staab and A. Maedche: CREAM- Creating relational metadata with a component-based, ontology-driven annotation framework. First International Conference on Knowledge Capture (K-CAP 2001), Victoria B.C., October 2001.
14. P. Hayes: RDF Model Theory, W3C Working Draft, February 2002 URL: http://www.w3.org/TR/rdf-mt/.
15. J. Heflin and J. Hendler: A Portrait of the Semantic Web in Action. IEEE Intelligent Systems, 16(2), 2001.
16. J. Kahan and M. Koivunen and E. Prud'Hommeaux and R. Swick: Annotea: Open RDF Infrastructure for Shared Web Annotations. In Proc. of the WWW10 International Conference. Hong Kong, 2001.
17. Y. Kalfoglou and J. Domingue and E. Motta.and M. Vargas-Vera and S. Buckingham Shum: MyPlanet: an ontology-driven Web based personalised news service. Proceedings of the IJCAI'01 workshop on Ontologies and Information Sharing, Seattle, WA, USA 2001.
18. P. Kogut and W. Holmes: AeroDAML: Applying Information Extraction to Generate DAML Annotations from Web Pages. First International Conference on Knowledge Capture (K-CAP 2001). Workshop on Knowledge Markup and Semantic Annotation, Victoria, B.C., Canada, October 2001.
19. N. Kushmerick and D. Weld and R. Doorenbos: Wrapper induction for information extraction, Proc. of 15th International Conference on Artificial Intelligence, IJCAI-97.
20. O. Lassila and R. Swick: Resource Description Framework (RDF): Model and Syntax Specification. Recommendation, World Wide Web Consortium, 1999. URL: http://www.w3.org/TR/REC-rdf-syntax/.
21. E. Riloff: An Empirical Study of Automated Dictionary Construction for Information Extraction in Three Domains. *The AI Journal,* 85, 101-134, 1996.

22. D. Maynard and V. Tablan and H. Cunningham and C. Ursu and O. Saggion and K. Bontcheva and Y. Wilks: Architectural Elements of Language Engineering Robustness. *Journal of* Natural Language Engineering – Special Issue on Robust Methods in Analysis of Natural Language Data ,forthcoming, 2002.
23. S. McIlraith and T. C. Son.and H. Zeng: Semantic Web Services, IEEE Intelligent Systems, Special Issue on the Semantic Web, Volume 16, No. 2, pp. 46-53, March/April, 2001.
24. R. S. Mickalski and I. Mozetic and J. Hong and H. Lavrack: The multi purpose incremental learning system AQ15 and its testing application to three medical domains', in Proceedings of the 5th National Conference on Artificial Intelligence, Philadelphia. Morgan Kaufmann publisher, 1986.
25. E. Motta: *Reusable Components for Knowledge Models*. IOS Press, Amsterdam, 1999.
26. E. Riloff: An Empirical Study of Automated Dictionary Construction for Information Extraction in Three Domains. *The AI Journal,* 85, 101-134, 1996.
27. S. Staab and A. Mädche and S. Handschuh: An Annotation Framework for the Semantic Web. In: S. Ishizaki (ed.), *Proc. of The First International Workshop on MultiMedia Annotation.* January, 30 - 31, 2001. Tokyo, Japan.
28. M. Vargas-Vera and J. Domingue and Y. Kalfoglou and E. Motta and S. Buckingham-Shum: Template-driven information extraction for populating ontologies. *Proc of the IJCAI'01 Workshop on Ontology Learning,* Seattle, WA, USA 2001.
29. M. Vargas-Vera and E. Motta and J. Domingue and S. Buckingham Shum and M. Lanzoni: Knowledge Extraction by using an Ontology-bases Annotation Tool. First International Conference on Knowledge Capture (K-CAP 2001). *Workshop on Knowledge Markup and Semantic Annotation ,* Victoria B.C., Canada, October 2001.

New Tools for the Semantic Web

Jennifer Golbeck, Michael Grove, Bijan Parsia,
Adtiya Kalyanpur, and James Hendler

Maryland Information and Network Dynamics Laboratory
University of Maryland, College Park
College Park, Maryland, 20742, USA
golbeck@cs.umd.edu, mhgrove@wam.umd.edu, bparsia@email.unc.edu,
aditkal@yahoo.com, hendler@cs.umd.edu
http://www.mindswap.org

Abstract. The Semantic Web will allow for significantly more machine-readable content to be available on the World Wide Web. Getting this content onto the web, and using it once it is there, requires new "metaphors" for working with Semantic Web data. In this paper, we describe the "Semantic Web Portal" an approach to using Semantic Web content, and some (open source) tools that we are developing to make it a reality.

1 Introduction

The Semantic Web [1,2] is based on making machine-readable content available on the World Wide Web, and designing the appropriate technologies to harness it. Currently, a number of tools developed for traditional artificial intelligence work are being adopted to the Semantic Web. Examples include tools such as Protégé-2000[7] and OILEd [6], which are used for creating ontologies, OntoEdit [10], used for marking up web pages with information from external ontologies, and Chimera [8], which can be used to find errors in ontologies. These tools all work with Semantic Web languages such as RDFS [3] and DAML+OIL[4], and are able to create ontologies and web pages containing semantic markup.

However, these tools are primarily the products of traditional AI research which have been transitioned to use on the World Wide Web. As such, they are very powerful tools, but only focus on some parts of the "lifecycle" of Semantic Web information. The Semantic Web Agents Projects at the Maryland Information and Network Dynamics Laboratory (MIND SWAP; http://www.mindswap.org) has been developing a set of tools aimed at creating an integrated system for authoring, searching, and browsing the Semantic Web. These tools are motivated by the idea of a "Semantic Web Portal" which provides a mechanism for tying together many Semantic Web components. In this paper, we first describe the idea of a Semantic Web Portal, and then describe some of the tools we are developing to make this vision a reality. These tools are available for download at the MIND SWAP web page.

A. Gómez-Pérez and V.R. Benjamins (Eds.): EKAW 2002, LNAI 2473, pp. 392–400, 2002.
© Springer-Verlag Berlin Heidelberg 2002

2   The Goal – A Semantic Web Portal

A particular focus of our group is the creation of Semantic Web Portal technology that will motivate researchers and students in many areas to add semantic markup to documents, images and data. Authors will be able to link their evolving web resources to terms from multiple ontologies (or to define terms that extend the ontological coverage). As these links are added, queries are made to various web back-ends that contain similar pointers from other documents, databases, image archives, etc. The results are displayed to the user, allowing a constant, dynamical web portal to be created.   This portal contains pointers to documents that are on similar topics, databases that can answer queries about conceptually related science, and images and other multimedia resources.

For example, if a scientist authoring a paper or web page uses a particular term from an online ontology, the semantic web portal will return other sources with similar markup. This includes links to related photos she can use in her documents, to database queries that can show recent results, and to other documents she might want to cite or link to.   By providing useful information and resources, users will be encouraged to mark up their documents so that they make take advantage of the portal.

What allows this system to work more fully is the integration of the markup process with the portal. The portal provides the most advantage to users while they are creating their own semantic web documents. Thus, not only does the portal provide information, but also it is able to create more links based on the user. If she chooses to link to certain terms provided by the portal, a semantic link is created between the two documents.

Research being done at MIND SWAP to implement such a system includes the development of inference engines that can find relationships between entities that are not explicitly stated, the development of backend "triple stores" that can integrate database and knowledge-base processing, and the development of presentation technologies that can present the information in the portals in a way that is appropriate to the needs of the specific user.   In addition, we are developing several tools to make it easier to develop Semantic Web content from existing web sources. In the next section, we discuss some tools being developed in MIND SWAP aimed at the eventual creation of a Semantic Web Portal system.

3   Tools at MIND SWAP

MIND SWAP has developed two tools for generating DAML and RDF from formatted documents: ConvertToRDF which works with delimited files, and the Web Scraper which looks at formatted HTML pages. For generating content from scratch, there are two more tools. The RDF Editor provides a variety of features to aide users in creating RDF in tandem with HTML documents. The RDF Instance Creator (RIC) provides a simple interface for creating RDF for other media, such as pictures.

Finally, the PARKA ontology manager works with triples to provide a fast interface for searching and finding relationships among data.

3.1   RDF Editor

The RDF editor (Fig. 1) provides users with the ability to create Semantic Web markup, using information from multiple ontologies, while they simultaneously create HTML documents. The aim of this software is as follows:

- To provide the user with a flexible environment in which he can create his web page without markup hindrances;
- To allow the user to semantically classify his data set for annotation and generate markup with minimal knowledge of RDF terms and syntax.;
- To provide a reference to existing ontologies on the Internet in order to use more precise references in his own web page/text;
- To ensure accurate and complete RDF markup with scope to make modifications easily.
- To allow extension to ontological concepts by the user, thus creating new ontological content [5].

To achieve these ends, the application has three functional parts.

1. HTML Editor with Preview Browser – This is a standard WYSIWYG editor for creating and deploying web pages. Users can write some HTML from scratch, or use the editor to add images and create content in a more natural way.

2. Ontology Browser - A particularly innovative feature of the RDF Editor is that it encourages users to work with multiple ontologies. Many existing tools allow users to create their own ontologies for use in RDF documents. This tool encourages users to work with and extend pre-existing ontologies, exploiting the distributed nature of the Semantic Web.

    This interface allows the user to browse through existing ontologies on the Internet with the aim of finding relevant terms and properties. The default starting page is the DAML Ontology web site (http://www.daml.org/ontologies) from where the user could issue search queries using Class/Property names as keys. Once the appropriate ontology has been located, the user can add it to the local database, and the properties of the ontology are automatically added to the Local Ontology Information where it can be managed.

3. Semantic Data Trees – This part of the interface is what allows users to classify the data semantically into one of four basic elements: Class, Object, Property and Value.

As an interface to the Semantic Web Portal, the RDF Editor is ideal. As users select classes from ontologies, the portal can return results to them in a separate window. The fetched data is then immediately available for reference or incorporation to the current document. When the user publishes their document, the portal can include all of the new references in its knowledge base.

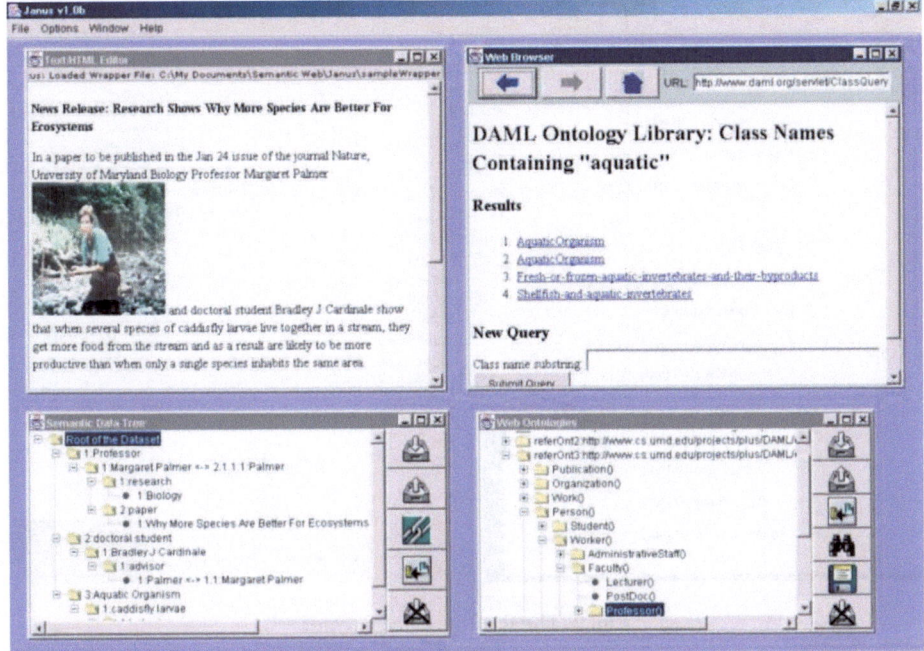

Fig 1. The RDF Editor Interface

3.2   RDF Instance Creator

The RDF Instance Creator (RIC), shown in Fig. 2, is a tool designed to ease the process of creating markup, particularly for non-text sources. RIC allows the user to generate RDF simply by filling a series of forms, thus freeing the user from needing to know RDF while still providing all the benefits that it has to offer.

RIC can use any valid ontology that is currently accessible through the Internet. After importing an ontology, the user is presented with a list of available classes from which they can create objects. When defining an object, its properties appear in the workspace. This provides a simple form interface where the user enters data for each of the object's properties. Some error checking is also built in. For example, a field has an integer range, the user cannot enter "3.2" or "two."

Using a tool like RIC to markup media that is not text based is particularly useful. Resources that cannot be described, let alone searched, in the current web framework suddenly become available and accessible to users who may be interested in them.

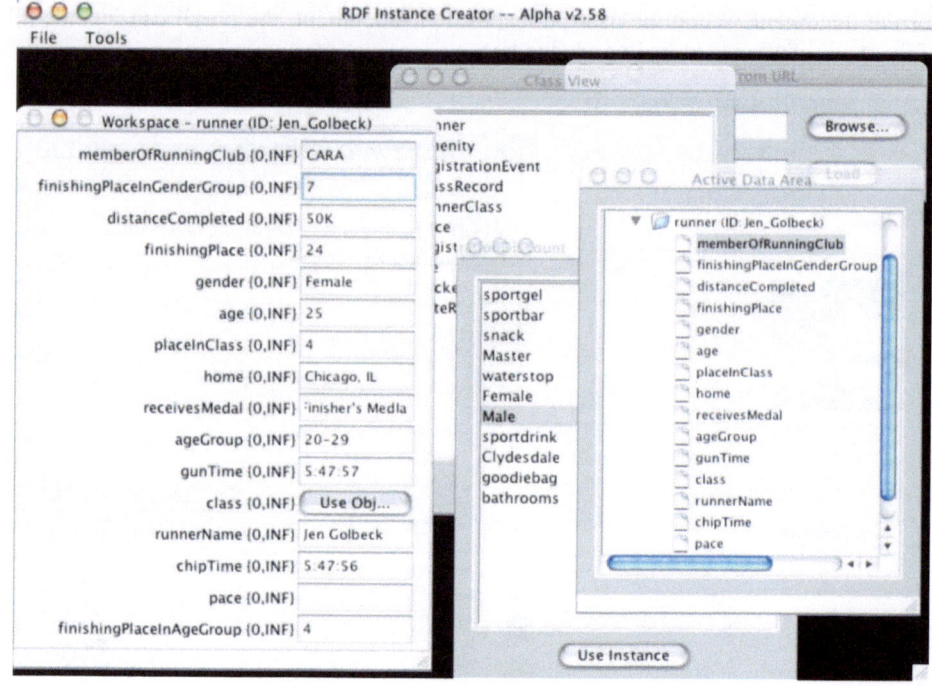

Fig. 2. The RDF Instance Creator

3.3   Scraper

Some web pages have regular structure with labeled fields, lists and tables. Often, an analyst can map these structures to an ontology and write a program to translate a portion of the web page into the semantic markup language. The RDF Web Scraper (Fig. 3) is a tool that helps users specify how to extract RDF markup from these kinds of web pages.

Users analyze the HTML in a page and create a wrapper that describes how the tag structure relates to the contents. The scraper parses the page based on the wrapper, and generates a table of data. The user can then indicate ontological specifications for each column of the table and generate the corresponding RDF.

This application has the ability to take information from between tags as well as from within them. This allows users to scrape the URI's of images or links and mark them up. For example, if a faculty list html document contains pictures of each faculty member, the scraper can grab the URI's of those pictures and include markup that indicates who is pictured in the image.

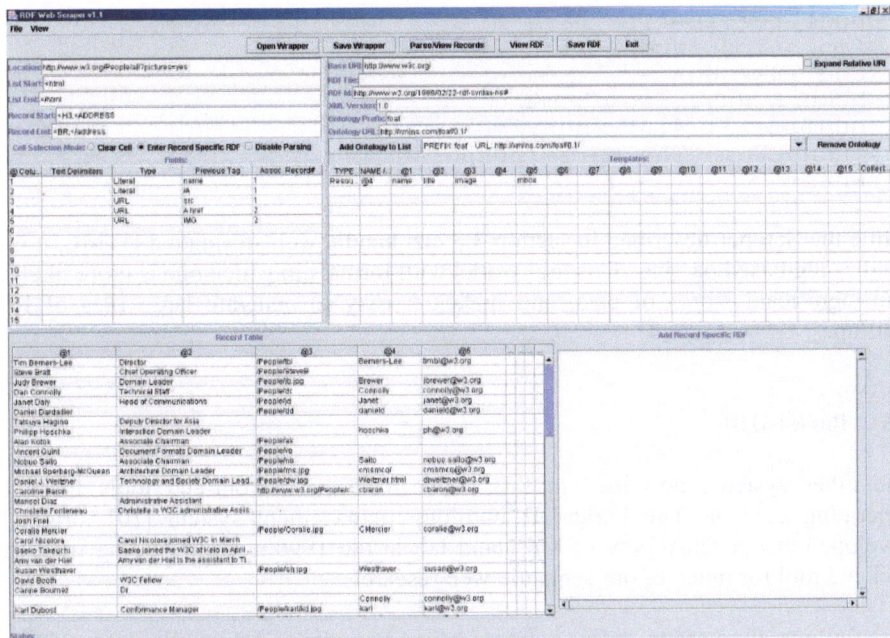

Fig. 3. The Screen Scraper

3.4 ConvertToRDF

ConvertToRDF is a tool that takes delimited data, from spreadsheets such as Microsoft Excel or from databases, and generates markup based on the column headers.

Consider this small table of data describing a race:

Name	Place	Time	Age	Hometown
The Tortoise	1	3:24:03	84	Shelton RI
The Hare	2	3:24:05	18	Bunnyville PA

By creating a simple mapping of column headings to ontological terms (from an ontology about running, in this case), this tool will generate the required headers as well as formatted RDF for each row:

```
<runner rdf:ID="The_Tortoise">
  <finishingPlace>1</finishingPlace>
  <age>84</age>
  <home>Shelton RI</home>
  <gunTime>3:24:03</gunTime>
  <runnerName>The Tortoise</runnerName>
</runner>
```

```
<runner rdf:ID="The_Hare">
  <finishingPlace>2</finishingPlace>
  <age>18</age>
  <home>Bunnyville</home>
  <gunTime>3:24:05</gunTime>
  <runnerName>The Hare</runnerName>
</runner>
```

While the Scraper described in section 3.3 can handle well--formatted HTML, it only handles tag based parsing. This tool works with formats in which one is more likely to find significant stores of data, and makes it easy to generate large files of RDF markup.

3.5   Parka-DB™

The other systems described in this paper have been front-end tools for users generating content. The Parka-DB ontology management system [10], originally developed at our University of Maryland lab in the 1990's, is now being used as a backend tool for much of our semantic web research.

Parka allows the user to define a frame-based knowledge base with class, subclass, and property links used to encode the ontology. Property values can themselves be frames, or alternatively can be string, numeric values, or specialized data structures (used primarily in the implementation). The Parka language allows exceptions, in the form of multiple-inheritance, and provides extremely efficient (and efficiently parallelizable) algorithms for performing inheritance using a true inferential-distance-ordering calculation.

Parka can effectively compute recognition, and handle extremely complex ``structure matching" queries -- a class of conjunctive queries relating a set of variable and constraints and unifying these against the larger KB. One of the key features of Parka is that it can   efficiently handle its inferencing on KB's containing millions of assertions. Parka uses DBMS technologies to support inferencing and data management.

The structure of the Parka system meshes nicely with the triple structure of DAML and RDF. RDF instances are easily converted into Parka assertions and loaded into the database. At that point, it is possible to extract information about relationships within the data that would not be accessible otherwise. Parka's inferencing mechanisms are then used to take advantage of the ontological information defined in DAML.

4   Conclusion

The Semantic Web requires new tools that can be used in new ways. One important use will be the semantic web portal, allowing people to dynamically create and use

Semantic Web information. Building such an application will need a number of new technologies, and we describe some tools aimed at providing this basis. Thus, the tools described in this paper are examples of some of the basic technologies that are needed to create this new portal technology. These include tools for generating Semantic Web instances from structured sources (ConvertToRDF) and from HTML pages (RDF Screen Scraper), a tool for creating marked up pages (RDF Editor) easily, a tool for creating instance data easily, especially for non-text sources (RIC) and a back-end ontology management tool (Parka-DB).

Downloads of the open source versions of all of these tools can be found on the MIND SWAP website -- http://www.mindswap.org.

Acknowledgements

This work was supported in part by grants from DARPA, the Air Force Research Laboratory, and the Navy Warfare Development Command. The Maryland Information and Network Dynamics Laboratory is supported by Industrial Affiliates including Fujitsu Laboratories of America, Lockheed Martin, and the Aerospace Corporation.

The programs described in this paper are available from the Maryland Information and Dynamics Laboratory, Semantic Web Agents Project (MIND SWAP) at http://www.mindswap.org.

References

1. Berners-Lee, T. and M. Fischetti, <u>Weaving the Web: The Original Design and Ultimate Destiny of the World Wide Web by its Inventor</u>, Harper, San Francisco, 1999.

2. Berners-Lee, T., Hendler, J. and Lassila, O. "The Semantic Web," *Scientific American,* May, 2001

3. Brickley, D and R.V. Guha, "Resource Description Framework (RDF) Model and Syntax Specification", W3C Recommendation submitted 22 February 1999, http://www.w3.org/TR/1999/REC-rdf-syntax-19990222/ (current May 2002).

4. Connolly, D, van Harmelen, F., Horrocks, I, McGuinness, D., Patel-Schneider, P., and Stein, L. DAML+OIL (March 2001) Reference Description, W3C Note 18 December 2001 (http://www.w3.org/TR/daml+oil-reference).

5. Hendler, Jim, "Agents and the Semantic Web," *IEEE Intelligent Systems.* March/April 2001 (Vol. 16, 2).

6. Horrocks, I. Et al – OilED, available on the WWW at http://img.cs.man.ac.uk/oil/

7. M. A. Musen, R. W. Fergerson, W. E. Grosso, N. F. Noy, M. Crubezy, & J. H. Gennari. "Component-Based Support for Building Knowledge-Acquisition Systems". In

Conference on Intelligent Information Processing (IIP 2000) of the International Federation for Information Processing World Computer Congress (WCC 2000), Beijing, 2000.

8. McGuinness, D. "Conceptual Modeling for Distributed Ontology Environments." *Proceedings of the Eighth International Conference on Conceptual Structures Logical, Linguistic, and Computational Issues (ICCS 2000)*. Darmstadt, Germany. August 14-18, 2000.

9. K. Stoffel, M. Taylor, J. Hendler. "Efficient Management of Very Large Ontologies." In *Proceedings of American Association for Artificial Intelligence Conference (AAAI-97)*, AAAI/MIT Press 1997.

10. Y. Sure, M. Erdmann, J. Angele, S. Staab, R. Studer, D.Wenke. OntoEdit: "Collaborative Ontology Development for the Semantic Web." In *Proceedings of the 1st International Semantic Web Conference - ISWC2002*, Springer, LNCS.

Author Index